INSIDE THIS IS

TWIC information
State / Federal DOT Contact Information
National Road Conditions
Highway Emergency Phone Numbers
Railroad Emergency Phone Numbers
Flagging / Signage Requirements by State
State Provisions - Summarized
Sunrise/Sunset Charts - Updated every 2 years
Truck Stops - M/LG/XLG (Including CAT scales)
EZ Record Keeping for Pilot Cars (Simple Forms to copy)
State Inspection lists
Equipment Lists
State-specific Route Survey / Requests Forms
Pilot Car Ads & Phone Directory - Detailed information
Articles

** State Provision updates can be found/added on pilotcarstoday.com or "The Overload Companion" page on Facebook

Some states are proposing changes regarding certification requirements, but the guidelines have not been officially posted Please stay alert and inform us w/ valuable information. Thank you

THE OVERLOAD ASSISTANT SERIES © 2013, 2014, 2015, 2016 Freda Barber Booth, owner - pilotcarstoday.com
THE OVERLOAD COMPANION SERIES © 2015, 2016, 2017 Freda Barber Booth, owner - pilotcarstoday.com
All rights reserved. No section of this publication may be reproduced, distributed, or transmitted in any form or by any means, including photocopying, recording, or other electronic or mechanical methods, without the prior written permission of the publisher, except in the case of brief quotations embodied in critical reviews and certain other noncommercial uses permitted by copyright law. Minimum file size PDF (non-printable edition) may be freely distributed to anyone without recourse. We charge reproduction fee of $100 per page. For permission requests, write to the publisher, addressed as written below.

Site Terms and Privacy Policy available on pilotcarstoday.com

Freda Barber Booth, Owner
Dba Pilot Cars Today,
401 Andrews Ave
Hartsville, TN 37074
pilotcarstoday.com
817-583-5503

STATE PROVISIONS are retrieved from individual state DOT websites and by other means. Any information is subject to change throughout the year for which this book is distributed. It is the sole responsibility of those involved in an Overdimensional Load movement to check with the permit along with the state's rules and regulations before traveling in that state.

While we strive to provide up-to-date information; this is merely a guide. All official information may be found at the listed websites per state contained within. State-controlled websites' URL may change or be removed - We recommend Google Search for the actual URL for state guidelines.

LITIGATION: This publication or any part within may not be used for litigation purposes.

SUNRISE/SUNSET CHART: Data retrieved from U. S. Naval Observatory, Washington, DC
ADVERTISING: All sponsors have submitted their information for advertising. Pilot Cars Today is not responsible for qualifications, rates or specials declared within any sponsor's ad.

Published by Freda Barber Booth
Printed by ClearSpace.com

FOCUS ON THE ROAD, NOT WHAT'S ABOVE IT.

Whether you're plotting a route or worrying about hazards and delays, transporting oversized loads can be stressful. But Kenco Bucket Trucks' high standards, certifications and well-equipped purple trucks make travel a snap. We make the safety of your cargo and personnel our highest priority. Plus we can assist with planning the route so there are no surprises, only smooth driving.

We ensure that when you choose HIGH LOADS, we give you OPEN ROADS.

KENCO MEANS:
- IMSA Work Zone Safety Certified
- IMSA Traffic Signal Technician Level I & II
- DISA Drug & Alcohol Tested Employees
- Professionalism, safety and reliability

TAKE A LOAD OFF. 1.877.459.3100 | HIGHLOADS.COM

FEATURED PILOT CAR COMPANY OF THE OVERLOAD COMPANION 2017

INDEX

INFORMATION AT YOUR FINGERTIPS

FIND YOUR NEXT CERTIFIED PILOT CAR/ESCORT - BEGINNING ON PAGE 117!

PAGE / SECTION BEGINS	PG
STATE - FEDERAL DOT CONTACT INFORMATION	8
TWIC INFORMATION	11
SAFETY EQUIPMENT LIST & MORE INFORMATION	12
FLAGGING / SIGNAGE REQUIREMENTS BY STATE	13
SAFE & EFFECTIVE FLAGGING	14
ROAD CONDITIONS PHONE DIRECTORY	18
STATE HWY EMERGENCY PHONE NUMBERS	19
RAILROAD EMERGENCY PHONE DIRECTORY	20
US REST AREAS BY STATE / HIGHWAYS	21
INVOICE FACTORING	36
STATE PROVISIONS PAGES	39
PILOT CAR COMPANIES	119
US TRUCKSTOPS	235
SUNRISE / SUNSET CHARTS BY STATE	293
CALENDAR	359
FORMS TO COPY / USE	371
RECORD KEEPING FOR PILOT CARS	380

THE OVERLOAD COMPANION 2017 © FREDA BARBER BOOTH

Need My Services? Pay Up!
By Freda Barber Booth

When a company or driver agrees to transport a permitted load, they have to make decisions based on their equipment on hand, time & costs involved. Additional fees may include normal costs as well as some surprise expenses - such as:
- State permits
- Route Surveys
- Law Enforcement Escorts
- Privately-Owned Pilot Car Escorts
- DOT fines
- Truck/Trailer Maintenance/Repairs
- Power-line Lifting or Removal Assistance
- Load Weighing (Scales)

Each and every above-mentioned service provider normally requires payment by Comcheck or Credit Card immediately before or after the service is performed - except one! Most of the time, privately-owned escorts are left out of the immediate payment category; and may be promised to be paid at a later date. Yet, privately owned escorts are the only companies listed above trying to continue business with the least running capital.

Why are they consistently broke? Escorts have their money tied up in expenses they haven't been paid for - and won't be for 30-60 days. Having one outstanding $500 invoice doesn't hurt the average pilot car escort's business much; but having 10 or more unpaid invoices will put them out of business - or stop them from working.

"Independent O/O" and "leased-on" drivers have been quite verbal about their "I'm not making any money on this run" excuses as they belittle an escort over his/her rates. Don't worry, Driver, We've heard your sorrowful stories. If you can't make money on that load, why did you agree to take it in the first place - knowing you were going to incur fees transporting it? And if you didn't know about all the fees, you didn't do your homework before agreeing to take the job.

In modern times, pilot car escorts are being held to a higher standard with more insurance liability and modern highly-equipped vehicles than ever before; but yet, companies, drivers and pilot-car brokers who contract them don't want to pay for that level of service, equipment and insurance the pilot car escort has to carry in order to meet that liability requirement. *News Flash!* The pilot car escort isn't a step-child to be stepped on. They help keep the load out of the grass, muck and traffic entanglements. They work hard to keep the public out of the spokes - and hopefully, keep everyone out of the grave.

Yes, pilot car escorts have lost their vehicles and/or lives protecting a load. So, what is that level of responsibility worth to you? Most likely, a lot less than what they're asking for. $1.50/mi to $1.70/mi is a fair rate nationwide for a standard lead/chase escort - no matter what's being paid at the pump. If you're needing a high pole operator or steering person? $1.75/mi to $2.25/mi is a fair rate while that escort is performing that particular specialty. Drivers & brokers telling a pilot car operator on the phone that you "can hire someone else" at a much lower rate" isn't a professional negotiating tactic. I would seriously question your business ethics. Negotiating is one method, belittling is another. Imagine being the one you're talking to!

Few pilot car brokers are fair in taking a small percentage for their services; and fewer pay the pilot car escort within days of finishing the job. Many pilot car brokers wait to pay the pilot car escort until after they've been paid; and zero if they don't get paid. *Another News Flash:* The contract is between the broker and the pilot car escort - a third party payment should never be added to the mix - and legally, it doesn't play well with a judge. It's never the pilot car escort's fault if the broker can't get their payment from the hauling company or driver. Maybe the broker should've asked for a deposit first - especially if they have no credit history with that hauling company or driver.

So, now you have the information you need to hire the best and most professional pilot car escorts in the industry. When they ask for a fair rate, you have every right to question their specialty skills, certifications, experience, equipment and the vehicle they will use in their job performance; but questioning their rate of pay based on your own theory or profit margin isn't the way to conduct good business. If you want it cheap, there are cheap pilot escorts out there with less than professional knowledge, experience, insurance and equipment to do the job. You better be careful of those. They can tell you anything to get hired - then when you get tangled up, you'll know what kind of muck you got yourself into.

Either way, company owners, drivers & brokers, you should pull out that credit card or Comchek and pay the bill! Let that pilot car escort continue onto their next job; to be available for another as he/she was available for you.

Freda Barber Booth is the owner and creator of The Overload Companion series. She holds 14 yrs in the industry. Her pilot-escorting, marketing, designing & publishing skills have helped to create this book.

SPONSOR AD

DEPARTMENT OF TRANSPORTATION CONTACT INFORMATION (STATE / FEDERAL)

IOWA
DEPARTMENT OF TRANSPORTATION
OFFICE OF MOTOR CARRIER SVCS
P.O. BOX 10382
DES MOINES, IA 50306-0382
PERMITS 515-237-3264

MOTOR FUEL TAX ADMIN / PERMITS

KANSAS
KANSAS TRUCKING CONNECTION
1500 SW ARROWHEAD
TOPEKA, KS 66614
785-271-3145 (OPTION 2)

TALLAHASSEE, FL 32303-5750

KENTUCKY
DEPARTMENT OF TRANSPORTATION
DIV OF MOTOR CARRIERS
200 METRO ST
FRANKFORT, KY 40622
502-564-7150 / FAX 502-564-0992

ATLANTA, GA 30316

LOUISIANA
DEPARTMENT OF TRANSPORTATION
1201 CAPITOL ACCESS RD
BATON ROUGE, LA 70802-4438
PERMITS OFFICE
225-343-2345 / 1-800-654-1433
WEIGHT ENFORCEMENT
225-377-7100
LOUISIANA TRUCK CENTER
225-925-4322 / 1-888-421-8757

DEPARTMENT OF TRANSPORTATION

MAINE
DEPT OF SECRETARY OF STATE
BMV - MOTOR CARRIER SVCS
29 HOUSE STATION - 101 HOSPITAL ST.
AUGUSTA, ME 04333-0029
207-624-9318 / FAX 207-622-5332

CDOT PERMIT OFFICE

MARYLAND
HAULING PERMIT UNIT
7491 CONNELLEY DR
HANOVER, MD 21076
1-800-846-6435 / 1-800-543-4564

MASSACHUSETTS
HIGHWAY TRUCKING PERMITS OFFICE
14 BEACH ST
MILFORD, MA 01757
508-473-4755

2150 South 1300 East, Ste. #100
Salt Lake City, UT 84106
801-488-0085 / FAX 801-463-6683
charley@cayias.com   www.cayias.com

We Insure Pilot Cars!

THE OVERLOAD COMPANION 2017 © FREDA BARBER BOOTH

DEPARTMENT OF TRANSPORTATION CONTACT INFORMATION (STATE / FEDERAL)

MICHIGAN
DEPARTMENT OF TRANSPORTATION
TRANSPORTS PERMITS UNIT
7050 W. SAGINAW, STE #2
LANSING, MI 48917
517-373-2120

MINNESOTA
DEPARTMENT OF TRANSPORTATION
OSOW PERMIT SECTION
395 JOHN IRELAND BLVD
ST PAUL, MN 55125
651-405-6000 / FAX 651-215-9677

MISSISSIPPI
DEPARTMENT OF TRANSPORTATION
PO BOX 1850
JACKSON, MS 39215
1-888-737-0061 / 601-359-1717
FAX 601-359-1709

MISSOURI
DEPARTMENT OF TRANSPORTATION
2211 ST MARY'S BLVD
PO BOX 1787
JEFFERSON CITY, MO 65109
1-888-275-6636 / 573-751-2551

MONTANA
DEPARTMENT OF TRANSPORTATION
MOTOR CARRIER SERVICES DIV
PO BOX 4639
HELENA, MT 59604-4639
406-444-6130 / FAX 406-444-7670

NEBRASKA
STATE DEPT OF ROADS - PERMITS
PO BOX 94759   LINCOLN, NE
402-471-0034
TWX/TELEX 402-479-3906
FAX 402-479-3907

NEVADA
DEPARTMENT OF TRANSPORTATION
1263 S STEWART ST
CARSON CITY, NV 89712
1-800-552-2127 / 775-888-7410
CLARK CO (LAS VEGAS) PERMITS
702-455-6100
AMBER LIGHT / HAZ-MAT PERMITS
775-684-4622

NEW JERSEY
DEPARTMENT OF TRANSPORTATION
PO BX 600
TRENTON, NJ 08625
609-530-6089 / FAX 609-633-9393

NEW HAMPSHIRE
DEPARTMENT OF TRANSPORTATION
ROOM 190, JOM BLDG
7 HAZEN DR
CONCORD, NH 03302
603-271-3734 / FAX 603-271-3914

NEW MEXICO
DEPARTMENT OF TRANSPORTATION
1120 CERRILLOS RD
SANTA FE, NM 87504-1149
505-827-5100
OSOW PERMITS
505-827-0376 / FAX 505-827-0384

NEW YORK
DEPARTMENT OF TRANSPORTATION
50 WOLF RD, 1ST FLOOR
ALBANY, NY 12232
1-888-783-1685

NORTH CAROLINA
DEPARTMENT OF TRANSPORTATION
OSOW PERMITS
(BY MAIL) 1568 MAIL SERVICE CTR
RALEIGH, NC 27699-1568
(DELIVERY) 1425 ROCK QUARRY RD
SUITES 109, 110
RALEIGH, NC 27610
SINGLE TRIP PERMIT - 919-733-7154
ANNUAL / SUPERLOAD 919-733-4740
FAX 919-733-7828 / 919-733-7921

NORTH DAKOTA
HIGHWAY PATROL HEADQUARTERS
600 EAST BLVD AVE - DEPT 504
BISMARCK, ND 58505
701-328-2455 / FAX 701-328-1717

OREGON
MOTOR CARRIER TRANSPORTATION DIV
OVER-DIMENSIONAL PERMIT UNIT
550 CAPITOL ST NE
SALEM, OR 97301
503-373-0000
WALK-IN SVC

PENNSYLVANIA
DEPARTMENT OF TRANSPORTATION
BUREAU OF MAINTENANCE & OPERATIONS
PO BOX 8210
HARRISBURG, PA 17105-8210
HAULING, SUPER & APRAS
717-787-7269 / 717-787-8645
HIGHWAY & BRIDGE OCCUPANCY
717-787-5368 / 717-705-1433

RHODE ISLAND
DIVISION OF MOTOR VEHICLES
286 MAIN ST
PAWTUCKET, RI 02860
401-588-3020
R.I. TURNPIKE & BRIDGE AUTHORITY
PO BOX 437
JAMESTOWN, RI 02835-0437
PERMITS 401-588-3011
401-423-0800 / FAX 401-423-0830

SOUTH CAROLINA
DEPARTMENT OF TRANSPORTATION
OSOW PERMIT OFFICE
1412 SHOP RD
COLUMBIA, SC 29201
BY MAIL: OSOW PERMIT OFFICE
PO BOX 191
COLUMBIA, SC 29202

SOUTH DAKOTA
HIGHWAY PATROL - MOTOR CARRIER SVCS
118 WEST CAPITOL AVE
PIERRE, SD 57501-2000
605-773-4578

TENNESSEE
DEPARTMENT OF TRANSPORTATION
COMMERCIAL VEHICLE DIVISION
1148 FOSTER AVE - COOPER HALL
NASHVILLE, TN 37210

TEXAS
DEPARTMENT OF TRANSPORTATION
125 EAST 11TH ST
AUSTIN, TX 78701-2483
512-486-5052 / FAX 512-486-5007

UTAH
DEPARTMENT OF TRANSPORTATION
4501 SOUTH 2700 WEST
PO BOX 141200
SALT LAKE CITY, UT 84114-1200
801-965-4000 / FAX 801-965-4936

THE OVERLOAD COMPANION 2017 © FREDA BARBER BOOTH

DEPARTMENT OF TRANSPORTATION CONTACT INFORMATION (STATE / FEDERAL)

UTAH
DEPARTMENT OF TRANSPORTATION
4501 SOUTH 2700 WEST
PO BOX 141200
SALT LAKE CITY, UT 84114-1200
801-965-4000 / FAX 801-965-4936

UTAH
DEPARTMENT OF TRANSPORTATION
4501 SOUTH 2700 WEST
PO BOX 141200
SALT LAKE CITY, UT 84114-1200
801-965-4000 / FAX 801-965-4936

WISCONSIN
DEPARTMENT OF TRANSPORTATION
MOTOR CARRIER SVCS
PO BOX 7980
MADISON, WI 53707-7980
608-266-7320 / FAX 608-264-7751

VERMONT
DEPARTMENT OF TRANSPORTATION
120 STATE STREET
MONTPELIER, VT 05603-0001
802-828-2064 / 802-828-5418

VERMONT
DEPARTMENT OF TRANSPORTATION
120 STATE STREET
MONTPELIER, VT 05603-0001
802-828-2064 / 802-828-5418

WYOMING
DEPARTMENT OF TRANSPORTATION
5300 BISHOP BLVD
CHEYENNE, WY
82009-3340
307-777-4735 / FAX 307-777-4289

VIRGINIA
DEPARTMENT OF MOTOR VEHICLES
MOTOR CARRIER SVCS
PO BOX 27412
RICHMOND, VA 23269
866-878-2582 / FAX 804-367-1073

VIRGINIA
DEPARTMENT OF MOTOR VEHICLES
MOTOR CARRIER SVCS
PO BOX 27412
RICHMOND, VA 23269
866-878-2582 / FAX 804-367-1073

FEDERAL TRANSPORTATION AGENCIES

FEDERAL MOTOR CARRIER SAFETY ADMINISTRATION (FMCSA)
1200 NEW JERSEY AVE S.E.
WASHINGTON, DC 20590
855-368-4200

FEDERAL HIGHWAY ADMINISTRATION (FHWA)
1200 NEW JERSEY AVE S.E.
202-366-4000

HOMELAND SECURITY
TRANSPORTATION SECURITY ADMINISTRATION
601 S 12TH STREET
ARLINGTON, VA 20598

NATIONAL TRANSPORTATION SAFETY BOARD HEADQUARTERS (NTSB)
1200 NEW JERSEY AVE. S.E.
WASHINGTON, DC 20590
202-314-6000

THE OVERLOAD COMPANION 2017 © FREDA BARBER BOOTH

TWIC®
(Transportation Worker Identification Credential)

Taken in part from the TSA website - for information purposes only - Refer to website for more information and links.

http://www.tsa.gov/stakeholders/transportation-worker-identification-credential-twic%C2%AE

Security Programs

A vital security measure that will ensure individuals who pose a threat do not gain unescorted access to secure areas of the nation's maritime transportation system.

TWIC enrollment centers have transitioned to a new enrollment provider as part of the TSA Universal Enrollment Services (UES) initiative. **https://universalenroll.dhs.gov/locator** for logistical information for enrollment centers (e.g., location updates, hours of operation).

Certified/cashier's checks, company checks, and money order payments for all services should be made out to "MorphoTrust USA". Personal checks are NOT accepted.

https://universalenroll.dhs.gov/faq - to get information about mobile and enroll your own services.

If you hold a TWIC that expires on or before December 31, 2014 and you are a U.S. citizen or U.S. national you will be able to replace your expiring TWIC with a 3-year Extended Expiration Date (EED) TWIC. To order an EED TWIC or a card replacement, you may contact the UES Call Center at 1-855-DHS-UES1 (1-855-347-8371) Monday through Friday from 8 AM - 10 PM Eastern. **(service.govdelivery.com)**

Transportation Workers

If you need further information, please contact the UES Call Center at 1-855-DHS-UES1 (1-855-347-8371) Monday through Friday from 8 AM - 10 PM Eastern.

- Site addresses, hours of operation, and directions
- Required Documentation for US Citizens
- Required Documentation for Non-US Citizens
- Renewal TWICs
- Check the status of your card and schedule a pickup
- Disqualifying offenses, appeals, and waivers
- Card technology and durability

Employers, Unions, and Facility Owner/Operators

If you have questions regarding TWIC enforcement and policy guidance, please contact the USCG Help Desk at **1-877-MTSA-AID (1-877-687-2243 - option #1)** or at **uscg-twic-helpdesk@uscg.mil.**

Note: Owners/operators/FSOs/VSOs/CSOs are encouraged to seek guidance directly from their local Captain of the Port TWIC action officer.

BASIC SAFETY EQUIPMENT & INFORMATION FOR PILOT CAR OPERATORS

RECOMMENDED SAFETY EQUIPMENT
(Check state requirements)

- Orange hard hat (original paint only)
- (2) Orange safety vest (Class 2 & Class 3)
- (2) 18"-24" STOP/SLOW paddle
- (9) Reflective triangles
- (8) Burn-style flares
- Flashlight w/minimum 1.5" lens (extra batteries)
- 6-in minimum traffic wand
- Gloves (Reflective / Safety Green / Safety Orange)
- (2) 10 lb. Fire Extinguishers
- (3) 18 in. orange cones w/ reflector
- (3) 36 in. orange cones w/ reflector (Florida)
- (4) 18-24 in. red/orange grommet flags
- (4) 18-24 in. red/orange flagstick
- (2) 18x72 Oversize Load signs
- 10" x 60" OVERSIZE LOAD sign Roof Mount - Viewed from front and rear
- (2) 10" x 60" OVERSIZE LOAD signs Bumper Mount
- 40 channel handheld CB radio *w/ backup*
- Emergency First Aid kit
- Reflective (Safety orange/green) Gloves

HEIGHT POLE EQUIPMENT / USAGE REQUIREMENTS

- Fiberglas pole - capable of withstanding high winds when extended.
- Must be attached securely to FRONT of vehicle.
- Video/Audio recording device is recommended.
- Height Measuring stick strongly recommended.
- Height pole to be set 6" above tallest point on load.
- Measure & check condition of Height Pole before use each day.

STEERING REQUIREMENTS

- Check state requirements for laws regarding who is eligible to operate a steering device in load movement.
- Some states require operator to hold a current Class A CDL license.
- Some states require operator to be separate from escort driver.
- Be certain your liability insurance covers steering before performing this duty.

Officially Recognized Defensive Driving Course
National Safety Council
8–HOUR Defensive Driving Course 8/6 (DDC 8/6)

INSURANCE
(Check state requirements)

Minimum of $1million Auto (Required)
$1M Business Liability (Recommended)
$1M Insurance for Flagging / Duties outside of vehicle
Pennsylvania - additional insured

Carrier companies & brokers may require to be listed as additionally insured on pilot car and contracted driver policies

Policy Declaration Sheet must state for "Pilot Car" duties

VEHICLE - EQUIPMENT - REQUIREMENTS

- Windshield free of large cracks/heavy pitting
- All-weather tires w/good tread
- Proper fuel and oil levels maintained
- Current state registration & inspections
- Commercial tags *(if required in your state)*
- Lights, horn, blinkers, brakes functioning properly
- *extra bulbs, fluids, etc.*
- Full-size Spare tire w/jack

CERTIFICATION REQUIRED

STATE	RECIPROCAL
ALABAMA	YES
ARIZONA	YES
COLORADO	YES
FLORIDA	YES
GEORGIA	YES
MINNESOTA	YES
OKLAHOMA	YES
NEVADA	YES
NEW YORK	NO
NORTH CAROLINA	YES
PENNSYLVANIA SUPERLOAD - SPECIAL	NO
UTAH	YES
VIRGINIA	YES
WASHINGTON	YES

VEHICLE INSPECTION SHEETS
New Mexico
Louisiana ($10 - Non-Res)
Utah

Florida - Scale Checklist
(Single Trip ONLY)

Amber Light Permits - Annual
Georgia - $2
Nevada - $2

NOTICE

Although we at pilotcarstoday.com work hard to keep up with current regulations within the industry; sometimes we may overlook something.

All those working with permitted loads are responsible for following STATE-issued papers and regulations.

This book is designed to give you a "heads up"
- but it's not the final word!

Please send updates or inquiries to:
fredabooth101@gmail.com

THE OVERLOAD COMPANION 2017 © FREDA BARBER BOOTH

FLAGGING - SIGNAGE REQUIREMENTS BY STATE

STATE	TRUCK SIGN	TRUCK FLAG	ESCORT SIGN	ESCORT FLAG	STATE	TRUCK SIGN	TRUCK FLAG	ESCORT SIGN	ESCORT FLAG
AK	12" x 48"	16"	12" x 48"	Not Stated	MT	8" Letters	Not Stated	8" Letters	Not Stated
AL	18" x 84"	18"	18" x 84"	18"	NC	18" x 84"	18"	10" Letters	18"
AR	10" Letters	18"	10" Letters	18"	ND	12" x 60"	12"	12" x 60"	Not Stated
AZ	12" x 72"	12"	12" x 60"	12"	NE	18" x 84"	18"	12" x 60"	18"
CA	10" Letters	16"	440 sq. in.	16"	NH	18" x 84"	12"	12" x 60"	Not Stated
CO	10" x 60"	12"	10" x 60"	12"	NJ	12" X 72"	18"	12" x 72"	18"
CT	18" x 84"	18"	8" Letters	18"	NM	12" x 60"	12"	12" x 60"	12"
DE	18" x 84"	18"	12" x 60"	18"	NV	10" Letters	18"	10" Letters	18"
FL	18" x 84"	18"	18" x 84"	18"	NY	18" x 84"	18"	12" x 60"	18"
GA	12" x 72"	18"	12" x 72"	18"	OH	18" x 84"	18"	12" x 60"	Not Stated
HI	12" x 72"	24"	12" x 72"	Not Stated	OK	14" x 60"	18"	10" x 60"	12"
IA	18" x 84"	18"	18" x 84"	18"	OR	18" x 84"	18"	10" x 60"	18"
ID	18" x 84"	18"	10" x 60"	Not Stated	PA	18" x 84"	18"	12" x 60"	Not Stated
IL	18" x 84"	18"	12" x 60"	Not Stated	RI	18" x 84"	18"	12" x 60"	Not Stated
IN	18" x 72"	18"	18" x 72"	18"	SC	12" Letters	12"	Not Stated	Not Stated
KS	18" x 84"	12"	12" x 60"	Not Stated	SD	18" x 84"	18"	12" Letters	12"
KY	18" x 72"	18"	18" x 72"	Not Stated	TN	18" x 84"	18"	10" Letters	18"
LA	18" x 84"	18"	18" x 84"	18"	TX	Not Stated	12"	12" x 60"	12"
MA	18" x 84"	12"	Not Stated	24"	UT	18" x 84"	18"	10" x 60"	Not Stated
MD	18" x 84"	18"	12" x 60"	Not Stated	VA	8" Letters	18"	8" Letters	18"
ME	18" x 84"	18"	12" x 60"	Not Stated	VT	18" x 84"	18"	12" x 60"	Not Stated
MI	18" x 84"	18"	12" x 60"	18"	WA	18" x 84"	18"	10" x 60"	12"
MN	18" x 72"	18"	12" x 60"	Not Stated	WI	18" x 84"	18"	12" x 60"	Not Stated
MO	18" x 84"	18"	12" x 60"	18"	WV	NS	18"	12" x 60"	18"
MS	18" x 84"	18"	Not Stated	Not Stated	WY	10" x 60"	12"	10" x 60"	12"

OVERSIZE LOAD

THE OVERLOAD COMPANION 2017 © FREDA BARBER BOOTH

DETAILED INSTRUCTIONS FOR SAFE & EFFECTIVE FLAGGING

As a flagger, you have a very important job. It should be carried out with authority and dignity, using proper flagging techniques. Your driver and the motoring public are relying on you to safely control traffic.

- You must have good sight, hearing, mobility, and physical stamina.
- You must be alert and able to react quickly in a dangerous situation to warn your co-workers and keep yourself safe.
- You must have the personal presence and people skills to gain respect and motorist compliance.
- You must have been properly trained in flagging procedures and they have become second nature to you

The Basic Functions
- To guide traffic safely around your load
- To protect the lives of traveling motorists as well as each other
- To avoid unreasonable delays to motorists.
- To answer questions courteously.

Equipment/ Clothing:
- 18" or 24" STOP/SLOW Paddle mounted on 5' Pole
- 2-Way Radio
- Reflective Gloves/ Flashlight or Traffic Wand
- Highway-Safety-Colored Hard Hat
- Reflective Safety Vest
- Durable reflective wear (recommended)
- Steel-Toed Boots
- No attire that could distract motorists.

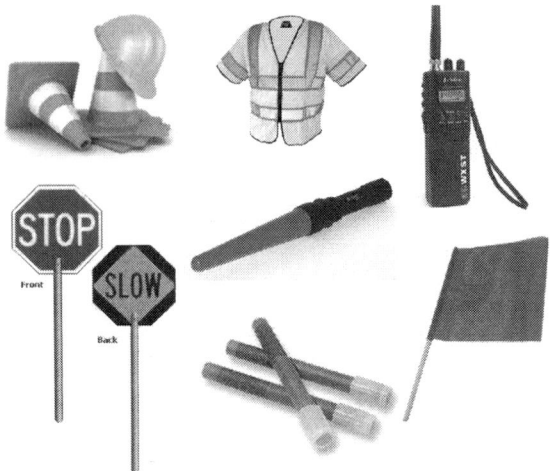

!•! NOTE: Windy conditions - Long hair / loose clothing can create visibility/miscommunication issues!
Flags should only be used in emergency situations. Experience has shown that it is very difficult to direct motorists by waving a flag.
HELPFUL HINT: Putting a rubber-band around a rolled up flag can create a high-visibility wand (daytime use only)

Flaggers
- Using a flagger at each end of the congested area to control traffic is the most common operation.
- One flagger should be designated lead flagger to coordinate the operation.
- Begin with both flaggers displaying STOP to approaching traffic.
- The lead flagger decides which direction to release first.
- Communication between flaggers is critical and can be maintained by:
- Visual contact Flaggers must be close enough to read each other's STOP/SLOW paddles and see each other's "all clear" signals.
- Use signals that can not be mistaken for flagging signals.
- Lifting the hat or raising and lowering the STOP/SLOW paddle are proper "all clear" signals.
- Two-way radio is the best means of communication, even when there is visual contact.

Position on Roadway
- You should stand on the shoulder adjacent to the traffic being controlled and be clearly visible to traffic.
- You should stand alone and never allow others to gather around you.
- Normally, after you have stopped the first vehicle, you will remain on the shoulder.
- If additional vehicles arrive and they cannot clearly see your paddle, you may walk toward the center of the
- road so they can.
- Stay at least 2 to 3 feet away from the centerline. Remember to watch out for traffic that may be coming from behind you.
* Never stand in the path of or turn your back on traffic. Always plan and maintain an escape path.

Single Flagger
For low volume situations (no more than three vehicles passing through the site in a five-minute period) and short traffic disruption areas on straight roads, a single flagger may sometimes be used to control traffic.
- The flagger must be visible to both directions of traffic.
- Standing on the shoulder opposite the work area, the flagger directs traffic with the STOP/SLOW paddle.
- When visibility is poor, or when one flagger cannot control traffic, use two flaggers. (Escort, truck driver or law enforcement)

Continued next page

SAFE & EFFECTIVE FLAGGING (CONT'D)

Hills and Curves
Never take a position over the crest of a hill or around a sharp curve.
When flagging near a hill or curve, take a position in advance of the hill or curve.
Law enforcement may be required for long-term back-up
Make sure you are visible to approaching traffic.

Stopping Traffic
- Stand in a safe position on the shoulder facing traffic.
- Hold the paddle away from your body and placed on or near the edge of the travel lane with the STOP sign facing traffic.
- Raise your free hand above shoulder height with the palm facing the approaching vehicle and make eye contact with the driver.
- Change to the STOP only if an approaching vehicle has plenty of distance to gradually stop.
- Avoid screeching halts.

Walking into the Road
- After you have stopped the first vehicle, you will usually remain on the shoulder of the road in your normal flagging location.
- If additional vehicles arrive and they cannot clearly see your STOP paddle, then you may walk out toward the center of the roadway.
- Do not cross the centerline. Stay at least 2 to 3 feet away from the centerline and remember to watch out for traffic that may be coming from behind you.
- To prepare to release traffic, move back to your normal position on the shoulder with the paddle remaining on STOP.

Releasing Traffic – Closed Lane
- Stand on the shoulder of the closed lane with your paddle turned to STOP facing traffic.
- Wait for an "all clear" signal from the other flagger.
- Once the "all clear" is received, turn the paddle to SLOW and with your free arm, signal drivers to proceed into the open lane.
- Be direct and clear with your hand signal. Point to the vehicle and then to the open lane

Releasing Traffic – Open lane
- Stand on the shoulder of the open lane with your paddle turned to STOP
- Wait for the "all clear" signal from the other flagger.
- Once the "all clear" is received, take a step or two back from the edge of the traffic lane and turn the paddle to SLOW.
- With your free arm, signal drivers to proceed in the open lane.
- Be direct and clear with your hand signal.
- Point to the vehicle and then to the open lane.
- After traffic clears, turn your paddle to STOP before returning to the shoulder position.

Slowing Traffic
- Stand on the shoulder facing traffic.
- With the SLOW sign turned toward traffic, you may slowly raise and lower your free arm with the palm facing down in front of your paddle.

Continued next page

SAFE & EFFECTIVE FLAGGING (CONT'D)

"All Clear" Signal
- When two or more flaggers are used, they must be able to communicate with one another.
- Two-way radios are necessary since waving a flag will only confuse drivers - confusion causes accidents
- Visual contact with the second flagger is always the preferred method

Flag Transfer - to signal "Last Vehicle to pass through Obstruction".
The driver of the last vehicle in the movement can be given a flag and instructed to give it to the flagger at the other end. This route should be one mile or less. DO NOT ALLOW A LATE VEHICLE TO TRY TO CATCH UP after the flag has been handed off!

Relay flagging
When distance/hill/curve inhibits radio or visual communication, a relay flagger should be positioned to be seen/heard by both of the other flaggers and relays the signals between flaggers. Cell phone communication can be useful if absolutely necessary, but signal-loss could create bigger problems and delays.

Night Flagging
Night flagging procedures are generally the same as daytime except for some necessary changes:
- Reflective STOP/SLOW paddles shall be used.
- ANSI CLASS 3 apparel should be used - offers more reflection / visibility.
- A flashlight with red glow-cone SHOULD be used to provide additional guidance to motorists
- Flares should be used in areas that allow them - battery-operated flares may be useful too

Procedure for Night Flagging
- To stop vehicles, stand on the shoulder and face traffic with the stop sign in the right hand and flashlight with red glow-cone in the left hand.
- Slowly wave the flashlight back and forth in front of your body.
- Don't let the arc extend beyond the base of the paddle staff.
- To release traffic, point from the driver to the open lane with the flashlight and hold in that position.
- Do not wave the flashlight when releasing traffic—this may confuse the driver

One-direction Control
- When loads occasionally block one lane of a two-lane, two-way road, such as when loading or unloading, a flagger can control just one direction of traffic. The other direction of traffic is not stopped.
- Stop traffic in the usual manner, and release the vehicles when the lane has been cleared.
- When releasing traffic, turn the paddle a quarter-turn so that the word STOP faces you. This way, the STOP message will not confuse the traffic coming from either direction.

Using Flags
Flags may be used to control traffic during emergency situations until STOP/SLOW paddles can be obtained.
- Use of hand movements without flag or paddle are prohibited except for law enforcement personnel or first responders.
- When used, flags shall be at least 24 inches square, of red or fluorescent orange/red material, and be attached to a staff approximately 36" long.
- The free edge of the flag should be weighted so the flag will hang vertically, even in heavy winds.
- To stop traffic, stand on the shoulder of the road and extend the flag across the traffic lane.
- Raise your free hand to the stop position.
- To release traffic, lower the flag to your side and with your free arm motion traffic to proceed.

DO NOT use the flag to motion traffic through

- To alert and slow traffic, extend the flag staff and slowly move your free hand up and down in a sweeping motion between shoulder height and straight down.
- Replace flags with STOP/SLOW paddles as soon as possible.

Continued next page

SAFE & EFFECTIVE FLAGGING (CONT'D)

The Do's of Flagging
- Stay alert at all times.
- Do Use clear and distinct hand signals when directing traffic.
- Do Stand on the shoulder of the road out of the path of oncoming traffic.
- Do Treat motorists courteously.
- Do Use proper equipment and warning signs.
- Do Wear proper clothing and shoes.
- Do Stand alone to be visible.
- Do Plan an escape route.
- Do Consult with driver and other escorts about flagging positions Before movement

The Don'ts of Flagging
- Don't Stand in an open lane.
- Don't Make unnecessary conversation with workers, pedestrians, or motorists.
- Don't Give flagging directions against a traffic signal.
- Don't Stand in the shade, over the crest of a hill, or around a sharp curve.
- Don't Sit down or flag from inside your vehicle.
- Don't Leave your station until someone takes your place.
- Don't Leave flagger signs in place when not flagging.
- Don't talk on a cellphone or text while on duty.
- Don't Stand near load
- Don't Stand with a group of people.
- Don't Stand next to a bridge railing, barrier, or wall.
- Don't Turn your back on traffic.

NATIONAL ROAD CONDITIONS
PHONE NUMBERS

Alabama (334) 242-4378

Alaska (907) 273-6037

Arizona (888) 411-7623

Arkansas (501) 569-2374

California (916) 445-7623

Colorado (303) 639-1111

Connecticut (800) 443-6817

Delaware (302) 739-4313

Florida (800) 749-7453

Georgia (404) 635-6800

Idaho (208) 336-6600

Illinois (800) 452-4368

Indiana (800) 261-7623

Iowa (800) 288-1047

Kansas (800) 585-7623

Kentucky (866) 737-3767

Louisiana (504) 379-1541

Maine (207) 287-3427

Maryland (800) 327-3125

Massachusetts (617) 374-1234

Michigan (800) 411-4823

Minnesota (800) 542-0220

Mississippi (601) 987-1212

Missouri (800) 222-6400

Montana (800) 226-7623

Nebraska (402) 479-4512

Nevada
- South (702) 486-3116
- Northwest (702) 793-1313
- Northeast (702) 738-8888

New Hampshire (603) 271-6900

New Jersey
- Turnpike (732) 247-0900
- Garden State Parkway (732) 727-5929

New Mexico (800) 432-4269

New York (800) 847-8929 (NY Thruway)

North Carolina (919) 549-5100 Ext. 7623

North Dakota (701) 328-7623

Ohio (614) 466-7170

Oklahoma (405) 425-2385

Oregon (503) 588-2941

Pennsylvania (814) 355-6044

Rhode Island (401) 277-2468

South Carolina (803) 896-9621

South Dakota (605) 367-5707

Tennessee (800) 858-6349

Texas (800) 452-9292

Utah (801) 964-6000

Vermont (802) 828-2648

Virginia (800) 367-7623

Washington (800) 695-7623

West Virginia (877) 982-7623

Wisconsin (866) 511-9472

Wyoming (307) 772-0824

STATE HIGHWAY EMERGENCY PHONE NUMBERS

Alabama	*47
Alaska	911
Arizona	911
Arkansas	*55
California	911
Colorado	*CSP (*277) or *DUI (384)
Connecticut	911
Delaware	911
Florida	*FHP (*347)
Georgia	*GSP (*477)
Idaho	*ISP (*477)
Illinois	*999
Indiana	911
Iowa	800-555-HELP (4357)
Kansas	911
• Salina, KS	*HP (*47)
• KTA or Wichita, KS	*KTA (*482)
Kentucky	911
Louisiana	*LHP (*547)
• Lake Ponchartrain	*27
Maine	*SP (*77)
Maryland	#SP (#77)
Massachusetts	
• In Area Code 413	*MSP (*677)
• Other Area Codes	*SP (*77)
Michigan	911
Minnesota	911
Mississippi	*HP (*47)
Missouri	*55
Montana	911
Nebraska	*55
Nevada	*NHP (*647)
New Hampshire	*SP (*77)
New Jersey	#77
New Mexico	911
New York	911
North Carolina	*HP (*47)
North Dakota	911
Ohio HP	800-525-5555
•Report erratic driving	800-GRAB-DUI
Oklahoma	*55
Oregon	911
Pennsylvania	*11
Rhode Island	*77
South Carolina	*HP (*47)
South Dakota	911
Tennessee	*THP (*847)
Texas	*DPS (*377)
Utah	*11
Vermont	911 or *DWI (*394)
Virginia	911
Washington	911
West Virginia	*SP (*77)
Wisconsin	911
Wyoming	Cell #HELP (4357)

WHEN IN DOUBT

EMERGENCY	911
OPERATOR ASST	"0" (ZERO)
LOCAL 411	411
NON-LOCAL 411	(AC) + 555-1212

THE OVERLOAD COMPANION 2017 © FREDA BARBER BOOTH

Railroad Emergency Phone Numbers

Call the local police or 911
if you cannot locate
the railroad emergency phone number at the site.

Be sure to specify that a vehicle is on the tracks!

Use these phone numbers
to report a vehicle stalled
or hung up on tracks - or a signal malfunction.

Provide:
Location
Crossing number (if posted)
Name of the road or highway that crosses the tracks.

Amtrak	1-800-331-0008
BNSF Railway	1-800-832-5452
CSX	1-800-232-0144
Canadian National	1-800-465-9239
Canadian Pacific	1-800-716-9132
Kansas City Southern	1-877-527-9464 or 1-800-892-6295
Norfolk Southern	1-800-453-2530
Union Pacific	1-888-877-7267

REST AREA LOCATIONS OF THE U.S.

REST AREAS BY STATE

ALABAMA

HIGHWAY	MM	DIRECTION
I-10	1.5	WB
I-10	65	EB
I-20/I-59	1	EB
I-20/I-59	38	EB/WB
I-20/I-59	84	EB/WB
I-59	165	NB
I-59	167	SB
I-59	240	SB
I-65	85	NB
I-65	89	SB
I-65	133	NB SB
I-65	213	NB SB
I-65	301	NB SB
I-65	364	SB
I-85	44	NB SB
I-85	78	SB
US-231	38	NB SB

ARIZONA

HIGHWAY	MM	DIRECTION
I-8	56	EB WB
I-8	84	EB WB
I-8	150	EB WB
I-10	4	EB WB
I-10	52	EB WB
I-10	86	EB WB
I-10	181	EB
I-10	183	WB
I-10	320	EB WB
I-10	388	EB WB
I-17	252	NB SB
I-17	297	NB SB
I-17	312	SB
I-19	54	NB SB
I-40	23	EB WB
I-40	155	WB
I-40	181	EB WB
I-40	235	EB WB
I-40	359	EB WB

ARKANSAS

HIGHWAY	MM	DIRECTION
I-30	7	EB
I-30	56	EB WB
I-30	13	EB WB

ARKANSAS (CONT'D)

HIGHWAY	MM	DIRECTION
I-30	92	EB WB
I-40	2	EB
I-40	36	EB WB
I-40	67	EB
I-40	72	WB
I-40	133	EB WB
I-40	199	EB WB
I-40	235	EB
I-40	243	WB
I-40	274	WB
I-55	35	SB
I-55	45	NB
I-55	68	SB
US-167	8	SB

CALIFORNIA

HIGHWAY	MM	DIRECTION
I-5	54A	NB SB
I-5	60	NB SB
I-5	105B	NB SB
I-5	206	NB SB
I-5	320	NB SB
I-5	386	NB SB
I-5	445	NB SB
I-5	529	SB
I-5	557	NB SB
I-5	583	NB SB
I-5	608	NB SB
I-5	633	NB SB
I-5	656	NB SB
I-5	667	NB SB
I-5	694	NB
I-5	705	SB
I-5	753	NB SB
I-5	786	NB SB
I-8	24	WB TURNOUT
I-8	51	EB WB
I-8	75	EB TURNOUT
I-8	108	EB WB
I-8	155	EB WB
I-10	86	EB
I-10	91	WB
I-10	113	EB WB
I-10	159	EB WB
I-10	222	EB WB

CALIFORNIA (CONT'D)

HIGHWAY	MM	DIRECTION
I-15	178	NB SB
I-15	217	NB SB
I-15	270	NB SB
I-40	28	EB WB
I-40	106	EB WB
I-80	143	EB WB
I-80	177	EB WB
I-280	36	NB
SR-36	LK ALMANOR	EB WB
SR-44	BOGARD	EB WB
SR-44	SHINGLETOWN	EB WB
SR-46	SHANDON	EB WB
SR-58	BORON	EB WB
SR-70	MASSACK	EB WB
SR-70	LT DAVIS	WB
SR-99	RAINE	NB SB
SR-99	WARLOW	NB
SR-99	CHRISTOFFERSON	NB SB
SR-299	HILLCREST	EB WB
SR-299	MATHEWS	EB WB
SR-299	LEE	EB
US-97	NA	NB SB
US-101	GRASS LAKE	NB
	GAVIOTA	SB
	CAMP ROBERTS	NB SB
	TRINIDAD	NB SB
	H DANA BOWER	NB
	EMPIRE CAMP	NB
	IRVINE LODGE	NB
	MOSS COVE	SB
US-199	COLLIER TUNNEL	NB SB
US-395	COSO JCT	NB SB
US-395	DIVISION CRK	NB SB
US-395	CRESTVIEW	NB SB
US-395	HONEY LAKE	NB SB
US-395	SECRET VALLEY	NB SB

COLORADO

HIGHWAY	MM	DIRECTION
I-25	1	NB
I-25	13B	NB SB
I-25	18	NB SB
I-25	74	NB SB
I-25	112	SB
I-25	115	NB

THE OVERLOAD COMPANION 2017 © FREDA BARBER BOOTH

REST AREAS BY STATE

COLORADO (CONT'D)

HIGHWAY	MM	DIRECTION
I-25	266	NB SB
I-25	434	NB SB
I-70	50	EB TURNOUT
I-70	90	EB WB
I-70	108	EB TURNOUT
I-70	115	EB
I-70	119	EB WB
I-70	121	EB WB
I-70	129	EB WB
I-70	163	EB WB
I-70	190	EB WB
I-70	213	EB TURNOUT
I-70	226	EB TURNOUT
I-70	306	EB WB
I-70	332	WB
I-70	383	EB WB
I-70	437	WB
I-76	66A	EB WB
I-76	125	EB WB
I-76	180	EB WB
CO-139	56	NB SB
US-40	101	EB WB
US-50	389	EB WB
US-50	467	EB WB
US-160	46	EB WB
US-160	191	EB WB
US-287	383	NB SB

CONNECTICUT

HIGHWAY	MM	DIRECTION
I-84	2	EB
I-84	42	EB
I-84	85	EB WB
I-91	15	SB
I-91	22	NB
I-95	9	SB
I-95	12	NB
I-95	23	NB SB
I-95	41	NB SB
I-95	53	NB SB
I-95	66	NB SB
I-95	74	NB
I-95	106	SB
I-395	8	SB
I-395	35	NB SB
CT-15	(5) 1 EVERY 11 MILES	

DELAWARE

HIGHWAY	MM	DIRECTION
I-95	5	NB SB

FLORIDA

HIGHWAY	MM	DIRECTION
I-4	46	EB WB
I-4	94	WB
I-4	96	EB
I-10	4	EB
I-10	29	EB WB
I-10	58	EB
I-10	61	WB
I-10	96	EB WB
I-10	133	EB WB
I-10	133	EB WB
I-10	162	EB WB
I-10	194	EB WB
I-10	233	EB WB
I-10	265	EB WB
I-10	294	EB
I-10	295	WB
I-10	318	EB WB
I-75	34	NB SB
I-75	63	NB SB
I-75	131	NB SB
I-75	238	NB SB
I-75	278	NB SB
I-75	307	NB
I-75	308	SB
I-75	345	NB
I-75	346	SB
I-75	382	SB
I-75	383	NB
I-75	413	NB SB
I-95	106	NB
I-95	107	SB
I-95	133	NB SB
I-95	168	NB
I-95	169	SB
I-95	225	NB
I-95	227	SB
I-95	302	NB
I-95	303	SB
I-95	331	NB
I-95	378	SB
I-275	7	NB SB

FLORIDA (CONT'D)

HIGHWAY	MM	DIRECTION
I-275	13	NB SB
US-27	0	NB SB
US-231	0	NB SB
FL TURNPIKE	19	NB SB
FL TURNPIKE	65	NB SB
FL TURNPIKE	94	NB SB
FL TURNPIKE	144	NB SB
FL TURNPIKE	184	NB SB
FL TURNPIKE	229	NB SB
FL TURNPIKE	263	NB SB
FL TURNPIKE	299	NB SB

GEORGIA

HIGHWAY	MM	DIRECTION
I-16	44	EB
I-16	46	WB
I-20	1	EB
I-20	103	EB
I-20	108	WB
I-20	181	EB WB
I-20	201	WB
I-75	3	NB
I-75	46	NB
I-75	76	SB
I-75	85	NB
I-75	107	NB
I-75	118	SB
I-75	179	SB
I-75	308	NB
I-75	319	SB
I-75	352	SB
I-85	1	NB
I-85	176	SB
I-95	1	NB
I-95	41	SB
I-95	111	SB
I-185	12	NB SB
I-475	7	NB

IDAHO

HIGHWAY	MM	DIRECTION
I-15	7	NB
I-15	25	SB
I-15	47	NB SB
IDAHO CONTINUED NEXT PAGE		

THE OVERLOAD COMPANION 2017 © FREDA BARBER BOOTH

REST AREAS BY STATE

IDAHO (CONT'D)

HIGHWAY	MM	DIRECTION
I-15	101	NB SB
I-15	167	NB SB
I-84	1	EB
I-84	62	EB WB
I-84	133	EB WB
I-84	171	EB
I-84	229	EB WB
I-84	269	EB WB
I-86	19	EB
I-86	31	WB
I-90	8	EB WB
US-12	28	EB WB
US-12	174	EB WB
US-20	178	EB WB
US-20	265	EB WB
US-26	265	EB WB
US-26	357	EB WB
US-30	184	EB WB
US-93	351	NB SB
US-95	101	NB SB
US-95	189	NB SB
US-95	371	NB SB
ID-75	178	NB SB

ILLINOIS

HIGHWAY	MM	DIRECTION
I-24	37	EB WB
I-39	85	NB SB
I-55	27	NB SB
I-55	64	NB SB
I-55	102	NB
I-55	104	SB
I-55	149	NB SB
I-55	194	NB SB
I-57	32	NB SB
I-57	74	NB
I-57	79	SB
I-57	114	NB SB
I-57	165	NB SB
I-57	222	NB SB
I-57	268	NB SB
I-57	333	NB SB
I-64	25	EB WB
I-64	82	EB
I-64	85	WB

ILLINOIS (CONT'D)

HIGHWAY	MM	DIRECTION
I-64	130	WB
I-70	27	EB WB
I-70	86	EB WB
I-70	149	WB
I-72	152	EB WB
I-74	28	EB
I-74	30	WB
I-74	62	EB WB
I-74	114	EB WB
I-74	156	EB WB
I-74	208	WB
I-80	1	EB
I-80	51	EB WB
I-80	117	EB
I-80	119	WB
I-80	160	EB WB
I-88	93	EB WB
I-90	2	EB
I-90	24	EB WB
I-90	74	EB WB
I-94	18	EB WB
I-294	1	NB SB
I-294	25	NB SB
I-294	38	NB SB

INDIANA

HIGHWAY	MM	DIRECTION
I-64	7	EB
I-64	58	EB WB
I-64	115	WB
I-65	22	NB SB
I-65	73	NB SB
I-65	148	NB
I-65	150	SB
I-65	196	NB SB
I-65	231	NB SB
I-69	251	NB SB
I-69	325	NB
I-69	345	SB
I-70	1	EB
I-70	65	EB WB
I-70	107	EB WB
I-70	143	WB
I-70	156	EB WB
I-74	1	EB

INDIANA (CONT'D)

HIGHWAY	MM	DIRECTION
I-74	57	EB WB
I-74	152	EB WB
I-80	22	EB WB
I-80	37	EB WB
I-80	56	EB WB
I-80	90	EB WB
I-80	108	EB WB
I-80	126	EB WB
I-90	56	EB WB
I-90	90	EB WB
I-94	43	WB
IN-TURNPIKE	22	EB WB
IN-TURNPIKE	37	EB WB
IN-TURNPIKE	56	EB WB
IN-TURNPIKE	90	EB WB
IN-TURNPIKE	108	EB WB
IN-TURNPIKE	126	EB WB

IOWA

HIGHWAY	MM	DIRECTION
I-29	38	NB SB
I-29	79	NB SB
I-29	91	NB SB
I-29	110	NB SB
I-29	132	NB
I-29	139	NB SB
I-35	7	NB SB
I-35	31	SB
I-35	33	NB SB
I-35	51	SB
I-35	53	NB
I-35	100	NB SB
I-35	105	NB
I-35	119	SB
I-35	120	NB SB
I-35	159	NB SB
I-35	196	NB SB
I-35	212	NB
I-35	214	NB SB
I-80	19	EB WB
I-80	32	EB WB
I-80	44	EB
I-80	80	WB
I-80	81	EB
I-80	147	EB WB

THE OVERLOAD COMPANION 2017 © FREDA BARBER BOOTH

REST AREAS BY STATE

IOWA (CONT'D)

HIGHWAY	MM	DIRECTION
I-80	180	EB WB
I-80	208	EB WB
I-80	237	EB WB
I-80	268	EB WB
I-80	270	EB WB
I-80	300	EB WB
I-380	13	NB SB
I-680	15	WB
I-680	16	EB

KANSAS

HIGHWAY	MM	DIRECTION
I-35	26	NB SB
I-35	65	NB SB
I-35	98	NB SB
I-35	175	NB SB
I-70	7	EB WB
I-70	48	EB WB
I-70	97	EB WB
I-70	132	EB WB
I-70	187	EB WB
I-70	224	EB WB
I-70	265	EB WB
I-70	294	EB WB
I-70	310	EB WB
I-70	336	EB WB
I-135	23	NB SB
I-135	68	NB SB
I-335	132	NB SB
I-70 / TRNPK	188	EB WB
I-70 / TRNPK	209	EB WB
I-70 / TRNPK	414	EB WB
KS-TURNPIKE	26	NB SB
KS-TURNPIKE	65	NB SB
KS-TURNPIKE	98	NB SB
KS-TURNPIKE	132	NB SB

KENTUCKY

HIGHWAY	MM	DIRECTION
I-24	7	EB WB
I-64	28	EB
I-64	60	EB WB
I-64	98	EB
I-64	108	WB
I-64	140	EB WB

KENTUCKY (CONT'D)

HIGHWAY	MM	DIRECTION
I-64	174	EB WB
I-65	0	NB
I-65	59	NB SB
I-65	113	SB
I-71	13	NB SB
I-71	176	NB SB
I-75	1	NB
I-75	127	NB SB
I-75	176	NB SB

LOUISIANA

HIGHWAY	MM	DIRECTION
I-10	1	EB
I-10	121	EB WB
I-10	270	WB
I-20	3	EB
I-20	95	EB
I-20	97	WB
I-20	184	WB
I-49	34	NB SB
I-49	94	NB SB

MAINE

HIGHWAY	MM	DIRECTION
I-95	3	NB
I-95	25	NB SB
I-95	59	NB SB
I-95	103	NB SB
I-95	175	NB
I-95	179	SB
I-95	199	NB SB
I-95	243	NB SB
I-95	302	NB SB
I-295	17	NB SB
I-295	51	NB SB

MARYLAND

HIGHWAY	MM	DIRECTION
I-68	6	EB
I-68	74	EB WB
I-70	39	EB WB
I-95	37	NB SB
I-95	81	NB SB
I-95	96	NB SB

MASSACHUSETTS

HIGHWAY	MM	DIRECTION
I-84	1	EB
I-84	4	WB
I-90	8	EB WB
I-90	29	EB WB
I-90	55	EB WB
I-90	80	EB
I-90	84	WB
I-90	104	WB
I-90	114	WB
I-90	117	EB
I-91	18	NB SB
I-91	34	NB SB
I-91	54	NB SB
I-95	2	NB
I-95	10	NB SB
I-95	16	SB
I-95	38	SB
I-95	46	NB
I-95	77	NB SB
I-95	90	SB
I-195	2	NB SB
I-495	11	NB SB
I-495	87	NB SB
I-495	110	NB
I-495	114	SB
MA-TURNPIKE	8	EB WB
MA-TURNPIKE	29	EB WB
MA-TURNPIKE	55	EB WB
MA-TURNPIKE	80	EB
MA-TURNPIKE	84	WB
MA-TURNPIKE	104	WB
MA-TURNPIKE	117	

MICHIGAN

HIGHWAY	MM	DIRECTION
I-69	6	NB
I-69	68	NB
I-69	40	SB
I-69	101	SB
I-69	126	NB
I-69	161	NB
I-69	174	SB
I-75	10	NB
I-75	94	SB

MICHIGAN CONTINUED NEXT PAGE

THE OVERLOAD COMPANION 2017 © FREDA BARBER BOOTH

25

REST AREAS BY STATE

MICHIGAN

HIGHWAY	MM	DIRECTION
I-75	96	NB
I-75	129	NB
I-75	130	SB
I-75	158	SB
I-75	175	NB
I-75	202	SB
I-75	210	NB
I-75	235	SB
I-75	252	NB
I-75	262	SB
I-75	277	NB
I-75	287	SB
I-75	317	NB
I-75	328	SB
I-75	338	NB SB
I-75	344	NB
I-75	348	SB
I-75	389	NB
I-75	394	NB SB
I-94	0	EB
I-94	42	WB
I-94	85	WB
I-94	96	EB
I-94	113	WB
I-94	135	EB
I-94	149	WB
I-94	161	EB
I-94	188	WB
I-94	250	WB
I-94	255	EB
I-96	8	WB
I-96	25	EB
I-96	63	EB
I-96	79	WB
I-96	87	EB
I-96	111	WB
I-96	135	EB
I-196	28	NB
I-196	43	SB
I-196	58	NB
I-275	4	SB
I-275	23	NB
US-2	39	EB WB
US-23	7	NB
US-23	48	SB

MICHIGAN (CONT'D)

HIGHWAY	MM	DIRECTION
US-23	82	NB
US-31	124	SB
US-31	135	NB
US-31	147	SB
US-31	163	NB
US-127	0	NB
US-127	89	SB
US-127	121	NB
US-127	160	NB SB
US-127	187	NB
US-131	43	SB
US-131	99	SB
US-131	122	NB
US-131	136	SB
US-131	169	SB
US-131	174	NB

MINNESOTA

HIGHWAY	MM	DIRECTION
I-90	250	NB SB
I-35	226	NB
I-35	208	SB
I-35	198	NB
I-35	154	NB
I-35	131	SB
I-35	75	SB
I-35	68	NB
I-35	35	NB SB
I-35	1	NB
I-90	0	EB
I-90	24	EB
I-90	25	WB
I-90	69	EB
I-90	72	WB
I-90	119	EB WB
I-90	162	EB
I-90	171	WB
I-90	202	EB
I-90	222	WB
I-90	224	EB
I-90	275	WB
I-94	2	EB
I-94	69	WB
I-94	100	EB
I-94	105	WB

MINNESOTA

HIGHWAY	MM	DIRECTION
I-94	152	EB WB
I-94	178	WB
I-94	187	EB
I-94	215	EB
I-94	256	WB
US-2	12	EB WB
US-2	59	EB WB
US-2	77	EB WB
US-2	131	EB WB
US-2	221	EB WB
US-10	55	EB WB
US-10	181	EB WB
US-10	218	EB WB
US-12	109	EB WB
US-53	20	NB SB
US-53	50	NB SB
US-53	109	NB SB
US-59	5	EB WB
US-59	256	NB SB
US-61	78	NB SB
US-61	4	WB
US-71	259	NB SB
US-169	80	NB SB
US-169	203	NB SB
US-169	246	NB SB
MN-60	5	EB WB
MN-60	74	EB WB
MN-61	18	NB SB
MN-61	39	NB SB
MN-61	59	NB SB
MN-61	79	NB SB
MN-61	104	NB SB
MN-61	146	NB SB
MN-61	148	NB SB
MN-95	101	NB SB
MN-210	173	NB SB
MN-371	20	NB SB

MISSISSIPPI

HIGHWAY	MM	DIRECTION
I-10	2	EB WB
I-10	63	EB WB
I-10	75	WB
I-20	1	EB WB
I-20	6	EB

REST AREAS BY STATE

MISSISSIPPI

HIGHWAY	MM	DIRECTION
I-20	75	WB
I-20	90	EB
I-20	164	WB
I-55	3	NB
I-55	54	NB SB
I-55	163	NB
I-55	173	SB
I-55	202	NB
I-55	204	SB
I-55	240	NB SB
I-55	276	NB
I-55	279	SB
I-59	3	NB
I-59	56	NB SB
I-59	106	NB
I-59	110	SB
I-59	164	SB

MISSOURI

HIGHWAY	MM	DIRECTION
I-29	24	SB
I-29	27	NB SB
I-29	108	SB
I-35	34	NB SB
I-35	81	NB SB
I-35	22	SB
I-35	112	SB
I-44	2	EB WB
I-44	52	EB WB
I-44	89	EB
I-44	110	EB WB
I-44	177	EB WB
I-44	235	EB WB
I-55	2	NB SB
I-55	21	NB
I-55	41	NB SB
I-55	110	NB SB
I-55	160	NB
I-57	18	NB
I-70	35	EB WB
I-70	57	EB WB
I-70	104	EB WB
I-70	168	EB WB
I-70	169	WB
I-70	198	EB WB
I-270	34	EB WB

MONTANA

HIGHWAY	MM	DIRECTION
I-15	108	NB SB
I-15	177	NB
I-15	178	SB
I-15	239	NB SB
I-15	318	NB SB
I-15	397	NB SB
I-90	4	EB WB
I-90	58	EB WB
I-90	72	EB WB
I-90	143	EB WB
I-90	167	WB
I-90	169	EB
I-90	208	EB WB
I-90	305	EB WB
I-90	380	EB
I-90	418	EB WB
I-90	475	WB
I-90	476	EB
I-94	38	EB
I-94	41	WB
I-94	64	EB WB
I-94	112	WB
I-94	113	EB
I-94	192	EB WB
I-94	242	EB WB
US-2	17	EB WB
US-2	255	EB WB
US-2	321	EB WB
US-2	527	EB WB
US-2	645	EB WB
US-12	0	EB WB
US-12	101	EB WB
US-87	71	EB WB
US-89	23	NB SB
US-89	76	NB SB
US-93	0	NB SB
US-93	17	NB SB
US-212	49	NB SB
US-212	84	NB SB
US-212	81	EB WB
US-287	0	NB SB
US-287	16	NB SB
US-287	49	NB SB
US-310	29	NB SB
MT-1	1	EB WB

MONTANA (CONT'D)

HIGHWAY	MM	DIRECTION
MT-5	42	EB WB
MT-41	42	NB SB
MT-200	32	EB WB
MT-200	158	EB WB
MT-200	248	EB WB

NEBRASKA

HIGHWAY	MM	DIRECTION
I-80	51	EB
I-80	61	WB
I-80	124	EB
I-80	132	WB
I-80	159	EB WB
I-80	193	WB
I-80	194	EB
I-80	226	EB
I-80	227	WB
I-80	269	EB
I-80	270	WB
I-80	314	EB
I-80	316	WB
I-80	350	EB
I-80	355	WB
I-80	375	WB
I-80	381	EB
I-80	425	EB
I-80	431	WB

NEW HAMPSHIRE

HIGHWAY	MM	DIRECTION
I-89	26	SB
I-89	40	NB
I-89	57	SB
I-93	1	NB
I-93	31	NB SB
I-93	51	NB
I-93	61	SB
I-93	125	NB SB
I-95	0	NB
NH TURNPIKE	31	NB

THE OVERLOAD COMPANION 2017 © FREDA BARBER BOOTH

REST AREAS BY STATE

NEW JERSEY

HIGHWAY	MM	DIRECTION
I-80	1	EB WB
I-80	7	EB
I-80	21	EB WB
I-80	32	EB WB
I-287	32	NB
I-295	3	NB
I-295	58	NB SB
NJ GS PKY	18	NB SB
NJ GS PKY	41	NB SB
NJ GS PKY	76	NB SB
NJ GS PKY	100	NB SB
NJ GS PKY	124	NB SB
NJ GS PKY	133	NB SB
NJ GS PKY	142	NB
NJ GS PKY	153	NB SB
NJ GS PKY	171	NB SB
NJ TURNPIKE	5	NB SB
NJ TURNPIKE	30	SB
NJ TURNPIKE	39	N
NJ TURNPIKE	58	NB SB
NJ TURNPIKE	78	N
NJ TURNPIKE	92	NB SB
NJ TURNPIKE	111	SB
NJ TURNPIKE	116	NB SB

NEW MEXICO

HIGHWAY	MM	DIRECTION
I-10	20	EB WB
I-10	54	EB
I-10	61	WB
I-10	111	WB
I-10	120	EB
I-10	135	EB
I-10	164	WB
I-25	23	NB SB
I-25	114	NB SB
I-25	167	NB SB
I-25	268	NB
I-25	376	NB SB
I-25	435	NB SB
I-40	3	EB
I-40	102	EB WB
I-40	207	EB WB
I-40	251	EB WB
I-40	302	EB WB

NEW MEXICO (CONT'D)

HIGHWAY	MM	DIRECTION
I-40	373	WB
US-64	242	EB WB
US-64	392	EB WB
US-82	143	EB WB
US-180	141	EB WB
US-285	150	NB SB
US-380	196	EB WB

NEW YORK

HIGHWAY	MM	DIRECTION
I-81	2	NB
I-81	33	SB
I-81	60	NB
I-81	101	SB
I-81	133	NB SB
I-81	147	SB
I-81	151	NB
I-81	159	NB SB
I-81	162	NB
I-81	166	SB
I-81	174	NB
I-81	177	SB
I-84	3	EB WB
I-84	17	EB
I-84	24	WB
I-84	55	EB WB
I-86	22	EB
I-86	38	WB
I-86	39	EB
I-86	72	WB
I-86	101	EB
I-86	147	WB
I-86	160	EB
I-86	167	WB
I-86	212	EB
I-86	222	WB
I-86	295	WB
I-86	313	EB
I-87	13	NB SB
I-87	33	NB SB
I-87	43	NB SB
I-87	83	NB SB
I-87	99	NB SB
I-87	123	NB SB
I-87	127	NB SB

NEW YORK (CONT'D)

HIGHWAY	MM	DIRECTION
I-87	162	NB SB
I-88	39	EB
I-88	40	WB
I-88	74	EB
I-88	79	WB
I-90	153	EB
I-90	168	WB
I-90	172	EB
I-90	184	EB WB
I-90	210	EB WB
I-90	227	WB
I-90	244	EB
I-90	250	EB
I-90	256	WB
I-90	266	WB
I-90	280	EB
I-90	292	WB
I-90	310	EB
I-90	318	WB
I-90	324	WB
I-90	350	WB
I-90	353	EB
I-90	366	EB
I-90	376	WB
I-90	397	EB
I-90	412	WB
I-90	443	EB WB
I-90	447	EB WB
I-390	38	NB SB
I-684	16	SB
I-684	25	NB

NORTH CAROLINA

HIGHWAY	MM	DIRECTION
I-26	6	EB
I-26	41	EB WB
I-26	68	WB
I-40	10	EB WB
I-40	82	EB WB
I-40	136	EB WB
I-40	139	EB WB
I-40	177	EB WB
I-40	324	EB WB
I-40	364	EB WB
I-74	60	NB SB

THE OVERLOAD COMPANION 2017 © FREDA BARBER BOOTH

REST AREAS BY STATE

NORTH CAROLINA

HIGHWAY	MM	DIRECTION
I-77	1	NB
I-77	39	NB SB
I-77	63	SB
I-77	72	NB
I-77	105	SB
I-85	2	NB
I-85	59	NB SB
I-85	99	NB SB
I-85	139	NB SB
I-85	199	NB SB
I-95	5	NB
I-95	48	NB SB
I-95	99	NB SB
I-95	142	NB SB
I-95	181	SB

NORTH DAKOTA

HIGHWAY	MM	DIRECTION
I-29	99	NB SB
I-29	178	NB SB
I-94	1	EB WB
I-94	32	EB WB
I-94	119	EB WB
I-94	168	WB
I-94	169	EB
I-94	221	EB
I-94	223	WB
I-94	254	WB
I-94	255	EB
I-94	304	EB WB
I-94	327	EB
I-94	337	WB
US-2	73	EB WB
US-2	168	EB WB
US-2	221	EB WB
US-2	277	EB WB
US-2	330	EB WB
US-52	208	EB WB
US-83	128	NB SB
US-281	39	NB SB
US-281	224	NB SB
ND-30	102	EB WB

OHIO

HIGHWAY	MM	DIRECTION
I-70	2	EB WB
I-70	70	EB WB
I-70	130	EB WB
I-70	163	WB
I-70	190	EB
I-70	210	EB WB
I-71	33	NB SB
I-71	67	NB SB
I-71	127	NB
I-71	129	SB
I-71	149	NB SB
I-71	179	NB SB
I-71	224	NB SB
I-75	27	NB SB
I-75	80	NB SB
I-75	114	NB SB
I-75	153	NB SB
I-75	179	NB SB
I-76	45	EB WB
I-77	3	NB
I-77	37	SB
I-77	39	NB
I-77	140	SB
I-77	141	NB
I-80	21	EB WB
I-80	77	EB WB
I-80	100	EB WB
I-80	139	EB WB
I-80	170	EB WB
I-80	197	EB WB
I-80	235	WB
I-90	198	EB WB
I-90	217	WB
I-271	7	NB SB
US-23	16	SB
US-23	73	SB
US-23	130	NB SB
US-23	161	NB
US-23	164	SB
US-30	9	EB WB
US-30	42	EB
US-30	43	WB
US-30	131	EB WB
US-33	30	EB WB
US-33	65	EB WB

OHIO (CONT'D)

HIGHWAY	MM	DIRECTION
US-33	98	EB WB
US-33	165	EB WB
US-33	215	EB WB
US-35	131	WB
US-35	163	EB WB
US-50	165	WB
US-50	197	EB
OH-2	114	WB
OH-2	141	EB WB
OH-7	47	EB WB
OH-7	197	EB WB
OH-7	230	EB WB
OH-11	73	SB
OH-32	34	EB WB
OH-32	71	EB WB
OH TURNPIKE	21	EB WB
OH TURNPIKE	77	EB WB
OH TURNPIKE	100	EB WB
OH TURNPIKE	139	EB WB
OH TURNPIKE	170	EB WB
OH TURNPIKE	197	EB WB
OH TURNPIKE	237	EB WB

OKLAHOMA

HIGHWAY	MM	DIRECTION
I-35	4	NB
I-35	46	NB SB
I-35	49	NB SB
I-35	59	NB SB
I-35	137	NB SB
I-35	171	NB
I-35	172	SB
I-35	195	NB SB
I-35	207	NB SB
I-35	225	SB
I-40	9	EB WB
I-40	110	EB
I-40	157	EB WB
I-40	197	EB WB
I-40	251	EB WB
I-40	283	EB WB
I-40	314	WB
I-40	316	EB

CONT'D NEXT PAGE

THE OVERLOAD COMPANION 2017 © FREDA BARBER BOOTH

REST AREAS BY STATE

OKLAHOMA (CONT'D)

HIGHWAY	MM	DIRECTION
I-44	20	EB WB
I-44	85	EB WB
I-44	157	WB
I-44	167	EB
I-44	178	EB WB
I-44	207	WB
I-44	288	EB WB
I-44	313	WB

OREGON

HIGHWAY	MM	DIRECTION
I-5	19	NB SB
I-5	22	SB
I-5	45	NB SB
I-5	62	NB SB
I-5	99	NB SB
I-5	142	NB SB
I-5	178	NB SB
I-5	206	NB SB
I-5	240	NB SB
I-5	281	NB SB
I-82	1	EB WB
I-84	65	WB
I-84	72	EB WB
I-84	160	EB WB
I-84	177	WB
I-84	186	EB WB
I-84	228	EB WB
I-84	252	EB WB
I-84	269	EB WB
I-84	295	EB WB
I-84	335	EB WB
I-84	374	EB WB
US-20	31	EB WB
US-20	42	EB WB
US-20	114	EB WB
US-20	155	EB WB
US-26	28	EB WB
US-26	48	EB WB
US-26	54	EB WB
US-26	155	EB WB
US-30	74	EB WB
US-97	68	NB SB
US-97	112	NB SB
US-97	206	NB SB

OREGON (CONT'D)

HIGHWAY	MM	DIRECTION
US-97	224	NB SB
US-97	282	NB SB
US-101	0	NB SB
US-101	28	NB SB
US-101	71	NB SB
US-101	97	NB SB
US-101	126	NB SB
US-101	153	NB SB
US-101	176	NB SB
US-101	220	NB SB
US-101	319	NB SB
US-101	355	NB SB
US-395	38	NB SB
US-395	50	NB SB
US-395	93	NB SB
US-395	126	NB SB
OR-99W	104	NB SB
OR-18	9	EB WB
OR-22	34	EB WB
OR-31	69	NB SB
OR-36	38	EB WB
OR-58	36	EB WB
OR-62	29	NB SB
OR-66	19	NB SB
OR-126	29	EB WB
OR-126	50	EB WB
OR-126	107	EB WB
OR-140	83	EB WB
OR-203	8	EB WB
OR-244	39	EB WB
OR-245	2	NB SB

PENNSYLVANIA

HIGHWAY	MM	DIRECTION
I-70	5	EB
I-70	77	WB
I-70	112	EB WB
I-70	147	EB WB
I-70	156	EB
I-70	171	WB
I-76	49	EB
I-76	77	WB
I-76	112	EB WB
I-76	147	EB WB
I-70	156	EB

PENNSYLVANIA (CONT'D)

HIGHWAY	MM	DIRECTION
I-70	171	WB
I-76	49	EB
I-76	77	WB
I-76	112	EB WB
I-76	147	EB WB
I-76	172	EB WB
I-76	202	WB
I-76	219	EB
I-76	249	EB
I-76	258	WB
I-76	289	EB
I-76	304	WB
I-76	324	EB
I-78	76	WB
I-79	5	NB
I-79	50	NB SB
I-79	108	NB
I-79	110	SB
I-79	135	NB SB
I-79	163	NB SB
I-80	1	EB
I-80	30	EB
I-80	31	WB
I-80	88	EB WB
I-80	146	EB WB
I-80	194	EB WB
I-80	219	EB
I-80	220	WB
I-80	246	EB WB
I-80	270	EB
I-80	295	EB
I-80	310	WB
I-81	1	NB
I-81	38	NB
I-81	39	SB
I-81	80	NB SB
I-81	157	NB
I-81	158	SB
I-81	203	NB
I-81	208	SB
I-81	232	SB
I-83	2	NB
I-84	26	EB WB
I-84	53	WB
CONTINUED NEXT PAGE		

THE OVERLOAD COMPANION 2017 © FREDA BARBER BOOTH

REST AREAS BY STATE

PENNSYLVANIA (CONT'D)

HIGHWAY	MM	DIRECTION
I-90	2	EB
I-90	46	WB
I-95	1	NB
I-276	328	WB
I-476	55	NB SB
I-476	86	NB SB

RHODE ISLAND

HIGHWAY	MM	DIRECTION
I-295	19	NB

SOUTH CAROLINA

HIGHWAY	MM	DIRECTION
I-20	0	EB
I-20	93	EB WB
I-26	3	EB
I-26	63	EB WB
I-26	123	EB WB
I-26	150	EB
I-26	152	WB
I-26	204	EB
I-77	65	NB SB
I-77	89	SB
I-85	0	NB
I-85	17	NB
I-85	24	SB
I-85	103	SB
I-95	4	NB
I-95	17	NB SB
I-95	47	NB SB
I-95	99	NB SB
I-95	139	NB SB
I-95	195	SB
I-385	5	NB SB

SOUTH DAKOTA

HIGHWAY	MM	DIRECTION
I-29	26	NB SB
I-29	121	NB SB
I-29	160	NB
I-29	161	SB
I-29	213	NB SB
I-90	1	EB
I-90	41	EB WB
I-90	98	EB WB
I-90	165	EB
I-90	166	WB
I-90	218	EB
I-90	221	WB
I-90	264	EB WB
I-90	301	EB WB
I-90	362	EB WB
I-90	412	EB WB

Lead / Chase Certified / Insured
S&W Pilot Car Escort Service, LLC
419-705-3500

THE OVERLOAD COMPANION 2017 © FREDA BARBER BOOTH

REST AREAS BY STATE

TENNESSEE

HIGHWAY	MM	DIRECTION
I-24	1	EB
I-24	133	EB WB
I-24	160	EB WB
I-24	171	EB
I-26	5	EB WB
I-26	46	EB WB
I-40	73	EB WB
I-40	130	EB
I-40	131	WB
I-40	170	EB WB
I-40	267	EB WB
I-40	324	EB
I-40	326	WB
I-40	420	EB
I-40	425	WB
I-40	446	WB
I-55	3	NB
I-65	3	NB
I-65	24	NB
I-65	25	SB
I-65	121	SB
I-75	1	NB
I-75	45	NB SB
I-75	161	SB
I-81	2	SB
I-81	38	NB
I-81	41	SB
I-81	75	SB
I-155	8	EB

TEXAS

HIGHWAY	MM	DIRECTION
I-10	1	EB
I-10	50	EB
I-10	51	WB
I-10	98	EB
I-10	99	WB
I-10	144	EB WB
I-10	185	EB WB
I-10	233	EB WB
I-10	279	EB
I-10	308	EB WB
I-10	346	EB
I-10	394	EB WB

TEXAS (CONT'D)

HIGHWAY	MM	DIRECTION
I-10	423	EB WB
I-10	514	EB WB
I-10	619	WB
I-10	621	EB
I-10	692	EB WB
I-10	814	EB
I-10	815	WB
I-10	880	WB
I-20	69	EB WB
I-20	191	EB
I-20	204	WB
I-20	256	EB WB
I-20	296	EB WB
I-20	353	EB
I-20	358	EB WB
I-20	390	EB WB
I-20	634	WB
I-27	29	NB SB
I-30	143	EB WB
I-30	223	WB
I-35	18	NB SB
I-35	130	NB SB
I-35	281	NB
I-35	282	SB
I-35	362	NB SB
I-35	502	SB
I-37	78	NB
I-37	82	SB
I-40	76	EB
I-40	129	EB
I-40	131	WB
I-44	1	NB SB
I-45	124	NB
I-45	125	SB
I-45	216	NB SB

UTAH

HIGHWAY	MM	DIRECTION
I-15	45	NB SB
I-15	88	NB SB
I-15	135	NB SB
I-15	167	NB SB
I-15	261	NB SB
I-15	361	NB
I-15	369	SB

UTAH (CONT'D)

HIGHWAY	MM	DIRECTION
I-70	86	EB WB
I-70	102	EB WB
I-70	114	EB
I-70	120	EB WB
I-70	141	EB WB
I-70	180	EB
I-70	188	WB
I-70	227	WB
I-80	10	EB WB
I-80	54	EB
I-80	55	WB
I-80	171	EB WB
I-84	91	EB
I-84	94	WB
I-84	361	WB
I-84	369	EB

VERMONT

HIGHWAY	MM	DIRECTION
I-89	8	NB SB
I-89	32	SB
I-89	64	NB
I-89	65	SB
I-89	82	NB SB
I-89	95	NB SB
I-89	110	NB
I-89	111	SB
I-91	0	NB
I-91	2	SB
I-91	6	NB
I-91	22	NB SB
I-91	39	NB SB
I-91	68	SB
I-91	100	NB SB
I-91	114	NB
I-91	115	SB
I-91	141	SB
I-91	142	NB
I-91	167	NB SB
I-91	176	SB
I-93	1	NB

REST AREAS BY STATE

VIRGINIA		
HIGHWAY	MM	DIRECTION
I-64	2	EB
I-64	105	EB
I-64	113	WB
I-64	168	WB
I-64	169	EB
I-64	213	EB WB
I-66	48	EB WB
I-77	1	NB
I-77	59	NB
I-77	61	SB
I-81	1	NB
I-81	13	NB
I-81	53	SB
I-81	61	NB
I-81	108	NB SB
I-81	129	NB
I-81	158	SB
I-81	199	SB
I-81	232	NB SB
I-81	262	NB SB
I-81	320	SB
I-85	1	NB
I-85	32	NB SB
I-85	55	NB SB
I-95	1	NB
I-95	37	NB
I-95	107	NB SB
I-95	131	SB
I-95	154	NB SB
I-95	155	NB SB
VA-13	1	NB SB

WASHINGTON		
HIGHWAY	MM	DIRECTION
I-5	11	NB
I-5	12	SB
I-5	54	NB SB
I-5	90	NB
I-5	93	SB
I-5	140	NB
I-5	188	SB
I-5	207	NB SB
I-5	238	NB SB
I-5	267	NB
I-5	269	SB
I-82	22	WB
I-82	24	EB
I-82	80	EB WB
I-90	89	EB WB
I-90	125	EB WB
I-90	161	EB WB
I-90	198	EB WB
I-90	241	EB
I-90	242	WB
US-2	58	EB WB
US-2	81	EB WB
US-2	238	EB WB
US-12	126	EB WB
US-12	391	EB WB
US-12	413	EB WB
US-195	60	NB SB
US-395	66	NB SB
WA-7	17	NB SB
WA-8	2	EB
WA-14	73	EB WB

WASHINGTON (CONT'D)		
HIGHWAY	MM	DIRECTION
WA-17	89	NB SB
WA-21	106	NB SB
WA-24	43	EB WB
WA-26	66	EB WB
WA-26	118	EB WB
WA-28	25	EB WB
WA-401	1	NB SB
WA-504	33	EB WB
WA-906	1	EB WB

WEST VIRGINIA		
HIGHWAY	MM	DIRECTION
I-64	10	EB
I-64	35	EB WB
I-64	45	EB WB
I-64	69	EB
I-64	72	WB
I-64	179	WB
I-68	31	WB
I-77	9	NB SB
I-77	18	NB SB
I-77	45	NB SB
I-77	69	SB
I-77	72	NB
I-77	166	NB SB
I-77	185	NB SB
I-79	49	NB SB
I-79	85	NB SB
I-79	123	NB SB
I-79	159	SB
I-81	2	NB
I-81	25	SB
WV TURNPIKE	9	NB SB
WV TURNPIKE	18	NB SB
WV TURNPIKE	45	NB SB
WV TURNPIKE	69	SB
WV TURNPIKE	72	NB

pilotcarstoday.com

THE OVERLOAD COMPANION 2017 © FREDA BARBER BOOTH

REST AREAS BY STATE

WISCONSIN		
HIGHWAY	MM	DIRECTION
I-39	113	NB SB
I-39	117	NB
I-39	120	SB
I-39	168	SB
I-39	187	NB
I-43	31	NB
I-43	32	SB
I-43	168	NB SB
I-90	1	EB
I-90	20	EB
I-90	21	WB
I-90	74	EB
I-90	75	WB
I-90	113	EB WB
I-90	168	EB
I-90	187	WB
I-94	43	EB WB
I-94	74	EB
I-94	75	WB
I-94	113	EB WB
I-94	121	WB
I-94	261	EB
I-94	263	WB
I-94	347	EB WB
US-51	117	NB
US-51	120	SB
US-53	122	SB
US-53	125	NB
US-53	162	NB SB

WYOMING		
HIGHWAY	MM	DIRECTION
I-25	7	NB SB
I-25	54	NB SB
I-25	92	NB SB
I-25	126	NB SB
I-25	254	NB SB
I-80	6	EB WB
I-80	41	EB WB
I-80	144	EB WB
I-80	228	EB WB
I-80	267	EB WB
I-80	323	EB WB
I-80	401	EB WB
I-90	23	EB WB
I-90	88	EB WB
I-90	153	EB WB
I-90	189	EB WB
I-90	199	EB WB
US-14A	58	EB WB
US-14	206	EB WB
US-16	221	EB WB
US-18	39	EB WB
US-18	196	EB WB
US-20	53	EB WB
US-26	0	NB SB
US-26	18	EB WB
US-26	96	EB WB
US-85	54	NB SB
US-287	62	NB SB
WY-28	34	NB SB
WY-59	43	EB WB
WY-120	37	NB SB
WY-220	63	EB WB
WY-387	0	EB WB
WY-487	45	NB SB

THE OVERLOAD COMPANION 2017 © FREDA BARBER BOOTH

CALIFORNIA PILOT CAR ASSOCIATION

A California Non-Profit Corporation
P.O. BOX 110, BLOOMINGTON, CA 92316

708-443-4164

FOR MORE INFORMATION - *capilotcar@gmail.com*

**Call Us for All
Your Pilot Car/Escort needs**
Chase, High Pole, Route Survey

www.capilotcarassoc.com

FACTORING - IT'S EASY

1. SAME DAY FUNDING.
2. PLANS CREATED SPECIFICALLY FOR YOU AND YOUR BUSINESS.
3. SIMPLE RATES THAT ARE DISCUSSED UPFRONT - NO HIDDEN FEES.
4. BILLING AND COLLECTIONS ARE MANAGED FOR YOU.
5. FUEL ADVANCES TO KEEP YOU MOVING FORWARD.
6. FREE CREDIT CHECKS FOR PEACE OF MIND.
7. MOST OF ALL - FRIENDLY SERVICE TO OUR CLIENTS.

ABOUT US

Century Finance, LLC was formed in 2004 as a factoring company dedicated to the transportation industry. Our goal has always been to provide flexible and easy factoring programs tailor-made to freight bill factoring. When you choose Century Finance as your factoring partner, you are choosing a company that believes in principals.

Century Finance has customers from all over the United States. We provide our customers with multiple methods of payment, multiple ways to submit freight invoices and online tracking of your information.
We're not only your factor; we are your business partner.

PLEASE SUPPORT Pilotcarstoday.com!
Tell them FREDA BOOTH sent you!

FACTORING 101

What is factoring? In factoring, a business sells its receivables in the form of an invoice to the factor, who makes an advance of 70-98% of the purchase price of the receivable amount. The factor collects the full amount from the customer in due course and pays the balance amount due to the business owner after deducting his commission and other charges.

How does factoring differ from bank funding?

- Factors make funding decisions based on the credit-worthiness of your customers; a bank makes a credit decision based on your company's financial history, cash flow and collateral.

- Factoring is not a loan. No liability appears on your balance sheet.

- A factor makes funding decisions in days or hours – while a bank may take weeks or even months.

- A reliable factor will also provide a personal account executive to assess risk and manage your account and quality credit information to check credit on your customers.

Why would a company sell accounts receivable?
Companies that need cash now to meet immediate financial demands such as payroll and fuel expenses often can't afford to wait 30, 60, or even 90 days to get paid. Factoring helps provide this cash by funding the purchase of accounts receivable, often within 24 hours. CALL CENTURY FINANCE TODAY AT 888/684-7195 TO GET "THE 411" ON HOW OUR PROGRAMS WILL MAKE YOUR BUSINESS MORE PRODUCTIVE, PROFITABLE AND MORE SECURE

We factor invoices for Pilot Cars & Truck Drivers

Application NEXT 2 PAGES
Just copy or cut out - and send to us!

Fax: 870-336-3078
Email: alma@centuryfinance.com

THE OVERLOAD COMPANION 2017 © FREDA BARBER BOOTH

1723 Executive Sq • Jonesboro, Arkansas 72401
Tel: 888-684-7195 • Fax: 870-336-3078 /E-mail: alma@centuryfinance.com

Century Finance, LLC

Accounts Receivable Factoring Application

Business Name: _____

State of Incorporation (if incorporated) _____

Physical Street Address: _____
City: _____ State: _____ Zip: _____
Parish/County: _____
Mailing address: _____
_____

Length of time at address: _____
Previous Address if less than 5 Yrs. _____
Cell: (___) _____ Home: (___) _____ Fax: (___) _____
Email address: _____
Federal I.D. No.: _____ Motor Carrier No.: _____
How did you hear about us? **The Overload Assistant** Who referred you? **Freda Booth**

Owner & Officer Names and Social Security Numbers:
Title   First   Middle   Last   SS#
Owner _____
_____
_____

Please complete the above information and fax to 870-336-3078.
Along with this form send back:
*your articles of incorporation (if incorporated)
*motor carrier authority (if you are a motor carrier)
*driver's license
*proof of insurance / Certificate of Insurance with Century Finance as Certificate Holder
*W-9
*Wiring or ACH instructions from your bank or a voided check (if you want us to wireor ach the money to you)
And we will generate your contract.

Our advance rate is 93% our fee is 7%. We charge back invoices at 90 days.

Need Extra Cash!!! Ask about our "Referral Plan". There is no limit to how much $$$$ you can make.

SIGNATURE: _____
By executing this form, I authorize Century Finance, LLC to verify the information provided in the application, to obtain personal credit reports, business reference reports, and any other information Century Finance deems necessary. All statements in this form are true and accurate to the best of my information and belief.

Notification of Assignment
CENTURY FINANCE

Attention: Accounts Payable

This letter is to inform you that the company named below uses Century Finance LLC as its factoring company.
Company: _____
City: _____ State: _____ MC: _____

Pursuant to a factoring contract with Century Finance LLC, the assignment includes all current and future invoices received for your company by the company stated above.

Please remit payment for all current and future invoices received by this company to Century Finance LLC. This Assignment may only be rescinded if formal written notice is provided by and confirmed with Century Finance LLC.

Release of this Assignment cannot be provided by any party other than Century Finance LLC. Payment in any other way will not discharge this legal obligation.

UNDER NO CIRCUMSTANCES SHOULD PAYMENT BE PROVIDED DIRECTLY TO THE ABOVE COMPANY

All payments for invoices received by this company should be mailed to Century Finance at the following address:

**Century Finance LLC
P.O. Box 16960
Jonesboro, AR 72403**

Should you have questions concerning this letter or payment instructions, please call Century Finance at (870) 910-0050.

Your cooperation is greatly appreciated

Company: _____
(Company Name)

Signature: _____

Print Name: _____ Date: _____

STATE PROVISIONS

The following pages include

* **When Permit is Required**
* **When Escort is Required**
* **Legal Travel Times**
* **Escort / Vehicle Requirements**

PIT ROW SERVICES

FRONT/REAR HIGH POLE STEERMAN ROUTE SURVEY

ASK YOURSELF

WHO'S PILOTING YOUR LOADS?
ARE THEY QUALIFIED?
ARE THEY CERTIFIED?
WHO'S REALLY RESPONSIBLE?

WE OFFER CERTIFICATION CLASSES!

FULLY INSURED INCLUDING PROFESSIONAL LIABILITY

HIGHLY EQUIPPED PROFESSIONAL FLEET OF VEHICLES. TRAINED & CERTIFIED NATIONWIDE. ESCORT YOUR OVERSIZED LOADS WITH THE BEST LOOKING & MOST PROFESSIONAL PILOT CARS IN THE COUNTRY.

(205) 763 - 9340

LINCOLN AL
MOBILE AL

WWW.PITROW.SERVICES

ALABAMA

WHEN A PERMIT IS NEEDED
- OVER 8'6" WIDE
- SEMI –TRAILER OVER 53'6" LONG,
LOAD OVER 13'6" HIGH

TIMES OF MOVEMENT
- 1/2 HOUR BEFORE SUNRISE, 1/2 HOUR AFTER SUNSET MONDAY THRU SATURDAY; NO TRAVEL ALLOWED ON SUNDAY
- LOADS 120'-150' RESTRICTED FROM 9AM –3PM M-F
- TRAVEL PROHIBITED ON THE FOLLOWING HOLIDAYS:
  NEW YEARS DAY, MEMORIAL DAY, JULY 4TH, LABOR DAY, THANKSGIVING DAY, CHRISTMAS
- PERMIT OFFICE CLOSED ON THE ABOVE HOLIDAYS AS WELL AS
MARTIN LUTHER KING DAY, WASHINGTON'S BIRTHDAY, COLUMBUS DAY, CONFEDERATE MEMORIAL DAY, JEFFERSON DAVIS' BIRTHDAY & VETERANS DAY
(TRAVEL NOT RESTRICTED)
- NO TRAVEL IS PERMITTED IN FOG, SNOW, ICE OR LESS THAN 500' OF VISIBILITY

CURFEWS (MAY NOT BE STATED ON PERMIT)
TUSCALOOSA & BIRMINGHAM - ALL ROADWAYS
NO TRAVEL BETWEEN 7AM-8:30AM - 4PM-6PM - DAYS NOT SPECIFIED IN ORDINANCES

WHEN ESCORT VEHICLE IS REQUIRED
- **OVER 12' WIDE** - 2 PILOT CARS - 1 FRONT - 1 REAR
- **OVER 85' LONG** - 1 PILOT CAR IN REAR;
- **OVER 105'** - 2 PILOTS (1 IN FRONT AND 1 IN THE REAR)
- **OVER 15'5" HIGH** - 1 PILOT CAR IN FRONT WITH HEIGHT POLE
- **OVERHANG IN REAR MORE THAN 5'** - 1 PILOT CAR IN REAR
- **OVERHANG IN FRONT MORE THAN 10'** - 1 PILOT CAR IN FRONT OF LOAD

** IMPORTANT **
PROPOSED CHANGES COULD AFFECT
WHEN ESCORT IS REQUIRED

REFER TO PERMIT

REQUIREMENTS FOR ESCORT VEHICLE
VEHICLE TO BE PASSENGER CAR, PICKUP, CARRYALL OR STATION WAGON
- **LIGHTS**—MUST BE EQUIPPED WITH A FLASHING OR REVOLVING AMBER LIGHT, ROOF MOUNT ONLY VISIBLE @ 1000' AND 120 DEGREE VISIBILITY
- **SIGNS**—MAY BE MODIFIED TO FIT VEHICLE WITH A YELLOW OR ORANGE BACKGROUND. WIDTH IS TO BE 48" OR MORE WITH 10" HIGH BY 2" WIDE BLOCK LETTERS. SIGN MUST READ " OVERSIZE LOAD" ONLY. SIGN IS TO BE MOUNTED TO EITHER THE ROOF OR FRONT AND REAR BUMBERS. SIGN MUST BE REMOVED , LAID DOWN OR COVERED WHEN NOT IN USE.
- **ADDITIONAL EQUIPMENT**—2 WAY RADIO WITH 1/2 MILE RANGE TO ALLOW COMMUNICATION BETWEEN PILOT/ESCORT AND LOAD

REQUIREMENTS FOR ESCORT VEHICLE OPERATOR
- ORANGE SAFETY VEST OR JACKET
- STOP/SLOW PADDLE
- 2 QTY 16" SQUARE HAND FLAGS

ALABAMA DEPT OF TRANSPORTATION PERMIT OFFICE – OFFICE HOURS 8am-4:45pm CT
(334) 834-1092 / (334) 242-6700 / 800-499-2782   Fax: (334) 832-9084

IMPORTANT PHONE NUMBERS
State Highway Patrol General Info (DPS):	(334) 242-4371
Overweight/Oversize Permits (ALDOT):	(334) 242-6358
Motor Carrier Services (IRP/IFTA):	(334) 242-2999
Trip Permits/Fuel Permits:	(334) 353-9135
Motor Carrier Safety Unit:	(334) 242-4395
Motor Carrier Enforcement:	(334) 242-5775
Alabama Traffic Service Center:	(866) 954-9399
Pre-Pass:	(800) 773-7277

CALL US TODAY!
CASH TODAY!
FACTORING MADE EASY FOR AMERICA'S TRUCKERS
1-888-684-7195
CENTURY FINANCE

ALASKA

WHEN A PERMIT IS NEEDED
- DISTANCE TO BE TRAVELED, ROUTE, AND OBSTRUCTIONS ON ROUTE TAKEN INTO CONSIDERATION WHEN DETERMINING NEED FOR PERMIT.

SPECIAL INFORMATION NEEDED FOR PERMIT
- COMPANY NAME, ADDRESS, LICENSE AND STATE ID FOR TRACTOR AND TRAILER, MAKE AND MODEL, NUMBER OF AXLES, LOAD DESCRIPTION WITH MAKE AND MODEL, DATES OF MOVEMENT, STARTING AND STOPPING POINTS, ROUTING DESIRED, AXLE SPACING AND WEIGHTS, TIRE WIDTH AND LOAD RATINGS, GROSS WEIGHT AND OVERALL DIMENSIONS

TIMES OF MOVEMENT
- 1/2 HOUR BEFORE DAY LIGHT UNTIL 1/2 HOUR AFTER SUNSET
- MONDAY THRU FRIDAY NOON. SUNDAY TRAVEL INCLUDED FOR VEHICLES LESS THAN 10' WIDE, 16' HIGH, and 85' LONG WITH LEGAL OVERHANG.
- OVERSIZED VEHICLES MAY TRAVEL DURING HOURS OF DARKNESS WITH SPECIAL LIGHTING AND TAPING
- **TRAVEL PROHIBITED** ON WEEKENDS OF **NEW YEAR'S DAY, MEMORIAL DAY, JULY 4TH, LABOR DAY, THANSGIVING DAY and CHRISTMAS DAY**
- **NO TRAVEL** IN URBAN AREAS FROM 7-8AM AND 4:30—6PM
- **SCHOOL YEAR RESTRICTIONS** FOR THE STERLING HIGHWAY, KENAI SPUR, AND KALIFORNSKI BEACH RD. FROM 6:45-9AM and FROM 2:15-4:30PM FOR LOADS GREATER THAN 14' WIDE

WHEN ESCORT VEHICLE IS REQUIRED
- 10' TO 12' - 1 PILOT CAR (FRONT)
- 12' TO 14' - 2 PILOT CARS (1 FRONT & 1 REAR)
- OVER 14' - 3 PILOT CARS (2 FRONT & 1 REAR)
- OVER 85' TO 100' IN LENGTH—1 PILOT CAR (FRONT)
- OVER 100' IN LENGTH—2 PILOT CARS (1 FRONT & 1 REAR)
- OVERHANG OVER 10' - 1 REAR PILOT CAR OR EXTENDED LIGHT BAR FOR UP TO 20' REAR OVERHANG
- OVERHANG OVER 35' - 2 PILOT CARS (1 FRONT & 1 REAR)
- OVERWEIGHT CROSSING BRIDGES STADDLING CENTER—2 PILOT CARS (1 FRONT & 1 REAR)

REQUIREMENTS FOR LOAD
- FLAGS REQUIRED ON VEHICLES WITH LOAD MORE THAN 10' WIDE OR A OVERHANG EXCEEDING STATE LEGAL LIMITS.
- "OVERSIZE" SIGN REQUIRED ON FRONT AND REAR ON LOADS EXCEEEDING 8'6" WIDE. SIGN SHOULD BE A MINUMOM OF 48" WIDE , WITH A YELLOW BACKGROUND WITH BLACK LETTERING 10" HIGH AND 2" BRUSH STROKES

REQUIREMENTS FOR ESCORT VEHICLE
- VEHICLE TO BE PASSENGER CAR OR PICKUP NOT EXCEED UNLADEN WEIGHT OF 10,000 LBS
- **LIGHTS**—MUST BE EQUIPPED WITH A FLASHING OR REVOLVING AMBER LIGHT, ROOF MOUNT ONLY VISIBLE @ 1000' AND 120 DEGREE VISIBILITY
- **SIGNS**—MUST BE MODIFIED TO FIT VEHICLE WITH A YELLOW OR ORANGE BACKGROUND. WIDTH IS TO BE 48" OR MORE WITH 10" HIGH BY 2" BRUSH STROKES.. SIGN MUST READ " OVERSIZE LOAD" ONLY. SIGN IS TO BE MOUNTED TO THE ROOF. SIGN MUST BE REMOVED , LAYED DOWN OR COVERED WHEN NOT IN USE.
- **ADDITIONAL EQUIPMENT**—2 WAY RADIO WITH 1/2 MILE RANGE TO ALLOW COMMUNICATION BETWEEN PILOT/ESCORT AND LOAD

REQUIREMENTS FOR ESCORT VEHICLE OPERATOR
- SHALL NOT BE LESS THAN 18 YRS OF AGE AND CAPABLE OF CARRY OUT FLAGGING RESPONSIBILITIES IN ACCORDANCE WITH THE ALASKA STATE TRAFFIC MANUAL REGULATIONS.
- ORANGE SAFETY VEST OR JACKET
- STOP/SLOW PADDLE
- 2 QTY 16" SQUARE HAND FLAGS

ALASKA DEPT. OF TRANSPORTATION PERMITS OFFICE – OFFICE HOURS: 8AM-5:00PM (ALASKA TIME)
(907)341-3200 / (800)478-7636 (within Alaska)
Fax: (907)341-3221; (866)345-2641 (within Alaska) Fax-on-demand: (907)348-9876

WHEN PERMIT IS NEEDED
- OVER 8'6" WIDE
- OVER 14' HIGH ON HIGHWAY'S
- 13'6" ON ALL OTHER ROADS
- TRAILER OVER 57'6" ON HIGHWAYS
- OVER 53' ON ALL OTHER ROADS

SPECIAL INFORMATION NEEDED FOR PERMIT
- DRIVER'S NAME
- ARIZONA MOTOR CARRIER # OR IFTA # (IFTA # IS STATE CODE + FEIN)
- ORIGIN, DESTINATION, ROUTE, DATE AND TIME OF MOVEMENT. TRUCK MAKE, LICENSE # AND STATE
- LOAD INFO
- IF USING A JEEP, STATE AND LICENSE #;
- EMPTY WEIGHT OF TRACTOR AND TRAILER
- OVERHANG, FIRST 7 DIGITS OF MOTOR CARRIER USE FUEL #

TIMES OF MOVEMENT
- SUNRISE TO SUNSET; NO TRAVEL SATURDAY—SUNDAY;
- OVERWEIGHT ONLY—NOT OVER 10' WIDE—OR NOT OVER 14' HIGH OR NOT MORE THAN 10' REAR OVERHANG OR 3' FRONT OVERHANG MAY BE GRANTED CONTUNUOUS OPERATION
- RESTRICTED TRAVEL ON THE FOLLOWING HOLIDAYS: **NEW YEAR'S DAY, MEMORIAL DAY, JULY 4TH, LABOR DAY, THANKSGIVING DAY, CHRISTMAS DAY**
- IF THE HOLIDAY FALL ON A MONDAY, MOVEMENT SHALL STOP BEFORE NOON THE FRIDAY PRECEDING THE HOLIDAY.
- PERMIT OFFICE CLOSED ON THE ABOVE HOLIDAYS PLUS **LINCOLN'S BIRTHDAY, WASHINGTON'S BIRTHDAY, COLUMBUS DAY AND VETERANS DAY** (NO TRAVEL RESTRICTIONS)
- LOADS NO GREATER THAN 16' WIDE, 16' HIGH, 120' LONG AND 250,000 LBS. CAN TRAVEL ON SPECIAL ROUTES FROM 3AM TO NOON ON WEEKENDS AND NIGHTS. ANY LOADS OVER 11' WIDE MUST HAVE A REAR ESCORT.

CURFEWS:
- 7-9AM & 4-6PM FOR THE FOLLOWING HIGHWAYS
- I-17/I-10/SR 360 WITHIN CITY LIMITS OF METROPOLITAN PHOENIX
- I-10/I-19 WITHIN CITY LIMITS OF METROPOLITAN TUCSON

WHEN ESCORT VEHICLE IS REQUIRED
- UNDER 14' WIDE, 16' HIGH, 120' LONG: NO PILOT CARS NEEDED
- OVER 14' WIDE—1 OR MORE PILOT CARS
- OVER 16' HIGH—1 OR MORE PILOT CARS
- OVER 120' LONG—1 OR MORE PILOT CARS

REQUIREMENTS FOR ESCORT VEHICLE
PASSENGER CAR OR 2 AXLE TRUCK NOT EXCEEDING 20,000 LBS
LIGHTS: WARNING LIGHTS ARE REQUIRED
SIGNS: "OVERSIZE LOAD" SIGN FACING TRAFFIC APPROACHING THE LOAD BEING ESCORTED, MUST BE 5' ABOVE THE GROUND; MOUNTED SECURELY TO THE VEHICLE, DIMENSION: 5' BY 1' WITH 1" BLACK LETTERS ON YELLOW BACKGROUND
FLAGS: 12" RED FLAGS ON ALL FOUR CORNERS OF THE VEHICLE
ADDITIONAL EQUIPMENT: 2 WAY RADIO WITH 1/2 MILE MIN RANGE, 8 FLARES, FIRST AID KIT, 2 RED EMERGENCY FLAGS ON A STAFF

REQUIREMENTS FOR ESCORT VEHICLE OPERATOR
- AT LEAST 18 YEARS OLD; HAVE A VALID DRIVERS LICENSE
- HAVE A VALID/LEGIBLE ESCORT VEHICLE OPERATOR CERTIFICATE ISSUED BY AZ OR IN ANOTHER STATE IN IMMEDIATE POSSESSION
- REPEAT TRAINING & CERTIFICATION REQUIREMENTS AT LEAST ONCE EVERY 4 YEARS

ARIZONA DEPT OF TRANSPORTATION PERMITS OFFICE HOURS 6AM—5PM MONDAY THRU FRIDAY
(623) 932-2257 / FAX—(623) 932-2441

ARKANSAS

WHEN A PERMIT IS NEEDED
- OVER 8'6" WIDE
- OVER 13'6" HIGH
- TRAILER OVER 53'6" LONG,
- OVER 80,000 LBS

SPECIAL INFORMATION NEEDED FOR PERMIT
- PHYSICAL ADDRESS IF STOPPING OR STARTING WITHIN STATE OF ARKANSAS
- OVERWEIGHT NEED ORIGIN AND DESTINATION
- CONTAINERIZED-NEED TO KNOW WHAT'S INSIDE CONTAINER
- COPY OF FREIGHT BILL / BILL OF LADING
- DATE AND TIME OF MOVEMENT
- MAKE OF TRUCK
- LICENSE PLATE # AND STATE

TIMES OF MOVEMENT
- **DAYLIGHT HOURS ONLY** UNLESS PERMIT ALLOWS TRAVEL ON HOLIDAYS AND AT NIGHT (OVERWEIGHT ONLY)
- PERMITS MUST BE ISSUED FOR OVERDIMENSIONAL LOADS TO MOVE ON SATURDAY AND SUNDAY
- LOADS NOT EXCEEDING 90' LONG MAY TRAVEL 24/7
- **CURFEW** FROM 7-9AM & 4-6PM IN LITTLE ROCK AREA ON I-30 (MILE MARKER 137-143, MILE MARKER 151-155) & ALL OF INTERSTATE 630
- TRAVEL PROHIBITED ON THE FOLLOWING HOLIDAYS: **NEW YEARS DAY, INDEPENDENCE DAY, LABOR DAY, THANKSGIVING, AND CHRISTMAS DAY**
- CAN TRAVEL, IF PERMIT ALLOWS, ON THE FOLLOWING HOLIDAYS: **MARTIN LUTHER KING DAY, ROBERT E. LEE'S BIRTHDAY, GEORGE WASHINGTON'S BIRTHDAY & VETERANS DAY.** (PERMIT OFFICE CLOSED ON ABOVE HOLIDAYS AS WELL AS CONFEDERATE MEMORIAL DAY AND THE DAY AFTER THANKSGIVING)

WHEN ESCORT VEHICLE IS REQUIRED

2 LANES
- WIDTH OVER 12' TO 14'1" - 1 FRONT PILOT CAR
- OVER 14'1" WIDE—1 FRONT AND 1 REAR PILOT CAR
- HEIGHT OVER 15'1" - 1 FRONT PILOT CAR WITH HEIGHT POLE
- OVER 16' HIGH—MUST OPTAIN SPECIAL APPROVAL

4 LANES
- 14' TO 16' WIDE—1 PILOT CAR IN REAR
- OVER 15' HIGH—1 FRONT PILOT CAR WITH HEIGHT POLE
- OVER 16'HIGH—MUST OPTAIN SPECIAL APPROVAL

REQUIREMENTS FOR ESCORT VEHICLE
- **VEHICLE**—TRUCK HAVING A RATED LOAD CAPACITY OF NOT LESS THAN 1/4 TONE OR AUTO HAVING A GROSS WEIGHT OF NOT LESS THAN 2000LBS. MUST BE LICENSED IN ARKANSAS STATE OR BY A STATE WITH RECIPROCAL AGREEMENTS
- **SIGNS**—"OVERSIZE LOAD" SIGN MUST BE CONTRUCTED OF A DURABLE MATERIAL WITH YELLOW BACKGROUND & BLACK LETTERS (2" BRUSH STROKE) WHICH ARE 10" HIGH. WHEN ESCORTING A MOBILE HOME SIGN MUST STATE "OVESIZE (WIDTH IN FEET) LOAD"
- **LIGHTS**—MUST BE MOUNTED ON TOP OF VEHICLE AND VISIBLE 360 DEGREES. MUST HAVE EITHER A ROTATING AMBER LIGHT WITH INCANDESCENT OR HALOGEN BULB LAMPS EMITTING 35,000 (MIN.) CANDLEPOWER FACTORY CERTIFIED STEADY BEAM; LENS HEIGHT 6" (MIN) OR STROBE-TYPE FLASHING (80 FLASES/MIN) AMBER LIGHT CAPABLE OF EMITTING 500,000 (MIN) TOTAL CANDLE POWER,; LENS HEIGHT 3 1/2" (MIN)
- **FLAGS**—2 SOLID RED FLAGS, 18" SQUARE, MOUNTED ON TOP OF VEHICLE, IN LINE WITH THE WARNING LIGHTS, AT AN ANGLE BETWEEN 40-70 DEGREE; SHALL NOT EXTEND 6" FROM SIDE OF VEHICLE; TOTAL SPREAD SHALL NOT EXCEED 8'
- **ADDITIONAL EQUIPMENT**—10LB. CLASS B, C FIRE EXTINGUISHER, 4—14 MINUTE FLARES, LIGHT STICKS OR TRIANGLES
- **MUST HAVE** THE NAME AND ADDRESS OR TELEPHONE NUMBER & CITY OF THE COMPANY/OWNER OF THE ESCORT ON EACH DOOR, LEGIBLE AND VISIBLE TO THE MOTORING PUBLIC.

CERTIFICATION / INSURANCE REQUIREMENTS FOR ESCORT VEHICLE OPERATOR
- NO CERTIFICATION REQUIRED
- DRIVER SHALL CARRY IN THE VEHICLE PROOF OF LIABILITY INSURANCE IN THE AMOUNT OF $100,000 EACH BODILY INJURY OR DEATH; $300,000 EACH ACCIDENT; $25,000 PROPERTY DAMAGE ($325,000 MINIMUM COMBINED SINGLE LIMIT COVERAGE)

ARKANSAS DEPT. OF TRANSPORTATION PERMITS OFFICE—
HOURS: 6AM—4:30PM; MONDAY THRU FRIDAY
STATE HWY & TRANS DEPT—PERMITS (501) 569-2381

CALIFORNIA PILOT CAR ASSOCIATION

A California Non-Profit Corporation
P.O. BOX 110, BLOOMINGTON, CA 92316

708-443-4164

FOR MORE INFORMATION - *capilotcar@gmail.com*

**Call Us for All
Your Pilot Car/Escort needs**
Chase, High Pole, Route Survey

www.capilotcarassoc.com

CALIFORNIA

WHEN A PERMIT IS NEEDED
- OVER 8'6" WIDE
- OVER 14' HIGH
- OVER 80,000 LBS
- OVER-LENGTH (SEE SIZE AND WEIGHT MANUAL. CAN BE DOWNLOADED FROM THE CALTRANS WEBSITE

SPECIAL INFORMATION NEEDED FOR PERMIT
- NAME, ADDRESS
- LOAD DESCRIPTION AND DIMENSIONS
- TRUCK INFO
- ROUTE (ADD DIRECTIONS TO THE ROUTE—EAST, WEST, NORTH, SOUTH)
- ALSO INCLUDE JUNCTION ONTO HIGHWAYS

WHEN ESCORT VEHICLE IS REQUIRED
- ALL LOADS OVER 12' WIDE—1 OR 2 PILOT CARS DEPENDING ON ROUTE
- LENGTH OVER 85' TO 135' (OVER 100' IN LA COUNTY & LA CITY)
- 1 FRONT / 1 REAR
- IF REQUESTED BY A PERMITTEE, A POLE CAR WILL BE PERMITTED AND IDENTIFIED AS A PERMITTEE REQUEST.
- OVERHANG (FRONT OR REAR) 25' OR MORE—1 PILOT CAR OR MORE
- MUST CHECK PERMIT FOR ESCORT REQUIREMENTS, DEPENDING ON LOCATION; MAY NEED ESCORT FOR UNDER 12' WIDE. PILOT CAR MAPS MAY BE DOWNLOADED FROM THE CALTRANS WEBSITE

TIMES OF MOVEMENT
- 24 HOURS A DAY 7 DAY A WEEK UNLESS: AN ESCORT VEHICLE IS REQUIRED OR LOAD EXCEEDS A 2 VEHICLE CONFIGURATION OR EXCEEDS GREEN LOADING WEIGHT OR A DETOUR IS NEEDED—THEN TRAVEL IS RESTRICTED TO **1/2 HOUR BEFORE SUNRISE TO 1/2 HOUR AFTER SUNSET**
- TRAVEL PROHIBITED (UNLESS EXEMPTED BY PERMIT) ON THE FOLLOWING HOLIDAYS: **NEW YEARS DAY, LINCOLN'S BIRTHDAY, WASHINGTON'S BIRTHDAY, MARTIN LUTHER KING DAY, MEMORIAL DAY, JULY 4TH, LABOR DAY, THANKSGIVING DAY, AND CHRISTMAS DAY.**
- IF A HOLIDAY FALLS ON A FRIDAY OR MONDAY, TRAVEL IS PROHIBITED DURING THE WEEKEND.

CURFEWS: LOADS 10' OR MORE IN WIDTH ARE RESTRICTED FROM TRAVELING MONDAY THRU FRIDAY AT THE FOLLOWING TIMES:

LOS ANGELES & SURROUNDING AREAS	6-9AM	3-6PM
SACRAMENTO & SURROUNDING AREAS	7-9AM	4-6PM
SAN DIEGO & SURROUNDING AREAS	7-9AM	4-6PM
SAN FRANCISCO/OAKLAND BAY BRIDGE	6:30-9AM	3:30-6:30PM
SAN FRANCISCO & SURROUNDING AREAS	7-9AM	4-6PM

CHP NEEDED WHEN LOADS IS OVER 15'WIDE ON 2-LANE; 16' WIDE ON YELLOW ROUTES AND ALL LOADS EXCEEDING 17' HIGH

REQUIREMENTS FOR ESCORT VEHICLE
- A VEHICLE AT LEAST 60" WIDE
- **SIGNS**: "OVERSIZE LOAD" SIGN SHALL BE 48" (MIN) FROM GROUND ; SHALL BE LEGIBLE AT 45 DEGREES FROM EITHER SIDE/ FRONT & BACK, YELLOW BACKGROUND, W LETTERS 6" HIGH (MIN); BRUSH STROKE 1 5/8" (MIN)
- **LIGHTS:** FLASHING AMBER WARNING LIGHTS VISIBLE 360 DEGREES - MUST BE COVERED WHEN NOT ESCORTING AN OVERSIZE LOAD
- **FLAGS:** AT LEAST 1 RED WARNING FLAG ON EACH SIDE OF VEHICLE; MUST BE AT LEAST 12" SQUARE; MUST BE VISIBLE FROM THE FRONT & REAR
- **ADDITIONAL EQUIPMENT:** 1 "STOP/SLOW" PADDLE, 1 ORANGE VEST/SHIRT/JACKET; 1 RED EMERGENCY FLAG (24" SQUARE); A 2 WAY RADIO WITH 1/2 MILE RANGE

CERTIFICATION REQUIREMENTS FOR ESCORT VEHICLE
- NO CERTIFICATION REQUIREMENTS AT THIS TIME

CALIFORNIA DEPT OF TRANSPORTATION PERMIT OFFICE
CATRANS (916) 322-1297 / FAX (916) 322-4966

COLORADO

WHEN PERMIT IS NEEDED
- OVER 8'6" WIDE
- OVER 13' HIGH
- TRAILER OVER 57'5" LONG
- WEIGHT OVER 80,000 LBS

SPECIAL INFORMATION NEEDED FOR PERMIT
- OVERHANG
- MOBILE HOME STARTING / STOPPING IN STATE—HUD #
- LAST 10 DIGITS OF SERIAL # FOR TRACTOR

TIMES OF MOVEMENT
- 7 DAYS A WEEK, 24 HOURS A DAY EXCEPT FOR VEHICLES / LOADS MORE THAN 14' WIDE AND ON **MEMORIAL DAY, JULY 4TH AND LABOR DAY**.
- SUPER LOADS— NO MOVEMENT ON WEEKENDS OR ACCORDING TO PERMIT.

WHEN ESCORT VEHICLE IS REQUIRED
- ESCORT REQUIREMENTS VARY ACCORDING TO ROUTES TRAVELED WITH THE STATE AND EACH MAJOR CITY. **PILOT CAR OVERSIZE RESTRICTION MAP, HEIGHT RESTRICTION MAP, AND BRIDGE WEIGHT LIMIT MAP** MUST BE CARRIED AT ALL TIMES BY ESCORT VEHICLE AND ARE AVAILABLE BY CALLING CDOT

REQUIREMENTS FOR ESCORT VEHICLE
- **SIGNS**: "WIDE LOAD", "LONG LOAD", "OVERSIZE LOAD" MOUNTED ON TOP OF VEHICLE; 5' WIDE (MIN) WITH 10" HIGH BY 1" WIDE BRUSH STROKE / BLACK LETTERS/ 8" HIGH (MIN) ON A YELLOW BACKGROUND OR 7' WIDE (MAX) / 18" HIGH / 1.41" BRUSH STROKE / BLACK LETTERS 10" HIGH (MIN) ON A YELLOW BACKGROUND. CLEARLY LEGIBLE & READABLE FROM FRONT ESCORT VEHICLE OR REAR ESCORT VEHICLE. "HEIGHT SURVEY IN PROGRESS" TO BE DISPLAYED WHEN CONDUCTING A ROUTE SURVEY (SAME DIMENSIONS OF SIGNS PREVIOUSLY NOTED)
- **LIGHTS**: 1-3 FLASHING (OR ROTATING/OSCILLATING/FLASHING) YELLOW/AMBER LIGHTS/LIGHT BAR VISIBLE FROM FRONT AND REAR; VISIBLE AT 500' IN NORMAL SUNLIGHT; AAMVA APPROVED
- **FLAGS**: AT LEAST 2 RED OR ORANGE FLAGS MOUNTED TO THE TOP OF THE VEHICLE AT APPROX 45 DEGREE ANGLES; NOT EXTENDING MORE THAN 6" ON EITHER SIDE.
- **RADIOS**: 2 WAY RADIO WITH 1/2 RANGE (MIN), 2 HANDHELD 2 –WAY SIMPLEX RADIOS FOR OUTSIDE VEHICLE OPERATIONS
- **ADDITIONAL EQUIPMENT**: STANDARD 18" STOP / SLOW PADDLE; 3 BI-DIRECTIONAL EMERGENCY REFLECTIVE TRIANGLES; 8 RED BURNING FLARES, GLOW STICKS OR EQUIVALENT; 1 5 LB B, C FIRE EXTINGUISHER; REFLECTIVE ORANGE TYPE 2 SAFETY VEST; ORANGE / WHITE HARD HAT; 1 ADDITIONAL "OVERSIZE LOAD " SIGN; IDENTIFICATION SIGNS ON BOTH SIDES OF VEHICLE; FLASHLIGHT, WHICH USES TWO OR MORE D CELL BATTERIES, WITH A MIN 1 1/2" LENS DIAMETER, WITH EXTRA BATTERIES OR CHARGER; AND A 9" MIN LENGTH RED OR ORANGE CONE FLASHLIGHT FOR USE WHEN DIRECTING TRAFFIC; 3 ORANGE REFLECTIVE TRAFFIC CONES—MIN 18" HIGH, CLEARLY MARKED FIRST AID KIT; SERVICEABLE SPARE TIRE, TIRE JACK, LUG WRENCH; HEIGHT POLE (MUST BE USED WHEN ESCORTING LOADS EXCEEDING 16' HIGH)

CERTIFICATION REQUIREMENTS FOR ESCORT VEHICLE OPERATOR
MUST OBTAIN / MAINTAIN CERTIFICATION TO ESCORT ON A STATE HIGHWAY (GOOD FOR 4 YEARS; RENEWABLE FOR 4 YEARS ONLINE OR BY MAIL) OR CERTIFICATION CARDS OR EQUIVALENT FROM OTHER STATES. A LIST OF PROVIDERS OF AN AUTHORIZED ESCORT VEHICLE CERTIFICATION PROGRAM CAN BE OBTAINED FROM THE DEPARTMENTS WEBSITE OR BY CALL THE PERMIT OFFICE.

ADDITIONAL REQUIREMENTS OF PILOT CAR OPERATOR
- MUST BE AT LEAST 18 YEARS OF AGE
- POSSESS A VALID DRIVERS LICENSE
- NO ONE UNDER THE AGE OF 16 ALLOWED IN PILOT CAR WHILE ESCORTING LOAD
- POSSESS A CURRENT CERTIFICATION OF INSURANCE / ENDORSEMENT WHICH INDICATES THAT THE OPERATOR, OR THE OPERATORS EMPLOYER, HAS IN FULL FORCE AND EFFECT COMMERICAL LIABILITY INSURANCE IN AT LEAST $1,000,000 COMBINED SINGLE LIMIT COVERAGE FOR BODILY INJURY & / OR PROPERTY DAMAGE FOR BODILY INJURY / PROPERTY DAMAGE CAUSED BY AN ACT OR OMISSION BY ESCORT VEHICLE OPERATOR OF THE ESCORT DUTIES REQUIRED BY THE RULES. SUCH INSURANCE OR INDORSEMENT, AS APPLICABLE, MUST BE MAINTAINED AT ALL TIMES DURING THE TERM OF THE CERTIFICATION. *INSURANCE DOCUMENT MUST INDICATE ON THE FACE OF THE DOCUMENT THAT THE POLICY IS FOR THE OPERATION OF PILOT ESCORT VEHICLE(S) AND PILOT ESCORT DUTIES/RESPONSIBILITIES AS REQUIRED BY THESE RULES.*
- TILLERMAN OPERATIONS WILL NOT BE PERFORMED BY THE PILOT ESCORT VEHICLE DRIVER/OPERATOR OR BY A PASSENGER IN THE PILOT ESCORT VEHICLE THAT IS ESCORTING THE EXTRA-LEGAL VEHICLE OR LOAD.

PILOT CAR OPERATOR MUST CARRY IN THE VEHICLE WHILE ESCORTING
- COPY OF THE EXTRA-LEGAL RULES
- HAZARDOUS AND NUCLEAR MATERIALS MAP
- PROOF OF INSURANCE

COLORADO DEPT OF TRANSPORTATION PERMITS OFFICE
HOURS - MOUNTAIN TIME: 7AM—5PM MONDAY THRU FRIDAY; SAT 8AM—NOON
(303) 757-9539 / (800) 350-3765 / FAX (303) 757-9719

BRECKENRIDGE PILOT CAR SERVICES
(COLORADO)

720-590-6541 **352-507-9146**
PRIMARY   CELL

Certified, Insured & Equipped
to meet State Requirements

GA/NV Amber Light
NM Inspection

CONNECTICUT

WHEN PERMIT IS NEEDED
- OVER 8'6" WIDE
- OVER 13' 6" HIGH
- TRAILER OVER 48' LONG
- WEIGHT OVER 80,000 LBS

SPECIAL INFORMATION NEEDED FOR PERMIT
- DATE AND TIME OF MOVEMENT
- TRUCK MAKE, LICENSE # AND STATE
- LOAD INFO

TIMES OF MOVEMENT
- 1/2 HOUR AFTER SUNRISE TO 1/2 HOUR BEFORE SUNSET; NO WEEKEND TRAVEL; NO TRAVEL FROM 6:30—9AM & 4—6PM
- LOADS OVER 13'6" WIDE OR OVER 14' HIGH CAN TRAVEL TUES THRU THUR 9AM TO 4PM
- NO TRAVEL **NEW YEAR'S DAY, MARTIN LUTHER KING DAY, LINCOLN'S BIRTHDAY, WASHINGTON'S BIRTHDAY, GOOD FRIDAY, MEMORIAL DAY, JULY 4TH, LABOR DAY, COLUMBUS DAY, VETERANS DAY, THANKSGIVING DAY AND CHRISTMAS DAY**

WHEN ESCORT VEHICLE IS REQUIRED
- OVER 14' HIGH—1 PILOT CAR WITH HEIGHT POLE
- OVER 15' HIGH & 15' WIDE—1 FRONT PILOT CAR & 2 REAR PILOT CARS

DIVIDED HIGHWAYS:
- 12' WIDE OR UNDER 100' LONG OR UNDER, MOBILE HOMES 10' WIDE OR UNDER, 80' LONG OR UNDER— NO PILOT CAR REQUIRED
- OVER 12' WIDE, 120' LONG, MOBILE HOMES OVER 12' WIDE—1 REAR PILOT CAR REQUIRED
- OVER 13'6" WIDE, OVER 120' LONG; MOBILE HOMES OVER 12' WIDE OR OVER 85' LONG—1 FRONT & 2 REAR PILOT CARS REQUIRED

UNDIVIDED HIGHWAYS:
- 12' WIDE OR UNDER, OVER 80' LONG, MOBILE HOMES 10' WIDE OR UNDER, OR OVER 80' LONG—1 REAR PILOT CAR REQUIRED
- OVER 12' WIDE, OVER 100' LONG, MOBILE HOMES OVER 10' WIDE, OVER 85' LONG—1 FRONT AND 1 REAR PILOT CAR REQUIRED

REQUIREMENTS FOR ESCORT VEHICLE
- **SIZE**: MIN 60: WIDE; MAX. CAPACITY 1 1/2 TON
- **SIGNS**: MOUNTED 48" ABOVE ROADWAY (MIN); BLACK LETTERS 8" HIGH (MIN) ON YELLOW BACKGROUND: "OVERSIZE LOAD FOLLOWING", "OVERSIZE LOAD AHEAD", "WIDE LOAD AHEAD", " WIDE LOAD FOLLOWING", " LONG LOAD AHEAD", " LONG LOAD FOLLOWING"
- **LIGHTS**: TOP MOUNTED FLASHING OR ROTATING AMBER LIGHTS VISIBLE FOR 1000'
- **FLAGS**: 18" SQUARE ON FRONT OR REAR CORNERS OF VEHICLE WHICHEVER IS APPROPRIATE
- **RADIOS**: 2 WAY RADIO WITH 1/2 RANGE (MIN), 2 HANDHELD 2 –WAY SIMPLEX RADIOS FOR OUTSIDE VEHICLE OPERATIONS
- **ADDITIONAL EQUIPMENT**: RED HAND FLAG AND SAFETY VEST / JACKET

CERTIFICATION REQUIREMENTS FOR ESCORT VEHICLE OPERATOR
- NO CERTIFICATION IS REQUIRED

CONNECTICUT DEPT OF TRANSPORTATION PERMITS OFFICE—HOURS: 8AM—4:30PM ET
(860) 594-2880 / FAX (860) 594-2949

MARTIN EMERSON
SABATTUS, MAINE

NEW YORK STATE CERTIFIED ESCORT

High Pole - Lead - Chase - Steer
Certified   Fully Insured   Passport

Heavy, Wide or Tall, We'll Help You Haul 'Em All

207-240-7876
emerson01@rocketmail.com

Emerson Pilot Car Services — EPCS

THE OVERLOAD COMPANION 2017 © FREDA BARBER BOOTH

PERMIT LIMITATIONS
- WEIGHT: SINGLE—20,000, TANDEM—34,000; 2 AXLES—40,000; 3 AXLES—54,000; 4 AXLES—74,000; 5 AXLES—80,000 OR THE BRIDGE FORMULA
- LENGTH—53'
- WIDTH—102"
- HEIGHT—13'6"

✓ *RESTRICTIONS AND MODIFICATIONS WILL BE NOTED ON THE PERMIT*

WHEN ESCORT VEHICLE IS REQUIRED
ONE ESCORT
- MORE THAN 12' IN WIDTH/ NOT EXCEEDING 14(FOURTEEN) FEET.
- 85' FEET OR MORE OVERALL LENGTH

TWO ESCORTS
- MORE THAN 14 (FOURTEEN) FEET IN WIDTH
- 100 (ONE HUNDRED) FEET OR MORE IN OVERALL LENGTH
- 15 (FIFTEEN) FEET OR MORE IN HEIGHT
- MORE THAN 120,000 LBS. IN WEIGHT

SEPARATE STATE POLICE ESCORT (3RD ESCORT)
- MORE THAN 15 (FIFTEEN) FEET IN WIDTH
- 120 (ONE HUNDRED TWENTY) OR MORE IN LENGTH
- 17'6" (SEVENTEEN FEET SIX INCHES) OR MORE IN HEIGHT
- MORE THAN 120,000 LBS. IN WIEGHT

TRAVEL TIMES
- PERMITTED VEHICLES MAY MOVE MONDAY THRU FRIDAY, FROM SUNRISE TO SUNSET, UNLESS OTHERWISE AUTHORIZED OR PROHIBITED BY THE PERMIT.
- PROHIBITED HOLIDAYS — **NEW YEARS DAY, MEMORIAL DAY, INDEPENDENCE DAY,**

LABOR DAY, THANKSGIVING DAY, ALONG WITH THE DAY AFTER THANKSGIVING DAY, AND CHRISTMAS DAY.

REQUIREMENTS FOR ESCORT VEHICLES
- VEHICLE NO SMALLER THAN A COMPACT CAR
- **SIGNS**: ROOF MOUNT ("OVERSIZE LOAD" ON BOTH SIDES) OR FRONT & REAR ("OVERSIZE LOAD" ON ONE SIDE); MINIMUM 5' X 12"; BLACK LETTERS 8" HIGH ON A YELLOW BACKGROUND
- **LIGHTS:** NOT REQURED IN DE , BUT MAY BE LOCATED ON ROOF & BE 43" - 52" LONG / 10" - 13" WIDE / 4" - 8" HIGH CONSISTING OF FLASHING OR STROBE LIGHTS (MIN. 4 LIGHTS—2 AT EACH END)
- **FLAGS:** NOT REQUIRED
- **ADDITIONAL EQUIPMENT**: 2 WAY RADIO

CERTIFICATION REQUIREMENTS FOR ESCORT VEHICLE OPERATOR
- NONE AT THIS TIME

DELAWARE DEPT. OF TRANSPORTATION
- DELAWARE DEPT. OF TRANSPORTATION **(**302) 760-2080
- DELAWARE DOT - PUBLIC SAFETY BLDG. - (302) 744-2700; FAX (302) 739-6299

CENTURY FINANCE

CASH TODAY!

FACTORING MADE EASY FOR AMERICA'S TRUCKERS

1-888-684-7195

FLORIDA

Acorn
Truck Safety Escort, LLC

MEMBER

National Pilot Car Association

www.npca.news
"So everyone gets home safe!"

Bill King
Owner / Operator

Cell: 740-823-1856
Office: 740-823-1169

HIGH POLE
CERTIFIED
INSURED - EQUIPPED
& READY TO ROLL!

FLORIDA

WHEN A PERMIT IS NEEDED
- OVER 8'6" WIDE
- OVER 13'6" HIGH
- TRAILER OVER 53' LONG

SPECIAL INFORMATION NEEDED FOR PERMIT
- OVERWEIGHT—GROSS WEIGHT, # OF AXLES, AXLE LOAD, AXLE SPACING AND MANUFACTURED TIRE LIMIT
- MAKE AND YEAR OF MOBILE HOME
- SEAL AND CONTAINER #

TIMES OF MOVEMENT
- 1/2 HR BEFORE SUNRISE TO 1/2 HR AFTER SUNSET; MONDAY THRU FRIDAY'; SATURDAY & SUNDAY: 1/2 HR BEFORE SUNRISE UNTIL NOON
- WEEKEND TRAVEL ALLOWED FOR OVERWEIGHT ONLY
- PROHIBITED HOLIDAYS: **NEW YEARS DAY, MEMORIAL DAY, JULY 4TH, LABOR DAY, THANGSGIVING DAY, CHRISTMAS DAY** AND DAYS OF OBSERVATION OTHER THAN CALENDAR DATE AS WELL AS ADDITIONAL DAYS OF OBSERVATION BEFORE/AFTER DATE.
- **CURFEWS:** NOTED ON PERMIT

WHEN ESCORT VEHICLE IS REQUIRED
2 LANE HIGHWAYS
- 1 FRONT ESCORT—LOADS OVER 12' UP 14' WIDE (IF PAVEMENT IS 24' OR LARGER WIDE)
- 1 FRONT/1 REAR ESCORT—LOADS OVER 12' WIDE (IF PAVEMENT IS LESS THAN 24' WIDE)
- 1 FRONT/1 REAR ESCORT—LOADS OVER 14' TO 15' WIDE (EACH LANE MUST BE 12' WIDE)
- LOADS 75' TO 95' LONG MAY REQUIRE 1 REAR ESCORT
- 1 REAR ESCORT—LOADS OVER 95' LONG
- 1 FRONT W/ HEIGHT POLE—LOADS 14'6" HIGH AND OVER (SURVEY REQUIRED IF OVER 15'0")
- 1 FRONT W/ HEIGHT POLE AND 1 REAR—LOADS OVER 16' HIGH (SURVEY REQUIRED)

4 LANE HIGHWAYS
- 1 FRONT ESCORT—LOADS 12' UP TO 14' WIDE
- 1 FRONT/1 REAR ESCORT—LOADS 14' TO 15' IN WIDTH
- LOADS 75' TO 95' MAY REQUIRE 1 REAR ESCORT
- 1 FRONT W/ HEIGHT POLE—LOADS 14'6" HIGH AND OVER (SURVEY REQUIRED IF OVER 15')
- 1 FRONT W/ HEIGHT POLE AND 1 REAR - OR POLICE ESCORT (LOCAL ROUTE)—LOADS OVER 16' HIGH (SURVEY REQUIRED)

REQUIREMENTS FOR ESCORT VEHICLE
- VEHICLE 2000 LBS—15,000 LBS GVW LICENSED AND OPERATED BY A QUALIFIED ESCORT
- BUMPER OR ROOF MOUNTED SIGNS ("OVERSIZE LOAD"): YELLOW W/ BLACK LETTERS 10" HIGH W/ 1 1/2 WIDE BRUSH STROKE ON FRONT & BACK
- PLACARDS OR SIGNS (8" X 12" MIN.) ON BOTH SIDES OF VEHICLE SHOWING NAME OF COMPANY, OWNER OR DRIVER OF VEHICLE W/ NAME & PHONE # OF OWNER/DRIVER
- CLASS 2 AMBER WARNING LIGHTS - VISIBLE ALL SIDES AT 500 FT
- 2 FLAGS (RED OR FLOURESCENT ORANGE) 18" X 18" MIN. MOUNTED AT A 40 TO 70 DEGREE ANGLE ON ROOF RACK

ADDITIONAL EQUIPMENT: 2-WAY COMMUNICATIONS DEVICE; 2—5 LB. FIRE EXTINQUISHERS; "STOP/SLOW" PADDLE (18" X 18") W/6" HIGH LETTERS, CLASS II SAFETY ORANGE VEST (DAYTIME) CLASS III SAFETY ORANGE VEST (NIGHT); HAND-HELD FLAG (RED OR FLOURESCENT ORANGE - 12"X12"); HARD HAT; 3 REFLECTIVE TRIANGLES, 2 SPARE WARNING SIGNS 7"X18" (YELLOW W/ BLACK LETTERS)
3-36" ORANGE CONES; HEIGHT POLE FOR HEIGHT LOADS (SET 6" ABOVE LOAD HEIGHT)

REQUIREMENTS FOR ESCORT VEHICLE OPERATOR
MUST BE ONE OF THE FOLLOWING
- FLORIDA LAW ENFORCEMENT OFFICER IN ENFORCEMENT VEHICLE
- PERSON MEETING THE FOLLOWING REQUIREMENTS:
- MUST HAVE SUCCESSFULLY COMPLETED THE FDOT PILOT/ESCORT FLAGGING COURSE (RE-QUALIFICATION REQUIRED EVERY 4 YEARS)
- MUST HAVE A VALID CDL CLASS A, B, OR MUST HAVE SUCCESSFULLY COMPLETED THE *NSC 8–HOUR DEFENSIVE DRIVING COURSE* (EVEN IF CERTIFIED BY ANOTHER STATE'S AUTHORIZING AGENCY)
- MUST BE A LEAST 18 YRS OF AGE
- A PERSON QUALIFIED BY ANOTHER STATE'S AUTHORIZING AGENCY - (*VIRGINIA CERTIFICATION NOT LISTED AS RECIPROCATED STATES LIST*)

FLAGGING COURSE OFFERED BY:
FLORIDA TECHNOLOGY TRANSFER CTR (352) 392-2371 X 298

FLORIDA DEPT OF TRANSPORTATION PERMITS OFFICE - (850) 410-5777 / FAX (850) 421-5779

Grant Pilot Cars
Runnin' for America

850-381-4959
Fax: 888-791-5090

www.grantpilotcars.com

Multiple Cars Based in Several States

High Pole - CDL - Steer/Tillerman
Lead - Chase - Traffic Control
Call Us for your Large & Small Projects

FL/GA/WA Certified - $1M GL+ PA - $1M PL
TWIC & Passport
Mobile Office - Cam - GPS Equipped
Permits & Equipment for All States

Fair Rates - Experienced - Professional

THE OVERLOAD COMPANION 2017 © FREDA BARBER BOOTH

ENFORCEMENT BULLETIN 2015-001

Escort Checklist (Single-Trip)

Motor Carrier Size and Weight (MCSAW) Inspectors will be issuing escort checklist for single trip escorts. This checklist will insure that necessary items are being checked per Florida Administrative Code Rule 14-26.012 and Florida Statutes 316.550 and 316.515. A copy of the checklist is attached.

If a single trip escort vehicle enters a MCSAW Scale Facility and is checked by a MCSAW Weight Inspector, the Inspector will complete and sign an Escort Checklist form for that trip. This completed form can be provided by the escort driver to other MCSAW Inspectors at other FDOT Scale locations in order to expedite the process by MCSAW Scale Facility personnel in checking for proper equipment and documents required for escorts.

Contact your immediate supervisor if you have any questions.

ESCORT CHECKLIST
(Single Trip)
Per Florida Administrative Code (FAC) 14-26.012

1. **ESCORT QUALIFICATION:**

   - [ ] At least 18 years of age and valid driver's license in the state of residence.
     - EITHER an eight hour defensive driving course (National Safety Council)
     - OR Valid Commercial Driver's License (Class A, B, or C).
   - [ ] Completed a minimum eight hour pilot/escort flagging course.
     - Qualification must be current. Acceptable States are: **Arizona; Colorado; Georgia; Minnesota; North Carolina; Oklahoma; Utah; Washington; and Wisconsin**
     - Qualified or refresher course within past four years.

2. **ESCORT VEHICLE:**

   - [ ] Single unit vehicle (GVWR 2,000 lbs – 25,999 lbs) w/valid registration.
   - [ ] Company/owner/driver ID placard both sides of vehicle. At least 8" x 12", w/telephone number.
   - [ ] Rotating, strobe or flashing amber warning lights visible by all approaching traffic within 500 feet.
   - [ ] "OVERSIZE LOAD" signs – black letters – 10" high and 1 ½ "wide – front and rear.
   - [ ] Two flags, red or fluorescent orange in color – at least 18" x 18" – 40 to 70 degree angle - mounted on roof rack.

3. **ON BOARD EQUIPMENT (MUST BE IN WORKING ORDER):**

   - [ ] Operable two-way electronic communication.
   - [ ] Two fire extinguishers – minimum 5 lbs each.
   - [ ] "STOP" and "GO" or "STOP" and "SLOW" paddles – 18" with 6" letters.
   - [ ] Class 2 safety vest for daytime hours or Class 3 safety vest for night.
   - [ ] One hand held flag, red or fluorescent orange, 12" x 12".
   - [ ] Two spare warning signs – 7' X 18", yellow with black lettering.
   - [ ] Three 36" traffic cones, reflective if used at night.
   - [ ] Height pole (for over height loads – 6" above load height).

ESCORT DRIVER NAME:_____

ESCORT COMPANY NAME:_____

DATE/TIME:_____

SCALE LOCATION:_____

INSPECTOR NAME & SIGNATURE:_____

GEORGIA

WHEN A PERMIT IS NEEDED
- OVER 8'6" WIDE
- OVER 13'6" HIGH
- OVER 100' LONG
- OVER 80,000 GROSS WEIGHT

TIMES OF MOVEMENT
- 1/2 HOUR AFTER SUNRISE TO 1/2 HOUR BEFORE SUNSET; MONDAY THRU SATURDAY
- NO SUNDAY TRAVEL
- PREMITED LOADS IN EXCESS OF 12' WIDE—NO TRAVEL WHEN VISIBILITY IS LESS THAN 600' OR WINDSPEED IS GREATER THAN 25 MPH
- PROHIBITED HOLIDAYS: **NEW YEAR'S DAY, MEMORIAL DAY, JULY 4TH, LABOR DAY, THANKSGIVING DAY, AND CHRISTMAS DAY**
- NO TRAVEL INTO/THROUGH ATLANTA AREA BOUNDED BY I-285 UNLESS PICKING UP OR DELIVERING IN THE CITY. CURFEWS: 7-9 AM & 4-6 PM; MONDAY THRU FRIDAY

WHEN ESCORT VEHICLE IS REQUIRED
2- LANE HIGHWAYS
- 1 REAR ESCORT—LOADS OVER 75' LONG
- 1 FRONT / 1 REAR—LOADS OVER 125' LONG & OVER 12' WIDE
- 1 FRONT W/ HEIGHT POLE—LOADS OVER 15'6" HIGH

4– LANE HIGHWAYS
- 1 REAR ESCORT—LOADS OVER 75' LONG & OVER 12' UP TO 13'11" WIDE
- 1 FRONT / 1 REAR—LOADS OVER 125' LONG & 14' UP TO AND INCLUDING 15' WIDE

REQUIREMENTS FOR ESCORT VEHICLE
- **GENERAL:** MUST BE A PICKUP OR AN AUTOMOBILE - 1/4 TON OR LESS - OR VEHICLE NOT LESS THAN 2,000 LBS
- **SIGNS:** MOUNTED ON FRONT OF FRONT ESCORT / ON BACK OF REAR ESCORT. SIZE: 6' X 1'; BLACK LETTERS 8" X 4" (MIN) ON ORANGE OR FEDERAL YELLOW BACKGROUND SAYING "OVERSIZE LOAD"
- **LIGHTS:** AMBER LIGHT OR STROBE LIGHT (8" IN DIAMETER MIN) LOCATED ON TOP OF VEHICLE W/ CANDLEPOWER OF 35,000 (MIN) AND 80 REVOLUTIONS/MIN. OR EQUIVALENT 4" STROBE LIGHT VISIBLE AT LEAST 1/4 MILE—
- **AMBER LIGHT PERMIT FROM DPS**
    P.O BOX 101072, ATLANTA, GA 30392; (678) 413-8786 - (FEE: $2.00 /YEAR)
- **FLAGS:** 2 RED FLAGS - 45 DEGREE ANGLE ON ROOF (NOT EXTENDED 6" PAST VEHICLE)

ADDITIONAL EQUIPMENT: 2 WAY RADIO, 18" OR LARGER STOP/SLOW PADDLE, FLUORESCENT VEST & HARDHAT, 9 REFLECTIVE TRIANGLES, 8 FLARES (GLOW STICKS),
3 ORANGE 18" CONES, 5-LB "BC" OR "ABC" FIRE EXTINGUISHER, FLASHLIGHT WITH GLOW-WAND (EXTRA BATTERIES), "FIRST AID" KIT, SPARE FULL-SIZE TIRE

http://www.dot.state.ga.us/dot/operations/permits/672-2.shtml

ADDITIONAL REGULATIONS / REQUIREMENTS FOR ESCORT VEHICLE OPERATORS
- NO PETS, NO UNCERTIFIED PASSENGERS
- **MUST HAVE CURRENT CERTIFICATION** FROM THE "ESCORT VEHICLE OPERATOR CERTIFICATION" PROGRAM
    CONTACT: GEORGIA DEPARTMENT OF TRANSPORTATION OVERSIZE/OVERWEIGHT PERMIT UNIT

ATTN: CERTIFIED VEHICLE ESCORT PROGRAM
935 E. CONFEDERATE AVE, BUILDING 24
P.O. BOX 17937 ATLANTA, GA 30316
(404) 635-8176; (888) 262-8306

- **RECIPROCAL AGREEMENTS** WITH OTHER STATES THAT DEMONSTRATE THE COURSE MATERIALS MEET THE MINIMUM REQUIREMENTS OUTLINED BY THE U.S. DOT FEDERAL HIGHWAY ADMINISTRATION PUBLICATION FHWA-HOP-04.028, BEST PRACTICES GUIDELINES. A LIST OF RECIPROCAL STATES MAY BE OBTAINED FROM THE DEPARTMENT'S WEBSITE LISTED BELOW

GEORGIA DEPT OF TRANSPORTATION PERMITS OFFICE
(888) 262-8306 (PERMIT CUSTOMER SERVICE)
(800) 570-5428 (SINGLE TRIP PERMIT LINE)
(404) 635-8176 (MAIN OFFICE)
FAX (404) 635-8501/8509

DRIVERS FIRST CHOICE

PROFESSIONAL **9 YRS** DEPENDABLE

"Professionally leading the industry - one load at a time"

HIGH POLE, PILOT AND ESCORT SERVICE
MINUTES FROM IN/KY LINE I-64 AND I-65

LISA
812-406-7169

driversfirstchoice@live.com

- GENERAL & PROFESSIONAL LIABILITY
- CERTIFIED AND EQUIPPED FOR 48 STATES
- ON BOARD GPS, DELORME MAPPING, ALL STATE ATTACH.
- PA LISTED, LA PERMIT, GA & NV AMBER LIGHT PERMITS
- MULTIPLE CARS AVAILABLE - NETWORKED WITH MANY OTHERS NATIONWIDE

APPROVED FOR MOST MAJOR COMPANIES INCLUDING:
LANDSTAR, GREENTREE, BENNETT, ATS/SENTINEL, MERCER, ADMIRAL MERCHANTS, AETNA, AMERICAN TRANSPORT, MARATHON TRANSPORT

THE OVERLOAD COMPANION 2017 © FREDA BARBER BOOTH

IDAHO

WHEN A PERMIT IS NEEDED
- OVER 8'6" WIDE
- OVER 14' HIGH
- TRAILER OVER 48' LONG
- OVER 80,000 LBS

SPECIAL INFORMATION NEEDED FOR PERMIT
- NO ADDITIONAL INFO NEEDED

TIMES OF MOVEMENT
- 1/2 HOUR BEFORE SUNRISE TO 1/2 HOUR AFTER SUNSET
- IF 10' WIDE OR LESS, TRAVEL IS ALLOWED 24/7
- LOADS 10' WIDE / 14'6" HIGH / 100' LONG ON 2-LANE OR 120' LONG ON 4-LANE MAY TRAVEL 24/7
- RESTRICTED HOLIDAYS: **NEW YEAR'S DAY, MEMORIAL DAY, JULY 4TH, LABOR DAY, THANKSGIVING DAY AND CHRISTMAS DAY**
- PERMIT OFFICE CLOSED THOSE DAYS PLUS **WASHINGTON'S BIRTHDAY, COLUMBUS DAY AND VETERAN'S DAY**

WHEN ESCORT VEHICLE IS REQUIRED
2– LANE HIGHWAY
- 1 FRONT ESCORT—LOADS OVER 12' WIDE OR 16' HIGH
- 1 REAR ESCORT—LOADS OVER 100' LONG
- 1 FRONT/1 REAR ESCORT—LOADS OVER 14' WIDE

ON INTERSTATES
- 1 REAR ESCORT—LOADS OVER 15' WIDE OR 115' LONG
- 1 FRONT ESCORT—LOADS OVER 16' HIGH

OVERSIZE LOADS WHICH INDIVIDUALLY REQUIRE AN ESCORT CAN TRAVEL IN CONVOY (NOT OVER 4 LOADS & NOT MOBILE HOMES) MAXIMUM DIMENSIONS FOR CONVOY UNITS ON INTERSTATE OR BLACK CODED ROUTES: 14'6" WIDE, 115' LONG. ON RED CODED ROUTES: 12'6" WIDE & 100' LONG

REQUIREMENTS FOR ESCORT VEHICLES
- **GENERAL:** PASSENGER CAR/LIGHT TRUCK/VEHICLE AUTHORIZED BY THE VEHICLE SIZE & WEIGHT SPECIALIST
- **SIGNS:** 5' X 10"; BLACK LETTERS (8" HIGH) ON YELLOW A YELLOW BACKGROUND—"OVERSIZE LOAD"
- **LIGHTS:** FLASHING OR ROTATING AMBER LIGHTS MOUNTED AT EACH END OF THE REQUIRED SIGN ABOVE THE ROOF. AS AN ALTERNATIVE A ESCORT VEHICLE MAY DISPLAY 1 (ONE) ROTATING OR FLASHING AMBER BEACON VISIBLE FROM A MINIMUM OF 500' FEET
- **FLAGS:** NONE REQUIRED
- **ADDITIONAL EQUIPMENT:** 18" STOP/SLOW PADDLE; 3 BI DIRECTIONAL REFLECTIVE TRIANGLES; 1-5 LB. B,C, FIRE EXTINGUISHER; A REFLECTIVE ORANGE VEST/SHIRT/JACKET; ADDITIONAL "OVERSIZE LOAD" SIGNS; NON-METALLIC HEIGHT POLE; 2-WAY RADIO

REQUIREMENTS FOR ESCORT VEHICLE OPERATOR
- VALID DRIVERS LICENSE

IDAHO DIVISION OF MOTOR VEHICLES/ PORT OF ENTRY & OVERLEGAL PERMITS
(208) 334-8420

THE OVERLOAD COMPANION 2017 © FREDA BARBER BOOTH

IDAHO

ASAP
PILOT CAR SERVICE
406-600-9703

Carolyn Johnson
Owner/Operator

montanatrafficcontrol.com

asappilotcarservice.com

**PROFESSIONAL ROUTE SURVEYS
TRAFFIC MGMT PLANS**

HIGH POLE
LEAD - CHASE
CANADA-LEGAL
WA CERTIFIED
$3MIL INSURED

Equipped w/ VHF Radio
Streets & Trips

ILLINOIS

MATT WALLACE ENTERPRISES
Bowling Green, KY

Lead - Chase - High Pole - Steer

270-320-5345

We have a Large Network across the US

CO/UT/NY CERT - CO/UT FLAGGING CERT
PERMITTED/EQUIPPED FOR 48 STATES
$1M - $2M INSURED W/ PA ADD-ON

Email: matthew3e@aol.com

Follow me on Facebook!

ILLINOIS

WHEN A PERMIT IS NEEDED
- OVER 8'6" WIDE
- OVER 13'6" HIGH
- TRAILER OVER 53' LONG

SPECIAL INFORMATION NEEDED FOR PERMIT
- ICC # IF FOR HIRE
- SINGLE OR ROUND TRIP
- MOBILE SERIAL #

TIMES OF MOVEMENT
- 1/2 HOUR BEFORE SUNRISE TO 1/2 HOUR AFTER SUNSET 7 DAYS/WEEK - IF UP TO 14' 6"W / 15'H / 145'L (UPDATE: 1-1-15)
- NO MOVEMENT ON **NEW YEAR'S DAY, MEMORIAL DAY, JULY 4TH, LABOR DAY, THANKSGIVING DAY AND CHRISTMAS DAY**
- PERMIT OFFICE CLOSED THOSE DAYS PLUS **MARTIN LUTHER KING DAY, LINCOLN'S BIRTHDAY, WASHINGTON'S BIRTHDAY, COLUMBUS DAY, ELECTION DAY, VETERAN'S DAY, AND THE DAY AFTER THANKSGIVING.**

WHEN ESCORT VEHICLE IS REQUIRED
- FOR ANY MOVE ACROSS, UPON OR ALONG A HIGHWAY WHEN ADDITIONAL WARNING IS REQUIRED TO ALERT THE TRAVELING PUBLIC. (IF REQUIRED TO MOVE DURING DARKNESS OR ON A WEEKEND TO RESPOND TO EMERGENCY SITUATION)
- A SEPARATE ESCORT MUST BE PROVIDED FOR EACH LOAD - CONVOYING IS PROHIBITED UNLESS POLICE ESCORT IS REQUIRED AND PERMIT OFFICE AUTHORIZES CONVOY MOVEMENT FOR MULTIPLE LOADS.
- 1 ESCORT REQUIRED—ALL MOVES THAT EXCEED 14'6' WIDE OR 14'6' HIGH OR 110' LONG
- 2 ESCORTS REQUIRED—MOVES THAT EXCEED **BOTH** 14'6" WIDE AND 14'6" HIGH
- 3 ESCORTS REQUIRED—MOVES EXCEEDING 16' WIDE OR 145' LONG AND 18' HIGH

- **STATE POLICE ESCORTS**—CALL (217) 786-7110 OR (217) 786-7107 24 HRS IN ADVANCE
- FOR ALL LOADS EXCEEDING 18' WIDE, 200' LONG, 18' HIGH, 230,000 LBS.
- FOR OVERWEIGHT MOVES WHERE BRIDGE RESTRICTIONS REQUIRE THAT ALL TRAFFIC BE KEPT OFF OF A STRUCTURE WHILE THE PERMITTED VEHICLE CROSSES
- FOR ANY MOVE OF AN UNUSUAL NATURE WHERE ADDITIONAL TRAFFIC CONTROL IS NECESSARY TO ALERT THE MOTORING PUBLIC TO THE PERMIT MOVEMENT.
- WHEN DEEMED NECESSARY BY THE DEPARTMENT'S BRIDGE OFFICE'S ANALYSIS OR BY THE DEPARTMENT'S DISTRICT INVESTIGATION.

REQUIREMENTS FOR ESCORT VEHICLES
- **GENERAL:** PASSENGER CAR/LIGHT TRUCK/VEHICLE NOT EXCEEDING 8,000 LBS GVW
- **INSURANCE:** MINIMUM AMOUNT OF $500,000 PER OCCURRENCE COMBINED BODILY INJURY & PROPERTY DAMAGE
- **SIGNS:** "OVERSIZE LOAD" SHALL BE DISPLAYED TO BE VISIBLE FROM FRONT (2-LANE) AND REAR (4-LANE)
- **LIGHTS:** FLASHING OR ROTATING AMBER LIGHTS MOUNTED ON TOP OF ROOF.
- **FLAGS:** NOT STIPULATED
- **ADDITIONAL EQUIPMENT:** 2-WAY RADIO; HEIGHT POLE

ESCORT VEHICLES SHALL TRAVEL APPROXIMATELY 300' IN FRONT OF THE LOAD (2-LANE) AND SAME IN REAR ON MULTI-LANE ROADS. A SEPARATE

REQUIREMENTS FOR ESCORT VEHICLE OPERATOR
- 18 YRS OF AGE OR OLDER W/ VALID DRIVER'S LICENSE

ILLINOIS DEPT OF TRANSPORTATION PERMITS OFFICE
(217) 785-1477

Express Pilot Services
Belvedere, IL   (IL/WI Line)

James Francey
847-489-4099
expresspilot1@gmail.com

High Pole - Chase - Steer
Superloads
Insured - Certified
CDL - Nationwide Service

Approved for: Greentree & Bennett

INDIANA

WHEN A PERMIT IS NEEDED
- OVER 8'6" WIDE
- OVER 13'6" HIGH
- TRAILER OVER 53' LONG
- OVER 80,000 LBS

SPECIAL INFORMATION NEEDED FOR PERMIT
- INDIANA ACCOUNT #
- MAKE OF TRUCK, SERIAL #, LICENSE # AND STATE, OVERALL LENGTH, WIDTH AND HEIGHT, NUMBER AND SIZE OF TIRES (OVERWEIGHT ONLY), AXLE SPACING (OVERWEIGHT ONLY), LOAD DESCRIPTION, ROUTE, IN COMPANY #

TIMES OF MOVEMENT
- LOADS OVER 110' LONG, 10' WIDE, 13'6" HIGH AND UNDER 200,000 LBS MAY TRAVEL CONTINUOUS 7 DAYS/WEEK
- LOADS OVER 16' WIDE, 15' HIGH, AND OVER 200,000 LBS MAY ONLY TRAVEL FROM 8:30 AM TO 3:30 PM MONDAY THRU FRIDAY
- LOADS 14'4" THRU 16' WIDE MAY TRAVEL 1/2 HOUR BEFORE SUNRISE—1/2 HOUR AFTER SUNSET
- RESTRICTED HOLIDAYS: **NEW YEAR'S DAY, MEMORIAL DAY, JULY 4TH, AND CHRISTMAS DAY (BEGINNING AT NOON ON THE LAST WEEKDAY PRECEDING THE HOLIDAY)**

WHEN ESCORTS ARE NEEDED
PERMITTED VEHICLES MUST HAVE ESCORTS WHEN THEY EXCEED:
- 12'4" IN WIDTH, 110' IN LENGTH OR 14'6" IN HEIGHT
- ONE ESCORT VEHICLE MUST BE IN FRONT WHEN ON UNDIVIDED
- HIGHWAY AND IN REAR WHEN ON DIVIDED HIGHWAYS
- IF OVER 14'6" HIGH, MUST HAVE AN ESCORT WITH A HEIGHT STICK
- TRAVELING IN FRONT OF LOAD
- IF BETWEEN 14"4" AND 17" WIDE, ONE REAR ESCORT ON A DUAL
- LANE DIVIDED HIGHWAY AND TWO ESCORTS (FRONT AND REAR) ON
- ALL OTHER ROADS. **HEIGHT POLE REQUIRED ABOVE 14'6".**

REQUIREMENTS FOR ESCORT VEHICLES
- **GENERAL:** PASSENGER CAR/LIGHT TRUCK/VEHICLE AUTHORIZED BY THE VEHICLE SIZE & WEIGHT SPECIALIST
- **SIGNS:** 5' X 10"; BLACK LETTERS (8" HIGH) ON YELLOW A YELLOW BACKGROUND—"OVERSIZE LOAD"
- **LIGHTS:** FLASHING OR ROTATING AMBER LIGHTS MOUNTED AT EACH END OF THE REQUIRED SIGN ABOVE THE ROOF. AS AN ALTERNATIVE A ESCORT VEHICLE MAY DISPLAY 1 (ONE) ROTATING OR FLASHING AMBER BEACON VISIBLE FROM A MINIMUM OF 500' FEET
- **FLAGS:** NONE REQUIRED
- **ADDITIONAL EQUIPMENT:** 18" STOP/SLOW PADDLE; 3 BI DIRECTIONAL REFLECTIVE TRIANGLES; 1-5 LB. B,C, FIRE EXTINGUISHER; A REFLECTIVE ORANGE VEST/SHIRT/JACKET; ADDITIONAL "OVERSIZE LOAD" SIGNS; NON-METALLIC HEIGHT POLE; 2-WAY RADIO

REQUIREMENTS FOR ESCORT VEHICLE OPERATOR
- VALID DRIVERS LICENSE

INDIANA DIVISION OF MOTOR VEHICLES/ PORT OF ENTRY & OVERLEGAL PERMITS
(208) 334-8420

DRIVERS FIRST CHOICE

PROFESSIONAL **9 YRS** DEPENDABLE

"Professionally leading the industry - one load at a time"

HIGH POLE, PILOT AND ESCORT SERVICE
MINUTES FROM IN/KY LINE I-64 AND I-65

LISA
812-406-7169

driversfirstchoice@live.com

- GENERAL & PROFESSIONAL LIABILITY
- CERTIFIED AND EQUIPPED FOR 48 STATES
- ON BOARD GPS, DELORME MAPPING, ALL STATE ATTACH.
- PA LISTED, LA PERMIT, GA & NV AMBER LIGHT PERMITS
- MULTIPLE CARS AVAILABLE - NETWORKED WITH MANY OTHERS NATIONWIDE

APPROVED FOR MOST MAJOR COMPANIES INCLUDING:
LANDSTAR, GREENTREE, BENNETT, ATS/SENTINEL, MERCER, ADMIRAL MERCHANTS, AETNA, AMERICAN TRANSPORT, MARATHON TRANSPORT

THE OVERLOAD COMPANION 2017 © FREDA BARBER BOOTH

INDIANA

J & H PILOT SERVICES
260-336-2412
Johnny Cole - CEO

HIGH POLE - LEAD - CHASE
WA / NY Certified
$2M Commercial Insurance
TWIC - Passport

WHEN A PERMIT IS NEEDED
- OVER 8'6" WIDE
- OVER 13'6" HIGH
- 14' HIGH FOR AUTO TRANSPORTERS
- TRAILER OVER 53' LONG
- OVER 80,000 LBS

SPECIAL INFORMATION NEEDED FOR PERMIT
- REGISTERED WEIGHT
- OVERHANG
- OVERWEIGHT—(MUST BE REGISTERED FOR THE AMOUNT OF WEIGHT BEING HAULED W/ COPY OF CAB CARD SENT TO STATE AS PROOF)

TIMES OF MOVEMENT
- MAY TRAVEL 1/2 HOUR BEFORE SUNRISE THRU 1/2 HOUR AFTER SUNSET 24 HOURS A DAY 7 DAYS A WEEK IF LOAD IS NOT OVER 11' WIDE, 100' LONG, OR 14'4" HIGH
- RESTRICTED HOLIDAYS: MEMORIAL DAY, JULY 4TH, AND LABOR DAY (BEGINNING AT NOON ON THE LAST WEEKDAY PRECEDING THE HOLIDAY)
- CURFEWS: DES MOINES I-235 FROM 7:00-9:00AM & FROM 4:00-6:00PM MONDAY THRU FRIDAY
- CONTINUOUS MOVES - LIMITED TO 11FT W; 14'6"H, 100'L & PERMITTED AXLE LIMITS

WHEN ESCORT VEHICLE IS REQUIRED
ALL HIGHWAYS
- 1 FRONT ESCORT W/ HEIGHT POLE—LOADS OVER 14'6" TO 20' HIGH
- OVER 20' HIGH - 1 ESCORT BUT NOT HEIGHT POLE; MUST CONTACT POWER & UTILITY COMPANIES TO ACCOMPANY LOAD OR THE CARRIER MUST HAVE AND CARRY A LETTER OF CLEARANCE FROM THEM
- 1 REAR ESCORT—LOADS OVER 120' LONG

ON 2-LANE HIGHWAYS
- 1 FRONT ESCORT—WIDTH EXCEEDS 14'6" AND TAKES UP 1/2 OF THE ROADWAY
- **OPTIONAL-** WIDTH EXCEEDS 14'6" - IF ROADWAY IS 12' OR MORE, LOAD MAY HAVE AMBER LIGHT ON POWER UNIT AND ON EXTREME REAR OF LOAD (VEHICLE)

ON 4-LANE HIGHWAYS/INTERSTATES
- 1 REAR ESCORT OVER 16'6" WIDE

REQUIREMENTS FOR ESCORT VEHICLES
- **GENERAL:** PASSENGER CAR/LIGHT TRUCK/VEHICLE AUTHORIZED BY THE VEHICLE SIZE & WEIGHT SPECIALIST
- **SIGNS:** "OVERSIZE LOAD" SIGN AT LEAST 18" X 7' WITH A MINUMUM OF 12", BLACK LETTERS, WITH A 1 1/2 " STROKE ON A YELLOW BACKGROUND, AND MOUNTED ON THE FRONT BUMPER AND ON THE REAR OF THE VEHICLE
- **LIGHTS:** AN AMBER REVOLVING LIGHT AT LEAST 7" HIGH AND 7" IN DIAMETER WITH AT LEAST A 100-CANDLEPOWER LAMP PROVIDING 360 DEGREE WARNING. A LIGHT OF SMALLER DIMENSIONS SHALL NOT BE PERMITTED UNLESS A STROBE LIGHT IS USED. MOBILES: MUST DISPLAY AMBER/STROBE/REVOLVING LIGHT ON REAR & 1 ON TOWED VEHICLE
- **FLAGS**: AN 18" X 18" RED OR ORANGE FLOURESCENT FLAG SHALL BE MOUNTED ON EACH CORNER OF THE FRONT BUMPER OF THE ESCORT VEHICLE

ADDITIONAL EQUIPMENT: NONE STIPULATED

REQUIREMENTS FOR ESCORT VEHICLE OPERATOR
- **A** PERSON AGED 18 YRS OR OVER AND WHO POSSESSES A CLASS A, B, C OR D DRIVER'S LICENSE, HAS A PROPERLY EQUIPPED VEHICLE, AND WHO CARRIES PROOF OF PUBLIC LIABILITY INSURANCE IN THE AMOUNTS OF $100,000/$200,000/$50,000

IOWA DEPT. OF TRANSPORTATION PERMITS OFFICE
(515) 244-8725 (GENERAL INFO)
(515) 237-3264; FAX (515) 237-3257 (PERMITS)

KANSAS

WHEN A PERMIT IS NEEDED
- OVER 8'6" WIDE
- OVER 14' HIGH
- TRAILER OVER 56' 6" LONG
- OVER 80,000 LBS

SPECIAL INFORMATION NEEDED FOR PERMIT
- TRUCK VIN (LAST 5)
- REGISTERED WEIGHT
- KCC# & KS FUEL # (FOR O/W ONLY)

TIMES OF MOVEMENT
- 1/2 HOUR BEFORE SUNRISE TO 1/2 HOUR AFTER SUNSET 7 DAYS A WEEK (INCLUDING HOLIDAYS); COULD BE SPECIAL CONDITIONS BUT WILL NOT BE NOTED ON THE PERMIT
- NIGHT MOVEMENT ALLOWED FOR OVERWEIGHT-ONLY LOADS
- PERMIT OFFICE CLOSED ON THE FOLLOWING HOLIDAYS: NEW YEARS DAY, MEMORIAL DAY, INDEPENDENCE DAY, LABOR DAY, THANKSGIVING DAY, AND CHRISTMAS DAY

WHEN ESCORT VEHICLE IS REQUIRED
ON HIGHWAYS LESS THAN 4 LANES:
- 1 REAR ESCORT —LOAD OVER 14' WIDE
- **ON ALL HIGHWAYS**
- 1 FRONT, 1 REAR ESCORT—MOBILE HOMES OVER 12'6" WIDE
- 1 FRONT, 1 REAR ESCORT—SUPERLOADS

REQUIREMENTS FOR ESCORT VEHICLES
- **GENERAL:** PASSENGER CAR OR 2 AXLE TRUCK; MINUMUM INSURANCE REQUIRED BY STATE IN WHICH VEHICLE IS LICENSED;
- MINUMUM 60" WIDE/MAX. 1 TONE CARRYING CAPACITY
- **SIGNS:** "OVERSIZE LOAD" SIGN AT LEAST 18" X 5' WITH A MINUMUM OF 8", BLACK LETTERS, WITH A 1 1/8 " STROKE ON A YELLOW BACKGROUND, VISIBLE 500' AND MOUNTED ON THE TOP OR FRONT OF VEHICLE
- **LIGHTS:** 2 AMBER FLASHING LIGHTS (6" OR LARGER) OR ONE ROTATING OR OSCILLATING LIGHT ON TOP OF VEHICLE; VISIBLE 1000'
- **FLAGS:** NO FLAGS REQUIRED - ** IF EQUIPPED, FLAGS MAY NOT EXCEED BEYOND MIRRORS WHEN EXTENDED STRAIGHT OUT
- **ADDITIONAL EQUIPMENT:** 18" OR 24" STOP/SLOW PADDLE SIGN; 8 REFLECTIVE TRAINGLES OR 8 RED-BURING FLARES; 3 18" HIGH ORANGE CONES; ORANGE HARD HAT; HEIGHT POLE (NON—CONDUCTIVE, FLEXIBLE OR FRANGIBLE MATERIAL) WHEN ESCORTING A LEAD EXCEEDING 17" HIGH; FIRST AID KIT; SPARE TIRE; TIRE JACK AND LUG WRENCH; ORANGE VEST/JACKET; 2(MIN) 12" RED/ORANGE HAND-HELD FLAGS; 1 5LB. B,C, FIRE EXTINGUISHER

REQUIREMENTS FOR ESCORT VEHICLE OPERATOR
- MUST HAVE IN VEHICLE A COPY OF "TRAVELING THROUGH KANSAS"
- KANSAS NO LONGER REQUIRES SUPERLOAD CERTIFICATION

KANSAS DEPT. OF TRANSPORTATION PERMITS OFFICE
Kansas no longer has updated pilot car requirements on the website.
Please contact KDOT (785) 271-3145 for more information

Kenco Bucket Trucks | HIGHLOADS.COM

FOCUS ON THE ROAD, NOT WHAT'S ABOVE IT.

Whether you're plotting a route or worrying about hazards and delays, transporting oversized loads can be stressful. But Kenco Bucket Trucks' high standards, certifications and well-equipped purple trucks make travel a snap. We make the safety of your cargo and personnel our highest priority. Plus we can assist with planning the route so there are no surprises, only smooth driving.

We ensure that when you choose HIGH LOADS, we give you OPEN ROADS.

KENCO MEANS:
- IMSA Work Zone Safety Certified
- IMSA Traffic Signal Technician Level I & II
- DISA Drug & Alcohol Tested Employees
- Professionalism, safety and reliability

KENCO Bucket Trucks
HIGH LOADS. OPEN ROADS.

TAKE A LOAD OFF. 1.877.459.3100 | HIGHLOADS.COM

30 YEARS OF SAFETY — THE SAFEST ROUTE. KENCO

THE OVERLOAD COMPANION 2017 © FREDA BARBER BOOTH

CHARLES JAMES CAYIAS INSURANCE INC.

801-488-0085

PROFESSIONAL PILOT CAR INSURANCE PACKAGE

Working in cooperation with North America's leading escort vehicle trainers, certifying entities, and insurance professionals who specialize in protecting the needs of escort operators all across the United States.

Whether an accident is your fault or not, without the right protection, you could pay tens of thousands out of pocket to defend yourself in a lawsuit brought against you by others. Be prepared by having the proper insurance protection!

The Professional Pilot Car Insurance Package offers the following insurance coverage(s):

- **Commercial Automobile**: As personal auto insurance policies exclude business operations, commercial insurance is essential. We offer $1,000,000 in bodily injury and property damage coverage, along with medical payments, personal injury protection (in those states where required), and uninsured motorists to protect you, your passengers and members of the public in case of an over the road accident. Comprehensive and collision coverage is also offered to protect your vehicle. We can provide commercial automobile coverage on a mono-line basis.
- **General Liability**: Will protect you against injuries to members of the public at your premises, and damages that you may cause to the property of others that does not involve an automobile. We offer limits of $1,000,000 each occurrence and $2,000,000 aggregate for losses occurring during the policy term. We can provide general liability coverage on a mono-line basis.
- **Professional Liability**: Will provide you with protection for those activities normally excluded under a general liability policy because they are considered to be a professional exposure. We offer $1,000,000 in coverage for flagging, height pole, route surveys and shunting services, subject to certain qualifications. No coverage is offered for rigging, steerables or tillerman services.
- **Inland Marine**: Will cover your miscellaneous equipment used in your operation such as small tools, magnetic vehicle signage, flags, cones, etc. We offer three limits of coverage $1,000; $2,500; $5,000 depending on your needs. Higher limits are available upon request.

Charles James Cayias Insurance, Inc.
2150 South 1300 East, Suite #100
Salt Lake City, UT 84106
PH: (801) 488-0085
Fax: (801) 463-6683
www.cayias.com

Program benefits include a combination of coverage specific to the pilot car industry, competitive pricing, expertise, and prompt friendly service. Simply put... our goal is to provide you with the best value for your money!

KENTUCKY

MATT WALLACE ENTERPRISES
Bowling Green, KY

Lead - Chase - High Pole - Steer

270-320-5345

We have a Large Network across the US

CO/UT/NY CERT - CO/UT FLAGGING CERT
PERMITTED/EQUIPPED FOR 48 STATES
$1M - $2M INSURED W/ PA ADD-ON

Email: matthew3e@aol.com

Follow me on Facebook!

KENTUCKY

WHEN A PERMIT IS NEEDED
- OVER 8' WIDE
- OVER 13' 6" HIGH
- TRAILER OVER 53' LONG
- OVER 80,000 LBS

SPECIAL INFORMATION NEEDED FOR PERMIT
- NEED COMPANY'S KYU NUMBER
- MANUFACTURER AND MODEL OF LOAD; OVERHANG (IF ANY)
- DOZER OVER 12' WIDE—DOES IT HAVE A BUCKET OR A BLADE?

TIMES OF MOVEMENT
- 1/2 HOUR BEFORE SUNRISE TO 1/2 HOUR AFTER SUNSET
- TRAVEL IS ALLOWED 24/7 UNLESS SPECIFIED OTHERWISE ON PERMIT
- MOBILE HOME MOVEMENT IS ALLOWED DURING DAYLIGHT HOURS ONLY, MON-SAT, WITH NO TRAVEL PERMITTED ON SUNDAY. WEEKEND TRAVEL ALLOWED EXCEPT FOR SUPERLOADS.
- NO LONGER A "HOLIDAY" RESTRICTION UNLESS IT IS A SUPERLOAD OR A HOUSE MOVE
- CURFEWS: NO OW/OD LOADS PERMITTED TO TRAVEL IN THE FOLLOWING COUNTIES: BOONE, KENTON, CAMPBELL, FAYETTE, JEFFERSON FROM 7-9 AM OR 4-6 PM M-F; (APPLIES TO OWENSBORO, KY 431 BRIDGE, AS WELL)

WHEN ESCORT VEHICLE IS REQUIRED

ON 2-LANE HIGHWAYS:
- 1 FRONT ESCORT —LOAD 10'6" TO 12' WIDE
- 1 FRONT & 1 REAR ESCORT—LOAD EXCEEDS 12' WIDE
- 1 REAR ESCORT—LOADS TRAVELING AT SPEEDS BELOW THE AVERAGE DRIVING SPEED OF SURROUNDING TRAFFIC
- 1 FRONT ESCORT—LOAD 75' TO 85' LONG
- 1 FRONT & 1 REAR ESCORT—LOADS OVER 85' LONG

4 OR MORE LANES (DIVIDED HIGHWAYS)
- 1 REAR ESCORT—LOADS OVER 12' WIDE
- 1 REAR ESCORT—TRAVELING SPEED AT LEAST 45MPH
- 1 REAR ESCORT—LOADS LENGTH 120'
- 1 FRONT, 1 REAR ESCORT—LOAD LENGTH OVER 120'
- 1 ESCORT at POINT OF OVERHANG WHEN OVER 10'

HEIGHT POLE REQUIREMENTS
- 1 FRONT ESCORT WITH HEIGHT POLE FOR HEIGHT OVER 15' - ALL ROADS

REQUIREMENTS FOR ESCORT VEHICLES
- ESCORT VEHICLES SHALL ACCOMPANY THE OVERSIZE VEHICLE AT A DISTANCE OF 300 FT ON OPEN HIGHWAYS AND WILL: MAINTAIN RADIO CONTACT WITH THE LOADED VEHICLE. VEHICLES CAPABLE OF CARRYING 2,000 LBS OR MORE REQUIRE DOT NUMBER
- **SIGNS:** POST APPROPRIATE SIGNS ON VEHICLE SHOWING NAME OF THE PILOT CAR ESCORT BUSINESS AND THE STATE OF BUSINESS OPERATION. SECURELY ATTACH A YELLOW BACKGROUND, 12" X 60", ROOF OR BUMPER MOUNTED "OVERSIZE LOAD" SIGN TO THE ESCORT VEHICLE THAT IS VISIBLE FROM A DISTANCE OF 100' FROM BOTH THE FRONT AND REAR
- **LIGHTS:** HAVE 2 OR MORE TOP MOUNTED HIGH INTENSITY FLASHING OR ROTATING AMBER LIGHTS VISIBLE FOR A FULL 360 DEGREES FOR A MIN OF 500FT IN DAYLIGHT CONDITIONS
- **FLAGS:** RED OR ORANGE FLUORESCENT FLAGS THAT ARE A MIN OF 18" SQUARE SHALL BE DISPLAYED ON ESCORT VEHICLE
- **ADDITIONAL EQUIPMENT:** 2-WAY RADIO

REQUIREMENTS FOR ESCORT VEHICLE OPERATOR
NONE AT THIS TIME

KENTUCKY DEPT. OF TRANSPORTATION PERMITS OFFICE
DIVISION OF MOTOR CARRIERS - OW/OD SECTION
(502) 564-7150; FAX (502) 564-0992

High Lines, LLC
Oversize Load Escorting
RIG MOVING SPECIALISTS

Janet Watson
Weston, WV
Fax 866-520-9531
highlines11@yahoo.com

304-203-9700

HIGH POLES - CHASE -LEAD - STEER
PERMIT WRITING ABILITY/ ACCTS - HANDS-FREE CELL BOOSTER
ON BOARD CAMERAS - GPS - DELORME / STREETS & TRIPS
LAPTOP / PRINTER

ALL STATES CERT & EQUIPPED - MULTIPLE OIL COMPANY CERTIFICATIONS
LA PERMIT - PRO-GL $2MIL - NV & GA AMBER LIGHT PERMITS

LOUISIANA

WHEN A PERMIT IS NEEDED
- OVER 8'6" WIDE
- OVER 13' 6" HIGH
- TRAILER OVER 59'6" LONG
- OVER 80,000 LBS

SPECIAL INFORMATION NEEDED FOR PERMIT
- YOU CHOOSE HOW MANY DAYS YOU WANT PERMIT TO BE VALID — PERMIT FEE'S ARE $10/DAY
- LOADS OVER 232, 000 LBS. MUST PROVIDE A DETAILED DRAWING AS PRESCRIBED BY LOUISIANA DEPARTMENT OF TRANSPORTATION AND DEVELOPMENT (DOTD)

TIMES OF MOVEMENT
- SUNRISE TO SUNSET UNLESS PROHIBITED UNDER RESTRICTION TRAVEL SECTION OF PERMIT
- **CURFEWS:** OVERSIZE LOADS OVER 12' WIDE MAY NOT TRAVEL ON THE INTERSTATE SYSTEM THROUGH SHREVEPORT, MONROE, LAKE CHARLES, BATON ROUGE AND NEW ORLEANS FROM 7-9AM AND FROM 3:30-5:30PM., MON-FRI
- TRAVEL IS PROHIBITED ON THE FOLLOWING HOLIDAYS: **MARDI GRAS DAY, MEMORIAL DAY, INDEPENDENCE DAY, LABOR DAY, THANKSGIVING DAY, CHRISTMAS DAY, AND NEW YEAR'S DAY**

WHEN ESCORT VEHICLE IS REQUIRED
PRIVATE ESCORTS:
- WIDTH OVER 12' AND UP TO 16' - 1 FRONT ESCORT IF ON 2 LANE; 1 REAR ESCORT IF ON MULTI-LANE
- LENGTH OVER 90' AND UP TO 125' - 1 REAR
- NO HEIGHT LIMIT—STATE WILL ROUTE LOADS ACCORDINGLY

NEW ORLEANS POLICE ESCORT: (504) 826-7525
- LOADS OVER 13'6" HIGH / OVER 12' WIDE/ OVER 90' LONG

STATE POLICE ESCORT:
- LOADS OVER 16' WIDE ON LANE HWY OR ON MULTI-LANE HWY
- LOADS OVER 125' LONG

AN ESCORT VEHICLE MAY ESCORT 2 OVER-LENGTH VEHICLES OR LOADS, BUT ONLY 1 OVER-WIDTH VEHICLE OR LOAD

REQUIREMENTS FOR ESCORT VEHICLES
- **GENERAL:** THE ESCORTING VEHICLE SHALL BE REGISTERED IN ACCORDANCE WITH LOUISIANA REVISED STATUTES OR RECIPROCAL AGREEMENT. CLOSED VANS, BUSES, CAMPERS, MOTOR HOMES, AND MOTOR DRIVEN CYCLES ARE NOT ACCEPTABLE
- **SIGNS:** 2 SIGNS WITH THE WORDING "OVERSIZE LOAD" ARE REQUIRED ON THE ESCORT VEHICLE. THESE SIGNS MUST BE 12" HIGH AND 5' IN LENGTH, THE LETTERING MUST BE BLACK ON A YELLOW BACKGROUND AND IS TO BE 10" HIGH WITH 1 5/8" BRUSH STROKE.
- **LIGHTS:** AN APPROVED AMBER 360 DEGREE "EMERGENCY WARNING LAMP"— INCLUDES LIGHT BAR, STROBE, ROTATING AND STATIONARY LAMPS. DOME TYPE LAMP MUST HAVE A LENS OF NOT LESS THAN 9" IN DIAMETER & 4" IN HEIGHT
- **FLAGS:** 2 RED/FLOURESCENT ORANGE FLAGS, 18" SQUARE MOUNTED ATOP THE VEHICLE IN LINE W/ WARNING LAMPS (APPROX 45 DEGREE ANGLE), EXTENDING MORE THAN 6" TO EITHER SIDE OF VEHICLE (TOTAL WIDTH NOT MORE THAN 8')
- **ADDITIONAL EQUIPMENT:** 2-WAY RADIO; IDENTIFICATION ON EACH SIDE OF VEHICLE (MUST HAVE NAME/ADDRESS OR PHONE# & CITY OF COMPANY/OWNER OF VEHICLE); 2 REAR-VIEW MIRRORS; 1 (ONE) 10 LB. BC DRY OR EQUIVALENT FIRE EXTINGUISHER; 4 15-MIN BURNING FLARES; 2 RED/FLOURESCENT ORANGE HAND-HELD FLAGS; 4 RED/FLOURESCENT ORANGE FLAGS (18" SQUARE); 2 "OVERSIZE LOAD" SIGNS (18" X 7') W/ BLACK LETTERING ON YELLOW BACKGROUND 10" HIGH W/ 1 1/2" BRUSH STROKE

REQUIREMENTS FOR ESCORT VEHICLE OPERATOR
- MUST HAVE A **LA APPROVED ESCORT VEHICLE PERMIT** (SEE FORMS AT END OF THIS BOOK) WHICH MAY BE OBTAINED FROM ANY WEIGHTS AND STANDARDS POLICE OFFICER AT A STATIONARY SCALE LOCATION OR THE LOUISIANA TRUCK CENTER. OUT-OF-STATE COMPANIES MUST PAY A $10 FEE. EACH DRIVER OF THE ESCORT VEHICLE MUST HAVE A VALID OPERATOR'S LICENSE ISSUED BY A STATE OR TERRITORY OF THE U.S. A **48-HOUR TRIP PERMIT** (FEE $10) IS REQUIRED FOR INTRASTATE MOVEMENTS, OTHERWISE ESCORTING IS LIMITED TO INTERSTATE MOVEMENT ONLY.
- EACH OUT-OF-STATE COMPANY WHICH OPERATES AN ESCORT SERVICE IN LA SHALL REGISTER ANNUALLY WITH THE SECRETARY
- APPLICANTS FOR ESCORT VEHICLES MUST HAVE PROOF TO THE DOT & DWSO OF INSURANCE FOR NOT LESS THAN $50,000 FOR BODILY INJURY TO OR DEATH OF ONE (1) PERSON IN ANY (1) ACCIDENT, $100,000 FOR BODILY INJURY OR DEATH OF TWO (2) OR MORE PERSONS IN ANY ONE (1) ACCIDENT, AND $50,000 FOR INJURY TO OR DESTRUCTION OF PROPERTY TO OTHERS IN ANY ONE (1) ACCIDENT.

LOUISIANA DEPT. OF TRANSPORTATION PERMITS OFFICE
TRUCK PERMIT SECTION
(225) 343-2345; (800) 654-1433 (NATIONWIDE)
FAX: (225) 377-7108

Grant Pilot Cars
Runnin' for America
850-381-4959
Fax: 888-791-5090
www.grantpilotcars.com

Multiple Cars Based in Several States
High Pole - CDL - Steer/Tillerman
Lead - Chase - Traffic Control
Call Us for your Large & Small Projects

FL/GA/WA Certified - $1M GL+ PA - $1M PL
TWIC & Passport
Mobile Office - Cam - GPS Equipped
Permits & Equipment for All States

Fair Rates - Experienced - Professional

MAINE

WHEN A PERMIT IS NEEDED
- OVER 8'6" WIDE
- OVER 13'6" HIGH
- TRAILER OVER 48' LONG
- OVER 80,000 LBS

SPECIAL INFORMATION NEEDED FOR PERMIT
- RW, # AXLES
- LOADS EXCEEDING 125,000 LBS. MUST SUBMIT VEHICLE CONFIGURATION WITH AXLE SPACING AND WEIGHTS FOR SPECIAL APPROVAL

TIMES OF MOVEMENT
- 1/2 HOUR BEFORE SUNRISE TO 1/2 HOUR AFTER SUNSET. TRAVEL PERMITTED SATURDAY 1/2 HOUR BEFORE SUNRISE TO 1/2 HOUR AFTER SUNSET EXCEPT DURING THE MONTHS OF JULY AND AUGUST. **THE MOVEMENT OF LOADS EXCEEDING THE LEGAL LIMITS ARE NOW PERMITED TO MOVE ON SATURDAYS AND SUNDAYS THROUGHOUT THE YEAR EXCEPT DURING THEMONTHS OF JULY AND AUGUST.**
- TRAVEL PROHIBITED: NEW YEARS DAY, MEMORIAL DAY, INDEPENDENCE DAY, LABOR DAY, COLUMBUS DAY, VETERANS DAY, THANKSGIVING DAY (AND DAY AFTER), CHRISTMAS EVE & CHRISTMAS DAY.
- MOBILE HOMES AND MODULAR UNITS OVER 13'6" TO 14'6" WIDE ARE EXCLUDED FROM MOVING FRIDAY AFTERNOONS, SATURDAYS, SUNDAYS AND MOBILE HOMES OVER 14'6" WIDE CAN ONLY MOVE ON MONDAYS, TUESDAYS, WEDNESDAYS & THURSDAYS.
- **MAINE TURNPIKE:** OVERSIZE LOADS MAY TRAVEL ON THE MAINE TURNPIKE FROM 1/2 HOUR BEFORE SUNRISE UNTIL 1/2 HOUR AFTER SUNDET (DAYLIGHT HOURS), EXCEPT FOR FRIDAY AFTERNOONS, SATURDAYS, SUNDAYS & HOLIDAYS. THE TOTAL HEIGHT IS LIMITED TO 13'6" AND TOTAL WIDTH IS LIMITED TO 14'6". FOR ADDITIONAL INFORMATION CONTACT MAINE TURNPIKE AUTHORITY, (800) 698-7747 OR (207) 871-7771
- **NIGHT MOVES:** AS DEFINED IN TITLE 29—A SECTION 101 SUB SECTION 78: MAY BE AUTHORIZED BY ANY MAINE STATE POLICE TROOP COMMANDER FOR TRAVEL AS SUCH TIMES AND PLACES, CHECK WITH MAINE STATE POLICE

WHEN ESCORT VEHICLE IS REQUIRED
ON HIGHWAYS WITH 2 LANES:
- 1 FRONT ESCORT —LOAD IS 12' TO 15'11" WIDE
- 1 FRONT ESCORT— LOAD IS 80' UP TO 124' LONG
- 1 FRONT ESCORT— LOAD OVERHANG IS 15' OR MORE
- 1 FRONT, 1 REAR ESCORT— LOAD OVERHANG IS 15' OR MORE AND WIDTH 12' OR MORE
- **ON 4 OR MORE LANES**
- SAME AS 2-LANES EXCEPT ESCORTS TRAVEL TO REAR OF LOADS

STATE POLICE ESCORTS
- MAY BE REQUIRED FOR A SUPER LOAD OF EXTREME LENGTH AND WIDTH. LENGTH OF 125' OR MORE; WIDTH OF 16' OR MORE; HEIGHT OVER 16'. CONTACT (207) 624-7000, MIN 3 DAY NOTICE REQUIRED.

MOBILE HOMES
- 1 FRONT ESCORT—LOAD IS 12' TO 14'6" WIDE
- 1 FRONT, 1 REAR ESCORT— LOAD IS 14'6" TO 16'8" WIDE
- 1 REAR ESCORT—LOAD WIDTH IS 11'6" TO 16'8" ON MULTI-LANE HIGHWAYS
- STATE POLICE ESCORT WITH DEEMED NECESSARY FOR LOADS 16' WIDE AT THE BASE AND OVER 16'8" WIDE AT ANY OTHER POINT

REQUIREMENTS FOR ESCORT VEHICLES
- **GENERAL:** PASSENGER CAR OR 2 AXLE TRUCK
- **SIGNS:** "OVERSIZE LOAD" SIGN AT LEAST 5' X 12" WITH BLACK LETTERING (8" HIGH AND 1.4" BRUSH STROKE / 1" MIN BORDER AROUND LETTERS); MOUNTED ON REAR BUMPER WHEN FOLLOWING LOAD / MOUNTED ON FRONT BUMPER WHEN PRECEDING LOAD (COULD BE MOUNTED ON ROOF)
- **LIGHTS:** 2 AMBER FLASHING LIGHTS (6" OR LARGER), ROTARY (2 AT LEAST 4" IN DIAMETER) OR LIGHT BAR (A MIN. OF 4 FLASHING, STROBE, COMBINATION)—EXTREME TOP LEFT & RIGHT OR LEFT TO RIGHT
- **FLAGS:** NOT STIPULATED
- **ADDITIONAL EQUIPMENT:** 2-WAY RADIO WITH 1 MILE RADIUS

REQUIREMENTS FOR ESCORT VEHICLE OPERATOR
- MUST BE AT LEAST 18 YRS OF AGE; MUST HAVE HAD AN OPERATORS LICENSE FOR 2 CONSECUTIVE YEARS

MAINE DEPT. OF TRANSPORTATION PERMITS OFFICE
OVERLIMIT PERMIT UNIT - (207)624-9318; FAX (207) 622-5332

High Pole / Steer
Lead - Chase
NY / WA Cert
Passport

207-240-2535

mpcs1243@gmail.com

THE OVERLOAD COMPANION 2017 © FREDA BARBER BOOTH

WASHINGTON STATE CERTIFICATION
By
SUE MISS

Certified Instructor

12 YRS ESCORTING EXPERIENCE

OWNER - PEGASUS PILOTS, LLC
HAGERSTOWN, MD

CLASSES HELD LOCALLY EVERY MONTH

AREA (I-70 & I-81 INTERCHANGE)
MOST REASONABLE PRICES
WE GIVE DISCOUNTS FOR GROUPS OF 10+
WILLING TO TRAVEL

PEGASUS PILOTS LLC
301-991-4406

MARYLAND

WHEN A PERMIT IS NEEDED
- OVER 8'6" WIDE
- OVER 13' 6" HIGH
- TRAILER OVER 48' LONG
- OVER 80,000 LBS

SUPER LOADS: 120' IN LENGTH; 16' WIDTH; 16' HEIGHT

SPECIAL INFORMATION NEEDED FOR PERMIT
- TYPE OF LOAD (MAKE, MODEL & SERIAL #)
- REGISTERED WEIGHT OF TRACTOR, TRAILER AND LOAD

SPECIAL LIGHTS, SIGNS, FLAGS: 2 RED LIGHTS DISPLAYED ON REAR OVERHANG EXCEEDING 4' AND ONE ON EACH SIDE OF LOAD.

TIMES OF MOVEMENT
- 1/2 HOUR BEFORE SUNRISE TO 1/2 HOUR AFTER SUNSET; SATURDAY UNTIL NOON
- NO TRAVEL ON SUNDAY
- UP TO 12' WIDE, 90' IN LENGTH, 14'6 TALL, 150,000 GVW - MON 12:01 AM TO NOON SAT.

NIGHT MOVES: LOADS UP TO WEIGHT 120K GVW, WIDTH 12', HEIGHT 14'6", LENGTH 75' MAY MOVE FROM 9PM TO 5AM EST

CURFEWS / RESTRICTIONS
- IF THE LOAD EXCEEDS 45 TONS GVW, 100' IN LENGTH, OR 12' IN WIDTH TRAVEL ON I-495 AND I-95 (CAPITAL BELTWAY) OR I-695 (BALTIMORE BELTWAY) FROM 9AM-3:30PM; IF 14' WIDE OR MORE, 9:00AM TO 3:30PM ON ANY HIGHWAY.
- BEFORE MAKING YOUR MOVE ACROSS FACILITIES OWNED AND OPERATED BY THE MARYLAND TRANSPORTATION AUTHORITY, PLEASE CALL THE FACILITIES LISTED FOR ADDITIONAL INFORMATION.
- ROUTE AND TRAVEL RESTRICTIONS AS WELL AS RESTRICTIONS ON THE HOURS OF MOVEMENT WILL BE LISTED ON YOUR PERMIT.
- TRAVEL IS PROHIBITED ON THE FOLLOWING HOLIDAYS: **NEW YEAR'S DAY, GOOD FRIDAY, MEMORIAL DAY, INDEPENDENCE DAY, LABOR DAY, THANKSGIVING DAY, CHRISTMAS DAY**
- **PERMIT OFFICES CLOSED:** PREVIOUSLY LISTED PLUS MLK DAY, COLUMBUS DAY, ELECTION DAY, DAY AFTER THANKSGIVING

TOLL ENTRANCES
- TOLL, BRIDGE & TUNNEL RESTRICTIONS - CALL 1-800-846-6435 (SEE ADD'L NUMBERS BELOW
- DRIVER MUST CONTACT TOLL FACILITIES AT LEAST ONE HR BEFORE ARRIVAL TOLL LANE IS FAR RIGHT ONLY - IF CLOSED - WAIT FOR MDTA TO OPEN FOR YOU

WHEN ESCORT VEHICLE IS REQUIRED
ON ALL HIGHWAYS:
- WIDTH OVER 13' AND UP TO 14' (EXCEPT MFG HOMES)- 1 PILOT/ESCORT
- WIDTH OVER 14' WIDE OR MORE (INCLUDING MFG HOMES) - 2 PILOT/ESCORTS
- OVER 85' - 140' LONG—1 PILOT/ESCORT
- OVER 100' LONG—2 PILOTS/ ESCORTS
- OVER 14'6" HIGH OR MORE—1 PILOT/ESCORT WITH HEIGHT POLE
- OVER 60 TONS GVW—1 PILOT/ESCORT
- IF ROAD IS TOO NARROW TO PASS SAFELY OR IF TRAFFIC WILL HAVE TO BE DIVERTED/STOPPED OR WEATHER/ROAD CONDITIONS REQUIRE IT —2 PILOT/ESCORTS NEEDED

POLICE ESCORTS NEEDED WHEN:
- 16' WIDE OR MORE
- OVER 75 TONS GVW
- OR IF TRAFFIC WILL HAVE TO BE DIVERTED OR STOPPED OR IF IT WILL AFFECT 2 OR MORE LANES OF TRAFFIC ON A HIGHWAY HAVING ONLY 1 LANE IN EACH DIRECTION

REQUIREMENTS FOR ESCORT VEHICLES
- **SIGNS:** "OVERSIZE LOAD"/"WIDE LOAD" SIGN W/ BLACK LETTERS (8"HIGH) ON A YELLOW BACKGROUND (5' X 12") MOUNTED ON THE ROOF OF VEHICLE
- **LIGHTS:** 1 (ONE) OSCILLATING OR ROTATING ROOF LIGHT, YELLOW IN COLOR, AT LEAST 3" IN DIAMETER AND VISIBLE FROM THE FRONT AND REAR. HEADLIGHTS SHALL BE ON WHILE CONDUCTING THE MOVE
- **FLAGS:** NOT STIPULATED
- **ADDITIONAL EQUIPMENT:** 2-WAY RADIO FOR CONSTANT COMMUNICATION

REQUIREMENTS FOR ESCORT VEHICLE OPERATOR
- IT IS REQUIRED THAT ALL ESCORT DRIVERS POSSESS A TRANSPORTATION WORKER IDENTIFICATION CREDENTIAL (TWIC) TO ENTER THE PORT OF BALTIMORE.

MARYLAND DEPT. OF TRANSPORTATION PERMITS OFFICE
STATE HIGHWAY ADMINISTRATION
HAULING PERMITS SECTION
(800) 543-4564; (410) 582-5727; (800) 846-6435; FAX: (410) 787-2863

http://www.roads.maryland.gov/Index.aspx?PageId=500

TOLL FACILITIES:

LANE BRIDGE (US 50)	(410) 757-1977
POTOMAC (NICE BRIDGE) (US 301)	(301) 259-4444
JFK MEMORIAL HIGHWAY	(410) 537-1108
CHESAPEAKE BAY BRIDGE (US50/301)	(410) 295-8150
FRANCIS SCOTT KEY BRDG	(410) 228-8573
HATEM BRIDGE (US 40)	(410) 537-1197
FORT MC HENRY TUNNEL	(410) 537-1230

High Lines, LLC
Oversize Load Escorting
RIG MOVING SPECIALISTS

Janet Watson
Weston, WV
Fax 866-520-9531
highlines11@yahoo.com

304-203-9700

HIGH POLES - CHASE -LEAD - STEER
PERMIT WRITING ABILITY/ ACCTS - HANDS-FREE CELL BOOSTER
ON BOARD CAMERAS - GPS - DELORME / STREETS & TRIPS
LAPTOP / PRINTER

ALL STATES CERT & EQUIPPED - MULTIPLE OIL COMPANY CERTIFICATIONS
LA PERMIT - PRO-GL $2MIL - NV & GA AMBER LIGHT PERMITS

MASACHUSETTS TUNNEL OS/OW RESTRICTIONS

A VEHICLE DOES NOT REQUIRE A SPECIAL PERMIT WITH RESPECT TO ITS SIZE IF THE VEHICLE DOES NOT EXCEED ANY OF THE FOLLOWING MAXIMUM DIMENSIONS:

VEHICLE WIDTH

WIDTH, INCLUDING LOAD IS NO GREATER THAN EIGHT FEET, SIX INCHES FOR USE OF THE TUNNELS.

VEHICLE HEIGHT

HEIGHT, INCLUDING LOAD, IS NO GREATER THAN THE FOLLOWING MAXIMUM VEHICLE HEIGHT FOR THE WAY UPON WHICH THE VEHICLE IS TRAVELING:

WAY	MAXIMUM VEHICLE HEIGHT
TURNPIKE	13' 6"
TED WILLIAMS TUNNEL	13' 6"
CALLAHAN TUNNEL	12' 6"
SUMNER TUNNEL	12' 6"
O'Neill Tunnel (I-93)	13' 6"
CANA (CITY SQUARE) TUNNELS	13' 6"
OTHER LOCATIONS NOT LISTED	13' 6"

VEHICLE LENGTH

TYPE OF VEHICLE	MAXIMUM VEHICLE LENGTH
MOTOR VEHICLE NOT LISTED	33'
VEHICLE COMBINATION NOT LISTED OTHER THAN SEMI TRAILER	60'
AUTO HOME	40'
AUTOMOBILE TRANSPORTER (TRADITIONAL)	65'
AUTOMOBILE TRANSPORTER (STINGER-STEERED)	75'
BOAT TRANSPORTER (TRADITIONAL)	65'
BOAT TRANSPORTER (STINGER-STEERED)	75'
BOAT TRANSPORTER (TRUCK TRAILER)	65'
HOUSE TRAILER	40'
SADDLEMOUNT COMBINATION	75'
TRAILER IN TRACTOR-TRAILER COMBINATION	53'
TRAILER NOT IN TRACTOR-TRAILER COMBINATION	33'
TRUCK	40'

MASSACHUSETTS

WHEN A PERMIT IS NEEDED
- OVER 8'6" WIDE
- OVER 13' 6" HIGH
- TRAILER OVER 53' LONG
- OVER 80,000 LBS

SPECIAL INFORMATION NEEDED FOR PERMIT
- MOBILE HOMES 100' LONG; 14'11" WIDE AND OVER 13'8" HIGH REQUIRED A ROUTE SURVEY

TIMES OF MOVEMENT
- ALL OVER DIMENSIONAL AND OVERWEIGHT VEHICLES MAY TRAVEL MONDAY 12:01AM—12:00 NOON SATURDAY; UNTIL NOON SUNDAY
- VEHICLES BETWEEN 12' AND 14' WIDE, OVER 80' BUT NOT LONGER THAN 115' & NOT OVER 14' HIGH MAY TRAVEL DURING DAYLIGHT HOURS ONLY EXCEPT BETWEEN THE HOURS OF 3:30-7:00PM
- VEHICLES OVER 14' WIDE AND/OR OVER 115' LONG MAY TRAVEL ONLY ON TUESDAY—THURSDAY FROM 9:30AM—3:30PM
- TRAVEL IS PROHIBITED ON THE FOLLOWING HOLIDAYS: **NEW YEAR'S DAY, GOOD FRIDAY, MEMORIAL DAY, INDEPENDENCE DAY, LABOR DAY, THANKSGIVING DAY, CHRISTMAS DAY (STARTS AT NOON THE DAY BEFORE THE HOLIDAY AND ENDS AT NOON THE DAY AFTER)**
- **CURFEWS & RESTRICTIONS:** MA HAS MANY TURNPIKE/TOLL RESTRICTIONS. FOR TRAVEL TIMES/SIZES CONTACT MA TURNPIKE (781) 431-5000 (M-F; 8AM-4:45PM)

WHEN ESCORT VEHICLE IS REQUIRED
ON ALL HIGHWAYS
- WIDTH OVER 12' AND UP TO 13'5" - 1 REAR PILOT CAR
- WIDTH OVER 13'6" - 1 FRONT & 1 REAR PILOT CAR
- OVER 13'6" HIGH (DEPENDING ON ROUTE)—1 FRONT PILOT CAR
- OVER 13'11" HIGH (DEPENDING ON ROUTE) - 1 FRONT & 1 REAR PILOT CAR
- OVER 13'8" - ROUTE SURVEY NEEDED
- 80' TO 95' LONG—1 REAR PILOT CAR
- OVER 95' LONG—1 FRONT & 1 REAR PILOT CAR
- OVER 115' LONG—MA STATE POLICE & 1 FRONT & 1 REAR PILOT CAR

IN BOSTON
- IF OVER LEGAL DIMENSIONS—AT LEAST 1 ESCORT & USUALLY CITY POLICE

ON MASSACHUSETTS TURNPIKE
- WIDTH OVER 12' —1 REAR PILOT CAR
- WIDTH OVER 13' - 1 FRONT & 1 REAR PILOT CAR
- WIDTH OVER 15' - 1 FRONT & 1 REAR PILOT CAR PLUS 2 POLICE
- OVER 80' LONG—1 REAR PILOT CAR
- OVER 85' LONG—1 FRONT & 1 REAR PILOT CAR
- OVER 135' LONG—1 FRONT & 1 REAR PILOT CAR PLUS 2 POLICE

ON CAPE COD
- WIDTH OVER 12' AT LEAST 1 STATE POLICE

REQUIREMENTS FOR ESCORT VEHICLES
- **GENERAL:** LIGHT TRUCK OR PASSENGER CAR
- **SIGNS:** "OVERSIZE LOAD" SIGN
- **LIGHTS:** 2 FLASHING AMBER LIGHTS VISIBLE FROM FRONT AND REAR
- **FLAGS:** 24" SQUARE RED FLAGS ON RIGHT AND LEFT REAR
- **ADDITIONAL EQUIPMENT:** NONE STIPULATED

MASSACHUSETTS DEPT. OF TRANSPORTATION PERMITS OFFICE
HIGHWAY DEPT (508) 473-4778; FAX (508) 473-0865

MARTIN EMERSON
SABATTUS, MAINE
NEW YORK STATE CERTIFIED ESCORT
High Pole - Lead - Chase - Steer
Certified   Fully Insured   Passport
Heavy, Wide or Tall, We'll Help You Haul 'Em All
207-240-7876
emerson01@rocketmail.com
EMERSON PILOT CAR SERVICES - EPCS

THE OVERLOAD COMPANION 2017 © FREDA BARBER BOOTH

MICHIGAN

Escorting America

EscortingAmerica@gmail.com

CERTIFIED, PROFESSIONAL, AND EXPERIENCED

Elizabeth - Mark - Alexandra
(330)413-4532   (330)313-5954   (443)206-1865

Hi-Pole - Lead - Chase - Steer

SIZE MATTERS

MEMBER
SC&RA — Specialized Carriers & Rigging Association

National Pilot Car Association

MICHIGAN

WHEN A PERMIT IS NEEDED
- OVER 8'6" WIDE
- OVER 13' 6" HIGH
- TRAILER OVER 50' LONG
- OVER 80,000 LBS. ON 5 AXLES

SPECIAL INFORMATION NEEDED FOR PERMIT
- LOAD DESCRIPTION; WEIGHT, WIDTH, HEIGHT, LENGTH
- TRACTOR WIDTH
- TRAILER LENGTH
- OVERALL WIDTH, HEIGHT, LENGTH, REAR OVERHANG
- TO AND FROM DESTINATION
- REQUESTED ROUTE

TIMES OF MOVEMENT
- 1/2 HOUR BEFORE SUNRISE TO 1/2 HOUR AFTER SUNSET; NO WEEKEND TRAVEL
- **CURFEWS:** MOVEMENT IS NOT ALLOWED FROM 7AM—9AM & FROM 3PM—6PM IN THE FOLLOWING COUNTIES: GENESEE, INGHAM, JACKSON, KALAMAZOO, KENT, MUSKEGON, MACOMB, OAKLAND, SAGINAW, WAYNE, AND WESTENAU
- TRAVEL IS PROHIBITED ON THE FOLLOWING HOLIDAYS: **MEMORIAL DAY, INDEPENDENCE DAY, GOOD FRIDAY, LABOR DAY, THANKSGIVING DAY, CHRISTMAS DAY, AND NEW YEAR'S DAY**

WHEN ESCORT VEHICLE IS REQUIRED
2 LANE HIGHWAYS:
- WIDTH OVER 12' AND UP TO 14' - 1 PILOT CAR
- WIDTH OVER 14' 2 (FRONT & REAR)
- 90' TO 100' LONG—1 REAR PILOT CAR
- OVER 100' LONG—2 (FRONT & REAR)
- OVER 14'5" HIGH—1 FRONT PILOT CAR W/ HEIGHT POLE
- OVER 15' HIGH—1 FRONT PILOT CAR W/ HEIGHT POLE & 1 REAR PILOT CAR
- OVERHANG OVER 15' - 1 REAR PILOT CAR

MOBILE HOMES/MODULAR LOADS
- 12' TO 14' WIDE—1 REAR PILOT CAR

REQUIREMENTS FOR ESCORT VEHICLES
- **GENERAL:** PASSENGER CAR OR PICKUP
- **SIGNS:** "OVERSIZE LOAD" SIGN (5' X 12") W/ BLACK LETTERS (8" HIGH) ON A YELLOW BACKGROUND MOUNTED ON ROOF OF VEHICLE
- **LIGHTS:** 1 (ONE) FLASHING/ROTATING AMBER LIGHT ON TOP OF VEHICLE VISIBLE FOR 500'
- **FLAGS:** NO STIPULATIONS
- **ADDITIONAL EQUIPMENT:** A HEIGHT POLE IS REQUIRED AND SET AT A HEIGHT TO ASSURE CLEARANCE OF THE LOAD IF HEIGHT OF LOAD EXCEEDS 14'6"

REQUIREMENTS FOR ESCORT VEHICLE OPERATOR
- NONE STIPULATED

MICHIGAN DEPT. OF TRANSPORTATION PERMITS OFFICE
PERMITS UNIT (517) 636-6915

INTERNATIONAL BRIDGE AUTHORITY:
- SAULT STE. MARIE, (906) 635-5255

MACKINAC BRIDGE AUTHORITY
- ST. IGNACE, (906) 643-7600 (MUST CALL 24HRS IN ADVANCE BEFORE CROSSING)

US CUSTOMS: BORDER CROSSING INFORMATION
- SAULT STE. MARIE (906) 632-2831
- DETROIT TUNNEL (313) 567-4422
- BLUE WATER BRIDGE (810) 984-3131
- AMBASSADOR BRIDGE (313) 226-3139 (10' WIDE RESTRICTION)

Dragonfly Pilot Car Service
Homeworth, Ohio

Connie Green - Owner

Lead, Chase, Site Survey
Certified / Fully Insured

330-614-8939

THE OVERLOAD COMPANION 2017 © FREDA BARBER BOOTH

MINNESOTA

WHEN A PERMIT IS NEEDED
- OVER 8'6" WIDE
- OVER 13' 6" HIGH
- TRAILER OVER 53' LONG
- OVER 80,000 LBS.

SPECIAL INFORMATION NEEDED FOR PERMIT
- FAX # NEAR MINNESOTA
- TRUCK MAKE, EMPTY WEIGHT, LICENSE AND STATE
- MINNESOTA REGISTERED WEIGHT
- TRAILER MAKE, DIMENSIONS, EMPTY WIEGHT AND LICENSE
- LOAD INFO, SERIAL #, NET WEIGHT
- ARE YOU FOR HIRE?
- WHAT CAN STRETCHED TRAILER BE REDUCED TO?
- KING PIN SETTING FOR O/W OR LONG TRAILERS

TIMES OF MOVEMENT
- 2AM UNTIL 10PM DAILY
- DURING SUMMER MONTHS NO TRAVEL FROM 2:00PM ON FRI. TO SUNRISE ON SAT
- TRAVEL IS PROHIBITED ON THE FOLLOWING HOLIDAYS: **NEW YEAR'S DAY, MAIN FISHING OPENING DAY, MEMORIAL DAY, INDEPENDENCE DAY, LABOR DAY, THANKSGIVING DAY, AND CHRISTMAS DAY.**
- NO TRAVEL 2:00PM THE DAY BEFORE A HOLIDAY TILL SUNRISE THE DAY AFTER THE HOLIDAY OR THE HOLIDAY WEEKEND
- NO MOVEMENT AFTER 2PM ON FRIDAYS, AND SUNDAYS STARTING WITH THE MEMORIAL DAY WEEKEND THROUGH THE LABOR DAY WEEKEND
- **NO MOVEMENT IN DULUTH FROM 7:30AM—8:30AM AND 4PM –5:30PM**
- PERMIT OFFICE IS CLOSED ON THE ABOVE HOLIDAYA PLUS : **MARTIN LUTHER KING DAY, PRESIDENT'S DAY, VETERAN'S DAY, AND THE DAY AFTER THANKSGIVING**

WHEN ESCORT VEHICLE IS REQUIRED
2 LANE HIGHWAYS:
- WIDTH OF 14'6" TO 16' ON SINGLE LANE RDS—2 PILOT CARS

ON MULTI-LANE DIVIDED HIGHWAYS:
- WIDTH OF 14'6" TO 16' - 1 PILOT CAR

LOADS REQUIRING ESCORTS
- OVER 16' WIDE—2 PILOT CARS
- 95' TO 110' LONG—1 PILOT CAR
- OVER 110' LONG—2 PILOT CARS
- OVER 15' 6" HIGH—ROUTE SURVEY REQUIRED

REQUIREMENTS FOR ESCORT VEHICLES
- **GENERAL:** PASSENGER CAR OR PICKUP
- **SIGNS:** "WIDE LOAD" OR "LONG LOAD" SIGN SHALL BE DISPLAYED ON **TOP** OF THE ESCORT VEHICLE. MINIMUM 12" X 60",; BLACK LETTERS (8" HIGH, 1 1/8" BRUSH STROKE) ON A YELLOW BACKGROUND. SIGNS SHALL NOT EXTEND BEYOUND THE LINE OF THE FENDORS ON THE LEFT SIDE NOR MORE THAN 6" BEYOND THE FENDOR LINE ON THE RIGHT SIDE OF THE PILOT CAR/ESCORT VEHICLE. FOR NIGHT TRAVEL THE SIGNS MUST BE LIGHTED OR REFLECTIVE.
- **LIGHTS:** SINGLE OR DUAL AMBER LIGHT MOUNTED AT THE TOP OR SIDES OF THE SIGN (AT LEAST 5' ABOVE THE ROAD SURFACE). LIGHTS SHALL FLASH AT A RATE OF 60-90 FLASHES/MINUTE; MAY BE DISC OR STROBE TYPE OR ROTATING BEACON; VISIBLE/READABLE FROM 500' AWAY. MUST BE LIGHTED FOR NIGHT TIME TRAVEL.
- **FLAGS:** NO STIPULATIONS
- **ADDITIONAL EQUIPMENT:** 2-WAY RADIO

REQUIREMENTS FOR ESCORT VEHICLE OPERATOR
- THE PILOT CAR /ESCORT DRIVER SHALL BE NOT LESS THAN 18YRS OF AGE
- MINNESOTA RESIDENTS MUST BE CERTIFIED IN MINNESOTA - ALL OTHERS MAY HAVE RECIPROCATING CERTIFICATE

MINNESOTA DEPT. OF TRANSPORTATION PERMITS OFFICE

MINNESOTA TRUCK CENTER
(800) 657-3959
(651) 405-6000
(651) 405-6024 (FAX)

THE OVERLOAD COMPANION 2017 © FREDA BARBER BOOTH

CHARLES JAMES CAYIAS INSURANCE INC.

801-488-0085

PROFESSIONAL PILOT CAR INSURANCE PACKAGE

Working in cooperation with North America's leading escort vehicle trainers, certifying entities, and insurance professionals who specialize in protecting the needs of escort operators all across the United States.

Whether an accident is your fault or not, without the right protection, you could pay tens of thousands out of pocket to defend yourself in a lawsuit brought against you by others. Be prepared by having the proper insurance protection!

The Professional Pilot Car Insurance Package offers the following insurance coverage(s):

- **Commercial Automobile**: As personal auto insurance policies exclude business operations, commercial insurance is essential. We offer $1,000,000 in bodily injury and property damage coverage, along with medical payments, personal injury protection (in those states where required), and uninsured motorists to protect you, your passengers and members of the public in case of an over the road accident. Comprehensive and collision coverage is also offered to protect your vehicle. We can provide commercial automobile coverage on a mono-line basis.
- **General Liability**: Will protect you against injuries to members of the public at your premises, and damages that you may cause to the property of others that does not involve an automobile. We offer limits of $1,000,000 each occurrence and $2,000,000 aggregate for losses occurring during the policy term. We can provide general liability coverage on a mono-line basis.
- **Professional Liability**: Will provide you with protection for those activities normally excluded under a general liability policy because they are considered to be a professional exposure. We offer $1,000,000 in coverage for flagging, height pole, route surveys and shunting services, subject to certain qualifications. No coverage is offered for rigging, steerables or tillerman services.
- **Inland Marine**: Will cover your miscellaneous equipment used in your operation such as small tools, magnetic vehicle signage, flags, cones, etc. We offer three limits of coverage $1,000; $2,500; $5,000 depending on your needs. Higher limits are available upon request.

Charles James Cayias Insurance, Inc.
2150 South 1300 East, Suite #100
Salt Lake City, UT 84106
PH: (801) 488-0085
Fax: (801) 463-6683
www.cayias.com

Program benefits include a combination of coverage specific to the pilot car industry, competitive pricing, expertise, and prompt friendly service. Simply put... our goal is to provide you with the best value for your money!

MISSISSIPPI

WHEN A PERMIT IS NEEDED
- OVER 8'6" WIDE
- OVER 13' 6" HIGH
- TRAILER OVER 53' LONG
- OVER 80,000 LBS.

SPECIAL INFORMATION NEEDED FOR PERMIT
- NEED TO HAVE A CERTIFICATE OF INSURANCE ON FILE LISTING THE STATE OF MISSISSIPPI AS A CERTIFICATE HOLDER
- ALL LOADS OVER 15'8" HIGH REQUIRE A ROUTE SURVEY W/ HEIGHT POLE

TIMES OF MOVEMENT
- 1/2 HOUR BEFORE SUNRISE TO 1/2 HOUR AFTER SUNSET; WEEKEND TRAVEL IS PERMITTED UNTIL 1/2 HOUR BEFORE SUNSET ON SAT. NO SUNDAY TRAVEL
- TRAVEL IS PROHIBITED ON THE FOLLOWING HOLIDAYS: **NEW YEAR'S DAY, MEMORIAL DAY, INDEPENDENCE DAY, LABOR DAY, THANKSGIVING DAY, AND CHRISTMAS DAY (NO MOVEMENT AFTER NOON ON DAY PRECEDING THESE HOLIDAYS)**
- **CURFEWS:** NO MOVEMENT FOR LOADS IN EXCESS OF 12' WIDE IN THE MAJOR URBAN AREAS OF MEMPHIS/SOUTH HAVEN, JACKSON & GULF COAST (EXCEPT I-10) 7AM-8:30AM & 4:30PM—5:30PM

WHEN ESCORT VEHICLE IS REQUIRED
ON ALL HIGHWAYS:
- OVERALL LENGTH 95' TO 105' - 1 REAR PILOT CAR
- OVER 105' LONG—2 (FRONT & REAR)
- OVER 12' WIDE—1 PILOT CAR
- OVERHANG OF 15' OR MORE IN FRONT—1 FRONT PILOT CAR
- OVERHANG OF 15' OR MORE IN REAR—1 REAR PILOT CAR

MOBILE HOMES/MODULAR LOADS
ON 2 LANE HIGHWAYS
- WIDTH UNDER 14' WIDE—1 FRONT PILOT CAR
- WIDTH 14'1" TO 16' - 2 PILOT CARS

ON 4 LANE OR MORE LANE HIGHWAYS
- 14' TO 16' WIDE—1 REAR PILOT CAR

NIGHT MOVEMENTS
- WHEN OPERATING ON 2-LANE ROADWAYS LOADS 10' WIDE OR GREATER WILL REQUIRE AT MIN THE USE OF A FRONT ESCORT AND FLASHING AMBER LIGHTS MOUNTED ON THE REAR OF THE LOAD.
- WHEN OPERATING ON DIVIDED HIGHWAYS LOADS 10' WIDE OR GREATER WILL REQUIRE AT MIN THE USE OF A REAR ESCORT AND FLASHING AMBER LIGHTS MOUNTED ON THE REAR OF THE LOAD
- LOADS LESS THAN 10' WIDE WILL REQUIRE, AT MIN, FLASHING AMBER LIGHTS MOUNTED ON THE REAR OF THE LOAD

(NO PILOT CAR REQUIRED)

REQUIREMENTS FOR ESCORT VEHICLES
- **GENERAL:** PASSENGER CAR OR PICKUP
- **SIGNS:** "OVERSIZE LOAD" SIGN MOUNTED ON FRONT OF LEAD ESCORT & ON REAR OF THE FOLLOWING ESCORT OR FRONT AND REAR OF SINGLE ESCORT
- **LIGHTS:** FLASHING OR REVOLVING AMBER LIGHT
- **FLAGS:** 2 RED FLAGS MOUNTED ON TOP OF THE VEHICLE
- **ADDITIONAL EQUIPMENT:** 2-WAY RADIO

MISSSSIPPI DEPT. OF TRANSPORTATION PERMITS OFFICE
(601) 359-1717 - (888) 737-0061 - (601) 459-1544 (FAX)

MISSOURI

WHEN A PERMIT IS NEEDED
- OVER 8'6" WIDE
- OVER 13' 6" HIGH
- TRAILER OVER 53' LONG
- OVER 80,000 LBS.

SPECIAL INFORMATION NEEDED FOR PERMIT
- MODEL AND SERIAL #
- TRAILER & LOAD LENGTH

TIMES OF MOVEMENT
- 1/2 HOUR BEFORE SUNRISE TO 1/2 HOUR AFTER SUNSET EXCEPT IN METROPOLITAN AND TOURIST AREAS
- TRAVEL PERMITED ALL DAY SATURDAY. NO SUNDAY MOVEMENT

CURFEWS: (SEE BOTTOM OF PAGE)
- ST. LOUIS CITY & COUNTY, EXCEPT ROUTE 370 - 6:30AM TO 9:00AM / 3:30PM TO 6:30PM
- ST. CHARLES COUNTY ON I-70, EASTBOUND TRAVEL BETWEEN THE JUNCTION WITH ROUTE 61 AND THE MISSOURI RIVER BRIDGE IS RESTRICTED FROM 6:30AM TO 9:00AM
- I-70 WESTBOUND BETWEEN THE MISSOURI BRIDGE JUNCTION WITH ROUTE 61 IS RESTRICTED FROM 3:30PM TO 6:30PM.
- ROUTE 40/61 (I-64) (BOTH DIRECTIONS) BETWEEN THE MISSOURI RIVER BRIDGE AND I-70 AND ROUTE 94 (BOTH DIRECTIONS) BETWEEN ROUTE 370 AND ROUTE 40/61 (I-64) ARE RESTRICTED FROM 6:30AM TO 9:00AM AND 3:30PM TO 6:30PM.
- JEFFERSON COUNTY ON I-55 (BOTH DIRECTIONS) BETWEEN THE ST. LOUIS COUNTY LINE AND ROUTE 67
- ROUTE 21 AND ROUTE 30 (BOTH DIRECTIONS) BETWEEN ST. LOUIS COUNTY LINE AND ROUTE BB; ROUTE 141 (BOTH DIRECTIONS BETWEEN THE ST. LOUIS COUNTY LINE AND ROUTE 61/67 IS RESTRICTED BETWEEN THE HOURS OF 6:30AM TO 9:00AM AND 3:30PM TO 6:30PM.
- IN THE KANSAS CITY AREA ON THE ROUTES OR INSIDE OF THE AREA BOUNDED BY ROUTES 150, 291, I-470, 152 W, TO I-435 (PLATTE COUNTY) EXIT 24 SOUTH TO THE KANSAS STATE LINE, TRAVEL IS RESTRICTED BETWEEN THE HOURS OF 7:00AM TO 9:00AM AND 4:00PM TO 6:00PM.
- INSIDE THE CITY LIMITS OF SPRINGFIELD, TRAVEL IS RESTRICTED ON ALL ROUTES ON THE STATE HIGHWAY SYSTEM BETWEEN THE HOURS OF 7:00AM TO 9:00AM AND 4:00PM TO 6:00PM, EXCEPT I-44— RESTRICTED BETWEEN 4:00PM AND 6:00PM ONLY.
- U.S. 60— RESTRICTED BETWEEN 4:00PM AND 6:00PM ONLY; U.S. 65— RESTRICTED BETWEEN 7:00AM TO 9:00AM AND BETWEEN 3:30PM AND 6:00PM

MISSOURI HOLIDAY TRAVEL RESTRICTIONS
TRAVEL IS PROHIBITED ON THE FOLLOWING HOLIDAYS:
- **MEMORIAL DAY, INDEPENDENCE DAY, LABOR DAY, THANKSGIVING DAY, CHRISTMAS DAY, NEW YEAR'S DAY.**
- RESTRICTIONS BEGIN AT NOON OF THE WEEKDAY BEFORE THE HOLIDAY AND LIGHTS THE DAY AFTER—OVERWEIGHT TRAVEL RESTRICTION LIFTED AT 12:01AM/OVERDIMENSION TRAVEL RESTRICTION LIFTED 30 MIN BEFORE SUNRISE.

WHEN ESCORT VEHICLE IS REQUIRED
2 LANE AND DIVIDED HIGHWAYS:
- WIDTH OVER 12'4" AND UP TO 14' ON 2-LANE - 1 FRONT PILOT CAR
- WIDTH OVER 12'4" AND UP TO 14' (ON DESIGNATED HIGHWAYS) - 2 (FRONT &REAR)
- WIDTH OVER 14' TO 16' - 2 (FRONT & REAR)
- OVER 90' LONG FOR A COMBO UNIT ON ALL HIGHWAYS EXCEPT DIVIDED– 1 REAR
- OVER 15'6" HIGH (& ROUTE SURVEY) - 1 PILOT CAR W/ HEIGHT POLE

ON INTERSTATE & DIVIDED MULTI-LANE HIGHWAYS:
- 12'4" TO 16' WIDE—1 REAR PILOT CAR
- OVER 15'6" HIGH (& ROUTE SURVEY) - 1 PILOT CAR W/ HEIGHT POLE

SUPERLOADS:
- LOADS EXCEEDING 16' WIDE, 16' HIGH, 150' LONG AND/OR 160,000 LB GW
- IF OVER 17'5" HIGH, TRANSPORTER MUST HAVE WRITTEN APPROVAL FROM THE APPROPRIATE UTILITY COMPANY SHOWING APPROVAL TO DISTURB LINES ACROSS ROUTE.
- NO MOVEMENT FROM 6:30AM—9:00AM AND 3:30PM– 6:00PM

STATE HIGHWAY PATROL:
- 1 FRONT AND 1 REAR CIVILIAN PILOT CAR
- ON 2-LANE HIGHWAYS IF LOAD EXCEEDS 16' WIDE—1 FRONT PLUS 2 REAR CIVILIAN
- WHEN LOAD EXCEEDS 16' WIDE ON ANY HIGHWAY OTHER THAN INTERSTATE/18' WIDE ON INTERSTATE/150' OVERALL LENGTH

REQUIREMENTS FOR ESCORT VEHICLES
- **GENERAL:** A PROPERLY LICENSED AUTOMOBILE COVERED BY AT LEAST THE MINIMUM AMOUNT OF INSURANCE AS REQUIRED BY LAW
- **SIGNS:** "OVERSIZE LOAD" SIGN (5' X 12") W/ BLACK LETTERS (8" HIGH) ON A YELLOW BACKGROUND MOUNTED ON FRONT AND OR REAR OF THE ESCORT VEHICLE
- **LIGHTS:** 1 (ONE) FLASHING/ROTATING AMBER LIGHT ON TOP OF VEHICLE VISIBLE FOR 500'
- **FLAGS:** AT LEAST 2 RED/ORANGE FLUORESCENT WARNING FLAGS MOUNTED ON A STAFF AT THE 2 FRONT EXTREMITIES OF THE ESCORT VEHICLE FOR A FRONT ESCORT AND AT THE REAR EXTREMITIES OF THE REAR ESCORT VEHICLE
- **ADDITIONAL EQUIPMENT:** HEIGHT POLE AND 2 WAY RADIO

REQUIREMENTS FOR ESCORT VEHICLE OPERATOR
PILOT CAR OPERATORS SHALL BE PROPERLY LICENSED, OBEY ALL TRAFFIC LAWS AND BE AT LEAST 18YRS OF AGE

MISSOURI DEPT. OF TRANSPORTATION PERMITS OFFICE (866) 831-6277; (573) 751-7100; FAX: (573) 751-7408
MISSOURI DOT/MOTOR CARRIER SERVICES/OS/OW PERMIT SECTION

THE OVERLOAD COMPANION 2017 © FREDA BARBER BOOTH

WHEN A PERMIT IS NEEDED
- OVER 8'6" WIDE
- OVER 14" HIGH
- OVER 17' HIGH—ROUTE SURVEY REQUIRED
- TRAILER OVER 53' LONG
- OVER 80,000 LBS.
- ANNUAL PERMIT ALLOWS FOR UP TO 15'6" TALL

SPECIAL INFORMATION NEEDED FOR PERMIT
- NAME OF INSURANCE COMPANY
- CITY, STATE, POLICY #, EXPIRATION DATE
- RW (REGISTERED WEIGHT)
- US DOT #
- DO YOU HAVE AUTHORITY IN MONTANA? (IF NOT YOU NEED FUEL & TRIP PERMIT)
- HOW MANY DAY ON THE PERMIT? LIMITS OF LIABILITY, OVERHANG

TIMES OF MOVEMENT
- CONTINUOUS TRAVEL IS ALLOWED FOR LOADS NOT OVER 10' WIDE (9'6" FOR BALED HAY & HAY RACKS)
- 14' 6" HIGH, 75' LONG W/ OVERHANG, 110' LONG W/ NO OVERHANG ON NON-INTERSTATE
- NON REDUCIBLE 10' OR LESS MAY TRAVEL ON INTERSTATES
- DAYLIGHT TRAVEL ONLY, 7 DAYS A WEEK, FOR LOADS NOT EXCEEDING 18'WIDE, 18' HIGH (OVER 17' HIGH MUST HAVE HELENA APPROVAL), 120' LONG W/ OVERHANG, 110' W/ O OVERHANG ON NON-INTERSTATE
- DAYLIGHT TRAVEL ONLY MON. THRU 3PM FRI (NO TRAVEL FROM 3PM FRIDAY UNTIL SUNRISE MON) FOR LOADS THAT EXCEED 18' WIDE, 120' LONG AND 18' HIGH (OVER 17' HIGH MUST HAVE HELENA APPROVAL). EXCEPTIONS: IMPLEMENTS OF HUSBANDRY
- TRAVEL IS PROHIBITED ON THE FOLLOWING HOLIDAYS: **MEMORIAL DAY, INDEPENDENCE DAY, GOOD FRIDAY, LABOR DAY, THANKSGIVING DAY, CHRISTMAS DAY, AND NEW YEAR'S DAY.**
- IF HOLIDAY FALLS ON WEEKEND OR FRIDAY—**NO TRAVEL ON FRI—SUN; IF HOLIDAY FALLS ON MONDAY—NO TRAVEL SAT—MON; IF HOLIDAY FALL ON TUES—THURS—NO TRAVEL ONLY ON THAT DAY**

WHEN ESCORT VEHICLE IS REQUIRED
ON INTERSTATE:
- WIDTH OVER 16'6"- 1 REAR PILOT CAR
- OVER 120' LONG—1 REAR PILOT CAR

ON 2-LANE OR MULTI-LANE NON-INTERSTATE
- OVER 12'6" TO 16'6" WIDE—1 FRONT PILOT CAR
- VEHICLE OR LOAD EXCEEDS 16'6" WIDE—2 (FRONT & REAR)
- OVER 110' LONG—1 REAR PILOT CAR
- OVER 10' WIDE & NOT EQUIPPED WITH LIGHT & SIGNS—2 (FRONT & REAR)
- OVER 17' HIGH—(BEFORE PERMIT—ROUTE SURVEY)

CONVOYS:
- NO MORE THAN 5 OS/OW LOADS NEEDING PILOT CARS MAY CONVOY IF WIDTH IS NOT OVER 14' (OR 15' W/ PROJECTIONS AND NOT OVER 120' LONG) - 2 (FRONT & REAR); NOT MORE THAN 5 MAY CONVOY IF LENGTH OF ANY UNIT IS OVER 110' LONG ON INTERSTATE HIGHWAYS
- **32-j MOVEMENT (MOVEMENT OF LARGE & UNUSUAL OBJECTS NOT COVERED BY OTHER RULES/REGULATIONS OF DOT)**
- **CLASS 1**: OVER 18'—34' WIDE; OVER 17'- 24' HIGH; OVER 150' - 200' LONG; WEIGHT DOESN'T REQUIRED BRIDGE BUREAU APPROVAL. TRAVEL TIMES SAME AS OTHER OS/OW VEHICLES ABOVE WIDTH REQUIRES 1 FRONT/2 REAR PILOT CARS; LENGTH REQUIRES 1 PILOT CAR
- **CLASS 2**: OVER 34' WIDE, OVER 24' HIGH OR ROUTE REQUIRES UTILITIES TO CUT POWER LINES, OVER 200' LONG - TRAVEL TIMES SAME AS OTHER OS/OW VEHICLES ABOVE

INTERSTATE: WIDTH REQUIRES 1 FRONT/2 REAR PILOT CARS; LENGTH REQUIRES 1 REAR PILOT CAR; HEIGHT REQUIRES 1 FRONT PILOT CAR IF POWER LINES NEED TO BE CUT

NON-INTERSTATE: WIDTH REQUIRES 2 FRONT/2 REAR PILOT CARS, LENGTH REQUIRES 1 FRONT/1 REAR; HEIGHT REQUIRES 1 FRONT/1 REAR PILOT CAR IF POWER LINES NEED TO BE CUT
- **CLASS 3:** WIDTH NOT OVER 18'; HEIGHT NOT OVER 17'; LENGTH NOT OVER 150'
- WEIGHT REQUIRES BRIDGE BUREAU APPROVAL

REQUIREMENTS FOR ESCORT VEHICLES
- **GENERAL:** ANY PASSENGER CAR/ 2 AXLE TRUCK; A MIN OF 60" WIDE; SHALL NOT EXCEED 2 TON GVW
- **SIGNS:** "OVERSIZE LOAD" SIGN (5' X 12") W/ BLACK LETTERS (8" HIGH) ON A YELLOW BACKGROUND MOUNTED ON ROOF OF VEHICLE
- **LIGHTS:** 1 (ONE) FLASHING/ROTATING AMBER LIGHT ON TOP OF VEHICLE VISIBLE FOR 500'
- **FLAGS:** NO STIPULATIONS
- **ADDITIONAL EQUIPMENT:** 2-WAY RADIO

MONTANA DEPT. OF TRANSPORTATION PERMITS OFFICE
(406) 444-6130; (406) 444-6130 (PERMITS); FAX (406) 444-7670/0800

MONTANA

ASAP PILOT CAR SERVICE
406-600-9703
Carolyn Johnson
Owner/Operator

asappilotcarservice.com

PROFESSIONAL ROUTE SURVEYS TRAFFIC MGMT PLANS

HIGH POLE
LEAD - CHASE
CANADA-LEGAL
WA CERTIFIED
$3MIL INSURED

Equipped w/ VHF Radio
Streets & Trips

Montana **T**raffic **C**ontrol

Carolyn Johnson
Owner/Operator
406-600-9703

ASAP
PILOT CAR SERVICE

What We Do

- Moving your load in Montana & surrounding states
- Traffic plans required for Montana state
- Surveys
- Certified and professional pilots
- Canadian legal

Montana Traffic Control is a professional traffic management/piloting company, dedicated to moving your super-load throughout Montana and the surrounding states.

Safety for the public and the load is our first priority and we strive for perfection.

Experienced pilots with over 1 million miles, plus years of piloting super-loads has provided us with the professional knowledge and insight to navigate you safely to your destination.

Being a non union affiliation, MTC can provide you with the best service and save your company unnecessary expenses.

Please call and find out how we can assist with your traffic plan/route survey, and movement.

THE OVERLOAD COMPANION 2017 © FREDA BARBER BOOTH

NEBRASKA

WHEN A PERMIT IS NEEDED
- OVER 8' 6" WIDE
- OVER 14' 6" HIGH
- OVERALL LENGTH EXCEEDS 40' LONG - EXCEPTIONS FOUND
- OVER 80,000 LBS

SPECIAL INFORMATION NEEDED FOR PERMIT
- MOBILE HOMES / MODULAR HOMES—NEED HUD # OR SEAL #, MANUFACTURED (OFFLINE) DATE & INSURANCE ON FILE - (FAX TO (402) 479-3906)
- 94,000 IS MAX RW IN NEBRASKA

HAULING VEHICLE: SPECIAL EQUIP REQUIRED
- IF OVER 85' IN LENGTH ON INTERSTATES - LIGHTBAR MUST BE ATTACHED ON BACK AT REAR OF TRAILER

TIMES OF MOVEMENT
- 1/2 HOUR BEFORE SUNRISE TO 1/2 HOUR AFTER SUNSET 7 DAYS/WEEK
- TRAVEL DURING INCLEMENT WEATHER CONDITIONS PROHIBITED (HIGH WINDS, LOW VISIBILITY OF 1/2 MILE, RAIN, SLEET, SNOW, SLIPPERY OR HAZARDOUS ROADWAY CONDITIONS

CURFEWS:
- **LINCOLN CITY LIMITS STATE HIGHWAYS (I-80 EXCLUDED):** NO TRAVEL 7AM—9AM & 4PM—6PM MON THRU FRI; NO TRAVEL AFTER NOON SAT—SUN;
- **CORNHUSKER HOME GAME DAY:** I-80 EXITS 395-405 RESTRICTED; STATE HWY SYSTEM CLOSED FROM IOWA LINE TO NE-14 & KS LINE NORTH TO NE-91.
- **OMAHA CITY LIMITS STATE HIGHWAYS/INTERSTATES:** - NO TRAVEL 7AM—9AM & 4AM—6PM MON THRU FRI, NO TRAVEL AFTER NOON SAT & SUN
- TRAVEL IS PROHIBITED ON THE FOLLOWING HOLIDAYS: **NEW YEAR'S DAY, GOOD FRIDAY, MEMORIAL DAY, INDEPENDENCE DAY, LABOR DAY, THANKSGIVING DAY AND CHRISTMAS DAY**

WHEN ESCORT VEHICLE IS REQUIRED
WIDTH
- WIDTH OVER 12' AND UP TO 14' - CHOICE OF AMBER LIGHT OR 1 PILOT CAR (*IF PERMIT ALLOWS IT)
- WIDTH OVER 14' WIDE - 2 PILOT CARS

HEIGHT:
- DEPENDS ON ROUTE; LOADS EXCEEDING 14'6" IN HEIGHT MAY REQUIRE A PILOT W/ HEIGHT POLE
- OVER 16' IN HEIGHT A PRE-RUN ROUTE SURVEY SHALL BE REQUIRED & SUBMITTED TO DEPARTMENT OF ROADS

LENGTH:
- ON INTERSTATE OR DIVIDED ROADWAY OVER 100' - 1 PILOT OR PROPER LIGHT BAR
- NO STIPULATIONS ON 2 LANES

REQUIREMENTS FOR ESCORT VEHICLES
- **GENERAL:** STANDARD TRUCK OR CAR AT LEAST 60" WIDE
- **SIGNS:** "OVERSIZE LOAD"/"WIDE LOAD" SIGN W/ BLACK LETTERS (8"HIGH) ON A YELLOW BACKGROUND (5' X 12") MOUNTED ON THE FRONT AND/OR REAR OF VEHICLE
- **LIGHTS:** REVOLVING OR ROTATING AMBER OR YELLOW LIGHT SUFFICIENT TO BE SEEN 800' (MIN OR 50 CANDLEPOWER BULB); 360 DEGREE VISIBILITY; NOT LESS THAN 6" IN DIAMETER; MOUNTED ON ROOF A MIN OF 53" ABOVE ROADWAY
- **FLAGS:** RED/FLOURESCENT ORANGE FLAGS (MIN 18" SQUARE) ON ALL 4 CORNERS OF VEHICLE
- **ADDITIONAL EQUIPMENT:** 2-WAY RADIO FOR CONSTANT COMMUNICATION

REQUIREMENTS FOR ESCORT VEHICLE OPERATOR
- NONE STIPULATED

NEBRASKA DEPT. OF TRANSPORTATION PERMITS OFFICE
(402) 471-0034 / FAX: (402) 479-3771

NEVADA

WHEN A PERMIT IS NEEDED
- OVER 8'6" WIDE
- OVER 14' HIGH
- VEHICLE OR COMBINATION OVER 70' LONG

SPECIAL INFORMATION NEEDED FOR PERMIT
- NEED EXACT ADDRESS WHEN STARTING OR STOPPING IN NEVADA

TIMES OF MOVEMENT
- 1/2 HOUR BEFORE SUNRISE TO 1/2 HOUR AFTER SUNSET; SATURDAY UNTIL NOON; NO TRAVEL ON SUNDAY
- TRAVEL IS PERMITTED 24 HOURS A DAY IF LEGAL HEIGHT AND WIDTH AND 75' OR LESS LONG, 10' OR LESS OVERHANG, ANY WEIGHT
- NIGHT TRAVEL IS ALLOWED ON 4-LANE HIGHWAYS FOR VEHICLES WHOSE WIDTH IS 8'6" TO 10', 14' HIGH, 75' LONG AND 10' OVERHANG
- VEHICLES BELOW THE FOLLOWING DIMENSIONS: 14' WIDE, 16' HIGH, 105' LONG, 15' OVERHANG CAN TRAVEL WEEKENDS BUT CANNOT TRAVEL I-80 BETWEEN RENO AND CA LINE & I-15 BETWEEN LAS VEGAS AND CA LINE UNLESS THEY MEET HOLIDAY TRAVEL RESTRICTIONS
- TRAVEL IS PROHIBITED ON THE FOLLOWING HOLIDAYS: **NEW YEAR'S DAY, GOOD FRIDAY, MEMORIAL DAY, INDEPENDENCE DAY, LABOR DAY, ADMISSION DAY, THANKSGIVING DAY CHRISTMAS DAY**

WHEN ESCORT VEHICLE IS REQUIRED
ON 2 LANE ROADS
- WIDTH OVER 12' AND UP TO 14' - 1 PILOT CAR
- WIDTH OVER 14' WIDE TO 16' - 1 FRONT & 1 REAR PILOT CAR
- WIDTH OVER 16' WIDE—3 (2 FRONT & 1 REAR PILOT CARS)
- OVER 105' LONG—1 PILOT CAR
- OVERHANG OVER 25' FRONT OR REAR—1 (FRONT OR REAR) PILOT CAR

ON INTERSTATE & 4 OR MORE LANES
- WIDTH OVER 14' AND UP TO 16' - 1 PILOT CAR
- WIDTH OVER 16' AND UP 17' - 1 FRONT & 1 REAR PILOT CAR
- WIDTH OVER 17' - REVIEWED ON AN INDIVIDUAL BASES
- OVER 17' HIGH—1 FRONT PILOT CAR W/ HEIGHT POLE
- OVER 105' LONG—1 REAR PILOT CAR
- OVERHANG OVER 25' FRONT OR REAR—1 (FRONT OR REAR) PILOT CAR

MOBILE HOMES
- 14' WIDE AND UP TO 2" EAVE TO RIGHT SIDE OF INTERSTATE—1 REAR PILOT CAR
- 14' WIDE AND UP TO 2" EAVE TO RIGHT SIDE ON ALL OTHER ROADS—1 FRONT & 1 REAR PILOT CAR

REQUIREMENTS FOR ESCORT VEHICLES
- **GENERAL:** MINIMUM VEHICLE WIDTH 60", MINUMIM WHEEL BASE 95"; NO LONGER THAN 1 1/2 TON TRUCK
- **SIGNS:** "OVERSIZE LOAD"/"WIDE LOAD" SIGN W/ BLACK LETTERS ON A YELLOW BACKGROUND MOUNTED ON THE ROOF OF VEHICLE
- **LIGHTS:** PERMIT REQUIRED TO USE LIGHTS IN NEVADA (CONTACT # BELOW) VALID FROM 7/1—6/30. MOUNTED ON ROOF ABOVE SIGN; REVOLVING OR BLINKING AMBER LIGHTS W/ MINIMUM 50 CANDLEPOWER; LENS SIZE MIN. 5" DIAMETER; FLASH FREQUENCY MIN. 50 FLASHES/MIN.; VISIBLE FROM DISTANCE OF AT LEAST 500' IN NORMAL SUNLIGHT
- **FLAGS:** NOT STIPULATED
- **ADDITIONAL EQUIPMENT:** A VALID DRIVERS LICENSE, THREE (3) REFLECTIVE TRIANGLES, THREE (3) 18" ORANGE TRAFFIC CONES, ONE (1) 5 LB. BC FIRE EXTINGUISHER, HARDHAT, AND A 2-WAY RADIO. FOR FLAGGING; SOLID FLOURESCENT YELLOW-GREEN VEST THAT COMPLETELY COVERS TORSO; RED FLAG; "STOP" PADDLE (WHITE LETTERS ON RED BACKGROUND)

REQUIREMENTS FOR ESCORT VEHICLE OPERATOR
- PILOT CAR DRIVER MUST BE AT LEAST 18 YEARS OF AGE
- PILOT CAR OPERATOR MUST BE **CERTIFIED** BY COMPLETING A CURRENT INSTRUCTIONAL COURSE SPECIFIC TO FLAGGER REQUIREMENTS AND PROCEDURES. NEVADA RECOGNIZES ALL OTHER CERTIFICATIONS FROM OTHER STATES THAT HAVE CERTIFICATION PROGRAMS.

NEVADA DEPT. OF TRANSPORTATION PERMITS OFFICE
(775) 888-7410; (800) 552-2127; FAX: (775) 888-7103

AMBER LIGHT SECTION, NV HIGHWAY PATROL
(775) 684-4622; FAX (775) 684-4649

YOU CAN GET THE AMBER LIGHT PERMIT ON THE INTERNET

NEW HAMPSHIRE

WHEN A PERMIT IS NEEDED
- OVER 8' 6" WIDE
- OVER 13' 6" HIGH
- TRAILER OVER 48' LONG
- OVER 80,000 LBS

- **SPECIAL INFORMATION NEEDED FOR PERMIT**
- IF A VEHICLE OR LOAD EXCEEDS 16' IN WIDTH, 16' HIGH, 115,000 POUNDS IN WEIGHT FOR A 5 AXLE UNIT, OR AT 150,000 POUNDS OR GREATER IN GROSS VEHICLE WEIGHT, THEN IT IS CONSIDERED A SUPER MOVE AND WILL REQUIRE AN ENGINEERING STUDY PERFORMED BY THE NHDOT. THERE WILL BE A FEE AND PROCESSING TIME COULD TAKE UP TO 7-10 BUSINESS DAYS TO COMPLETE.
- ALL LOADS GREATER THAN 13'6" HIGH, THE CARRIER IS RESPONSIBLE FOR SECURING A CERTIFIED HEIGHT SURVEY

TIMES OF MOVEMENT
- 1/2 HOUR BEFORE SUNRISE TO 1/2 HOUR AFTER SUNSET - NO WEEKEND TRAVEL ALLOWED
- VEHICLES THAT ARE OVERWEIGHT ONLY SHALL NOT BE RESTRICTED TO THE TIME OF TRAVEL
- TRAVEL IS PROHIBITED ON THE FOLLOWING HOLIDAYS: **NEW YEAR'S DAY, MARTIN LUTHER KING JR. DAY, PRESIDENTS DAY, MEMORIAL DAY, INDEPENDENCE DAY, LABOR DAY, COLUMBUS DAY, VETERANS DAY, THANKSGIVING DAY AND CHRISTMAS DAY**

WHEN ESCORT VEHICLE IS REQUIRED
- **LESS THAN 4-LANE HIGHWAYS:**
- WIDTH OVER 12' AND OVER - 1 FRONT PILOT CAR
- 80' LONG AND OVER—1 FRONT PILOT CAR
- OVERHANG 15' AND OVER W/ 12' WIDTH—2 (FRONT & REAR)
- **4 LANE HIGHWAYS**
- 12' WIDE AND OVER—1 REAR PILOT CAR
- 80' LONG AND OVER—1 REAR PILOT CAR
- OVERHANG 15' AND OVER W/ 12' WIDTH—2 (FRONT & REAR)

POLICE ESCORT REQUIRED WHEN:
- OVER 18' WIDE & OVER 100' LONG
- MOBILES AND MODULARS ARE RESTRICTED TO 16' WIDE & 95' LONG
- **LESS THAN 4-LANE HIGHWAYS**
- 12' WIDE OR LESS—1 FRONT PILOT CAR
- 12' TO 14'6" WIDE—1 FRONT PILOT CAR
- WIDTH 14'6" TO 16' W/ APPROVED ROUTES—2 SP+
- **4-LANE HIGHWAYS:**
- 12' WIDE TO 14'6" (WITHIN MILES OF AN EXIT FROM SUCH HWY) - 1 REAR
- WIDTH 14'6" WITH APPROVED ROUTE– 2 SP+

REQUIREMENTS FOR ESCORT VEHICLES
- **GENERAL:** NO SMALLER THAN A COMPACT CAR OR PICKUP TRUCK
- **SIGNS:** SHAPE MAY BE VARIED TO FIT VEHICLE (MIN 5' X 12'); "OVERSIZE LOAD" W/ BLACK LETTERS (10" HIGH W/ 1.4" BRUSH STROKE) ON A YELLOW BACKGROUND MOUNTED ON FRONT AND /OR ON REAR OF VEHICLE
- **LIGHTS:** TOP MOUNTED FLASHING OR ROTATING AMBER LIGHT
- **FLAGS**: NOT STIPULATED
- **ADDITIONAL EQUIPMENT:** 2-WAY RADIO FOR CONSTANT COMMUNICATION

REQUIREMENTS FOR ESCORT VEHICLE OPERATOR
- NONE STIPULATED

NEW HAMPSHIRE DEPT. OF TRANSPORTATION PERMITS OFFICE
(603) 271-2691 / FAX: (603) 271-5990

MARTIN EMERSON
SABATTUS, MAINE
High Pole - Lead - Chase - Steer
Certified Fully Insured Passport
NEW YORK STATE CERTIFIED ESCORT
Heavy, Wide or Tall, We'll Help You Haul 'Em All
207-240-7876
emerson01@rocketmail.com
EMERSON PILOT CAR SERVICES — EPCS

THE OVERLOAD COMPANION 2017 © FREDA BARBER BOOTH

NEW JERSEY

WHEN A PERMIT IS NEEDED
- OVER 8' 6" WIDE
- OVER 13' 6" HIGH
- TRAILER OVER 48' LONG
- OVER 80,000 LBS

SPECIAL INFORMATION NEEDED FOR PERMIT
- NEED CERTIFICATION OF INSURANCE ON FILE, LISTING THE STATE OF NEW JERSEY DOT AS A CERTIFICATED HOLDER

TIMES OF MOVEMENT
- SUNRISE TO SUNSET; MAY TRAVEL SAT. UNTIL 12:00 NOON; NO SUNDAY TRAVEL
- OVERWEIGHT AND LEGAL DIMENSION LOADS CAN TRAVEL 7 DAYS A WEEK 24 HOURS A DAY
- OVER 14' LOADS ARE NOT ALLOWED ON TURN PIKE OR TOLL ROADS.
- NO OVERSIZE (8'6" WIDE OR 13' 6" HIGH) AND OVERWEIGHT (80,000LBS GROSS WEIGHT) VEHICLES ARE ALLOWED ON NEW JERSEY TURN PIKE OR GARDER STATE PARKWAY.
- OS/OW LOADS ARE PERMITTED ON NON-TOLLED SECTIONS OF NEW JERSEY TURNPIKE FROM EXIT #18W TO THE GEORGE WASHINGTON BRIDGE
- TRAVEL IS PROHIBITED ON THE FOLLOWING HOLIDAYS: **NEW YEAR'S DAY, MEMORIAL DAY, INDEPENDENCE DAY, LABOR DAY, VETERANS DAY, THANKSGIVING DAY AND CHRISTMAS DAY**

WHEN ESCORT VEHICLE IS REQUIRED
2-LANE HIGHWAYS:
- WIDTH OVER 14' - 1 FRONT PILOT CAR
- WIDTH OVER 16' - 1 FRONT AND 1 REAR PILOT CAR
- OVER 100' LONG—1 FRONT PILOT CAR
- OVER 120' LONG—1 FRONT AND 1 REAR PILOT CAR
- OVER 14' HIGH—1 FRONT PILOT CAR

4 OR MORE LANE HIGHWAYS:
- WIDTH OVER 14' - 1 REAR PILOT CAR
- WIDTH OVER 16' - 1 FRONT AND 1 REAR PILO T CAR
- OVER 100' LONG—1 REAR PILOT CAR
- OVER 120' LONG—1 FRONT AND 1 REAR PILOT CAR

REQUIREMENTS FOR ESCORT VEHICLES
- **GENERAL:** NOT STIPULATED
- **SIGNS:** "OVERSIZE LOAD"/"WIDE LOAD" SIGN W/ BLACK LETTERS (10"HIGH) ON A YELLOW BACKGROUND (6' X 12") MOUNTED ON THE FRONT AND REAR OF VEHICLE
- **LIGHTS:** NOT STIPULATED
- **FLAGS:** RED/FLOURESCENT ORANGE FLAGS (MIN 18" SQUARE) ON ALL 4 CORNERS OF VEHICLE
- **ADDITIONAL EQUIPMENT:** 2-WAY RADIO FOR CONSTANT COMMUNICATION

REQUIREMENTS FOR ESCORT VEHICLE OPERATOR
- NONE STIPULATED

NEW JERSEY DEPT. OF TRANSPORTATION PERMITS OFFICE
BUREAU OF MOTOR CARRIERS
(609) 530-6089 / FAX: (609) 530-5270

New Mexico Inspection

ATTENTION:

PILOT CAR MUST HAVE CURRENT INSPECTION <u>BEFORE</u> BRINGING PERMITTED LOAD THROUGH PORT OF ENTRY

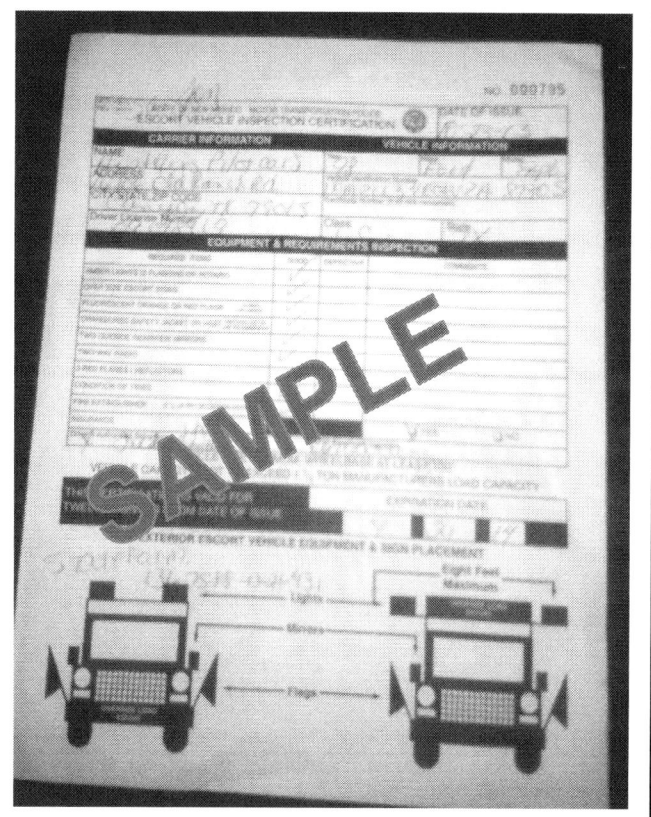

EQUIPMENT CHECKED BY INSPECTOR

- **AMBER LIGHTS - FLASHING OR ROTARY**

Must be full lightbar (or beacons) on outer edges - 360° Visibility

- **OVERSIZE ESCORT SIGNS**

May be displayed on both bumpers, roof, rear window, tailgate

- **FLUORESCENT ORANGE OR RED FLAGS (12 IN OR LARGER)**

May be mounted on bumper or roof

- **ORANGE/RED SAFETY VEST OR JACKET**

Matching hard hat recommended

- **TWO OUTSIDE REARVIEW MIRRORS**
- **TWO-WAY RADIO**
- **3 RED FLARES / REFLECTORS**
- **GOOD CONDITION TIRES** (CHECKED WITH A PENNY)
- **FIRE EXTINGUISHER (2 LB)**
- **INSURANCE (25K/50K/10K)**

<u>ATTENTION</u>

DRIVER'S LICENSE / WARRANTS / REGISTRATION CHECKED BY TROOPER

NEW MEXICO

WHEN A PERMIT IS NEEDED
- OVER 8' 6" WIDE
- OVER 14' HIGH
- TRAILER OVER 57'6" LONG
- OVER 80,000 LBS

SPECIAL INFORMATION NEEDED FOR PERMIT
- NEED INSURANCE ON FILE

TIMES OF MOVEMENT
- SUNRISE TO SUNSET MONDAY THRU SATURDAY; NO SUNDAY TRAVEL
- **CURFEWS:** ALBUQUERQUE AND ESPANOLA: 7-9AM AND 4-6PM; SANTA FE: 7-9AM; 11:30AM-1:30PM; 4-6PM
- TRAVEL IS PROHIBITED ON THE FOLLOWING HOLIDAYS: **NEW YEAR'S DAY, MEMORIAL DAY, INDEPENDENCE DAY, LABOR DAY, THANKSGIVING DAY AND CHRISTMAS DAY**

WHEN ESCORT VEHICLE IS REQUIRED
ON ALL HIGHWAYS
- WIDTH OVER 8'6", IF DEEMED A HAZARD—1 PILOT CAR
- WIDTH OVER 14' - 1 PILOT CAR
- WIDTH OVER 20' FOR 5 OR MORE MILES—POLICE ESCORT + FLAGMAN
- OVER 90' LONG UP TO 110' LONG—1 PILOT CAR
- OVER 110' LONG—1 FRONT AND 1 REAR PILOT CAR
- HEIGHT 16' & OVER—1 PILOT CAR W/ HEIGHT POLE (+ EXTRA MAN OR PILOT CAR TO CHECK FOR OVERHEAD CLEARANCE)
- HEIGHT 18' & OVER - 1 PILOT CAR W/ HEIGHT POLE (+CLEARANCE FROM UTILITIES, MUNICIPAL & LOCAL AUTHORITIES)

REQUIREMENTS FOR ESCORT VEHICLES
- **GENERAL:** MUST BE INSPECTED BY DOT ON AN ANNUAL BASIS AND SHOW INSPECTION CERTIFICATE AT ALL NMPOE.
- **VEHICLE REQUIREMENTS:** WHEELBASE AT LEAST 100"; MUST NOT EXCEED 1 1/2 TON CAPACITY; INSURANCE IN THE AMOUNT 25/50/10 MIN. (PROOF MUST BE CARRIED IN VEHICLE)
- **SIGNS:** "OVERSIZE LOAD" SIGN W/ BLACK LETTERS (10"HIGH AND 1" BRUSH STROKE) ON A YELLOW BACKGROUND (5' X 12') MOUNTED ON THE FRONT AND REAR OF VEHICLE OR TOP OF VEHICLE
- **LIGHTS:** 2 AMBER LIGHTS (ROTATING, FLASHING OR STROBE) ON TOP OF ESCORT VEHICLE AT VEHICE WIDTH OR AT WIDTH NOT TO EXCEED 8'; SUFFICIENT INTENSITY TO BE VISIBLE AT A DISTANCE OF 1000' MIN. IN NORMAL SUNLIGHT. LIGHTS MUST BE COVERED OR REMOVED WHEN NOT IN USE
- **FLAGS:** 2 RED/FLOURESCENT ORANGE FLAGS (MIN 18" SQUARE) ON ALL 4 CORNERS OF VEHICLE OR ON TOP OF VEHICLE
- **ADDITIONAL EQUIPMENT:** AT PORT OF ENTRY YOU WILL BE ASKED TO DISPLAY THE FOLLOWING EQUIPMENT FOR INSPECTION: AMBER LIGHTS (2 FLASHING, ROTATING OR STROBE), OVERSIZE ESCORT SIGNS, 2 FLOURESCENT ORANGE OR RED FLAGS (12" OR LARGER), ORANGE/RED SAFTEY JACKET OR VEST, 2 OUTSIDE REAR VIEW MIRRORS, 2-WAY RADIO, 3 RED FLARES/REFLECTORS, CONDITION OF TIRES, FIRE EXTINGUISHER (2 1/2 LB DRY OR CARBON DIOXIDE),

SEE LEFT PAGE FOR PILOT CAR INSPECTION INFORMATION
←

REQUIREMENTS FOR ESCORT VEHICLE OPERATOR
- AT LEAST 18 YEARS OF AGE

NEW MEXICO DEPT. OF TRANSPORTATION PERMITS OFFICE
DEPT OF PUBLIC SAFETY
(505) 827--0376
FAX: (505) 827-0071

SEE PAGE ACROSS

NEW YORK

Rowley's Pilot Cars

Cortland, NY

Larry & Steph Rowley

607-745-9850

607-745-4668

HIGH POLE - LEAD - CHASE

NEW YORK

WHEN A PERMIT IS NEEDED
- OVER 8' 6" WIDE
- OVER 13'6" HIGH
- TRAILER OVER 53' LONG
- OVER 80,000 LBS

SPECIAL INFORMATION NEEDED FOR PERMIT
- PERMITS FOR LOADS 160,000 LBS OR MORE MUST GO TO THE STRUCTURES DIVISION FOR APPROVAL.
- LOADS 14' HIGH AND OVER MUST HAVE A HEIGHT SURVEY AND REQUIRE A HEIGHT POLE
- MUST USE A COMMERCIAL PERMIT SERVICE TO OBTAIN NEW YORK STATE PERMIT
- MUST HAVE 6" CLEARANCE ABOVE A 14' HEIGHT AND 3" BELOW A 14' HEIGHT WHEN DOING A ROUTE SURVEY

TIMES OF MOVEMENT
- MON-FRI 1/2 HOUR BEFORE SUNRISE TO 1/2 HOUR AFTER SUNSET; OD/OW MOVES LESS THAN 12' WIDE & 85' LONG & CAN MAINTAIN TRAFFIC FLOW SPEED ARE ALLOWED TO MOVE UNTIL NOON SAT
- NIGHT TRAVEL IS REQUIRED ON LONG ISLAND FOR MOBILES, MODULAR SECTIONS, & OFFICE TRAILERS WIDER THAN 12'
- CONTINUOUS TRAVEL MAY BE OBTAINED WHEN THE VEHICLE DOES NOT EXCEED LEGAL DIMENSIONS AND DOES NOT GO OVER 125% OF LEGAL WEIGHT
- MAY TRAVEL ON SAT UNTIL NOON, IF NOT OVER 12' WIDE OR 72' LONG (85' ON APPROVED ROUTES)
- **CURFEWS:** DEPENDS UPON THE SIZE AND WEIGHT OF THE LOAD. IT WILL BE LISTED ON YOUR TRANSPORTATION PERMIT. ALSO NO TRAVEL IN BUSINESS DISTRICT BETWEEN 7-9AM AND 4-6PM. 15' AND OVER. NO TRAVEL IN NEW YORK CITY BETWEEN 7-9AM AND 4-6PM
- TRAVEL IS PROHIBITED ON THE FOLLOWING HOLIDAYS: **NEW YEAR'S DAY, MEMORIAL DAY, INDEPENDENCE DAY, LABOR DAY, THANKSGIVING DAY AND CHRISTMAS DAY**

WHEN ESCORT VEHICLE IS REQUIRED
ON 2-LANE HIGHWAYS
- IF OVER 12' WIDE, 80' OR MORE LONG, OVERHANG OVER 10' LONG AND HEIGHT OVER 14' - 1 FRONT PILOT CAR W/ HEIGHT POLE
- IF 16' WIDE OR MORE OR OVER 140' LONG—4 PILOT CARS (2 FRONT & 1 REAR + POLICE)
- LENGTH 100' OR MORE—2 FRONT & 1 REAR PILOT CAR
- HEIGHT 16' OR MORE—1 FRONT PILOT CAR W/ HEIGHT POLE + POLICE ESCORT
- WEIGHT OVER 200,000 LBS—POLICE ESCORT

(POLICE REQUIRE 2 BUSINESS DAYS NOTICE FOR POLICE ESCORTS BEGINNING WHEN PERMIT APPLICATION IS TURNED IN)

ON 4-LANES OR MORE
- OVER 12' WIDE, 80' LONG +, OVERHANG 10' +, OR IF VEHICLE IS SLOW MOVING OR SPEED RESTRICTIONS ARE REQUIRED—1 REAR PILOT
- IF 18' WIDE & OVER, OR 200' OR MORE LONG—2 FRONT & 1 REAR + POLICE
- HEIGHT 14' TO 16' - 1 FRONT PILOT CAR W/ HEIGHT POLE
- HEIGHT 16' OR MORE—1 FRONT PILOT CAR W/ HEIGHT POLE + POLICE

REQUIREMENTS FOR ESCORT VEHICLES
- **GENERAL:** 1997 OR NEWER VEHICLE WITH A 100" WHEELBASE MIN. UNLESS UTILITY VEHICLE
- **SIGNS:** "OVERSIZE LOAD" SIGN W/ BLACK LETTERS (10"HIGH AND 1.41" BRUSH STROKE) ON A YELLOW BACKGROUND (5' X 12") MOUNTED ON THE FRONT AND REAR OF VEHICLE OR TOP OF VEHICLE
- **LIGHTS:** FLASHING/STROBE SINGLE UNIT WARNING LIGHT BAR SHALL BE A MIN. OF 43" AND A MAX. OF 52" LONG, A MIN. OF 10" AND A MAX OF 13" WIDE AND A MIN. OF 4" WITH A MAX. OF 8" HIGH. WARNING LIGHT BAR SHALL CONSIST OF A MIN. OF 4 LIGHTS. IF FLASHING LIGHTS ARE USED THEY SHALL CONSIST OF AT LEAST 2-95 AND 2-150 MIN. FPM ROTATORS, MIRRORS SHALL BE PLACED DIAGONALLY BETWEEN LIGHTS (MIRRORS TO BE REFLECTIVE ON BOTH SIDES). ALL LIGHTS SHALL BE VISIBLE ON A 360 DEGREE BASIS FROM THE VEHICLE FOR A DISTANCE OF 1000' AND ARRANGED WITH AT LEAST TWO LIGHTS ON EACH SIDE OF THE LIGHTBAR. THE DOME COVER SHALL BE AMBER. **THE LIGHTBAR MUST BE MANUFACTURED AS A SINGLE UNIT, 2 MINI LIGHTBARS ARE NOT ACCEPTABLE**.
- **FLAGS:** NOT STIPULATED
- **ADDITIONAL EQUIPMENT:** STATE MANDATED INSIGNIA (ONE ON EACH SIDE OF VEHICLE); 2-WAY RADIO, CELL PHONE, 3 EMERGENCY TRIANGLES AND /OR FLARES; 3 EMERGENCY FLARES (FOR NIGHT MOVES), FLOURESCENT VEST W/ CERTIFIED ESCORT INSIGNIA ON LEFT CHEST OF VEST, STOP PADDLE, 3 18" SQUARE RED/FLOURESCENT ORANGE FLAGS ON STAFFS (1 MUST BE WEIGHTED), FIRE EXTINGUISHER CLASS 5BC OR LARGER AND A HEIGHT POLE

CERTIFICATION REQUIREMENTS FOR ESCORT VEHICLE OPERATOR
- MUST BE CERTIFIED BY NEW YORK NO MATTER WHERE YOU LIVE.

NEW YORK DEPT OF TRANSPORTATION
(518) 457-1155
FAX: (518) 457-0367

NY CITY DOT PERMITS
(212) 643-2816

NY STATE POLICE HEADQUARTERS
(518) 457-3258

NY THRUWAY PERMITS
(518) 436-2793

High Pole / Steer
Lead - Chase
NY / WA Cert
Passport

207-240-2535

mpcs1243@gmail.com

THE OVERLOAD COMPANION 2017 © FREDA BARBER BOOTH

NORTH CAROLINA

WHEN A PERMIT IS NEEDED
- OVER 8' 6" WIDE
- OVER 13'6" HIGH
- TRAILER OVER 53' LONG
- OVER 80,000 LBS

SPECIAL INFORMATION NEEDED FOR PERMIT
- REGISTERED WEIGHT OF TRACTOR
- OVERHANG (IF ANY)
- ANYTHING ABOVE NORMAL PERMIT ISSUE MAY BE CONSIDERED AS A SUPERLOAD. (WEIGHTS IN EXCESS OF 132,000 LBS, OVER 60,000 OBS PER 3 OR MORE AXLE GROUPINGS). PLEASE ALLOW UP TO 10 WORKING DAYS FOR PERMIT APPLICATION TO BE PROCESSED.

TIMES OF MOVEMENT
- SUNRISE TO SUNSET MONDAY THRU SATURDAY; NO SUNDAY TRAVEL
- **CURFEWS:** CHECK YOUR PERMIT AND SPECIAL PROVISIONS SHEET. LOADS MAY TRAVEL FROM MONDAY THROUGH SATURDAY, MAXIMUM 15' WIDE. NO MOVEMENT TO BE MADE ON SUNDAY OR BETWEEN SUNSET AND SUNRISE WHEN GROSS WEIGHT EXCEEDS 112,000 OR VEHICLE COMBINATION EXCEEDS LEGAL DIMENSIONS ALLOWED BY LAW UNLESS OTHERWISE SPECIFIED, VIA ROUTE SECTION OF YOUR PERMIT. CANNOT MOVE WHEN VISIBILITY IS LESS THAN 500' OR WIND VELOCITY IS GREATER THAN 25 M.P.H. CONTINUOUS TRAVEL- (24 HRS/7DAYS) IS AUTHORIZED IF: THE PERMITTED GROSS WEIGHT DOES NOT EXCEED 112,000 LBS AND IF NO OVERDIMENSION OF WIDTH, LENGTH OR HEIGHT IS PART OF THE PERMITTED MOVEMENT
- TRAVEL IS PROHIBITED ON THE FOLLOWING HOLIDAYS: **NEW YEAR'S DAY, MEMORIAL DAY, INDEPENDENCE DAY, LABOR DAY, THANKSGIVING DAY AND CHRISTMAS DAY**

WHEN ESCORT VEHICLE IS REQUIRED
FOR ALL OVER WIDTH MOVEMENTS ON MULTI-LANE HIGHWAYS:
- ANYTHING OVER 12' WIDE—1 PILOT CAR
- LOADS OVER 14'5" HIGH—1 FRONT PILOT CAR W/ HEIGHT POLE
- OVER 110' LONG (SUPERLOADS-100') - 1 REAR PILOT CAR
- OVERHANG OVER 14' - 1 PILOT CAR
- WEIGHT OVER 149,999 LBS—1 PILOT CAR
- MULTIPLE ESCORTS POSSIBLE FOR COMBINATION OF OVER-DIMENSIONS
- 16' WIDE MOBILES WITH LEGAL HEIGHT AND A MAX OF 3" GUTTER EDGE ARE REQUIRED TO HAVE 2 PILOT CARS ON ALL CONTROLLED ACCESS HIGHWAYS. 3 PILOT CARS ON ALL OTHER MULTI-LANE HIGHWAYS, AND 3 ESCORTS (1 BEING A LAW ENFORCEMENT OFFICER) ON ALL 2LANE/2WAY TRAFFIC ROADS PLUS PROOF OF FINAL DESTINATION
- SUPERLOADS OVER 15' WIDE—3 PILOTS (1 NC HIGHWAY PATROL)

REQUIREMENTS FOR ESCORT VEHICLES
- **GENERAL:** VEHICLE NOT LESS THAN 2000 LBS,; LOAD CAPACITY OF 17,000 LBS OR LESS
- **SIGNS:** "OVERSIZE LOAD" SIGN W/ BLACK LETTERS (10"HIGH AND 1 1/2" BRUSH STROKE) ON A YELLOW BACKGROUND (5' X 12") MOUNTED ON THE FRONT AND REAR OF VEHICLE OR TOP OF VEHICLE. *MUST BE ROOF MOUNT IF ESCORTING 16' WIDE MOBILE HOMES.*
- **LIGHTS:** FLASHING AMBER LIGHTS (ROTATING SEALED BEAM OR STROBE); 5" MIN. DIAMETER BASE; 4" MIN HEIGHT; MOUNTED ON TOP OF VEHICLE
- **FLAGS:** NOT STIPULATED
- **ADDITIONAL EQUIPMENT:** IDENTIFICATION SIGNS (8" X 12" MIN) W/ NAME AND PHONE # OF OWNER/OPERATOR

REQUIREMENTS FOR ESCORT VEHICLE OPERATOR
- MUST BE CERTIFIED BY NCDOT: MUST BE AT LEAST 21 YEARS OF AGE OR 18 W/ CDL (CLASS A) DRIVERS LICENSE AND POSSESSES DOCUMENTATION OF COMPLETION OF A DEFENSICVE DRIVING COURSE APPROVED BY THE NATIONAL SAFETY COUNCIL OR DEPARTMENT OF TRANSPORTATION OVERSIZE/OVERWEIGHT LOAD ESCORT VEHICLE OPERATOR CERTIFICATION PROGRAM OFFERED BY THE NORTH CAROLINA COMMUNITY COLLEGE SYSTEM WITH A CERTIFICATION EXAMINATION SCORE OF AT LEAST 75% CORRECT TO OBTAIN AN ESCORT CERTIFICATION FROM THE DEPARTMENT. THE CERTIFICATION SHALL BE EFFECTIVE FOR 4 YEARS FROM THE ISSUE DATE. UPON SATIFACTORY COMPLETION OF THE COURSE, THE NORTH CAROLINA DEPARTMENT OF TRANSPORTATIN AT NO FEE WILL ISSUE A CERTIFICATION TO EACH INDIVIDUAL.
- NO DRIVER OR PASSENGER OTHER THAN A CERTIFIED ESCORT VEHICLE OPERATOR WILL BE ALLOWED TO TRAVEL IN THE ESCORT VEHICLE
- NORTH CAROLINA WILL RECOGNIZE ESCORT VEHICLE OPERATOR CERTIFICATIONS FROM OTHER STATES FOR OPERATORS THAT CURRENTLY HAVE A VALID OUT-OF-STATE DRIVERS LICENSE AND CERTIFICATION

NORTH CAROLINA DOT OS/OW PERMIT UNIT
GENERAL INFO/ANNUALS/SUPERLOADS (919) 733-4740
SINGLE TRIP PERMITS (919) 733-7154
FAX: (919) 733-7828

CAROLINA REO SERVICES

CHRIS SHUPE
(704) 202-3127

STACY MORTON
(704) 754-2911

For Your Pilot Car Needs to, through and from North Carolina!

MULTIPLE CARS

carolinareoservices@hotmail.com

WIDE LOAD
OVERSIZE LOAD
LONG LOAD

High pole
WA-NY-NC Cert
GA Amber
LA-NM Inspected
Insured - $1M

THE OVERLOAD COMPANION 2017 © FREDA BARBER BOOTH

NORTH DAKOTA

WHEN A PERMIT IS NEEDED
- OVER 8' 6" WIDE
- OVER 14' HIGH
- TRAILER OVER 53' LONG
- OVER 80,000 LBS

SPECIAL INFORMATION NEEDED FOR PERMIT
- FOR MOBILE HOMES ENDING IN NORTH DAKATO—NEED TO KNOW DESTINATION (FACTORY, CUSTOMER ADDRESS, ETC.) AND TIRE SIZE
- LOADS EXCEEDING 18' WIDE, 18' HIGH, 120' LONG, 150,000 LBS OR EXCEED BRIDGE STRUCTION LIMITATIONS REQUIRE SPECIAL
-   PERMIT APPLICATION FOR SUPERLOADS..

TIMES OF MOVEMENT
- 1/2 HOUR BEFORE SUNRISE TO 1/2 HOUR AFTER SUNSET; NIGHT TIME MOVEMENT FOR UPTO 10' IN WIDTH OR OVERWEIGHT ONLY; LOADS NOT EXCEEDING 16' WIDE/110' LONG TRAVEL M-F & UNTIL NOON SATURDAY
- VEHICLE AND LOAD MOVEMENTS EXCEEDING 16' IN WIDTH ARE NOT AUTHORIZED TO TRAVEL AFTER 12 NOON ON SATURDAY, SUNDAY , AND ON HOLIDAYS.
- TRAVEL IS PROHIBITED ON THE FOLLOWING HOLIDAYS: **NEW YEAR'S DAY, MEMORIAL DAY, INDEPENDENCE DAY, LABOR DAY, THANKSGIVING DAY AND CHRISTMAS DAY**

WHEN ESCORT VEHICLE IS REQUIRED
2-LANE HIGHWAYS:
- OVER 14'6" TO 16' - 1 FRONT PILOT CAR

4 OR MORE LANE DIVIDED HIGHWAYS:
- OVER 16' WIDE—1 REAR PILOT CAR

ON ALL HIGHWAYS:
- OVER 18' WIDE—OFFICIAL ESCORT (UNLESS EXEMPTED BY HIGHWAY PATROL)
- OVER 18' HIGH—1 FRONT PILOT CAR (& WRITTEN PERMISSION FROM UTILITY COMPANY)
- OVER 120' LONG—1 REAR PILOT CAR
- WEIGHT OF EARTH MOVING EQUIPMENT THAT EXCEEDS LEAGAL AXLE WEIGHT—1 REAR PILOT CAR
- WEIGHT OF ANY LOAD THAT EXCEEDS NORMAL ALLOWABLE WEIGHTS—1 OR 2 PILOT CARS MAY BE REQUIRED

MOBILE/MODULARS:
2 LANE HIGHWAY:
- FROM 14'6" TO 16' WIDE—1 FRONT PILOT CAR
- OVER 16' - 2 (FRONT & REAR)

4 OR MORE LANE DIVIDED HIGHWAYS:
- WIDTH OVER 16' - 1 REAR PILOT CAR

REQUIREMENTS FOR ESCORT VEHICLES
- **GENERAL:** 2-AXLE TRUCK OR PASSENGER VEHICLE ONLY; MUST MEET REQUIREMENTS OF ND CENTURY CODE, TITLE 39
- **SIGNS:** "OVERSIZE LOAD" SIGN W/ BLACK LETTERS (8"HIGH AND 1" BRUSH STROKE) ON A YELLOW BACKGROUND (5' X 12") MOUNTED ON THE FRONT AND REAR OF VEHICLE OR TOP OF VEHICLE
- **LIGHTS:** FLASHING AMBER LIGHTS MOUNTED ON ENDS OF SIGN OR 1 CENTRALLY MOUNTED REVOLVING AMBER LIGHT ON TOP OF SIGN
- **FLAGS:** NOT STIPULATED
- **ADDITIONAL EQUIPMENT:** 2–WAY RADIO COMMUNICATION

REQUIREMENTS FOR ESCORT VEHICLE OPERATOR
- MUST HAVE A VALID DRIVERS LICENSE
- BE 18 YEARS OLD MIN
- ALL PILOT CARS NOT REGISTERED IN NORTH DAKOTA SHALL BE REQUIRED TO PURCHASE TEMPORARY REGISTRATION WHEN ESCORTING INTRASTATE MOVEMENTS

NORTH DAKOTA DEPT. OF TRANSPORTATION PERMITS OFFICE
HIGHWAY PATROL
(701) 328-2621 / (FAX: (701) 328-1642

ASAP PILOT CAR SERVICE
Carolyn Johnson
Owner/Operator
406-600-9703
Asappilotcarservice.com
Montanatrafficcontrol.com

HIGH POLE PROFESSIONAL SURVEYS MONTANA TRAFFIC CONTROL

EQUIPPED VHF RADIO
CANADA-LEGAL
WA CERTIFIED
$3M INSURED

THE OVERLOAD COMPANION 2017 © FREDA BARBER BOOTH

OHIO

CHARLES JAMES CAYIAS
INSURANCE INC.
801-488-0085

PROFESSIONAL PILOT CAR INSURANCE PACKAGE

Working in cooperation with North America's leading escort vehicle trainers, certifying entities, and insurance professionals who specialize in protecting the needs of escort operators all across the United States.

Whether an accident is your fault or not, without the right protection, you could pay tens of thousands out of pocket to defend yourself in a lawsuit brought against you by others. Be prepared by having the proper insurance protection!

The Professional Pilot Car Insurance Package offers the following insurance coverage(s):

- **Commercial Automobile**: As personal auto insurance policies exclude business operations, commercial insurance is essential. We offer $1,000,000 in bodily injury and property damage coverage, along with medical payments, personal injury protection (in those states where required), and uninsured motorists to protect you, your passengers and members of the public in case of an over the road accident. Comprehensive and collision coverage is also offered to protect your vehicle. We can provide commercial automobile coverage on a mono-line basis.
- **General Liability**: Will protect you against injuries to members of the public at your premises, and damages that you may cause to the property of others that does not involve an automobile. We offer limits of $1,000,000 each occurrence and $2,000,000 aggregate for losses occurring during the policy term. We can provide general liability coverage on a mono-line basis.
- **Professional Liability**: Will provide you with protection for those activities normally excluded under a general liability policy because they are considered to be a professional exposure. We offer $1,000,000 in coverage for flagging, height pole, route surveys and shunting services, subject to certain qualifications. No coverage is offered for rigging, steerables or tillerman services.
- **Inland Marine**: Will cover your miscellaneous equipment used in your operation such as small tools, magnetic vehicle signage, flags, cones, etc. We offer three limits of coverage $1,000; $2,500; $5,000 depending on your needs. Higher limits are available upon request.

Charles James Cayias Insurance, Inc.
2150 South 1300 East, Suite #100
Salt Lake City, UT 84106
PH: (801) 488-0085
Fax: (801) 463-6683
www.cayias.com

Program benefits include a combination of coverage specific to the pilot car industry, competitive pricing, expertise, and prompt friendly service. Simply put... our goal is to provide you with the best value for your money!

OHIO

DRIVERS FIRST CHOICE

"Professionally leading the Industry - One load at a Time"

PROFESSIONAL   **10 YRS**   **DEPENDABLE**

HIGH POLE, PILOT & ESCORT SERVICE

MINUTES FROM KY/IN LINE I-64 & I-65

LISA: 812-406-7169

driversfirstchoice@live.com

FULLY INSURED INCL. GENERAL/PROFESSIONAL LIABILITY
CERTIFIED & EQUIPPED FOR 48 CONTINENTAL STATES

ON BOARD GPS, DELORME MAPPING, ALL STATE ATTACHMENTS
PA LISTED, LA PERMIT, GA/NV AMBER PERMITS

MULTIPLE CARS AVAILABLE

APPROVED FOR MOST MAJOR COMPANIES INCLUDING: LANDSTAR, GREENTREE, BENNETT, ATS/SENTINEL, MERCER, ADMIRAL MERCHANTS, AETNA, AMERICAN TRANSPORT & MARATHON TRANSPORT

WE WORK WITH A NETWORK OF PROFESSIONAL COMPANIES LOCALLY & NATIONWIDE

WHEN A PERMIT IS NEEDED
- OVER 8' 6" WIDE
- OVER 13'6" HIGH
- TRAILER OVER 53' LONG
- OVER 80,000 LBS

SPECIAL INFORMATION NEEDED FOR PERMIT
- LOAD DIMENSIONS, TIRE SIZE AND AXLE WEIGHTS IF OVERWEIGHT
- DIMENSIONS OF TRACTOR/TRAILER, OVERHANG I
- EXACT ADDRESS IF START OR END POINT IS IN OHIO
- OS-32 INSURANCE CERTIFICATE ON FILE
- **FOR UP-TO-DATE REQUIREMENTS REFER TO OHIO STATE PROVISION SHEET OS-1A 2198, 10/08. PROVISION SHEET MUST BE ATTACHED TO OVERSIZE TRUCK PERMIT**

TIMES OF MOVEMENT
- 1/2 HOUR BEFORE SUNRISE UNTIL 1/2 HOUR AFTER SUNSET
- TRAVEL IS PERMITTED 24/7 FOR OVERWEIGHT LOADS, DIMENSIONS MUST BE LEGAL
- LOADS UP TO 12' WIDE MAY RUN DAYLIGHT HOURS 7 DAYS A WEEK
- LOADS OVER 12' WIDE ARE PERMITTED UNTIL 3PM ON SATURDAY AND SUNDAY
- **CURFEWS:** MOVEMENT OF ALL VEHICLES/LOADS EXCEEDING 12' WIDE IS PROHIBITED WITH A 25 MILE RADIUS OF CINCINNATI, CLEVELAND, AND COLUMBUS & WITHIN THE CORPORATE LIMITS OF AKRON, CANTON, DAYTON, LIMA, TOLEDO & YOUNGSTOWN FROM 6:30-9AM & 4:30-6PM MONDAY THROUGH FRIDAY UNLESS OTHERWISE SPECIFIED BY THE SPECIAL HAULING PERMIT SECTION
- MOVEMENT OF ALL VEHICLES/LOADS IN EXCEED OF 12' WIDE SHALL BE PROHIBITED WITHIN BUTLER, CLERMONT, CUYAHOGA, DELAWARE, FAIRFIELD, GEAUGA, HAMILTON, LAKE LICKING, LORAIN, LUCAS, MADISON, MAHONING, MEDINA, MONTGOMERY, PICKAWAY, STARK, SUMMIT, UNION, WARREN AND WOOD COUNTIES BETWEEN THE HOURS OF 6:30-9:00AM AND 4:30—6:00PM MONDAY THRU FRIDAY.
- **APRIL 1 - NOV 1:** MOVEMENT OF ALL VEHICLES/LOADS IN EXCEED OF 12' WIDE SHALL BE PROHIBITED IN BUTLER, CLERMONT, CUYAHOGA, DELAWARE, FAIRFIELD, GEAUGA, HAMILTON, LAKE LICKING, LORAIN, LUCAS, MADISON, MAHONING, MEDINA, MONTGOMERY, PICKAWAY, STARK, SUMMIT, UNION, WARREN AND WOOD COUNTIES BETWEEN THE HOURS OF 6:30-9:00AM AND 3:00—6:00PM
- TRAVEL IS PROHIBITED ON THE FOLLOWING HOLIDAYS: **NEW YEAR'S DAY, MEMORIAL DAY, INDEPENDENCE DAY, LABOR DAY, THANKSGIVING DAY AND CHRISTMAS DAY**

WHEN ESCORT VEHICLE IS REQUIRED
- OVERALL LENGTH IN EXCESS OF 90' - 1 REAR PILOT CAR
- OVERALL WIDTH IN EXCESS OF 13' - 1 LEAD PILOT CAR (REAR ON MULTI LANE HIGHWAYS)
- OVERALL HEIGHT IN EXCESS OF 14'6" - 1 LEAD PILOT CAR W/ HEIGHT POLE
- OVERALL WIDTH IN EXCESS OF 14'6" - 1 LEAD PILOT CAR AND 1 REAR PILOT CAR
- OVERALL HEIGHT IN EXCESS OF 14'10" - 1 LEAD PILOT CAR W/ HEIGHT POLE AND 1 REAR PILOT CAR
- MORE THAN ONE OF THE ABOVE CONDITIONS—1 LEAD PILOT CAR AND 1 REAR PILOT CAR

REQUIREMENTS FOR ESCORT VEHICLES
- **GENERAL:** SHALL BE A SINGLE UNIT VEHICLE WITH UNOBSTRUCTED VISION FROM THE FRONT AND REAR
- **SIGNS:** "OVERSIZE LOAD" SIGN W/ BLACK LETTERS (8"HIGH AND 1" BRUSH STROKE) ON A YELLOW BACKGROUND (5' X 12") MOUNTED ON THE FRONT AND REAR OF VEHICLE OR TOP OF VEHICLE
- **LIGHTS:** ROOF MOUNTED AMBER FLASHING OR ROTATING LIGHTS
- **FLAGS: NOT STIPULATED**
- **ADDITIONAL EQUIPMENT:** 2-WAY RADIO, HEIGHT POLE (WHEN REQUIRED)

REQUIREMENTS FOR ESCORT VEHICLE OPERATOR
- NONE STIPULATED

OHIO DEPT. OF TRANSPORTATION PERMITS OFFICE
SPECIAL HAULING PERMITS
(614) 351-2300 / FAX: (614) 728-4099
SPECIAL LIMITATIONS FOR SUPERLOADS
(614) 351-2300—SUPERLOAD SECTION

CENTURY FINANCE

CASH TODAY!

FACTORING MADE EASY FOR AMERICA'S TRUCKERS

1-888-684-7195

OKLAHOMA

Blue Star Pilot Car Service LLC
Moore, OK

Ross Legg, Owner - 405-464-5802

LEAD - CHASE - STEER

CDL with Doubles/Triples
Current medical card
TWIC Card
Fully equipped
Fully insured w/ CO & PA add-on

GA / NV Amber light permits
LA / NM Permits
OK / NY Certified
Hands-Free Cell
Garmin GPS - Dash Camera

Service is a little thing that makes a BIG difference!

OKLAHOMA

WHEN A PERMIT IS NEEDED
- OVER 8'6" WIDE
- OVER 13' 6" HIGH
- TRAILER OVER 53' LONG
- OVER 80,000 LBS

SPECIAL INFORMATION NEEDED FOR PERMIT
- TYPE OF TRAILER
- REGISTERED WEIGHT OF TRACTOR
- USED MOBILE HOMES STARTING/STOPPING IN OKLAHOMA NEED HUD#

TIMES OF MOVEMENT
- 1/2 HOUR BEFORE SUNRISE TO 1/2 HOUR AFTER SUNSET 7 DAYS A WEEK
- **CURFEWS:** MOVEMENT NOT ALLOWED ON THE INTERSTATE SYSTEM IN OKLAHOMA, TULSA AND CLEVELAND COUNTIES FROM 7AM-9AM AND 3:30PM TO 6:30PM MON—FRI
- TRAVEL IS PROHIBITED ON THE FOLLOWING HOLIDAYS: **MEMORIAL DAY, INDEPENDENCE DAY, LABOR DAY, THANKSGIVING DAY AND DAY AFTER, CHRISTMAS EVE, CHRISTMAS DAY, AND NEW YEAR'S DAY**

WHEN ESCORT VEHICLE IS REQUIRED
2 LANE HIGHWAYS:
- WIDTH OVER 12' AND UP TO 14' - 1 FRONT PILOT CAR
- WIDTH OVER 14' 2 (FRONT & REAR)
- OVER 80' LONG—1 FRONT PILOT CAR
- OVER 100' LONG—2 (FRONT & REAR)
- EVERY VEHICLE AND OR LOAD EXCEEDING 15'9" IN HEIGHT SHALL BE ACCOMPANIED BY TWO ESCORTS. ONE TRAVELING IN FRONT OF SUCH LOAD WITH A HEIGHT POLE 6"ABOVE THE FOLLOWING OVERHEIGHT VEHICLE, AND ONE REAR ESCORT

MULTI-LANE HIGHWAYS
- LOADS OVER 12' WIDE UP TO 16'- 1 REAR PILOT CAR
- WIDTH OVER 14' BUT NOT OVER 16' - 1 REAR PILOT CAR
- WIDTH OVER 16' (ON ALL HIGHWAYS AND ROADS) - 2 (FRONT & REAR)
- EVERY VEHICLE AND OR LOAD EXCEEDING 15'9" IN HEIGHT SHALL BE ACCOMPANIED BY TWO ESCORTS. ONE TRAVELING IN FRONT OF SUCH LOAD WITH A HEIGHT POLE 6"ABOVE THE FOLLOWING OVERHEIGHT VEHICLE, AND ONE REAR ESCORT
- LOADS OVER 15'9" HIGH MUST CONTACT ALL PUBLIC UTILITIES AND RAILROADS ALONG THE ROUTE IN ADVANCE OF THE MOVE

MOBILE HOMES AND BOATS ON 2-LANE HIGHWAYS AND ROADS
- OVER 80' LONG—1 PILOT CAR
- WIDTH OVER 12' BUT NOT OVER 14'—1 FRONT PILOT CAR
- WIDTH OVER 14' BUT NOT OVER 16'—2 (FRONT & REAR)

REQUIREMENTS FOR ESCORT VEHICLES
- **GENERAL:** PICKUP TRUCK NOT LESS THAN 1/4 TON RATED LOAD CAPACITY OR AN AUTOMOBILE NOT LESS THAN 2000LBS.; PROPERLY LICENSED IN OKLAHOMA OR LICENSED IN ANY OTHE STATE IF PROVIDING INTERSTATE ESCORT SERVICES
- **SIGNS:** "OVERSIZE LOAD" SIGN (5' X 12") W/ BLACK LETTERS (10" HIGH X 1 1/2" BRUSH STROKE) ON A YELLOW BACKGROUND MOUNTED IN FRONT OR ON TOP OF THE FRONT ESCORT VEHICLE & ON REAR OF ESCORT
- **LIGHTS:** ROTATING OR FLASHING AMBER BEACON OR FLASHING AMBER LIGHT BAR SYSTEM MOUNTED ON TOP (VISIBLE 500'); 10" IN DIAMETER MIN. X 8" HIGH
- **FLAGS:** 2 REDFLAGS, 12" SQUARE MIN. ATTACHED TO STANDARDS ANGLED UPWARD AT A 45 DEGREE ANGLE'; MOUNTED ON CAB AND TO UPRIGHT STANDARDS ON REAR CORNERS OF VEHICLE
- **ADDITIONAL EQUIPMENT:** 2-WAY RADIO TRANSMITTING OVER A DISTANCE OF 1/2 MILE MIN.; HEIGHT POLE; 10 LB. BC FIRE EXTINGUISHER OR 2-5 LB CHEMICAL FIRE EXTINGUISHER; 4-15 MIN. FLARES; 2 RED HAND-HELD FLAGS OR 4 REFLECTIVE TRIANGLES; DISPLAY ON EACH SIDE OF VEHICLE W/ THE NAME/CITY OF ESCORT COMPANY, THE OWNER OF VEHICLE, OR BOTH; TWO 18" REFLECTIVE STOP/SLOW PADDLES; ORANGE HARD HAT; FLUORESCENT ORANGE VEST; FLASHLIGHT W/ 2 D-CELL BATTERIES; FULL-SIZE SPARE TIRE W/ TIRE JACK & LUG WRENCH

REQUIREMENTS FOR ESCORT VEHICLE OPERATOR
- OK Residents MUST BE CERTIFIED BY DPS;
- OK Residents MUST MAINTAIN A VALID OK INSURANCE POLICY NOT LESS THAN $1,000,000 COMBINED SINGLE LIMIT COVERAGE FOR BODILY INJURY AND /OR PROPERTY DAMAGE AS A RESULT OF THE OPERATION OF THE ESCORT VEHICLE, THE ESCORTED VEHICLE, OR BOTH (
- OUT OF STATE ESCORTS MUST HAVE SAME LIABILITY OF INSURANCE AS IN-STATE RESIDENTS
- OUT OF STATE ESCORTS MAY BE CERTIFIED IN ANOTHER STATE WITH RECIPROCAL AGREEMENT WITH OKLAHOMA. **(CURRENTLY CO, UT, NC, VA, FL, GA, WA)**

OKLAHOMA DEPT. OF TRANSPORTATION PERMITS OFFICE
DEPT. OF PUBLIC SAFETY
(877) 425-2390; FAX (405) 424-0943
http://www.dps.state.ok.us/ohp.chapter14.pdf

OVERSIZE LOAD OVERSIZE LOAD OVERSIZE LOAD OVERSIZE LOAD OVERSIZE LOAD OVERSIZE LOAD OVERSIZE LOAD OVERSIZE LOAD OVERSIZE LOAD

DRIVERS FIRST CHOICE
PROFESSIONAL   **9 YRS**   DEPENDABLE

"Professionally leading the industry - one load at a time"

HIGH POLE, PILOT AND ESCORT SERVICE
MINUTES FROM IN/KY LINE I-64 AND I-65

LISA
812-406-7169

driversfirstchoice@live.com

- GENERAL & PROFESSIONAL LIABILITY
- CERTIFIED AND EQUIPPED FOR 48 STATES
- ON BOARD GPS, DELORME MAPPING, ALL STATE ATTACH.
- PA LISTED, LA PERMIT, GA & NV AMBER LIGHT PERMITS
- MULTIPLE CARS AVAILABLE - NETWORKED WITH MANY OTHERS NATIONWIDE

APPROVED FOR MOST MAJOR COMPANIES INCLUDING:
LANDSTAR, GREENTREE, BENNETT, ATS/SENTINEL, MERCER, ADMIRAL MERCHANTS, AETNA,
AMERICAN TRANSPORT, MARATHON TRANSPORT

THE OVERLOAD COMPANION 2017 © FREDA BARBER BOOTH

OREGON

WHEN A PERMIT IS NEEDED
- OVER 8' 6" WIDE
- OVER 14' HIGH
- TRAILER OVER 53' LONG
- OVER 80,000 LBS

SPECIAL INFORMATION NEEDED FOR PERMIT
- OREGON PUC #

TIMES OF MOVEMENT
- 1/2 HOUR BEFORE SUNRISE TO 1/2 HOUR AFTER SUNSET
- DAYLIGHTS HOURS SATURDAY AND SUNDAY, EXCEPT BETWEEN MEMORIAL DAY TO LABOR DAY, THEN ALLOWED SATURDAY UNTIL NOON, NO TRAVEL ON SUNDAY
- **CURFEWS:** REFER TO AS CITY HOURS. ADDITIONAL RESTRICTION IN PORTLAND ON INTERSTATE 5 FROM THE OREGON/WASHINGTON BORDER TO THE JUNCTION OF OR@17 AND NEAR MEDFORD ON INTERSTATE 5 BETWEEN EXITS 24 AND 33 TRAVEL IS NOT ALLOWED BETWEEN 7 AND 9AM AND FROM 4 TO 6PM.
- TRAVEL IS PROHIBITED ON THE FOLLOWING HOLIDAYS: **NEW YEAR'S DAY, MEMORIAL DAY, INDEPENDENCE DAY, LABOR DAY, THANKSGIVING DAY AND CHRISTMAS DAY**

WHEN ESCORT VEHICLE IS REQUIRED
- EACH CASE IS DETERMINED BY DISTRICT - MUST REFER TO LOCAL / STATE PERMITS

REQUIREMENTS FOR ESCORT VEHICLES
- **GENERAL:** A PASSENGER CAR, PICKUP, TRUCK, OR TRUCK TRACTOR OF LEGAL SIZE & WEIGHT
- **SIGNS:** "OVERSIZE LOAD" SIGN W/ BLACK LETTERS (8"HIGH AND 1" BRUSH STROKE) ON A YELLOW BACKGROUND (5' X 10") MOUNTED ON THE FRONT AND REAR OF VEHICLE OR TOP OF VEHICLE
- **LIGHTS:** 2 AMBER FLASHING LIGHTS (AS WIDELY SPACED LATERALLY AS PROCTICAL) W/ 4" LENDS DIAMETER MIN (35 CANDLEPOWER RATING MIN 30 FLASHES/MINUTE) OR REVOLVING LIGHT (W/ MIN OF 125 SQ IN OF DOME SURFACE/EMITTING 30 FLASHES/MINUTE) OR STROBE LIGHTS W/ 360 DEGREE VISIBILITY MOUNTED ABOUVEE ROOF (VISIBLE 500')
- **FLAGS:** 2 HAND-HELD RED FLAGS 18" SQUARE MOUNTED ON 3' LONG STAFFS
- **ADDITIONAL EQUIPMENT:** 2-WAY RADIO, 8 SAFETY FLARES OR REFLECTORS

REQUIREMENTS FOR ESCORT VEHICLE OPERATOR
- NONE STIPULATED

OREGON DEPT. OF TRANSPORTATION PERMITS OFFICE
OS/OD PERMIT UNIT
(503) 373-0000 / FAX: (503) 378-2873

OREGON HIGHWAY EMERGENCY NUMBER
(503) 588-9610

http://egov.oregon.gov/ODOT/MCT/OD.shtml#od

PORTS OF ENTRY

ASHLAND, OR	1-5 N/B	(541) 776-6117
FREWELL BEND, OR	1-84 W/B	(541) 869-2293
UMATILLA, OR		(541) 922-3761
PORTLAND BRIDGE		(503) 283-5700

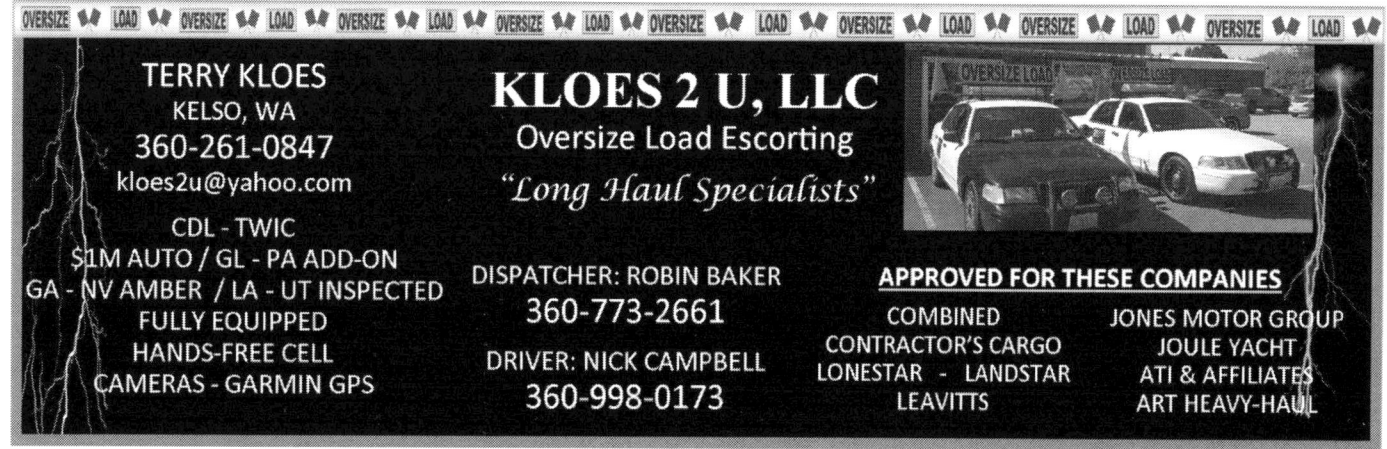

TERRY KLOES
KELSO, WA
360-261-0847
kloes2u@yahoo.com

CDL - TWIC
$1M AUTO / GL - PA ADD-ON
GA - NV AMBER / LA - UT INSPECTED
FULLY EQUIPPED
HANDS-FREE CELL
CAMERAS - GARMIN GPS

KLOES 2 U, LLC
Oversize Load Escorting
"Long Haul Specialists"

DISPATCHER: ROBIN BAKER
360-773-2661

DRIVER: NICK CAMPBELL
360-998-0173

APPROVED FOR THESE COMPANIES
COMBINED
CONTRACTOR'S CARGO
LONESTAR - LANDSTAR
LEAVITTS
JONES MOTOR GROUP
JOULE YACHT
ATI & AFFILIATES
ART HEAVY-HAUL

THE OVERLOAD COMPANION 2017 © FREDA BARBER BOOTH

PENNSYLVANIA

CHARLES JAMES CAYIAS INSURANCE INC.
801-488-0085

PROFESSIONAL PILOT CAR INSURANCE PACKAGE

Working in cooperation with North America's leading escort vehicle trainers, certifying entities, and insurance professionals who specialize in protecting the needs of escort operators all across the United States.

Whether an accident is your fault or not, without the right protection, you could pay tens of thousands out of pocket to defend yourself in a lawsuit brought against you by others. Be prepared by having the proper insurance protection!

The Professional Pilot Car Insurance Package offers the following insurance coverage(s):

- **Commercial Automobile**: As personal auto insurance policies exclude business operations, commercial insurance is essential. We offer $1,000,000 in bodily injury and property damage coverage, along with medical payments, personal injury protection (in those states where required), and uninsured motorists to protect you, your passengers and members of the public in case of an over the road accident. Comprehensive and collision coverage is also offered to protect your vehicle. We can provide commercial automobile coverage on a mono-line basis.
- **General Liability**: Will protect you against injuries to members of the public at your premises, and damages that you may cause to the property of others that does not involve an automobile. We offer limits of $1,000,000 each occurrence and $2,000,000 aggregate for losses occurring during the policy term. We can provide general liability coverage on a mono-line basis.
- **Professional Liability**: Will provide you with protection for those activities normally excluded under a general liability policy because they are considered to be a professional exposure. We offer $1,000,000 in coverage for flagging, height pole, route surveys and shunting services, subject to certain qualifications. No coverage is offered for rigging, steerables or tillerman services.
- **Inland Marine**: Will cover your miscellaneous equipment used in your operation such as small tools, magnetic vehicle signage, flags, cones, etc. We offer three limits of coverage $1,000; $2,500; $5,000 depending on your needs. Higher limits are available upon request.

Charles James Cayias Insurance, Inc.
2150 South 1300 East, Suite #100
Salt Lake City, UT 84106
PH: (801) 488-0085
Fax: (801) 463-6683
www.cayias.com

Program benefits include a combination of coverage specific to the pilot car industry, competitive pricing, expertise, and prompt friendly service. Simply put... our goal is to provide you with the best value for your money!

PENNSYLVANIA

A1 Escort Services
No load too big...No road too far

John T Widrig
Owner/Operator

john.widrig@gmail.com
484-560-3589

2253 Irma Drive
Allentown, PA 18109

FULLY CERTIFIED & INSURED

PENNSYLVANIA

WHEN A PERMIT IS NEEDED
- OVER 8' WIDE
- OVER 13'6" HIGH
- TRAILER OVER 53' LONG
- OVER 80,000 LBS

SPECIAL INFORMATION NEEDED FOR PERMIT
- AXLE WEIGHTS & SPACING
- REGISTERED WEIGHT
- MAKE, MODEL, SERIAL # OF LOAD AND # OF PIECES
- COMPANY FEIN
- SPECIFIC MILES & DIRECTION FROM NEAREST INTERSECTION WHERE MOVEMENT BEGINS/ENDS (EX: 3.7 MILES SOUTH OF I-81).

TIMES OF MOVEMENT
- 7 DAYS/ WEEK - SEE PERMIT FOR TRAVEL TIMES IN URBAN AREA
- IF NOT OVERSIZE AND IF GROSS WEIGHT DOES NOT EXCEED 100,000 LBS. VEHICLES OPERATING AT PREVAILING SPEEDS MAY OPERATE CONTINUOUSLY, EXCEPT DURING HOLIDAY PERIODS OR DURING INCLEMENT WEATHER
- SEE PERMIT FOR MOBILE HOMES 16' WIDE
- **CURFEWS:** WILL BE NOTED ON PERMIT
- TRAVEL IS PROHIBITED ON THE FOLLOWING HOLIDAYS: **NEW YEAR'S DAY, MEMORIAL DAY, INDEPENDENCE DAY, LABOR DAY, THANKSGIVING DAY AND CHRISTMAS DAY**

WHEN ESCORT VEHICLE IS REQUIRED
ON ALL HIGHWAYS:
- WIDTH OVER 13' - 1 (REAR IF MULTI-LANE) (2 FRONT IF 2-LANE)
- WIDTH OVER 16' - POLICE ESCORT
- LENGTH OVER 90' - 1 REAR PILOT CAR
- LENGTH OVER 160' - POLICE ESCORT
- REAR OVERHANG OVER 15' - 1 REAR PILOT CAR
- HEIGHT OVER 14'6" - 1 FRONT PILOT CAR W/ HEIGHT POLE
- OVERWEIGHT MORE THAN 201,000 LBS—POLICE ESCORT
- OVERWEIGHT IF REQUIRED TO TRAVEL AT REDUCED SPEEDS OVER BRIDGES—1 REAR PILOT CAR
- OVERWEIGHT IF PERMIT REQUIRED LOAD MUST BE THE ONLY VEHICLE ON A BRIDGE OR TO OCCUPY MORE THAN 1 LANE TO CROSS ON 2-DIRECTIONAL BRIDGE—2(FRONT & REAR)
- IF BRIDGES SUPPORTS ONLY 1-LANE OF TRAFFICE—1 REAR PILOT CAR
- URBAN AREAS:
- OVERSIZE LOADS ALLOWED TO RUN 3:00AM TO SUNRISE—2 (FRONT & REAR) PILOT CARS
- PERMITTED LOADS NOT ABLE TO RUN 40 MPH ON LIMITED ACCESS HIGHWAYS ALLOWED BETWEEN 9AM TO 4PM—1 REAR PILOT CAR
- NON-URBANIZED AREAS:
- PERMITTED LOADS NOT ABLE TO MAINTAIN 40 MPH ON LIMITED ACCESS HIGHWAYS—1 REAR PILOT CAR

REQUIREMENTS FOR ESCORT VEHICLES
- **GENERAL:** NOT SPECIFIED
- **SIGNS:** "OVERSIZE LOAD" SIGN W/ BLACK LETTERS (8"HIGH AND 1 1/2" BRUSH STROKE) ON A YELLOW BACKGROUND (5' X 12") MOUNTED ON THE FRONT AND REAR OF VEHICLE OR TOP OF VEHICLE
- **LIGHTS:** 1 OR 2 FLASHING LIGHTS
- **FLAGS:** NOT NEEDED ON PILOT CARS
- **ADDITIONAL EQUIPMENT:** 2-WAY RADIO

REQUIREMENTS FOR ESCORT VEHICLE OPERATOR
- LIABILITY INSURANCE IN THE COMBINED AMOUNT OF $1,00,000 & PROOF THEREOF
- MUST SHOW THE COMMONWEALTH OF PENNSYLVANIA AS ADDITIONALLY INSURED
- MUST HAVE A GENERAL CONDITIONS PROVISION SHEET M-938 REVISED 3-05 IN YOUR POSSESSION WHEN ESCORTING OR
- PERMITTING AN OVERSIZE OR OVERWEIGHT LOAD

PENNSYLVANIA DEPT. OF TRANSPORTATION PERMITS OFFICE
(717) 787-4680 / FAX: (717) 787-9890

www.states.pa.us

High Lines, LLC
Oversize Load Escorting
RIG MOVING SPECIALISTS

Janet Watson
Weston, WV
Fax 866-520-9531
highlines11@yahoo.com

304-203-9700

HIGH POLES - CHASE -LEAD - STEER
PERMIT WRITING ABILITY/ ACCTS - HANDS-FREE CELL BOOSTER
ON BOARD CAMERAS - GPS - DELORME / STREETS & TRIPS
LAPTOP / PRINTER

ALL STATES CERT & EQUIPPED - MULTIPLE OIL COMPANY CERTIFICATIONS
LA PERMIT - PRO-GL $2MIL - NV & GA AMBER LIGHT PERMITS

THE OVERLOAD COMPANION 2017 © FREDA BARBER BOOTH

RHODE ISLAND

WHEN A PERMIT IS NEEDED
- OVER 8'6" WIDE
- OVER 13' 6" HIGH
- TRAILER OVER 48'6" LONG
- OVER 80,000 LBS

SPECIAL INFORMATION NEEDED FOR PERMIT
- REGISTERED WEIGHT
- TRAILER LICENSE PLATE

TIMES OF MOVEMENT
- 1/2 HOUR BEFORE SUNRISE TO 1/2 HOUR AFTER SUNSET; NO WEEKEND TRAVEL
- RED ROUTES PROHIBIT ONLY MOVES OVER 12' WIDE BETWEEN 7-9AM AND AFTER 3:30PM ON MULTI-STATE PERMIT MAPS AND PROVISION SHEET.
- TRAVEL IS PROHIBITED ON THE FOLLOWING HOLIDAYS: **MEMORIAL DAY, INDEPENDENCE DAY, LABOR DAY, THANKSGIVING DAY AND DAY AFTER, CHRISTMAS EVE, CHRISTMAS DAY, AND NEW YEAR'S DAY**

WHEN ESCORT VEHICLE IS REQUIRED
- WIDTH OVER 12' AND UP TO 14'6" - 1 PILOT CAR
- WIDTH OVER 14'6" 2 (FRONT & REAR)
- OVER 80' UP TO 90' LONG—1 PILOT CAR
- OVER 90' LONG—2 (FRONT & REAR)
- HEIGHT OVER 14' - 1 PILOT CAR
- OVERHANG OF 15' OR MORE—1 PILOT CAR
- ONE 2-LANE HIGHWAY IF OVER 12' WIDE—2 PILOT CARS

REQUIREMENTS FOR ESCORT VEHICLES
- **GENERAL:** AT LEAST AS LARGE AS A COMPACT CAR OR LARGER
- **SIGNS:** "OVERSIZE LOAD" SIGN ON ROOF
- **LIGHTS:** YELLOW LIGHTS (VISIBLE FROM FRONT & REAR) IN OPERATION ABOVE THE HIGHEST POINT OF THE VEHICLE
- **FLAGS:** NOT STIPULATED
- **ADDITIONAL EQUIPMENT:** 2-WAY RADIO

REQUIREMENTS FOR ESCORT VEHICLE OPERATOR
- NO STIPULATIONS

RHODE ISLAND DEPT. OF TRANSPORTATION PERMITS OFFICE
DIVISION OF MOTOR VEHICLES
(401) 462-5745

www.dmv.ri.gov

RHODE ISLAND TURN PIKE & BRIDGE AUTHORITY
(401) 423-0800

SOUTH CAROLINA

WHEN A PERMIT IS NEEDED
- OVER 8'6" WIDE
- OVER 13' 6" HIGH
- TRAILER OVER 53" LONG
- OVER 80,000 LBS

SPECIAL INFORMATION NEEDED FOR PERMIT
- LENGTH OF TRAILER AND OVERHANG
- **SUPER LOADS** ARE CONSIDERED TO BE ALL LOADS OVER 130,000 LBS ON 7 AXLES, 125' LONG, 14' WIDE. HEIGHT RESTRICTIONS WILL DEPEND ON ROUTES TO BE TAKEN. IN EXCESS OF 130,000 LBS THE APPLICATION GOES TO THE BRIDGE DEPARTMENT FOR APPROVAL.

TIMES OF MOVEMENT
- 1/2 HR BEFORE SUNRISE TO 1/2 AFTER SUNSET MONDAY THRU SATURDAY FOR STANDARD ISSUE
- **WEEKEND TRAVEL:** LOADS 14' WIDE OR LESS MAY TRAVEL SUNRISE TO SUNSET ON SATURDAY. LOADS 16' WIDE MAY TRAVEL 9AM-3PM ON SATURDAY
- **TRAVEL TIMES:** LOADS OVER 15' WIDE & MOBILE HOMES OVER 14' - SCHOOL DAYS 9-3; NON-SCHOOL DAYS 9-4
- TRAVEL IS PROHIBITED ON SUNDAY OR BETWEEN NOON BEFORE/NOON AFTER THE FOLLOWING HOLIDAYS: **MEMORIAL DAY, INDEPENDENCE DAY, LABOR DAY, THANKSGIVING DAY AND DAY AFTER, CHRISTMAS EVE, CHRISTMAS DAY, AND NEW YEAR'S DAY**
- **SUMMER TRAVEL TIMES:** MOVEMENT IS PROHIBITED ON FRIDAY AND SATURDAY FROM MEMORIAL DAY THROUGH LABOR DAY OVER ROUTES INCLUDING, BUT NOT LIMITED TO, US-378, SC-327, US- 76, SC-576, US-501, SC-22, SC-31 AND SC-9 EAST OF I-95 TO AND FROM THE MYRTLE BEACH AREA AND ON US-17 FROM THE NORTH CAROLINA LINE TO POINTS SOUTH OF MYRTLE BEACH (GEORGETOWN) AND ON ANY OTHER ROUTES IN THE MYRTLE BEACH VICINITY.

WHEN ESCORT VEHICLE IS REQUIRED
ON 2-LANE HIGHWAYS:
- WIDTH 12'-14' - 1 FRONT ONLY- UNLESS OTHERWISE STATED
- (NO MOVEMENT ON STATE HIGHWAYS IN CLOSE PROXIMITY OF LARGE URBAN AREAS FROM 7-9AM OR 3-6PM SCHOOL DAYS OR 7-9AM OR 4:30-6PM OTHER DAYS)
- WIDTH OVER 14' TO 16' - 2 PILOT CARS
- MON-FRI - 9AM-3PM; SAT - 9AM-4PM ONLY. MUST TRAVEL ON FOUR-LANE HIGHWAYS.
- OVER 16' HEIGHT – FRONT ESCORT (HEIGHT POLE) - ROUTE SURVEY REQUIRED
- OVERLENGTH - OVER 125' - FRONT & REAR PILOT CAR
- REAR OVERHANG OF 15' - FRONT & REAR PILOT CAR

REQUIREMENTS FOR ESCORT VEHICLES
- **SIGNS:** "OVERSIZE LOAD" OR "WIDE LOAD" SIGN ON FRONT AND/OR REAR - DEPENDING ON LEAD / FOLLOW STATUS
- **LIGHTS:** ROTATING AMBER BEACON OR LIGHT DISPLAYED ON TOP OF VEHICLE
- **FLAGS:** NO STIPULATIONS
- **ADDITIONAL EQUIPMENT:** 2-WAY RADIO

REQUIREMENTS FOR ESCORT VEHICLE OPERATOR
- NO STIPULATIONS

SOUTH CAROLINA DEPT. OF TRANSPORTATION PERMITS OFFICE
DEPARTMENT OF TRANSPORTATION
(803) 737-6769
(803) 737-2199—FAX

Flying Squirrel Escorts Service

Bill Musall - Owner
Fingerville, SC
(864) 208-4752
HIGH POLE - STEER (CLASS A CDL)
TWIC - PASSPORT - $1M INSURED + PA
LANDSTAR APPROVED
ALL LIGHT PERMITS

Multiple cars located in the South to Midwest

THE OVERLOAD COMPANION 2017 © FREDA BARBER BOOTH

SOUTH DAKOTA

ASAP
PILOT CAR SERVICE
406-600-9703

Carolyn Johnson
Owner/Operator

montanatrafficcontrol.com

asappilotcarservice.com

PROFESSIONAL ROUTE SURVEYS
TRAFFIC MGMT PLANS

HIGH POLE
LEAD - CHASE
CANADA-LEGAL
WA CERTIFIED
$3MIL INSURED

Equipped w/ VHF Radio
Streets & Trips

SOUTH DAKOTA

WHEN A PERMIT IS NEEDED
- OVER 8'6" WIDE
- OVER 14' HIGH
- TRAILER OVER 53' LONG
- OVER 80,000 LBS

SPECIAL INFORMATION NEEDED FOR PERMIT
- SERIAL NUMBER OF TRUCK

TIMES OF MOVEMENT
- 1/2 HOUR BEFORE SUNRISE TO 1/2 HOUR AFTER SUNSET
- MOVEMENT OF LOAD OR WIDE FARM MACHINERY DURING DARKNESS IS A CLASS 2 MISDEMEANOR.
- **CURFEW:** BLACK HILLS AREA– WHEN LOAD EXCEEDS WIDTH OF 10' ONE FRONT ESCORT REQUIRED.
- TRAVEL IS PROHIBITED ON THE FOLLOWING HOLIDAYS: **MEMORIAL DAY, INDEPENDENCE DAY, LABOR DAY, THANKSGIVING DAY AND DAY AFTER, CHRISTMAS EVE, CHRISTMAS DAY, AND NEW YEAR'S DAY**

WHEN ESCORT VEHICLE IS REQUIRED
ON STATE HIGHWAYS:
- WIDTH OVER 20' - 1 PILOT CAR (FRONT IF 2-LANE, REAR IF MULTI-LANE)

ON INTERSTATE:
- WIDTH OVER 16' - 1 REAR. IN BLACK HILLS AREA SEE PERMIT
- MOBILE HOMES: PILOT CARS ARE AT THE DISCRETION OF THE PERMIT AUTHORITY

BLACK HILLS AREA:
- WIDTH EXCEEDS 10' - 1 FRONT PILOT CAR

REQUIREMENTS FOR ESCORT VEHICLES
- **GENERAL:** LICENSED MOTOR VEHICLES—NO MOTORCYCLES
- **SIGNS:** "WIDE LOAD AHEAD" (MOUNTED ON FRONT OF LEADING ESCORT) OR "WIDE LONG LOAD" (MOUNTED ON BACK OF TRAILING ESCORT) WITH 12" HIGH LETTERING
- **LIGHTS:** REVOLVING (OR 2 2-WAY FLASHING) AMBER LIGHTS AT LEAST 4" IN DIAMETER
- **FLAGS:** BRIGHT RED OR ORANGE FLAGS; 12" SQUARE MIN.; MOUNTED ON BRACKETS OR STANDARDS ON EACH SIDE OF THE SIGNS
- **ADDITIONAL EQUIPMENT:** 2-WAY RADIO

TAX REQUIREMENTS FOR ESCORT VEHICLE OPERATOR
! PILOT CAR SERVICES ARE TAXABLE SERVICES IN SOUTH DAKOTA SUBJECT TO 4% STATE AND APPLICABLE MUNICIPAL SALES TAX.
! PILOT CAR SERVICES THAT ORIGINATE IN ANOTHER STATE BUT PASS THROUGH OR END IN SOUTH DAKOTA ARE NOT SUBJECT TO SOUTH DAKOTA SALES TAX.

SOUTH DAKOTA DEPT. OF TRANSPORTATION PERMITS OFFICE
HIGHWAY PATROL
(605) 698-3925 / FAX (605) 698-7665

TENNESSEE

PIT ROW SERVICES

FRONT/REAR HIGH POLE STEERMAN ROUTE SURVEY

ASK YOURSELF
WHO'S PILOTING YOUR LOADS?
ARE THEY QUALIFIED?
ARE THEY CERTIFIED?
WHO'S REALLY RESPONSIBLE?

WE OFFER CERTIFICATION CLASSES!

FULLY INSURED INCLUDING PROFESSIONAL LIABILITY

HIGHLY EQUIPPED PROFESSIONAL FLEET OF VEHICLES. TRAINED & CERTIFIED NATIONWIDE. ESCORT YOUR OVERSIZED LOADS WITH THE BEST LOOKING & MOST PROFESSIONAL PILOT CARS IN THE COUNTRY.

(205) 763 - 9340 LINCOLN AL
MOBILE AL   **WWW.PITROW.SERVICES**

Tennessee

WHEN A PERMIT IS NEEDED
- OVER 8'6" WIDE
- OVER 13' 6" HIGH
- TRUCK/TRAILER COMBINATION OVER 50' LONG
- OVER 80,000 LBS
- OVERHANG OVER 60" FRONT OR REAR
- WEIGHT: OVER 20,000 LBS (SINGLE AXLE) & 34,000 (DOUBLE AXLE)
- ANNUAL PERMIT UP TO 165,000 LBS (FEE INCREASES)
- SINGLE-TRIP PERMIT (VALID FOR 10 DAYS)

SPECIAL INFORMATION NEEDED FOR PERMIT
- MOVEMENT WITH GROSS WEIGHT EXCEEDING 150,000 LBS MUST BE APPROVED BY THE STRUCTURE DIVISION BEFORE A SPECIAL PERMIT CAN BE ISSUED.
- LENGTH: 120', WIDTH: 16'; LOAD IN EXCEED OR 15' IN HEIGHT WILL REQUIRE AN ESCORT WITH HEIGHT POLE.
- IF LOAD EXCEEDS ANY OF THE ABOVE DIMENSIONS OR WEIGHTS, REFER TO THE STATE ON SUPER LOADS.
- LOADS WEIGHING 150,000LBS OR MORE MUST GO TO THE BRIDGE DEPARTMENT.

TIMES OF MOVEMENT
- SUNRISE TO SUNSET MON - SAT; NO SUNDAY TRAVEL
- CURFEWS: LOADS GREATER THAN 12'6" WIDE OR 85' OR MORE LONG MAY NOT TRAVEL IN CITY LIMITS OR HEAVILY TRAVELED AREAS FROM 6-9AM & 3-6PM MONDAY THRU FRIDAY
- OVERWEIGHT ONLY MAY HAVE CONTINUOUS MOVEMENT
- TRAVEL IS PROHIBITED: **MEMORIAL DAY, INDEPENDENCE DAY, LABOR DAY, THANKSGIVING DAY, CHRISTMAS DAY -** (PERMIT MAY INCLUDE OTHER HEAVY-TRAFFIC DAYS)

WHEN ESCORT VEHICLE IS REQUIRED
- INTERSTATE / 4-LANE - OVER 12'6" - 14' WIDE - 1 REAR PILOT CAR
- INTERSTATE / 4-LANE - OVER 14' WIDE - 1 FRONT & 1 REAR PILOT CAR
- 2-LANE HIGHWAYS (UNDER 24' PAVEMENT) - OVER 10' - 14' - 1 PILOT CAR IN FRONT OF LOAD
- 2-LANE HIGHWAYS (UNDER 24' PAVEMENT) - OVER 14' WIDE - 1 FRONT & 1 REAR PILOT CAR
- LENGTH 85' LONG—1 REAR PILOT CAR; 120' LONG—2 PILOT CARS
- HEIGHT 15' OR MORE—1 FRONT PILOT CAR W/ HEIGHT POLE
- FLAG PERSON REQUIRED ON ALL BRIDGES LESS THAN 20' WIDE

REQUIREMENTS FOR ESCORT VEHICLES
- **GENERAL:** PROPERLY-LICENSED, SINGLE-UNIT VEHICLE (PASSENGER AUTOMOBILE, PICKUP TRUCK, OR SUV) THAT ALLOWS AN UNOBSTRUCTED 360° VIEW FOR SAFETY.
- NO FLATBED TRUCKS, SERVICE VEHICLES, AND NO VEHICLE TOWING A TRAILER CAN BE USED AS AN ESCORT VEHICLE.
- **SIGNS:** "OVERSIZE LOAD" (BUMPER OR ROOF MOUNTED - 12 X 5) W/ BLACK LETTERS (10" HIGH X 1.5" BRUSH STROKE) ON YELLOW BACKGROUND - MAY NOT OBSCURE VISIBILITY OF LIGHTS OR REAR SIGNALS.
- **LIGHTS:** ROTATING OR STROBE TYPE AMBER LIGHT VISIBLE FROM 500'; HORIZONTAL PLACEMENT VISIBLE 360 DEGREES
- **FLAGS:** 2 - 18" RED/FLOURESCENT ORANGE FLAGS MOUNTED ON ROOF OF ESCORT VEHICLE
- **ADDITIONAL EQUIPMENT:** 2-WAY ELECTRONIC COMMUNICATION; 2-5LB FIRE EXTINGUISHERS; "STOP/SLOW PADDLE (18" W/ 6" LETTERS); SAFETY ORANGE VEST/SHIRT/JACKET; 18" HAND HELD RED FLAG; 2 "OVERSIZE LOAD" BANNERS (BLACK LETTERS ON YELLOW BACKGROUND); HARD HAT; REFLECTING TRI-ANGLES OR 18" TRAFFIC CONES. ADDITIONAL EQUIPMENT RECOMMENDED, BUT NOT REQUIRED: HAND-HELD 2-WAY RADIO, FLARES, MAP(S), HEIGHT POLE.
- **LIGHTS/FLAGS REQUIREMENTS FOR OVERSIZED VEHICLE:** "OVERSIZE LOAD SIGN PLACED ON FRONT & REAR OF OS/OW VEHICLE - ROTATING OR STROBE TYPE AMBER LIGHT VISIBLE FROM 500'; HORIZONTAL PLACEMENT VISIBLE 360 DEGREES

REQUIREMENTS FOR ESCORT VEHICLE OPERATOR
- NO CERTIFICATION OR SPECIAL PERMITS REQUIRED

TENNESSEE DEPT. OF TRANSPORTATION PERMITS OFFICE
(615) 741-3821 / (615) 741-1159

Papa's Pilot Car Service
Chattanooga, TN
Harold McClure - Owner
423-530-1116

$1M GL/PL/BL Insurance
Louisiana Permit
GA / WA Certs
GA/NV Amber

DDC Cert
GPS / Dash Cam
Full Mobile Office

*No load too big, no trip too long....
We'll be there to get the job done.*

THE OVERLOAD COMPANION 2017 © FREDA BARBER BOOTH

TENNESSEE

AA Pilot Escort Service

Tim: 865-680-4248
Rick: 865-680-7692

East TN

LEAD - CHASE - HIGH POLE
(We use "Wonder Pole")

FL / WA / NY Certified

$1M GL / PL Insured

Equipped for All States!

TEXAS

Blue Star Pilot Car Service LLC
Moore, OK

Ross Legg, Owner - 405-464-5802

LEAD - CHASE - STEER

CDL with Doubles/Triples
Current medical card
TWIC Card
Fully equipped
Fully insured w/ CO & PA add-on

GA / NV Amber light permits
LA / NM Permits
OK / NY Certified
Hands-Free Cell
Garmin GPS - Dash Camera

Service is a little thing that makes a BIG difference!

TEXAS

WHEN A PERMIT IS NEEDED
- OVER 8'6" WIDE
- OVER 14' HIGH
- TRAILER OVER 59' LONG
- REAR OVERHANG OVER 4'
- OVER 80,000 LBS

SPECIAL INFORMATION NEEDED FOR PERMIT
- ID, ICC/MC#, SERIAL # ON TRUCK, HUD #

TIMES OF MOVEMENT
- 1/2 HOUR BEFORE SUNRISE TO 1/2 HOUR AFTER SUNSET
- VEHICLES NOT EXCEEDING 10' WIDE OR 100' LONG MAY OPERATE ON THE INTERSTATE 24-7
- TRAVEL IS PROHIBITED FOR LOADS EXCEEDING 14' WIDE, 16' HIGH & 110' LONG ON THE FOLLOWING HOLIDAYS: **MEMORIAL DAY, INDEPENDENCE DAY, LABOR DAY, THANKSGIVING DAY AND DAY AFTER, CHRISTMAS EVE, CHRISTMAS DAY, AND NEW YEAR'S DAY**
- **CURFEWS:** PERMIT NOT VALID WITH CURFEW SHEET ATTACHED. TO VIEW CURFEWS, GO TO THE TEXAS DEPARTMENT OF TRANSPORTATION WEBSITE AT www.txdot.gov.

WHEN ESCORT VEHICLE IS REQUIRED
- WIDTH OF 14' UP TO AND INCLUDING 16' - 1 PILOT CAR
- WIDTH OVER 16'- 2 (FRONT & REAR)
- WIDTH OVER 20' - MUST HAVE A ROUTE SURVEY
- OVER 110' UP TO 125' LONG—1 PILOT CAR
- OVER 125' LONG—2 (FRONT & REAR)
- HEIGHT OVER 17' - 1 PILOT CAR W/ HEIGHT POLE (CONTACT UTILITY COMPANIES)
- HEIGHT OVER 18' - 2 (FRONT & REAR + HEIGHT POLE)
- HEIGHT OVER 19' - MUST HAVE ROUTE SURVEY
- REAR OVERHANG 20' UP TO 30' —1 PILOT CAR
- OVERHANG OVER 30' - 2 (FRONT & REAR + SPECIAL APPROVAL)

MANUFACTURED HOMES:
- WIDTH OVER 16' UP TO 18' (ON 2-LANE HIGHWAYS 1 FRONT); (ON MULTI-LANE HIGHWAYS—1 REAR)
- REFER TO PERMIT IN REGARD TO CONVOYING OF MOBILE HOMES
- WIDTH OVER 18' ON ALL HIGHWAYS—2 (FRONT & REAR)

POLICE MOTORCYCLE ESCORTS:
- AN OFFICIAL LAW ENFORCEMENT MOTORCYCLE MAY BE USED AS A PRIMARY ESCORT VEHICLE FOR A PERMITTED LOAD TRAVELING WITH THE LIMITS OF AN INCORPORATED CITY. AN ESCORT MOTORCYCLE MUST MAINTAIN 2-WAY RADIO COMMUNICATION WITH THE PERMITTED VEHICLE AND OTHER ESCORT VEHICLES WHILE MOVING PERMITTED LOAD.

CONVOY ESCORT REQUIREMENTS
- 110', 1" TO 125' - ONE PILOT CAR PER LOAD, OR CONVOY 2 TO 4 LOADS WITH 1 FRONT AND 1 REAR PILOT CAR
- 125', 1" TO 150' - FRONT AND REAR PILOT CARS PER LOAD, OR CONVOY 2 TO 4 LOADS WITH 1 FRONT AND 1 REAR PILOT CAR
- 150', 1" TO 180' - FRONT AND REAR PILOT CARS PER LOAD, OR CONVOY UP TO 2 LOADS WITH 1 FRONT AND 1 REAR PILOT CAR
- SPACING AND LIGHTING OF A LOAD: EACH PERMITTED LOAD IN THE CONVOY MUST: TRAVEL AT LEAST 1000', BUT NOT MORE THAN 2000', FROM ANY OTHER PERMITTED LOAD IN THE CONVOY, HAVE A ROTATING AMBER BEACON OR AN AMBER PULSATING LIGHT NOT LESS THAN 8" IN DIAMETER MOUNTED AT THE TOP REAR OF THE LOAD

REQUIREMENTS FOR ESCORT VEHICLES
- **GENERAL:** SINGLE UNIT W/ GVW OF 1000LBS MIN TO 10,000 LBS MAX
- **SIGNS:** "OVERSIZE LOAD" OR "WIDE LOAD" SIGN MOUNTED ON EITHER THE ROOF OF THE VEHICLE OR THE FRONT & REAR OF THE VEHICLE; MUST BE VISIBLE FROM THE FRONT & REAR; (5'-7"X12"-18") W/ BLACK LETTERS (8" - 10" HIGH W/ 1.41" BRUSH STROKE) ON A YELLOW BACKGROUND
- **LIGHTS:** 2 FLASHING OR 1 ROTATING AMBER LIGHT; 8" IN DIAMETER MIN; MOUNTED ON THE ROOF OF VEHICLE; VISIBLE 360 DEGREES
- **FLAGS:** NOT STIPULATED
- **ADDITIONAL EQUIPMENT:** 2-WAY RADIO

REQUIREMENTS FOR ESCORT VEHICLE OPERATOR
- NO STIPULATIONS

TEXAS DEPT. OF TRANSPORTATION PERMITS OFFICE
(512) 465-3500
(800) 299-1700, PERMITS ONLY

Grant Pilot Cars
Runnin' for America
850-381-4959
Fax: 888-791-5090
www.grantpilotcars.com

Multiple Cars Based in Several States

High Pole - CDL - Steer/Tillerman
Lead - Chase - Traffic Control
Call Us for your Large & Small Projects

FL/GA/WA Certified - $1M GL+ PA - $1M PL
TWIC & Passport
Mobile Office - Cam - GPS Equipped
Permits & Equipment for All States

Fair Rates - Experienced - Professional

THE OVERLOAD COMPANION 2017 © FREDA BARBER BOOTH

UTAH

WHEN A PERMIT IS NEEDED
- OVER 8'6" WIDE
- OVER 14' HIGH
- TRAILER OVER 48' LONG
- OVER 80,000 LBS

SPECIAL INFORMATION NEEDED FOR PERMIT
- NEED A CURRENT CERTIFICATE OF INSURANCE ON FILE (MIN COVERAGE OF $750,000 COMBINED SINGLE LIMIT)
- LENGTH OF OVERHANG
- LOAD HEIGHTS OF 16' OR MORE REQUIRE A PILOT CAR W/ HEIGHT POLE
- LOAD HEIGHTS OF 17'7" OR MORE REQUIRED SPECIAL DOT APPROVAL

TIMES OF MOVEMENT
- 1/2 HOUR BEFORE SUNRISE TO 1/2 HOUR AFTER SUNSET; 7 DAY A WEEK
- LOADS 10' WIDE, 92' LONG AND LEGAL HEIGHT MAY TRAVEL 24/7
- CURFEWS: TRAVEL IS PROHIBITED FOR LOADS IN EXCESS OF 10' WIDE, 105' LONG, AND 14' HIGH MONDAY THRU FRIDAY BETWEEN 6-9AM AS WELL AS 3:30 TO 6PM ON THE FOLLOWING HIGHWAYS: ALL HIGHWAYS SOUTH OF PERRY INTERCHANGE, 1-15, EXIT #357. ALL HIGHWAYS IN WEBER, DAVIS AND SALT LAKE COUNTIES. ALL HIGHWAYS NORTH OF IRONTON INTERCHANGE, 1-15, EXIT 261. SR 68, NORTH OF MILE POST 16 IN UTAH COUNTY
- NIGHT TIME TRAVEL: LOADS MAY NOT EXCEED 12' WIDE ON SECONDARY HIGHWAYS, 14' ON INTERSTATES, AND 14' HIGH ON ALL ROADWAYS. LOADS EXCEEDING 10' WIDE, 105' LONG, OR 10' FRONT AND REAR OVERHANG ARE REQUIRED TO HAVE ONE CERTIFIED PILOT CAR ON INTERSTATE HIGHWAYS AND 2 PILOT CARS ON ALL SECONDARY HIGHWAYS. LOADS EXCEEDING 92' LONG ARE REQUIRED TO HAVE PROPER LIGHTING EVERY 25'. WITH AMBER LIGHTS TO THE FRONT AND SIDES OF THE LOAD MARKING EXTREME WIDTH, AND REAR TO THE REAR.
- TRAVEL IS PROHIBITED ON THE FOLLOWING HOLIDAYS: **MEMORIAL DAY, INDEPENDENCE DAY, LABOR DAY, THANKSGIVING DAY AND DAY AFTER, CHRISTMAS EVE, CHRISTMAS DAY, AND NEW YEAR'S DAY**

WHEN ESCORT VEHICLE IS REQUIRED
- WIDTH OVER 12' - 1 PILOT CAR
- WIDTH OVER 14' OR MORE—2 (FRONT & REAR)
- WIDTH OVER 17' - 2 (FRONT & REAR) + 2 POLICE CARS
- OVER 105' UP TO 120' LONG—1 PILOT CAR
- OVER 120' LONG—2 (FRONT & REAR)
- HEIGHT OVER 16' OR MORE– 2 (FRONT & REAR) + HEIGHT POLE
- OVERHANG OF 20' OR MORE—1 PILOT CAR
- AS REQUIRED BY UDOT

REQUIREMENTS FOR ESCORT VEHICLES
- **GENERAL:** WHEELBASE 95" MIN; WEIGHT 12,000 MAX
- **SIGNS:** "OVERSIZE LOAD" SIGN (5' X 10") W/ BLACK LETTERS (8" HIGH W/ 1" BRUSH STROKE) ON A YELLOW BACKGROUND MOUNTED ON TOP OF PILOT CAR
- **LIGHTS:** 2 6" OR LARGER AMBER WARNING LIGHTS MOUNTED 1 ON EACH SIDE OF SIGN OR AN AAMVA APPROVED AMBER ROTATING,
-     OSCILLATING OR FLASHING BEACON/LIGHT BAR MOUNTED ON TOP OF THE VEHICLE & VISIBLE FOR 360 DEGREES
- **FLAGS:** NOT STIPULATED
- **ADDITIONAL EQUIPMENT:** 2-WAY RADIO (MIN 4 WATTS) CAPABLE OF TRANSMITTING 1/2 MILE; "24" "STOP/SLOW PADDLE; 9 REFLECTIVE TRIANGLES; 8 BURNING FLARES OR APPROVED ALTERNATIVE; 3 18" (OR LARGER) ORANGE CONES; ORANGE HARD HAT; ORANGE VEST; FLASH LIGHT W/ MIN 1 1/2" LENS WITH RED OR ORANGE CONE (MIN 9"); HEIGHT POLE (NON-CONDUCTIVE MATERIAL); FIRE EXTINGUISHER; FIRST AID KIT (CLEARLY LABELED); 1 "OVERSIZE LOAD" SIGN (7' X 18"); SPARE TIRE; TIRE JACK; LUG WRENCH

REQUIREMENTS FOR ESCORT VEHICLE OPERATOR
- MINIMUM 18 YEARS OF AGE; POSSESS A VALID DRIVER'S LICENSE FOR THE STATE IN WHICH THE DRIVER RESIDES; A CERTIFICATION CARD WILL BE ISSUED BY AN AUTHORIZED QUALIFIED CERTIFICATION PROGRAM THAT IS VALID FOR 4 YEARS THEN 1 ADDITIONAL 4 YEAR CERTIFICATION MAY BE OBTAINED BY MAIL OR ONLINE. NON RESIDENT DRIVERS MAY OPERATE AS A CERTIFIED DRIVER WITH ANOTHER STATE'S CERTIFICATION PROVIDED THE COURSE MEETS THE MINIMUM REQUIREMENTS OUTLINED BY UDOT. UTAH CURRENTLY RECOGNIZES CERTIFICATIONS FROM THE STATES OF WA, NC, CO, OK, FL, UT.
- PILOT CAR OPERATOR MUST HAVE A MINIMUM LIABILITY INSURANCE OF $750,000 ON VEHICLE

UTAH DEPT. OF TRANSPORTATION PERMITS OFFICE
(801) 965-4508 / (801) 965-4399

PORTS OF ENTRY

ST. GEORGE	(435) 673-9651	PEERLESS	(435) 472-3401
WENDOVER	(435) 665-2274	DANIELS	(435) 654-1091
ECHO	(435) 289-3122	PERRY	(425) 734-9414
KANAB	(435) 644-5871	MONTICELLO	(435) 587-2662

CALL US TODAY!

CASH TODAY!

FACTORING MADE EASY FOR AMERICA'S TRUCKERS

1-888-684-7195

CENTURY FINANCE

THE OVERLOAD COMPANION 2017 © FREDA BARBER BOOTH

CHARLES JAMES CAYIAS INSURANCE INC.

801-488-0085

PROFESSIONAL PILOT CAR INSURANCE PACKAGE

Working in cooperation with North America's leading escort vehicle trainers, certifying entities, and insurance professionals who specialize in protecting the needs of escort operators all across the United States.

Whether an accident is your fault or not, without the right protection, you could pay tens of thousands out of pocket to defend yourself in a lawsuit brought against you by others. Be prepared by having the proper insurance protection!

The Professional Pilot Car Insurance Package offers the following insurance coverage(s):

- **Commercial Automobile**: As personal auto insurance policies exclude business operations, commercial insurance is essential. We offer $1,000,000 in bodily injury and property damage coverage, along with medical payments, personal injury protection (in those states where required), and uninsured motorists to protect you, your passengers and members of the public in case of an over the road accident. Comprehensive and collision coverage is also offered to protect your vehicle. We can provide commercial automobile coverage on a mono-line basis.
- **General Liability**: Will protect you against injuries to members of the public at your premises, and damages that you may cause to the property of others that does not involve an automobile. We offer limits of $1,000,000 each occurrence and $2,000,000 aggregate for losses occurring during the policy term. We can provide general liability coverage on a mono-line basis.
- **Professional Liability**: Will provide you with protection for those activities normally excluded under a general liability policy because they are considered to be a professional exposure. We offer $1,000,000 in coverage for flagging, height pole, route surveys and shunting services, subject to certain qualifications. No coverage is offered for rigging, steerables or tillerman services.
- **Inland Marine**: Will cover your miscellaneous equipment used in your operation such as small tools, magnetic vehicle signage, flags, cones, etc. We offer three limits of coverage $1,000; $2,500; $5,000 depending on your needs. Higher limits are available upon request.

Charles James Cayias Insurance, Inc.
2150 South 1300 East, Suite #100
Salt Lake City, UT 84106
PH: (801) 488-0085
Fax: (801) 463-6683
www.cayias.com

Program benefits include a combination of coverage specific to the pilot car industry, competitive pricing, expertise, and prompt friendly service. Simply put... our goal is to provide you with the best value for your money!

VERMONT

WHEN A PERMIT IS NEEDED
- OVER 8'6" WIDE
- OVER 13' 6" HIGH
- TRAILER OVER 68' LONG
- OVER 80,000 LBS

SPECIAL INFORMATION NEEDED FOR PERMIT
- VERMONT HUT #

TIMES OF MOVEMENT
- 1/2 HOUR BEFORE SUNRISE TO 1/2 HOUR AFTER SUNSET;
- VEHICLES WHICH ARE OVER WEIGHT ONLY AND ARE CAPABLE OF TRAVELING WITH THE FLOW OF TRAFFIC MAY TRAVEL 24 HRS
- NO WEEKEND TRAVEL FOR LOADS GREATER THAN 108,000 LBS, 10'6" WIDE, 100' LONG OR ON FRIDAY AFTERNOONS (7/1-LABOR DAY) OR ON THE FOLLOWING HOLIDAYS: **MEMORIAL DAY, COLUMBUS DAY, MARTIN LUTHER KING DAY, INDEPENDENCE DAY, VETERANS DAY, LABOR DAY, THANKSGIVING DAY AND DAY AFTER, CHRISTMAS EVE, CHRISTMAS DAY, PRESIDENTS DAY, AND NEW YEAR'S DAY**
- SEE PROVISION SHEET OR PERMIT FOR SPECIAL INSTRUCTIONS/CURFEWS OR CALL (802) 282-2064
- **CURFEWS** — RUTLAND—US 4 NO TRAVEL BETWEEN 7—9AM AND 3—6PM. ROUTE 107 SCHOOL DAY
- RESTRICTION ONLY. NO TRAVEL ALLOWED BEFORE 8:30AM AND BETWEEN 11—12:30PM AND 2-5PM.

WHEN ESCORT VEHICLE IS REQUIRED
- WIDTH OVER 12' OR MORE - 1 PILOT CAR
- HEIGHT GREATER THAN 14' - 1 PILOT CAR W/ HEIGHT POLE (AS DETERMINED BY DOT)
- LENGTH OF 80' OR MORE—1 PILOT CAR
- HEIGHT OVER 14' - 1 PILOT CAR
- OVERHANG OF 15' OR MORE—1 PILOT CAR
- LARGE OR HAZARDOUS MOVES—2 (FRONT & REAR; MAY NEED POLICE ESCORT)

REQUIREMENTS FOR ESCORT VEHICLES
- **GENERAL:** AT LEAST AS LARGE AS A COMPACT CAR OR LARGER
- **SIGNS:** "OVERSIZE LOAD" SIGN ON FRONT AND/OR REAR DEPENDING ON VEHICLE AND LOAD (5' X 12" W/ 10" HIGH/1 5/8 WIDE LETTERS)
- **LIGHTS:** YELLOW LIGHTS (VISIBLE FROM FRONT & REAR) IN OPERATION ABOVE THE HIGHEST POINT OF THE VEHICLE
- **FLAGS:** NOT STIPULATED
- **ADDITIONAL EQUIPMENT:** 2-WAY RADIO

REQUIREMENTS FOR ESCORT VEHICLE OPERATOR
- PILOT CARS MUST TRAVEL WITH LOW BEAM HEADLIGHTS ON WHEN ESCORTING LOADS

VERMONT DEPT. OF TRANSPORTATION PERMITS OFFICE
DIVISION OF MOTOR VEHICLES
(802) 828-2064 / (802) 828-5418—FAX

MARTIN EMERSON
SABATTUS, MAINE
High Pole - Lead - Chase - Steer
Certified   Fully Insured   Passport
Heavy, Wide or Tall, We'll Help You Haul 'Em All
207-240-7876
emerson01@rocketmail.com
NEW YORK STATE CERTIFIED ESCORT
EMERSON PILOT CAR SERVICES — EPCS

VIRGINIA

WHEN A PERMIT IS NEEDED
- OVER 8'6" WIDE
- OVER 13' 6" HIGH
- TRAILER OVER 48' LONG
- OVER 80,000 LBS

SPECIAL INFORMATION NEEDED FOR PERMIT
- TRAILER SERIAL #
- NEED INTERSECTING ROUTES IF ORIGIN AND DESTINATION IS INSIDE VA
- NEED FEDERAL ID #

TIMES OF MOVEMENT
- 1/2 HOUR BEFORE SUNRISE TO 1/2 HOUR AFTER SUNSET MONDAY THRU 12 NOON ON SATURDAY.
- OVERWEIGHT ONLY CAN TRAVEL 24/7
- VEHICLES EXCEEDING 12' BUT NO GREATER THAN 14' WIDE AND 105' LONG ARE PERMITTED TO TRAVEL BETWEEN THE HOURS OF 9:00 TO 12 NOON SATURDAY.
- **CURFEWS**—NO PERMTTED TRAVEL IS ALLOWED WITHIN THE CORPORATE LIMITS OF CITIES/TOWNS BETWEEN THE HOURS OF 7-9AM AND 4-6PM EXCEPT FOR CONFIGURATIONS THAT ARE OVERWEIGHT OR OVERHEIGHT ONLY OR ANY COMBINATION OF THE 2
- **CURFEWS WILL BE ATTACHED TO YOUR PERMIT FOR TIMES OF TRAVEL UNDER SPECIAL CONDITIONS**
- TRAVEL IS PROHIBITED ON THE FOLLOWING HOLIDAYS: **MEMORIAL DAY, INDEPENDENCE DAY, LABOR DAY, THANKSGIVING DAY AND DAY AFTER, CHRISTMAS EVE, CHRISTMAS DAY, AND NEW YEAR'S DAY**

WHEN ESCORT VEHICLE IS REQUIRED
ON 2-LANE HIGHWAYS:
- WIDTH OVER 10' ON ALL 2 & 3 LANE—1 FRONT PILOT CAR
- WIDTH OVER 12' OR OVER 75' LONG NEED AMBER FLASHING LIGHTS LOCATED ON TOP OF TOWING VEHICLE OR PILOT CARS WITH AMBER FLASHING LIGHTS

WIDTH OVER 12':
- THROUGH BIG WALKER TUNNEL & EAST RIVER MT. TUNNER—1 PILOT CAR
- LENGTH OVER 85' - 1 FRONT PILOT CAR
- HEIGHT—PERMITEE IS RESPONSIBLE FOR ALL HORIZONTAL & VERTICAL CLEARANCES, ROUTES DETERMINE ESCORT NEEDS
- WIDTH OVER 14'7" - 2 (FRONT & REAR ON SOME ROUTES)

- **ON 4-LANE/INTERSTATE HIGHWAYS:**
- WIDTH OVER 10', LENGTH OVER 75', HEIGHT UNDER & OVER 14'6" ALL DEPEND ON ROUTES

REQUIREMENTS FOR ESCORT VEHICLES
- **GENERAL:** AT LEAST AS LARGE AS A COMPACT CAR OR LARGER
- **SIGNS:** SIGN (VISIBLE DAY OR NIGHT) MUST IDENTIFY THE TYPE OF LOAD BEING ESCORTED (I.E. "WIDE LOAD", "OVERSIZE LOAD", "OVERDIMENSIONAL LOAD", OVERWEIGHT LOAD"). SIGNS MUST HAVE BLACK LETTERS 10" X 1 1/2" BRUSH STROKE & MUST BE 60" LONG X 12" HIGH
- **LIGHTS:** MUST HAVE FLASHING AMBER LIGHTS W/ STROBE OR ROTATING SEALED BEAM; 5" DIAMETER BASE; MIN 4" LENS HEIGHT
- **FLAGS:** NOT STIPULATED
- **ADDITIONAL EQUIPMENT:** 2-WAY RADIO

REQUIREMENTS FOR ESCORT VEHICLE OPERATOR
- VIRGINIA CERTIFCATION MANDATORY FOR ALL ESCORT DRIVERS REGARDLESS OF RESIDENCY FOR LOADS 12'-14' WIDE.
- MULTIPLE CHOICE QUESTIONS ON ESCORTS DRIVER'S TEST BASED ON **VIRGINIA DRIVER'S MANUAL & VIRGINIA HAULING PERMIT MANUAL,**
- ADMINISTERED THROUGH DMV'S KNOWLEDGE AUTOMATED TESTING SYSTEM (KATS)
- TEST MAY BE TAKEN AT ANY OF THE 14 DOH OFFICES
- RE-TESTING REQUIRED TO REMAIN CERTIFIED BEFORE EXPIRATION DATE ON BACK OF CERTIFICATION CARD
- IF LOADS ARE LESS THAN 12' WIDE, NO CERTIFICATION IS REQUIRED

VIRGINIA DEPT. OF TRANSPORTATION PERMITS OFFICE
(804) 786-3495

PEGASUS PILOTS, LLC
SMITHSBURG, MARYLAND
301-991-4406
12 Years

Tired of Working with Non-Professional Escorts?

We have 8 Professional Drivers with fully equipped vehicles!

CDL Experience
60 mi. to Port of Baltimore / 100 mi. to MD/WV Line I-68
Equipped / Legal for All States
Courteous, Professional, Reliable, Dependable

Access to Nationwide High Quality
High-Polers & Steer-people

WASHINGTON STATE CERTIFIED INSTRUCTOR

WASHINGTON

WHEN A PERMIT IS NEEDED
- OVER 8'6" WIDE
- OVER 14' HIGH
- TRAILER OVER 53' LONG
- OVER 80,000 LBS

SPECIAL INFORMATION NEEDED FOR PERMIT
- MILE POSTS REQUIRED FOR EACH SECTION OF HIGHWAY COVERED BY AN OVERWEIGHT PERMIT

TIMES OF MOVEMENT
- 1/2 HOUR BEFORE SUNRISE TO 1/2 HOUR AFTER SUNSET; 7 DAYS A WEEK
- NIGHT MOVEMENTS: VEHICLES OR COMBINATIONS OPERATING UNDER SPECIAL MOTER VEHICLE PERMITS THAT ARE OVERDIMENSIONAL, NOT EXCEEDING 12' WIDE, 100' LONG AND 14'6" HIGH MAY BE PERMITTED TO MOVE AT NIGHT ON STATE HIGHWAYS DURING NORMAL ATMOSPHERIC CONDITIONS WITH PROPER LIGHTING.
- OVERWEIGHT VEHICLES WITH LEGAL DIMENSIONS CAN OPERATE 24/7 PROVIDING THEM CAN MAINTAIN THEIR SPEED IN TRAFFIC.
- TRAVEL IS PROHIBITED ON THE FOLLOWING HOLIDAYS: **MEMORIAL DAY, INDEPENDENCE DAY, LABOR DAY, THANKSGIVING DAY AND DAY AFTER, CHRISTMAS EVE, CHRISTMAS DAY, AND NEW YEARS DAY**

WHEN ESCORT VEHICLE IS REQUIRED
2-LANE HIGHWAYS:
- WIDTH OVER 11' - 2 (FRONT & REAR) PILOT CARS
- OVER 105' LONG (OR REAR OVERHANG EXCEEDS 1/3 TOTAL LENGTH—1 REAR PILOT CAR
- OVER 14'6" HIGH—1 FRONT + COUNTY OR CITY AUTHORIZATION
- FRONT OVERHANG (DEPENDING ON ROUTE) - 1 REAR PILOT CAR
- THE TRUCK DRIVER CAN'T SEE 200' TO THE REAR OF THE LOAD W/ MIRRORS

MULTI-LANE HIGHWAYS:
- WIDTH OVER 14' TO 20' - 1 REAR PILOT CAR
- WIDTH OVER 20' - 2 (FRONT & REAR) PILOT CARS
- LENGTH OVER 125' - 1 REAR PILOT CAR
- HEIGHT OVER 14'6" - 1 FRONT PILOT CAR W/ HEIGHT POLE + COUNTY OR CITY AUTHORIZATION
- FRONT OVERHANG OVER 20' - 1 FRONT PILOT CAR
- REAR OVERHANG GREATER THAN 20' - 1 REAR PILOT CAR
- THE TRUCK DRIVER CAN'T SEE 200' TO THE REAR OF THE LOAD W/ MIRRORS

MOBILE HOMES:
- OVER 15' HIGH—1 FRONT PILOT CAR W/ HEIGHT POLE

FARM IMPLEMENTS:
- WIDTH OVER 12'6" ON 2-LANE STATE HIGHWAYS—2 (FRONT & REAR)
- WIDTH OVER 14' ON MULTIPLE LANE STATE HIGHWAYS—1 REAR PILOT CAR

REQUIREMENTS FOR ESCORT VEHICLES
- **GENERAL:** AT LEAST AS LARGE AS A COMPACT CAR OR LARGER
- **SIGNS:** "OVERSIZE LOAD" SIGN DIMENSIONS: 5' WIDE X 10" HIGH; 1" BRUSH STROKE BLACK LETTERS (8" HIGH) ON A
- YELLOW BACKGROUND
- **LIGHTS:** 2 FLASHING OR ROTATING AMBER LIGHTS ABOVE THE ROOF LINE
- **FLAGS:** NOT STIPULATED
- **ADDITIONAL EQUIPMENT:** HEIGHT POLE IN USE AT ALL TIMES WHEN LOAD IS OVER 14'6" IN HEIGHT (EXTENDED NOT LESS THAN 3" NOR MORE THAN 6" ABOVE THE LOAD MAX HEIGHT); EXTERIOR REAR VIEW MIRRORS ON RIGHT & LEFT SIDES; STANDARD 18" STOP/SLOW PADDLE SIGN; 3 BI-DIRECTIONAL EMERGENCY REFLECTIVE TRIANGLES; 1 5LB B.C. FIRE EXTINGUISHER, OR EQUIVALENT; HIGH VISIBILITY SAFETY GARMENT (FLOURESCENT YELLOW-GREEN, FLOURESCENT ORANGE-RED OR FLOURESCENT RED); FIRST AID KIT, FLASHLIGHT W/ RED NOSE CONE, 2-WAY RADIO

REQUIREMENTS FOR ESCORT VEHICLE OPERATOR
- MUST POSSESS A VALID WA STATE PILOT/ESCORT VEHICLE OPERATOR CERTIFICATE/CARD OR CERTIFICATION FROM ANOTHER JURISDICTION APPROVED BY THE DEPARTMENT, SUBJECT TO THE PERIODIC REVIEW OF THE ISSUING JURISDICTION'S CERTIFICATION PROGRAM. WA'S OPERATOR CARDS MUST BE RENEWED EVERY 3 YEARS. CERTIFICATION TEST MAY BE TAKEN BY CONTACTING THE PILOT ESCORT AND FLAGGING INSTRUCTOR AT (509) 684-7632. WASHINGTON STATE CURRENTLY RECOGNIZES CERTIFICATIONS FROM UT, FL, NC, OK AND CO

WASHINGTON DEPT. OF TRANSPORTATION PERMITS OFFICE
(360) 704-6340 / (360) 704-6350

WASHINGTON DC

WHEN A PERMIT IS NEEDED
- OVER 8'6" WIDE
- OVER 13' 6" HIGH
- ANY VEHICLE, OTHER THAN A BUS, OVER 40' LONG
- VEHICLE WITH A COMBINED OVERALL LENGTH OF OVER 55' LONG
- A BUS LONGER THAN 60' OR WIDER THAN 8'6"
- OVER 80,000 LBS

SPECIAL INFORMATION NEEDED FOR PERMIT
- APPLY ONLINE ON TOPS, THE DDOT ONLINE PERMITTING SYSTEM, AT tops.ddot.dc.gov
- COMPANY NAME, TAX ID #, COMPANY STREET ADDRESS AND PHONE #
- TRACTOR AND TRAILER INFORMATION; GROSS WEIGHT; AXLE WEIGHTS; AXLE SPACINGS; ORIGIN AND DESTINATION
- ALLOW UP TO 2 WEEKS FOR AN ANNUAL PERMIT
- ALLOW 1 WEEK FOR SINGLE HAUL PERMIT

TIMES OF MOVEMENT
- TRAVEL IS PERMITTED FROM SUNRISE TO SUNSET 7 DAYS A WEEK
- OVERWIDTH VEHICLES AND OVER HIEGHT VEHICLES MAY BE RESTRICTED TO NIGHT TRAVEL BETWEEN THE HOURS OF 10PM TO 5AM. TRAVEL IS ALLOWED ON WEEKENDS.
- TRAVEL NOT RESTRICTED ON HOLIDAYS

WHEN ESCORT VEHICLE IS REQUIRED
- REQUIREMENTS WILL BE STATED ON A PERMIT UPON APPLICATION
- VEHICLES OVER 79,000 LBS., 15' IN WIDTH OR HEIGHT, OR 80' IN LENGTH MUST BE ACCOMPANIED BY A LEAD ESCORT

A POLICE ESCORT IS REQUIRED FOR:
- ANY VEHICLE AND LOAD THAT IS 75' IN LENGTH OR LINGER
- ANY VEHICLE AND LOAD 12' WIDE OR WIDER
- ANY VEHICLE AND LOAD EXCEEDING 13'6" HIGH
- ANY VEHICLE WITH A TOTAL GROSS WEIGHT OF 120,000 OR MORE
- ANY VEHICLE CARRY ANY CLASS 1 EXPLOSIVES—DIVISION 1.1, 1.2, 1.3

REQUIREMENTS FOR ESCORT VEHICLES
- NOT STIPULATED

REQUIREMENTS FOR ESCORT VEHICLE OPERATOR
- NOT STIPULATED

WASHINGTON D.C. DEPT. OF TRANSPORTATION PERMITS OFFICE
TOPS PERMITTING SYSTEM
(202) 442-4670

WEST VIRGINIA

WHEN A PERMIT IS NEEDED
- OVER 8'6" WIDE
- OVER 13' 6" HIGH
- TRAILER OVER 53' LONG
- OVER 80,000 LBS

SPECIAL INFORMATION NEEDED FOR PERMIT
- OVERHANG; MFG MODEL/SERIAL # OF LOAD
- DRIVERS NAME
- IF HAULING MOBILE HOME, WEIGHT OF LOAD

TIMES OF MOVEMENT
- SUNRISE TO SUNSET FOR VEHICLES 14' WIDE OR LESS, 75' LONG OR LESS, 10' OR LESS OVERHANG, AND A HEIGHT OF 14' OR LESS, 7DAYS A WEEK
- TRAVEL ONLY ON INTERSTATE OR APD ROUTES FROM SUNRISE TO SUNSET, 7 DAYS A WEEK, W/DIMENSIONS LESS THAN 14' WIDE, 95' LONG, 15' OVERHANG AND 14'6 HIGH
- OVERSIZE VEHICLES EXCEEDING THE ABOVE DIMENSIONS UP TO & INCLUDING 16' WIDE CAN TRAVEL SUNRISE TO SUNSET, MONDAY THRU FRIDAY
- OVERSIZE VEHCILES EXCEEDING 16' WIDE MAY ONLY TRAVEL ON SUNDAY MORNING
- OVERWEIGHT VEHICLES UP TO & INCLUDING 110,000 LBS MAY TRAVEL 24/7.
- TRAVEL IS PROHIBITED ON THE FOLLOWING HOLIDAYS: **GOOD FRIDAY, MEMORIAL DAY, INDEPENDENCE DAY, LABOR DAY, THANKSGIVING DAY AND DAY AFTER, CHRISTMAS EVE, CHRISTMAS DAY, AND NEW YEAR'S DAY**

WHEN ESCORT VEHICLE IS REQUIRED
ON 2-LANE HIGHWAYS:
- WIDTH OVER 10'6" AND UP TO 12' - 1 FRONT PILOT CAR, 7 DAYS
- WIDTH OVER 12' UP TO 14' - 2 (FRONT & REAR), 7 DAYS
- WIDTH OVER 14' UP TO 15' - 2 (FRONT & REAR), MON—FRI
- WIDTH OVER 15' UP TO 16' - 2 FRONT & 1 REAR
- WIDTH OVER 16' - AS REQUIRED BY PERMIT—SUNDAY (MUST BE ACCOMPANIED BY WV DOT)
- OVER 75' UP TO 95' LONG—1 REAR PILOT CAR, MON-FRI
- OVER 95' UP TO 100' LONG—2 (FRONT & REAR), MON—FRI
- OVER 100' LONG—1 FRONT & 1 REAR PILOT CAR, MON—FRI
- OVERHANG OVER 10' (FRONT) - 1 FRONT PILOT CAR, MON—FRI
- OVERHANG OVER 10' (REAR) - 1 REAR PILOT CAR, MON—FRI
- HEIGHT OVER 15' - 1 FRONT PILOT CAR W/ HEIGHT POLE IN ADDITION TO ANY OTHER ESCORT

4 OR MORE LANE HIGHWAYS
- WIDTH OVER 12' UP TO 14' - 1 REAR PILOT CAR, 7 DAYS
- WIDTH OVER 14' UP TO 15' - 1 FRONT & 1 REAR PILOT CAR, MON—FRI (EXCEPT WV PARKWAY AUTHORITY, M-TH & SUN TILL NOON; NO MOVEMENT ON FRI)
- WIDTH OVER 15' UP TO 16' - 1 FRONT & 2 REAR PILOT CARS (SAME AS ABOVE)
- WIDTH OVER 16' - SAME AS 2 LANE EXCEPT OVER 16' NOT ALLOWED ON PARKWAY
- LENGTH OVER 95' UP TO 100' - 1 REAR PILOT CAR, MON-FRI
- LENGTH OVER 100' - 1 FRONT & 1 REAR PILOT CAR, MON-FRI
- OVERHANG OVER 10' (FRONT) - 1 FRONT PILOT CAR, MON—FRI
- OVERHANG OVER 10' (REAR) - 1 REAR PILOT CAR, MON—FRI
- HEIGHT OVER 15' - 1 FRONT PILOT CAR W/ HEIGHT POLE IN ADDITION TO OTHER PILOT CARS REQUIRED (PARKWAY (I-77/64) YEAGER BRIDGE—MAX HEIGHT 15'10")

REQUIREMENTS FOR ESCORT VEHICLES
- **GENERAL:** AT LEAST AS LARGE AS A COMPACT CAR OR LARGER
- **SIGNS:** "OVERSIZE LOAD" SIGN MOUNTED TO BUMPER OR ROOF; 5' X 12", 10" HIGH BLACK LETTERING W/ 1 1/2" BRUSH STROKE
- **LIGHTS:** ROTATING/STROBE AMBER PLASTIC OR ACRYLIC OR GLASS COVERED FLASHING LIGHT—VISIBLE AT LEAST 500' & 360 DEGREES
- **FLAGS:** 2 FLAGS (RED OR SAFETY ORANGE), 18" SQUARE; MOUNTED AT A 40-70 DEGREE ANGLE ON VEHICLES ROOF OR ALL 4 CORNERS OF THE PILOT CAR
- **ADDITIONAL EQUIPMENT:** 2-WAY RADIO, (2) 5 LB FIRE EXTINGUISHERS, 18" " STOP/SLOW" PADDLE W/ 6" LETTERS, SAFETY ORANGE VEST/ SHIRT/JACKET, RED HAND-HELD FLAG (18"), (2) "OVERSIZE LOAD" BANNERS, 3 REFLECTIVE TRIANGLES OR 18" TRAFFIC CONES, SIGNS/ PLACARDS (MIN 8" X 12") SHOWING NAME OF COMPANY OR OWNER AND PHONE # ON BOTH SIDES OF VEHICLE

REQUIREMENTS FOR ESCORT VEHICLE OPERATOR
- NO STIPULATIONS

WEST VIRGINIA DEPT. OF TRANSPORTATION PERMITS OFFICE
(304) 558-0384; FAX: (304) 558-0591

High Lines, LLC
Oversize Load Escorting
RIG MOVING SPECIALISTS

Janet Watson
Weston, WV
Fax 866-520-9531
highlines11@yahoo.com

304-203-9700

HIGH POLES - CHASE -LEAD - STEER
PERMIT WRITING ABILITY/ ACCTS - HANDS-FREE CELL BOOSTER
ON BOARD CAMERAS - GPS - DELORME / STREETS & TRIPS
LAPTOP / PRINTER

ALL STATES CERT & EQUIPPED - MULTIPLE OIL COMPANY CERTIFICATIONS
LA PERMIT - PRO-GL $2MIL - NV & GA AMBER LIGHT PERMITS

THE OVERLOAD COMPANION 2017 © FREDA BARBER BOOTH

WISCONSIN

WHEN A PERMIT IS NEEDED
- OVER 8'6" WIDE
- OVER 13' 6" HIGH
- TRAILER OVER 40' LONG
- OVER 80,000 LBS

SPECIAL INFORMATION NEEDED FOR PERMIT
- LOAD INFO
- LOAD DIMENSIONS BROKEN DOWN

TIMES OF MOVEMENT
- SUNRISE TO SUNSET—MONDAY THRU FRIDAY & SATURDAY TILL NOON
- NIGHT TIME TRAVEL IS PERMITTED FOR LOADS NOT EXCEEDING 100' LONG, 12' WIDE OR 13' 6" HIGH
- TRAVEL IS ALLOWED UNTIL 12:00 NOON SATURDAY ONLY ON LOADS OVER 100' LONG, 12' WIDE AND 13' 6" HIGH
- LOADS LESS THAN THE ABOVE DIMENSIONS ARE ALLOWED TO TRAVEL ALL WEEKEND, FROM MEMORIAL DAY TO LABOR DAY, UNLESS SPECIFIED ON THE PERMIT
- TRAVEL IS PROHIBITED ON THE FOLLOWING HOLIDAYS: **MEMORIAL DAY, INDEPENDENCE DAY, LABOR DAY, THANKSGIVING DAY, CHRISTMAS EVE, CHRISTMAS DAY, AND NEW YEAR'S DAY**

WHEN ESCORT VEHICLE IS REQUIRED
ON 2-WAY, 2-LANE HIGHWAYS
- WHEN ANY PART OF THE LOAD OR VEHICLE EXTENDS BEYOND THE LEFT OF ROADWAY CENTERLINE—1 PILOT CAR
- WIDTH OVER 15' UP TO 16" (FREQUENTLY) - 1 FRONT PILOT CAR
- ON ANY HIGHWAY DESIGNATED BY PERMIT—1 OR MORE PILOT CARS
- WIDTH OVER 16' - 1 FRONT & 1 REAR PILOT CAR
- OVER 125' LONG—1 FRONT & 1 REAR PILOT CAR

ON MULTI-LANE HIGHWAYS:
- SAME AS 2-LANE EXCEPT WHEN ANY PART OF THE VEHICLE EXTENDS BEYONG THE LEFT OF THE RIGHT HAND LANE

MOBILES HOMES:
- WIDTH OVER 14' (ON CERTAIN HIGHWAYS) - 1 PILOT CAR
- WIDTH OVER 16' - POLICE/PRIVATE ESCORT: 1 REAR ON DIVIDED HIGHWAYS; 1 FRONT & 1 REAR ON NON-DIVIDED HIGHWAYS

REQUIREMENTS FOR ESCORT VEHICLES
- **GENERAL:** AT LEAST AS LARGE AS A COMPACT CAR OR LARGER
- **SIGNS:** "OVERSIZE LOAD" SIGN MOUNTED ON ROOF OF THE PILOT CAR; SIGN MUST MEASURE 5' X 12" W/ BLACK LETTERS 10" HIGH (BRUSH STROKE WIDTH OF NOT LESS THAN 1 1/2") ON A SOLID YELLOW/AMBER BACKGROUND
- **LIGHTS:** 2 AMBER WARNING LIGHTS MOUNTED ON OR ABOVE THE VEHICLE ROOF; IT SHALL INCLUDE A SINGLE OR MULTIPLE PULSE STROBE LIGHT AND SHALL FLASH, PULSE OR ROTATE BETWEEN 30 & 120 TIMES/MIN; SHALL BE VISIBLE AT A DISTANCE OF 500' FOR 360 DEGREES
- **FLAGS:** 2 BRIGHT RED OR ORANGE FLAGS AT LEAST 18" SQUARE ON A SHORT STAFF MOUNTED ON THE FRONT BUMPER (ONE ON EACH SIDE)
- **ADDITIONAL EQUIPMENT:** 2-WAY RADIO

REQUIREMENTS FOR ESCORT VEHICLE OPERATOR
- MUST BE AT LEAST 18 YEARS OF AGE
- MUST HAVE AN OPERATOR'S LICENSE ISSUED TO THE VEHICLE OPERATOR AND VALID IN WISCONSIN
- A NON-RESIDENT MUST HAVE A DRIVERS LICENSE OR CERTIFICATION ISSUED IN ANOTHER JURISDICTION THAT ALLOWS THAT PERSON TO OPERATE A PILOT CAR IN THAT JURISDICTION

WISCONSIN DEPT. OF TRANSPORTATION PERMITS OFFICE
(608) 266-7320 / FAX (608) 264-7751

THE OVERLOAD COMPANION 2017 © FREDA BARBER BOOTH

WYOMING

WHEN A PERMIT IS NEEDED
- OVER 8'6" WIDE
- OVER 14' HIGH
- TRAILER OVER 60' LONG
- OVER 80,000 LBS

SPECIAL INFORMATION NEEDED FOR PERMIT
- COMPANY MUST CALL FOR CLEARANCE WHEN 150 MILES FROM WYOMING STATE LINE

TIMES OF MOVEMENT
- DAYLIGHT HOURS ONLY EXCEPT FOR THE FOLLOWING (WHICH MUST BE PROPERLY SIGNED & LIGHTED): A COMBO MORE THAN 60' LONG UP TO 85', UP TO 10' WIDE ON INTERSTATE HIGHWAYS ONLY
- TRAVEL IS PROHIBITED FOR LOADS REQUIRING PILOT CARS ON THE FOLLOWING HOLIDAYS: **MEMORIAL DAY, INDEPENDENCE DAY, LABOR DAY, THANKSGIVING DAY, CHRISTMAS DAY, AND NEW YEAR'S DAY**

WHEN ESCORT VEHICLE IS REQUIRED
ON PRIMARY & SECONDARY HIGHWAYS:
- WHEN ANY PORTION OF VEHICLE EXTENDS TO THE LEFT OF THE HIGHWAY CENTERLINE—1 FRONT & 1 REAR PILOT CAR
- WIDTH 14' OR MORE—1 FRONT & 1 REAR PILOT CAR
- WIDTH: WYOMING HIGHWAY PATROL MAY REQUIRE MORE ESCORTS AT ITS DISCRETION
- LENGTH 100' OR MORE—1 FRONT & 1 REAR PILOT CAR
- HEIGHT 17'6" OR MORE—1 FRONT PILOT CAR W/ HEIGHT POLE

ON INTERSTATE (4 OR MORE LANES)
- WIDTH OVER 15' OR MORE—1 REAR PILOT CAR
- LENGTH 110' OR MORE—1 FRONT & 1 REAR PILOT CAR
- HEIGHT 17'6" OR MORE—1 FRONT PILOT CAR W/ HEIGHT POLE
- WIDTH: WYOMING HIGHWAY PATROL MAY REQUIRE MORE ESCORTS AT ITS DISCRETION

REQUIREMENTS FOR ESCORT VEHICLES
- **GENERAL:** AT LEAST AS LARGE AS A COMPACT CAR OR LARGER
- **SIGNS:** "OVERSIZE LOAD" SIGN VISIBLE TO ONCOMING TRAFFIC; 5' X 10" HIGH, 1" BRUSH STROKE BLACK LETTERING 8" HIGH, ON A YELLOW BACKGROUND
- **LIGHTS:** REVOLVING AMBER, AMBER STROBE, OR 2-WAY FLASHING AMBER LIGHTS MOUNTED ON TOP OF VEHICLE
- **FLAGS:** 2 RED OR FLOURESCENT ORANGE FLAGS MOUNTED ON A STAFF AT EACH SIDE OF SIGN; AT LEAST 12" SQUARE
- **ADDITIONAL EQUIPMENT:** LEFT OUTSIDE MIRRORS, 2-WAY RADIO, EMERGENCY TRIANGLES, EXTRA FLAGS, 5 LB B,C, FIRE EXTINGUISHER

REQUIREMENTS FOR ESCORT VEHICLE OPERATOR
- NO STIPULATIONS

WYOMING DEPT. OF TRANSPORTATION PERMITS OFFICE
DEPT OF TRANSPORTATION
(307) 777-4376 / FAX (307) 777-4399

PORTS OF ENTRY

ALPINE	(307) 654-7569	GILLETTE	(307) 682-4030
CASPER	(307) 265-3532	KEMMERER	(307) 877-4229
CHEYENNE (I-80)	(307) 777-4894	LARAMIE	(307) 745-2200
CHEYENNE (I-25)	(307) 777-4896	LUSK	(307) 334-3814
CHEYENNE (US 85)	(307) 777-4895	SHERIDAN	(307) 674-2350
EVANSTON	(307) 789-3538	SUNDANCE	(307) 283-1616
FRANNIE	(307) 664-2389	TORRINGTON	(307) 532-2519

ASAP PILOT CAR SERVICE
Carolyn Johnson
Owner/Operator
406-600-9703
Asappilotcarservice.com
Montanatrafficcontrol.com

HIGH POLE
PROFESSIONAL SURVEYS
MONTANA TRAFFIC CONTROL

EQUIPPED VHF RADIO
CANADA-LEGAL
WA CERTIFIED
$3M INSURED

PILOT CARS 2017

THE OVERLOAD COMPANION 2017 © FREDA BARBER BOOTH - PILOTCARSTODAY.COM

WANT TO ADVERTISE?
READ THIS FIRST!

When you purchase ANY ad space in THE OVERLOAD COMPANION 2018-19
You will automatically receive ONE state listing directing the viewer to YOUR Detailed Ad!
You may purchase additional listing within another state!

EACH listing will be specifically pointed to the *AD/PAGE* **YOU** specify.

Example: You have a PROV ad on pg. 93; a FULL ad on pg. 132; & a QTR ad on pg. 325
You can direct ANY listing to ANY page containing your ad!
Mix/Match works!

SEE SAMPLE & PRICES BELOW!

MONTANA		
COMPANY	CONTACT	DETAILS
ASAP PILOT CAR SERVICE	406-600-9703	PG 124
BARB'S PILOT CAR	406-860-3856	PG 312
ROBINS PILOT CAR SERVICE	406-207-3933	PG

PRICES

SIZE - LOCATION OF AD SPACE - PRICED "EACH" ** ANY AD SPACE PURCHASED GIVES **ONE** FREE STATE LISTING		DISCOUNT FOR MULTIPLE ORDERS
STATE PROVISIONS PAGE - FIRST COME, FIRST SERVE	$450	20% DISCOUNT
FULL PAGE AD - OR - TRUCKSTOP PAGE AD (SIZED TO FIT)	$450	20% DISCOUNT
QTR PAGE AD - LIMIT <u>ONE</u> PER CUSTOMER	$200	20% DISCOUNT
STATE LISTINGS (EACH)	$100	20% DISCOUNT

TO ORDER

PLEASE EMAIL THE FOLLOWING TO
fredabooth101@gmail.com

SUBJECT: OVERLOAD COMPANION 18-19
WE WILL CONTACT YOU!

MED. SIZE PICTURE(S): VEHICLE, LOAD, LOGO, ETC.

COMPANY CONTACT INFORMATION

LIST OF CREDENTIALS / SPECIALTIES / ETC
YOU WANT DISPLAYED IN YOUR AD

(SEE ADS IN BOOK FOR SUGGESTIONS)

ALL ORDERS MUST BE PLACED AND PAID FOR BY DEC 1, 2017

ALL SPECIAL OFFERS MUST BE PAID
WITHIN 72 HRS - OR FORFEIT THE SPECIAL PRICE

ACCEPTED METHOD OF PAYMENT

- CREDIT / DEBIT
- COMPANY CHECK (BUSINESS)
- STORE-PURCHASED PRE-PAID DEBIT (MAILED
- COMCHEK - EFS

** CALL BEFORE MAILING / SHIPPING PAYMENTS!!

"PILOT CARS TODAY"
FREDA BOOTH, OWNER

401 ANDREWS AVE
HARTSVILLE, TN 37074

817-583-5503

THE OVERLOAD COMPANION 2017 © FREDA BARBER BOOTH - PILOTCARSTODAY.COM

KLOES 2 U, LLC
Oversize Load Escorting

"Long Haul Specialists"

DISPATCHER: ROBIN BAKER
360-773-2661

DRIVER: NICK CAMPBELL
360-998-0173

MET APPROVAL FOR:
COMBINED
CONTRACTOR'S CARGO
LONESTAR - LANDSTAR
LEAVITTS - JONES MOTOR GROUP
JOULE YACHT - ATI & AFFILIATES
ART HEAVY-HAUL

TERRY KLOES
KELSO, WA
360-261-0847
kloes2u@yahoo.com

CDL - TWIC
$1M AUTO / GL - PA ADD-ON
GA - NV AMBER
LA - UT INSPECTED
FULLY EQUIPPED
HANDS-FREE CELL
CAMERAS - GARMIN GPS

We Network with These Companies!

B-LINE PILOT CAR SERVICES
OFFICE: 541-889-5770
RICHARD BUNN: 208-739-1609
LORRI GONZALEZ-BUNN: 208-739-1961

MARK'S PILOT/ESCORT SERVICE
MARK BIERRE: 702-375-6275

EBJB PILOT CAR
HOME: 208-233-5196
JEANNE: 208-251-8891
ED: 208-251-8892

HD2 PILOT CAR SERVICES
PETER HAUGEN CELL: 651-336-9261

HIGH DESERT PILOT
MARK KENNEDY: 760-947-9917

FULL SAIL PILOT CAR SERVICE
ROB ANGERMAN: 208-215-4457

NOAH'S PILOT CAR SERVICE
ROD NOAH: 308-440-3757
JANE NOAH: 308-233-2190

MCKEE PILOT CAR SERVICE
MOBILE: 951-314-3838

A+ ESCORT / PILOT SERVICE
GENE SCHLAKE: 402-239-5107

ALABAMA

MATT WALLACE ENTERPRISES
Bowling Green, KY

Lead - Chase - High Pole - Steer

270-320-5345

We have a Large Network across the US

CO/UT/NY CERT - CO/UT FLAGGING CERT
PERMITTED/EQUIPPED FOR 48 STATES
$1M - $2M INSURED W/ PA ADD-ON

Email: matthew3e@aol.com

Follow me on Facebook!

ALABAMA

Flying Squirrel Escorts Service

Bill Musall - Owner
Fingerville, SC
(864) 208-4752

HIGH POLE - STEER (CLASS A CDL)
TWIC - PASSPORT - $1M INSURED + PA
LANDSTAR APPROVED
ALL LIGHT PERMITS

Multiple cars located in the South to Midwest

Papa's Pilot Car Service
Chattanooga, TN
423-530-1116

*No load too big, no trip too long....
We'll be there to get the job done.*

$1M GL/PL/BL Insurance
Louisiana Permit
GA / WA Certs
GA/NV Amber

DDC Cert
GPS / Dash Cam
Full Mobile Office

National Pilot Car Association

JLS PILOT CAR SERVICE — MULTIPLE CARS

WA CERTIFIED   **HIGH POLE - LEAD - CHASE**   FULLY INSURED

CELL: 678-873-5016   ALT: 470-239-8776   FAX 678-807-5751

Lucky Ladies Pilot Cars, LLC

Cassandra Bostock
931-241-2241

Jodi Hurd-Cavanagh
231-388-0813

Lead / Chase
High Pole
Route Survey
$1M GL/PL/Commercial

ALABAMA

PIT ROW SERVICES

FRONT/REAR HIGH POLE STEERMAN ROUTE SURVEY

ASK YOURSELF

WHO'S PILOTING YOUR LOADS?
ARE THEY QUALIFIED?
ARE THEY CERTIFIED?
WHO'S REALLY RESPONSIBLE?

WE OFFER CERTIFICATION CLASSES!

FULLY INSURED INCLUDING PROFESSIONAL LIABILITY

HIGHLY EQUIPPED PROFESSIONAL FLEET OF VEHICLES. TRAINED & CERTIFIED NATIONWIDE. ESCORT YOUR OVERSIZED LOADS WITH THE BEST LOOKING & MOST PROFESSIONAL PILOT CARS IN THE COUNTRY.

(205) 763 - 9340

LINCOLN AL
MOBILE AL

WWW.PITROW.SERVICES

ARIZONA

Elliott's Pilot Car
Corona, California

Cell: 951-543-3407 **Office: 909-930-1936**
Fax: 909-673-0901

Coming In or Leaving - Call Us First - 24/7!

$1M Insured
NM / UT Inspection
NV / GA Amber Permit
TWIC

33 YRS - CDL   9 YRS - ESCORT/FLAGGER

HIGH POLE - LEAD - CHASE

APPROVED FOR
LANDSTAR, MERCER,
ADMIRAL MERCHANTS, TII GROUP
Etc, Etc, Etc

THOM HEAVY HAUL ESCORT, LLC
Detroit Lakes, MN
Gold Canyon, AZ

Height pole - Lead - Chase - Surveys
Fully Insured & Certified
UT / NM inspected
NV / GA Amber Permits
218-329-7606

thomheavyhaul@yahoo.com   www.thomheavyhaul.com

A1 Escort Services
No Load Too Big...No Road Too Far

John T Widrig
484-560-3589
john.widrig@gmail.com

NORTHEAST PA
LG NATIONWIDE NETWORK

LA/NM PERMITS
GA / NV AMBER
$1M INSURED
NY / FL / NDDC CERT.
EXT. DELORME NAV. SOFTWARE
DASHCAMS

HIGH POLE - SURVEYS
LEAD/CHASE/3RD CAR

ARKANSAS

J & J Pilot Car Service, Inc.
Salado, AR

30 YEARS

Jessie Smith - Owner/Contractor

Big or small - We do them all!

High pole - Route Surveys - Lead/Chase
Fully Insured

Office: 870-376-0000
Fax: 1-800-251-9768

Here Today Gone Tomorrow Pilot Service

WA / NY Cert
$1M Insured
TWIC
CDL

Brian Webb - Owner   731-415-8557

ARKANSAS

CON-SPEC, LLC

Tom or Toni
405-604-7828
405-474-2181

3 OK-Certified Operators
$2M insured / PA add-on
LandStar / ATS approved
GA, LA & NV permits
NM, UT, & OH Inspections

LEAD - CHASE - HIGH POLE

BackBone Pilot Car Services

Paul Muller
Owner
936-689-5581

17858 Crystalwood Circle
New Caney, TX 77357

Insured up to 2 Million
24/7 Any State

brianmuller70@yahoo.com

MATT WALLACE ENTERPRISES

Bowling Green, KY

We have a Large Network across the US

CO/UT/NY CERT - CO/UT FLAGGING CERT
PERMITTED/EQUIPPED FOR 48 STATES
$1M - $2M INSURED W/ PA ADD-ON

Email: matthew3e@aol.com

270-320-5345

Lead - Chase - High Pole - Steer

CALIFORNIA

Elliott's Pilot Car
Corona, California

Cell: 951-543-3407   Office: 909-930-1936
Fax: 909-673-0901

Coming In or Leaving - Call Us First - 24/7!

33 YRS - CDL

9 YRS - ESCORT/FLAGGER

HIGH POLE - LEAD - CHASE

$1M Insured
NM / UT Inspection
NV / GA Amber Permit
TWIC

APPROVED FOR
LANDSTAR, MERCER,
ADMIRAL MERCHANTS, TII GROUP
Etc, Etc, Etc.

CALIFORNIA

PIRCH PILOT CAR SERVICE

Southern California
Andrey Sr.
951-442-4476
pirchandrey@yahoo.com

Northern California
Andrey Jr.
951-587-5080
andrepirch@gmail.com

Quality Service
- Since 2004 -

10-Car Family Team of Drivers

HIGH POLE - STEERMAN - ROUTE SURVEY
LEAD - CHASE

Certified & Equipped for 48 States
Approved for All Major Companies - including Bennett & LandStar

In or Out of State - Make Us Your First Choice!
Call Us Anytime 24/7

Current CDL - TWIC - Passport
$1M / $2M GL - $1M PL Insured
NM / UT Inspections - Amber Permits
NSC DDC-8 (Defensive Driving Course)
Dash-Cam - Delorme GPS System

Reasonable Rates - Free Deadhead

WILLY B PILOT CAR SERVICE

CALIFORNIA

951-704-5436
Cell: 714-321-6965

Utah DOT Pilot/Flagger Certified
Certified NY Escort Vehicle
Nevada and Georgia Amber Light Permits
Louisiana Pilot Car Permit
$1M GL & $1M Commercial Liability Insurance

TWIC Card
On-board GPS
Front facing Camera recordings (upon request)
Full credit card services with email or text receipts and emailed invoices.

CALIFORNIA

BOBBI'S PILOT CAR SERVICE
209-810-5238

HIGH POLE

UT CERT

TWIC

GA/NV AMBER

NM/LA PERMITS

15 YRS EXPERIENCE

Delgado Family PCS

Los Angeles Area - California

Dolores Delgado - Owner/Operator

626-893-1277

LEAD - CHASE

GA / NV AMBER

NM / LA PERMITS

UT CERT

$1M GL/PL/COMMERCIAL

PASSPORT - TWIC

Approved for LandStar, Bennett & TII Group

Reasonable Rates, Reliable & Ready to Roll!

CALIFORNIA

TERRY KLOES
KELSO, WA
360-261-0847
kloes2u@yahoo.com

CDL - TWIC
$1M AUTO / GL - PA ADD-ON
GA - NV AMBER
LA - UT INSPECTED
FULLY EQUIPPED
HANDS-FREE CELL
CAMERAS - GARMIN GPS

APPROVED FOR:
COMBINED
CONTRACTOR'S CARGO
LONESTAR - LANDSTAR
LEAVITTS
JONES MOTOR GROUP
JOULE YACHT
ATI & AFFILIATES
ART HEAVY-HAUL

KLOES 2 U, LLC
Oversize Load Escorting
"Long Haul Specialists"

DISPATCHER: ROBIN BAKER
360-773-2661

DRIVER: NICK CAMPBELL
360-998-0173

CALIFORNIA PILOT CAR ASSN.
CPCA
EST. 1995
OVERSIZE LOAD

A California Non-Profit Organization
PO Box 110 Bloomington, CA 92316

708-443-4164

FOR MORE INFORMATION
capilotcar@gmail.com
www.capilotcarassoc.com

Call us for all your pilot car/escort needs

Chase - High Pole - Route Survey

COLORADO

Legacy Pilot Car Services, LLC

James: 970-396-5538
Erin: 970-396-6496

Located in Northern Colorado

HIGH POLE - LEAD - CHASE

Local and Long Haul
Single trip or full project
CO certified
$1M CA/GL/PL Insurance
CDL - TWIC - Passport
Fully equipped
On board office
Fuel Transfer Tank
(All required PPE / FR if needed)
*Prompt, professional
& safety oriented*

BRECKENRIDGE PILOT CAR SERVICES
(COLORADO)

720-590-6541   **352-507-9146**
PRIMARY   CELL

Certified, Insured & Equipped
to meet State Requirements

GA/NV Amber Light
NM Inspection

CONNECTICUT

SABATTUS, ME

LEAD - CHASE - HIGH POLE - STEER
NY/WA CERT - PASSPORT

f Mikespilotcar   mpcs1243@gmail.com

MARTIN EMERSON

SABATTUS, MAINE

NEW YORK STATE CERTIFIED ESCORT

207-240-7876
emerson01@rocketmail.com

EMERSON PILOT CAR SERVICES — EPCS

High Pole - Lead - Chase - Steer

Certified   Fully Insured   Passport

Heavy, Wide or Tall, We'll Help You Haul 'Em All

DELAWARE

Deb's Pilot Car
443-866-1408

OVERSIZE LOAD AHEAD

Angel's Pilot Car
717-752-7750

4 Cars Available

All NY/WA Certified

$1M Pro-Liability

$1M Insured w/ PA add-on

GA Amber Light Stickers

Grant Pilot Cars

Runnin' for America

Tallahassee, FL

850-381-4959

Fax: 888-791-5090

www.grantpilotcars.com

Multiple Cars Offering Nationwide Service

Lead - Chase - Steer - Traffic Control

FL/GA/WA Certified - $1M GL+ PA - $1M PL
TWIC & Passport
Mobile Office (Laptop, Printer, Fax)
Cam - GPS Equipped
Permits / Equipped for All States

Call us Today for your Large & Small Project Needs!

We offer fair rates, experience and professionalism

FLORIDA

PHA TAZZ
Pilot Service
Mayo, FL
386-688-4429

HIGH POLE
ROUTE SURVEYS
LEAD / CHASE

Since 1986

UT & NY Certified
Insured for US & Canada
Passport - GPS
Mobile Office

MEMBER
NATIONAL PILOT CAR Association

FLORIDA

Acorn
Truck Safety Escort, LLC

MEMBER

National Pilot Car Association

www.npca.news
"So everyone gets home safe!"

Bill King
Owner / Operator

Cell: 740-823-1856
Office: 740-823-1169

HIGH POLE
CERTIFIED
INSURED - EQUIPPED
& READY TO ROLL!

FLORIDA

Flying Squirrel Escorts Service

Bill Musall - Owner
Fingerville, SC
(864) 208-4752

HIGH POLE - STEER (CLASS A CDL)
TWIC - PASSPORT - $1M INSURED + PA
LANDSTAR APPROVED
ALL LIGHT PERMITS

Multiple cars located in the South to Midwest

Erazo's Pilot Services Inc
Kissimmee, FL
407-235-6873

WE RECORD YOUR LOAD FOR YOUR SAFETY

GREENTREE, LANDSTAR, BENNETT APPROVED

WE ACCEPT CREDIT CARDS, COMCHECK AND PAY PAL

FL, GA, & NY CERTIFIED - INSURED
CLASS A CDL DRIVER
TWIC - PASSPORT
GA, NV AMBER PERMITS - LA PERMIT

JLS PILOT CAR SERVICE — MULTIPLE CARS

WA CERTIFIED   **HIGH POLE - LEAD - CHASE**   FULLY INSURED

CELL: 678-873-5016   ALT: 470-239-8776   FAX 678-807-5751

Cheyenne Escort Service, LLC
386-854-5109 or 386-288-0150

18 YEARS

HIGH POLE - STEER - LEAD - CHASE

CERTIFIED ALL STATES   NATIONWIDE SERVICE   FULLY EQUIPPED
$2M INSURED   MOBILE OFFICE

www.cheyenneescortservice.com

FLORIDA

BOYD'S PILOT CARS
Saint Matthews, SC
803-457-1956

Lead - Chase - High Pole - Steer - Route Surveys

Alternate Phone: 803-596-1544

Lucky Ladies Pilot Cars, LLC

Cassandra Bostock
931-241-2241

Jodi Hurd-Cavanagh
231-388-0813

Lead / Chase
High Pole
Route Survey
$1M GL/PL/Commercial

Papa's Pilot Car Service
Chattanooga, TN
423-530-1116

No load too big, no trip too long....
We'll be there to get the job done.

$1M GL/PL/BL Insurance
Louisiana Permit
GA / WA Certs
GA/NV Amber

DDC Cert
GPS / Dash Cam
Full Mobile Office

NATIONAL PILOT CAR Association

This spot could have been yours.

Beginning 2018 - This will be a 2-yr book.

Will you be in it?

PilotCars TODAY ™
We get you noticed
pilotcarstoday.com

GEORGIA

TeeCee Logistics
Escort Services

LEAD / CHASE ☆ HIGH POLE

Fully Certified, Equipped & Insured for 48 States

JOYCE
Owner / Operator
478-387-5078

CATHY
Mgr / Dispatch
478-251-7583

GEORGIA

Lucky Ladies Pilot Cars, LLC

Cassandra Bostock
931-241-2241

Jodi Hurd-Cavanagh
231-388-0813

Lead / Chase
High Pole
Route Survey
$1M GL/PL/Commercial

Flying Squirrel Escorts Service

Bill Musall - Owner
Fingerville, SC
(864) 208-4752

HIGH POLE - STEER (CLASS A CDL)
TWIC - PASSPORT - $1M INSURED + PA
LANDSTAR APPROVED
ALL LIGHT PERMITS

Multiple cars located in the South to Midwest

JLS PILOT CAR SERVICE — MULTIPLE CARS

WA CERTIFIED   **HIGH POLE - LEAD - CHASE**   FULLY INSURED

CELL: 678-873-5016   ALT: 470-239-8776   FAX 678-807-5751

Cheyenne Escort Service, LLC
386-854-5109 or 386-288-0150

18 YEARS

HIGH POLE - STEER - LEAD - CHASE

CERTIFIED ALL STATES   NATIONWIDE SERVICE   FULLY EQUIPPED
$2M INSURED   MOBILE OFFICE

www.cheyenneescortservice.com

THE OVERLOAD COMPANION 2017 © FREDA BARBER BOOTH - PILOTCARSTODAY.COM

GEORGIA

Papa's Pilot Car Service
Chattanooga, TN
423-530-1116

No load too big, no trip too long....
We'll be there to get the job done.

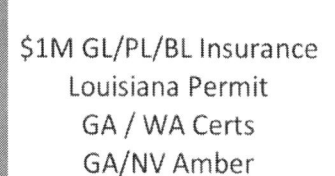

$1M GL/PL/BL Insurance
Louisiana Permit
GA / WA Certs
GA/NV Amber

DDC Cert
GPS / Dash Cam
Full Mobile Office

BOYD'S PILOT CARS
Saint Matthews, SC
803-457-1956

Lead - Chase - High Pole - Steer - Route Surveys

Alternate Phone: 803-596-1544

DRIVERS FIRST CHOICE

PROFESSIONAL — **8 YRS** — **DEPENDABLE**

"Professionally leading the industry - One load at a time"

HIGH POLE, PILOT AND ESCORT SERVICE
MINUTES FROM IN/KY LINE I-64 AND I-65

LISA 812-406-7169
MIKE 502-380-6049

driversfirstchoice@live.com

FULLY INSURED INCLUDED GEN & PRO LIABILITY - CERTIFIED AND EQUIPPED FOR 48 CONTINENTAL STATES

ON BOARD GPS, DELORME MAPPING, ALL STATE ATTACHMENTS
PA LISTED, LA PERMIT, GA & NV AMBER LIGHT PERMITS

MULTIPLE CARS AVAILABLE
WE WORK WITH A NETWORK OF OTHER PROFESSIONAL COMPANIES - LOCALLY AND NATIONWIDE

APPROVED FOR MOST MAJOR COMPANIES INCLUDING:
LANDSTAR, GREENTREE, BENNETT, ATS/SENTINEL, MERCER, ADMIRAL MERCHANTS,
AETNA, AMERICAN TRANSPORT, MARATHON TRANSPORT

IDAHO

ASAP PILOT CAR SERVICE

Carolyn Johnson
Owner/Operator

406-600-9703

Asappilotcarservice.com
Montanatrafficcontrol.com

**HIGH POLE
PROFESSIONAL SURVEYS
MONTANA TRAFFIC CONTROL**

**EQUIPPED VHF RADIO
CANADA-LEGAL
WA CERTIFIED
$3M INSURED**

TERRY KLOES
KELSO, WA
360-261-0847
kloes2u@yahoo.com

CDL - TWIC
$1M AUTO / GL - PA ADD-ON
GA - NV AMBER
LA - UT INSPECTED
FULLY EQUIPPED
HANDS-FREE CELL
CAMERAS - GARMIN GPS

APPROVED FOR:
COMBINED
CONTRACTOR'S CARGO
LONESTAR - LANDSTAR
LEAVITTS
JONES MOTOR GROUP
JOULE YACHT
ATI & AFFILIATES
ART HEAVY-HAUL

KLOES 2 U, LLC
Oversize Load Escorting
"Long Haul Specialists"

DISPATCHER: ROBIN BAKER
360-773-2661

DRIVER: NICK CAMPBELL
360-998-0173

IDAHO

KLOES 2 U, LLC
Oversize Load Escorting

"Long Haul Specialists"

MET APPROVAL FOR:
COMBINED
CONTRACTOR'S CARGO
LONESTAR - LANDSTAR
LEAVITTS - JONES MOTOR GROUP
JOULE YACHT - ATI & AFFILIATES
ART HEAVY-HAUL

TERRY KLOES
KELSO, WA
360-261-0847
kloes2u@yahoo.com

DISPATCHER: ROBIN BAKER
360-773-2661

DRIVER: NICK CAMPBELL
360-998-0173

CDL - TWIC
$1M AUTO / GL - PA ADD-ON
GA - NV AMBER
LA - UT INSPECTED
FULLY EQUIPPED
HANDS-FREE CELL
CAMERAS - GARMIN GPS

We Network with These Companies!

B-LINE PILOT CAR SERVICES
OFFICE: 541-889-5770
RICHARD BUNN: 208-739-1609
LORRI GONZALEZ-BUNN: 208-739-1961

MARK'S PILOT/ESCORT SERVICE
MARK BIERRE: 702-375-6275

EBJB PILOT CAR
HOME: 208-233-5196
JEANNE: 208-251-8891
ED: 208-251-8892

HD2 PILOT CAR SERVICES
BUSINESS: 507-829-6406
PETER HAUGEN CELL: 651-336-9261

HIGH DESERT PILOT
MARK KENNEDY: 760-947-9917

FULL SAIL PILOT CAR SERVICE
ROB ANGERMAN: 208-215-4457

NOAH'S PILOT CAR SERVICE
ROD NOAH: 308-440-3757
JANE NOAH: 308-233-2190

MCKEE PILOT CAR SERVICE
MOBILE: 951-314-3838

A+ ESCORT / PILOT SERVICE
GENE SCHLAKE: 402-239-5107

THE OVERLOAD COMPANION 2017 © FREDA BARBER BOOTH - PILOTCARSTODAY.COM

IOWA

S&W Pilot Car Escort Service, LLC

15 Minutes from Toledo, OH

419-705-3500

Lead / Chase

UT Certified / Insured

Nationwide Network

ILLINOIS

MATT WALLACE ENTERPRISES
Bowling Green, KY

Lead - Chase - High Pole - Steer

270-320-5345

We have a Large Network across the US

CO/UT/NY CERT - CO/UT FLAGGING CERT
PERMITTED/EQUIPPED FOR 48 STATES
$1M - $2M INSURED W/ PA ADD-ON

Email: matthew3e@aol.com

Follow me on Facebook!

ILLINOIS

Express Pilot Services
Belvedere, IL (IL/WI Line)

James Francey
847-489-4099

expresspilot1@gmail.com

High Pole - Chase - Steer
Superloads
Insured - Certified
CDL - Nationwide Service

Approved for: Greentree & Bennett

Jack Enterprises, Inc
Pilot Car Service

Mike Jack - Owner
Greenfield, In
Cell: 317-514-8043
Fax: 317-326-2166

Email: mljack4039@hotmail.com

25 yrs OTR
Owner/Operator

Utah Certified
$1M Insured
Wide - Long - High - Heavy

VISA MasterCard DISCOVER AMERICAN EXPRESS

S&W Pilot Car Escort Service, LLC
419-705-3500

Lead / Chase
Certified / Insured

INDIANA

DRIVERS FIRST CHOICE

"Professionally leading the Industry - One load at a Time"

PROFESSIONAL   **10 YRS**   **DEPENDABLE**

HIGH POLE, PILOT & ESCORT SERVICE

MINUTES FROM KY/IN LINE I-64 & I-65

LISA: 812-406-7169

driversfirstchoice@live.com

**FULLY INSURED INCL. GENERAL/PROFESSIONAL LIABILITY
CERTIFIED & EQUIPPED FOR 48 CONTINENTAL STATES**

ON BOARD GPS, DELORME MAPPING, ALL STATE ATTACHMENTS
PA LISTED, LA PERMIT, GA/NV AMBER PERMITS

MULTIPLE CARS AVAILABLE

APPROVED FOR MOST MAJOR COMPANIES INCLUDING: LANDSTAR, GREENTREE, BENNETT, ATS/SENTINEL, MERCER, ADMIRAL MERCHANTS, AETNA, AMERICAN TRANSPORT & MARATHON TRANSPORT

WE WORK WITH A NETWORK OF PROFESSIONAL COMPANIES LOCALLY & NATIONWIDE

INDIANA

J & H PILOT SERVICES
260-336-2412
Johnny Cole - CEO

HIGH POLE - LEAD - CHASE

WA / NY Certified

$1M Commercial Insurance

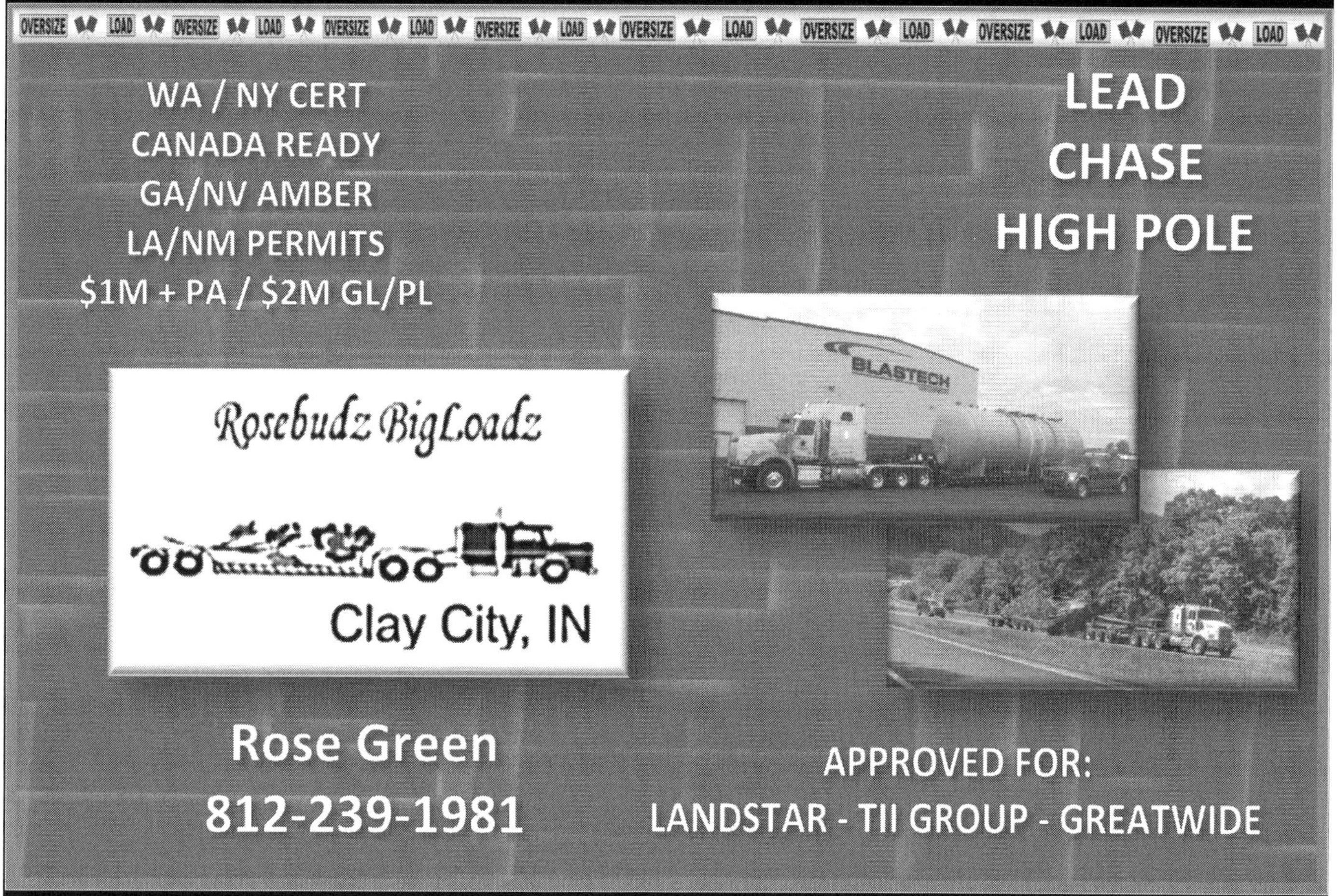

INDIANA

WA / NY CERT
CANADA READY
GA/NV AMBER
LA/NM PERMITS
$1M + PA / $2M GL/PL

LEAD
CHASE
HIGH POLE

Rosebudz BigLoadz
Clay City, IN

Rose Green
812-239-1981

APPROVED FOR:
LANDSTAR - TII GROUP - GREATWIDE

Lead / Chase
Certified / Insured

S&W Pilot Car Escort Service, LLC
419-705-3500

INDIANA

KyPilotCars
Walton, KY

LEAD - CHASE
HIGH POLE

Office: 859-400-0101
Website: Kypilotcars.com
Email: Dispatch@kypcs.com

Jack Enterprises, Inc
Pilot Car Service

Mike Jack - Owner
Greenfield, In
Cell: 317-514-8043
Fax: 317-326-2166

Email: mljack4039@hotmail.com

25 yrs OTR
Owner/Operator

Utah Certified
$1M Insured
Wide - Long - High - Heavy

VISA MasterCard DISCOVER AMERICAN EXPRESS

MATT WALLACE ENTERPRISES
Bowling Green, KY

We have a Large Network across the US

CO/UT/NY CERT - CO/UT FLAGGING CERT
PERMITTED/EQUIPPED FOR 48 STATES
$1M - $2M INSURED W/ PA ADD-ON

Email: matthew3e@aol.com

270-320-5345

Lead - Chase - High Pole - Steer

Pilotcarstoday.com

KANSAS

Located in Liberal, KS
Available for OK Panhandle Loads
As well as Mid-Western Region

580-523-1522
620-482-0803

High Pole
Multiple Cars

NM Permit
GA / FL Cert

John's Flag Car, LLC
Jessica Schupman

Safety, Professionalism, and Integrity

CON-SPEC, LLC

Tom or Toni
405-604-7828
405-474-2181

3 OK Cert Operators

$2M Insured + PA

LandStar & ATS approved

All Permits & Inspections

(NM, UT, OH, LA, GA, NV)

KENTUCKY

DRIVERS FIRST CHOICE

"Professionally leading the Industry - One load at a Time"

PROFESSIONAL **10 YRS** **DEPENDABLE**

HIGH POLE, PILOT & ESCORT SERVICE

MINUTES FROM KY/IN LINE I-64 & I-65

LISA: 812-406-7169

driversfirstchoice@live.com

FULLY INSURED INCL. GENERAL/PROFESSIONAL LIABILITY
CERTIFIED & EQUIPPED FOR 48 CONTINENTAL STATES

ON BOARD GPS, DELORME MAPPING, ALL STATE ATTACHMENTS
PA LISTED, LA PERMIT, GA/NV AMBER PERMITS

MULTIPLE CARS AVAILABLE

APPROVED FOR MOST MAJOR COMPANIES INCLUDING: LANDSTAR, GREENTREE, BENNETT, ATS/SENTINEL, MERCER, ADMIRAL MERCHANTS, AETNA, AMERICAN TRANSPORT & MARATHON TRANSPORT

WE WORK WITH A NETWORK OF PROFESSIONAL COMPANIES LOCALLY & NATIONWIDE

KENTUCKY

M & R FLAG CARS

Charleston, WV

Mary Jones
304-549-8743

Randy Jones
304-541-8737

Fax: 304-744-0365

$1M Commercial Auto w/ PA add-on
Cert. PC/FLAGGER: NC, NY, UT
NSC Defensive Driving Cert
GA Amber Light Permit

8 CARS AVAILABLE

C&L Pilot Escort

Lori Hill
Sole Proprietor

WA. Cert
GL / PL Insured
TWIC
Passport
NSC DDC
LA / GA/ NV PERMITS
DASH CAM
DELORME GPS
MOBILE OFFICE

317-490-7376

Hartsville, TN
midway between
I-65 KY/TN Line
I-40 (Gordonsville)

cnlpcs4u@gmail.com

KENTUCKY

Jack Bloodworth Pilot Car Service

270-556-3462

LEAD/CHASE
HIGH POLE

TWIC
CDL - 38 YRS OTR
WA / NY CERTIFIED
FULLY INSURED

Here Today Gone Tomorrow Pilot Service

WA / NY Cert
$1M Insured
TWIC
CDL

Brian Webb - Owner   **731-415-8557**

KENTUCKY

KyPilotCars
Walton, KY

LEAD - CHASE HIGH POLE

Office: 859-400-0101
Website: Kypilotcars.com
Email: Dispatch@kypcs.com

MATT WALLACE ENTERPRISES
Bowling Green, KY

We have a Large Network across the US

CO/UT/NY CERT - CO/UT FLAGGING CERT
PERMITTED/EQUIPPED FOR 48 STATES
$1M - $2M INSURED W/ PA ADD-ON

Email: matthew3e@aol.com

270-320-5345

Lead - Chase - High Pole - Steer

High Lines, LLC
Oversize Load Escorting
RIG MOVING SPECIALISTS

Janet Watson
Weston, WV
Fax 866-520-9531
highlines11@yahoo.com

HIGH POLES - CHASE - LEAD - STEER
PERMIT WRITING ABILITY/ ACCTS - HANDS-FREE CELL BOOSTER
ON BOARD CAMERAS - GPS - DELORME / STREETS & TRIPS
LAPTOP / PRINTER

ALL STATES CERT & EQUIPPED - MULTIPLE OIL COMPANY CERTIFICATIONS
LA PERMIT - PRO-GL $2MIL - NV & GA AMBER LIGHT PERMITS

304-203-9700

M & H FLAG CAR SERVICE
MAYFIELD, KY

270-970-7431

Lead - Chase - High Pole - Route Surveys
GPS & Cameras
Certified - $1M insurance
20 Yrs experience

LOUISIANA

MOPED EXPRESS
CERTIFIED AND INSURED — HIGH POLE AND CHASE

pamelaalwell2000@gmail.com
Charles and Pam Alwell 225-236-2998
225-200-0265

AM KEMP
PILOT CAR SERVICES
NATCHEZ, MS
(Previously located in Texas)

940-389-9475

HIGH POLE - LEAD - CHASE

$1M / $2M GL/PL $1M COMMERCIAL

WA/NY CERTIFIED

TX & MS

LOUISIANA

Flying Squirrel Escorts Service

Bill Musall - Owner
Fingerville, SC
(864) 208-4752

HIGH POLE - STEER (CLASS A CDL)
TWIC - PASSPORT - $1M INSURED + PA
LANDSTAR APPROVED
ALL LIGHT PERMITS

Multiple cars located in the South to Midwest

MAY BABY P.C.S.
918-385-1034

Lead / Chase

$1 million Ins
UT / NY Certs - CDL
GA/NV/LA Permits

BackBone Pilot Car Services

Paul Muller
Owner
936-689-5581

17858 Crystalwood Circle
New Caney, TX 77357

Insured up to 2 Million
24/7 Any State

brianmuller70@yahoo.com

Elk Mountain Transfer, Inc
Located TX/LA Line - Midway to I-10 / I-20 / I-30

Kris: 406-551-3796   Sandy: 505-280-7932

LEAD/CHASE - HIGH POLE - STEERMAN

OK/NY Cert - Equipped for 48 States
GL/PL/Commercial Insurance - CDL-30 yrs - TWIC
All Permits for GA / NV / LA / NM
Mobile Office / Internet - Dash-Cam - GPS

*A small family company
dedicated to professional service.*

MAINE

MARTIN EMERSON
MONMOUTH, MAINE

NEW YORK STATE CERTIFIED ESCORT

207-240-7876
emerson01@rocketmail.com

Emerson Pilot Car Services - EPCS

High Pole - Lead - Chase - Steer

Certified   Fully Insured   Passport

Heavy, Wide or Tall, We'll Help You Haul 'Em All

SABATTUS, ME

MPC - MIKE'S PILOT CAR
"CHECK YOUR MIRRORS"
NEW YORK AND WASHINGTON STATE CERTIFIED
207-240-2535

LEAD - CHASE - HIGH POLE - STEER
NY/WA CERT - PASSPORT

f Mikespilotcar   mpcs1243@gmail.com

THE OVERLOAD COMPANION 2017 © FREDA BARBER BOOTH - PILOTCARSTODAY.COM   160

MARYLAND

PEGASUS PILOTS, LLC

SMITHSBURG, MARYLAND

301-991-4406

12 YEARS

Tired of Working with Non-Professional Escorts?

We have 8 Professional Drivers with fully equipped vehicles!

CDL EXPERIENCE
60 MI. to PORT OF BALTIMORE / 100 MI. to MD/WV LINE I-68
EQUIPPED / LEGAL for ALL STATES
COURTEOUS, PROFESSIONAL, RELIABLE, DEPENDABLE

ACCESS TO NATIONWIDE HIGH QUALITY HI POLERS & STEERMEN

WASHINGTON STATE CERTIFIED INSTRUCTOR - *SEE INSTRUCTOR AD PAGE* -

---

Rig Moving Specialists

"Your Safety is OUR Priority!"

High Lines, LLC
Oversize Load Escorting
304-203-9700

Janet Watson
Weston, WV
Fax 866-520-9531
highlines11@yahoo.com

NATIONWIDE SERVICES

HIGH POLES - CHASE
LEAD - STEER
PERMIT WRITING ABILITY/ ACCTS

MOBILE OFFICES/EQUIPMENT

HANDS-FREE CELL BOOSTER
ON BOARD CAMERAS
GPS - DELORME / STREETS & TRIPS
LAPTOP / PRINTER

CREDENTIALS

All States Certified
NY / KS-Super / LA
Auto $1MIL
Insured w/ PA
PRO-GL $2MIL
NV & GA Amber
Equipped
Experienced

COMPANY APPROVED

ATSSA
SAFE LAND
SHELL
WHIPSTOCK
PATTERSON
STONE ENERGY
NOBLE
HESS
CHESAPEAKE

MARYLAND

RICHARD'S FLAG CAR SERVICE

Richard R. Bitts, Jr., Owner — Lancaster, PA

Easy access to Harrisburg, York, Hanover, Carlisle, Philadelphia PA, NJ, DE & Port of Baltimore, MD

- UT & NY Cert
- Passport
- PA Insured $1Mil
- LandStar Approved

LEAD - CHASE

- CDL License
- TWIC
- Dual Dash Cams
- GPS

Deadhead up to 100 miles with approved mileage rate

610-960-8437

richardsflagcar@comcast.net

T-N-T Pilot Car, LLC

We go the extra mile for you!

Terry Miller - Owner
Corapeake, NC
Cell: 813-401-3447
Office: 252-465-2036
www.tntpilotcar.webs.com
tntpilotcar@gmail.com

NC, VA, NY, FL Certified
Fully insured w/ PA add-on
High Pole
GA/ NV light - LA Permit
FL 36" cones
GPS Equipped
TWIC
LandStar & Greentree Approved

We have cars where you need them!

Deb's Pilot Car   443-866-1408

Angel's Pilot Car   717-752-7750

4 Cars Available
All NY/WA Certified
$1M Pro-Liability
$1M Insured w/ PA add-on
GA Amber Light Stickers

OVERSIZE LOAD AHEAD

CALL US TODAY!

CASH TODAY!

FACTORING MADE EASY FOR AMERICA'S TRUCKERS

1-888-684-7195

CENTURY FINANCE

MASSACHUSETTS

SABATTUS, ME

MPC - MIKE'S PILOT CAR
"CHECK YOUR MIRRORS"
207-240-2535
NEW YORK AND WASHINGTON STATE CERTIFIED

LEAD - CHASE - HIGH POLE - STEER
NY/WA CERT - PASSPORT

f Mikespilotcar   mpcs1243@gmail.com

MARTIN EMERSON

MONMOUTH, MAINE

NEW YORK STATE CERTIFIED ESCORT

207-240-7876
emerson01@rocketmail.com

EPCS - EMERSON PILOT CAR SERVICES

High Pole - Lead - Chase - Steer
Certified   Fully Insured   Passport

Heavy, Wide or Tall, We'll Help You Haul 'Em All

MASSACHUSETTS

Green's Flag Car Service
Newark Valley, NY
607-761-7495   607-323-5140
High Pole - Chase - Lead
NY/WA Certified

A1 Escort Services
No Load Too Big, No Road Too Far

John T Widrig
Owner/Operator

john.widrig@gmail.com
484-560-3589

2253 Irma Drive
Allentown, PA 18109

FULLY CERTIFIED & INSURED

HIGH POLE - SURVEYS   LEAD/CHASE/3RD CAR

NORTHEAST PA
LG NATIONWIDE NETWORK

LA/NM PERMITS - GA / NV AMBER
$1M INSURED
NY / FL / DDC CERT.
LAPTOP W/ EXT. DELORME NAV. SOFTWARE
DASHCAMS

facebook.com/A1escorServices/

MICHIGAN

Escorting America

EscortingAmerica@gmail.com

OVERSIZE LOAD

OVERSIZE LOAD

CERTIFIED, PROFESSIONAL, AND EXPERIENCED

Elizabeth - Mark - Alexandra
(330)413-4532   (330)313-5954   (443)206-1865

Hi-Pole - Lead - Chase - Steer

SIZE MATTERS

MEMBER SC&RA
Specialized Carriers & Rigging Association

National Pilot Car Association

OVERSIZE LOAD

MICHIGAN

Bill Jameson Pilot Car Service, LLC

Taylor, Michigan

313-291-5393
CELL: 313-590-3356

Certified & Equipped
to run ALL states
Plus Canada!

MICHIGAN

Dragonfly Pilot Car Service

Homeworth, OH

Connie Green - Owner

330-614-8939

Lead   Chase   Surveys

Certified & Fully Insured

MINNESOTA

THOM HEAVY HAUL ESCORT, LLC
Detroit Lakes, MN
Gold Canyon, AZ

Height pole - Lead - Chase - Surveys

Fully Insured & Certified
UT / NM inspected
NV / GA Amber Permits

218-329-7606

thomheavyhaul@yahoo.com

www.thomheavyhaul.com

Legacy Pilot Car Services, LLC

James: 970-396-5538   Erin: 970-396-6496

Located in Northern Colorado
Local and Long Haul - Single trip or full project
CO certified - $1M CA/GL/PL Insurance
CDL - TWIC - Passport - High Pole - Lead - Chase
Fully equipped - On board office
Fuel transfer tank - All required PPE / FR if needed
Prompt, professional and safety oriented

Jack Bloodworth Pilot Car Service

270-556-3462

LEAD/CHASE
HIGH POLE

TWIC
CDL - 38 YRS OTR
WA / NY CERTIFIED
FULLY INSURED

MINNESOTA

**Lead / Chase
Certified / Insured**

S&W Pilot Car Escort Service, LLC
419-705-3500

Call Us! We're Ready to Roll!

Bill Jameson Pilot Car Service, LLC
313-291-5393 Taylor, MI

Certified & Equipped to run All States Plus Canada!

MISSISSIPPI

AM KEMP
PILOT CAR SERVICES
NATCHEZ, MS
(Previously located in Texas)

940-389-9475

HIGH POLE - LEAD - CHASE

$1M / $2M GL/PL $1M COMMERCIAL

WA/NY CERTIFIED

TX & MS

ADVERTISING IN THIS SPACE COULD GIVE YOU THE FIELD ADVANTAGE!

MISSISSIPPI

Flying Squirrel Escorts Service

Bill Musall - Owner
Fingerville, SC
(864) 208-4752

HIGH POLE - STEER (CLASS A CDL)
TWIC - PASSPORT - $1M INSURED + PA
LANDSTAR APPROVED
ALL LIGHT PERMITS

Multiple cars located in the South to Midwest

MAY BABY P.C.S.
918-385-1034

Lead / Chase

$1 million Ins
UT / NY Certs - CDL
GA/NV/LA Permits

MATT WALLACE ENTERPRISES

Bowling Green, KY

We have a Large Network across the US

CO/UT/NY CERT - CO/UT FLAGGING CERT
PERMITTED/EQUIPPED FOR 48 STATES
$1M - $2M INSURED W/ PA ADD-ON

Email: matthew3e@aol.com

270-320-5345

Lead - Chase - High Pole - Steer

Maynard First Choice Pilot Car Service

OPERATING IN TX & MS

Kathy: 361-489-9266

LEAD - CHASE

CERTIFIED & INSURED

MISSOURI

Here Today Gone Tomorrow Pilot Service

WA / NY Cert
$1M Insured
TWIC
CDL

Brian Webb - Owner   731-415-8557

Jack Bloodworth Pilot Car Service

270-556-3462

LEAD/CHASE
HIGH POLE

TWIC
CDL - 38 YRS OTR
WA / NY CERTIFIED
FULLY INSURED

MONTANA

ASAP PILOT CAR SERVICE

Carolyn Johnson
Owner/Operator

406-600-9703

Asappilotcarservice.com
Montanatrafficcontrol.com

**HIGH POLE
PROFESSIONAL SURVEYS
MONTANA TRAFFIC CONTROL**

**EQUIPPED VHF RADIO
CANADA-LEGAL
WA CERTIFIED
$3M INSURED**

Captain Harloch's Pilot Service

Casper, Wyoming

Lead - Chase - High Pole - Blade Steering

Will deadhead for the right job

Business# 307-797-7971
Personal cell# 405-365-3141
Email address captainharloch@gmail.com

This spot could have been yours.

Beginning 2018 - This will be a 2-yr book.

Will you be in it?

pilotcarstoday.com

NEBRASKA

Legacy Pilot Car Services, LLC

James: 970-396-5538
Erin: 970-396-6496

Located in Northern Colorado

HIGH POLE - LEAD - CHASE

Local and Long Haul
Single trip or full project
CO certified
$1M CA/GL/PL Insurance
CDL - TWIC - Passport
Fully equipped
On board office
Fuel Transfer Tank
(All required PPE / FR if needed)
*Prompt, professional
& safety oriented*

CON-SPEC, LLC

Tom or Toni
405-604-7828
405-474-2181

3 OK Cert Operators

$2M Insured + PA

LandStar & ATS approved

All Permits & Inspections

(NM, UT, OH, LA, GA, NV)

CALIFORNIA PILOT CAR ASSOCIATION

A California Non-Profit Corporation
P.O. BOX 110, BLOOMINGTON, CA 92316

708-443-4164

FOR MORE INFORMATION - *capilotcar@gmail.com*

**Call Us for All
Your Pilot Car/Escort needs**
Chase, High Pole, Route Survey

www.capilotcarassoc.com

NEVADA

KLOES 2 U, LLC
Oversize Load Escorting

"Long Haul Specialists"

DISPATCHER: ROBIN BAKER
360-773-2661

DRIVER: NICK CAMPBELL
360-998-0173

MET APPROVAL FOR:
COMBINED
CONTRACTOR'S CARGO
LONESTAR - LANDSTAR
LEAVITTS - JONES MOTOR GROUP
JOULE YACHT - ATI & AFFILIATES
ART HEAVY-HAUL

TERRY KLOES
KELSO, WA
360-261-0847
kloes2u@yahoo.com

CDL - TWIC
$1M AUTO / GL - PA ADD-ON
GA - NV AMBER
LA - UT INSPECTED
FULLY EQUIPPED
HANDS-FREE CELL
CAMERAS - GARMIN GPS

We Network with These Companies!

B-LINE PILOT CAR SERVICES
OFFICE: 541-889-5770
RICHARD BUNN: 208-739-1609
LORRI GONZALEZ-BUNN: 208-739-1961

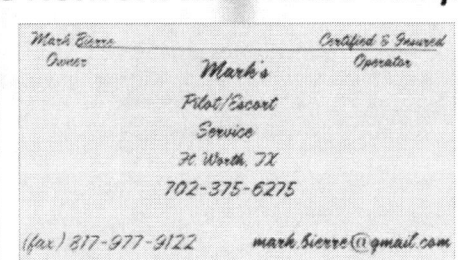

MARK'S PILOT/ESCORT SERVICE
MARK BIERRE: 702-375-6275

EBJB PILOT CAR
HOME: 208-233-5196
JEANNE: 208-251-8891
ED: 208-251-8892

HD2 PILOT CAR SERVICES
PETER HAUGEN CELL: 651-336-9261

HIGH DESERT PILOT
MARK KENNEDY: 760-947-9917

FULL SAIL PILOT CAR SERVICE
ROB ANGERMAN: 208-215-4457

NOAH'S PILOT CAR SERVICE
ROD NOAH: 308-440-3757
JANE NOAH: 308-233-2190

MCKEE PILOT CAR SERVICE
MOBILE: 951-314-3838

A+ ESCORT / PILOT SERVICE
GENE SCHLAKE: 402-239-5107

NEVADA

BOBBI'S PILOT CAR SERVICE
209-810-5238

HIGH POLE

UT / NY CERT

TWIC

GA/NV AMBER

NM/LA PERMITS

15 YRS EXPERIENCE

Delgado Family PCS

Los Angeles Area - California

Dolores Delgado - Owner/Operator

626-893-1277

LEAD - CHASE

GA / NV AMBER

NM / LA PERMITS

UT CERT

$1M GL/PL/COMMERCIAL

PASSPORT - TWIC

Approved for LandStar, Bennett & TII Group

Reasonable Rates, Reliable & Ready to Roll!

NEW HAMPSHIRE

MARTIN EMERSON

MONMOUTH, MAINE

NEW YORK STATE CERTIFIED ESCORT

207-240-7876

emerson01@rocketmail.com

EMERSON PILOT CAR SERVICES — EPCS

High Pole - Lead - Chase - Steer

Certified   Fully Insured   Passport

Heavy, Wide or Tall, We'll Help You Haul 'Em All

SABATTUS, ME

"CHECK YOUR MIRRORS"

MPC — MIKE'S PILOT CAR

207-240-2535

NEW YORK AND WASHINGTON STATE CERTIFIED

LEAD - CHASE - HIGH POLE - STEER
NY/WA CERT - PASSPORT

f Mikespilotcar   mpcs1243@gmail.com

NEW HAMPSHIRE

Green's Flag Car Service

Newark Valley, NY

607-761-7495 607-323-5140

High Pole - Chase - Lead

NY/WA Certified

Century Finance

Money Problems Got You Stuck On The Side Of The Road?

Need "CASH" Fast?

Call 888-684-7195 "QUICK PAY"

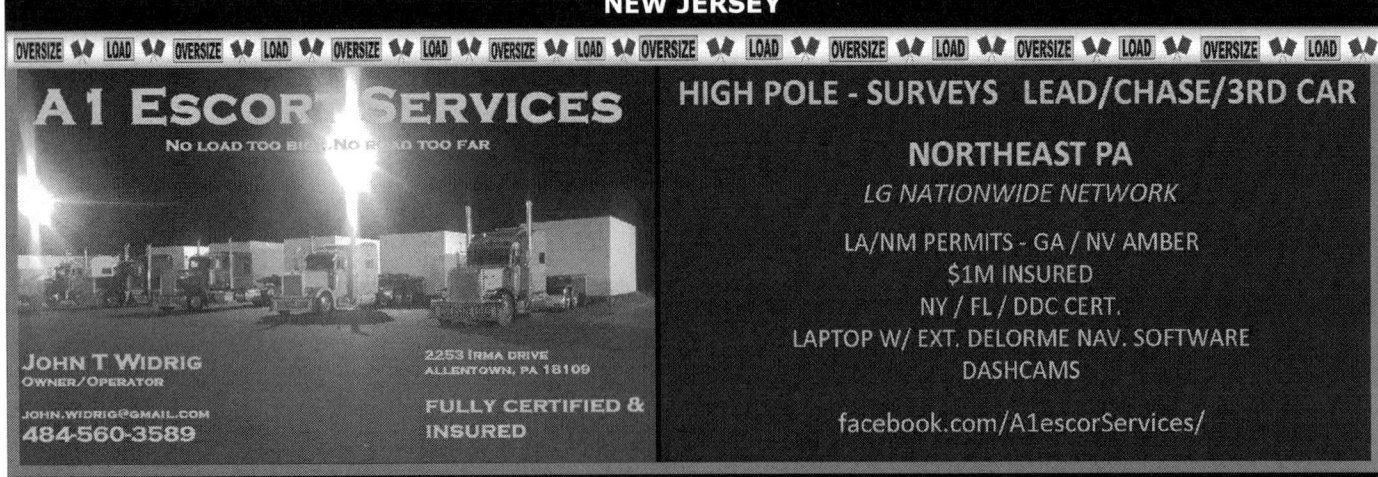

NEW JERSEY

A1 Escort Services
No Load Too Big, No Road Too Far

John T Widrig
Owner/Operator

john.widrig@gmail.com
484-560-3589

2253 Irma Drive
Allentown, PA 18109

FULLY CERTIFIED & INSURED

HIGH POLE - SURVEYS   LEAD/CHASE/3RD CAR

NORTHEAST PA
LG NATIONWIDE NETWORK

LA/NM PERMITS - GA / NV AMBER
$1M INSURED
NY / FL / DDC CERT.
LAPTOP W/ EXT. DELORME NAV. SOFTWARE
DASHCAMS

facebook.com/A1escorServices/

Green's Flag Car Service
Newark Valley, NY

607-761-7495   607-323-5140

High Pole - Chase - Lead
NY/WA Certified

Are you hiding?

PilotCars TODAY
We get you noticed

pilotcarstoday.com

The UN-Hider!

THE OVERLOAD COMPANION 2017 © FREDA BARBER BOOTH - PILOTCARSTODAY.COM

NEW MEXICO

John's Flag Car, LLC
Jessica Schupman

Located in Liberal, KS
Available for OK Panhandle Loads
As well as Mid-Western Region

580-523-1522
620-482-0803

High Pole
Multiple Cars

NM Permit
GA / FL Cert

Safety, Professionalism, and Integrity

Elliott's Pilot Car
Corona, California

Cell: 951-543-3407   **Office: 909-930-1936**
Fax: 909-673-0901

Coming In or Leaving - Call Us First - 24/7!

$1M Insured
NM / UT Inspection
NV / GA Amber Permit
TWIC

33 YRS - CDL   9 YRS - ESCORT/FLAGGER

HIGH POLE - LEAD - CHASE

APPROVED FOR
LANDSTAR, MERCER,
ADMIRAL MERCHANTS, TII GROUP
Etc, Etc, Etc

NEW YORK

Rowley's Pilot Cars
Cortland, NY

Larry & Steph Rowley
607-745-9850
607-745-4668

HIGH POLE - LEAD - CHASE

NEW YORK

Green's Flag Car Service
Newark Valley, NY
607-761-7495 **607-323-5140**
High Pole - Chase - Lead
NY/WA Certified

A1 Escort Services
No Load Too Big, No Road Too Far

John T Widrig
Owner/Operator

2253 Irma Drive
Allentown, PA 18109

john.widrig@gmail.com
484-560-3589

FULLY CERTIFIED & INSURED

HIGH POLE - SURVEYS   LEAD/CHASE/3RD CAR

NORTHEAST PA
LG NATIONWIDE NETWORK

LA/NM PERMITS - GA / NV AMBER
$1M INSURED
NY / FL / DDC CERT.
LAPTOP W/ EXT. DELORME NAV. SOFTWARE
DASHCAMS

facebook.com/A1escorServices/

SABATTUS, ME

"CHECK YOUR MIRRORS"

MPC - MIKE'S PILOT CAR
207-240-2535

LEAD - CHASE - HIGH POLE - STEER
NY/WA CERT - PASSPORT

f Mikespilotcar   mpcs1243@gmail.com

FOCUS ON THE ROAD, NOT WHAT'S ABOVE IT.

Whether you're plotting a route or worrying about hazards and delays, transporting oversized loads can be stressful. But Kenco Bucket Trucks' high standards, certifications and well-equipped purple trucks make travel a snap. We make the safety of your cargo and personnel our highest priority. Plus we can assist with planning the route so there are no surprises, only smooth driving.

We ensure that when you choose HIGH LOADS, we give you OPEN ROADS.

KENCO MEANS:
- IMSA Work Zone Safety Certified
- IMSA Traffic Signal Technician Level I & II
- DISA Drug & Alcohol Tested Employees
- Professionalism, safety and reliability

KENCO Bucket Trucks
HIGH LOADS. OPEN ROADS.

20 YEARS OF SAFETY — THE SAFEST ROUTE. KENCO

TAKE A LOAD OFF. 1.877.459.3100 | HIGHLOADS.COM

NORTH CAROLINA

HIGH POLE LEAD CHASE STEER ROUTE SURVEYS

BOYD'S PILOT CARS
Saint Matthews, SC
803-457-1956

Alternate Phone: 803-596-1544

T-N-T Pilot Car, LLC

Terry Miller - Owner
Corapeake, NC

Cell: 813-401-3447   **Office: 252-465-2036**

We have cars where you need them!

Certified NC - VA - NY - FL
Fully Insured
High Pole - Lead - Chase
GA / NV Light Permit
LA Inspection Permit
FL - 36" Cones
BPS Equipped
TWIC

LandStar & Greentree Approved

Website: www.tntpilotcar.webs.com
Email: tntpilotcar@gmail.com

We Go the Extra Mile for You!

NORTH CAROLINA

Al's Big Rig Pilot Car Service
Allen Lohr
343 Banks Fort Road
Stasburg, Va 22657
Phone: 540-683-0000
E-mail: Al_lohr@yahoo.com

U.S. Passport & certified/permitted/equipped for all 48 states.
Providing experienced Hi-pole/Lead/Chase cars.
30 miles from VA/WV. Line for that extra car in WV.
Located near the VA/WVA/MD/PA line at the I-81/I-66 split.

NORTH CAROLINA

J & W TORRENCE PILOT CAR, LLC

FAYETTEVILLE, NC

405-476-8006

LEAD - CHASE - HIGH POLE

$1M INSURANCE GA/NV AMBER PERMIT OK & GA CERTIFIED

PEGASUS PILOTS, LLC

SMITHSBURG, MARYLAND

301-991-4406

12 YEARS

Tired of Working with Non-Professional Escorts?

We have 8 Professional Drivers with fully equipped vehicles!

CDL EXPERIENCE
60 MI. to PORT OF BALTIMORE / 100 MI. to MD/WV LINE I-68
EQUIPPED / LEGAL for ALL STATES
COURTEOUS, PROFESSIONAL, RELIABLE, DEPENDABLE

ACCESS TO NATIONWIDE HIGH QUALITY HI POLERS & STEERMEN

WASHINGTON STATE CERTIFIED INSTRUCTOR - *SEE INSTRUCTOR AD PAGE -*

NORTH CAROLINA

CAROLINA REO SERVICES

CHRIS SHUPE
(704) 202-3127

STACY MORTON
(704) 754-2911

For Your Pilot Car Needs to, through and from North Carolina!

MULTIPLE CARS

carolinareoservices@hotmail.com

WIDE LOAD
OVERSIZE LOAD
LONG LOAD

High pole
WA-NY-NC Cert
GA Amber
LA-NM Inspected
Insured - $1M

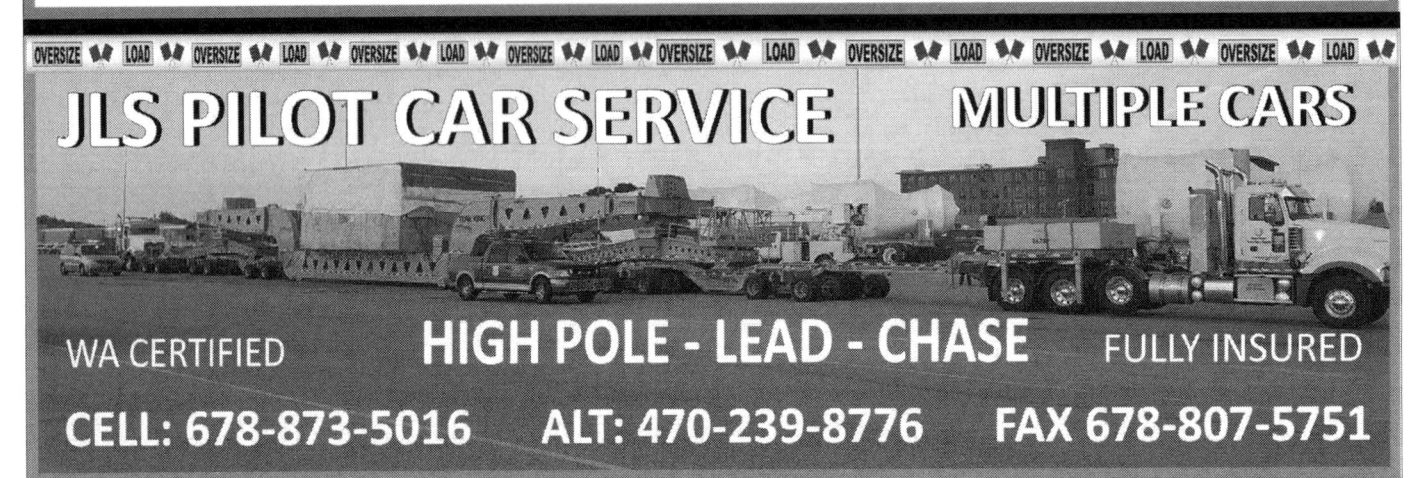

JLS PILOT CAR SERVICE — MULTIPLE CARS

WA CERTIFIED   **HIGH POLE - LEAD - CHASE**   FULLY INSURED

CELL: 678-873-5016   ALT: 470-239-8776   FAX 678-807-5751

Flying Squirrel Escorts Service

Bill Musall - Owner
Fingerville, SC
(864) 208-4752

HIGH POLE - STEER (CLASS A CDL)
TWIC - PASSPORT - $1M INSURED + PA
LANDSTAR APPROVED
ALL LIGHT PERMITS

Multiple cars located in the South to Midwest

Blazin' Trailz Pilot Car Services LLC

NC/SC Line on I-85 and I-77

Shiree Peak, Owner

704-460-4799

LEAD - CHASE

NC/NY/UT Certified - 1 Million ins.
PA additional insured - GA / LA permits - TWIC card

NORTH DAKOTA

ASAP
PILOT CAR SERVICE
406-600-9703

Carolyn Johnson
Owner/Operator

PROFESSIONAL ROUTE SURVEYS
TRAFFIC MGMT PLANS

HIGH POLE
LEAD - CHASE
CANADA-LEGAL
WA CERTIFIED
$3MIL INSURED

Equipped w/ VHF Radio
Streets & Trips

montanatrafficcontrol.com

asappilotcarservice.com

OHIO

Escorting America

EscortingAmerica@gmail.com

CERTIFIED, PROFESSIONAL, AND EXPERIENCED

Elizabeth - Mark - Alexandra
(330)413-4532 (330)313-5954 (443)206-1865

Hi-Pole - Lead - Chase - Steer

SIZE MATTERS

MEMBER
S&RA Specialized Carriers & Rigging Association

National Pilot Car Association

OHIO

S&W Pilot Car Escort Service, LLC

15 Minutes from Toledo, OH

419-705-3500

Lead / Chase

UT Certified / Insured

Nationwide Network

Acorn Truck Safety Escort, LLC

MEMBER — National Pilot Car Association

www.npca.news
"So everyone gets home safe!"

Bill King
Owner / Operator

Cell: 740-823-1856
Office: 740-823-1169

HIGH POLE
CERTIFIED
INSURED - EQUIPPED
& READY TO ROLL!

OHIO

Dragonfly Pilot Car Service

Homeworth, OH
Connie Green - Owner

330-614-8939

Lead   Chase   Surveys

Certified & Fully Insured

OHIO

Lead / Chase
Certified / Insured

S&W Pilot Car Escort Service, LLC
419-705-3500

Call Us! We're Ready to Roll!

Bill Jameson Pilot Car Service, LLC
313-291-5393 Taylor, MI

Certified & Equipped to run All States Plus Canada!

OHIO

High Lines, LLC
Oversize Load Escorting
304-203-9700

Janet Watson
Weston, WV
Fax 866-520-9531
highlines11@yahoo.com

Rig Moving Specialists

CREDENTIALS

ALL STATES CERTIFIED
NY / KS-SUPER / LA
AUTO $1MIL
INSURED W/ PA
PRO-GL $2MIL
NV & GA AMBER
EQUIPPED
EXPERIENCED

APPROVED FOR:

ATSSA
SAFE LAND
SHELL
PATTERSON
STONE ENERGY
NOBLE
HESS

NATIONWIDE SERVICES

HIGH POLES - ROUTE SURVEYS
CHASE - LEAD
PERMIT WRITING ABILITY/ ACCTS

MOBILE OFFICES/EQUIPMENT

HANDS-FREE CELL BOOSTER
ON BOARD CAMERAS
GPS DELORME / STREETS & TRIPS
LAPTOP / PRINTER

"Your SAFETY is Our PRIORITY!"

OHIO

A1 Escort Services
No load too big...No road too far

John T Widrig
Owner/Operator

john.widrig@gmail.com
484-560-3589

2253 Irma Drive
Allentown, PA 18109

FULLY CERTIFIED & INSURED

M&R Flag Cars

Charleston, WV

Mary Jones
304-549-8743

Randy Jones
304-541-8737

Fax: 304-744-0365

$1M Commercial Auto w/ PA add-on
Cert. PC/FLAGGER: NC, NY, UT
NSC Defensive Driving Cert
GA Amber Light Permit

8 CARS AVAILABLE

OHIO

ANGIE'S PILOT CAR
740-600-5138

HIGH POLE
CO / NY CERTIFIED
$1M GL / PL / Auto + PA

ADD-MAN PILOT CARS
adammcglaughlin@gmail.com
304-639-6305

Washington State Certified
High Pole - Lead - Chase
GPS - Dash Cam

ROSCH PILOT CAR SERVICES, LLC
NEWARK, OHIO

NANCY ROSCH - OWNER
614-554-0872

WA CERT - $1M INS + PA - $2M GL/PL
GA / NV / LA PERMITS

nrosch07@aol.com   FAX: 740-763-7213

KyPilotCars
Walton, KY

LEAD - CHASE
HIGH POLE

Office: 859-400-0101
Website: Kypilotcars.com
Email: Dispatch@kypcs.com

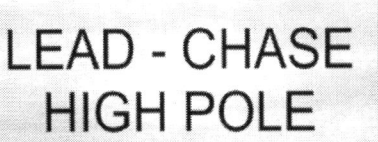

OKLAHOMA

Blue Star Pilot Car Service LLC
Moore, OK

Ross Legg, Owner - 405-464-5802

LEAD - CHASE - STEER

CDL with Doubles/Triples
Current medical card
TWIC Card
Fully equipped
Fully insured w/ CO & PA add-on

GA / NV Amber light permits
LA / NM Permits
OK / NY Certified
Hands-Free Cell
Garmin GPS - Dash Camera

Service is a little thing that makes a BIG difference!

OKLAHOMA

CON-SPEC, LLC

Tom or Toni
405-604-7828
405-474-2181

3 OK Cert Operators
$2M Insured + PA
LandStar & ATS approved
All Permits & Inspections
(NM, UT, OH, LA, GA, NV)

Located in Liberal, KS
Available for OK Panhandle Loads
As well as Mid-Western Region

580-523-1522
620-482-0803

High Pole
Multiple Cars

NM Permit
GA / FL Cert

John's Flag Car, LLC
Jessica Schupman

Safety, Professionalism, and Integrity

OKLAHOMA

BackBone Pilot Car Services

Paul Muller — Owner
936-689-5581
17858 Crystalwood Circle
New Caney, TX 77357
brianmuller70@yahoo.com

Insured up to 2 Million
24/7 Any State

L J'S PILOT CAR SERVICE
North Texas Area

Tina Kemp, Office Manager: 940-577-2621
Larry J Kemp, Owner Operator: 940-393-5965

Chase/Lead, Route Survey & Traffic Control

Safety and Professionalism First and Foremost!

DRIVERS FIRST CHOICE

PROFESSIONAL **9 YRS** DEPENDABLE

"Professionally leading the industry - one load at a time"

HIGH POLE, PILOT AND ESCORT SERVICE
MINUTES FROM IN/KY LINE I-64 AND I-65

LISA
812-406-7169

driversfirstchoice@live.com

- GENERAL & PROFESSIONAL LIABILITY
- CERTIFIED AND EQUIPPED FOR 48 STATES
- ON BOARD GPS, DELORME MAPPING, ALL STATE ATTACH.
- PA LISTED, LA PERMIT, GA & NV AMBER LIGHT PERMITS
- MULTIPLE CARS AVAILABLE - NETWORKED WITH MANY OTHERS NATIONWIDE

APPROVED FOR MOST MAJOR COMPANIES INCLUDING:
LANDSTAR, GREENTREE, BENNETT, ATS/SENTINEL, MERCER,
ADMIRAL MERCHANTS, AETNA,
AMERICAN TRANSPORT, MARATHON TRANSPORT

Gigglers Pilot Car Services

WA Cert~ Insured

Lead ~ Chase ~ High Pole ~ Bulldog

OVERSIZE LOAD

Lisa Nichols
903-394-8651

Mike Nichols
903-221-4045

gigglerspcs@gmail.com

OKLAHOMA

J & J Pilot Car Service, Inc.
Salado, AR

30 YEARS

Jessie Smith - Owner/Contractor
Big or small - We do them all!

High pole - Route Surveys - Lead/Chase
Fully Insured

Office: 870-376-0000
Fax: 1-800-251-9768

Pilotcarstoday.com

OREGON

Elliott's Pilot Car
Corona, California

Cell: 951-543-3407 **Office: 909-930-1936**

Fax: 909-673-0901

Coming In or Leaving - Call Us First - 24/7!

33 YRS - CDL
9 YRS - ESCORT/FLAGGER
HIGH POLE - LEAD - CHASE

$1M Insured
NM / UT Inspection
NV / GA Amber Permit
TWIC

APPROVED FOR
LANDSTAR, MERCER,
ADMIRAL MERCHANTS, TII GROUP
Etc, Etc, Etc.

OREGON

KLOES 2 U, LLC
Oversize Load Escorting
"Long Haul Specialists"

TERRY KLOES
KELSO, WA
360-261-0847
kloes2u@yahoo.com

CDL - TWIC
$1M AUTO / GL - PA ADD-ON
GA - NV AMBER
LA - UT INSPECTED
FULLY EQUIPPED
HANDS-FREE CELL
CAMERAS - GARMIN GPS

APPROVED FOR:
COMBINED
CONTRACTOR'S CARGO
LONESTAR - LANDSTAR
LEAVITTS
JONES MOTOR GROUP
JOULE YACHT
ATI & AFFILIATES
ART HEAVY-HAUL

DISPATCHER: ROBIN BAKER
360-773-2661

DRIVER: NICK CAMPBELL
360-998-0173

BOBBI'S PILOT CAR SERVICE
209-810-5238

HIGH POLE

UT / NY CERT

TWIC

GA/NV AMBER

NM/LA PERMITS

15 YRS EXPERIENCE

THE OVERLOAD COMPANION 2017 © FREDA BARBER BOOTH - PILOTCARSTODAY.COM

WANT TO ADVERTISE?
READ THIS FIRST!

When you purchase ANY ad space in THE OVERLOAD COMPANION 2018-19
You will automatically receive ONE state listing directing the viewer to YOUR Detailed Ad!
You may purchase additional listing within another state!

EACH listing will be specifically pointed to the *AD/PAGE* **YOU** specify.

Example: You have a PROV ad on pg. 93; a FULL ad on pg. 132; & a QTR ad on pg. 325
You can direct ANY listing to ANY page containing your ad!
Mix/Match works!

SEE SAMPLE & PRICES BELOW!

MONTANA		
COMPANY	CONTACT	DETAILS
ASAP PILOT CAR SERVICE	406-600-9703	PG 124
BARB'S PILOT CAR	406-860-3856	PG 312
ROBINS PILOT CAR SERVICE	406-207-3933	PG

PRICES

SIZE - LOCATION OF AD SPACE - PRICED "EACH" ** ANY AD SPACE PURCHASED GIVES **ONE** FREE STATE LISTING		DISCOUNT FOR MULTIPLE ORDERS
STATE PROVISIONS PAGE - FIRST COME, FIRST SERVE	$450	20% DISCOUNT
FULL PAGE AD - OR - TRUCKSTOP PAGE AD (SIZED TO FIT)	$450	20% DISCOUNT
QTR PAGE AD - LIMIT <u>ONE</u> PER CUSTOMER	$200	20% DISCOUNT
STATE LISTINGS (EACH)	$100	20% DISCOUNT

TO ORDER

PLEASE EMAIL THE FOLLOWING TO
fredabooth101@gmail.com

SUBJECT: OVERLOAD COMPANION 18-19
WE WILL CONTACT YOU!

MED. SIZE PICTURE(S): VEHICLE, LOAD, LOGO, ETC.
COMPANY CONTACT INFORMATION
LIST OF CREDENTIALS / SPECIALTIES / ETC YOU WANT DISPLAYED IN YOUR AD   *(SEE ADS IN BOOK FOR SUGGESTIONS)*

ALL ORDERS MUST BE PLACED AND PAID FOR BY DEC 1, 2017

ALL SPECIAL OFFERS MUST BE PAID WITHIN 72 HRS - OR FORFEIT THE SPECIAL PRICE

ACCEPTED METHOD OF PAYMENT
- CREDIT / DEBIT
- COMPANY CHECK (BUSINESS)
- STORE-PURCHASED PRE-PAID DEBIT (MAILED
- COMCHEK - EFS

** CALL BEFORE MAILING / SHIPPING PAYMENTS!!

"PILOT CARS TODAY"
FREDA BOOTH, OWNER
401 ANDREWS AVE
HARTSVILLE, TN 37074

817-583-5503

PENNSYLVANIA

A1 Escort Services
No load too big...No road too far

John T Widrig
Owner/Operator

john.widrig@gmail.com
484-560-3589

2253 Irma Drive
Allentown, PA 18109

FULLY CERTIFIED & INSURED

PENNSYLVANIA

Terry's Flag Car Service
Trevorton, PA

PHONE: 570-898-1095
FAX: 570-797-4794
terrylaforme@yahoo.com

HIGH POLE - LEAD - CHASE

15 Yrs in Business
5 Yrs Rig Moving Experience
PA Insured
NY/ WA CERTIFIED

All Certified - Qualified Pilots

PENNSYLVANIA

JDMD Escort Services

536 16th St.
Niagara Falls, NY 14301

jdmdescortsvcs@yahoo.com
www.jdmdescortsvcs.com

Phone: 602-284-1618
Fax: 716-284-1618

Certified in Every State in America including NY

PENDOT Super Load Certified
Pennsylvania Certified Escort Vehicle Driver

Passport in hand. Canada Accessible

****

High Pole - Lead - Chase - Route Surveys

****

Utah with Utah Flagging Certificate
ATSSA Flagging Certificate
National Safety Course Defensive Driving Course

GA & NV Light Bar Permits
Current Louisiana / New Mexico Permits / Inspections

Landstar Approved

NEW YORK — NEW YORK STATE CERTIFIED ESCORT VEHICLE

PENNSYLVANIA — STATE CERTIFIED ESCORT VEHICLE

PENNSYLVANIA

High Lines, LLC
Oversize Load Escorting
304-203-9700

Janet Watson
Weston, WV
Fax 866-520-9531
highlines11@yahoo.com

Rig Moving Specialists

CREDENTIALS
ALL STATES CERTIFIED
NY / KS-SUPER / LA
AUTO $1MIL
INSURED W/ PA
PRO-GL $2MIL
NV & GA AMBER
EQUIPPED
EXPERIENCED

APPROVED FOR:
ATSSA
SAFE LAND
SHELL
PATTERSON
STONE ENERGY
NOBLE
HESS

NATIONWIDE SERVICES
HIGH POLES - ROUTE SURVEYS
CHASE - LEAD
PERMIT WRITING ABILITY/ ACCTS

MOBILE OFFICES/EQUIPMENT
HANDS-FREE CELL BOOSTER
ON BOARD CAMERAS
GPS DELORME / STREETS & TRIPS
LAPTOP / PRINTER

"Your SAFETY is Our PRIORITY!"

PENNSYLVANIA

Charleston, WV

Mary Jones
304-549-8743

Randy Jones
304-541-8737

Fax: 304-744-0365

$1M Commercial Auto w/ PA add-on

Cert. PC/FLAGGER: NC, NY, UT

NSC Defensive Driving Cert

GA Amber Light Permit

8 CARS AVAILABLE

PEGASUS PILOTS, LLC

SMITHSBURG, MARYLAND

301-991-4406

12 YEARS

Tired of Working with Non-Professional Escorts?

We have 8 Professional Drivers with fully equipped vehicles!

CDL EXPERIENCE

60 MI. to PORT OF BALTIMORE / 100 MI. to MD/WV LINE I-68

EQUIPPED / LEGAL for ALL STATES

COURTEOUS, PROFESSIONAL, RELIABLE, DEPENDABLE

ACCESS TO NATIONWIDE HIGH QUALITY HI POLERS & STEERMEN

WASHINGTON STATE CERTIFIED INSTRUCTOR - *SEE INSTRUCTOR AD PAGE -*

PENNSYLVANIA

Chappies Piloting Service
Boalsburg, PA

814-548-6243

Lead - Chase - Third car

$1M Insured   NY / WA Certified

Give Chappies a call today!

RICHARD'S FLAG CAR SERVICE
Richard R. Bitts, Jr., Owner   Lancaster, PA

Easy access to Harrisburg, York, Hanover, Carlisle, Philadelphia PA, NJ, DE & Port of Baltimore, MD

Goes Anywhere - Anytime

610-960-8437

LEAD - CHASE

OVERSIZE & SUPER-SIZE

- UT & NY Cert
- Passport
- PA Insured $1Mil
- LandStar Approved

- CDL License
- TWIC
- Dual Dash Cams
- GPS

Deadhead up to 100 miles with approved mileage rate

richardsflagcar@comcast.net

Green's Flag Car Service
Newark Valley, NY

607-761-7495   607-323-5140

High Pole - Chase - Lead

NY/WA Certified

Deb's Pilot Car   443-866-1408

Angel's Pilot Car   717-752-7750

4 Cars Available
All NY/WA Certified
$1M Pro-Liability
$1M Insured w/ PA add-on
GA Amber Light Stickers

OVERSIZE LOAD AHEAD

RHODE ISLAND

A1 Escort Services
No load too big...No road too far

John T Widrig
Owner/Operator

john.widrig@gmail.com
484-560-3589

2253 Irma Drive
Allentown, PA 18109

FULLY CERTIFIED & INSURED

SOUTH CAROLINA

A.R. CHANEY PILOT CAR SERVICE

UTAH CERTIFIED

GASTON, SC
803-422-2361
Email: archaneypcs@gmail.com

$1M GL-PL Insured   -   Class A CDL   -   GA Amber - LA Permit

Approved for LandStar, Turner Transportation & Comdata

J & W TORRENCE PILOT CAR, LLC

FAYETTEVILLE, NC

405-476-8006

LEAD - CHASE - HIGH POLE

$1M INSURANCE   GA/NV AMBER PERMIT   OK & GA CERTIFIED

SOUTH CAROLINA

Flying Squirrel Escorts Service

Bill Musall - Owner
Fingerville, SC
(864) 208-4752
HIGH POLE - STEER (CLASS A CDL)
TWIC - PASSPORT - $1M INSURED + PA
LANDSTAR APPROVED
ALL LIGHT PERMITS

Multiple cars located in the South to Midwest

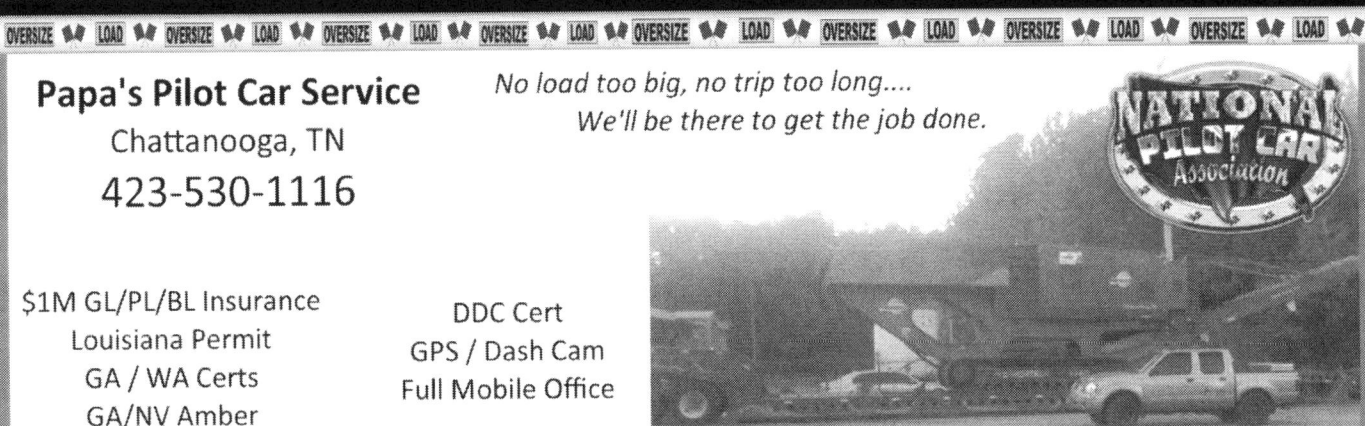

JLS PILOT CAR SERVICE — MULTIPLE CARS

WA CERTIFIED   **HIGH POLE - LEAD - CHASE**   FULLY INSURED
CELL: 678-873-5016   ALT: 470-239-8776   FAX 678-807-5751

BOYD'S PILOT CARS
Saint Matthews, SC
803-457-1956

Lead - Chase - High Pole - Steer - Route Surveys

Alternate Phone: 803-596-1544

Papa's Pilot Car Service
Chattanooga, TN
423-530-1116

*No load too big, no trip too long....
We'll be there to get the job done.*

$1M GL/PL/BL Insurance
Louisiana Permit
GA / WA Certs
GA/NV Amber

DDC Cert
GPS / Dash Cam
Full Mobile Office

National Pilot Car Association

THE OVERLOAD COMPANION 2017 © FREDA BARBER BOOTH - PILOTCARSTODAY.COM

SOUTH DAKOTA

ASAP PILOT CAR SERVICE

Carolyn Johnson
Owner/Operator

406-600-9703

Asappilotcarservice.com
Montanatrafficcontrol.com

**HIGH POLE
PROFESSIONAL SURVEYS
MONTANA TRAFFIC CONTROL**

**EQUIPPED VHF RADIO
CANADA-LEGAL
WA CERTIFIED
$3M INSURED**

Legacy Pilot Car Services, LLC

James: 970-396-5538   Erin: 970-396-6496

Located in Northern Colorado
Local and Long Haul - Single trip or full project
CO certified - $1M CA/GL/PL Insurance
CDL - TWIC - Passport - High Pole - Lead - Chase
Fully equipped - On board office
Fuel transfer tank - All required PPE / FR if needed
Prompt, professional and safety oriented

Captain Harloch's Pilot Service

Casper, Wyoming

Lead - Chase - High Pole - Blade Steering

Will deadhead for the right job

Business# 307-797-7971
Personal cell# 405-365-3141
Email address captainharloch@gmail.com

TENNESSEE

MATT WALLACE ENTERPRISES
Bowling Green, KY

Lead - Chase - High Pole - Steer

270-320-5345

We have a Large Network across the US

CO/UT/NY CERT - CO/UT FLAGGING CERT
PERMITTED/EQUIPPED FOR 48 STATES
$1M - $2M INSURED W/ PA ADD-ON

Email: matthew3e@aol.com

Follow me on Facebook!

TENNESSEE

Gigglers
Pilot Car Services

WA Cert~ Insured

Lead ~ Chase ~ High Pole ~ Bulldog

OVERSIZE LOAD

Lisa Nichols
903-394-8651

Mike Nichols
903-221-4045

gigglerspcs@gmail.com

TENNESSEE

AA Pilot Escort Service

Tim: 865-680-4248
Rick: 865-680-7692

East TN

LEAD - CHASE - HIGH POLE
(We use "Wonder Pole")

FL / WA / NY Certified
$1M GL / PL Insured
Equipped for All States!

TENNESSEE

Cell: 740-823-1856
Office: 740-823-1169

Member NPCA
www.npca.news
"So everyone gets home safe!"

Acorn Truck Safety Escort, LLC

Here Today
Gone Tomorrow
Pilot Service

WA / NY Cert
$1M Insured
TWIC
CDL

OVERSIZED LOAD
Pilot Service

Brian Webb - Owner   731-415-8557

TENNESSEE

Papa's Pilot Car Service
Chattanooga, TN
423-530-1116

No load too big, no trip too long....
We'll be there to get the job done.

$1M GL/PL/BL Insurance
Louisiana Permit
GA / WA Certs
GA/NV Amber

DDC Cert
GPS / Dash Cam
Full Mobile Office

Jack Bloodworth Pilot Car Service
270-556-3462

HIGH POLE / LEAD / CHASE

TWIC
CDL - 38 YRS OTR
WA / NY CERTIFIED
FULLY INSURED

JLS PILOT CAR SERVICE
MULTIPLE CARS

WA CERTIFIED   HIGH POLE - LEAD - CHASE   FULLY INSURED

CELL: 678-873-5016   ALT: 470-239-8776   FAX 678-807-5751

Lucky Ladies Pilot Cars, LLC

Cassandra Bostock
931-241-2241

Jodi Hurd-Cavanagh
231-388-0813

Lead / Chase
High Pole
Route Survey
$1M GL/PL/Commercial

TEXAS

Blue Star Pilot Car Service LLC
Moore, OK

Ross Legg, Owner - 405-464-5802

LEAD - CHASE - STEER

CDL with Doubles/Triples
Current medical card
TWIC Card
Fully equipped
Fully insured w/ CO & PA add-on

GA / NV Amber light permits
LA / NM Permits
OK / NY Certified
Hands-Free Cell
Garmin GPS - Dash Camera

Service is a little thing that makes a BIG difference!

TEXAS

A1 Escort Services
No load too big...No road too far

John T Widrig
Owner/Operator

john.widrig@gmail.com
484-560-3589

2253 Irma Drive
Allentown, PA 18109

Fully Certified & Insured

TEXAS

Gigglers
Pilot Car Services

WA Cert~ Insured

Lead ~ Chase ~ High Pole ~ Bulldog

OVERSIZE LOAD

Lisa Nichols
903-394-8651

Mike Nichols
903-221-4045

gigglerspcs@gmail.com

TEXAS

MOPED EXPRESS
CERTIFIED AND INSURED — HIGH POLE AND CHASE

pamelaalwell2000@gmail.com
Charles and Pam Alwell 225-236-2998
225-200-0265

J & J Pilot Car Service, Inc.
Salado, AR

30 YEARS

Jessie Smith - Owner/Contractor

Big or small - We do them all!

High pole - Route Surveys - Lead/Chase
Fully Insured

Office: 870-376-0000
Fax: 1-800-251-9768

TEXAS

BackBone Pilot Car Services
Paul Muller — Owner
936-689-5581
17858 Crystalwood Circle
New Caney, TX 77357
brianmuller70@yahoo.com
Insured up to 2 Million
24/7 Any State

Flying Squirrel Escorts Service
Bill Musall - Owner
Fingerville, SC
(864) 208-4752
HIGH POLE - STEER (CLASS A CDL)
TWIC - PASSPORT - $1M INSURED + PA
LANDSTAR APPROVED
ALL LIGHT PERMITS

Multiple cars located in the South to Midwest

L J'S PILOT CAR SERVICE
North Texas Area
Tina Kemp, Office Manager: 940-577-2621
Larry J Kemp, Owner Operator: 940-393-5965

Chase/Lead, Route Survey & Traffic Control

Safety and Professionalism First and Foremost!

Maynard First Choice Pilot Car Service
OPERATING IN TX & MS
Kathy: 361-489-9266

LEAD - CHASE
CERTIFIED & INSURED

UTAH

Elliott's Pilot Car
Corona, California

Cell: 951-543-3407 **Office: 909-930-1936**
Fax: 909-673-0901

Coming In or Leaving - Call Us First - 24/7!

$1M Insured
NM / UT Inspection
NV / GA Amber Permit
TWIC

33 YRS - CDL   9 YRS - ESCORT/FLAGGER

HIGH POLE - LEAD - CHASE

APPROVED FOR
LANDSTAR, MERCER,
ADMIRAL MERCHANTS, TII GROUP
Etc, Etc, Etc

BRECKENRIDGE PILOT CAR SERVICES
(COLORADO)

720-590-6541   **352-507-9146**
PRIMARY   CELL

Certified, Insured & Equipped
to meet State Requirements
GA/NV Amber Light
NM Inspection

Legacy Pilot Car Services, LLC

James: 970-396-5538   **Erin: 970-396-6496**

Located in Northern Colorado
Local and Long Haul - Single trip or full project
CO certified - $1M CA/GL/PL Insurance
CDL - TWIC - Passport - High Pole - Lead - Chase
Fully equipped - On board office
Fuel transfer tank - All required PPE / FR if needed
Prompt, professional and safety oriented

VERMONT

MARTIN EMERSON

MONMOUTH, MAINE

NEW YORK STATE CERTIFIED ESCORT

207-240-7876

emerson01@rocketmail.com

EMERSON PILOT CAR SERVICES — EPCS

High Pole - Lead - Chase - Steer

Certified   Fully Insured   Passport

Heavy, Wide or Tall, We'll Help You Haul 'Em All

Green's Flag Car Service

Newark Valley, NY

607-761-7495   607-323-5140

High Pole - Chase - Lead

NY/WA Certified

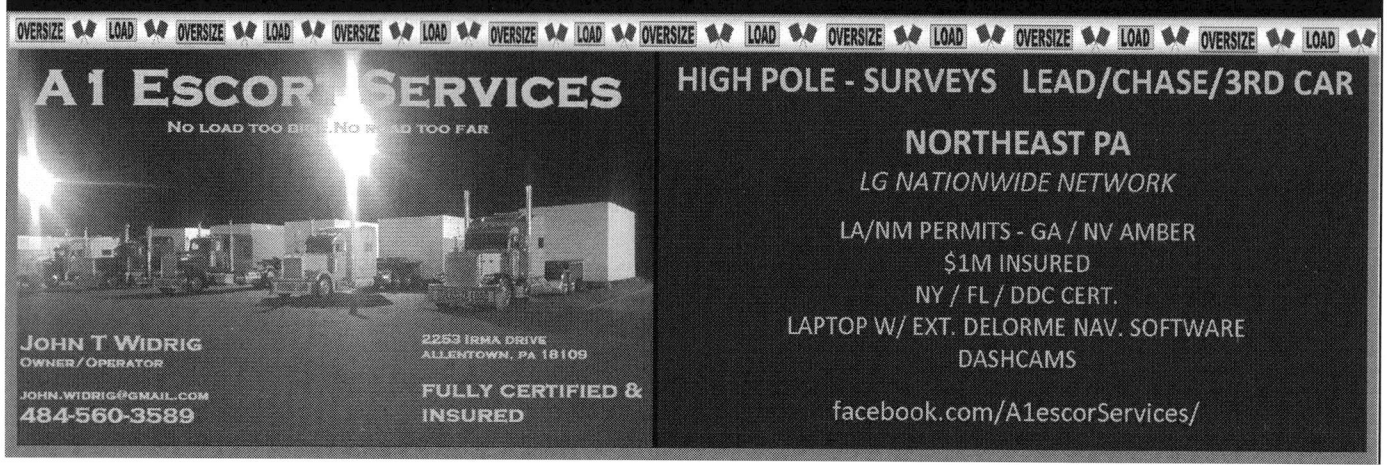

A1 Escort Services

No Load Too Big, No Road Too Far

John T Widrig
Owner/Operator

john.widrig@gmail.com
484-560-3589

2253 Irma Drive
Allentown, PA 18109

FULLY CERTIFIED & INSURED

HIGH POLE - SURVEYS   LEAD/CHASE/3RD CAR

NORTHEAST PA

LG NATIONWIDE NETWORK

LA/NM PERMITS - GA / NV AMBER
$1M INSURED
NY / FL / DDC CERT.
LAPTOP W/ EXT. DELORME NAV. SOFTWARE
DASHCAMS

facebook.com/A1escorServices/

VIRGINIA

Al's Big Rig Pilot Car Service
Allen Lohr
343 Banks Fort Road
Stasburg, Va 22657
Phone: 540-683-0000
E-mail: Al_lohr@yahoo.com

U.S. Passport & certified/permitted/equipped for all 48 states.
Providing experienced Hi-pole/Lead/Chase cars.
30 miles from VA/WV. Line for that extra car in WV.
Located near the VA/WVA/MD/PA line at the I-81/I-66 split.

VIRGINIA

PEGASUS PILOTS, LLC

SMITHSBURG, MARYLAND

301-991-4406

12 YEARS

Tired of Working with Non-Professional Escorts?

We have 8 Professional Drivers with fully equipped vehicles!

CDL EXPERIENCE
60 MI. to PORT OF BALTIMORE / 100 MI. to MD/WV LINE I-68
EQUIPPED / LEGAL for ALL STATES
COURTEOUS, PROFESSIONAL, RELIABLE, DEPENDABLE

ACCESS TO NATIONWIDE HIGH QUALITY HI POLERS & STEERMEN

WASHINGTON STATE CERTIFIED INSTRUCTOR - *SEE INSTRUCTOR AD PAGE* -

---

JLS PILOT CAR SERVICE — MULTIPLE CARS

WA CERTIFIED   **HIGH POLE - LEAD - CHASE**   FULLY INSURED

CELL: 678-873-5016   ALT: 470-239-8776   FAX 678-807-5751

T-N-T Pilot Car, LLC

We go the extra mile for you!

Terry Miller - Owner
Corapeake, NC
Cell: 813-401-3447
Office: 252-465-2036
www.tntpilotcar.webs.com
tntpilotcar@gmail.com

NC, VA, NY, FL Certified
Fully insured w/ PA add-on
High Pole
GA/ NV light - LA Permit
FL 36" cones
GPS Equipped
TWIC
LandStar & Greentree Approved

We have cars where you need them!

THE OVERLOAD COMPANION 2017 © FREDA BARBER BOOTH - PILOTCARSTODAY.COM

WASHINGTON

TERRY KLOES
KELSO, WA
360-261-0847
kloes2u@yahoo.com

CDL - TWIC
$1M AUTO / GL - PA ADD-ON
GA - NV AMBER
LA - UT INSPECTED
FULLY EQUIPPED
HANDS-FREE CELL
CAMERAS - GARMIN GPS

APPROVED FOR:
COMBINED
CONTRACTOR'S CARGO
LONESTAR - LANDSTAR
LEAVITTS
JONES MOTOR GROUP
JOULE YACHT
ATI & AFFILIATES
ART HEAVY-HAUL

KLOES 2 U, LLC
Oversize Load Escorting
"Long Haul Specialists"

DISPATCHER: ROBIN BAKER
360-773-2661

DRIVER: NICK CAMPBELL
360-998-0173

ADVERTISING IN THIS SPACE COULD GIVE YOU THE FIELD ADVANTAGE!

WEST VIRGINIA

High Lines, LLC
Oversize Load Escorting
304-203-9700

Janet Watson
Weston, WV
Fax 866-520-9531
highlines11@yahoo.com

Rig Moving Specialists

CREDENTIALS
ALL STATES CERTIFIED
NY / KS-SUPER / LA
AUTO $1MIL
INSURED W/ PA
PRO-GL $2MIL
NV & GA AMBER
EQUIPPED
EXPERIENCED

APPROVED FOR:
ATSSA
SAFE LAND
SHELL
PATTERSON
STONE ENERGY
NOBLE
HESS

NATIONWIDE SERVICES
HIGH POLES - ROUTE SURVEYS
CHASE - LEAD
PERMIT WRITING ABILITY/ ACCTS

MOBILE OFFICES/EQUIPMENT
HANDS-FREE CELL BOOSTER
ON BOARD CAMERAS
GPS DELORME / STREETS & TRIPS
LAPTOP / PRINTER

"Your SAFETY is Our PRIORITY!"

WEST VIRGINIA

M&R FLAG CARS

Charleston, WV

Mary Jones
304-549-8743

Randy Jones
304-541-8737

Fax: 304-744-0365

$1M Commercial Auto w/ PA add-on

Cert. PC/FLAGGER: NC, NY, UT

NSC Defensive Driving Cert

GA Amber Light Permit

8 CARS AVAILABLE

PEGASUS PILOTS, LLC

SMITHSBURG, MARYLAND

301-991-4406

12 YEARS

Tired of Working with Non-Professional Escorts?

We have 8 Professional Drivers with fully equipped vehicles!

CDL EXPERIENCE
60 MI. to PORT OF BALTIMORE / 100 MI. to MD/WV LINE I-68
EQUIPPED / LEGAL for ALL STATES
COURTEOUS, PROFESSIONAL, RELIABLE, DEPENDABLE

ACCESS TO NATIONWIDE HIGH QUALITY HI POLERS & STEERMEN

WASHINGTON STATE CERTIFIED INSTRUCTOR - *SEE INSTRUCTOR AD PAGE* -

WEST VIRGINIA

ADD-MAN PILOT CARS
adammcglaughlin@gmail.com
304-639-6305

Washington State Certified
High Pole - Lead - Chase
GPS - Dash Cam

AL'S BIG RIG PILOT CAR SERVICE
Allen Lohr
Owner / Operator
Stasburg, VA
540-683-0000
VA/WV/MD/PA @ I-81/I-66 Split
Call us for your 3rd car across WV!

HIGH POLE - LEAD - CHASE

Multiple Cars to Serve Your Needs

MATT WALLACE ENTERPRISES
Bowling Green, KY

We have a Large Network across the US

CO/UT/NY CERT - CO/UT FLAGGING CERT
PERMITTED/EQUIPPED FOR 48 STATES
$1M - $2M INSURED W/ PA ADD-ON

Email: matthew3e@aol.com

270-320-5345
Lead - Chase - High Pole - Steer

KyPilotCars
Walton, KY

**LEAD - CHASE
HIGH POLE**

Office: 859-400-0101
Website: Kypilotcars.com
Email: Dispatch@kypcs.com

WYOMING

AAA Pilot Service LLC

Gillette, WY 82717

307-682-1296

307-680-3552 (Joyce cell)

307-660-3552 (Ed cell)

Lead, chase Certified
Hi-pole Insured

19 Years Runnin'

Legacy Pilot Car Services, LLC

James: 970-396-5538

Erin: 970-396-6496

Located in Northern Colorado

HIGH POLE - LEAD - CHASE

Local and Long Haul
Single trip or full project
CO certified
$1M CA/GL/PL Insurance
CDL - TWIC - Passport
Fully equipped
On board office
Fuel Transfer Tank
(All required PPE / FR if needed)
*Prompt, professional
& safety oriented*

WYOMING

ASAP PILOT CAR SERVICE

Carolyn Johnson
Owner/Operator

406-600-9703

Asappilotcarservice.com
Montanatrafficcontrol.com

HIGH POLE
PROFESSIONAL SURVEYS
MONTANA TRAFFIC CONTROL

EQUIPPED VHF RADIO
CANADA-LEGAL
WA CERTIFIED
$3M INSURED

Captain Harloch's Pilot Service

Casper, Wyoming

Lead - Chase - High Pole - Blade Steering

Will deadhead for the right job

Business# 307-797-7971
Personal cell# 405-365-3141
Email address captainharloch@gmail.com

BRECKENRIDGE PILOT CAR SERVICES
(COLORADO)

720-590-6541 **352-507-9146**
PRIMARY CELL

Certified, Insured & Equipped
to meet State Requirements

GA/NV Amber Light
NM Inspection

THE OVERLOAD COMPANION 2017 © FREDA BARBER BOOTH - PILOTCARSTODAY.COM

TRUCK STOPS FOR LARGE LOADS

A general listing of truckstops in America that should accommodate an oversize load while giving the drivers additional services they may require.
(showers, food and scales)

This is not a complete listing, but it's close.

CAT SCALE INCLUDED!

THE OVERLOAD COMPANION 2017 © FREDA BARBER BOOTH - PILOTCARSTODAY.COM

ALABAMA TRUCK STOPS

CITY	HIGHWAY	EXIT	TRUCK STOP	PHONE	FAX	LOT	SCALES
PHENIX CITY	410 US 431 S	NA	MARATHON	334-291-1416	334-297-0607	M	CAT
GRAND BAY	I-10	4	TA	251-865-6175	251-865-3278	M	CAT
THEODORE	I-10	13	PILOT TRAVEL	251-653-8834	251-653-9556	M	CAT
LOXLEY	I-10	44	LOVES	251-964-2090	251-964-2090	M	CAT
ROBERTSDALE	I-10	53	OASIS TRAVEL	251-960-1150	251-960-1140	XL	SCALES
LINCOLN	I-20	165	PILOT TRAVEL CENTER	205-763-2225	205-763-2229	M	CAT
LINCOLN	I-20	165	I-20 TRUCKSTOP	205-763-7626	205-763-2880	LG	CAT
LINCOLN	I-20	168	TA	205-763-2771	205-763-2774	XLG	CAT
LINCOLN	I-20	168	PIT ROW TRUCK PLAZA	205-763-9340	205-763-9341	LG	
HEFLIN	I-20	205	STATE LINE FUEL CENTER	256-463-5747	256-463-2796	M	CAT
YORK	I-20/59	8	YORK TRUCK PLAZA	205-392-7400	205-392-7795	XL	CAT
LIVINGSTON	I-20/59	17	L & B TRAVEL PLAZA	205-652-6460	205-652-1106	M	
TUSCALOOSA	I-20/59	76	PILOT TRAVEL	205-553-9710	205-553-3089	LG	CAT
COTTONDALE	I-20/59	77	WILCO-HESS TRAVEL PLAZA	205-633-2155	205-633-2158	M	CAT
COTTONDALE	I-20/59	77	TA	205-554-0215	205-553-5337	XL	CAT
BUCKSVILLE	I-20/59	100	PETRO STOPPING CENTER	205-477-9178	205-477-0124	XL	SCALES
MCALLA	I-20/I-59	104	FLYING J	205-477-9181	205-477-6870	XL	SCALES
BIRMINGHAM	I-20/59	128	KANGAROO EXPRESS	205-808-3879	205-808-3881	M	CAT
BIRMINGHAM	I-20/59	123	PILOT TRAVEL CENTER	205-324-4532	205-324-5897	L	CAT
STEELE	I-59	175	LOVES	256-538-1964	256-538-7226	LG	CAT
GADSDEN	I-59	181	PETRO 2	256-413-7135	256-413-7330	XL	CAT
SATSUMA	I-65	19	PILOT TRAVEL	251-679-6260	251-679-6235	M	CAT
EVERGREEN	I-65	93	LOVES	251-578-4496	251-578-4831	LG	CAT
EVERGREEN	I-65	96	MCINTYRE	251-578-3588	251-578-3883	LG	
HOPE HULL	I-65	158	FLYING J	334-613-0212	334-613-0849	M	CAT
HOPE HULL	I-65	164	SAVEWAY TRAVEL CENTER	334-281-9100	334-281-9123	LG	CAT
MONTGOMERY	I-65	168	TA	334-288-3700	334-281-6462	LG	CAT
CLANTON	I-65	208	LOVES	205-755-8104	205-755-8694	M	CAT
JEMISON	I-65	219	JEMISON EXXON	205-688-1022	205-688-2690	M	
DODGE CITY	I-65	299	PETRO	256-287-1299	256-734-1596	LG	CAT
CULLMAN	I-65	304	JACKS TRUCKSTOP	256-739-0220	256-739-2680	XL	SCALES
FALKVILLE	I-65	322	LOVES	256-784-6106	256-784-6100	LG	CAT
PRICEVILLE	I-65	334	PILOT TRAVEL	256-353-5252	256-353-5235	XL	CAT
ELKMONT	I-65	361	PAM'S TRUCKSTOP	256-423-6030	256-423-6034	M	
BIRMINGHAM	I-65 & SR 94	264	FLYING J	205-323-2177	205-323-7885	XL	CAT
SHORTER	I-85	22	PETRO 2	334-727-3354	334-727-3576	M	CAT
TUSKEGEE	I-85	42	TORCH 85 TRUCK	334-727-7993	334-727-7993	M	CAT
CUSSETA	I-85	70	BRIDGES TRAVEL PLAZA	334-756-3161	334-756-3276	M	CAT
HAMILTON	US 78	16	MOORES SUPER STORE	205-921-4713	205-921-2013	M	SCALES
PIKE ROAD	US 231/82	NA	MAVRICKS	334-288-1540	334-288-1651	LG	SCALES
DOTHAN	US 431/231 BYPS		FLYING J	334-792-5152	334-792-5293	XL	CAT

If we need to make a change, add or subtract - please text 817-583-5503

PIT ROW SERVICES

FRONT/REAR HIGH POLE STEERMAN ROUTE SURVEY

ASK YOURSELF

WHO'S PILOTING YOUR LOADS?
ARE THEY QUALIFIED?
ARE THEY CERTIFIED?
WHO'S REALLY RESPONSIBLE?

WE OFFER CERTIFICATION CLASSES!

FULLY INSURED INCLUDING PROFESSIONAL LIABILITY

HIGHLY EQUIPPED PROFESSIONAL FLEET OF VEHICLES. TRAINED & CERTIFIED NATIONWIDE. ESCORT YOUR OVERSIZED LOADS WITH THE BEST LOOKING & MOST PROFESSIONAL PILOT CARS IN THE COUNTRY.

(205) 763 - 9340 LINCOLN AL / MOBILE AL **WWW.PITROW.SERVICES**

ALASKA - ARIZONA TRUCK STOPS

ALASKA

CITY	HIGHWAY	EXIT	TRUCK STOP	PHONE	FAX	LOT	SCALES
FOX	AK2	5.5	HILLTOP TRUCK STOP	907-389-7600	907-389-7601	M	
FAIRBANKS	3569 S CUSHMAN		TESORO TRUCK STOP	907-456-1122	907-456-1122	M	SCALES

If we need to make a change, add or subtract - please text 817-583-5503

ARIZONA

CITY	HIGHWAY	EXIT	TRUCK STOP	PHONE	FAX	LOT	SCALES
EHRENBERG	I-10	1	FLYING J	928-923-9600	928-923-7735	XL	CAT
EHRENBERG	I-10	5	SUNMART	928-927-6568	928-927-3990	M	CAT
QUARTZSITE	I-10	17	PILOT TRAVEL CENTER	928-927-7777	928-927-7000	LG	CAT
VICKSBURG	I-10	45	TOMAHAWK A/T PLAZA	928-859-3843	928-859-4432	XL	SCALES
TONOPAH	I-10	103	TA	623-386-6443	623-386-6490	XL	CAT
BUCKEYE	I-10	114	LOVES	623-386-6926	623-386-7462	M	CAT
AVONDALE	I-10	133	PILOT TRAVEL CENTER	623-936-0900	623-936-7376	XL	CAT
PHOENIX	I-10	137	FLYING J	623-936-1118	623-936-3611	XL	SCALES
PHOENIX	I-10	138	LIBERTY FUEL	602-233-1196	602-233-1635	XL	
CHANDLER	I-10	162	LOVES	520-796-1185	520-796-1228	M	CAT
ELOY	I-10	200	PETRO STOPPING CENTER	520-836-3983	520-423-2726	XL	CAT
ELOY	I-10	203	TA ELOY	520-466-7363	520-466-7536	XL	CAT
ELOY	I-10	208	PILOT TRAVEL CENTER	520-466-7550	520-466-7575	XL	CAT
ELOY	I-10	208	FLYING J	520-466-9204	520-466-9588	XL	CAT
TUCSON	I-10	268	TUCSON TRUCK TERM (TTT)	520-574-0050	520-574-9606	XL	CAT
BENSON	I-10	302	LOVES	520-586-8702	520-586-8707	XL	
SAN SIMON	I-10	378	SUNMART (CHEVRON)	520-845-2251	520-845-2483	XL	CAT
RIO RICO	I-19	12	PILOT TRAVEL CENTER	520-377-0001	520-377-0003	LG	
LAKE HAVASU CITY	I-40	9	LOVES	928-764-1505	928-764-1533	LG	CAT
LAKE HAVASU CITY	I-40	9	PILOT TRAVEL CENTER	928-764-2416	928-764-2021	M	CAT
KINGMAN	I-40	48	TA	928-753-7600	928-753-4577	LG	CAT
KINGMAN	I-40	53	FLYING J	928-757-7300	928-757-1085	LG	CAT
KINGMAN	I-40	66	PETRO STOPPING CENTER	928-757-2799	928-681-5245	XL	CAT
BELLEMONT	I-40	185	PILOT TRAVEL CENTER	928-773-0180	928-773-0205	M	CAT
FLAGSTAFF	I-40	198	LITTLE AMERICA T/C	928-779-7942	928-779-7978	M	SCALES
WINSLOW	I-40	255	FLYING J	928-289-2081	928-289-3798	XL	CAT
JOSEPH CITY	I-40	277	LOVES	928-288-3726	928-288-3738	M	CAT
HOLBROOK	I-40	283	FUEL EXPRESS	928-524-3006	928-524-9181	XL	
HOLBROOK	I-40	292	HOPI TRAVEL PLAZA	928-524-6243	928-524-3317	XL	SCALES
LUPTON	I-40	359	SPEEDYS LANDMARK	928-688-2775	928-688-2231	XL	
YUMA	I-8	3	LOVES	928-341-9100	928-341-9105	M	CAT
YUMA	I-8	12	FLYING J	928-342-2696	928-342-1619	LG	CAT
GILA BEND	I-8	115	LOVES	928-683-2210	928-683-2230	M	CAT

THE OVERLOAD COMPANION 2017 © FREDA BARBER BOOTH - PILOTCARSTODAY.COM

ARKANSAS TRUCK STOPS

CITY	HIGHWAY	EXIT	TRUCK STOP	PHONE	FAX	LOT	SCALES
CLARKSVILLE	3309 AR-109		HIGHWAY 109 TRK PLAZA	479-705-1410	479-705-0214	LG	
TEXARKANA	I-30	7	FLYING J	870-774-3595	870-774-3595	XL	CAT
PRESCOTT	I-30	44	TA	870-887-3414	870-887-8920	XL	CAT
PRESCOTT	I-30	44	EXIT 44 TRUCK STOP	870-887-5811	870-887-8920	LG	
PRESCOTT	I-30	46	LOVES	870-887-1744	870-887-8715	M	CAT
GURDON	I-30	63	SOUTHFORK TS	870-353-4363	870-353-2066	XL	
BENTON	I-30	121	PILOT TRAVEL CENTER	501-794-5900	501-794-5904	LG	CAT
RUSSELLVILLE	I-40	84	FLYING J	479-890-6161	479-890-2639	XL	CAT
RUSSELLVILLE	I-40	84	PILOT TRAVEL CENTER	479-967-7414	479-964-0112	LG	CAT
N LITTLE ROCK	I-40	142	MORGAN	501-851-8615	501-851-6494	M	SCALES
N LITTLE ROCK	I-40	161	LOVES	501-945-5400	501-945-5427	M	
N LITTLE ROCK	I-40	161	PETRO STOPPING CENTER	501-945-3206	501-955-4008	XL	CAT
N LITTLE ROCK	I-40	161	PILOT TRAVEL CENTER	501-945-2226	501-945-2282	LG	CAT
N LITTLE ROCK	I-40	161	TRUCKOMAT	501-945-2899	501-945-4368	M	CAT
PALESTINE	I-40	233	LOVES	870-581-5004	870-581-5089	LG	CAT
EARLE	I-40	260	TA	870-657-2105	870-657-2536	XL	CAT
WEST MEMPHIS	I-40 EXIT 280 / I-55 EXIT 4		PILOT TRAVEL CENTER	870-732-1202	870-732-1202	XL	CAT
WEST MEMPHIS	I-40 EXIT 280 / I-55 EXIT 4		FLYING J	870-735-8200	870-735-3300	XL	CAT
WEST MEMPHIS	I-40 EXIT 280 / I-55 EXIT 4		LOVES	870-732-1272	870-732-1280	LG	CAT
WEST MEMPHIS	I-40 EXIT 280 / I-55 EXIT 4		PETRO STOPPING CENTER	870-702-5540	870-702-5547	XL	CAT
FORT SMITH	I-540	12	SHORT STOP TS	479-646-8186	479-648-3195	M	CAT
ALMA	I-540	24	HILLTOP TRAVEL CENTER	479-632-1356	479-632-1359	LG	
SPRINGDALE	I-540	72	PILOT TRAVEL CENTER	479-872-6100	479-872-6103	M	CAT
JONESBORO	US 63/AR 18	39	SNAPPY MART	870-934-8462	870-934-8464	M	SCALES
PINE BLUFF	US 65/		CIRCLE N #55	870-247-9663	870-247-1761	M	
DUMAS	US 65/165		CASH'S TRAVEL PLZ CITGO	870-382-3262	870-382-3263	LG	
BELLEFONTE	US 65S / US62-412E		WHITE OAK STATION	870-743-3875	870-743-3862	M	CAT
BALD KNOB	US 67-167	55	BALD KNOB TRAVEL CENTER	501-724-1385	501-724-1389	M	CAT

If we need to make a change, add or subtract - please text 817-583-5503

Kenco Bucket Trucks | HIGHLOADS.COM

HIGH LOAD TRANSPORTATION.

KENCO Bucket Trucks
HIGH LOADS. OPEN ROADS.

1.877.459.3100 | HIGHLOADS.COM

THE OVERLOAD COMPANION 2017 © FREDA BARBER BOOTH - PILOTCARSTODAY.COM

CALIFORNIA TRUCK STOPS

CITY	HIGHWAY	EXIT	TRUCK STOP	PHONE	FAX	LOT	SCALES
CASTIC	I-5	176	PILOT TRAVEL CENTER	661-257-2800	661-257-2800	M	CAT
FRAZIER PARK	I-5	205	FLYING J	661-248-2600	661-248-2610	XL	SCALES
WHEELER RIDGE	I-5	219A	TA	661-858-2804	661-858-2804	XL	SCALES
WHEELER RIDGE	I-5	219B	PETRO STOPPING CENTER	661-663-4341	661-663-4348	XL	CAT
BUTTONWILLOW	I-5	257	TA	661-764-5266	661-764-5410	XL	CAT
LOST HILLS	I-5	278	LOVES	661-797-1800	661-797-1220	M	CAT
LOST HILLS	I-5	278	PILOT TRAVEL CENTER	661-797-2122	661-797-9772	M	CAT
SANTA NELLA	I-5	407	LOVES	209-827-1399	209-827-1033	M	CAT
SANTA NELLA	I-5	407	ROTTEN ROBBIES	209-826-4418	209-826-2032	M	CAT
SANTA NELLA	I-5	407	TA	209-826-0741	209-826-6399	XL	CAT
WESTLEY	I-5	441	JOE'S TRAVEL PLAZA	209-894-3040	209-894-3154	LG	SCALES
STOCKTON	I-5	471	VANCO TRUCK/AUTO PLAZA	209-466-0833	209-466-2740	M	CAT
LODI	I-5	485	3 B'S TRUCK/AUTO PLAZA	209-369-6391	209-365-0715	M	CAT
LODI	I-5	485	FLYING J	209-339-4066	209-339-4287	XL	CAT
DUNNIGAN	I-5	554	PILOT TRAVEL CENTER	530-724-3060	530-724-3029	LG	CAT
CORNING	I-5	630	LOVES	530-824-8767	530-824-8776	XL	CAT
CORNING	I-5	630	PETRO STOPPING CENTER	530-824-4685	530-824-1973	LG	CAT
CORNING	I-5	630	TA	530-824-4646	530-824-0547	XL	CAT
REDDING	I-5	673	TA	530-221-4760	530-221-8269	XL	CAT
WEED	I-5	745	PILOT TRAVEL CENTER	530-938-9600	530-938-9700	LG	CAT
EL CENTRO	I-8	115	SUPER STOP TRAVEL CENTER	760-352-0044	760-312-9451	XL	CAT
EL CENTRO	I-8	118	TRUCK STOP 111	760-353-3303	760-353-6027	M	CAT
ONTARIO	I-10	57	TA - EAST	909-390-7800	909-390-7298	XL	CAT
ONTARIO	I-10	57	TA - WEST	909-390-2525	909-605-6765	XL	CAT
FONTANA	I-10	61	THREE SISTERS TRUCK STOP	909-822-4415	909-822-8378	M	SCALES
FONTANA	I-10	61	TRUCK TOWN PLAZA	909-823-0635	909-823-4794	XL	SCALES
RIALTO	I-10	68	I-10 TRUCK STOP	909-877-1171	909-877-6085	$ M	CAT
COLTON	I-10	73	ROYAL TRUCK STOP	909-825-5190	760-329-0083	M	SCALES
PALM SPRINGS	I-10	120	PILOT TRAVEL CENTER	760-329-5562	760-329-0083	M	CAT
THOUSAND PALMS	I-10	130	FLYING J	760-343-1500	760-343-1330	LG	SCALES
COACHELLA	I-10	146	LOVES	760-775-3401	760-775-3409	XL	CAT
COACHELLA	I-10	146	TA	760-342-6200	760-342-6208	XL	CAT
BLYTHE	I-10	232	BB TRAVEL CENTER	760-922-5109	760-922-7580	XL	CAT
HESPERIA	I-15	141	PILOT TRAVEL CENTER	760-956-2844	760-956-1198	XL	CAT
BARSTOW	I-15	178	LOVES	760-253-4080	760-253-4091	LG	CAT
BARSTOW	I-15	178	FLYING J	760-253-7043	760-253-7051	XL	CAT
BARSTOW	I-15	178	PILOT TRAVEL CENTER	760-253-2861	760-253-2863	M	CAT
BARSTOW	I-15	178	TA	760-253-2922	760-253-7959	XL	CAT
SACRAMENTO	I-80	85	PILOT TRAVEL CENTER	916-927-4774	916-927-6641	XL	SCALES
SAN DIEGO	I-805	1B	PILOT TRAVEL CENTER	619-661-9558	619-661-9814	LG	CAT
MECCA	66TH AVE		MECCA TRAVEL CENTER	760-396-5243	760-396-5247	LG	CAT
SANTA NELLA	CA-33/CA 152		PETRO	209-827-8025	209-826-2730	XL	CAT

CALIFORNIA (CONT'D)
CONNECTICUT - DELAWARE TRUCK STOPS

CALIFORNIA (CONT'D)

CITY	HIGHWAY	EXIT	TRUCK STOP	PHONE	FAX	LOT	SCALES
SANTA NELLA	CA 152 CA 133		PETRO	209-827-8025	209-826-2730	XL	CAT
TEHACHAPI	CA 58	151	LOVES	661-823-1484	661-823-1486	LG	CAT
BAKERSFIELD	CA 58 & CA 184		24/7 TRAVEL PLAZA	661-364-0630	661-364-0718	LG	CAT
BAKERSFIELD	CA 58 & CA 184		KIMBER RENEGAD SHELL	661-366-1860	661-366-1871	M	CAT
BAKERSFIELD	CA 58 & CA 184		BRUCE'S TRUCKSTOP	661-366-5314	661-366-1215	M	CAT
BAKERSFIELD	CA 99	13	BEAR MTN TRAVEL STOP	661-834-5733	661-834-5039	M	CAT
BAKERSFIELD	CA 99	39	FLYING J	661-392-5300	661-392-5307	XL	CAT
TULARE	CA 99	85	LOVES	559-686-1400	559-686-3049	LG	CAT
TRAVER	CA 99	106	RJ TRAVEL CENTER	559-238-3801	559-238-3850	XL	CAT
FOWLER	CA 99	121	BUFORD STAR MART	559-834-3634	559-834-3684	XL	CAT
FRESNO	CA 99	127	5TH WHEEL TRUCK STOP	559-485-0701	559-485-0019	M	SCALES
FRESNO	CA 99	142	EZ TRIP GOLDEN TRAVEL PLAZA	559-276-8001	559-276-8600	XL	SCALES
MADERA	CA 99	159	PILOT TRAVEL CENTER	559-673-3878	559-673-7679	XL	CAT
LIVINGSTON	CA 99	203	TA	209-394-4418	209-394-1419	LG	CAT
RIPON	CA 99	237	LOVES	209-599-0740	209-599-3680	LG	CAT
RIPON	CA 99	237	FLYING J	209-599-4141	209-599-4265	XL	CAT
YUBA CITY	CA 99	342??	HIGHWAY 99 TRVL CTR	530-790-0588	530-790-6871	LG	CAT
SALINAS	US 101	326B	PILOT TRAVEL CENTER	831-775-0380	831-775-0360	LG	CAT
GILROY	US 101	NA	GARLIC FARM CENTER	408-847-5172	408-847-9904	XL	CAT
KRAMER JUNCTION	US 395/CA-58		PILOT TRAVEL CENTER	760-762-0041	760-762-5231	M	CAT

If we need to make a change, add or subtract - please text 817-583-5503

CONNECTICUT - DELAWARE TRUCK STOPS

CONNECTICUT

CITY	HIGHWAY	EXIT	TRUCK STOP	PHONE	FAX	LOT	SCALES
MILLDALE	I-84	28	TA	860-621-0106	860-628-6735	$ LG	CAT
WILLINGTON	I-84	71	TA	860-684-0499	860-684-1213	$ XL	CAT
MILFORD	I-95	40	PILOT TRAVEL STOP	203-876-1266	203-876-9473	XL	CAT
BRANFORD	I-95	56	TA	203-481-0301	203-481-3049	LG	CAT
NORTH STONINGTON	I-95	93	SPICER FOOD & FUEL	860-599-3894	860-599-1634	M	CAT
NORTH STONINGTON	I-95	93	PILOT TRAVEL STOP	860-599-2020	860-599-5771	LG	CAT

DELAWARE

CITY	HIGHWAY	EXIT	TRUCK STOP	PHONE	FAX	LOT	SCALES
FELTON	US 13 S/DE 286		UNCLE WILLIES	302-284-2193	302-284-2194	M	CAT
MIDDLETOWN	US 301 S	N/A	301 PLAZA	302-376-4301	302-876-4300	M	CAT
NEW CASTLE	US 13/40 NB		DELAWARE TRUCK PLAZA	302-322-0978	302-322-5458	LG	

If we need to make a change, add or subtract - please text 817-583-5503

COLORADO TRUCK STOPS

CITY	HIGHWAY	EXIT	TRUCK STOP	PHONE	FAX	LOT	SCALES
WALSENBURG	I-25	52	ACORN TRAVEL PLAZA	719-738-5733	719-738-3950	XL	
PUEBLO	I-25	104	LOVES	719-253-1338	719-253-1341	M	CAT
FOUNTAIN	I-25	128	TOMAHAWK TRUCK STOP	719-382-5473	719-382-5476	LG	SCALES
MONUMENT	I-25	158	DIAMOND SHAMROCK	719-481-3628	719-488-0660	M	SCALES
LONGMONT	I-25	240	LONGMONT TRUCK STOP	303-776-9396	303-485-8407	LG	CAT
JOHNSTOWN	I-25	254	JOHNSONS CORNER TRUCK STOP	970-667-2069	970-667-8669	LG	CAT
FRUITA	I-70	19	LOCO TRAVEL STOP	970-858-8006	970-858-4640	M	CAT
WHEATRIDGE	I-70	266	TA - DENVER WEST	303-423-8250	303-426-4694	XL	CAT
DENVER	I-70	276A	PILOT TRAVEL CENTER	303-292-6303	303-292-3647	LG	CAT
AURORA (DENVER)	I-70	285	FLYING J	303-366-7600	303-367-5657	LG	CAT
WATKINS	I-70	295	TOMAHAWK TRUCK STOP	303-261-9677	303-261-9615	LG	SCALES
BENNETT	I-70	304	LOVES	303-644-3585	303-644-3412	LG	CAT
LIMON	I-70	359	TA	719-775-9317	719-775-2713	LG	CAT
LIMON	I-70	359	FLYING J	719-775-9286	719-775-9306	XL	CAT
BURLINGTON	I-70	437	TRAVEL SHOPPE	719-346-8515	719-346-5196	M	
COMMERCE CITY	I-70 X-278/I-270 X-4		SAPP BROS	303-289-3900	303-289-3936	XL	SCALES
COMMERCE CITY	I-70 X-278/I-270 X-4		TA - DENVER EAST	303-286-0123	303-286-6781	XL	CAT
HUDSON	I-76	31	LOVES	303-536-9900	303-536-9904	LG	CAT
EVANS	665 US 85		SUNMART	970-330-5028	970-339-8276	LG	CAT
TOWAOC	US 160/491		UTE MTN TRAVEL CENTER	970-565-5364	970-565-6991	M	
LAMAR	US 50/US 287		PORTS TO PLAINS TRAVEL PLAZA	719-336-3445	719-336-3449	XL	CAT

CONNECTICUT - DELAWARE TRUCK STOPS ON PREVIOUS PAGE

BRECKENRIDGE PILOT CAR SERVICES
(COLORADO)

720-590-6541 PRIMARY **352-507-9146** CELL

Certified, Insured & Equipped to meet State Requirements

GA/NV Amber Light
NM Inspection

THE OVERLOAD COMPANION 2017 © FREDA BARBER BOOTH - PILOTCARSTODAY.COM

FLORIDA TRUCK STOPS

CITY	HIGHWAY	EXIT	TRUCK STOP	PHONE	FAX	LOT	SCALES
SEFFNER/TAMPA	I-4	10	TA	813-262-1560	813-262-1548	$ LG	CAT
POLK CITY	I-4	44	LOVES	863-984-7030	863-984-2268	XL	CAT
COTTONDALE	I-10	130	LOVES	850-352-2041	850-352-2043	LG	CAT
MARIANNA	I-10	142	TA	850-526-3303	850-482-8953	LG	CAT
MARIANNA	I-10	142	PILOT	850-482-2148	850-482-2136	LG	CAT
MIDWAY	I-10	192	FLYING J	850-574-1299	850-574-6546	XL	CAT
MIDWAY	I-10	192	PILOT	850-576-3200	850-576-3213	LG	CAT
LLOYD	I-10	217	CAPITOL CITY TRAVEL CENTER	850-997-3538	850-997-8986	LG	SCALES
LEE	I-10	262	JIMMYS AUTO/TRUCK PLAZA	850-971-4200	850-971-5152	M	CAT
LEE	I-10	262	LOVES	850-971-4115	850-971-4117	LG	CAT
BALDWIN	I-10	343	PILOT TRAVEL CENTER	904-266-4238	904-266-9820	M	CAT
BALDWIN	I-10	343	TA	904-266-4281	904-266-9614	LG	CAT
FORT MYERS	I-75	139	PILOT	239-693-6868	239-693-1253	M	CAT
PUNTA GORDA	I-75	161	PILOT	941-637-3974	941-637-5729	M	CAT
SAN ANTONIO	I-75	285	FOUR STAR FUEL MART	352-588-2006	352-588-3757	M	SCALES
SAN ANTONIO	I-75	285	FLYING J	352-588-5444	352-588-4629	XL	CAT
LAKE PANASOFFKEE	I-75	321	SPIRIT TRAVEL CENTER	352-793-1233	352-793-1233	M	CAT
WILDWOOD	I-75	329	TA	352-784-2501	352-748-2390	XL	CAT
BELLEVIEW	I-75	341	PILOT	352-347-8555	352-347-3082	M	CAT
OCALA	I-75	358	PILOT TRAVEL CENTER # 092	352-402-9081	352-622-5233	XL	CAT
OCALA	I-75	358	PILOT # 424	352-867-8300	352-867-8448	LG	CAT
OCALA	I-75	358	LOVES	352-368-5719	352-368-5910	M	CAT
REDDICK	I-75	368	PETRO STOPPING CENTER	352-591-1881	352-591-8639	XL	CAT
JASPER	I-75	460	J&J TRUCK PLAZA	386-792-1497	386-792-2850	M	
FORT PIERCE	I-95	129	PILOT	772-460-0611	772-460-4252	LG	CAT
FORT PIERCE	I-95	129	LOVES	772-460-5777	772-460-8901	LG	CAT
FORT PIERCE	I-95	129	FALCON TS	772-466-7160	561-466-5179	$ XL	CAT
FORT PIERCE	I-95	131	FLYING J	772-461-0091	772-461-0291	XL	CAT
VERO BEACH	I-95	147	TA	772-562-1791	772-569-0433	XL	CAT
ORMOND BEACH	I-95	273	LOVES	386-671-9585	386-671-9587	M	CAT
ST AUGUSTINE	I-95	305	FLYING J	904-794-0426	904-794-7582	XL	CAT
JACKSONVILLE	I-95	329	TA	904-829-3946	904-824-4115	LG	CAT
HAINES CITY	US 27		PILOT TRAVEL CENTER	863-421-3571	863-421-6302	LG	CAT
SOUTH BAY	US 27 N		GR'S TRAVEL MART	561-996-6599	561-992-4098	LG	NEARBY
WESTON	US-27		SEMINOLE TRUCK STOP	954-434-0662	954-434-0844	$ LG	CAT
PERRY	FL 19/27/17		WACO TRAVEL CENTER	850-838-1852	850-838-8254	M	CAT
HIALEAH GARDENS	FL 826 - US27		USA TRUCK SERV PLAZA	305-822-8851	305-557-3251	$ LG	CAT
POMPANO BEACH	FLTP	67	POMPANO TRUCK STOP	954-971-5051	954-917-7099	$ M	

If we need to make a change, add or subtract - please text 817-583-5503

CHARLES JAMES CAYIAS INSURANCE INC.

801-488-0085

PROFESSIONAL PILOT CAR INSURANCE PACKAGE

Working in cooperation with North America's leading escort vehicle trainers, certifying entities, and insurance professionals who specialize in protecting the needs of escort operators all across the United States.

Whether an accident is your fault or not, without the right protection, you could pay tens of thousands out of pocket to defend yourself in a lawsuit brought against you by others. Be prepared by having the proper insurance protection!

The Professional Pilot Car Insurance Package offers the following insurance coverage(s):

- **Commercial Automobile**: As personal auto insurance policies exclude business operations, commercial insurance is essential. We offer $1,000,000 in bodily injury and property damage coverage, along with medical payments, personal injury protection (in those states where required), and uninsured motorists to protect you, your passengers and members of the public in case of an over the road accident. Comprehensive and collision coverage is also offered to protect your vehicle. We can provide commercial automobile coverage on a mono-line basis.
- **General Liability**: Will protect you against injuries to members of the public at your premises, and damages that you may cause to the property of others that does not involve an automobile. We offer limits of $1,000,000 each occurrence and $2,000,000 aggregate for losses occurring during the policy term. We can provide general liability coverage on a mono-line basis.
- **Professional Liability**: Will provide you with protection for those activities normally excluded under a general liability policy because they are considered to be a professional exposure. We offer $1,000,000 in coverage for flagging, height pole, route surveys and shunting services, subject to certain qualifications. No coverage is offered for rigging, steerables or tillerman services.
- **Inland Marine**: Will cover your miscellaneous equipment used in your operation such as small tools, magnetic vehicle signage, flags, cones, etc. We offer three limits of coverage $1,000; $2,500; $5,000 depending on your needs. Higher limits are available upon request.

Charles James Cayias Insurance, Inc.
2150 South 1300 East, Suite #100
Salt Lake City, UT 84106
PH: (801) 488-0085
Fax: (801) 463-6683
www.cayias.com

Program benefits include a combination of coverage specific to the pilot car industry, competitive pricing, expertise, and prompt friendly service. Simply put... our goal is to provide you with the best value for your money!

GEORGIA TRUCK STOPS

CITY	HIGHWAY	EXIT	TRUCK STOP	PHONE	FAX	LOT	SCALES
MACON	I-16	6	OCMULGEE CHEVRON	478-750-4331	478-750-4328	LG	CAT
DUBLIN	I-16	49	LOVES	478-296-1368	478-296-1396	M	CAT
TALLAPOOSA	I-20	5	PILOT TRAVEL CENTER	770-574-9922	770-574-9697	LG	CAT
TALLAPOOSA	I-20	5	NEWBORN A/T PLAZA	770-574-5082	770-574-8941	XL	CAT
WACO	I-20	9	LOVES	770-824-5040	770-824-5531	LG	CAT
TEMPLE	I-20	19	PILOT TRAVEL CENTER	770-562-9773	770-562-2269	LG	CAT
TEMPLE	I-20	19	FLYING J	770-562-4009	770-562-3571	XL	CAT
VILLA RICA	I-20	26	WILCO-HESS TRAVEL PLAZA	770-456-9941	770-456-9942	XL	CAT
MADISON	I-20	114	TA	706-342-4176	706-342-2390	LG	CAT
MADISON	I-20	114	PILOT TRAVEL CENTER	706-343-1455	706-343-1033	LG	CAT
SILOAM	I-20	138	FLYING J	706-486-4835	706-486-4845	XL	CAT
THOMPSON	I-20	172	LOVES	706-843-9833	706-843-9835	LG	CAT
AUGUSTA	I-20	200	PILOT TRAVEL CENTER	706-667-6557	706-481-9940	LG	CAT
RISING FAWN	I-59	4	PILOT TRAVEL CENTER	706-462-2455	706-462-2702	XL	CAT
LAKE PARK	I-75	2	TA	229-559-5113	229-559-4864	M	CAT
LAKE PARK	I-75	2	FLYING J	229-559-6500	229-559-3008	XL	CAT
VALDOSTA	I-75	11	WILCO-HESS TRAVEL PLAZA	229-293-0388	229-293-0350	LG	CAT
VALDOSTA	I-75	11	PILOT TRAVEL CENTER	229-244-8034	229-244-6020	LG	CAT
ADEL	I-75	39	ADEL TRUCK PLAZA (CITGO)	229-896-7453	229-896-2163	XL	CAT
TIFTON	I-75	59	LOVES	229-382-9118	229-382-9136	LG	CAT
TIFTON	I-75	60	PILOT TRAVEL CENTER	229-382-7295	229-382-4910	XL	CAT
TIFTON	I-75	61	SHELL TRAVEL PLAZA	229-388-0543	229-387-8632	LG	
CORDELE	I-75	101	PILOT TRAVEL CENTER	229-271-5775	229-271-5774	M	CAT
VIENNA	I-75	109	PILOT TRAVEL CENTER	229-268-1414	229-268-4880	M	CAT
UNADILLA	I-75	121	ALLSTATE TRUCK STOP	478-627-3218	678-601-5960	XL	SCALES
BYRON	I-75	146	PILOT TRAVEL CENTER	478-956-5316	478-956-3726	XL	CAT
JACKSON	I-75	201	FLYING J	770-775-0138	770-775-1134	XL	CAT
JACKSON	I-75	201	LOVES	678-752-0041	678-752-9931	M	CAT
JACKSON	I-75	201	WILCO-HESS TRAVEL PLAZA	770-504-9206	770-504-9209	LG	CAT
JACKSON	I-75	201	TA	770-775-2076	770-775-2807	XL	CAT
FOREST PARK	I-75	237	PATRIOT TRUCK STOP	404-366-4562	404-366-0218	$ M	CAT
EMERSON	I-75	283	LOVES	770-382-4141	770-382-4107	LG	CAT
CARTERSVILLE	I-75	296	TA	770-607-8885	770-607-7265	XL	CAT
CARTERSVILLE	I-75	296	PILOT TRAVEL CENTER	770-607-7835	770-607-7873	M	CAT
CALHOUN	I-75	318	WILCO-HESS TRAVEL PLAZA	706-625-5580	706-625-3639	LG	CAT
RESACA	I-75	320	FLYING J	706-629-1541	706-629-2003	XL	CAT
DALTON	I-75	326	PILOT TRAVEL CENTER	706-370-4060	706-370-5769	XL	CAT
DALTON	I-75	328	PILOT TRAVEL CENTER	706-277-7934	706-277-3337	LG	CAT
RINGGOLD	I-75	345	COCHRAN'S T/P	706-935-2351	706-965-2922	LG	CAT
RINGGOLD	I-75	345	CHOO-CHOO	706-935-5107	706-965-6374	LG	SCALES
LAGRANGE	I-85	13	PILOT TRAVEL CENTER	706-884-6318	706-884-1872	M	CAT
HOGANSVILLE	I-85	28	LOVES	706-637-4311	706-637-6090	M	CAT
NEWNAN	I-85	41	PILOT TRAVEL CENTER	770-252-3551	770-252-2197	LG	CAT
FAIRBURN	I-85	61	FAIRBURN FAMILY TRVL CTR	770-306-8319	770-306-2127	XL	CAT
BRASELTON	I-85	129	PILOT TRAVEL CENTER	706-654-2820	706-654-9326	M	CAT
COMMERCE	I-85	149	TA	706-335-5198	706-335-6729	LG	CAT

GEORGIA TRUCK STOPS

CITY	HIGHWAY	EXIT	TRUCK STOP	PHONE	FAX	LOT	SCALES
CARNESVILLE	I-85	160	FLYING J	706-335-6656	706-335-4432	XL	CAT
CARNESVILLE	I-85	160	PETRO STOPPING CENTER	706-335-1980	706-335-2075	$ XL	CAT
CARNESVILLE	I-85	166	ECHO A/T PLAZA	706-384-7331		M	SCALES
CARNESVILLE	I-85	166	WILCO-HESS TRAVEL PLAZA	706-384-3084	706-384-3202	M	CAT
KINGSLAND	I-95	1	WILCO-HESS TRAVEL PLAZA	912-576-7858	912-576-7861	XL	CAT
KINGSLAND	I-95	3	PETRO STOPPING CENTER	912-882-3111	912-882-3050	XL	CAT
WOODBINE	I-95	14	SUNSHINE TRAVEL PLAZA	912-882-8440	912-882-8671	M	CAT
BRUNSWICK	I-95	29	LOVES	912-264-2777	912-264-6003	LG	CAT
BRUNSWICK	I-95	29	FLYING J	912-280-0006	912-280-9555	XL	CAT
RICHMOND HILL	I-95	87	TA	912-756-3381	912-756-3273	XL	CAT
RICHMOND HILL	I-95	90	LOVES	912-756-5394	912-756-6501	LG	CAT
PORT WENTWORTH	I-95	109	PILOT TRAVEL CENTER	912-966-2723	912-964-7808	XL	CAT
ATLANTA	I-285	12	PETRO STOPPING CENTER	404-794-7772	404-792-6941	$ XL	CAT
SMYRNA	I-285	16	PILOT TRAVEL CENTER	770-434-9949	770-434-8341	M	CAT
CONLEY/ATLANTA	I-285	51	PILOT TRAVEL CENTER	404-212-8733	404-212-8568	LG	CAT
BAINBRIDGE	US-84 W		KANGAROO EXPRESS	229-243-0300		XL	CAT
ALBANY	GA-300		PILOT TRAVEL CENTER	229-878-1355	229-878-1302	M	CAT

If we need to make a change, add or subtract - please text 817-583-5503

A.R. CHANEY PILOT CAR SERVICE

GASTON, SC
803-422-2361
Email: archaneypcs@gmail.com

$1M GL-PL Insured - Class A CDL - GA Amber - LA Permit

UTAH CERTIFIED

Approved for LandStar, Turner Transportation & Comdata

THE OVERLOAD COMPANION 2017 © FREDA BARBER BOOTH - PILOTCARSTODAY.COM

IDAHO - ILLINOIS TRUCK STOPS

IDAHO

CITY	HIGHWAY	EXIT	TRUCK STOP	PHONE	FAX	LOT	SCALES
DOWNY	I-15	31	FLAGS WEST T/S	208-897-5238	208-897-5612	M	
MCCAMMON	I-15	47	FLYING J	208-254-9845	208-254-9106	LG	CAT
FORT HALL	I-15	80	TP TRUCK STOP	208-237-9064	208-637-1151	M	
CALDWELL	I-84	29	FLYING J	208-453-9225	208-453-9409	LG	CAT
CALDWELL	I-84	29	SAGE TRAVEL PLAZA	208-454-2084	208-454-3766	LG	
NAMPA	I-84	35	JACKSON FOOD STORE	208-466-0802	208-466-0802	LG	
BOISE	I-84	54	FLYING J	208-385-9745	208-344-3624	M	
BOISE	I-84	54	TA	208-344-1091	208-345-7560	LG	CAT
BOISE (S)	I-84	71	BOISE STAGE STOP	208-343-1367	208-343-1999	XL	SCALES
MOUNTAIN HOME	I-84	95	PILOT TRAVEL CENTER	208-587-4465	208-587-3071	LG	CAT
TWIN FALLS (JEROME)	I-84	173	FLYING J	208-324-3442	208-324-4097	XL	CAT
EDEN	I-84	182	TRAVELERS OASIS T/P	208-825-4147	208-825-5720	XL	CAT
HEYBURN	I-84	211	LOVES	208-434-8777	208-434-8779	M	CAT
POST FALLS	I-90	2	FLYING J	208-773-0593	208-773-0404	LG	CAT
POST FALLS	I-90	2	LOVES	208-773-4577	208-773-4425	M	CAT

If we need to make a change, add or subtract - please text 817-583-5503

ILLINOIS

CITY	HIGHWAY	EXIT	TRUCK STOP	PHONE	FAX	LOT	SCALES
NOTICE: Many truckstops are located at conjoining highways							
METROPOLIS	I-24	37	METROPOLIS T/T PLAZA	618-524-4831	NA	M	
ALORTON	I-255	17	FLYING J	618-337-4579	618-337-4851	XL	CAT
PONTOON BEACH	I-270	6B	FLYING J	618-931-1580	618-931-3587	XL	CAT
ROCHELLE	I-39	99	PETRO STOPPING CENTER	815-562-3716	815-562-5225	XL	SCALES
ROCKFORD	I-39	115	JOHNSON OIL	815-874-0323	NA	XL	CAT
ROSCOE	I-39/90	3	LOVES	815-389-1923	815-389-0848	L	CAT
SOUTH BELOIT	I-39/I-90	1	PILOT TRAVEL PLAZA	815-389-2190	815-398-3917	M	CAT
SPRINGFIELD	I-55	100	ROAD RANGER T/C	217-789-9637	217-789-9746	LG	CAT
WILLIAMSVILLE	I-55	109	LOVES	217-566-3448	217-566-3465	M	CAT
LINCOLN	I-55	126	THORTONS TRAVEL PLAZA	217-732-3915	217-732-4875	L	CAT
MCLEAN	I-55	145	DIXIE T/P	309-874-2323	309-874-3335	XL	CAT
WILMINGTON	I-55	240	MOBILE T/P	815-476-4271	815-476-5427	M-$	CAT
CHANNAHON	I-55	248	PILOT TRAVEL PLAZA	815-467-4455	815-467-0972	M	
BOLINGBROOK	I-55	267	I-55 TRUCKSTOP	630-739-7006	630-739-0168	$ XL	CAT
BLOOMINGTON	I-55, I-74, I-39	160	TA	309-827-4676	309-828-6651	L	CAT
EAST ST LOUIS	I-55/70	4	PILOT TRAVEL PLAZA	618-875-5800	618-875-4234	XL	CAT
TROY	I-55/70	18	PILOT TRAVEL PLAZA	618-667-0946	618-667-0966	XL	CAT
EFFINGHAM	I-55/70	162	PILOT TRAVEL PLAZA	217-342-3787	217-342-6672	M	CAT
BLOOMINGTON	I-55/74	160	PILOT TRAVEL PLAZA	309-827-7867	309-827-2355	XL	CAT
TROY	I-55-70	18	TA	618-667-9931	618-667-8051	L	CAT
INA	I-57	83	LOVES	618-437-5275	618-437-5278	M	CAT

ILLINOIS TRUCK STOPS (CONT'D)

CITY	HIGHWAY	EXIT	TRUCK STOP	PHONE	FAX	LOT	SCALES
\multicolumn{8}{c}{NOTICE: Many truckstops are located at conjoining highways}
CHAMPAIGN	I-57	240	ROAD RANGER T/C	217-643-4991	217-643-2355	XL	CAT
GILMAN	I-57	283	K&H T/P	815-265-7625	815-265-7982	M	CAT
GILMAN	I-57	283	PILOT TRAVEL PLAZA	815-265-4754	815-265-4754	L	CAT
KANKAKEE	I-57	308	LOVES	815-929-1549	915-929-1728	LG	CAT
MONEE	I-57	335	PILOT TRAVEL PLAZA	708-534-2483	708-534-3980	M	CAT
MONEE	I-57	335	PETRO STOPPING CENTER	708-534-0400	708-534-8489	XL	CAT
MARION	I-57	54-B	MARION TRUCK PLAZA	618-993-2697	618-997-9082	M	SCALES
MOUNT VERNON	I-57/64	95	HUCKS TRAVEL CENTER	618-244-2616	618-244-3248	XL	SCALES
MOUNT VERNON	I-57/64	95	PILOT TRAVEL PLAZA	618-244-1216	618-244-1262	L	SCALES
MOUNT VERNON	I-57/64	95	TA	618-244-4242	618-244-9182	XL	CAT
EFFINGHAM	I-57-70	160	TA	217-347-7183	217-342-4029	L	CAT
NASHVILLE	I-64	50	LITTLE NASHVILLE T/S	618-478-5777	618-478-5583	M	SCALES
GREENVILLE	I-70	45	LOVES	618-664-9287	618-664-9622	L	CAT
VANDALIA	I-70	61	FAST STOP	618-283-1557	618-283-5393	M	CAT
EFFINGHAM	I-70 & I-57	160	FLYING J	217-347-7161	217-347-5815	XL	CAT
EFFINGHAM	I-70/I-57	159	PETRO STOPPING CENTER	217-347-0480	217-540-2939	XL	CAT
DECATUR	I-72	144	PILOT TRAVEL PLAZA	217-876-0208	217-876-0522	M	CAT
WOODHULL	I-74	32	HOMESTEAD	309-334-2844	NA	L	CAT
MORTON	I-74	102	MORTON TRAVEL CENTER	309-266-5450	309-263-5350	M	CAT
LE ROY	I-74	149	LOVES	309-962-3060	309-962-3093	L	CAT
OAKWOOD	I-74	206	PILOT TRAVEL PLAZA	217-354-4270	217-354-4047	XL	CAT
DANVILLE	I-74	220	MARATHON STATION	217-446-8239	217-446-8250	M	CAT
GENESEO	I-80	19	BECK'S	309-944-6040	309-944-1186	XL	CAT
PRINCETON	I-80	56	PILOT TRAVEL PLAZA	815-315-4951	815-875-1718	XL	CAT
PERU	I-80	73	SAPP BROS	815-224-1065	815-224-4562	XL	SCALES
PERU	I-80	77	FLYING J	815-220-0611	815-220-0617	XL	CAT
UTICA	I-80	81	LOVES	815-667-4572	815-667-4659	M	CAT
OTTAWA	I-80	93	OASIS CLOCKTOWER SHELL	815-434-7581	815-434-7585	XL	CAT
MORRIS	I-80	112	TA	815-942-5690	815-942-4371	XL	CAT
MINOOKA	I-80	122	PILOT TRAVEL PLAZA	815-467-4416	815-467-5409	L	CAT
HILLSDALE	I-88	10	EXPRESS LANE (SHELL)	309-658-2345	309-658-2817	M	CAT
DIXON	I-88	54	PILOT	815-516-1998	815-284-0469	M	CAT
ELGIN	I-90	365	TA	847-683-4558	847-683-4059	LG	CAT
HAMPSHIRE	I-90	365	PILOT TRAVEL PLAZA	815-209-9013	847-683-7609	M	CAT
SOUTH BELOIT	I-90/39	1	FLYING J	815-389-4760	815-389-4793	XL	CAT
N CHICAGO	I-94	1	TA	847-395-5580	847-395-6092	XL	CAT
JACKSONVILLE	US 67/IL 104 W		HANNELS TRUCK STOP	217-243-3541	217-243-6904	M	

If we need to make a change, add or subtract - please text 817-583-5503

INDIANA TRUCK STOPS

CITY	HIGHWAY	EXIT	TRUCK STOP	PHONE	FAX	LOT	SCALES
HAUBSTADT	I-64	25	FLYING J TRAVEL PLAZA	812-768-5304	812768-9215	XL	CAT
HAUBSTADT	I-64	25B	LOVES	812-768-5838	812-768-5427	LG	CAT
HAUBSTADT	I-64	25B	PILOT TRAVEL CENTER	812-868-1048	812-868-1050	LG	CAT
LEAVENWORTH	I-64	92	PILOT TRAVEL CENTER	812-739-2002	812-739-4034	M	CAT
MEMPHIS	I-65	16	LOVES	812-294-1379	812-2941408	XL	CAT
MEMPHIS	I-65	16	PILOT TRAVEL CENTER	812-294-4233	812-294-4237	LG	CAT
SEYMOUR	I-65	50A	TA	812-522-6622	812-523-6699	XL	CAT
WHITELAND	I-65	95	FLYING J	317-535-1124	317-535-4123	XL	CAT
WHITELAND	I-65	95	PILOT TRAVEL CENTER	317-535-7656	317-535-3058	LG	CAT
WHITELAND	I-65	95	LOVES	317-535-8686	317-535-9126	LG	CAT
GREENWOOD	I-65	99	ROAD RANGER	815-315-4987	317-865-4867	M	CAT
WHITESTOWN	I-65	130	TA	317-769-3291	317-769-6899	XL	CAT
WHITESTOWN	I-65	133	LOVES	317-769-2330	317-769-2333	M	CAT
LEBANON	I-65	139	FLYING J	765-483-9755	765-483-9762	XL	CAT
REMINGTON	I-65	201	PETRO STOPPING CENTER	219-261-2172	219-261-2025	XL	CAT
REMINGTON	I-65	201	PILOT TRAVEL CENTER	219-261-3786	219-261-3986	LG	CAT
DEMOTTE	I-65	230	LOVES	219-987-2202	219-987-2347	LG	CAT
DEMOTTE	I-65	230	TA	219-987-7520	219-987-7692	M	CAT
HEBRON	I-65	240	FLYING J	219-696-6446	219-696-2456	XL	CAT
HEBRON	I-65	240	PILOT TRAVEL CENTER	219-696-8265	219-696-8281	XL	CAT
FORTVILLE	I-69	14	PILOT TRAVEL CENTER	317-485-6211	317-485-4527	M	CAT
DALEVILLE	I-69	34	PILOT TRAVEL CENTER #446	765-378-0246	765-378-4248	LG	
GASTON	I-69	45	PETRO STOPPING CENTER	765-358-3326	765-358-0207	XL	CAT
MARION	I-69	64	LOVES	765-662-6462	765-662-6778	M	CAT
WARREN	I-69	78	WARREN TRAVEL CENTER	260-375-2888	260-375-7011	XL	CAT
FORT WAYNE	I-69	109A	FORT WAYNE T/P	260-482-7814	260-482-7780	XL	CAT
FREMONT	I-69	157	PETRO STOPPING CENTER	260-495-2523	260-495-2221	XL	CAT
FREMONT	I-69/I-80	157	PILOT TRAVEL CENTER	260-833-1987	260-833-6794	XL	CAT
TERRE HAUTE	I-70	11	PILOT TRAVEL CENTER	812-877-9977	812-877-9978	M	CAT
BRAZIL	I-70	23	PETRO STOPPING CENTER	812-446-2296	812-448-1440	LG	CAT
BRAZIL	I-70	23	PILOT TRAVEL CENTER	812-446-9400	812-446-6116	LG	CAT
CLOVERDALE	I-70	41	CLOVERDALE T/P	765-795-3223	765-795-3243	M	SCALES
BELLEVILLE	I-70	59	LOVES	317-539-5473	317-539-5516	LG	CAT
CLAYTON	I-70	59	TA INDIANAPOLIS WEST	317-539-6515	317-539-5370	LG	CAT
GREENFIELD	I-70	96	PILOT TRAVEL CENTER	317-894-1910	317-894-3499	XL	CAT
SPICELAND	I-70	123	FLYING J	765-987-1833	765-987-7836	XL	CAT
NEW LISBON	I-70	131	HOOSIER HEARTLAND T/C	765-332-2172	765-332-2051	LG	CAT
CAMBRIDGE CITY	I-70	137	AMERICAN PETROLEUM	765-478-5555	765-478-4082	LG	SCALES
RICHMOND	I-70	149-B	LOVES	765-939-8136	765-939-0749	M	CAT
COVINGTON	I-74	4	PILOT TRAVEL CENTER	765-793-7307	765-793-2155	M	CAT
CRAWFORDSVILLE	I-74	39	PILOT TRAVEL CENTER	765-361-9603	765-361-9601	LG	CAT
PITTSBORO	I-74	61	LOVES	317-892-2938	317-892-2956	M	CAT
FAIRLAND	I-74	109	PILOT TRAVEL CENTER	317-392-8771	317-392-8721	M	CAT
SAINT PAUL	I-74	123	LOVES	765-525-6808	765-525-6814		CAT
GREENSBURG	I-74	143	PETRO STOPPING CENTER	812-663-2333	812-663-4270	LG	CAT
SOUTH BEND	I-80/I-90	72	PILOT TRAVEL CENTER	574-272-8212	574-272-9914	M	CAT
MIDDLEBURY	I-80 / I-90	107	TOBACCO TOWN	574-825-7472	574-825-2968	XL	CAT

THE OVERLOAD COMPANION 2017 © FREDA BARBER BOOTH - PILOTCARSTODAY.COM

INDIANA TRUCK STOPS

CITY	HIGHWAY	EXIT	TRUCK STOP	PHONE	FAX	LOT	SCALES
GARY	I-80/I-94	9	PETRO STOPPING CENTER	219-884-1133	219-884-1456	XL	CAT
GARY	I-80/I-94	9	LOVES	219-981-4646	913-752-9679	XL	CAT
LAKE STATION	I-80/I-94	15/16	TA TRAVEL CENTER	619-962-6552	219-962-4573	XL	CAT
LAKE STATION	I-80/I-94	15/16	EXIT 16 WB FLYING J	219-962-8502	219-962-3259	XL	CAT
BURNS HARBOR	I-94	22A	PILOT TRAVEL CENTER	219-787-5705	219-787-9656	LG	CAT
PORTER	I-94	22-B	TA	219-926-4871	219-921-0726	XL	CAT
PORTER	I-94	22-B	TA	219-926-8566	219-395-8477	LG	CAT
MICHIGAN CITY	I-94	34	421 TRAVEL CENTER	219-879-1385	219-871-6024	XL	CAT
GROVERTOWN	US 30	56	GROVERTOWN T/P	574-867-2810	574-867-4815	LG	CAT
ROCHESTER	US-31 BYPS		PARADISE AUTO/TRUCK PLAZA	574-223-5005	574-223-8926	M	
MUNCIE	US-35 S		SOUTHSIDE HOOSIER PETE	765-282-1556	765-281-6423	M	CAT
CARLISLE	US-41 S		CARLISLE PLAZA	812-398-2526	812-398-4207	LG	SCALES
PLYMOUTH	US-30		PILOT TRAVEL CENTER	574-936-6525	574-936-4348	LG	CAT
PERU	US-31/US-24		GALLAGHAN T/P	765-472-1963	765-472-3690	LG	CAT
INDIANAPOLIS	I-465	4	FLYING J	317-783-5543	317-783-5648	XL	CAT
INDIANAPOLIS	I-465	4	PILOT TRAVEL CENTER	317-783-1033	317-783-0851	LG	CAT

If we need to make a change, add or subtract - please text 817-583-5503

WA / NY CERT
CANADA READY
GA/NV AMBER
LA/NM PERMITS
$1M + PA / $2M GL/PL

Rosebudz BigLoadz

Clay City, IN

Rose Green
812-239-1981

LEAD
CHASE
HIGH POLE

APPROVED FOR:
LANDSTAR - TII GROUP - GREATWIDE

THE OVERLOAD COMPANION 2017 © FREDA BARBER BOOTH - PILOTCARSTODAY.COM

IOWA TRUCK STOPS

CITY	HIGHWAY	EXIT	TRUCK STOP	PHONE	FAX	LOT	SCALES
PERCIVAL	I-29	10	PILOT TRAVEL CENTER	712-382-2224	712-382-1556	M	CAT
PERCIVAL	I-29	10	SAPP BROS	712-382-1101	712-382-1145	LG	SCALES
ONAWA	I-29	112	DAVE'S WORLD	712-433-3283	712-433-1413	M	SCALES
DES MOINES	I-35/I-80	125	LOVES TRAVEL STOP	515-276-5200	913-752-9687	XL	CAT
DES MOINES	I-35/I-80	126	PILOT TRAVEL CENTER	515-376-1509	515-276-8599	XL	CAT
DES MOINES	I-35/I-80	136	QUIK TRIP	515-266-1630	515-266-2015	M	CAT
OSCEOLA	I-35	34	PILOT TRAVEL CENTER	641-342-8658	641-342-1782	M	CAT
WILLIAMS	I-35	144	BOONDOCKS	515-854-2411	515-854-2411	M	
WILLIAMS	I-35	144	BROADWAY/FLYING J	515-854-2238	515-854-9124	M	CAT
CLEAR LAKE	I-35	194	PILOT TRAVEL CENTER	641-357-3124	641-357-4939	M	CAT
COUNCIL BLUFFS	I-80	1B	PILOT TRAVEL CENTER	712-322-0088	712-322-0236	M	CAT
COUNCIL BLUFFS	I-80	1B	SAPP BROS	712-366-3000	712-322-6072	L	CAT
COUNCIL BLUFFS	I-80	3	TA	712-366-2217	712-366-6939	M	CAT
AVOCA	I-80	40	WINGS AMERICA TRVL CTR	712-343-4007	712-343-5026	XL	CAT
STUART	I-80	93	CASEY'S	515-523-1003	515-523-1377	M	CAT
ALTOONA	I-80	142	FLYING J	515-967-7878	515-967-5276	XL	
NEWTON	I-80	168	LOVES TRAVEL STOP	641-791-2410	641-791-2438	M	CAT
BROOKLYN	I-80	201	PILOT TRAVEL CENTER	319-685-4221	319-685-4574	M	CAT
BROOKLYN	I-80	201	KWIK STAR	319-685-4411	319-685-6863	XL	CAT
WALCOTT	I-80	284	IOWA 80 TA TRUCKSTOP	563-284-6961	563-284-6989	XL	CAT
WALCOTT	I-80	284	PILOT TRAVEL CENTER	563-284-4100	563-284-4103	XL	
DAVENPORT	I-80	292	FLYING J TRAVEL PLAZA	563-386-7710	563-386-8243	L	CAT
ATALISSA	I-80	265	PILOT TRAVEL CENTER	563-946-3761	563-946-3871	M	CAT
CENTER POINT	I-380	35	CENTER POINT TRAVEL PLAZA	319-849-2700	319-849-1768	L	CAT
ELK RUN HEIGHTS	I-380	68	FLYING J TRAVEL PLAZA	319-291-7714	319-291-7720	M	CAT
ELK RUN HEIGHTS	I-380	68	ROAD RANGER	319-232-0249	319-232-1071	L	CAT
ALGONA	US 18		CHROME TRUCK STOP	515-295-9191	515-295-7000	XL	
AINSWORTH	US 218		FOUR CORNERS	319-657-3200	319-657-4422	L	CAT
FORT DODGE	US-20		AMPRIDE ALL-AROUND T/S	515-573-7512	515-573-8819	L	SCALES
WELTON	US-61	145	QC MART	563-659-8884	563-659-1998	M	CAT
MAQUOKETA	US-61	156	TIMBER CITY TRAVEL PLAZA	563-652-1100	563-652-1105	M	CAT

If we need to make a change, add or subtract - please text 817-583-5503

THE OVERLOAD COMPANION 2017 © FREDA BARBER BOOTH - PILOTCARSTODAY.COM

KANSAS TRUCK STOPS

CITY	HIGHWAY	EXIT	TRUCK STOP	PHONE	FAX	LOT	SCALES
EMPORIA	I-35	127	FLYING J TRAVEL PLAZA	620-343-2717	620-343-3692	L	CAT
BETO JUNCTION	I-35	155	TA BETO JUNCTION	620-265-6311	620-256-6275	XL	CAT
OTTAWA	I-35	183	LOVES TRAVEL STOP	785-242-2882	785-242-2608	M	CAT
OLATHE	I-35	215	STAR FUEL CENTER	913-780-2009	913-780-6503	M	CAT
COLBY	I-70	53	PETRO	785-460-0044	785-460-0045	L	CAT
COLBY	I-70	54	PILOT TRAVEL CENTER	785-460-5832	785-460-5875	L	CAT
OAKLEY	I-70	70	J-J OIL	785-672-3900	785-672-3422	M	CAT
OAKLEY	I-70	76	TA	785-672-4111	785-672-4532	XL	CAT
WAKEENEY	I-70	127	24/7 TRAVEL STORE	785-743-2157	785-743-2267	L	
SALINA	I-70	252	PILOT TRAVEL CENTER	785-825-6787	785-827-3394	XL	CAT
SALINA	I-70	252	PETRO STOPPING CENTER	785-827-9275	785-827-2405	XL	SCALE
SALINA	I-70	253	FLYING J TRAVEL PLAZA	785-825-5300	785-452-9221	L	CAT
JUNCTION CITY	I-70	295	SAPP BROS	785-238-1600	785-238-1601	M	CAT
NEWTON	I-135	31	NEWELL TRUCK PLAZA	316-283-4000	316-283-3789	M	SCALE
DODGE CITY	US-400/US-283		FLYING J TRAVEL PLAZA	620-338-8888	620-338-8829	M	CAT
GARDEN CITY	US-50		U PUMP IT COUNTRY CORNER	620-276-3923	620-275-6251	L	CAT
IOLA	US-54		JUMPSTART TRAVEL CENTER	620-365-8280	620-365-8363	M	CAT
MEADE	US-54 W		MEADE TRUCK PLAZA	620-873-2316	620-873-2062	M	CAT
STAFFORD	US-60	202	STAFFORD AMPRIDE	620-234-6119	620-234-5556		CAT
GARDEN CITY	US-83		GARDEN CITY TRAVEL PLAZA	620-275-4404	620-275-1005	XL	CAT

If we need to make a change, add or subtract - please text 817-583-5503

CON-SPEC, LLC

Tom or Toni
405-604-7828
405-474-2181

3 OK Cert Operators
$2M Insured + PA
LandStar & ATS approved
All Permits & Inspections
(NM, UT, OH, LA, GA, NV)

KENTUCKY TRUCK STOPS

CITY	HIGHWAY	EXIT	TRUCK STOP	PHONE	FAX	LOT	SCALES
PENDLETON	I-21	28	PILOT TRAVEL CENTER	502-743-5496	502-743-5228	XL	CAT
PADUCAH	I-24	3	PILOT TRAVEL CENTER	270-443-2044	270-442-8538	M	CAT
PADUCAH	I-24	16	SOUTHERN PRIDE	270-898-6753	270-898-2754	L	SCALES
CALVERT CITY	I-24	27	LOVES TRAVEL STOP	270-395-0546	270-395-0597	L	CAT
KUTTAWA	I-24	40	HUCK'S TRAVEL CENTER	270-388-8111	270-388-8084	XL	CAT
OAK GROVE	I-24	86	FLYING J TRAVEL PLAZA	270-640-7000	270-640-7060	L	CAT
OAK GROVE	I-24	86	PILOT TRAVEL CENTER	270-439-0153	270-439-0765	L	CAT
OAK GROVE	I-24	89	PILOT TRAVEL CENTER	270-439-1776	270-439-7624	L	CAT
MOUNT STERLING	I-61	113	PILOT TRAVEL CENTER	859-497-4041	859-497-8709	M	CAT
SIMSONVILLE	I-64	28	PILOT TRAVEL CENTER	502-722-5636	502-722-5630	M	CAT
WADDY	I-64	43	FLYING J TRAVEL PLAZA	502-829-9100	502-829-5600	L	CAT
WADDY	I-64	43	LOVES TRAVEL STOP	502-829-0157	502-829-0159	L	CAT
WINCHESTER	I-64	94	APPLE MARKET	859-744-8252	859-744-9756	M	CAT
WINCHESTER	I-64	96	96 TRUCK STOP	859-744-9611	859-744-0904	L	SCALES
MOREHEAD	I-64	133	EAGLE TRAVEL PLAZA	606-783-1828	606-783-1860	M	
GRAYSON	I-64	172	SUPER QUIK	606-474-5142	606-474-8260	XL	
GRAYSON	I-64	172	LOVES TRAVEL STOP	606-474-6009	606--474-0436	M	CAT
RICKWOOD	I-64	175	TA CINCINNATI	859-485-4111	859-485-4772	L	CAT
CANNONSBURG	I-64	185	FLYING J TRAVEL PLAZA	606-928-8383	606-928-4546	XL	CAT
FRANKLIN	I-65	2	FLYING J TRAVEL PLAZA	270-586-3343	270-586-8984	XL	CAT
FRANKLIN	I-65	6	SUDDEN SERVICE	270-586-3248	270-586-0979	XL	SCALES
SMITHS GROVE	I-65	38	SMITH GROVE TRAVEL CENTER	270-563-4713	270-563-4211	XL	CAT
HORSE CAVE	I-65	58	LOVES TRAVEL STOP	270-786-4000	270-786-4201	L	CAT
GLENCOE	I-65	62	EXIT 62 FUEL STOP	859-643-4811	859-643-4826	M	
SONORA	I-65	81	PILOT TRAVEL CENTER	270-369-7300	270-369-8596	XL	CAT
GLENDALE	I-65	86	PETRO STOPPING CENTER	270-369-6579	270-369-6848	XL	CAT
RICHMOND	I-65	95	LOVES TRAVEL STOP	859-624-0882	859-624-0953	M	CAT
LEBANON JUNCTION	I-65	105	PILOT TRAVEL CENTER	502-833-2727	502-833-2729	XL	CAT
SHEPHERDSVILLE	I-65	116	LOVES TRAVEL STOP	502-543-7000	502-543-7080	L	CAT
BROOKS	I-65	121	PILOT TRAVEL CENTER	502-955-5049	502-955-9717	L	CAT
PENDLETON	I-71	28	PILOT TRAVEL CENTER	502-743-5222	502-743-5123	L	CAT
SPARTA	I-71	55	LOVES TRAVEL STOP	859-567-1140	859-567-1713	L	CAT
GLENDALE	I-71	86	PILOT TRAVEL CENTER	270-369-7360	270-369-6991	L	CAT
GEORGETOWN	I-71	129	PILOT TRAVEL CENTER	502-868-7427	502-867-1847	M	CAT
FLORENCE	I-71/I-75	181	TA FLORENCE	859-371-7166	859-283-5743	L	CAT
FRANKLIN	I-75	6	PILOT TRAVEL CENTER	270-586-4149	270-586-9887	M	CAT
WILLIAMSBURG	I-75	11	PILOT TRAVEL CENTER	606-549-0162	606-549-0166	M	CAT

If we need to make a change, add or subtract - please text 817-583-5503

KENTUCKY TRUCK STOPS

CITY	HIGHWAY	EXIT	TRUCK STOP	PHONE	FAX	LOT	SCALES
CORBIN	I-75	29	LOVES TRAVEL STOP	606-526-8099	606-526-1057	L	CAT
CORBIN	I-75	29	PILOT TRAVEL CENTER	606-528-0631	606-379-6480	L	CAT
LONDON	I-75	38	EXIT 38 TRUCK PLAZA	606-864-2163	606-864-6966	M	
LONDON	I-75	41	LONDON A/T CENTER	606-864-6426	606-864-9850	XL	SCALES
LIVINGSTON	I-75	49	49ER FUEL CENTER	606-843-9042	606-843-2004	M	
BEREA	I-75	76	76 FUEL CENTER	859-985-1834	859-985-0484	M	
GEORGETOWN	I-75	129	PILOT TRAVEL CENTER	502-863-2708	502-863-5012	XL	CAT
WALTON	I-75	171	FLYING J TRAVEL PLAZA	859-485-4400	859-485-6886	XL	CAT
MAYSVILLE	KY 9		TOWN-N-COUNTRY BP	606-883-3265	606-883-3575	L	
MORGANTOWN	NATCHER PKWY	26	JUMPIN' JACKS TRAVEL PLAZA	270-526-6227	270-526-6911	M	
MORTONS GAP	US-41	37	PILOT TRAVEL CENTER	270-258-5213	270-258-5387	M	CAT
OWENSBORO	US-60		HILLBILLY'S	270-685-6001	CALL FIRST	XL	CAT
BEAVER DAM	W KY PKWY	75	WK TRUCK STOP	270-274-7991	270-274-7618	M	
CANEYVILLE	W KY PKWY	94	PARKWAY MARATHON	270-879-8517	270-879-8517	M	

MATT WALLACE ENTERPRISES

Bowling Green, KY

We have a Large Network across the US

CO/UT/NY CERT - CO/UT FLAGGING CERT
PERMITTED/EQUIPPED FOR 48 STATES
$1M - $2M INSURED W/ PA ADD-ON

Email: matthew3e@aol.com

Follow me on Facebook!

Lead - Chase - High Pole - Steer

270-320-5345

LOUISIANA TRUCK STOPS

CITY	HIGHWAY	EXIT	TRUCK STOP	PHONE	FAX	LOT	SCALES
VINTON	I-10	4	CASH MAGIC TRUCK STOP	337-589-3989	337-589-4079	M	
VINTON	I-10	7	LOVES TRAVEL STOP	337-589-9858	337-589-9856	M	CAT
SULPHUR	I-10	23	KANGAROO EXPRESS	337-882-1405	337-882-1669	M	
LAKE CHARLES	I-10	36	CHARDELE'S TRUCK PLAZA	337-433-1366	337-433-1350	M	
LAKE CHARLES	I-10	36	CASH MAGIC	337-491-9293	337-493-1088	M	SCALE
IOWA	I-10	43	KING'S TRAVEL STOP	337-582-5464	337-582-4297	M	
IOWA	I-10	43	LOVES TRAVEL STOP	337-582-4528	337-582-3650	M	CAT
JENNINGS	I-10	64	JENNING'S TRAVEL CENTER	337-616-9989	337-616-9992	M	SCALE
EGAN	I-10	76	PETRO 2	337-783-0424	337-783-6946	L	CAT
CROWLEY	I-10	80	EXIT 80 TRAVEL PLAZA	337-783-9792	337-783-3714	M	SCALE
DUSON	I-10	92	SHOP RITE TOBACCO PLUS	337-873-8100	337-873-8462	XL	
LAFAYETTE	I-10	101	TA LAFAYETTE	337-237-0176	337-235-1713	L	CAT
BREAUX BRIDGE	I-10	109	SILVER'S TRAVEL CENTER	337-507-3440	337-507-3449	M	
BREAUX BRIDGE	I-10	109	PILOT TRAVEL CENTER	337-332-1253	337-332-0618	L	CAT
HENDERSON	I-10	115	HENDERSON TRAVEL PLAZA	337-332-2090	337-332-2101	M	
HENDERSON	I-10	115	I-10 TRAVEL CENTER	337-332-6608	337-332-6737	M	
GROSSE TETE	I-10	139	TIGER TRUCK STOP	225-648-2312	225-648-2935	M	
PORT ALLEN	I-10	151	CASH'S TRUCK PLAZA	225-387-3100	225-387-3177	L	SCALE
PORT ALLEN	I-10	151	NINO'S TRUCK STOP	225-383-0799	225-343-3420	M	
PORT ALLEN	I-10	151	LOVES TRAVEL STOP	225-389-9111	225-389-9144	M	CAT
LAPLACE	I-10	209	LAPLACE TRAVEL CENTER	985-651-1800	985-651-1802	XL	SCALE
LAPLACE	I-10	209	PILOT TRAVEL CENTER	985-652-0531	985-652-4141	XL	CAT
NEW ORLEANS	I-10	254	IRISH BAYOU TRAVEL CENTER	504-254-1869	504-254-1822	M	
SLIDELL	I-10	266	TA SIDELL	985-643-9974	985-649-1676	XL	CAT
NEW ORLEANS	I-10	236 B	MARDI GRAS TRUCK STOP	504-945-1204	504-945-3835	L $	SCALE
NEW ORLEANS	I-10	236 B	BIG EASY TRAVEL PLAZA	504-945-5000	504-942-2415	M $	SCALE
SORRENTO	I-10	182	SORRENTO SUPER STOP	225-675-5393	225-675-6820	M	CAT
BATON ROUGE	I-110	8	MADE 2 GO TRUCK STOP	225-775-0069	225-775-0005	M	CAT
DENHAM SPRINGS	I-12	10	PILOT TRAVEL CENTER	225-665-4151	225-665-4122	M	CAT
HAMMON	I-12	40	PETRO STOPPING CENTER	985-542-4981	985-429-5951	XL	CAT
HAMMON	I-12	42	PILOT TRAVEL CENTER	985-345-5476	985-542-5028	M	CAT
GREENWOOD	I-20	3	FLYING J TRAVEL PLAZA	318-938-7744	318-938-5697	XL	CAT
GREENWOOD	I-20	3	LOVES TRAVEL STOP	318-938-8312	318-938-8314	M	CAT
VINTON	I-20	4	LONGHORN TRUCK PLAZA	337-589-5647	337-589-5642	L	SCALE
GREENWOOD	I-20	5	TA GREENWOOD	318-938-5411	318-938-5003	XL	CAT
SHREVEPORT	I-20	8	PETRO STOPPING CENTER	318-686-6111	318-671-6534	XL	CAT
MINDEN	I-20	38	GET-N-GEAUX	318-371-1717	318-377-6927	M	
MINDEN	I-20	49	LOVES TRAVEL STOP	318-371-3790	318-371-3792	L	CAT
MINDEN	I-20	49	TRUCKER'S PARADISE	318-371-1310	318-371-1531	L	
CALHOUN	I-20	103	USA TRAVEL PLAZA	318-644-1559	318-644-5704	M	
WEST MONROE	I-20	112	PILOT TRAVEL CENTER	318-329-3590	318-329-3592	M	CAT
RAYVILLE	I-20	138	PILOT TRAVEL CENTER	318-728-4100	318-728-4236	L	CAT
TALLULAH	I-20	171	TALLULAH TRUCK STOP	318-574-1325	318-574-8787	M	SCALE
TALLULAH	I-20	171	LOVES TRAVEL STOP	318-574-6413	318-574-6416	M	CAT
HAUGHTON	I-20	33P	PILOT TRAVEL CENTER	318-390-9709	318-390-9713	L	CAT
TALLULAH	I20	171	TA TALLULAH	318-574-5900	318-574-4671	L	CAT

LOUISIANA TRUCK STOPS

CITY	HIGHWAY	EXIT	TRUCK STOP	PHONE	FAX	LOT	SCALES
OPELOUSAS	I-49	23	I-49 TRUCK STOP	337-948-3212	337-942-8090	M	
OPELOUSAS	I-49	23	THE QUARTERS	337-948-1946	337-948-6912	M	CAT
OPELOUSAS	I-49	23	167 TRUCK STOP	337-594-8782	337-594-8783	M	
NATCHITOCHES	I-49	138	SHOP-A-LOT	318-357-0365	318-357-0110	M	CAT
FRIERSON	I-49	186	RELAY STATION	318-872-1900	318-872-2317	M	CAT
WHITEVILLE	I-49	40	TIGER TRAX	318-838-7788	318-838-9581	M	
NEW ORLEANS	I-510	2 C	PALACE TRUCK STOP	504-241-0409	504-241-1712	XL	CAT
GREENSBURG	LA-10		BRIDGEMART	225-222-4518	225-222-4898	M	
DEQUINCY	LA-12		TIGERLAND	337-786-3065	337-786-3510	M	
AMITE	LA-16	46	AMITE PLAZA TRUCK STOP	985-748-7870	985-748-4054	XL	CAT
SAINT MARTINVILLE	LA-31		HWY 31 TRUCK STOP	337-394-8428	337-394-4278	M	
SAREPTA	LA-371		TIMBERLAND TRUCK STOP	318-994-3701	318-994-3307	M	CAT
HOUMA	LA-57		HOUMA TRUCK PLAZA	985-857-8070	985-857-9527	M	SCALE
DONALDSONVILLE	LA-70		LUCKY STAR TRUCK STOP	225-473-0903	225-473-0719	M	CAT
ERWINVILLE	US-190		LA EXPRESS	225-627-9200	225-627-6593	M	
PORT ALLEN	US-190		TMI FUEL STOP	225-383-6500	225-336-9753	M	CAT
PORT ALLEN	US-190		PORT ALLEN CHEVRON	225-377-2012	225-387-2776	L	
GRAMERCY	US-61		GOLDEN GROVE SUPER STOP	225-8691212	225-869-6242	M	CAT
SAINT ROSE	US-61		SAINT ROSE TRAVEL CENTER	504-472-0772	504-472-0773	L	CAT
JEANERETTE	US-90	143.5	LANDRY'S AUTO/TRUCK STOP	337-276-3592	337-276-3971	M	CAT
AVONDALE	US-90		AVONDALE TRUCK STOP	504-342-8111	504-342-8112	L $	SCALE
BROUSSARD	US-90		VEGAS STYLE NORTH	337-857-0078	337-857-8526	M	

If we need to make a change, add or subtract - please text 817-583-5503

MAINE - MARYLAND - MASSACHUSETTS TRUCK STOPS

MAINE

CITY	HIGHWAY	EXIT	TRUCK STOP	PHONE	FAX	LOT	SCALES
KITTERY	I-95	2	CIRCLE K	207-451-9780	207-451-9782	M	CAT
AUBURN	I-95	75	CIRCLE K	207-795-5052	207-782-0716	M	CAT
FAIRFIELD	I-95	132	CIRCLE K	207-238-9979	207-238-9918	M	
BANGOR/HERMON	I-95	180	DYSART'S SERVICE	207-942-4878	207-947-3559	XL	SCALE
HOULTON	I-95	302	IRVING BIG STOP	207-532-2948	207-532-2948	M	CAT
BAILEYVILLE	US-1/ME-9		IRVING BIG STOP	207-454-8129	207-454-8370	M	CAT
FARMINGTON	US-2		IRVING OIL	207-778-3701	207-778-4264	M	CAT

MARYLAND

CITY	HIGHWAY	EXIT	TRUCK STOP	PHONE	FAX	LOT	SCALES
GRANTSVILLE	I-68	22	PILOT TRAVEL CENTER	301-895-4536	301-895-4548	M	CAT
GRANTSVILLE	I-68	22	FUEL CITY	301-895-3233	301-895-5876	LG	CAT
HAGERSTOWN	I-70	24	PILOT TRAVEL CENTER	301-582-9004	301-582-9008	LG	CAT
HANCOCK	I-70 / MD 144 E	3	LITTLE SANDY'S HANCOCK TS	301-678-7111	301-678-7336	LG	
HAGERSTOWN	I-81	5B	PILOT TRAVEL CENTER	301-582-6111	301-582-5004	LG	CAT
HAGERSTOWN	I-81	5B	AC&T FUEL CENTER	301-582-2702	301-582-3314	$ XL	CAT
BALTIMORE	I-95	57	TA	410-633-4611	410-633-4613	XL	CAT
PERRYVILLE	I-95	93	PILOT TRAVEL CENTER	410-642-2883	410-378-4941	M	CAT
NORTH EAST	I-95	100	FLYING J	410-287-7110	410-287-7116	XL	CAT
ELKTON	I-95	109A	PATRIOT FARMS FLYING J	443-245-4229	443-485-2048	XL	CAT
ELKTON	I-95	109B	TA	410-398-7000	410-398-9124	XL	CAT
JESSUP	I-95	41A	TA BALTIMORE SOUTH	410-799-3835	410-799-7736	$ XL	CAT
MILLERSVILLE	I-97	10	NEW TRANSIT TS	410-987-1444	410-279-3346	$ M	CAT
NEWBURG	US 301 S	MM 3	ONE STOP TRAVEL PLAZA	301-259-2693	301-259-4861	XL	SCALES
CENTREVILLE	US 301/MD304		TRAILWAY TRUCK STOP	410-758-2444	410-758-0782	LG	SCALES

If we need to make a change, add or subtract - please text 817-583-5503

MASSACHUSETTS

CITY	HIGHWAY	EXIT	TRUCK STOP	PHONE	FAX	LOT	SCALES
STURBRIDGE	I-84	1	PILOT TRAVEL CENTER	508-347-9104	508-347-9165	XL	
STURBRIDGE	I-90/I-84	9/3-A	NEW ENGLAND TRUCK STOP	508-347-7363	508-347-9842	M	SCALE
CHICOPEE	I-90	6	PRIDE TRAVEL CENTER	413-592-6190	413-731-5852	XL	
WESTBOROUGH	I-90	55	WESTBOROUGH PLAZA	508-366-4941	508-366-4237	M	
SPRINGFIELD	I-91	9	PRIDE TRAVEL CENTER	413-733-6126	413-733-2430	M	
WHATELY	I-91	24	WHATELY TRUCK STOP	413-665-8727	413-665-2109	L	
PEABODY	I-95	44	J&H BEST AUTO	978-535-9870	978-535-2889	M $	
LEOMINSTER	I-190	7	MR MIKE'S MINI MART	978-537-9531	978-466-3946	M	
PLAINVILLE	I-495	14	CITCO TRAVEL PLAZA	508-316-0840	508-316-0836	L $	SCALE
WRENTHAM	I-495	14-A	INTERSTATE TRAVEL PLAZA	508-384-9501	508-384-2902	L $	
SHREWSBURY	US-20 / MA140		FLYNN'S TRUCK STOP	508-753-9698	508-753-1532	XL	SCALE

MICHIGAN TRUCK STOPS

CITY	HIGHWAY	EXIT	TRUCK STOP	PHONE	FAX	LOT	SCALES
TEKONSHA	I-69	25	TE-KON TRAVEL PLAZA	517-767-4740	517-767-3430	L	CAT
PERRY	I-69	105	ROAD TRIP OASIS	517-625-1112	517-625-1170	M	CAT
GRAND LEDGE	I-69/I-96	90/81	FLYING J TRAVEL PLAZA	517-627-7504	517-622-4960	XL	CAT
MONROE	I-75	15	TA	734-384-7952	734-240-0453	XL	CAT
MONROE	I-75	18	PILOT TRAVEL CENTER	734-457-3500	734-457-2835	M	CAT
WOODHAVEN	I-75	32	FLYING J TRAVEL PLAZA	734-675-0222	734-675-4973	$ XL	CAT
SAGINAW	I-75	144B	TA	989-777-7650	989-777-9770	M	CAT
SAGINAW	I-75	151	M-81 EXPRESS STOP	989-755-6081	989-755-2473	L	
SAGINAW	I-75	151	FLYING J TRAVEL PLAZA	989-752-6350	989-752-6842	M	CAT
GRAYLING	I-75	251	CHARLIE'S C C	989-348-2700	989-348-5818	XL	CAT
SAWYER	I-94	12	TA SAWYER	269-426-4884	269-426-3719	XL	CAT
SAWYER	I-94	12	DUNES TRUCK PLAZA	269-426-3246	269-426-4209	M	SCALE
BENTON HARBOR	I-94	30	PILOT TRAVEL CENTER	269-925-7547	269-925-7508	L	CAT
MATTAWAN	I-94	66	SPEEDWAY	269-668-3341	269-668-2000	M	CAT
MARSHALL	I-94	110	PIONEER	269-781-6900	269-781-3384	XL	
MARSHALL	I-94	112	LOVES TRAVEL STOP	269-781-9203	269-781-9245	L	CAT
MARSHALL	I-94	115	THE 115 TRUCK STOP	269-781-9616	269-781-7842	L	
PARMA	I-94	128	PARMA TRAVEL CENTER	517-531-8800	517-531-8300	M	CAT
DEXTER	I-94	167	PILOT TRAVEL CENTER	734-426-4618	734-426-7836	L	CAT
DEXTER	I-94	167	PILOT TRAVEL CENTER	734-426-0065	734-426-0339	M	CAT
DEXTER	I-94	167	TA ANN ARBOR	734-426-3951	734-426-8558	XL	CAT
ROMULUS	I-94	200	MADCO TRUCK PLAZA	313-292-2500	313-292-2503	$ XL	CAT
MARYSVILLE	I-94	266	SUNRISE	810-364-5115	810-364-2872	M	CAT
GRAND LEDGE	I-69/I-96	90/81	FLYING J TRAVEL PLAZA	517-627-7504	517-622-4960	XL	CAT
HOLLAND	I-196	49	TULIP CITY TRUCK STOP	616-396-2538	616-3964739	L	CAT
BELLEVILLE	I-275	20	MOBIL TRAVEL CENTER	734-394-1974	734-394-2594	M	CAT
OTTAWA LAKE	US-23	1	23 FUEL STOP	734-856-4674	734-854-6789		CAT
OTTAWA LAKE	US-23	5	PILOT TRAVEL CENTER	734-854-1772	734-854-6912	XL	CAT
NILES	US-31	3	J & D'S TRUCK STOP	269-683-9558	269-695-3165	L	SCALE
GRAND RAPIDS	US-131	75	76 STREET TRUCK PLAZA	616-455-3600	616-281-0905	XL	CAT
HOWARD CITY	US-131	120	M-46 MOBIL TRUCK STOP	231-937-4090	231-937-6194	M	CAT

If we need to make a change, add or subtract - please text 817-583-5503

MINNESOTA TRUCK STOPS

CITY	HIGHWAY	EXIT	TRUCK STOP	PHONE	FAX	LOT	SCALES
ALBERT LEE	I-35	11	LOVES TRAVEL STOP	507-373-3200	507373-3204	M	CAT
ALBERT LEE	I-35/I-90	11	TRAIL'S TA	507-373-4200	507-379-2646	XL	CAT
FAIRBAULT	I-35	59	TRUCKER'S INN TRAVEL PLAZA	507-334-3333	507-334-4688	L	CAT
NORTHFIELD	I-35	69	FLYING J	507-645-6082	507-645-2494	L	CAT
LAKEVILLE	I-35	81	MEGA STOP	952-469-1998	952-469-4637	L	CAT
CARLTON	I-35	235	JUNCTION OASIS	218-384-3531	218-384-4035	M	SCALE
WORTHINGTON	I-90	45	BLUE LINE TRAVEL CENTER	507-372-4038	507-372-4920	M	SCALE
WORTHINGTON	I-90	45	WORTHINTON TRAVEL PLAZA	507-376-4848	507-376-4119	M	CAT
AUSTIN	I-90	179	AUSTIN TRUCK STOP	507-437-6702	507-437-0089	M	CAT
FERGUS FALLS	I-94	50	BIG CHIEF TRUCK STOP	218-739-9648	218-739-4743	M	
ALEXANDRIA	I-94	100	PILOT TRAVEL PLAZA	320-759-3083	320-763-2339	L	CAT
SAUK CENTRE	I-94	127	TRUCKER'S INN	320-352-3692	320-352-5104	XL	CAT
CLEARWATER	I-94	178	PETRO STOPPING CENTER	320-558-2261	320-558-6505	L	CAT
HASTY	I-94	183	OLSON'S TRUCK STOP	763-878-1655	763-878-1675	L	CAT
ROGERS	I-94	207	TA ROGERS	763-428-2277	763-428-2007	L	CAT
SAINT PAUL	I-494	64	STOCKMANS TRUCK STOP	651-455-3044	651-455-1193	L	CAT
SAUK RAPIDS	MN-23 E		SHORT STOP	320-251-4144	320-251-1106	M	
CLARA CITY	MN-7/MN-23		DONNER'S CROSSROADS	320-847-3200	320-847-3200	M	
MOTLEY	US-10/MN-210		BRICKS TRAVEL CENTER	218-385-4620	218-352-6047	M	
SHAKOPEE	US-169/CR-41		HOLIDAY STATION	952-445-2926	952-445-2699	M	CAT
SHAKOPEE	US-169/CR-78		SUPER AMERICA	952-445-4303	952-445-4303	L	
CANNON FALLS	US-52 S/CR-24 E		CANNONBALL TRAVEL PLAZA	507-263-3396	507-263-4698	M	
INNER GROVE	US-52/MN-55		PILOT TRAVEL PLAZA	651-438-3397	651-480-4800	L	CAT

If we need to make a change, add or subtract - please text 817-583-5503

MISSISSIPPI TRUCK STOPS

CITY	HIGHWAY	EXIT	TRUCK STOP	PHONE	FAX	LOT	SCALES
GULFPORT	I-10	31	FLYING J TRAVEL PLAZA	228-868-2711	228-868-3711	XL	CAT
BILOXI	I-10	44	LOVES TRAVEL STOP	228-396-5646	228-396-5648	L	CAT
ESCATAWPA	I-10	69	CONE TRUCK PLAZA	228-474-9492	228-474-8685	XL	CAT
JACKSON	I-20/ EX 45 EB / EX 45A WB		PETRO STOPPING CENTER	601-292-0940	601-292-0947	XL	CAT
JACKSON	I-20/ EX 45 EB / EX 45A WB		PILOT TRAVEL CENTER	601-968-9491	601-968-0699	M	CAT
FLOWOOD	I-20 / EX 47B EB / EX 47 WB		LOVES TRAVEL STOP	601-420-8324	601-420-3581	L	CAT
FLOWOOD	I-20 / EX 47B EB / EX 47 WB		FLYING J TRAVEL PLAZA	601-936-0190	601-936-0196	XL	CAT
MERIDIAN	I-20	129	SPACEWAY TRUCK STOP	601-693-5104	601-693-5169	XL	SCALE
MERIDIAN	I-20/ I-59	150	QUEEN CITY TRUCK STOP	601-482-0233	601-482-0633	M	SCALE
MERIDIAN	I-20/ I-59	151	PILOT TRAVEL CENTER	601-484-5106	601-484-7370	M	CAT
RUSSELL	I-20/ I-59	160	TA MERIDAN	601-483-7611	601-483-8269	L	CAT
TOOMSUBA	I-20/ I-59	165	LOVES TRAVEL STOP	601-632-4006	601-632-0096	M	CAT
McCOMB	I-55	13	LOVES TRAVEL STOP	601-684-3353	601-684-7456	M	CAT
BROOKHAVEN	I-55	42	KASKO TRAVEL CENTER	601-835-0091	601-835-0106	L	CAT
WESSON	I-55	51	COUNTRY JUNCTION	601-643-5705	601-649-5801	XL	
CANTON	I-55	119	LOVES TRAVEL STOP	601-859-9370	601-859-9372	M	CAT
WINONA	I-55	185	PILOT TRAVEL CENTER	662-283-5985	662-283-5906	L	CAT
BATESVILLE	I-55	246	LOVES TRAVEL STOP	662-536-1852	662-563-1855	M	CAT
SENATOBIA	I-55	265	PILOT TRAVEL CENTER	662-560-1973	662-560-0153	M	CAT
LAUREL	I-59	97	84 E TRUCK STOP	601-649-9398	601-649-0809	L	CAT
CORINTH	US-45		45 SOUTH TRUCK STOP	662-287-7784	662-665-9930	M	CAT
COLUMBUS	US-45/MS-182		SPRINT MART	662-241-4996	662-241-4996	M	SCALE
HATTIESBURG	US-49		CORNER FUEL CENTER	601-544-7527	601-544-8909	M	CAT
OLIVE BRANCH	BETHEL ROAD		FLYING J TRAVEL PLAZA	662-895-1001	662-895-0008	M	CAT
NEW ALBANY	US-78	64	PILOT TRAVEL CENTER	662-539-0222	662-539-0212	L	CAT
LUCEDALE	US-98/MS-198		FOUR MILE TRUCKSTOP	601-947-3085	601-947-8299	M	

If we need to make a change, add or subtract - please text 817-583-5503

MISSOURI TRUCK STOPS

CITY	HIGHWAY	EXIT	TRUCK STOP	PHONE	FAX	LOT	SCALES
FAUCETT	I-29	35	FARRIS TRUCK STOP	816-238-5666	816-238-0903	XL	SCALE
SAINT JOSEPH	I-29	44	LOVES TRAVEL STOP	816-279-8870	816-279-8725	L	CAT
SAINT JOSEPH	I-29	44	WIEDMAIER TRUCK STOP	816-232-6701	816-323-6195	M	SCALE
KEARNEY	I-35	26	PILOT TRAVEL CENTER	816-635-4015	816-635-4116	XL	CAT
CAMERON	I-35	54	JONES TRAVEL MART	816-632-7561	816-632-1083	L	CAT
JOPLIN	I-44	4	PETRO STOPPING CENTER	417-624-3400	417-623-0759	XL	CAT
JOPLIN	I-44	4	PILOT TRAVEL CENTER	417-781-0255	417-781-0179	L	CAT
JOPLIN	I-44	11A	FLYING J TRAVEL PLAZA	417-626-7600	417-626-8802	XL	CAT
MOUNT VERNON	I-44	46	TA	417-466-2930	417-466-3587	XL	SCALE
BOIS D' ARC	I-44	61	HOOD'S SERVICE CENTER	417-732-6818	417-732-6820	L	SCALE
STRAFFORD	I-44	88	LOVES TRAVEL STOP	417-736-9043	417-736-9045	L	CAT
STRAFFORD	I-44	88	TA SPRINGFIELD EAST	417-736-2161	417-736-3486	L	SCALE
LEBANON	I-44	127	CLAYTON'S CONOCO	417-588-3869	417-588-1310	XL	SCALE
RICHLAND	I-44	145	PRIME TIME OASIS	573-765-4880	573-765-3669	XL	
SAINT ROBERT	I-44	163	ROAD RANGER	573-336-8703	573-336-8704	XL	CAT
ROLLA	I-44	189	LOVES TRAVEL STOP	573-426-5683	573-426-5402	L	CAT
CUBA	I-44	208	MIDWEST PETROLEUM	573-885-3992	573-885-4892	XL	SCALE
SULLIVAN	I-44	226	FLYING J TRAVEL PLAZA	573-860-8880	573-860-8892	XL	CAT
PACIFIC	I-44	257	PILOT TRAVEL CENTER	636-257-4100	636-257-4107	M	CAT
STEELE	I-55	8	DEERFIELD TRAVEL CENTER	573-695-2810	573-695-2819	L	CAT
HAYTI	I-55	19	PILOT TRAVEL CENTER	573-359-2007	573-359-2031	L	CAT
HAYTI	I-55	19	HAYTI TRAVEL CENTER	573-359-2020	573-359-6285	M	
MARSTON	I-55	40	PILOT TRAVEL CENTER	573-643-2320	573-643-2252	M	CAT
NEW MADRID	I-55	52	BJ's TRAVEL CENTER	573-748-9710	573-748-5099	M	
MATTHEWS	I-55	58	FLYING J TRAVEL PLAZA	573-472-3336	573-471-1161	XL	CAT
MATTHEWS	I-55	58	TA MATTHEWS	573-471-8644	573-471-6927	L	CAT
MATTHEWS	I-55	58	LOVES TRAVEL STOP	573-471-4944	573-471-3155	L	CAT
SCOTT CITY	I-55	91	RHODES TRAVEL CENTER	573-335-8200	573-335-7789	XL	SCALE
HERCULANEUM	I-55	178	QUIK TRIP	636-937-3813	636-937-3813	M	CAT
CHARLESTON	I-57	10	PILOT TRAVEL CENTER	573-683-6056	573-683-6016	M	CAT
CHARLESTON	I-57	12	FLYING J TRAVEL PLAZA	573-683-4153	573-683-4196	LG	CAT
GRAIN VALLEY	I-70	24	CONOCO TRAVEL CENTER	816-443-2027	816-443-2522	M	CAT
OAK GROVE	I-70	28	PETRO STOPPING CENTER	816-690-4455	816-625-4596	XL	CAT
OAK GROVE	I-70	28	TA	816-690-4115	816-625-4555	L	CAT
OAK GROVE	I-70	28	QUIK TRIP	816-690-8569	816-625-3149	M	SCALE
HIGGINSVILLE	I-70	49	PILOT TRAVEL CENTER	660-584-8484	660-584-8486	L	CAT
CONCORDIA	I-70	58	TA	660-463-2001	660-463-2046	L	CAT
BOONVILLE	I-70	101	LOVES TRAVEL STOP	660-882-7770	660-882-7448	L	CAT
BOONVILLE	I-70	101	PILOT TRAVEL CENTER	660-882-9120	660-882-9710	XL	CAT
COLUMBIA	I-70	121	MIDWAY TRUCK PLAZA	573-445-9466	573-445-1040	L	
KINGDOM CITY	I-70	148	GASPER'S TRAVEL PLAZA	573-642-6641	573-642-6124	XL	SCALE
KINGDOM CITY	I-70	148	PETRO STOPPING CENTER	573-642-0676	573-592-1832	XL	CAT
WARRENTON	I-70	188	FLYING J TRAVEL PLAZA	636-456-2001	636-456-2016	XL	CAT
FORISTELL	I-70	203	TA	636-673-2295	636-673-2821	L	CAT
SAINT PETERS	I-70	222	QUIK TRIP	636-970-3029	636-279-3002	M	CAT

MISSOURI (CONT'D) - MONTANA TRUCK STOPS

MISSOURI - PG 2 OF 2

CITY	HIGHWAY	EXIT	TRUCK STOP	PHONE	FAX	LOT	SCALES
KANSAS CITY	I-435	57	FLYING J TRAVEL PLAZA	816-483-7600	816-483-1492	XL	CAT
COLLINS	MO-13		PILOT TRAVEL CENTER	417-275-4796	417-275-4796	M	CAT
WAYLAND	US-136/27		FLYING J TRAVEL PLAZA	660-754-1550	660-754-1556	L	CAT
PALMYRA	US-24-61 S		WILCO FAST BREAK	573-769-3638	573-769-3670	L	CAT
CABOOL	US-60		EL RANCHO TRUCK PLAZA	417-962-3817	417-962-3177	L	CAT
TAYLOR	US-61/6		FAST LANE	573-769-2861	573-769-2657	XL	SCALE
NEELYVILLE	US-67		STATE LINE TRAVEL CENTER	573-989-6494	573-989-6480	XL	
POPLAR BLUFF	US-67/M		HEARTLAND EXPRESS	573-778-0772	573-686-6545	M	CAT
NEVADA	US-71	54	PILOT TRAVEL CENTER	417-667-3271	417-667-4843	M	SCALE
LAMAR	US-71/160		LAMARTI'S TRAVEL CENTER	417-682-6034	417-682-6035	L	SCALE
PECULIAR	US-71/J		FLYING J TRAVEL PLAZA	816-779-8000	816-779-4441	XL	CAT

MONTANA

CITY	HIGHWAY	EXIT	TRUCK STOP	PHONE	FAX	LOT	SCALES
GREAT FALLS	I-15	277	PILOT TRAVEL CENTER	406-452-0342	406-452-0547	LG	CAT
SHELBY	I-15	363	PILOT TRAVEL CENTER	406-434-5491	406-434-7019	XL	CAT
MISSOULA	I-90	96	PILOT TRAVEL CENTER	406-542-0400	406-327-0802	XL	CAT
MISSOULA	I-90	96	CROSSROADS TRAVEL CENTER	406-549-2327	406-721-3719	XL	
MISSOULA	I-90	96	MURALT'S TRAVEL PLAZA	406-728-4700	406-728-1271	LG	CAT
MILLTOWN	I-90	109	TOWN PUMP	406-258-6588	406-258-6693	LG	CAT
ROCKER	I-90	122	TOWN PUMP	406-723-0088	406-723-4940	XL	CAT
THREE FORKS	I-90	274	TOWN PUMP	406-285-3807	406-497-6702	LG	CAT
BELGRADE	I-90	298	FLYING J TRAVEL PLAZA	406-388-4124	406-388-4231	XL	CAT
COLUMBUS	I-90	408	TOWN PUMP	406-322-4833	406-322-5273	LG	
LAUREL	I-90	437	PELICAN TRUCK PLAZA	406-628-4324	406-628-8442	M	CAT
BILLINGS	I-90	455	TOWN PUMP	406-256-8826	406-238-9825	M	SCALE
HARDIN	I-90	495	FLYING J TRAVEL PLAZA	406-665-1237	406-665-3123	M	SCALE
MILES CITY	I-94	138	TOWN PUMP	406-232-2582	406-232-4967	LG	
GLENDIVE	I-94	213	TRAIL STAR TRUCK STOP	406-377-3901	406-377-3901	M	

If we need to make a change, add or subtract - please text 817-583-5503

NEBRASKA - NEVADA TRUCK STOPS

NEBRASKA

CITY	HIGHWAY	EXIT	TRUCK STOP	PHONE	FAX	LOT	SCALES
SIDNEY	I-80	59	SAPP BROS	308-254-3096	308-254-5380	M	
BIG SPRINGS	I-80	107	FLYING J TRAVEL PLAZA	308-889-3686	308-889-3352	XL	CAT
OGALLALA	I-80	126	TA	308-284-3667	308-284-3823	L	CAT
HERSHEY	I-80	164	WESTERN CONVENIENCE	308-368-7368	308-368-7634	M	SCALE
NORTH PLATTE	I-80	179	FLYING J TRAVEL PLAZA	308-532-4555	308-532-8077	L	CAT
NORTH PLATTE	I-80	179	LOVE'S TRAVEL STOP	308-534-4610	308-534-4627	L	CAT
LEXINGTON	I-80	237	NEBRASKALAND	308-324-6374	308-324-3005	XL	
ELM CREEK	I-80	257	PILOT TRAVEL CENTER	308-856-4330	308-856-4457	M	CAT
WOOD RIVER	I-80	300	PILOT TRAVEL CENTER	308-583-2493	308-583-2115	M	
ALDA	I-80	305	TA	308-382-5902	308-382-1229	M	CAT
GRAND ISLAND	I-80	312	BOSSELMAN TRAVEL CENTER	308-382-2288	308-381-7464	XL	CAT
AURORA	I-80	332	LOVE'S TRAVEL STOP	402-694-2802	402-694-2807	M	CAT
YORK	I-80	353	PETRO STOPPING CENTER	402-362-1776	402-362-4424	XL	CAT
LINCOLN	I-80	395	DON&RANDY SHOEMAKER'S	402-438-4800	402-474-2630	XL	SCALE
GREENWOOD	I-80	420	CUBBY'S TRAVEL PLAZA	402-944-7055	402-944-2844	M	CAT
GRETNA	I-80	432	FLYING J TRAVEL PLAZA	402-332-4483	402-332-4576	XL	CAT
OMAHA	I-80	440	SAPP BROS	402-895-2121	402-895-2123	XL	SCALE
SCOTTS BLUFF	NE-71		WESTERN TRAVEL TERMINAL	308-635-7374	308-635-9651	M	SCALE
FREMONT	US-30/US-77		SAPP BROS	402-721-7620	402-721-7142	M	SCALE
NORFOLK	US-81		CUBBY'S TRAVEL PLAZA	402-371-5337	402-371-1126	M	SCALE
COLUMBUS	US-81/US-30		T-BONE TRUCK STOP	402-563-2933	402-564-2886	M	

NEVADA

CITY	HIGHWAY	EXIT	TRUCK STOP	PHONE	FAX	LOT	SCALES
PRIMM	I-15	1	WHISKEY PETE'S TRUCK STOP	702-679-6614	702-874-1510	XL	CAT
LAS VEGAS	I-15	33	TA LAS VEGAS	702-361-1176	702-361-6349	L	CAT
LAS VEGAS	I-15	37	WILD WEST TRUCK PLAZA	702-736-2289	702-739-6099	XL	SCALE
LAS VEGAS	I-15	46	MORTEN'S TRUCK STOP	702-649-2001	702-649-7964	XL	SCALE
LAS VEGAS	I-15	48	PILOT TRAVEL CENTER	702-644-1600	702-644-8432	M	CAT
LAS VEGAS	I-15	54	PETRO STOPPING CENTER	702-632-2636	702-632-2641	XL	CAT
LAS VEGAS	I-15	64	LOVES TRAVEL STOP	702-643-7398	702-643-8567	M	CAT
SPARKS	I-80	19	TA SPARKS	775-359-0550	775-359-2068	XL	CAT
SPARKS	I-80	21	PETRO STOPPING CENTER	775-355-8888	775-353-8605	XL	CAT
FERNLEY	I-80	46	PILOT TRAVEL CENTER	775-575-5115	775-575-4619	L	CAT
FERNLEY	I-80	46	LOVES TRAVEL STOP	775-575-2200	775-575-2215	M	CAT
MILL CITY	I-80	149	TA MILL CITY	775-538-7311	775-538-7319	XL	CAT
WINNEMUCCA	I-80	173	PILOT TRAVEL CENTER	775-625-2800	775-625-2814	XL	CAT
WINNEMUCCA	I-80	176	FLYING J TRAVEL PLAZA	775-623-0111	775-6230120	L	SCALE
BATTLE MOUNTAIN	I-80	231	FLYING J TRAVEL PLAZA	775-635-5424	775-635-0371	L	CAT
CARLIN	I-80	280	PILOT TRAVEL CENTER	775-754-6384	775-754-6025	M	CAT
WELLS	I-80	352	FLYING J TRAVEL PLAZA	775-752-2400	775-752-2406	XL	SCALE
WELLS	I-80	352	LOVES TRAVEL STOP	775-752-9915	775-752-9917	M	CAT
WEST WENDOVER	I-80	410	PILOT TRAVEL CENTER	775-664-3400	775-664-3347	L	CAT
HAWTHORNE	US-95		HAWTHORNE SHELL	775-945-4664	775-945-4461	M	
SEARCHLIGHT	US-95		TERRIBLE HERBS	702-298-1080	702-297-1913	M	

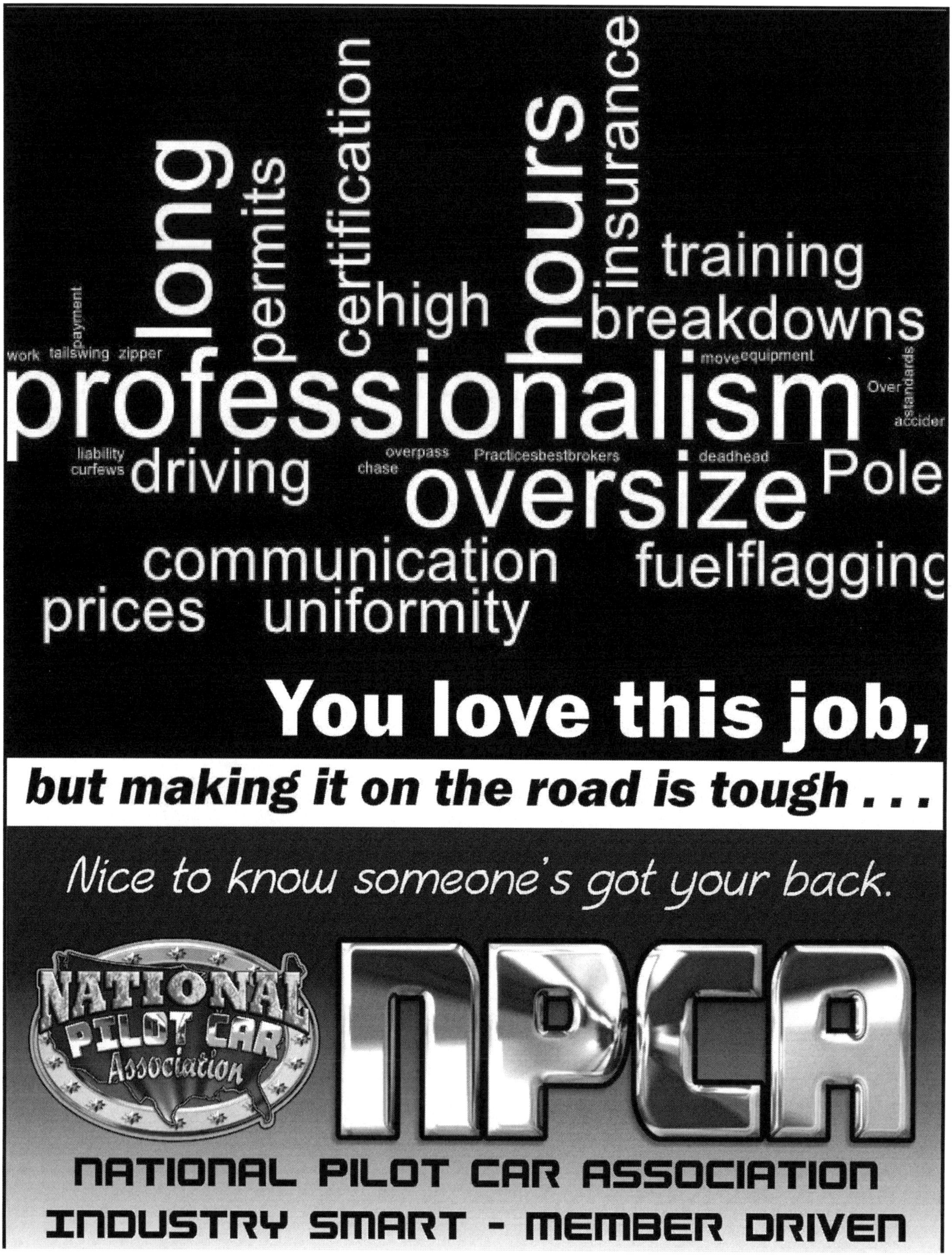
long
permits
certification
high
hours
insurance
training
breakdowns
payment
work tailswing zipper
move equipment
standards
professionalism
Over
accider
liability
curfews
driving
overpass
chase
Practicesbestbrokers
deadhead
oversize
Pole
communication
fuelflagging
prices
uniformity
You love this job,
but making it on the road is tough . . .
Nice to know someone's got your back.
NATIONAL PILOT CAR Association
NPCA
NATIONAL PILOT CAR ASSOCIATION
INDUSTRY SMART - MEMBER DRIVEN

NEW HAMPSHIRE - NEW JERSEY TRUCK STOPS

NEW HAMPSHIRE

CITY	HIGHWAY	EXIT	TRUCK STOP	PHONE	FAX	LOT	SCALES
LEBANON	I-89	18	EXIT 18 JIFFY MART	603-448-5510	603-443-5182	M	CAT
LONDONDERRY	I-93	5	RMZ TRUCKSTOP	603-437-9929	603-435-4008	M	
BOW JUNCTION	I-93	11	PILOT TRAVEL CENTER	603-223-6885	603-223-6884	M	
BOW JUNCTION	I-93	12	BOW JUNCTION IRVING	603-228-6175	603-226-1934	M	
GREENLAND	I-95	3	TA	603-436-3636	603-436-1575	L	CAT

NEW JERSEY

CITY	HIGHWAY	EXIT	TRUCK STOP	PHONE	FAX	LOT	SCALES
BLOOMSBURY	I-78	7	TA	908-479-4136	908-479-4533	LG	CAT
COLUMBIA	I-80	4C	TA	908-496-4124	908-496-4809	XLG	CAT
PAULSBORO	I-295	18	TA	856-423-5500	856-423-6261	XLG	CAT
CARNEY'S POINT	I-295	2C	ALL AMERICAN GAS	856-299-9300	856-299-4253	LG	CAT
CARNEY'S POINT	I-295	2C	FLYING J	856-351-0080	856-351-0293	XLG	CAT
BORDENTOWN	I-295	57	LOVES	609-324-1005	609-324-1933	LG	CAT
BORDENTOWN	NJ TPK / I-295	7	PETRO STOPPING CENTER	609-298-6070	609-227-5033	XLG	CAT

If we need to make a change, add or subtract - please text 817-583-5503

SABATTUS, ME
"CHECK YOUR MIRRORS"
MPC - MIKE'S PILOT CAR
207-240-2535
NEW YORK AND WASHINGTON STATE CERTIFIED

**LEAD - CHASE - HIGH POLE - STEER
NY/WA CERT - PASSPORT**

f Mikespilotcar   mpcs1243@gmail.com

NEW MEXICO TRUCK STOPS

CITY	HIGHWAY	EXIT	TRUCK STOP	PHONE	FAX	LOT	SCALES
LORDSBURG	I-10	24	PILOT	575-542-3100	575-542-3111	LG	CAT
LORDSBURG	I-10	24	FLYING J	575-542-3320	575-542-3324	XLG	SCALES
DEMING	I-10	68	PETRO	575-544-2222	575-544-2230	XLG	SCALES
LAS CRUCES	I-10	139	TA	505-527-7400	505-523-6876	XLG	CAT
VADO	I-10	155	NATIONAL	575-233-3695	575-233-4550	LG	
VADO	I-10	155	SUNMART	575-233-2988	575-233-4096	LG	
LEMITAR	I-25	156	ROADRUNNER TRVL PLAZA	575-838-1400	575-835-2302	LG	
SAN FELIPE PUEBLO	I-25	252	SAN FELIPE TRVL CTR	505-867-4706	505-867-4709	LG	
SPRINGER	I-25	419	RUSSELL'S TRUCK STOP	575-483-5004	575-483-2824	M	CAT
GALLUP	I-40	16	TA	505-863-6801	505-722-5106	M	CAT
JAMESTOWN	I-40	39	PILOT	505-722-6655	505-722-2674	XLG	CAT
MILAN	I-40	79	PETRO	505-285-6648	505-876-2830	XLG	CAT
PUEBLO OF ACOMA	I-40	102	SKY CITY TRUCKSTOP / CASINO	505-552-5700	505-552-5702	XLG	
CASA BLANCA	I-40	108	DANCING EAGLE TRVL CTR / CASINO	505-552-7477	505-552-7721	XLG	
RIO PUERCO	I-40	140	ROUTE 66 TRUCKSTOP/CASINO	505-352-7876	505-352-7868	XLG	TIGHT CURVE
ALBUQUERQUE	I-40	153	FLYING J	505-831-2001	505-833-0464	XLG	CAT
MORIARTY	I-40	194	TA	505-832-4421	505-832-6643	XLG	CAT
MORIARTY	I-40	197	LISA'S TRUCK STOP	505-832-4455	505-832-6641	LG	
SANTA ROSA	I-40	277	TA	575-472-3432	505-472-3717	XLG	CAT
SANTA ROSA	I-40	277	LOVES	575-472-1160	575-472-1162	LG	
TUCUMCARI	I-40	333	FLYING J	575-461-6590	575-461-3879	XLG	SCALES
TUCUMCARI	I-40	333	LOVES	575-461-1900	575-461-1910	XLG	CAT
SAN JON	I-40	356	CHISUM TRAVEL CTR	575-576-9252	575-576-2107	M	
SAN JON	I-40	356	DHILLON TRAVEL CTR	575-576-2444	575-576-2791	XLG	
GLEN RIO	I-40	369	RUSSELL'S TRUCK STOP	575-576-8700	575-576-0008	XLG	CAT
ALBUQUERQUE	I-40 / I-25 TA		TA	505-884-1066	505-881-0245	LG	CAT
CARLSBAD	US-285 S		UNITED FUEL TRUCK STOP	575-885-6130	575-887-0466	M	
ALAMOGORDO	US-54		KENT TRAVEL CENTER	575-437-0000	575-437-3750	M	CAT
BLOOMFIELD	US-64 W		GIANT	505-632-2975	505-632-2975	M	
CLOVIS	4700 US-60		LOVES	575-762-2966	575-763-0050	M	CAT
ROSWELL	US-285 / US 70		CHISUM TRAVEL CTR	575-623-9930	575-627-2036	M	CAT

If we need to make a change, add or subtract - please text 817-583-5503

NEW YORK TRUCK STOPS

CITY	HIGHWAY	EXIT	TRUCK STOP	PHONE	FAX	LOT	SCALES
MEXICO	I-81	34	SUNUP TRUCK PLAZA	315-625-4238	315-625-4800	LG	CAT
BINGHAMTON	I-81 X-2 WB; X-3 SB		LOVES	607-651-9153	607-651-9286	LG	CAT
BINGHAMTON	I-81 X-2 WB; X-3 SB		TA	607-775-3500	607-775-1528	LG	CAT
SYRACUSE	I-81 X-25; I-90 X-36		PILOT	315-424-0124	315-424-0126	M	CAT
MAYBROOK	I-84	5	TA	845-457-3163	845-457-3492	XLG	CAT
NEWBURGH	I-84	6	PILOT TRAVEL CENTER	845-567-1722	845-567-1773	M	CAT
KANONA	I-86	37	PILOT TRAVEL CENTER	607-776-2012	607-776-4179	LG	CAT
KANONA	I-86	37	WILSON FARMS	607-776-7634	607-776-2884	LG	CAT
WILTON	I-87	16	WILTON TRAVEL PLAZA	518-584-1444	518-584-1376	XLG	CAT
LEWIS	I-87	32	BETTY BEAVER TRUCK STOP	518-873-2083	518-873-9588	LG	
PLATTSBURGH	I-87	36	EXIT 36 TRUCKSTOP	518-561-3256	518-563-6463	M	SCALES
CHAMPLAIN	I-87	43	PETERBILT / CHAMPLAIN T/C	518-298-3835	518-298-2375	LG	CAT
CANAAN	I-90	3B	CANAAN SUPER STOP	518-781-4144	518-781-4695	$M	CAT
ROTTERDAM	I-88 X-25 I-90 X-25A		PILOT TRAVEL CENTER	518-356-5616	518-356-5634	M	CAT
FULTONVILLE	I-90	28	FULTONVILLE SUPER STOP	518-853-4601	518-853-4934	$M	CAT
FULTONVILLE	I-90	28	TA	518-853-3411	518-853-4523	LG	CAT
LIVERPOOL	I-90	36	PILOT TRAVEL CENTER	315-424-0124	315-424-0126	M	CAT
WATERLOO	I-90	41	PETRO	315-220-6550	315-539-9350	XLG	CAT
PEMBROKE	I-90	48A	FLYING J	585-599-4430	585-599-4436	XLG	CAT
PEMBROKE	I-90	48A	TA	585-599-4577	585-599-3456	LG	CAT
BUFFALO CHEEKTOWAGA	I-90	52E	JIM'S TRUCK PLAZA	716-683-9931	716-684-5450	LG	SCALES
DANSVILLE	I-390	5	TA	585-335-6023	585-335-2090	LG	CAT
HENRIETTA	I-390	12	WESTERN TRUCK STOP	585-334-7510	585-334-6017	$M	CAT
SYRACUSE	I-690 8EB 10WB		QUICK WAY	315-422-6818	315-472-0118	M	
ALBANY	NY TPK X-23; I-787 X-2 NB		PLAZA 23	518-462-1234	518-462-2103	M	CAT

If we need to make a change, add or subtract - please text 817-583-5503

Green's Flag Car Service

Newark Valley, NY

607-761-7495   607-323-5140

High Pole - Chase - Lead

NY/WA Certified

NORTH CAROLINA TRUCK STOPS

CITY	HIGHWAY	EXIT	TRUCK STOP	PHONE	FAX	LOT	SCALES
DUNN	I-95	71	KANGAROO	910-892-3642	910-980-2364	M	CAT
NAPLES	I-26	44	MOUNTAIN ENERGY	828-687-0402	828-654-8771	XL	CAT
LAKE JUNALUSKA	I-40	24	PILOT TRAVEL CENTER	828-627-8611	828-627-9499	M	CAT
CANDLER	I-40	37	TA	828-665-1156	828-665-2569	M	CAT
MARION	I-40	86	LOVES	828-652-3422	828-652-3806	M	CAT
CONOVER	I-40	133	WILCO-HESS TRAVEL PLAZA	828-465-2525	828-465-2504	M	CAT
MOCKSVILLE	I-40	170	HORN'S AMBEST TRVL CTR	336-751-3815	336-751-4994	XL	SCALES
WHITSETT	I-40 / I-85	138	TA	336-449-6060	336-449-0301	XL	CAT
HAW RIVER	I-40 / I-85	150	WILCO-HESS TRAVEL PLAZA	336-578-2610	336-578-2334	XL	CAT
HAW RIVER	I-40 / I-85	150	FLYING J	336-578-2427	336-578-0804	XL	CAT
MEBANE	I-40 / I-85	152	PILOT TRAVEL CENTER	919-563-4999	919-563-4929	LG	CAT
MEBANE	I-40 / I-85	157	PETRO	919-304-7476	919-304-8136	XL	CAT
CHARLOTTE	I-77	16 B	CHARLOTTE TRAVEL PLAZA	704-597-7980	704-597-2492	M	CAT
TROUTMAN	I-77	42	WILCO-HESS TRAVEL PLAZA	704-528-4104	704-528-6876	M	CAT
MT AIRY	I-77 EX-100, I-74 EX-6		BRINTLE TRAVEL PLAZA	336-352-3161	336-352-3169	XL	SCALES
CHARLOTTE	I-85	39	PILOT TRAVEL CENTER	704-358-1006	704-358-1506	M	CAT
KANNAPOLIS	I-85	63	PILOT TRAVEL CENTER	704-938-6800	704-938-6900	M	CAT
SALISBURY	I-85	71	WILCO-HESS TRAVEL PLAZA	704-638-0855	704-637-0314	M	CAT
LINWOOD	I-85	86	BILLS TRUCK STOP	336-956-4494	336-956-3588	M	CAT
HENDERSON	I-85	220	CHEX TRUCK STOP	252-492-7031	252-492-6170	$ LG	CAT
DUNN	I-95	75	PILOT TRAVEL CENTER	910-892-0106	910-892-2084	XL	CAT
DUNN	I-95	77	LOVES	910-892-7230	910-892-2623	M	CAT
KENLY	I-95	105	BIG BOYS TRUCK STOP	919-284-4046	919-284-4161	XL	SCALES
KENLY	I-95	106	FLYING J	919-284-4548	919-284-4214	LG	CAT
KENLY	I-95	106	PETRO	919-284-5121	919-284-5121	XL	CAT
KENLY	I-95	106	WILCO-HESS TRAVEL PLAZA	919-284-6109	919-284-3153	XL	CAT

If we need to make a change, add or subtract - please text 817-583-5503

CAROLINA REO SERVICES

CHRIS SHUPE
(704) 202-3127

STACY MORTON
(704) 754-2911

For Your Pilot Car Needs to, through and from North Carolina!

MULTIPLE CARS

carolinareoservices@hotmail.com

WIDE LOAD
OVERSIZE LOAD
LONG LOAD

High pole
WA-NY-NC Cert
GA Amber
LA-NM Inspected
Insured - $1M

THE OVERLOAD COMPANION 2017 © FREDA BARBER BOOTH - PILOTCARSTODAY.COM

NORTH DAKOTA TRUCK STOPS

CITY	HIGHWAY	EXIT	TRUCK STOP	PHONE	FAX	LOT	SCALES
FARGO	I-29	62	LOVES	701-281-0761	701-281-0763	LG	CAT
FARGO	I-29	62	FLYING J	701-282-7766	701-282-7259	XLG	CAT
FARGO	I-29	66	STAYMART TRAVEL CENTER	701-298-3500	701-235-0797	XLG	
GRAND FORKS	I-29	138	FLYING J	701-738-0017	701-746-4342	LG	CAT
GRAND FORKS	I-29	141	STAYMART TRAVEL CENTER	701-746-1356	701-772-4414	M	CAT
PAMBINA	I-29	215	GASTRAK	701-825-6275	701-825-6278	M	CAT
BEACH	I-94	1	FLYING J	701-872-4737	701-872-4985	M	CAT
MANDAN	I-94	147	FREEWAY 147 TRUCKSTOP	701-663-6922	701-663-2565	LG	SCALES
BISMARCK	I-94	161	STAYMART TRAVEL CENTER	701-222-1675	701-222-0268	M	CAT
JAMESTOWN	I-94	258	SUPER PUMPER	701-252-4732	701-252-3865	M	
JAMESTOWN	I-94	260	JAMESTOWN TRUCK PLAZA	701-252-3523	701-252-6321	M	SCALES
TOWER CITY	I-94	307	TOWER TRAVEL CENTER	701-749-6000	701-749-6004	M	
FARGO	I-94	348	PETRO	701-282-8105	701-282-9382	XLG	SCALES
FARGO	I-94	349	FLYING J	701-282-7766	701-282-7259	XLG	CAT
WILLISTON	US-85		LOVES	701-572-3578	701-572-3987	XLG	CAT

If we need to make a change, add or subtract - please text 817-583-5503

ASAP PILOT CAR SERVICE

Carolyn Johnson
Owner/Operator

406-600-9703

Asappilotcarservice.com
Montanatrafficcontrol.com

**HIGH POLE
PROFESSIONAL SURVEYS
MONTANA TRAFFIC CONTROL**

**EQUIPPED VHF RADIO
CANADA-LEGAL
WA CERTIFIED
$3M INSURED**

OHIO TRUCK STOPS - PG 1 OF 2

CITY	HIGHWAY	EXIT	TRUCK STOP	PHONE	FAX	LOT	SCALES
NEW PARIS	I-70	1	PETRO	937-437-8593	937-437-1066	XL	CAT
EATON	I-70	10	PILOT TRAVEL CENTER	937-456-6303	937-456-6497	M	CAT
EATON	I-70	10	TA	937-456-5521	937-456-1273	XL	CAT
LONDON	I-70	79	PILOT TRAVEL CENTER	614-879-4128	64-879-4137	XL	CAT
LONDON	I-70	79	TA (COLUMBUS WEST)	740-852-3810	740-852-4559	XL	CAT
COLUMBUS	I-70	94	PILOT TRAVEL CENTER	614-308-9195	614-308-9673	LG	CAT
KIRKERSVILLE	I-70	122	FLYING J	740-964-9601	740-964-9611	XL	CAT
HEBRON	I-70	126	PILOT TRAVEL CENTER	740-928-5588	740-928-6032	M	CAT
HEBRON	I-70	126	TA	740-467-2900	740-467-3358	XL	CAT
SONORA	I-70	160	LOVES	740-453-8506	740-453-8579	LG	CAT
JEFFERSONVILLE	I-71	65	TA	740-948-2365	740-948-2564	XL	CAT
JEFFERSONVILLE	I-71	65	LOVES	740-948-2342	740-948-2372	LG	CAT
JEFFERSONVILLE	I-71	69	FLYING J	740-426-9136	740-426-9156	LG	CAT
BERKSHIRE	I-71	131	FLYING J	740-965-9835	740-965-9770	XL	CAT
BERKSHIRE	I-71	131	PILOT TRAVEL CENTER	740-965-5540	740-965-5641	M	CAT
MARENGO	I-71	140	PILOT TRAVEL CENTER	419-253-1400	419-253-1402	M	CAT
BURBANK	I-71	204	PILOT TRAVEL CENTER	330-948-4571	330-948-4575	LG	CAT
BURBANK	I-71	204	LOVES	330-624-1000	330-624-1003	M	CAT
SEVILLE	I-71	209B	TA LODI	330-769-2053	330-769-4609	XL	CAT
SEVILLE	I-71	209B	PILOT TRAVEL CENTER	330-769-4220	330-769-2202	XL	CAT
MONROE	I-75	29	STONY RIDGE TRAVEL CENTER	513-539-7700	513-539-7254	XL	CAT
FRANKLIN	I-75	36	PILOT TRAVEL CENTER	937-746-4488	937-743-3006	XL	CAT
WAPAKONETA	I-75	111	TA	419-738-2550	419-738-8996	LG	CAT
BEAVER DAM	I-75	135	FLYING J	419-643-8001	419-643-8106	XL	CAT
BEAVER DAM	I-75	135	PILOT TRAVEL CENTER	419-463-6023	419-643-6085	LG	CAT
VAN BUREN	I-75	164	PILOT TRAVEL CENTER	419-299-3381	419-299-3096	M	CAT
NORTH BALTIMORE	I-75	167	LOVES	419-257-2600	419-257-2797	M	CAT
NORTH BALTIMORE	I-75	167	PETRO STOPPING CENTER	419-257-3744	419-257-5128	XL	CAT
TOLEDO	I-75	210	PILOT TRAVEL CENTER	419-729-3985	419-729-0905	M	CAT
NORTH LIMA	I-76	232	PILOT TRAVEL CENTER	330-549-9203	330-549-1930	M	CAT
CALDWELL	I-77	25	PILOT TRAVEL CENTER	740-732-5656	740-732-1404	M	CAT
NEWCOMERSTOWN	I-77	65	NEWCOMERSTOWN TRUCK STOP	740-498-5161	740-498-4302	LG	SCALES
NEW PHILADELPHIA	I-77	81	EAGLE AUTO/TRUCK PLAZA	330-339-4157	330-339-4141	M	CAT
NORTH CANTON	I-77	111	TA	330-494-7507	330-494-7911	LG	CAT
RICHFIELD	I-77	146	PILOT TRAVEL CENTER	330-659-2020	330-659-2021	LG	CAT
LEAVITTSBURG	I-80	14	SHORT STOP TRUCK PLAZA	330-898-7505	330-898-7505	LG	CAT
AUSTINTOWN	I-80	223B	PILOT TRAVEL CENTER	330-505-3532	330-505-3548	XL	CAT
YOUNGSTOWN	I-80	223A	TA YOUNGSTOWN	330-793-4426	330-793-7889	XL	CAT
GIRARD	I-80	226	PETRO STOPPING CENTER	330-544-6400	330-505-3742	XL	CAT
GIRARD	I-80	226	PILOT TRAVEL CENTER	330-530-8500	330-530-8318	M	CAT
HUBBARD	I-80	234	LOVES	330-534-1800	330-534-1810	LG	CAT
HUBBARD	I-80	234	TRUCK WORLD	330-534-8166	330-534-0448	XL	SCALES
HUBBARD	I-80	234	FLYING J	330-534-3774	330-543-4372	XL	CAT

If we need to make a change, add or subtract - please text 817-583-5503

OHIO TRUCK STOPS - PG 2 OF 2

CITY	HIGHWAY	EXIT	TRUCK STOP	PHONE	FAX	LOT	SCALES
MILLBURY	I-80	1B	PETRO STOPPING CENTER	419-837-9725	419-837-3326	XL	CAT
MILLBURY	I-280	1B	LOVES	419-837-0071	419-837-0076	LG	CAT
STONY RIDGE	I-80 / I-90	71	TA TOLEDO	419-837-5017	419-837-6186	XL	CAT
STONY RIDGE	I-80 / I-90	71	PILOT TRAVEL CENTER	419-837-5091	419-837-5658	M	CAT
AVON	I-90	151	PILOT TRAVEL CENTER	440-934-0110	440-934-1168	M	CAT
AUSTINBURG	I-90	223	PILOT TRAVEL CENTER	440-275-3303	440-275-3311	LG	CAT
AUSTINBURG	I-90	223	FLYING J	440-275-1515	440-275-3289	XL	CAT
KINGSVILLE	I-90	235	TA	440-224-2035	440-224-0446	XL	CAT
CONNEAUT	I-90	241	LOVES	440-593-6816	440-593-6815	M	CAT
AUSTINBURG	I-90	223	FLYING J	440-275-1515	440-275-3289	XL	CAT
MILLBURY	I-80	1B	PETRO STOPPING CENTER	419-837-9725	419-837-3326	XL	CAT
MILLBURY	I-280	1B	LOVES	419-837-0071	419-837-0076	LG	CAT
LAKE TOWNSHIP	I-280	1B	FLYING J	419-837-2100	419-837-2199	XL	CAT
SARDINIA	OH 32	13	TANKERS TRAVEL CENTER	937-446-3740	937-446-2090	M	CAT
MERCER	US 127 / US 33		MOTOR INN TRUCK PLAZA	419-363-3376	419-363-2106	LG	
CIRCLEVILLE	US 23		PILOT TRAVEL CENTER	740-420-8942	740-420-3972	M	CAT
JACKSON	US 35/CR 41 S		A & A TRUCKSTOP	740-286-1288	740-286-2340	XL	CAT
NAPOLEON	US 6/24 BYP	41	PETRO STOPPING CENTERS	419-599-3835	419-599-3833	LG	CAT
NAPOLEON	US 6/24 BYP	41	PILOT TRAVEL CENTER	419-599-0043	419-599-0051	M	CAT
NAPOLEON	US 6/24 BYP	41	TA	419-599-0065	419-592-0988	LG	CAT
UPPER SANDUSKY	US-30 E		PILOT TRAVEL CENTER	419-294-2971	419-294-3812	M	CAT

If we need to make a change, add or subtract - please text 817-583-5503

A1 Escort Services
NO LOAD TOO BIG...NO ROAD TOO FAR

John T Widrig
Owner/Operator

JOHN.WIDRIG@GMAIL.COM
484-560-3589

2253 Irma Drive
Allentown, PA 18109

FULLY CERTIFIED & INSURED

OKLAHOMA TRUCK STOPS

CITY	HIGHWAY	EXIT	TRUCK STOP	PHONE	FAX	LOT	SCALES
ARDMORE	I-35	32	LOVES	580-226-0973	580-226-0833	LG	CAT
ARDMORE	I-35	33	FLYING J	580-226-3833	580-226-3546	LG	CAT
BILLINGS	I-35	203	CIMARRON TRAVEL PLAZA	580-725-3252	580-725-3514	XLG	SCALE
TONKAWA	I-35	211	LOVES	580-628-5335	580-628-3449	M	CAT
TONKAWA	I-35	214	CASEY'S	580-628-2828	580-628-2271	M	SCALE
BRAMAN	I-35	231	KANZA TRAVEL PLAZA	580-385-2137	580-385-2159	LG	SCALE
OKLAHOMA CITY	I-35/ I-40	127	PETRO	405-228-7040	405-228-7047	XLG	CAT
OKLAHOMA CITY	I-35/I-44	137	FLYING J	405-475-9440	405-475-9435	LG	CAT
ERICK	I-40	7	LOVES	580-526-3345	580-526--3302	M	CAT
SAYRE	I-40	20	FLYING J	580-928-2216	580-928-2354	XLG	CAT
SAYRE	I-40	26	TA	580-928-5571	580-928-3087	M	CAT
CLINTON	I-40	66	DOMINO FOOD/FUEL	580-323-0341	NA	M	
WEATHERFORD	I-40	84	FAST LANE TRAVEL PLAZA	580-772-5618	580-772-8815	LG	CAT
HINTON	I-40	101	LOVES	405-542-3836	405-542-3847	LG	CAT
OKLAHOMA CITY	I-40	140	FLYING J	405-324-5000	405-324-7181	XLG	CAT
OKLAHOMA CITY	I-40	140	PILOT TRAVEL CENTER	405-440-1048	405-440-1093	XLG	CAT
OKLAHOMA CITY	I-40	140	TA	405-324-5376	405-324-8037	LG	CAT
OKLAHOMA CITY	I-40	142	TA	405-787-7411	405-789-2561	XLG	CAT
WEBBERS FALLS	I-40	287	LOVES	918-464-2865	918-464-2866	M	
ROLAND	I-40	325	PILOT TRAVEL CENTER	918-427-0895	918-427-0862	LG	CAT
ROLAND	I-40	325	CHEROKEE NATION TRVL PLAZA	918-427-2650	918-427-2904	M	CAT
CHECOTAH	I-40	264B	CHECOTAH TRUCK STOP	918-473-4551	918-473-4551	LG	
CHECOTAH	I-40 / US-69	264B	FLYING J	918-473-1243	918-473-1957	LG	CAT
TULSA	I-44	222A	QUIKTRIP	918-446-5500	918-446-6888	M	CAT
TULSA	I-44	238	QUIKTRIP	918-234-0380	918-438-9328	M	CAT
TULSA	I-44 X-236/ I-244 X-15 E		FLYING J	918-437-5477	918-437-5660	XLG	CAT

If we need to make a change, add or subtract - please text 817-583-5503

CON-SPEC, LLC

Tom or Toni
405-604-7828
405-474-2181

3 OK-Certified Operators
$2M insured / PA add-on
LandStar / ATS approved
GA, LA & NV permits
NM, UT, & OH Inspections

LEAD - CHASE - HIGH POLE

OREGON TRUCK STOPS

CITY	HIGHWAY	EXIT	TRUCK STOP	PHONE	FAX	LOT	SCALES
PHOENIX	I-5	24	PETRO	541-535-3372	541-512-3041	LG	CAT
MEDFORD	I-5	30	WITHAM TRUCK STOP	541-779-0792	541-779-0751	M	SCALES
CENTRAL POINT	I-5	33	PILOT	541-664-7001	541-664-7006	LG	CAT
CANYONVILLE	I-5	99	SEVEN FEATHERS T/C	541-839-4868	541-839-3101	XL	SCALES
ROSEBURG	I-5	119	LOVES	541-679-1916	541-679-2083	M	CAT
RICE HILL	I-5	148	PILOT	541-849-2133	541-849-2137	XL	CAT
COBURG	I-5	199	TA	541-485-2137	541-683-2301	XL	SCALES
HALSEY	I-5	216	PIONEER VILLA TRUCK PLAZA	541-369-2801	541-369-2356	XL	
BROOKS	I-5	263	PILOT	503-463-1114	503-463-0409	LG	CAT
AURORA	I-5	278	TA	503-678-2111	503-678-2571	XL	CAT
PORTLAND	I-5	307	JUBITZ TRAVEL CENTER	503-283-1111	503-240-5830	XL	SCALES
TROUTDALE	I-84	17	LOVES	503-665-7741	503-666-4999	XL	CAT
TROUTDALE	I-84	17	TA	503-666-1588	503-669-4148	XL	CAT
BIGGS JUNCTION	I-84	104	PILOT	541-739-2174	541-739-2479	M	CAT
HERMISTON	I-84	180	SHELL	541-567-5900	541-567-6056	LG	
HERMISTON	I-84	182	SPACE AGE TRUCK CENTER	541-564-6254	541-564-8583	LG	SCALES
STANFIELD	I-84	188	PILOT	541-449-1403	541-449-1430	LG	CAT
MISSION	I-84	216	ARROWHEAD TRUCK PLAZA	541-276-8080	541-276-8765	XL	SCALES
LAGRANDE	I-84	265	FLYING J	541-963-3432	541-663-9822	M	SCALES
BAKER CITY	I-84	304	BAKER TRUCK CORRAL	541-523-3952	541-523-2048	XL	SCALES
ONTARIO	I-84	374	LOVES	541-823-8282	541-823-2514	M	CAT
ONTARIO	I-84	376A	PILOT	541-889-3580	541-889-4117	LG	CAT
HINES	US-20		EDDIE'S TRUCK/AUTO CTR	541-573-2639	541-573-1765	M	SCALES
CHEMULT	US 97		PILOT	541-365-0991	541-365-0995	M	CAT
LAPINE	US-97		GORDY'S TRUCK STOP	541-536-6055	541-536-6110	XL	SCALES

If we need to make a change, add or subtract - please text 817-583-5503

TERRY KLOES
KELSO, WA
360-261-0847
kloes2u@yahoo.com

CDL - TWIC
$1M AUTO / GL - PA ADD-ON
GA - NV AMBER / LA - UT INSPECTED
FULLY EQUIPPED
HANDS-FREE CELL
CAMERAS - GARMIN GPS

KLOES 2 U, LLC
Oversize Load Escorting
"Long Haul Specialists"

DISPATCHER: ROBIN BAKER
360-773-2661

DRIVER: NICK CAMPBELL
360-998-0173

APPROVED FOR THESE COMPANIES
COMBINED — JONES MOTOR GROUP
CONTRACTOR'S CARGO — JOULE YACHT
LONESTAR - LANDSTAR — ATI & AFFILIATES
LEAVITTS — ART HEAVY-HAUL

PENNSYLVANIA TRUCK STOPS - PG 1 OF 2

CITY	HIGHWAY	EXIT	TRUCK STOP	PHONE	FAX	LOT	SCALES
CLAYSVILLE	I-70	6	PETRO	724-663-7718	724-663-5013	XL	CAT
BENTLEYVILLE	I-70	32B	PILOT TRAVEL CENTER	724-239-5855	724-239-5801	LG	CAT
SMITHTON	I-70	49	SMITHTON TRUCK STOP	724-872-4224	724-872-7885	XL	CAT
SMITHTON	I-70	49	FLYING J	724-872-4050	724-872-9471	LG	CAT
BREEZEWOOD	I-70/I-76	161	PILOT TRAVEL CENTER	814-735-4076	814-735-4823	XL	CAT
BREEZEWOOD	I-70/I-76	161	TA	814-735-4011	814-735-4494	XL	CAT
CARLISLE	I-76	226	LOVES	717-240-0055	717-240-0057	LG	CAT
CARLISLE	I-76	226	FLYING J	717-243-6659	717-243-2510	XL	CAT
CARLISLE	I-76	226	PETRO	717-249-1919	717-258-2339	XL	CAT
FRYSTOWN	I-78	10	PILOT TRAVEL CENTER	717-933-4146	717-933-5008	XL	CAT
HAMBURG	I-78	23	LOVES	610-488-8840	610-488-8843	M	CAT
ALLENTOWN	I-78	49B	TREXLAR PLAZA	610-395-6000	610-398-3600	$ LG	CAT
MT MORRIS	I-79	1	BFS TRUCK AUTO PLAZA	724-324-5385	724-324-9148	M	CAT
PORTERSVILLE	I-79	99	PILOT TRAVEL CENTER	724-368-3028	724-368-3059	M	CAT
BARKEYVILLE	I-80	29	TA	814-786-7988	814-786-9000	LG	CAT
EMLENTON	I-80	42	EMLENTON TRAVEL PLAZA	724-867-1511	724-867-6882	M	SCALES
BROOKVILLE	I-80	78	TA	814-849-3051	814-849-5259	XL	CAT
BROOKVILLE	I-80	78	FLYING J	814-849-2992	814-849-4715	XL	CAT
FALLS CREEK	I-80	97	PILOT TRAVEL CENTER	814-375-6046	814-375-6047	LG	CAT
CLEARFIELD	I-80	120	SAPP BROS	814-765-5321	814-765-2650	XL	SCALES
KYLERTOWN	I-80	133	KWIK FILL A/T PLAZA	814-345-6119	814-345-6469	LG	SCALES
MILESBURG	I-80	158	TA	814-355-7561	814-355-3197	LG	CAT
LAMAR	I-80	173	FLYING J	570-726-4080	570-726-4363	XL	CAT
LAMAR	I-80	173	PILOT TRAVEL CENTER	570-726-7618	570-726-5092	M	CAT
LAMAR	I-80	173	TA	570-726-4996	570-726-4172	XL	CAT
MILTON	I-80	215	FLYING J	570-742-2663	877-395-0850	XL	SCALES
BLOOMSBURG	I-80	232	TA	570-784-9400	570-784-9441	M	CAT
MIFFLINVILLE	I-80	242	LOVES	570-752-9013	570-752-9015	M	CAT
SYBERTSVILLE	I-80	256	PILOT TRAVEL CENTER	570-788-3262	570-788-2163	M	CAT
HICKORY RUN	I-80	274	HICKORY RUN TRAVEL PLAZA	570-443-4437	570-443-4430	LG	CAT

If we need to make a change, add or subtract - please text 817-583-5503

RICHARD'S FLAG CAR SERVICE

Richard R. Bitts, Jr., Owner   Lancaster, PA

Easy access to Harrisburg, York, Hanover, Carlisle, Philadelphia PA, NJ, DE & Port of Baltimore, MD

Goes Anywhere - Anytime

610-960-8437

LEAD - CHASE

OVERSIZE & SUPERLOADS

Deadhead up to 100 miles with approved mileage rate

- UT & NY Cert
- Passport
- PA Insured $1Mil
- LandStar Approved

- CDL License
- TWIC
- Dual Dash Cams
- GPS

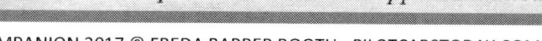

richardsflagcar@comcast.net

PENNSYLVANIA TRUCK STOPS - PG 2 OF 2

CITY	HIGHWAY	EXIT	TRUCK STOP	PHONE	FAX	LOT	SCALES
GREENCASTLE	I-81	5	TA	717-597-7762	717-597-3506	XL	CAT
CARLISLE	I-81	52	FLYING J	717-243-6659	717-243-2510	XL	CAT
CARLISLE	I-81	52	PETRO	717-249-1919	717-258-2339	XL	CAT
HARRISBURG	I-81	77	TA	717-652-4556	717-657-5012	LG	CAT
HARRISBURG	I-81	77	WILCO-HESS	717-545-5517	717-901-6191	LG	CAT
JONESTOWN	I-81	90	LOVES	717-861-7390	717-861-7393	M	CAT
PINE GROVE	I-81	100	GOOSEBERRY FARMS T/C	570-345-8800	570-345-8855	LG	CAT
RAVINE	I-81	104	RACEWAY TRUCK STOP	570-345-2498	570-345-4760	M	CAT
DORRANCE	I-81	155	BLUE RIDGE PLAZA	570-868-3117	570-868-6094	M	
DUPONT	I-81	175	PILOT TRAVEL CENTER	570-655-4116	570-655-2479	M	CAT
HARFORD	i-81	217	LIBERTY TRAVEL PLAZA	570-434-2330	570-434-9330	M	
HARFORD	I-81	217	PENN-CAN SERVICE	570-434-2608	570-434-9091	M	
GIBSON	I-81	219	FLYING J	570-465-2974	570-465-2979	LG	CAT
DUPONT	I-81	178B	PETRO	570-654-5111	570-657-3682	XL	CAT
STERLING	I-84	17	HOWE'S TRUCK PLAZA	570-689-4345	570-689-2347	LG	CAT
ERIE	I-90	27	PILOT	814-864-8536	814-866-0332	LG	CAT
HARBORCREEK	I-90	35	TA	814-899-1919	814-899-7918	XL	CAT
NORTH EAST	I-90	45	KWIK FILL A/T PLAZA	814-725-9661	814-725-2594	M	CAT
WILAWANA	NY-17	59A	DANDY MINIMART	570-888-4320	570-688-6545	M	CAT
COOPERSBURG	PA-309		309 TRUCK STOP	610-282-4011	610-282-4011	$ M	
LIBERTY	US-15/PA-414		LIBERTY EXXON	570-324-5440	570-324-6310	M	CAT
MILROY	US-322		TOM'S TRAVEL CENTER	717-667-6002	717-667-6093	LG	CAT
EAST EARL	US-322/PA 897		MARTIN'S TRAILSIDE EXPRESS	717-354-9486	717-354-0225	M	

If we need to make a change, add or subtract - please text 817-583-5503

Chappies Piloting Service
Boalsburg, PA

814-548-6243

Lead - Chase - Third car

$1M Insured   NY / WA Certified

Give Chappies a call today!

RHODE ISLAND - SOUTH CAROLINA (PG 1 OF 2) TRUCK STOPS

RHODE ISLAND

CITY	HIGHWAY	EXIT	TRUCK STOP	PHONE	FAX	LOT	SCALES
W GREENWICH	I-95	5B	RI'S ONLY 24 HR TA PLAZA	401-397-4580	401-397-3844	$ XLG	SCALES

SOUTH CAROLINA 1 OF 2

CITY	HIGHWAY	EXIT	TRUCK STOP	PHONE	FAX	LOT	SCALES
GRANITEVILLE	I-20	11	KENT'S KORNER	803-232-1732	803-564-5938	M	CAT
BATESBURG	I-20	39	HILL VIEW T/S	803-657-6383	803-657-6583	L	CAT
GILBERT	I-20	44	TRUCKSTOP 44	803-657-5542	803-657-6414	M	
COLUMBIA	I-20	70	FLYING J	803-735-9006	803-735-0917	XL	CAT
COLUMBIA	I-20	71	COLUMBIA T/P	803-786-7680	803-735-8065	L	CAT
LUGOFF	I-20	92	PILOT TRAVEL CENTER	803-438-5175	803-438-3947	M	CAT
BISHOPVILLE	I-20	116	WILCO-HESS T/P	803-428-2248	803-428-2004	M	CAT
CAMPOBELLO	I-26	5	PILOT TRAVEL CENTER	864-472-2128	803-333-3333	M	CAT
INMAN	I-26	10	HOT SPOT	864-472-3199	864-472-9559	XL	CAT
ENOREE	I-26	38	HOT SPOT	864-969-7081	864-969-7214	M	CAT
CLINTON	I-26	52	PILOT TRAVEL CENTER	864-833-4555	864-833-3765	M	CAT
NEWBERRY	I-26	76	LOVES	803-321-1125	803-321-3952	LG	CAT
POMARIA	I-26	82	KANGAROO EXPRESS	803-405-0409	803-405-1841	XL	CAT
POMARIA	I-26	82	WILCO-HESS	803-321-2392	803-321-2549	M	CAT
ST MATTHEWS	I-26	139	WILLCO-HESS	803-874-4340	803-874-1695	M	CAT
ORANGEBURG	I-26	154A	LOVES	803-534-1663	803-534-1636	M	CAT
BOWMAN	I-26	159	PILOT TRAVEL CENTER	803-829-3541	803-829-3352	LG	CAT
HARLEYVILLE	I-26	172A	E-Z SHOP	843-636-9740	843-563-4022	M	SCALES
SUMMERVILLE	I-26	199B	PILOT TRAVEL CENTER	843-486-5770	843-486-5702	M	CAT
CAYCE	I-26/I-77	115/1	PILOT TRAVEL CENTER	803-739-2921	803-739-4521	LG	CAT
GREAT FALLS	I-77	48	GRAND CENTRAL STATION	803-482-2118	803-482-7118	LG	SCALES
GREAT FALLS	I-77	48	WILLCO-HESS	803-482-6844	803-482-6353	LG	CAT
RICHBURG	I-77	65	CRENCO AUTO TRUCK STOP	803-789-6484	803-789-6484	LG	
ROCK HILL	I-77	73	FLYING J	803-328-5700	803-909-5800	LG	CAT
FORT MILL	I-77	83	LOVES	803-802-7130	803-802-7134	M	CAT
FAIR PLAY	I-85	4	BUBBA'S TRUCK STOP	864-287-8520	864-287-8530	M	CAT
FAIR PLAY	I-85	4	LOVES	864-287-5589	864-287-5983	LG	CAT
PIEDMONT	I-85	35	PILOT TRAVEL CENTER	864-845-8177	864-845-8178	M	CAT
DUNCAN	I-85	63	PILOT TRAVEL CENTER	864-433-1221	864-433-1210	M	CAT
DUNCAN	I-85	63	TA	864-433-0711	864-433-1495	XL	CAT
COWPENS	I-85	83	MR WAFFLE A/T/P	864-463-6464	864-463-6471	XL	SCALES
GAFFNEY	I-85	90	PILOT TRAVEL CENTER	864-206-0050	864-206-0052	LG	CAT
GAFFNEY	I-85	96	KANGAROO EXPRESS	864-487-5641	864-487-7253	M	

If we need to make a change, add or subtract - please text 817-583-5503

Flying Squirrel Escorts Service

Bill Musall - Owner
Fingerville, SC

(864) 208-4752

HIGH POLE - STEER (CLASS A CDL)

TWIC - PASSPORT - $1M INSURED + PA

LANDSTAR APPROVED

ALL LIGHT PERMITS

Multiple cars located in the South to Midwest

SOUTH CAROLINA (PG 2 OF 2) & SOUTH DAKOTA TRUCK STOPS

SOUTH CAROLINA

CITY	HIGHWAY	EXIT	TRUCK STOP	PHONE	FAX	LOT	SCALES
BLACKSBURG	I-85	102	FLYING J	864-839-5934	864-839-5942	XL	CAT
BLACKSBURG	I-85	104	LOVES	864-839-1543	434-589-4259	L	CAT
BLACKSBURG	I-85	106	WILCOHESS T/P	864-936-9984	864-936-9397	M	CAT
CANADAYS	I-95	68	CIRCLE C T/S	843-538-5443	843-538-3520	L	SCALES
DUNN	I-95	75	SADLER	910-892-0106	910-892-2084	M	SCALES
ST GEORGE	I-95	77	FLYING J	843-563-8989	843-563-8986		SCALES
ST GEORGE	I-95	82	WILCO-HESS	843-563-6306	843-563-6307	XL	CAT
MANNING	I-95	119	TA	803-473-2568	803-473-2822	M	CAT
FLORENCE	I-95	164	TA	843-292-0386	843-667-6976	M	CAT
FLORENCE	I-95	164	PILOT TRAVEL CENTER	843-662-2646	843-662-2893	M	CAT
FLORENCE	I-95	169	FLYING J	843-669-5736	843-269-2079	XL	CAT
FLORENCE	I-95	170	PILOT TRAVEL CENTER	843-662-6972	843-662-7013	M	CAT
LATTA	I-95	181A	FLYING J	843-752-5047	843-752-7265	XL	CAT
LATTA	I-95	181B	WILCO-HESS	843-752-9169	843-752-9157	XL	CAT
DILLON	I-95	190	LOVES	843-774-2255	843-774-2292	L	CAT
ORANGEBURG	US-301/601		HENRY'S	803-534-5808	803-533-1243	M	CAT

SOUTH DAKOTA

CITY	HIGHWAY	EXIT	TRUCK STOP	PHONE	FAX	LOT	SCALES
VERMILLION	I-29	26	COFFEE CUP FUEL STOP	605-624-2062	605-624-4840	LG	SCALES
SIOUX FALLS	I-29	83	FLYING J	605-977-1438	605-977-1538	XL	CAT
WATERTOWN	I-29	177	STONES TRUCKSTOP	605-882-1484	605-886-0925	LG	
RAPID CITY	I-90	55	PILOT TRAVEL CENTER	605-348-7070	605-348-3438	LG	CAT
RAPID CITY	I-90	61	FLYING J	605-342-5450	605-342-3011	XL	CAT
MURDO	I-90	192	PILOT TRAVEL CENTER	605-669-2465	605-669-2859	M	
MITCHELL	I-90	332	I-90 PILOT TRAVEL CENTER	605-996-3371	605-996-3910	XL	CAT
SPENCER	I-90	353	FUEL MART	605-449-4626	605-449-4627	M	
SIOUX FALLS	I-90	399	LOVES	605-332-7611	605-335-1567	LG	CAT
ELKTON	SD-13/US-14		SKYVIEW JUNCTION	605-542-4961	605-542-4971	M	
HERMOSA	SD-79/SD-40		FLYING J	605-255-4555	605-255-4522	M	
BRISTOL	US-12W		DALE'S SVC HOT SPOT	605-492-3681	605-492-3682	M	
ABERDEEN	US-12W / US281		STARLITE TRUCK STOP	605-225-5913	605-226-9072	M	
WOLSEY	US-14/281	331	281 TRAVEL CENTER	605-883-4586	605-883-4588	M	
BELLE FOURCHE	US-85 N / US 212 W		MID-AMERICA TRAVEL PLAZA	605-892-2063	605-892-2267	M	

If we need to make a change, add or subtract - please text 817-583-5503

TENNESSEE TRUCK STOPS - PG 1 OF 2

CITY	HIGHWAY	EXIT	TRUCK STOP	PHONE	FAX	LOT	SCALES
NASHVILLE	I-24	48	TA	615-244-3682	615-244-9419	XL	CAT
ANTIOCH	I-24	62	TA	615-641-6731	615-641-3353	LG	CAT
MURFREESBORO	I-24	81	PILOT TRAVEL CENTER	615-907-9595	615-907-3982	LG	CAT
CHRISTANA	I-24	89	LOVES	615-904-7303	615-904-1634	LG	CAT
MANCHESTER	I-24	114	I-24 TRUCK PLAZA	931-728-6710	93-172-8669	M	CAT
MONTEAGLE	I-24	135	WILCO-HESS	931-924-5111	931-924-2964	XL	CAT
LONGTOWN	I-40	35	LONGTOWN	901-594-5103	901-594-5272	LG	CAT
STANTON	I-40	42	PILOT TRAVEL CENTER	901-466-3535	901-465-7822	LG	CAT
DENMARK	I-40	68	TA	731-424-5591	731-4247160	XL	CAT
JACKSON	I-40	85	PILOT TRAVEL CENTER	731-422-5545	731-422-5780	LG	CAT
JACKSON	I-40	87	LOVES	731-422-0901	731-421-0405	LG	CAT
HOLLADAY	I-40	126	NORTH 40 TRUCK STOP	731-584-5163	731-584-5163	XL	SCALES
HURRICANE MILLS	I-40	143	PILOT TRAVEL CENTER	931-296-7180	931-296-7719	XL	CAT
DICKSON	I-40	172	PILOT TRAVEL CENTER	615-446-4600	615-446-0763	M	CAT
FAIRVIEW	I-40	182	FLYING J	615-799-4116	615-799-4120	XL	CAT
KINGSTON SPRINGS	I-40	188	PETRO	615-952-3208	615-952-6917	M	CAT
LEBANON	I-40	238	PILOT TRAVEL CENTER	615-453-8866	615-453-8860	XL	CAT
LEBANON	I-40	239A	UNCLE PETE'S	615-449-0030	615-443-1725	LG	CAT
GORDONSVILLE	I-40	258	WILCO-HESS	615-683-3417	615-683-3415	M	CAT
BAXTER	I-40	280	LOVES	931-858-6150	931-858-6157	M	CAT
COOKEVILLE	I-40	288	SUPER TRUCK & TRAVEL	931-526-3314	931-528-8278	XL	SCALES
CROSSVILLE	I-40	320	PILOT TRAVEL CENTER	931-787-1901	931-787-1905	LG	CAT
CROSSVILLE	I-40	320	PLATEAU TRAVEL PLAZA	931-484-7498	931-484-7498	M	SCALES
KNOXVILLE	I-40	398	PILOT TRAVEL CENTER	865-544-1067	865-544-1138	LG	CAT
DANDRIDGE	I-40	412	LOVES	865-397-5040	865-397-0620	M	CAT
DANDRIDGE	I-40	417	PILOT TRAVEL CENTER	865-397-3547	865-397-3699	M	CAT
KNOXVILLE	I-40/ I-75	374	TA	865-966-6781	865-966-4401	LG	CAT
KNOXVILLE	I-40/ I-75	374	PILOT TRAVEL CENTER	865-966-0445	865-966-2918	M	CAT
KNOXVILLE	I-40/75	369	FLYING J	865-531-7400	865-531-7982	XL	CAT
KNOXVILLE	I-40/75	369	PETRO	865-693-6542	865-560-3730	XL	CAT
KNOXVILLE	I-40/75	369	TA	865-531-7676	865-531-8701	XL	CAT

If we need to make a change, add or subtract - please text 817-583-5503

Lucky Ladies Pilot Cars, LLC

Cassandra Bostock
931-241-2241
Jodi Hurd-Cavanagh
231-388-0813

Lead / Chase
High Pole
Route Survey
$1M GL/PL/Commercial

MATT WALLACE ENTERPRISES
Bowling Green, KY

Lead - Chase - High Pole - Steer

270-320-5345

We have a Large Network across the US

CO/UT/NY CERT - CO/UT FLAGGING CERT
PERMITTED/EQUIPPED FOR 48 STATES
$1M - $2M INSURED W/ PA ADD-ON

Email: matthew3e@aol.com

Follow me on Facebook!

TENNESSEE TRUCK STOPS - PG 2 OF 2

CITY	HIGHWAY	EXIT	TRUCK STOP	PHONE	FAX	LOT	SCALES
NEWPORT	I-40	432B	TIME-OUT TRAVEL CTR	423-623-7440	423-623-2823	M	CAT
CORNERSVILLE	I-65	22	TENNESSEAN TRUCK STOP	931-293-4171	931-293-2490	LG	CAT
COLUMBIA	I-65	46	LOVES	931-388-1217	931-388-1257	LG	CAT
FRANKLIN	I-65	61	TA	615-794-8406	615-790-6510	LG	CAT
MCDONALD	I-75	20	PILOT TRAVEL CENTER	423-476-3892	423-476-5430	LG	CAT
CHARLESTON	I-75	33	LOVES	423-780-9171	423-780-9173	LG	CAT
NIOTA	I-75	56	WILCO-HESS	423-568-2529	423-568-2715	XL	CAT
PIONEER	I-75	141	PILOT TRAVEL CENTER	423-562-5000	423-566-1335	XL	CAT
WHITE PINE	I-81	4	PILOT TRAVEL CENTER	865-674-8570	865-674-8572	LG	CAT
WHITE PINE	I-81	4	WILCO-HESS	865-674-2900	865-674-2066	LG	CAT
BAILEYTON	I-81	36	TA	423-234-4451	423-234-6201	XL	CAT
NASHVILLE	TN-155		PILOT TRAVEL CENTER	615-350-7225	615-350-7318	LG	CAT
CAPLEVILLE	US-78		PILOT TRAVEL CENTER	901-202-5520	901-202-5522	LG	CAT
CAPLEVILLE	US-78		PILOT TRAVEL CENTER	901-366-0337	901-366-1712	M	CAT

If we need to make a change, add or subtract - please text 817-583-5503

T-N-T Pilot Car, LLC

Terry Miller - Owner
Corapeake, NC

Cell: 813-401-3447   **Office: 252-465-2036**

We have cars where you need them!

Certified NC - VA - NY - FL
Fully Insured
High Pole - Lead - Chase
GA / NV Light Permit
LA Inspection Permit
FL - 36" Cones
BPS Equipped
TWIC

LandStar & Greentree Approved

Website: www.tntpilotcar.webs.com
Email: tntpilotcar@gmail.com

We Go the Extra Mile for You!

TEXAS TRUCK STOPS - PG 1 OF 3

CITY	HIGHWAY	EXIT	TRUCK STOP	PHONE	FAX	LOT	SCALES
ANTHONY	I-10	0	FLYING J	915-886-2737	915-886-3522	M	CAT
ANTHONY	I-10	0	PILOT TRAVEL CENTER	915-886-3090	915-886-3404	M	CAT
ANTHONY	I-10	0	LOVES	915-886-3915	915-886-3634	LG	CAT
VINTON	I-10	2	PETRO 2 -	915-886-5761	915-886-5767	M	CAT
EL PASO	I-10	37	FLYING J	915-852-4141	915-852-4101	LG	CAT
EL PASO	I-10	37	LOVES	915-852-4021	915-852-2370	LG	CAT
EL PASO	I-10	37	PETRO STOPPING CENTER	915-859-3911	915-790-4528	XL	CAT
VAN HORN	I-10	138	CHEVRON TRUCK STOP	432-283-2343	432-283-1003	LG	
VAN HORN	I-10	140A	PILOT TRAVEL CENTER	432-283-8067	432-283-8071	M	CAT
VAN HORN	I-10	140B	LOVES	432-283-2881	432-283-2883	M	CAT
FORT STOCKTON	I-10	257	STRIPES	432-336-8861	432-336-8568	LG	
OZONA	I-10	372	CIRCLE BAR TRUCK CORRAL	325-392-2637	325-392-5880	XL	CAT
JUNCTION	I-10	456	GENES GO TRUCK STOP	325-446-9528	325-446-8110	LG	
SAN ANTONIO	I-10	582	PETRO STOPPING CENTER	210-661-9416	210-662-5325	XL	CAT
SAN ANTONIO	I-10	582	PILOT TRAVEL CENTER	210-661-5353	210-661-4660	M	CAT
SAN ANTONIO	I-10	583	TA	210-310-0145	210-661-3109	XL	CAT
SAN ANTONIO	I-10	583	FLYING J	210-666-2266	210-666-2280	XL	CAT
CONVERSE	I-10	585	SAN ANTONIO TRAVEL CENTER	210-661-2336	210-310-7722	M	SCALES
BROOKSHIRE	I-10	732	FLYING J	281-934-4133	281-934-4153	LG	CAT
KATY	I-10	737	LOVES	281-391-5556	281-391-3559	M	CAT
BAYTOWN	I-10	789	LOVES	281-426-6569	281-426-6982	XL	CAT
BAYTOWN	I-10	789	FLYING J	281-424-7226	281-424-7730	XL	CAT
BAYTOWN	I-10	789	TA	281-424-7772	281-424-3372	XL	CAT
BAYTOWN	I-10	793	I-10 TRAVEL CENTER	281-421-2283	281-421-7879	M	SCALES
BAYTOWN	I-10	797	CONOCO TRAVEL STOP	281-576-4472	281-576-0193	LG	CAT
BEAUMONT	I-10	848	PETRO STOPPING CENTER	409-842-9600	409-842-7228	XL	CAT
BEAUMONT	I-10	858	GATEWAY TRUCK PLAZA	409-783-2755	409-783-2765	M	CAT
ORANGE	I-10	873	FLYING J	409-883-9465	409-886-8224	XL	CAT
ORANGE	I-10	873	PILOT TRAVEL CENTER	409-745-1124	409-745-3336	LG	CAT
PECOS	I-20	42	FLYING J	432-445-9436	432-445-7171	XL	SCALES
ODESSA	I-20	115	LOVES	432-335-7062	432-335-7064	M	CAT
BIG SPRING	I-20	177	TA	432-264-4444	432-263-0418	LG	CAT
SWEETWATER	I-20	242	TA	325-235-8488	325-235-3703	XL	SCALES
MERKEL	I-20	270	BIG COUNTRY TRUCK STOP	325-928-5584	325-928-5582	XL	
TYE	I-20	277	FLYING J	325-691-9974	325-691-5365	XL	CAT
TYE	I-20	278	WES-T-GO TRUCK STOP	325-692-8736	325-692-0501	XL	CAT
WEATHERFORD	I-20	406	PILOT TRAVEL CENTER	817-341-4600	817-341-4602	LG	CAT
WEATHERFORD	I-20	406	TRUCK & TRAVEL	817-596-3096	817-599-4505	LG	
WEATHERFORD	I-20	409	PETRO STOPPING CENTER	817-599-9411	817-598-5524	XL	CAT

Kenco Bucket Trucks | HIGHLOADS.COM

HIGH LOAD TRANSPORTATION.

KENCO Bucket Trucks
HIGH LOADS. OPEN ROADS.

1.877.459.3100 | HIGHLOADS.COM

THE OVERLOAD COMPANION 2017 © FREDA BARBER BOOTH - PILOTCARSTODAY.COM

CHARLES JAMES CAYIAS INSURANCE INC.

801-488-0085

PROFESSIONAL PILOT CAR INSURANCE PACKAGE

Working in cooperation with North America's leading escort vehicle trainers, certifying entities, and insurance professionals who specialize in protecting the needs of escort operators all across the United States.

Whether an accident is your fault or not, without the right protection, you could pay tens of thousands out of pocket to defend yourself in a lawsuit brought against you by others. Be prepared by having the proper insurance protection!

The Professional Pilot Car Insurance Package offers the following insurance coverage(s):

- **Commercial Automobile**: As personal auto insurance policies exclude business operations, commercial insurance is essential. We offer $1,000,000 in bodily injury and property damage coverage, along with medical payments, personal injury protection (in those states where required), and uninsured motorists to protect you, your passengers and members of the public in case of an over the road accident. Comprehensive and collision coverage is also offered to protect your vehicle. We can provide commercial automobile coverage on a mono-line basis.
- **General Liability**: Will protect you against injuries to members of the public at your premises, and damages that you may cause to the property of others that does not involve an automobile. We offer limits of $1,000,000 each occurrence and $2,000,000 aggregate for losses occurring during the policy term. We can provide general liability coverage on a mono-line basis.
- **Professional Liability**: Will provide you with protection for those activities normally excluded under a general liability policy because they are considered to be a professional exposure. We offer $1,000,000 in coverage for flagging, height pole, route surveys and shunting services, subject to certain qualifications. No coverage is offered for rigging, steerables or tillerman services.
- **Inland Marine**: Will cover your miscellaneous equipment used in your operation such as small tools, magnetic vehicle signage, flags, cones, etc. We offer three limits of coverage $1,000; $2,500; $5,000 depending on your needs. Higher limits are available upon request.

Charles James Cayias Insurance, Inc.
2150 South 1300 East, Suite #100
Salt Lake City, UT 84106
PH: (801) 488-0085
Fax: (801) 463-6683
www.cayias.com

Program benefits include a combination of coverage specific to the pilot car industry, competitive pricing, expertise, and prompt friendly service. Simply put... our goal is to provide you with the best value for your money!

TEXAS TRUCK STOPS - PG 2 OF 3

CITY	HIGHWAY	EXIT	TRUCK STOP	PHONE	FAX	LOT	SCALES
DALLAS	I-20	470	USA TRAVEL CENTER	469-567-4000		$ LG	CAT
DALLAS	I-20	470	PILOT TRAVEL CENTER	972-228-2467	972-228-4386	XL	CAT
DALLAS	I-20	472	FLYING J	972-225-3566	972-225-3681	XL	CAT
DALLAS	I-20	472	TA	469-941-3150	469-941-3158	$ LG	CAT
TERRELL	I-20	503	TA	972-563-6939	972-563-7239	XL	CAT
VAN	I-20	540	LOVES	903-963-7341	903-963-8137	LG	CAT
TYLER	I-20	562	PILOT TRAVEL CENTER	903-593-5466	903-593-3204	LG	CAT
LONGVIEW	I-20	599	NATIONAL T/S	903-753-3631	903-247-1000	XL	CAT
MARSHALL	I-20	617	PONY EXPRESS TRAVEL CENTER	903-938-3466	903-938-7718	XL	SCALES
LUBBOCK	I-27	1C	RIP GRIFFIN	806-747-2505	806-762-2141	M	CAT
LUBBOCK	I-27	4	FLYING J	806-744-0539	806-744-7423	M	CAT
TULIA	I-27	74	RIP GRIFFIN / PILOT	806-995-4567	806-995-3501	M	SCALES
ROCKWALL	I-30	68	TA	972-722-7450	972-722-7458	LG	CAT
ROCKWALL	I-30	70	LOVES	972-722-3178	972-772-3180	M	CAT
CADDO MILLS	I-30	87	PILOT TRAVEL CENTER	903-527-2150	903-527-2103	M	CAT
SULPHUR SPRINGS	I-30	122	PILOT TRAVEL CENTER	903-885-0020	903-885-1580	M	CAT
MOUNT VERNON	I-30	147	LOVES	930-537-7695	903-537-2085	M	CAT
LEARY	I-30	213	LOVES	903-838-0856	903-838-0387	LG	CAT
LAREDO	I-35	12	FLYING J	956-712-3265	956-791-3057	XL	CAT
LAREDO	I-35	12	TA	956-724-2016	956-724-2511	$ XL	CAT
LAREDO	I-35	12	PILOT TRAVEL CENTER	956-717-5006	956-717-5012	XL	CAT
ENCINAL / LAREDO	I-35	39	LOVES	956-948-7044	956-948-7048	LG	CAT
PEARSALL	I-35	101	PEARSALL TRAVEL CENTER	830-334-8222	830-334-2395	XL	CAT
SAN ANTONIO	I-35	140	PILOT TRAVEL CENTER	210-622-9384	210-622-9302	LG	
SAN ANTONIO	I-35	144	LOVES	210-623-2329	210-623-2527	LG	CAT
NEW BRAUNFELS	I-35	184	PILOT TRAVEL CENTER	830-629-1424	830-629-1254	M	CAT
NEW BRAUNFELS	I-35	193	TA	830-608-9395	830-608-9064	XL	CAT
JARRELL	I-35	275	FLYING J	512-746-4341	512-746-4390	LG	SCALES
TEMPLE	I-35	304	CEFCO TRAVEL CENTER	254-778-3000	254-778-5692	M	CAT
HEWITT	I-35	328	PILOT TRAVEL CENTER	254-662-4771	254-662-4951	XL	CAT
WACO	I-35	331	FLYING J	254-714-0313	254-714-1798	XL	CAT
ELM MOTT	I-35	343	EDS TRUCK STOP	254-829-2133	254-829-1604	M	CAT
CARL'S CORNER	I-35 E	374	PETRO STOPPING CENTER	254-714-3000	254-714-3002	LG	CAT
DENTON	I-35	471	TA	940-383-1455	940-898-1527	XL	CAT
FORT WORTH	I-35 W	65	PILOT TRAVEL CENTER	817-337-5324	817-337-5137	XL	CAT
AMARILLO	I-40	74	LOVES	806-373-7775	806-373-5848	M	CAT
AMARILLO	I-40	74	TA	806-342-3080	806-371-8486	XL	CAT
AMARILLO	I-40	75	PETRO STOPPING CENTER	806-372-4899	806-378-3634	XL	CAT
AMARILLO	I-40	75	PILOT	806-335-3323	806-335-2868	LG	CAT
AMARILLO	I-40	76	FLYING J	806-335-1475	806-335-1058	XL	CAT
HOUSTON	I-45	50A	LOVES	713-694-9898	713-699-0434	XL	CAT
HOUSTON	I-45	64	FLYING J	281-893-0423	281-893-9368	XL	CAT

If we need to make a change, add or subtract - please text 817-583-5503

THE OVERLOAD COMPANION 2017 © FREDA BARBER BOOTH - PILOTCARSTODAY.COM

FOCUS ON THE ROAD, NOT WHAT'S ABOVE IT.

Whether you're plotting a route or worrying about hazards and delays, transporting oversized loads can be stressful. But Kenco Bucket Trucks' high standards, certifications and well-equipped purple trucks make travel a snap. We make the safety of your cargo and personnel our highest priority. Plus we can assist with planning the route so there are no surprises, only smooth driving.

We ensure that when you choose HIGH LOADS, we give you OPEN ROADS.

KENCO MEANS:
- IMSA Work Zone Safety Certified
- IMSA Traffic Signal Technician Level I & II
- DISA Drug & Alcohol Tested Employees
- Professionalism, safety and reliability

KENCO Bucket Trucks
HIGH LOADS. OPEN ROADS.

TAKE A LOAD OFF. 1.877.459.3100 | HIGHLOADS.COM

20 YEARS OF SAFETY
THE SAFEST ROUTE.
KENCO

TEXAS TRUCK STOPS

CITY	HIGHWAY	EXIT	TRUCK STOP	PHONE	FAX	LOT	SCALES
WILLIS	I-45	95	LOVES	936-856-5085	936-856-8170	LG	CAT
HUNTSVILLE	I-45	118	PILOT TRAVEL CENTER	936-291-1125	936-291-2421	LG	CAT
HUTCHINS	I-45	272	LOVES	972-225-3560	972-225-3532	LG	CAT
HOUSTON	I-610	24	LOVES	713-670-0235	713-670-0299	LG	CAT
HOUSTON	I-610	24	TRUCKER PARADISE	713-670-3000	713-670-8500	LG	CAT
HOUSTON	I-610	24	PILOT TRAVEL CENTER	713-675-3375	713-670-7629	LG	CAT
THE FOLLOWING ARE LISTED BY CITY							
ANNA	US 75	48	DRIVERS TRAVEL MART	972-924-3832	972-924-2866	XL	CAT
CLEVELAND	US-59		LOVES	281-593-0239	281-593-0906	LG	CAT
EAGLE PASS	US 57		MR CARTENDER	830-758-1712	830-757-5971	XL	CAT
EDINBURG	HWY 281		FLYING J	956-316-0149	956-316-4732	XL	CAT
EDINBURG	US 281		TA	956-383-0788	956-383-2310	LG	SCALES
EDINBURG	US 281		LOVES	956-316-1782	956-316-3968	M	CAT
EDNA	US 59		LOVES	361-782-6700	361-782-2786	M	CAT
FORNEY	US 80 W/FM 460		KNOX SUPER STOP	972-552-9021	972-552-4821	M	CAT
GANADO	US 59		TA	361-771-3504	361-771-1984	LG	CAT
HARROLD	US 287		FINA 7-11	940-886-2661	940-886-2655	M	CAT
HEARNE	TX-6/FM485		LOVES	979-279-9700	979-279-9665	M	CAT
KINGSVILLE	US 77 N		LOVES	361-592-7210	361-592-3641	M	CAT
LAPORTE	TX 146		LAPORTE TRAVEL CENTER	281-842-7200	281-842-7210	M	SCALES
LUFKIN	LP 287		LOVES	936-637-4928	936-637-6286	M	CAT
MEMPHIS	US 287		LOVES	806-259-2300	806-259-2304	M	SCALES
MIDLOTHIAN	US 67		LOVES	972-775-2820	972-775-4375	M	CAT
NACOGDOCHES	US 59		MORGAN OIL FUEL STOP	936-560-0558	936-564-6512	LG	
NEW CANEY	US 59		FLYING J	281-689-8065	281-689-8271	XL	CAT
PERRYTON	US 83 S		WATERHOLE	806-435-4777	806-435-9222	M	
RHOME	US-81 / 287		LOVES	817-636-0270	817-636-2296	M	CAT
ROBSTOWN	US 77/FM 892		ROADRUNNER TRUCK STOP	361-387-5558	361-387-9528	LG	CAT
SHEPHARD	US 59		CHAMPION TRAVEL PLAZA	281-593-1300	381-593-2600	$ XL	
VICTORIA	US 87/US 59		BIG VIC TRUCK STOP	361-575-7138	361-575-1915	LG	CAT
WALLER	US 290		LOVES	936-372-3449	936-372-3473	M	CAT
WICHITA FALLS	US 287		FLYING J	940-720-0598	940-720-0725	M	

If we need to make a change, add or subtract - please text 817-583-5503

L J'S PILOT CAR SERVICE
North Texas Area
Tina Kemp, Office Manager: 940-577-2621
Larry J Kemp, Owner Operator: 940-393-5965

Chase/Lead, Route Survey & Traffic Control

Safety and Professionalism First and Foremost!

UTAH - VERMONT TRUCK STOPS

UTAH

CITY	HIGHWAY	EXIT	TRUCK STOP	PHONE	FAX	LOT	SCALES
ST GEORGE	I-15	4	FLYING J	435-674-7104	435-652-3627	M	CAT
CEDAR CITY	I-15	62	LOVES	435-867-9888	435-867-9890	M	CAT
CEDAR CITY	I-15	62	JR'S TRUCK STOP	435-586-0498	435-586-3756	M	SCALES
PAROWAN	I-15	78	TA	435-477-3311	435-477-8713	LG	CAT
NEPHI	I-15	222	FLYING J	435-623-2400	435-623-2421	LG	CAT
NEPHI	I-15	222	TOP STOP TRUCK PLAZA	435-623-2085	435-623-2549	M	CAT
SPRINGVILLE	I-15	261	FLYING J	801-489-3622	801-489-3059	M	CAT
OGDEN	I-15	343	FLYING J	801-399-5577	801-399-9353	XL	CAT
OGDEN	I-15	344	PILOT TRAVEL CENTER	801-731-2900	801-731-2380	M	CAT
WILLARD	I-15	357	FLYING J	435-723-1010	435-723-1044	M	
SALT LAKE CITY	I-15 EX 305B I-80 EX 122		FLYING J	801-972-3711	801-972-6174	LG	CAT
RICHFIELD	I-70	40	FLYING J	435-896-5050	435-896-4044	M	
GREEN RIVER	I-70	160	PILOT TRAVEL CENTER	435-564-3495	435-564-3282	XL	CAT
WENDOVER	I-80	4	WENDOVER T/S	435-665-2243	435-665-2929	LG	SCALES
LAKE POINT	I-80	99	FLYING J	801-508-7400	801-508-7404	XL	CAT
LAKE POINT	I-80	99	TA	801-250-8585	801-252-2224	XL	CAT
SALT LAKE CITY	I-80	118	LOVES	801-239-1100	801-239-1692	LG	CAT
SNOWVILLE	I-84	7	FLYING J	435-872-8181	435-872-8171	M	
TREMONTON	I-84	40	RJ'S FUEL STOP	435-257-3530	435-257-0658	LG	SCALES
SALT LAKE CITY	I-215	28	FLYING J	801-936-1408	801-936-1457	M	
PANGUITCH	US-89		OWEN'S TRAVEL CTR	435-676-8986	435-676-8943	M	

VERMONT

CITY	HIGHWAY	EXIT	TRUCK STOP	PHONE	FAX	LOT	SCALES
FAIR HAVEN	US-4	2	FAIR HAVEN TRAVEL CENTER	802-265-3009	802-265-7924	M	
SAINT ALBANS	I-89	19	THE JOLLEY SHORT STOP	802-527-0104	802-524-2821	L	SCALE
SWANTON	I-89	21	CHAMPLAIN FARMS	802-868-7790	802-868-6461	M	
SPRINGFIELD	I-91	7	IRVING	802-885-2266	802-885-2266	M	CAT
WELLS RIVER	I-91	17	P&H TRUCK STOP	802-429-2141	802-429-2002	L	SCALE

If we need to make a change, add or subtract - please text 817-583-5503

CALL US TODAY!

CASH TODAY! FACTORING MADE EASY FOR AMERICA'S TRUCKERS

1-888-684-7195

CENTURY FINANCE

VIRGINIA TRUCK STOPS - PG 1 OF 2

CITY	HIGHWAY	EXIT	TRUCK STOP	PHONE	FAX	LOT	SCALES
TALLYSVILLE	I-64	211	PILOT	804-966-1880	804-966-9231	M	CAT
VIRGINIA BEACH	I-64	282	BIG CHARLIE'S TRUCK PLAZA	757-460-2032	757-363-9522	$ XL	SCALES
LAMBSBURG	I-77	1	LOVES	276-755-3117	276-755-3159	LG	CAT
WYTHEVILLE	I-77/81	41	TA	276-228-8676	276-228-8504	LG	CAT
WYTHEVILLE	I-77/81	77	FLYING J	276-228-7110	276-228-9010	XL	CAT
WYTHEVILLE	I-77/81	77	WILCO-HESS	276-228-2421	276-228-2463	M	CAT
FT CHISWELL	I-77/81	80	FLYING J	276-637-4115	276-637-6968	XL	CAT
GLADE SPRING	I-81	29	PETRO	276-429-5100	276-429-2985	XL	CAT
MAX MEADOWS	I-81	84	LOVES	276-637-3124	276-637-3271	M	CAT
ELLISTON	I-81	128	STOP IN FOOD STORE	540-268-9500	540-268-2440	M	
TROUTVILLE	I-81	150A	TA	540-992-3100	540-992-5069	LG	CAT
LEXINGTON	I-81	195	TA	540-463-3478	540-463-1543	XL	CAT
LEXINGTON	I-81	195	LEE HI T/S		540-463-2294	XL	CAT
RAPHINE	I-81	205	PETRO	540-377-2111	540-377-5729	XL	CAT
RAPHINE	I-81	205	WILCO-HESS	540-377-9239	540-377-6304	XL	CAT
GREENVILLE	I-81	213	PILOT TRAVEL CENTER	540-324-0714	540-324-0718	LG	CAT
GREENVILLE	I-81	251	PILOT TRAVEL CENTER	540-434-2529	540-343-2076	LG	CAT
MT JACKSON	I-81	273	SHEETZ TRAVEL CTR	540-477-3110	540-477-9447	LG	SCALES
MT JACKSON	I-81	273	SHENANDOAH TRAVEL CTR	540-477-2991	540-477-2824	XL	CAT
TOMS BROOK	I-81	291	WILCO-HESS	540-436-3121	540-436-3966	XL	CAT
TOMS BROOK	I-81	291	LOVES	540-436-8048	540-436-3465	LG	CAT
CLEAR BROOK	I-81	323	FLYING J	540-678-3641	540-678-3651	LG	CAT
SOUTH HILL	I-85	15	LOVES	434-584-0077	434-584-0020	M	CAT
WARFIELD	I-85	39	DAVIS TRAVEL CENTER	804-478-4403	804-478-4982	M	CAT

If we need to make a change, add or subtract - please text 817-583-5503

JLS PILOT CAR SERVICE — MULTIPLE CARS

WA CERTIFIED — HIGH POLE - LEAD - CHASE — FULLY INSURED

CELL: 678-873-5016   ALT: 470-239-8776   FAX 678-807-5751

VIRGINIA (PG 2 OF 2) & WASHINGTON TRUCK STOPS

VIRGINIA (PG 2)

CITY	HIGHWAY	EXIT	TRUCK STOP	PHONE	FAX	LOT	SCALES
SKIPPERS	I-95	4	LOVES	434-336-0203	434-336-0584	M	CAT
EMPORIA	I-95	8	SIMMON'S TRAVEL CTR	434-634-9296	434-634-2376	LG	CAT
EMPORIA	I-95	11B	SADLER TRAVEL PLAZA	434-634-4312	434-634-5397	XL	CAT
STONY CREEK	I-95	33	DAVIS TRAVEL CENTER	434-246-2881	434-246-2519	LG	CAT
COLONIAL HEIGHTS	I-95	58	PILOT TRAVEL CENTER	804-524-9556	804-524-9554	LG	CAT
ASHLAND	I-95	89	TA	804-798-6021	804-752-6665	XL	CAT
ASHLAND	I-95	92	TA	804-798-6011	804-798-7342	XL	CAT
RUTHER GLEN	I-95	104	FLYING J	804-448-9047	804-448-5592	XL	CAT
RUTHER GLEN	I-95	104	LOVES	804-448-0102	804-448-1222	M	CAT
RUTHER GLEN	I-95	104	FLYING J	804-448-3077	804-448-3210	XL	CAT
DISPUTANTA	I-295	3A	WILCO-HESS	804-863-4612	804-463-4616	LG	CAT
BOWERS HILL	I-664	13B	FRANK'S TRUCKING CTR	757-488-8337	757-488-0570	LG	SCALES
OPAL	US-15/17/29		QUARLES TRUCKSTOP	540-439-3000	540-439-1472	LG	
RUSTBURG	US-29		GOLDY'S TRUCK STOP	434-821-1513	434-821-1522	LG	CAT
AMELIA	US-360		360 TRUCK STOP	804-561-2802	804-561-6484	$ LG	
SUFFOLK	US-460		MILLER MART	757-539-0897	757-539-4060	M	CAT
SOUTH BOSTON	US-58		STOP IN FOOD STORE	434-575-1900	434-575-1177	LG	CAT

WASHINGTON

CITY	HIGHWAY	EXIT	TRUCK STOP	PHONE	FAX	LOT	SCALES
TOLEDO	I-5	57	GEE GEE'S TRUCK STOP	360-864-4300	360-864-4303	XL	CAT
CHEHALIS	I-5	72	RUSH ROAD TRUCKSTOP	360-748-0204	360-740-0150	M	CAT
TUMWATER	I-5	99	PILOT TRAVEL CENTER	360-754-0151	360-754-0159	LG	CAT
TACOMA	I-5	136	LOVES	253-922-8884	913-752-9622	M	CAT
MOUNT VERNON	I-5	224	TRUCK CITY	360-428-3070	360-428-3555	M	SCALES
FERNDALE	I-5	262	PILOT TRAVEL CENTER	360-312-1822	360-312-1851	$ M	CAT
UNION GAP	I-82	36	GEARJAMMER TRUCKSTOP	509-248-9640	509-575-0108	XL	CAT
NORTH BEND	I-90	34	TA	425-888-1119	425-888-9392	LG	CAT
ELLENSBURG	I-90	106	LOVES	509-925-5200	509-925-5308	M	CAT
ELLENSBURG	I-90	109	FLYING J	509-925-6161	509-925-5748	M	CAT
MOSES LAKE	I-90	179	ERNIE'S TRUCK STOP	509-765-4470	509-766-1830	XL	SCALES
RITZVILLE	I-90	220	JAKE'S EXXON	509-659-0815	509-659-4255	M	
SPOKANE	I-90	272	PETRO	509-842-1100	509-842-1105	XL	CAT
SPOKANE	I-90	286	FLYING J	509-535-3028	509-535-7589	M	CAT
PASCO	US-395		KHALSA KING CITY T/S	509-547-0373	509-542-0585	XL	SCALES
SUMNER	WA-167 N		MUSTARD SEED MKT/DELI	253-863-9916	253-863-9370	$ M	CAT
ROCK ISLAND	WA-28		BJ'S AUTO TRUCK PLAZA	509-886-0230	509-884-1398	M	SCALES

If we need to make a change, add or subtract - please text 817-583-5503

WEST VIRGINIA TRUCK STOPS

CITY	HIGHWAY	EXIT	TRUCK STOP	PHONE	FAX	LOT	SCALES
HURRICANE	I-64	39	TA	304-757-7600	304-757-7818	M	CAT
NITRO	I-64	45	PILOT TRAVEL CENTER	304-755-8654	304-755-8655	M	CAT
VALLEY GROVE/WHEELING	I-70	11	TA	304-547-1521	304-547-9454	XL	CAT
BECKLEY	I-77	45	BECKLEY PLAZA	304-253-8284	304-253-9826	LG	
RIPLEY	I-77	132	LOVES	304-372-5250	304-372-4247	M	CAT
MINERAL WELLS	I-77	170	LIBERTY TRUCK STOP	304-489-9201	304-489-2490	XL	SCALES
FLATWOODS	I-79	67	67 TRUCKSTOP / MOTEL	304-765-2288	304-765-7051	LG	
JANE LEW	I-79	105	JANE LEW TRUCK STOP	304-884-7876	304-884-8219	LG	SCALES
FAIRMONT	I-79	139	K & T TRUCK STOP	304-367-1517	304-367-9721	M	CAT
MORGANTOWN	I-79	146	PILOT TRAVEL CENTER	304-284-8518	304-284-8509	M	CAT
MOUNT NEBO	US 19 / WV129		U SAVE T/P	304-872-8377	304-872-8376	XL	SCALES

If we need to make a change, add or subtract - please text 817-583-5503

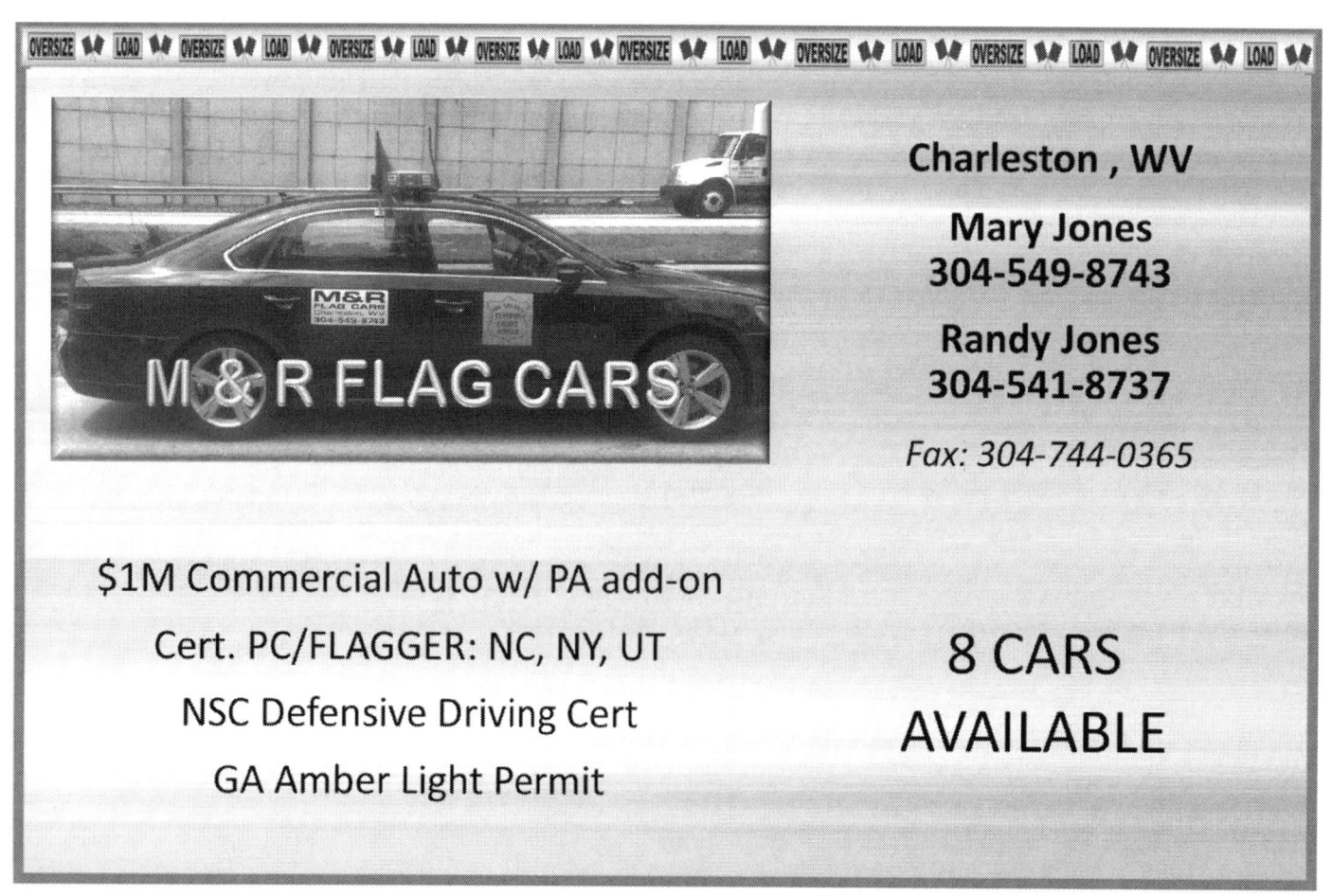

M & R FLAG CARS

Charleston, WV

Mary Jones
304-549-8743

Randy Jones
304-541-8737

Fax: 304-744-0365

$1M Commercial Auto w/ PA add-on

Cert. PC/FLAGGER: NC, NY, UT

NSC Defensive Driving Cert

GA Amber Light Permit

8 CARS AVAILABLE

THE OVERLOAD COMPANION 2017 © FREDA BARBER BOOTH - PILOTCARSTODAY.COM

WISCONSIN TRUCK STOPS

CITY	HIGHWAY	EXIT	TRUCK STOP	PHONE	FAX	LOT	SCALES
PLAINFIELD	I-39	136	PLAINFIELD TRAVEL PLAZA	715-335-7339		M	SCALES
PLOVER	I-39	151	SUPER 39 SHELL	715-344-5400	715-344-5432	LG	CAT
JANESVILLE	I-39 / I-90	171C	TA	608-752-8700	608-752-4604	LG	CAT
WAUSAU	I-39	188	RIB MOUNTAIN TRVL CTR	715-355-5600	715-359-8728	M	CAT
BELGIUM	I-43	107	HOW-DEA SVC CTR	262-285-3435	262-285-3471	LG	CAT
FRANCIS CREEK	I-43	157	FRANCIS CREEK TRVL PLAZA	920-684-4300	920-684-0716	M	SCALES
DEPERE	I-43	180	COUNTY EXPRESS TRUCKSTOP	920-336-6402	920-336-9071	LG	CAT
OAKDALE	I-90/ I-94	48	LOVES	608-372-3820	608-372-3829	M	CAT
OAKDALE	I-90/ I-94	48	PILOT TRAVEL CENTER	815-209-9040	608-3742001	M	CAT
MAUSTON	I-90 / I-94	69	KWIKTRIP	608-847-2333	608-547-2340	LG	SCALES
MAUSTON	I-90 / I-94	69	PILOT TRAVEL CENTER	608-847-3321	608-847-3316	M	CAT
PORTAGE	I-90 / I-94	108A	PETRO	608-742-6551	608-742-6534	XL	CAT
DEFOREST	I-90/ I-94	132	TA	608-249-9000	608-246-0359	LG	CAT
HUDSON	I-94	4	TA	715-386-5835	715-386-1149	M	CAT
HUDSON	I-94	10	FLYING J	715-749-4238	715-749-4241	M	CAT
BALDWIN	I-94	28	KWIK TRIP	715-772-4283	715-772-3281	LG	
WILSON	I-94	45	CENEX 45	715-235-1166	715-235-2820	M	CAT
MANOMONIE	I-94	45	KWIKTRIP	715-235-8755	715-235-8912	LG	SCALES
MANOMONIE	I-94	59	HOLIDAY STATION	715-874-6930	715-874-0563	M	SCALES
OSSEO	I-94	116	FLYING J	715-284-4341	715-284-1551	XL	CAT
BLACK RIVER FALLS	I-94	143	KWIK TRIP	608-372-5776	608-372-5065	M	SCALES
TOMAH	I-94	267	PINECONE TRAVEL PLAZA	920-699-2766	920-699-8171	LG	CAT
JOHNSON CREEK	I-94	322	LOVES	414-761-0482	414-761-0709	XL	CAT
OAK CREEK	I-94	322	PILOT TRAVEL CENTER	414-761-0939	414-761-0165	XL	CAT
OAK CREEK	I-94	329	PILOT TRAVEL CENTER	262-835-2292	262-835-2564	M	CAT
FRANKSVILLE	I-94	333	PETRO	262-884-7500	262-884-0778	XL	CAT
COLUMBUS	US-2/53		NEMADJI TRAVEL PLAZA	715-398-6668	715-398-2346	M	CAT
SUPERIOR	US-41	101	STRETCH TRUCK STOP	920-921-1500	920-273-0291	LG	SCALES
FOND DU LAC	US-41	113	PLANEVIEW TRAVEL PLAZA	920-426-2641	920-426-6330	XL	CAT
LITTLE CHUTE	US-41		RIVER CITIES TRAVEL PLAZA	715-732-9620	715-732-9641	M	SCALES
MARINETTE	US-41		EAGLE EXPRESS TRUCK STOP	715-582-0180	715-582-0129	M	CAT
PESHTIGO	US-41/45	57	RICHFIELD TRUCK STOP	262-628-1134	262-628-0036	M	CAT
RICHFIELD	US-41/WI-145		PIONEER TRAVEL PLAZA	262-628-3344	NA	LG	SCALES
BELMONT	US-151	118	COLUMBUS WEST TRAVEL CTR	920-623-9740	920-623-9681	M	CAT

If we need to make a change, add or subtract - please text 817-583-5503

WYOMING TRUCK STOPS

CITY	HIGHWAY	EXIT	TRUCK STOP	PHONE	FAX	LOT	SCALES
CHEYENNE	I-25	7	FLYING J	307-635-2918	307-634-2794	XL	CAT
CHEYENNE	I-25	7	LOVES	307-632-7902	307-632-7929	M	CAT
EVANSVILLE	I-25	182	EASTGATE TRAVEL PLAZA	307-234-0504	307-234-0619	XL	SCALES
EVANSTON	I-80	3	FLYING J	307-789-9129	307-789-5461	M	SCALES
EVANSTON	I-80	6	PILOT TRAVEL CENTER	307-783-5930	307-783-5916	M	CAT
FORT BRIDGER	I-80	30	TA	307-782-3814	307-782-6623	XL	CAT
LITTLE AMERICA	I-80	68	LITTLE AMERICA TRAVEL CTR	307-872-2686	307-872-2666	XL	SCALES
ROCK SPRINGS	I-80	104	FLYING J	307-362-4231	307-362-9710	M	CAT
WAMSUTTER	I-80	173	LOVES	307-324-0087	307-324-3675	M	CAT
RAWLINS	I-80	209	FLYING J	307-328-0158	307-328-1668	XL	CAT
RAWLINS	I-80	214	TA	307-328-2103	307-238-1523	XL	CAT
QUEALYDOM	I-80	290	A & C TRUCK STOP	307-745-1653	307-745-8156	LG	
LARAMIE	I-80	310	PILOT TRAVEL CENTER	307-742-6443	307-742-2576	LG	CAT
LARAMIE	I-80	310	PETRO	307-745-6480	307-721-6741	XL	CAT
CHEYENNE	I-80	367	PILOT	307-635-5744	307-635-5746	LG	CAT
CHEYENNE	I-80	370	SAPP BROS	307-632-6600	307-635-8549	XL	
HILLSDALE	I-80	377	TA	307-547-3557	307-547-3420	LG	CAT
GILLETTE	I-90	126	FLYING J	307-682-3562	307-682-5038	M	CAT
CASPER	US-20/26		GHOST TOWN FUEL STOP	307-472-0200	307-235-7933	LG	
TORRINGTON	US-26		TORRINGTON TRVL TERMINAL	307-532-8164	307-532-4950	M	SCALES
COKEVILLE	US-30/WY-232		FLYING J	307-279-3050	307-279-3041	LG	SCALES

AAA Pilot Service LLC

Gillette, WY 82717

307-682-1296

307-680-3552 (Joyce cell)

307-660-3552 (Ed cell)

Lead, chase
Hi-pole

Certified
Insured

19 Years Runnin'

SUNRISE SUNSET CHARTS

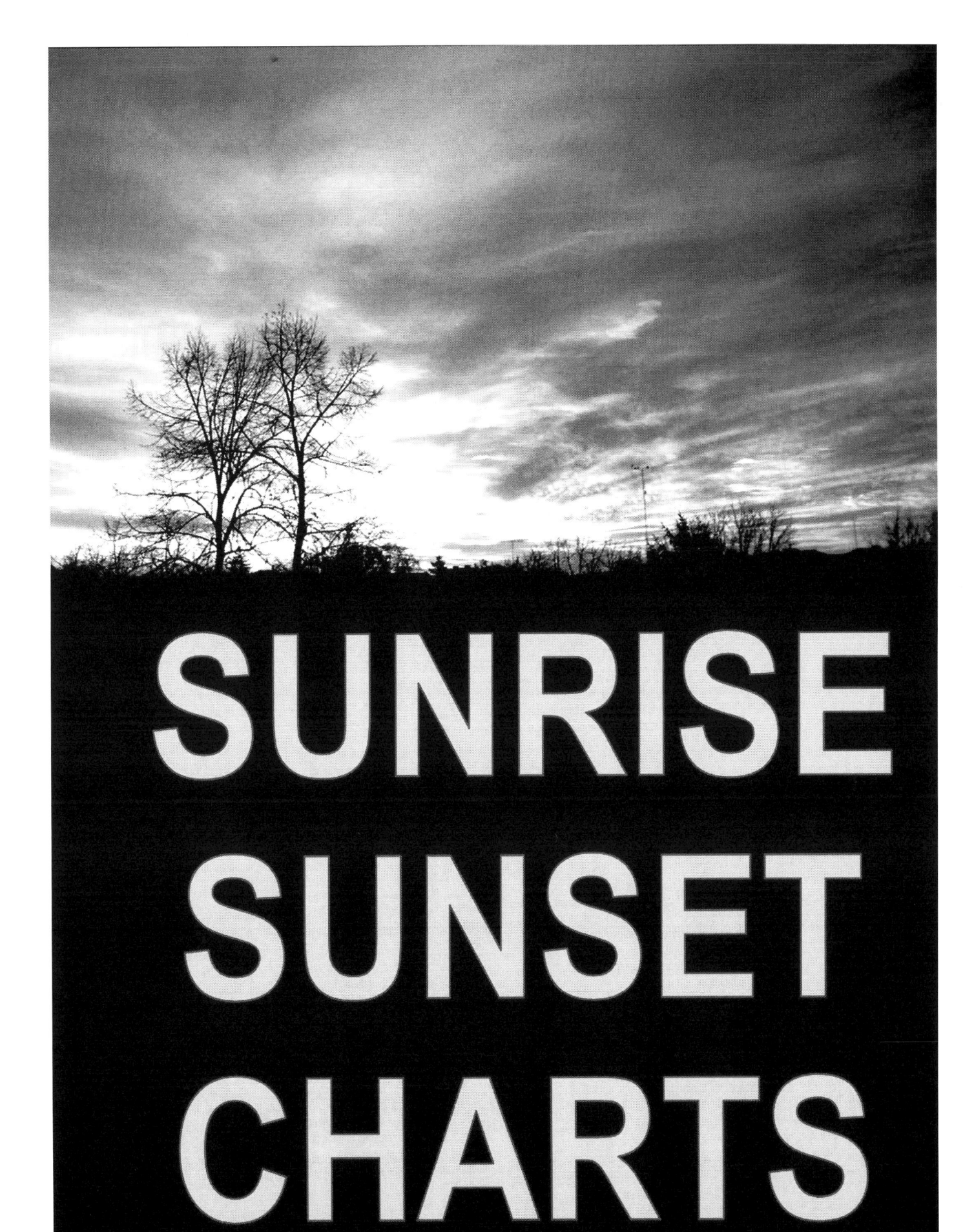

Astronomical Applications Dept
Location: W086 49, N33 32

Rise and Set for the Sun for 2017
BIRMINGHAM, ALABAMA

U. S. Naval Observatory, Washington, DC
Central Standard Time

	JAN		FEB		MAR		APR		MAY		JUN		JUL		AUG		SEP		OCT		NOV		DEC	
	AM	PM	AM	PM	AM	PM	AM	PM	AM	PM	AM	PM	AM	PM	AM	PM	AM	PM	AM	PM	AM	PM	AM	PM
1	6 51	4 50	6 44	5 18	6 15	5 44	5 34	6 08	4 58	6 31	4 38	6 53	4 41	7 01	5 00	6 47	5 22	6 12	5 42	5 31	6 07	4 55	6 34	4 39
2	6 52	4 51	6 43	5 19	6 14	5 45	5 33	6 09	4 57	6 31	4 38	6 53	4 42	7 01	5 01	6 46	5 22	6 11	5 43	5 30	6 07	4 54	6 35	4 39
3	6 52	4 52	6 42	5 20	6 12	5 46	5 32	6 10	4 56	6 32	4 38	6 54	4 42	7 01	5 01	6 45	5 23	6 09	5 43	5 28	6 08	4 53	6 36	4 39
4	6 52	4 52	6 42	5 21	6 11	5 47	5 30	6 10	4 55	6 33	4 37	6 54	4 43	7 01	5 02	6 44	5 24	6 08	5 44	5 27	6 09	4 52	6 36	4 39
5	6 52	4 53	6 41	5 22	6 10	5 48	5 29	6 11	4 55	6 34	4 37	6 55	4 43	7 01	5 03	6 43	5 24	6 07	5 45	5 26	6 10	4 51	6 37	4 39
6	6 52	4 54	6 40	5 23	6 09	5 48	5 28	6 12	4 54	6 34	4 37	6 55	4 44	7 01	5 04	6 42	5 25	6 05	5 46	5 24	6 11	4 50	6 38	4 39
7	6 52	4 55	6 39	5 24	6 07	5 49	5 26	6 13	4 53	6 35	4 37	6 56	4 44	7 01	5 04	6 41	5 25	6 04	5 46	5 23	6 12	4 50	6 39	4 39
8	6 52	4 56	6 38	5 25	6 06	5 50	5 25	6 13	4 52	6 36	4 37	6 56	4 45	7 00	5 05	6 40	5 26	6 02	5 47	5 22	6 13	4 49	6 39	4 39
9	6 52	4 56	6 37	5 26	6 05	5 51	5 24	6 14	4 51	6 37	4 37	6 57	4 45	7 00	5 06	6 39	5 27	6 01	5 48	5 20	6 14	4 48	6 40	4 39
10	6 52	4 57	6 37	5 27	6 04	5 52	5 22	6 15	4 50	6 37	4 37	6 57	4 46	7 00	5 06	6 38	5 28	6 00	5 49	5 19	6 15	4 47	6 41	4 40
11	6 52	4 58	6 36	5 28	6 02	5 53	5 21	6 16	4 49	6 38	4 37	6 57	4 46	6 59	5 07	6 37	5 28	5 58	5 49	5 18	6 16	4 47	6 42	4 40
12	6 52	4 59	6 35	5 29	6 01	5 53	5 20	6 16	4 49	6 39	4 37	6 58	4 47	6 59	5 08	6 36	5 29	5 57	5 50	5 17	6 17	4 46	6 42	4 40
13	6 52	5 00	6 34	5 30	6 00	5 54	5 19	6 17	4 48	6 40	4 37	6 58	4 47	6 58	5 08	6 35	5 30	5 56	5 51	5 15	6 17	4 45	6 43	4 40
14	6 52	5 01	6 33	5 31	5 58	5 55	5 17	6 18	4 47	6 40	4 37	6 59	4 48	6 58	5 09	6 34	5 30	5 54	5 52	5 14	6 18	4 45	6 44	4 41
15	6 52	5 02	6 32	5 31	5 57	5 56	5 16	6 19	4 46	6 41	4 37	6 59	4 49	6 57	5 09	6 33	5 31	5 53	5 52	5 13	6 19	4 44	6 44	4 41
16	6 51	5 03	6 31	5 32	5 56	5 56	5 15	6 19	4 46	6 42	4 37	6 59	4 49	6 57	5 10	6 32	5 32	5 52	5 53	5 12	6 20	4 44	6 45	4 41
17	6 51	5 04	6 30	5 33	5 54	5 57	5 14	6 20	4 45	6 43	4 37	7 00	4 50	6 56	5 11	6 30	5 32	5 50	5 54	5 11	6 21	4 43	6 46	4 42
18	6 51	5 05	6 29	5 34	5 53	5 58	5 13	6 21	4 44	6 43	4 37	7 00	4 50	6 56	5 12	6 29	5 33	5 49	5 55	5 09	6 22	4 43	6 46	4 42
19	6 50	5 06	6 28	5 35	5 52	5 59	5 11	6 22	4 44	6 44	4 37	7 00	4 51	6 55	5 13	6 28	5 34	5 47	5 56	5 08	6 23	4 42	6 47	4 43
20	6 50	5 07	6 27	5 36	5 50	5 59	5 10	6 22	4 43	6 45	4 38	7 00	4 52	6 55	5 13	6 27	5 34	5 46	5 56	5 07	6 24	4 42	6 47	4 43
21	6 50	5 08	6 25	5 37	5 49	6 00	5 09	6 23	4 43	6 45	4 38	7 01	4 52	6 54	5 14	6 26	5 35	5 45	5 57	5 06	6 25	4 41	6 48	4 44
22	6 49	5 08	6 24	5 38	5 48	6 01	5 08	6 24	4 42	6 46	4 38	7 01	4 53	6 54	5 15	6 25	5 36	5 43	5 58	5 05	6 26	4 41	6 48	4 44
23	6 49	5 09	6 23	5 39	5 46	6 02	5 07	6 25	4 42	6 47	4 38	7 01	4 54	6 53	5 15	6 23	5 36	5 42	5 59	5 04	6 27	4 41	6 49	4 45
24	6 48	5 10	6 22	5 39	5 45	6 02	5 06	6 25	4 41	6 48	4 38	7 01	4 54	6 53	5 16	6 22	5 37	5 40	6 00	5 03	6 28	4 40	6 49	4 45
25	6 48	5 11	6 21	5 40	5 44	6 03	5 05	6 26	4 41	6 48	4 39	7 01	4 55	6 52	5 17	6 21	5 38	5 39	6 00	5 02	6 29	4 40	6 50	4 46
26	6 47	5 12	6 20	5 41	5 42	6 04	5 04	6 27	4 40	6 49	4 39	7 01	4 56	6 51	5 18	6 20	5 38	5 38	6 01	5 01	6 29	4 40	6 50	4 46
27	6 47	5 13	6 19	5 42	5 41	6 04	5 02	6 28	4 40	6 50	4 39	7 01	4 57	6 51	5 18	6 18	5 39	5 36	6 02	5 00	6 30	4 40	6 50	4 47
28	6 46	5 14	6 17	5 43	5 40	6 05	5 01	6 28	4 39	6 50	4 40	7 01	4 57	6 50	5 19	6 17	5 40	5 35	6 03	4 58	6 31	4 39	6 51	4 48
29	6 46	5 15			5 38	6 06	5 00	6 29	4 39	6 51	4 40	7 01	4 58	6 49	5 20	6 16	5 41	5 34	6 04	4 58	6 32	4 39	6 51	4 48
30	6 45	5 16			5 37	6 06	4 59	6 30	4 39	6 51	4 41	7 01	4 59	6 48	5 20	6 14	5 41	5 32	6 05	4 57	6 33	4 39	6 51	4 49
31	6 44	5 17			5 36	6 07			4 38	6 52			4 59	6 47	5 21	6 13			6 06	4 56			6 51	4 50

Add one hour for daylight time, if and when in use.
East Bound - Subtract 1 min/10 mi from center   West Bound - Add 1 min/10 mi from center

BIRMINGHAM, ALABAMA

THE OVERLOAD COMPANION 2017 © FREDA BARBER BOOTH

Astronomical Applications Dept
Location: W149 52, N61 13

Rise and Set for the Sun for 2017
ANCHORAGE, ALASKA

U. S. Naval Observatory, Washington, DC
Alaska Standard Time

	JAN AM	JAN PM	FEB AM	FEB PM	MAR AM	MAR PM	APR AM	APR PM	MAY AM	MAY PM	JUN AM	JUN PM	JUL AM	JUL PM	AUG AM	AUG PM	SEP AM	SEP PM	OCT AM	OCT PM	NOV AM	NOV PM	DEC AM	DEC PM
1	10 14	3 53	9 20	5 06	7 58	6 27	6 20	7 47	4 49	9 06	3 35	10 21	3 28	10 38	4 34	9 36	5 53	8 04	7 08	6 29	8 29	4 56	9 47	3 51
2	10 13	3 54	9 18	5 09	7 55	6 29	6 17	7 50	4 46	9 09	3 33	10 23	3 30	10 37	4 36	9 33	5 55	8 01	7 10	6 25	8 32	4 53	9 49	3 49
3	10 12	3 56	9 15	5 12	7 52	6 32	6 14	7 52	4 43	9 11	3 32	10 25	3 31	10 36	4 39	9 31	5 58	7 57	7 13	6 22	8 35	4 50	9 51	3 48
4	10 11	3 58	9 13	5 15	7 49	6 35	6 11	7 55	4 40	9 14	3 30	10 27	3 32	10 35	4 41	9 28	6 00	7 54	7 15	6 19	8 37	4 48	9 53	3 47
5	10 11	3 59	9 10	5 18	7 46	6 37	6 08	7 58	4 37	9 17	3 29	10 28	3 34	10 33	4 44	9 25	6 03	7 51	7 18	6 16	8 40	4 45	9 55	3 46
6	10 10	4 01	9 08	5 20	7 42	6 40	6 05	8 00	4 34	9 19	3 28	10 30	3 35	10 32	4 46	9 22	6 05	7 48	7 20	6 13	8 43	4 42	9 57	3 45
7	10 08	4 03	9 05	5 23	7 39	6 42	6 02	8 03	4 32	9 22	3 27	10 31	3 37	10 31	4 49	9 19	6 08	7 45	7 23	6 10	8 46	4 40	9 58	3 44
8	10 07	4 05	9 02	5 26	7 36	6 45	5 58	8 05	4 29	9 25	3 26	10 33	3 39	10 29	4 52	9 16	6 10	7 42	7 26	6 07	8 48	4 37	10 00	3 43
9	10 06	4 07	8 59	5 29	7 33	6 48	5 55	8 08	4 26	9 27	3 25	10 34	3 41	10 28	4 54	9 14	6 13	7 38	7 28	6 04	8 51	4 35	10 02	3 42
10	10 05	4 09	8 57	5 32	7 30	6 50	5 52	8 11	4 24	9 30	3 24	10 35	3 43	10 26	4 57	9 11	6 15	7 35	7 31	6 01	8 54	4 32	10 03	3 42
11	10 03	4 12	8 54	5 34	7 27	6 53	5 49	8 13	4 21	9 33	3 23	10 36	3 45	10 24	4 59	9 08	6 18	7 32	7 33	5 57	8 57	4 30	10 05	3 41
12	10 02	4 14	8 51	5 37	7 24	6 56	5 46	8 16	4 18	9 35	3 22	10 37	3 47	10 22	5 02	9 05	6 20	7 29	7 36	5 54	8 59	4 27	10 06	3 41
13	10 00	4 16	8 48	5 40	7 21	6 58	5 43	8 18	4 16	9 38	3 22	10 38	3 49	10 21	5 05	9 02	6 23	7 26	7 38	5 51	9 02	4 25	10 07	3 40
14	9 59	4 19	8 45	5 43	7 17	7 01	5 40	8 21	4 13	9 40	3 21	10 39	3 51	10 19	5 07	8 59	6 25	7 22	7 41	5 48	9 05	4 23	10 09	3 40
15	9 57	4 21	8 43	5 46	7 14	7 03	5 37	8 24	4 11	9 43	3 21	10 40	3 53	10 17	5 10	8 56	6 28	7 19	7 44	5 45	9 07	4 20	10 10	3 40
16	9 55	4 23	8 40	5 48	7 11	7 06	5 34	8 26	4 08	9 45	3 20	10 41	3 55	10 15	5 12	8 53	6 30	7 16	7 46	5 42	9 10	4 18	10 11	3 40
17	9 54	4 26	8 37	5 51	7 08	7 09	5 30	8 29	4 06	9 48	3 20	10 41	3 57	10 13	5 15	8 50	6 33	7 13	7 49	5 39	9 13	4 16	10 12	3 40
18	9 52	4 29	8 34	5 54	7 05	7 11	5 27	8 32	4 03	9 50	3 20	10 42	3 59	10 10	5 17	8 47	6 35	7 10	7 52	5 36	9 15	4 14	10 12	3 40
19	9 50	4 31	8 31	5 57	7 02	7 14	5 24	8 34	4 01	9 53	3 20	10 42	4 02	10 08	5 20	8 44	6 38	7 07	7 54	5 33	9 18	4 11	10 13	3 41
20	9 48	4 34	8 28	5 59	6 58	7 16	5 21	8 37	3 59	9 55	3 20	10 42	4 04	10 06	5 23	8 41	6 40	7 03	7 57	5 30	9 20	4 09	10 14	3 41
21	9 46	4 36	8 25	6 02	6 55	7 19	5 18	8 40	3 56	9 58	3 20	10 42	4 06	10 04	5 25	8 38	6 43	7 00	7 59	5 27	9 23	4 07	10 14	3 42
22	9 44	4 39	8 22	6 05	6 52	7 21	5 15	8 42	3 54	10 00	3 21	10 42	4 09	10 01	5 28	8 35	6 45	6 57	8 02	5 24	9 26	4 05	10 15	3 42
23	9 42	4 42	8 19	6 08	6 49	7 24	5 12	8 45	3 52	10 02	3 21	10 42	4 11	9 59	5 30	8 32	6 48	6 54	8 05	5 21	9 28	4 04	10 15	3 43
24	9 39	4 44	8 16	6 10	6 46	7 27	5 09	8 48	3 50	10 05	3 22	10 42	4 14	9 57	5 33	8 29	6 50	6 51	8 07	5 18	9 31	4 02	10 15	3 44
25	9 37	4 47	8 13	6 13	6 43	7 29	5 06	8 50	3 48	10 07	3 22	10 42	4 16	9 54	5 35	8 26	6 53	6 48	8 10	5 16	9 33	4 00	10 15	3 45
26	9 35	4 50	8 10	6 16	6 39	7 32	5 03	8 53	3 46	10 09	3 23	10 41	4 18	9 52	5 38	8 22	6 55	6 44	8 13	5 13	9 35	3 58	10 15	3 46
27	9 33	4 52	8 07	6 18	6 36	7 34	5 00	8 56	3 44	10 11	3 23	10 41	4 21	9 49	5 40	8 19	6 58	6 41	8 16	5 10	9 38	3 56	10 15	3 47
28	9 30	4 55	8 04	6 21	6 33	7 37	4 57	8 58	3 42	10 13	3 24	10 40	4 23	9 47	5 43	8 16	7 00	6 38	8 18	5 07	9 40	3 55	10 15	3 48
29	9 28	4 58			6 30	7 40	4 54	9 01	3 40	10 15	3 26	10 40	4 26	9 44	5 45	8 13	7 03	6 35	8 21	5 04	9 42	3 53	10 15	3 49
30	9 25	5 01			6 27	7 42	4 52	9 03	3 38	10 17	3 27	10 39	4 28	9 41	5 48	8 10	7 05	6 32	8 24	5 01	9 45	3 52	10 14	3 51
31	9 23	5 04			6 24	7 45			3 36	10 19			4 31	9 39	5 50	8 07			8 26	4 59			10 14	3 52

Add one hour for daylight time, if and when in use.

East Bound - Subtract 1 min/10 mi from center   West Bound - Add 1 min/10 mi from center

ANCHORAGE, ALASKA

THE OVERLOAD COMPANION 2017 © FREDA BARBER BOOTH

Rise and Set for the Sun for 2017
PHOENIX, ARIZONA

Astronomical Applications Dept
U. S. Naval Observatory, Washington, DC
Location: W112 05, N33 30
Mountain Standard Time

	JAN AM	JAN PM	FEB AM	FEB PM	MAR AM	MAR PM	APR AM	APR PM	MAY AM	MAY PM	JUN AM	JUN PM	JUL AM	JUL PM	AUG AM	AUG PM	SEP AM	SEP PM	OCT AM	OCT PM	NOV AM	NOV PM	DEC AM	DEC PM
1	7 32	5 31	7 25	5 59	6 56	6 26	6 15	6 49	5 39	7 12	5 19	7 34	5 22	7 42	5 41	7 28	6 03	6 53	6 23	6 12	6 48	5 36	7 15	5 20
2	7 33	5 32	7 24	6 00	6 55	6 26	6 14	6 50	5 38	7 12	5 19	7 34	5 23	7 42	5 42	7 27	6 03	6 52	6 24	6 11	6 49	5 35	7 16	5 20
3	7 33	5 33	7 23	6 01	6 53	6 27	6 13	6 51	5 38	7 13	5 19	7 35	5 23	7 42	5 43	7 26	6 04	6 50	6 24	6 09	6 49	5 34	7 17	5 20
4	7 33	5 34	7 23	6 02	6 52	6 28	6 11	6 51	5 37	7 14	5 19	7 35	5 24	7 42	5 43	7 25	6 05	6 49	6 25	6 08	6 50	5 33	7 17	5 20
5	7 33	5 34	7 22	6 03	6 51	6 29	6 10	6 52	5 36	7 15	5 18	7 36	5 24	7 42	5 44	7 24	6 05	6 48	6 26	6 07	6 51	5 32	7 18	5 20
6	7 33	5 35	7 21	6 04	6 50	6 30	6 09	6 53	5 35	7 16	5 18	7 36	5 25	7 42	5 45	7 23	6 06	6 46	6 27	6 05	6 52	5 31	7 19	5 20
7	7 33	5 36	7 20	6 05	6 48	6 30	6 07	6 54	5 34	7 16	5 18	7 37	5 25	7 41	5 45	7 22	6 07	6 45	6 27	6 04	6 53	5 31	7 20	5 20
8	7 33	5 37	7 19	6 06	6 47	6 31	6 06	6 54	5 33	7 17	5 18	7 37	5 26	7 41	5 46	7 21	6 07	6 43	6 28	6 03	6 54	5 30	7 21	5 20
9	7 33	5 38	7 18	6 07	6 46	6 32	6 05	6 55	5 32	7 18	5 18	7 38	5 26	7 41	5 47	7 20	6 08	6 42	6 29	6 01	6 55	5 29	7 21	5 21
10	7 33	5 39	7 17	6 08	6 45	6 33	6 03	6 56	5 31	7 19	5 18	7 38	5 27	7 41	5 48	7 19	6 09	6 41	6 30	6 00	6 56	5 29	7 22	5 21
11	7 33	5 39	7 17	6 09	6 43	6 34	6 02	6 57	5 31	7 19	5 18	7 39	5 27	7 40	5 48	7 18	6 09	6 39	6 31	5 59	6 57	5 28	7 23	5 21
12	7 33	5 40	7 16	6 10	6 42	6 34	6 01	6 57	5 30	7 20	5 18	7 39	5 28	7 40	5 49	7 17	6 10	6 38	6 31	5 58	6 58	5 27	7 23	5 21
13	7 33	5 41	7 15	6 11	6 41	6 35	6 00	6 58	5 29	7 21	5 18	7 39	5 29	7 39	5 50	7 16	6 11	6 37	6 32	5 56	6 59	5 27	7 24	5 21
14	7 33	5 42	7 14	6 12	6 39	6 36	5 59	6 59	5 28	7 21	5 18	7 40	5 29	7 39	5 50	7 15	6 11	6 35	6 33	5 55	6 59	5 26	7 25	5 22
15	7 33	5 43	7 13	6 13	6 38	6 37	5 57	7 00	5 28	7 22	5 18	7 40	5 30	7 39	5 51	7 14	6 12	6 34	6 33	5 54	7 00	5 25	7 25	5 22
16	7 33	5 44	7 12	6 13	6 37	6 37	5 56	7 00	5 27	7 22	5 18	7 40	5 30	7 38	5 52	7 13	6 13	6 32	6 34	5 53	7 01	5 25	7 26	5 22
17	7 32	5 45	7 11	6 14	6 35	6 38	5 55	7 01	5 26	7 23	5 18	7 41	5 31	7 38	5 52	7 11	6 13	6 31	6 35	5 52	7 02	5 24	7 27	5 23
18	7 32	5 46	7 10	6 15	6 34	6 39	5 54	7 02	5 26	7 24	5 18	7 41	5 32	7 37	5 53	7 10	6 14	6 30	6 36	5 50	7 03	5 24	7 27	5 23
19	7 31	5 47	7 09	6 16	6 33	6 40	5 52	7 03	5 25	7 25	5 19	7 41	5 32	7 37	5 54	7 09	6 15	6 28	6 37	5 49	7 04	5 23	7 28	5 24
20	7 31	5 48	7 08	6 17	6 31	6 40	5 51	7 03	5 24	7 26	5 19	7 41	5 33	7 36	5 55	7 08	6 15	6 27	6 37	5 48	7 05	5 23	7 28	5 24
21	7 31	5 49	7 06	6 18	6 30	6 41	5 50	7 04	5 24	7 26	5 19	7 42	5 34	7 36	5 55	7 07	6 16	6 26	6 38	5 47	7 06	5 22	7 29	5 25
22	7 30	5 50	7 05	6 19	6 29	6 42	5 49	7 05	5 23	7 27	5 19	7 42	5 34	7 35	5 56	7 06	6 17	6 24	6 39	5 46	7 07	5 22	7 29	5 25
23	7 30	5 51	7 04	6 20	6 27	6 43	5 48	7 06	5 23	7 27	5 19	7 42	5 35	7 34	5 57	7 04	6 17	6 23	6 40	5 45	7 08	5 22	7 30	5 26
24	7 29	5 52	7 03	6 21	6 26	6 43	5 47	7 06	5 22	7 28	5 19	7 42	5 36	7 34	5 57	7 03	6 18	6 21	6 41	5 44	7 09	5 21	7 30	5 26
25	7 29	5 53	7 02	6 21	6 25	6 44	5 46	7 07	5 22	7 29	5 20	7 42	5 36	7 33	5 58	7 02	6 19	6 20	6 42	5 43	7 10	5 21	7 31	5 27
26	7 28	5 54	7 01	6 22	6 23	6 45	5 45	7 08	5 21	7 30	5 20	7 42	5 37	7 32	5 59	7 01	6 19	6 19	6 42	5 42	7 10	5 21	7 31	5 28
27	7 28	5 55	7 00	6 23	6 22	6 46	5 44	7 08	5 21	7 30	5 20	7 42	5 37	7 32	5 59	7 00	6 20	6 17	6 43	5 41	7 11	5 21	7 31	5 28
28	7 27	5 56	6 58	6 24	6 21	6 46	5 42	7 09	5 21	7 31	5 21	7 42	5 38	7 31	6 00	6 58	6 21	6 16	6 44	5 40	7 12	5 21	7 32	5 29
29	7 27	5 56			6 19	6 47	5 41	7 10	5 20	7 32	5 21	7 42	5 39	7 30	6 01	6 57	6 22	6 15	6 45	5 39	7 13	5 20	7 32	5 30
30	7 26	5 57			6 18	6 48	5 40	7 11	5 20	7 32	5 22	7 42	5 39	7 29	6 01	6 55	6 22	6 13	6 46	5 38	7 14	5 20	7 32	5 30
31	7 25	5 58			6 17	6 49			5 20	7 33			5 40	7 28	6 02	6 54			6 47	5 37			7 32	5 31

Add one hour for daylight time, if and when in use.
East Bound - Subtract 1 min/10 mi from center   West Bound - Add 1 min/10 mi from center

PHOENIX, ARIZONA

THE OVERLOAD COMPANION 2017 © FREDA BARBER BOOTH

Astronomical Applications Dept

Rise and Set for the Sun for 2017

U. S. Naval Observatory, Washington, DC

Location: W092 19, N34 44

LITTLE ROCK, ARKANSAS

Central Standard Time

	JAN		FEB		MAR		APR		MAY		JUN		JUL		AUG		SEP		OCT		NOV		DEC	
	AM	PM	AM	PM	AM	PM	AM	PM	AM	PM	AM	PM	AM	PM	AM	PM	AM	PM	AM	PM	AM	PM	AM	PM
1	7 17	5 09	7 08	5 38	6 38	6 06	5 56	6 31	5 18	6 55	4 57	7 18	5 00	7 26	5 20	7 11	5 43	6 35	6 04	5 53	6 30	5 15	6 59	4 58
2	7 17	5 10	7 07	5 39	6 37	6 07	5 54	6 32	5 17	6 56	4 57	7 18	5 00	7 26	5 20	7 10	5 43	6 34	6 05	5 51	6 31	5 14	7 00	4 58
3	7 17	5 11	7 06	5 40	6 35	6 07	5 53	6 32	5 16	6 56	4 57	7 19	5 01	7 26	5 21	7 09	5 44	6 32	6 06	5 50	6 32	5 13	7 00	4 58
4	7 17	5 11	7 06	5 41	6 34	6 08	5 51	6 33	5 15	6 57	4 56	7 19	5 01	7 26	5 22	7 08	5 45	6 31	6 07	5 48	6 33	5 12	7 01	4 58
5	7 17	5 12	7 05	5 42	6 33	6 09	5 50	6 34	5 14	6 58	4 56	7 20	5 02	7 26	5 23	7 07	5 45	6 29	6 07	5 47	6 34	5 11	7 02	4 58
6	7 17	5 13	7 04	5 43	6 31	6 10	5 49	6 35	5 13	6 59	4 56	7 20	5 02	7 26	5 23	7 06	5 46	6 28	6 08	5 46	6 35	5 10	7 03	4 58
7	7 17	5 14	7 03	5 44	6 30	6 11	5 47	6 36	5 12	7 00	4 56	7 21	5 03	7 25	5 24	7 05	5 47	6 27	6 09	5 44	6 36	5 10	7 04	4 58
8	7 17	5 15	7 02	5 45	6 29	6 12	5 46	6 36	5 11	7 00	4 56	7 21	5 03	7 25	5 25	7 04	5 48	6 25	6 10	5 43	6 37	5 09	7 05	4 58
9	7 17	5 16	7 01	5 46	6 27	6 12	5 45	6 37	5 10	7 01	4 56	7 22	5 04	7 25	5 26	7 03	5 48	6 24	6 11	5 42	6 38	5 08	7 05	4 59
10	7 17	5 17	7 00	5 47	6 26	6 13	5 43	6 38	5 09	7 02	4 56	7 22	5 05	7 25	5 26	7 02	5 49	6 22	6 12	5 40	6 39	5 07	7 06	4 59
11	7 17	5 17	6 59	5 48	6 25	6 14	5 42	6 39	5 08	7 03	4 56	7 23	5 05	7 24	5 27	7 01	5 50	6 21	6 12	5 39	6 40	5 07	7 07	4 59
12	7 17	5 18	6 58	5 49	6 23	6 15	5 41	6 40	5 08	7 03	4 56	7 23	5 06	7 24	5 28	7 00	5 50	6 20	6 13	5 38	6 41	5 06	7 08	4 59
13	7 17	5 19	6 57	5 50	6 22	6 16	5 40	6 40	5 07	7 04	4 56	7 24	5 06	7 24	5 29	6 59	5 51	6 18	6 14	5 36	6 42	5 05	7 08	4 59
14	7 17	5 20	6 56	5 51	6 21	6 17	5 38	6 41	5 07	7 05	4 56	7 24	5 07	7 23	5 29	6 58	5 52	6 17	6 15	5 35	6 43	5 05	7 09	5 00
15	7 17	5 21	6 55	5 52	6 19	6 17	5 37	6 42	5 06	7 06	4 56	7 24	5 08	7 23	5 30	6 57	5 53	6 15	6 15	5 34	6 44	5 04	7 10	5 00
16	7 16	5 22	6 54	5 53	6 18	6 18	5 36	6 43	5 05	7 07	4 56	7 25	5 08	7 22	5 31	6 55	5 53	6 14	6 16	5 33	6 45	5 03	7 10	5 00
17	7 16	5 23	6 53	5 54	6 16	6 19	5 34	6 44	5 04	7 07	4 56	7 25	5 09	7 22	5 32	6 54	5 54	6 12	6 17	5 31	6 46	5 03	7 11	5 01
18	7 16	5 24	6 52	5 55	6 15	6 20	5 33	6 44	5 04	7 08	4 56	7 25	5 10	7 21	5 33	6 53	5 55	6 11	6 18	5 30	6 47	5 02	7 11	5 01
19	7 15	5 25	6 51	5 56	6 14	6 21	5 32	6 45	5 03	7 09	4 56	7 25	5 10	7 21	5 34	6 52	5 56	6 10	6 19	5 29	6 48	5 02	7 12	5 01
20	7 15	5 26	6 50	5 57	6 12	6 21	5 31	6 46	5 03	7 10	4 56	7 26	5 11	7 20	5 34	6 51	5 56	6 08	6 20	5 28	6 49	5 01	7 12	5 02
21	7 14	5 27	6 49	5 58	6 11	6 22	5 30	6 47	5 02	7 10	4 56	7 26	5 12	7 19	5 35	6 49	5 57	6 07	6 21	5 27	6 50	5 01	7 13	5 02
22	7 14	5 28	6 48	5 58	6 09	6 23	5 28	6 48	5 01	7 11	4 57	7 26	5 12	7 19	5 35	6 48	5 58	6 05	6 22	5 25	6 51	5 00	7 13	5 03
23	7 13	5 29	6 46	5 59	6 08	6 24	5 27	6 48	5 01	7 12	4 57	7 26	5 13	7 18	5 36	6 47	5 58	6 04	6 22	5 24	6 52	5 00	7 14	5 04
24	7 13	5 30	6 45	6 00	6 07	6 25	5 26	6 49	5 00	7 13	4 57	7 26	5 14	7 17	5 37	6 46	5 59	6 02	6 23	5 23	6 53	5 00	7 14	5 04
25	7 12	5 31	6 44	6 01	6 05	6 25	5 25	6 50	5 00	7 14	4 58	7 26	5 15	7 17	5 38	6 44	6 00	6 01	6 24	5 22	6 53	4 59	7 15	5 05
26	7 12	5 32	6 43	6 02	6 04	6 26	5 24	6 51	4 59	7 14	4 58	7 26	5 15	7 16	5 38	6 43	6 01	6 00	6 25	5 21	6 54	4 59	7 15	5 06
27	7 11	5 33	6 42	6 03	6 02	6 27	5 23	6 52	4 59	7 15	4 58	7 27	5 16	7 15	5 39	6 42	6 01	5 58	6 26	5 20	6 55	4 59	7 16	5 06
28	7 11	5 34	6 40	6 04	6 01	6 28	5 22	6 53	4 58	7 16	4 59	7 27	5 17	7 14	5 40	6 40	6 02	5 57	6 27	5 19	6 56	4 59	7 16	5 07
29	7 10	5 35			6 00	6 29	5 20	6 53	4 58	7 16	4 59	7 27	5 17	7 14	5 40	6 39	6 03	5 55	6 28	5 18	6 57	4 58	7 15	5 07
30	7 09	5 36			5 58	6 29	5 19	6 54	4 58	7 17	5 00	7 26	5 18	7 13	5 41	6 38	6 04	5 54	6 28	5 17	6 58	4 58	7 16	5 08
31	7 09	5 37			5 57	6 30			4 57	7 17			5 19	7 12	5 42	6 36			6 29	5 16			7 16	5 09

Add one hour for daylight time, if and when in use.

East Bound - Subtract 1 min/10 mi from center   West Bound - Add 1 min/10 mi from center

LITTLE ROCK, ARKANSAS

THE OVERLOAD COMPANION 2017 © FREDA BARBER BOOTH

Astronomical Applications Dept
Rise and Set for the Sun for 2017
U. S. Naval Observatory, Washington, DC
LOCATION: W121 28, N38 34
SACRAMENTO, CALIFORNIA
Pacific Standard Time

	JAN AM	JAN PM	FEB AM	FEB PM	MAR AM	MAR PM	APR AM	APR PM	MAY AM	MAY PM	JUN AM	JUN PM	JUL AM	JUL PM	AUG AM	AUG PM	SEP AM	SEP PM	OCT AM	OCT PM	NOV AM	NOV PM	DEC AM	DEC PM
1	7 23	4 55	7 12	5 28	6 37	6 00	5 50	6 30	5 08	6 58	4 43	7 25	4 46	7 34	5 08	7 16	5 36	6 35	6 02	5 48	6 33	5 05	7 05	4 45
2	7 24	4 56	7 11	5 29	6 36	6 01	5 48	6 31	5 07	6 59	4 43	7 25	4 46	7 34	5 09	7 14	5 37	6 33	6 03	5 46	6 34	5 04	7 06	4 45
3	7 24	4 57	7 10	5 30	6 34	6 02	5 47	6 32	5 06	7 00	4 43	7 26	4 47	7 34	5 10	7 13	5 37	6 32	6 04	5 45	6 35	5 03	7 07	4 45
4	7 24	4 58	7 09	5 31	6 33	6 03	5 45	6 33	5 05	7 01	4 42	7 27	4 47	7 33	5 11	7 12	5 38	6 30	6 05	5 43	6 36	5 02	7 08	4 45
5	7 24	4 59	7 08	5 32	6 31	6 04	5 44	6 34	5 03	7 02	4 42	7 27	4 48	7 33	5 12	7 11	5 39	6 29	6 06	5 42	6 38	5 01	7 09	4 45
6	7 24	5 00	7 07	5 33	6 30	6 05	5 42	6 35	5 02	7 03	4 42	7 28	4 48	7 33	5 13	7 10	5 40	6 27	6 07	5 40	6 39	5 00	7 10	4 45
7	7 24	5 01	7 06	5 34	6 28	6 06	5 41	6 36	5 01	7 04	4 42	7 28	4 49	7 33	5 13	7 09	5 41	6 26	6 08	5 38	6 40	4 59	7 11	4 45
8	7 24	5 01	7 05	5 36	6 27	6 07	5 39	6 37	5 00	7 05	4 41	7 29	4 49	7 32	5 14	7 08	5 42	6 24	6 09	5 37	6 41	4 58	7 11	4 45
9	7 24	5 02	7 04	5 37	6 25	6 08	5 38	6 38	4 59	7 06	4 41	7 29	4 50	7 32	5 15	7 07	5 43	6 22	6 10	5 35	6 42	4 57	7 12	4 45
10	7 23	5 03	7 03	5 38	6 24	6 09	5 36	6 39	4 58	7 07	4 41	7 30	4 50	7 32	5 16	7 05	5 44	6 21	6 11	5 34	6 43	4 56	7 13	4 45
11	7 23	5 04	7 02	5 39	6 22	6 10	5 35	6 40	4 57	7 08	4 41	7 30	4 51	7 31	5 17	7 04	5 44	6 19	6 12	5 33	6 44	4 55	7 14	4 45
12	7 23	5 05	7 01	5 40	6 21	6 11	5 33	6 41	4 56	7 09	4 41	7 31	4 51	7 31	5 18	7 03	5 45	6 18	6 13	5 31	6 45	4 55	7 15	4 45
13	7 23	5 06	7 00	5 41	6 19	6 12	5 32	6 42	4 55	7 10	4 41	7 31	4 52	7 30	5 19	7 02	5 46	6 16	6 14	5 30	6 46	4 54	7 15	4 45
14	7 22	5 07	6 59	5 42	6 18	6 13	5 30	6 43	4 55	7 11	4 41	7 32	4 53	7 30	5 20	7 00	5 47	6 15	6 15	5 28	6 47	4 53	7 16	4 46
15	7 22	5 09	6 58	5 43	6 16	6 14	5 29	6 44	4 54	7 12	4 41	7 32	4 54	7 29	5 21	6 59	5 48	6 13	6 16	5 27	6 48	4 52	7 17	4 46
16	7 22	5 10	6 56	5 45	6 15	6 16	5 28	6 45	4 53	7 13	4 41	7 32	4 54	7 29	5 22	6 58	5 49	6 11	6 17	5 25	6 50	4 52	7 17	4 46
17	7 21	5 11	6 55	5 46	6 13	6 16	5 26	6 46	4 52	7 14	4 41	7 33	4 55	7 28	5 23	6 56	5 50	6 10	6 18	5 24	6 51	4 51	7 18	4 47
18	7 21	5 12	6 53	5 47	6 11	6 17	5 25	6 47	4 51	7 15	4 41	7 33	4 56	7 27	5 24	6 55	5 51	6 08	6 19	5 23	6 52	4 50	7 18	4 47
19	7 21	5 13	6 52	5 48	6 10	6 18	5 23	6 48	4 50	7 16	4 42	7 33	4 57	7 27	5 25	6 54	5 51	6 07	6 20	5 21	6 53	4 50	7 19	4 48
20	7 20	5 14	6 51	5 49	6 08	6 19	5 22	6 49	4 50	7 16	4 42	7 33	4 58	7 26	5 26	6 52	5 52	6 05	6 21	5 20	6 54	4 49	7 20	4 48
21	7 19	5 15	6 49	5 50	6 07	6 20	5 21	6 50	4 49	7 17	4 42	7 34	4 59	7 25	5 27	6 51	5 53	6 03	6 22	5 19	6 55	4 49	7 20	4 49
22	7 19	5 16	6 48	5 51	6 05	6 20	5 19	6 51	4 48	7 18	4 42	7 34	5 00	7 24	5 28	6 50	5 54	6 02	6 23	5 17	6 56	4 48	7 21	4 49
23	7 18	5 17	6 47	5 52	6 04	6 21	5 18	6 52	4 47	7 19	4 42	7 34	5 00	7 24	5 29	6 48	5 55	6 00	6 24	5 16	6 57	4 48	7 21	4 50
24	7 18	5 18	6 45	5 53	6 02	6 22	5 17	6 53	4 47	7 20	4 43	7 34	5 01	7 23	5 29	6 47	5 56	5 59	6 25	5 15	6 58	4 47	7 21	4 50
25	7 17	5 19	6 44	5 54	6 01	6 23	5 15	6 54	4 46	7 21	4 43	7 34	5 02	7 22	5 30	6 45	5 57	5 57	6 26	5 13	6 59	4 47	7 22	4 51
26	7 16	5 21	6 43	5 55	5 59	6 24	5 14	6 55	4 46	7 22	4 43	7 34	5 03	7 21	5 31	6 44	5 58	5 55	6 27	5 12	7 00	4 46	7 22	4 51
27	7 16	5 22	6 41	5 56	5 58	6 25	5 13	6 55	4 45	7 23	4 44	7 34	5 04	7 20	5 32	6 42	5 59	5 54	6 28	5 11	7 01	4 46	7 22	4 52
28	7 15	5 23	6 40	5 57	5 56	6 26	5 12	6 56	4 45	7 23	4 44	7 34	5 05	7 19	5 32	6 41	5 59	5 52	6 29	5 10	7 02	4 46	7 23	4 53
29	7 14	5 24			5 54	6 27	5 10	6 57	4 44	7 23	4 45	7 34	5 06	7 19	5 33	6 39	6 00	5 51	6 30	5 09	7 03	4 45	7 23	4 54
30	7 13	5 25			5 53	6 28	5 09	6 57	4 44	7 23	4 45	7 34	5 06	7 18	5 34	6 38	6 01	5 49	6 31	5 07	7 04	4 45	7 23	4 54
31	7 13	5 26			5 51	6 29			4 44	7 24			5 07	7 17	5 35	6 36			6 32	5 06			7 23	4 55

Add one hour for daylight time, if and when in use.
East Bound - Subtract 1 min/10 mi from center   West Bound - Add 1 min/10 mi from center

SACRAMENTO, CALIFORNIA

THE OVERLOAD COMPANION 2017 © FREDA BARBER BOOTH

Astronomical Applications Dept
LOCATION: W117 08, N32 45

Rise and Set for the Sun for 2017
SAN DIEGO, CALIFORNIA

U. S. Naval Observatory, Washington, DC
Pacific Standard Time

	JAN AM	JAN PM	FEB AM	FEB PM	MAR AM	MAR PM	APR AM	APR PM	MAY AM	MAY PM	JUN AM	JUN PM	JUL AM	JUL PM	AUG AM	AUG PM	SEP AM	SEP PM	OCT AM	OCT PM	NOV AM	NOV PM	DEC AM	DEC PM
1	6 51	4 53	6 44	5 21	6 16	5 46	5 36	6 09	5 01	6 31	4 41	6 52	4 45	7 00	5 03	6 46	5 24	6 12	5 43	5 32	6 07	4 57	6 33	4 42
2	6 51	4 54	6 43	5 22	6 14	5 47	5 35	6 10	5 00	6 31	4 41	6 52	4 45	7 00	5 04	6 46	5 24	6 11	5 44	5 31	6 08	4 56	6 34	4 42
3	6 51	4 55	6 42	5 23	6 13	5 48	5 33	6 11	4 59	6 32	4 41	6 53	4 45	7 00	5 04	6 45	5 25	6 10	5 44	5 30	6 09	4 55	6 35	4 42
4	6 51	4 56	6 42	5 24	6 12	5 49	5 32	6 11	4 58	6 33	4 41	6 54	4 46	7 00	5 05	6 44	5 26	6 09	5 45	5 28	6 09	4 55	6 36	4 42
5	6 52	4 56	6 41	5 25	6 11	5 49	5 31	6 12	4 57	6 33	4 41	6 54	4 46	7 00	5 06	6 43	5 26	6 07	5 46	5 27	6 10	4 54	6 37	4 42
6	6 52	4 57	6 40	5 26	6 10	5 50	5 29	6 13	4 56	6 34	4 40	6 55	4 47	7 00	5 06	6 42	5 27	6 06	5 47	5 26	6 11	4 53	6 37	4 42
7	6 52	4 58	6 39	5 27	6 08	5 51	5 28	6 13	4 55	6 35	4 40	6 55	4 47	7 00	5 07	6 41	5 28	6 05	5 47	5 25	6 12	4 52	6 38	4 42
8	6 52	4 59	6 38	5 27	6 07	5 52	5 27	6 14	4 55	6 36	4 40	6 56	4 48	6 59	5 08	6 40	5 28	6 03	5 48	5 23	6 13	4 51	6 39	4 43
9	6 52	5 00	6 38	5 28	6 06	5 53	5 26	6 15	4 54	6 36	4 40	6 56	4 48	6 59	5 08	6 39	5 29	6 02	5 49	5 22	6 14	4 51	6 40	4 43
10	6 52	5 01	6 37	5 29	6 04	5 53	5 24	6 15	4 53	6 37	4 40	6 56	4 49	6 59	5 09	6 38	5 29	6 01	5 49	5 21	6 15	4 50	6 40	4 43
11	6 52	5 01	6 36	5 30	6 03	5 54	5 23	6 16	4 52	6 38	4 40	6 57	4 50	6 58	5 10	6 37	5 30	5 59	5 50	5 20	6 16	4 49	6 41	4 43
12	6 52	5 02	6 35	5 31	6 02	5 55	5 22	6 17	4 51	6 39	4 40	6 57	4 50	6 58	5 10	6 36	5 31	5 58	5 51	5 18	6 16	4 49	6 42	4 43
13	6 51	5 03	6 34	5 32	6 01	5 56	5 21	6 18	4 51	6 40	4 40	6 58	4 51	6 58	5 11	6 35	5 31	5 57	5 52	5 17	6 17	4 48	6 43	4 44
14	6 51	5 04	6 33	5 33	5 59	5 56	5 19	6 18	4 50	6 40	4 40	6 58	4 51	6 58	5 12	6 34	5 32	5 55	5 52	5 16	6 18	4 48	6 43	4 44
15	6 51	5 05	6 32	5 34	5 58	5 57	5 18	6 19	4 49	6 41	4 40	6 58	4 52	6 57	5 12	6 33	5 33	5 54	5 53	5 15	6 19	4 47	6 44	4 44
16	6 51	5 06	6 31	5 35	5 57	5 58	5 17	6 20	4 49	6 42	4 40	6 59	4 52	6 57	5 13	6 32	5 33	5 53	5 54	5 14	6 20	4 47	6 44	4 45
17	6 51	5 07	6 30	5 36	5 55	5 58	5 16	6 21	4 48	6 43	4 40	6 59	4 53	6 56	5 14	6 31	5 34	5 51	5 55	5 12	6 21	4 46	6 45	4 45
18	6 50	5 08	6 29	5 36	5 54	5 59	5 15	6 21	4 47	6 43	4 41	6 59	4 54	6 56	5 15	6 29	5 35	5 50	5 55	5 11	6 22	4 46	6 46	4 46
19	6 50	5 09	6 28	5 37	5 53	6 00	5 14	6 22	4 47	6 44	4 41	6 59	4 54	6 55	5 15	6 28	5 35	5 48	5 56	5 10	6 23	4 45	6 46	4 46
20	6 50	5 10	6 27	5 38	5 52	6 01	5 12	6 23	4 46	6 45	4 41	7 00	4 55	6 55	5 16	6 27	5 36	5 47	5 57	5 09	6 24	4 45	6 47	4 47
21	6 49	5 11	6 26	5 39	5 50	6 01	5 11	6 23	4 46	6 46	4 41	7 00	4 56	6 54	5 16	6 26	5 36	5 46	5 58	5 08	6 25	4 44	6 47	4 47
22	6 49	5 11	6 25	5 40	5 49	6 02	5 10	6 24	4 45	6 46	4 41	7 00	4 56	6 54	5 17	6 25	5 37	5 44	5 58	5 07	6 26	4 44	6 48	4 48
23	6 49	5 12	6 24	5 41	5 48	6 03	5 09	6 25	4 45	6 47	4 41	7 00	4 57	6 53	5 18	6 24	5 38	5 43	5 59	5 06	6 26	4 44	6 48	4 48
24	6 48	5 13	6 23	5 41	5 46	6 03	5 08	6 26	4 44	6 48	4 42	7 00	4 58	6 53	5 18	6 22	5 38	5 42	6 00	5 05	6 27	4 43	6 49	4 49
25	6 48	5 14	6 22	5 42	5 45	6 04	5 07	6 26	4 44	6 48	4 42	7 00	4 58	6 52	5 19	6 21	5 39	5 40	6 01	5 04	6 28	4 43	6 49	4 49
26	6 47	5 15	6 21	5 43	5 44	6 05	5 06	6 27	4 43	6 49	4 43	7 00	4 59	6 51	5 20	6 20	5 40	5 39	6 02	5 03	6 29	4 43	6 49	4 50
27	6 47	5 16	6 20	5 44	5 42	6 06	5 05	6 28	4 43	6 50	4 43	7 00	5 00	6 50	5 20	6 19	5 40	5 38	6 03	5 02	6 30	4 43	6 50	4 50
28	6 46	5 17	6 19	5 45	5 41	6 06	5 04	6 29	4 42	6 51	4 44	7 01	5 00	6 50	5 21	6 17	5 41	5 36	6 03	5 01	6 31	4 43	6 50	4 51
29	6 46	5 18			5 40	6 07	5 03	6 29	4 42	6 51	4 44	7 01	5 01	6 49	5 22	6 16	5 42	5 35	6 04	5 00	6 32	4 42	6 51	4 52
30	6 45	5 19			5 38	6 08	5 02	6 30	4 42	6 51	4 44	7 01	5 02	6 48	5 22	6 15	5 42	5 34	6 05	4 59	6 33	4 42	6 51	4 52
31	6 44	5 20			5 37	6 08			4 42	6 51			5 02	6 47	5 23	6 14			6 06	4 58			6 51	4 53

Add one hour for daylight time, if and when in use.
East Bound - Subtract 1 min/10 mi from center   West Bound - Add 1 min/10 mi from center

SAN DIEGO, CALIFORNIA

THE OVERLOAD COMPANION 2017 © FREDA BARBER BOOTH

Astronomical Applications Dept
Location: W104 38, N38 17

Rise and Set for the Sun for 2017
PUEBLO, COLORADO

U. S. Naval Observatory, Washington, DC
Mountain Time Zone

	JAN AM	JAN PM	FEB AM	FEB PM	MAR AM	MAR PM	APR AM	APR PM	MAY AM	MAY PM	JUN AM	JUN PM	JUL AM	JUL PM	AUG AM	AUG PM	SEP AM	SEP PM	OCT AM	OCT PM	NOV AM	NOV PM	DEC AM	DEC PM
1	7 23	4 55	7 12	5 28	6 37	6 00	5 50	6 30	5 08	6 58	4 43	7 25	4 46	7 34	5 08	7 16	5 36	6 35	6 02	5 48	6 33	5 05	7 05	4 45
2	7 24	4 56	7 11	5 29	6 36	6 01	5 48	6 31	5 07	6 59	4 43	7 25	4 46	7 34	5 09	7 14	5 37	6 33	6 03	5 46	6 34	5 04	7 06	4 45
3	7 24	4 57	7 10	5 30	6 34	6 02	5 47	6 32	5 06	7 00	4 43	7 26	4 47	7 34	5 10	7 13	5 37	6 32	6 04	5 45	6 35	5 03	7 07	4 45
4	7 24	4 58	7 09	5 31	6 33	6 03	5 45	6 33	5 05	7 01	4 42	7 27	4 47	7 33	5 11	7 12	5 38	6 30	6 05	5 43	6 36	5 02	7 08	4 45
5	7 24	4 59	7 08	5 32	6 31	6 04	5 44	6 34	5 03	7 02	4 42	7 27	4 48	7 33	5 12	7 11	5 39	6 29	6 06	5 42	6 38	5 01	7 09	4 45
6	7 24	5 00	7 07	5 33	6 30	6 05	5 42	6 35	5 02	7 03	4 42	7 28	4 48	7 33	5 13	7 10	5 40	6 27	6 07	5 40	6 39	5 00	7 10	4 45
7	7 24	5 01	7 06	5 34	6 28	6 06	5 41	6 36	5 01	7 04	4 42	7 28	4 49	7 33	5 13	7 09	5 41	6 26	6 08	5 38	6 40	4 59	7 11	4 45
8	7 24	5 01	7 05	5 36	6 27	6 07	5 39	6 37	5 00	7 05	4 41	7 29	4 50	7 32	5 14	7 08	5 42	6 24	6 09	5 37	6 41	4 58	7 11	4 45
9	7 24	5 02	7 04	5 37	6 25	6 08	5 38	6 38	4 59	7 06	4 41	7 29	4 50	7 32	5 15	7 07	5 43	6 22	6 10	5 35	6 42	4 57	7 12	4 45
10	7 23	5 03	7 03	5 38	6 24	6 09	5 36	6 39	4 58	7 07	4 41	7 30	4 51	7 32	5 16	7 05	5 44	6 21	6 11	5 34	6 43	4 56	7 13	4 45
11	7 23	5 04	7 02	5 39	6 22	6 10	5 35	6 40	4 57	7 08	4 41	7 30	4 51	7 31	5 17	7 04	5 44	6 19	6 12	5 33	6 44	4 55	7 14	4 45
12	7 23	5 05	7 01	5 40	6 21	6 11	5 33	6 41	4 56	7 09	4 41	7 31	4 52	7 31	5 18	7 03	5 45	6 18	6 13	5 31	6 45	4 55	7 15	4 45
13	7 23	5 06	6 59	5 41	6 19	6 12	5 32	6 42	4 55	7 10	4 41	7 31	4 53	7 30	5 19	7 02	5 46	6 16	6 14	5 30	6 46	4 54	7 15	4 45
14	7 22	5 07	6 58	5 42	6 18	6 13	5 30	6 43	4 54	7 11	4 41	7 32	4 54	7 30	5 20	7 00	5 47	6 15	6 15	5 28	6 47	4 53	7 16	4 46
15	7 22	5 09	6 57	5 43	6 16	6 14	5 29	6 44	4 53	7 12	4 41	7 32	4 54	7 29	5 21	6 59	5 48	6 13	6 16	5 27	6 48	4 52	7 17	4 46
16	7 22	5 10	6 56	5 45	6 15	6 15	5 28	6 45	4 52	7 13	4 41	7 32	4 55	7 29	5 22	6 58	5 49	6 11	6 17	5 25	6 50	4 51	7 17	4 47
17	7 21	5 11	6 55	5 46	6 13	6 16	5 26	6 46	4 51	7 14	4 41	7 33	4 56	7 28	5 23	6 56	5 50	6 10	6 18	5 24	6 51	4 51	7 18	4 47
18	7 21	5 12	6 53	5 47	6 11	6 17	5 25	6 47	4 50	7 15	4 41	7 33	4 57	7 27	5 24	6 55	5 51	6 08	6 19	5 23	6 52	4 50	7 18	4 47
19	7 21	5 13	6 52	5 48	6 10	6 18	5 23	6 48	4 50	7 16	4 42	7 33	4 58	7 27	5 25	6 54	5 52	6 07	6 20	5 21	6 53	4 50	7 19	4 48
20	7 20	5 14	6 51	5 49	6 08	6 19	5 22	6 49	4 49	7 16	4 42	7 34	4 59	7 26	5 26	6 52	5 53	6 05	6 21	5 20	6 54	4 49	7 20	4 48
21	7 19	5 15	6 49	5 50	6 07	6 20	5 21	6 50	4 48	7 17	4 42	7 34	4 59	7 25	5 26	6 51	5 54	6 03	6 22	5 19	6 55	4 49	7 20	4 49
22	7 19	5 16	6 48	5 51	6 05	6 21	5 19	6 51	4 48	7 18	4 42	7 34	5 00	7 24	5 27	6 50	5 55	6 02	6 23	5 17	6 56	4 48	7 21	4 49
23	7 18	5 17	6 47	5 52	6 04	6 22	5 18	6 52	4 47	7 19	4 43	7 34	5 00	7 24	5 28	6 48	5 55	6 00	6 24	5 16	6 57	4 48	7 21	4 50
24	7 18	5 18	6 45	5 53	6 02	6 23	5 17	6 53	4 47	7 20	4 43	7 34	5 01	7 23	5 29	6 47	5 56	5 59	6 25	5 15	6 58	4 47	7 21	4 50
25	7 17	5 20	6 44	5 54	6 01	6 24	5 15	6 54	4 46	7 21	4 43	7 34	5 02	7 22	5 30	6 45	5 57	5 57	6 26	5 13	6 59	4 47	7 22	4 51
26	7 16	5 21	6 43	5 55	5 59	6 25	5 14	6 55	4 46	7 22	4 44	7 34	5 03	7 21	5 31	6 44	5 58	5 55	6 27	5 12	7 00	4 46	7 22	4 51
27	7 16	5 22	6 41	5 56	5 58	6 26	5 13	6 55	4 45	7 22	4 44	7 34	5 04	7 20	5 32	6 42	5 59	5 54	6 28	5 11	7 01	4 46	7 22	4 52
28	7 15	5 23	6 40	5 57	5 56	6 27	5 12	6 56	4 45	7 23	4 44	7 34	5 05	7 19	5 33	6 41	5 59	5 52	6 29	5 10	7 02	4 46	7 23	4 53
29	7 14	5 24			5 54	6 28	5 10	6 57	4 44	7 24	4 45	7 34	5 06	7 18	5 34	6 39	6 00	5 51	6 30	5 09	7 03	4 45	7 23	4 54
30	7 13	5 25			5 53	6 28	5 09	6 57	4 44	7 24	4 45	7 34	5 06	7 17	5 34	6 38	6 01	5 49	6 31	5 07	7 04	4 45	7 23	4 54
31	7 13	5 26			5 51	6 29			4 44	7 24			5 07	7 17	5 35	6 36			6 32	5 06			7 23	4 55

Add one hour for daylight time, if and when in use.
East Bound - Subtract 1 min/10 mi from center   West Bound - Add 1 min/10 mi from center

PUEBLO, COLORADO

THE OVERLOAD COMPANION 2017 © FREDA BARBER BOOTH

Astronomical Applications Dept
Location: W072 41, N41 46

Rise and Set for the Sun for 2017
HARTFORD, CONNECTICUT

U. S. Naval Observatory, Washington, DC
Eastern Standard Time

	JAN AM	JAN PM	FEB AM	FEB PM	MAR AM	MAR PM	APR AM	APR PM	MAY AM	MAY PM	JUN AM	JUN PM	JUL AM	JUL PM	AUG AM	AUG PM	SEP AM	SEP PM	OCT AM	OCT PM	NOV AM	NOV PM	DEC AM	DEC PM
1	7 18	4 30	7 03	5 06	6 25	5 42	5 33	6 17	4 47	6 50	4 18	7 19	4 20	7 29	4 45	7 08	5 17	6 23	5 48	5 32	6 24	4 45	6 59	4 21
2	7 18	4 31	7 02	5 07	6 23	5 43	5 31	6 18	4 45	6 51	4 18	7 20	4 21	7 29	4 46	7 07	5 18	6 22	5 49	5 30	6 25	4 43	7 00	4 21
3	7 18	4 32	7 01	5 08	6 22	5 44	5 29	6 19	4 44	6 52	4 17	7 21	4 21	7 29	4 47	7 06	5 19	6 20	5 50	5 28	6 26	4 42	7 01	4 20
4	7 18	4 33	7 00	5 09	6 20	5 45	5 28	6 20	4 43	6 53	4 17	7 22	4 22	7 29	4 48	7 05	5 20	6 18	5 51	5 27	6 27	4 41	7 02	4 20
5	7 18	4 34	6 59	5 11	6 18	5 46	5 26	6 21	4 42	6 54	4 17	7 22	4 22	7 28	4 49	7 03	5 21	6 16	5 52	5 25	6 28	4 40	7 03	4 20
6	7 18	4 35	6 58	5 12	6 17	5 48	5 24	6 22	4 40	6 55	4 17	7 23	4 23	7 28	4 50	7 02	5 22	6 15	5 54	5 23	6 30	4 39	7 04	4 20
7	7 18	4 36	6 57	5 13	6 15	5 49	5 23	6 23	4 39	6 56	4 16	7 23	4 24	7 28	4 51	7 01	5 23	6 13	5 55	5 22	6 31	4 38	7 05	4 20
8	7 18	4 37	6 56	5 15	6 13	5 50	5 21	6 24	4 38	6 57	4 16	7 24	4 24	7 27	4 52	7 00	5 24	6 11	5 56	5 20	6 32	4 37	7 06	4 20
9	7 18	4 38	6 55	5 16	6 12	5 51	5 20	6 26	4 37	6 58	4 16	7 25	4 25	7 27	4 53	6 58	5 25	6 10	5 57	5 18	6 33	4 35	7 07	4 20
10	7 17	4 39	6 53	5 17	6 10	5 52	5 18	6 27	4 36	6 59	4 16	7 25	4 26	7 26	4 54	6 57	5 26	6 08	5 58	5 17	6 35	4 34	7 08	4 20
11	7 17	4 40	6 52	5 18	6 09	5 53	5 16	6 28	4 35	7 00	4 16	7 26	4 27	7 26	4 55	6 56	5 27	6 06	5 59	5 15	6 36	4 33	7 09	4 20
12	7 17	4 41	6 51	5 20	6 07	5 55	5 15	6 29	4 34	7 01	4 16	7 26	4 27	7 25	4 57	6 54	5 28	6 04	6 00	5 13	6 37	4 33	7 10	4 21
13	7 17	4 42	6 50	5 21	6 05	5 56	5 13	6 30	4 33	7 02	4 15	7 27	4 28	7 25	4 58	6 53	5 29	6 03	6 01	5 12	6 38	4 32	7 10	4 21
14	7 16	4 44	6 48	5 22	6 03	5 57	5 11	6 31	4 32	7 03	4 15	7 27	4 29	7 24	4 59	6 51	5 30	6 01	6 02	5 10	6 39	4 31	7 11	4 21
15	7 16	4 45	6 47	5 23	6 02	5 58	5 10	6 32	4 31	7 04	4 15	7 27	4 30	7 23	5 00	6 50	5 31	5 59	6 04	5 09	6 41	4 30	7 11	4 21
16	7 15	4 46	6 46	5 25	6 00	5 59	5 08	6 33	4 30	7 05	4 16	7 28	4 30	7 23	5 01	6 48	5 32	5 58	6 05	5 07	6 42	4 29	7 12	4 21
17	7 15	4 47	6 44	5 26	5 58	6 00	5 07	6 34	4 29	7 06	4 16	7 28	4 31	7 22	5 02	6 47	5 33	5 56	6 06	5 06	6 43	4 28	7 13	4 22
18	7 14	4 48	6 43	5 27	5 57	6 01	5 05	6 35	4 28	7 07	4 16	7 28	4 32	7 21	5 03	6 45	5 34	5 54	6 07	5 04	6 44	4 27	7 13	4 22
19	7 14	4 49	6 41	5 28	5 55	6 02	5 04	6 37	4 27	7 08	4 16	7 29	4 33	7 21	5 04	6 44	5 35	5 52	6 08	5 02	6 45	4 27	7 14	4 23
20	7 13	4 51	6 40	5 30	5 53	6 04	5 02	6 38	4 26	7 09	4 16	7 29	4 34	7 20	5 05	6 42	5 36	5 51	6 09	5 01	6 47	4 26	7 14	4 23
21	7 13	4 52	6 39	5 31	5 52	6 05	5 01	6 39	4 25	7 10	4 16	7 29	4 35	7 19	5 06	6 41	5 37	5 49	6 10	5 00	6 48	4 25	7 15	4 24
22	7 12	4 53	6 37	5 32	5 50	6 06	4 59	6 40	4 24	7 11	4 17	7 29	4 36	7 18	5 07	6 39	5 38	5 47	6 12	4 58	6 49	4 25	7 15	4 24
23	7 11	4 54	6 36	5 33	5 48	6 07	4 58	6 41	4 24	7 12	4 17	7 29	4 37	7 17	5 08	6 38	5 39	5 45	6 13	4 57	6 50	4 24	7 16	4 25
24	7 10	4 55	6 34	5 35	5 46	6 08	4 56	6 42	4 23	7 13	4 17	7 29	4 38	7 16	5 09	6 36	5 40	5 44	6 14	4 55	6 51	4 24	7 16	4 25
25	7 10	4 57	6 33	5 36	5 45	6 09	4 55	6 43	4 22	7 14	4 17	7 30	4 39	7 15	5 10	6 35	5 42	5 42	6 15	4 54	6 52	4 23	7 16	4 26
26	7 09	4 58	6 31	5 37	5 43	6 10	4 53	6 44	4 22	7 15	4 18	7 30	4 39	7 14	6 11	6 33	5 43	5 40	6 16	4 52	6 54	4 23	7 17	4 26
27	7 08	4 59	6 30	5 38	5 41	6 11	4 52	6 45	4 21	7 16	4 18	7 29	4 40	7 13	5 12	6 31	5 44	5 38	6 18	4 51	6 55	4 22	7 17	4 27
28	7 07	5 00	6 28	5 39	5 40	6 12	4 51	6 46	4 21	7 17	4 18	7 29	4 41	7 12	5 13	6 30	5 45	5 37	6 19	4 50	6 56	4 22	7 17	4 28
29	7 06	5 02			5 38	6 13	4 49	6 47	4 20	7 17	4 19	7 29	4 42	7 11	5 14	6 28	5 46	5 35	6 20	4 48	6 57	4 21	7 18	4 29
30	7 05	5 03			5 36	6 15	4 48	6 49	4 19	7 18	4 20	7 29	4 43	7 10	5 15	6 27	5 47	5 33	6 21	4 47	6 58	4 21	7 18	4 29
31	7 04	5 04			5 35	6 16			4 19	7 19			4 44	7 09	5 16	6 25			6 22	4 46			7 18	4 30

Add one hour for daylight time, if and when in use.
East Bound - Subtract 1 min/10 mi from center   West Bound - Add 1 min/10 mi from center

HARTFORD, CONNECTICUT

Astronomical Applications Dept
Location: W075 32, N39 10

Rise and Set for the Sun for 2017
DOVER, DELAWARE

U. S. Naval Observatory, Washington, DC
Eastern Standard Time

	JAN AM	JAN PM	FEB AM	FEB PM	MAR AM	MAR PM	APR AM	APR PM	MAY AM	MAY PM	JUN AM	JUN PM	JUL AM	JUL PM	AUG AM	AUG PM	SEP AM	SEP PM	OCT AM	OCT PM	NOV AM	NOV PM	DEC AM	DEC PM
1	7 21	4 50	7 09	5 22	6 34	5 55	5 46	6 26	5 03	6 56	4 38	7 23	4 40	7 32	5 03	7 13	5 31	6 32	5 59	5 44	6 30	5 01	7 03	4 40
2	7 22	4 51	7 08	5 24	6 33	5 56	5 44	6 27	5 02	6 57	4 37	7 23	4 40	7 32	5 04	7 12	5 32	6 30	6 00	5 42	6 31	4 59	7 04	4 40
3	7 22	4 51	7 07	5 25	6 31	5 57	5 43	6 28	5 01	6 58	4 37	7 24	4 41	7 32	5 05	7 11	5 33	6 29	6 00	5 41	6 33	4 58	7 05	4 39
4	7 22	4 52	7 06	5 26	6 30	5 58	5 41	6 29	5 00	6 59	4 37	7 24	4 41	7 32	5 06	7 10	5 34	6 27	6 01	5 39	6 34	4 57	7 06	4 39
5	7 22	4 53	7 05	5 27	6 28	5 59	5 40	6 30	4 59	7 00	4 36	7 25	4 42	7 31	5 07	7 09	5 35	6 26	6 02	5 38	6 35	4 56	7 07	4 39
6	7 22	4 54	7 04	5 28	6 27	6 00	5 38	6 31	4 57	7 00	4 36	7 25	4 42	7 31	5 07	7 08	5 36	6 24	6 03	5 36	6 36	4 55	7 08	4 39
7	7 22	4 55	7 03	5 29	6 25	6 01	5 37	6 32	4 56	7 01	4 36	7 26	4 43	7 31	5 08	7 07	5 37	6 22	6 04	5 35	6 37	4 54	7 08	4 39
8	7 22	4 56	7 02	5 31	6 24	6 03	5 35	6 33	4 55	7 02	4 36	7 27	4 44	7 30	5 09	7 05	5 38	6 21	6 05	5 33	6 38	4 53	7 09	4 39
9	7 21	4 57	7 01	5 32	6 22	6 04	5 34	6 34	4 54	7 03	4 36	7 28	4 45	7 30	5 10	7 04	5 38	6 19	6 06	5 32	6 39	4 52	7 10	4 39
10	7 21	4 58	7 00	5 33	6 20	6 05	5 32	6 35	4 53	7 04	4 36	7 28	4 45	7 30	5 11	7 03	5 39	6 18	6 07	5 30	6 40	4 51	7 11	4 39
11	7 21	4 59	6 59	5 34	6 19	6 06	5 31	6 36	4 52	7 05	4 36	7 28	4 46	7 29	5 12	7 02	5 40	6 16	6 08	5 29	6 41	4 51	7 12	4 40
12	7 21	5 00	6 58	5 35	6 17	6 07	5 29	6 37	4 51	7 06	4 36	7 29	4 47	7 29	5 13	7 00	5 41	6 14	6 09	5 27	6 43	4 50	7 12	4 40
13	7 21	5 01	6 57	5 36	6 16	6 08	5 28	6 38	4 50	7 07	4 35	7 29	4 47	7 28	5 14	6 59	5 42	6 13	6 10	5 26	6 44	4 49	7 13	4 40
14	7 20	5 02	6 56	5 38	6 14	6 09	5 26	6 39	4 49	7 08	4 35	7 30	4 48	7 28	5 15	6 58	5 43	6 11	6 11	5 24	6 45	4 48	7 14	4 40
15	7 20	5 03	6 54	5 39	6 13	6 10	5 25	6 40	4 48	7 09	4 35	7 30	4 49	7 27	5 16	6 57	5 44	6 10	6 12	5 23	6 46	4 47	7 15	4 40
16	7 20	5 04	6 53	5 40	6 11	6 11	5 23	6 41	4 47	7 10	4 35	7 30	4 50	7 27	5 17	6 55	5 45	6 08	6 13	5 21	6 47	4 47	7 15	4 41
17	7 19	5 05	6 52	5 41	6 10	6 12	5 22	6 42	4 46	7 11	4 35	7 31	4 50	7 26	5 18	6 54	5 46	6 06	6 14	5 20	6 48	4 46	7 16	4 41
18	7 19	5 06	6 51	5 42	6 08	6 13	5 20	6 43	4 45	7 12	4 36	7 31	4 51	7 25	5 18	6 53	5 47	6 05	6 15	5 18	6 49	4 45	7 16	4 42
19	7 18	5 07	6 49	5 43	6 06	6 14	5 19	6 44	4 45	7 13	4 36	7 31	4 52	7 25	5 19	6 51	5 47	6 03	6 16	5 17	6 50	4 45	7 17	4 42
20	7 18	5 09	6 48	5 44	6 05	6 15	5 18	6 45	4 44	7 14	4 36	7 31	4 53	7 24	5 20	6 50	5 48	6 02	6 17	5 16	6 51	4 44	7 18	4 42
21	7 17	5 10	6 47	5 45	6 03	6 16	5 16	6 46	4 43	7 15	4 36	7 32	4 53	7 23	5 21	6 48	5 49	6 00	6 18	5 14	6 53	4 44	7 18	4 43
22	7 17	5 11	6 45	5 47	6 02	6 17	5 15	6 47	4 43	7 16	4 36	7 32	4 54	7 22	5 22	6 47	5 50	5 58	6 20	5 13	6 54	4 43	7 18	4 43
23	7 16	5 12	6 44	5 48	6 00	6 18	5 13	6 48	4 42	7 16	4 36	7 32	4 55	7 22	5 23	6 45	5 51	5 57	6 21	5 12	6 55	4 42	7 19	4 44
24	7 15	5 13	6 43	5 49	5 59	6 19	5 12	6 49	4 42	7 17	4 37	7 32	4 56	7 21	5 24	6 44	5 52	5 55	6 22	5 10	6 56	4 42	7 19	4 45
25	7 15	5 14	6 41	5 50	5 57	6 20	5 11	6 50	4 41	7 18	4 37	7 32	4 57	7 20	5 25	6 43	5 53	5 53	6 23	5 09	6 57	4 42	7 20	4 45
26	7 14	5 15	6 40	5 51	5 55	6 21	5 09	6 51	4 41	7 19	4 38	7 32	4 58	7 19	5 26	6 41	5 54	5 52	6 24	5 08	6 58	4 41	7 20	4 46
27	7 13	5 17	6 38	5 52	5 54	6 22	5 08	6 52	4 40	7 20	4 38	7 32	4 59	7 18	5 27	6 40	5 55	5 50	6 25	5 06	6 59	4 41	7 20	4 47
28	7 13	5 18	6 37	5 53	5 52	6 23	5 07	6 53	4 40	7 21	4 39	7 32	4 59	7 17	5 28	6 38	5 56	5 49	6 26	5 05	7 00	4 40	7 21	4 47
29	7 12	5 19			5 51	6 23	5 06	6 54	4 39	7 21	4 39	7 32	5 00	7 16	5 28	6 37	5 57	5 47	6 27	5 04	7 01	4 40	7 21	4 48
30	7 11	5 20			5 49	6 24	5 04	6 55	4 39	7 21	4 39	7 32	5 01	7 15	5 29	6 35	5 58	5 46	6 28	5 03	7 02	4 40	7 21	4 49
31	7 10	5 21			5 47	6 25			4 38	7 22			5 02	7 14	5 30	6 33			6 29	5 02			7 21	4 50

Add one hour for daylight time, if and when in use.

East Bound - Subtract 1 min/10 mi from center   West Bound - Add 1 min/10 mi from center

DOVER, DELAWARE

Astronomical Applications Dept
Location: W081 23, N28 32

Rise and Set for the Sun for 2017
ORLANDO, FLORIDA

U. S. Naval Observatory, Washington, DC
Eastern Standard Time

	JAN AM	JAN PM	FEB AM	FEB PM	MAR AM	MAR PM	APR AM	APR PM	MAY AM	MAY PM	JUN AM	JUN PM	JUL AM	JUL PM	AUG AM	AUG PM	SEP AM	SEP PM	OCT AM	OCT PM	NOV AM	NOV PM	DEC AM	DEC PM
1	7 18	5 40	7 14	6 05	6 50	6 26	6 15	6 44	5 44	7 01	5 28	7 19	5 32	7 27	5 47	7 16	6 04	6 46	6 19	6 11	6 38	5 40	7 01	5 28
2	7 18	5 41	7 13	6 06	6 49	6 27	6 14	6 44	5 44	7 02	5 28	7 19	5 32	7 27	5 48	7 15	6 04	6 45	6 19	6 10	6 39	5 39	7 02	5 28
3	7 19	5 41	7 13	6 06	6 48	6 27	6 13	6 45	5 43	7 02	5 28	7 20	5 32	7 27	5 49	7 14	6 05	6 44	6 20	6 08	6 39	5 39	7 03	5 28
4	7 19	5 42	7 12	6 07	6 47	6 28	6 12	6 46	5 42	7 03	5 28	7 20	5 33	7 27	5 49	7 14	6 05	6 43	6 20	6 07	6 40	5 38	7 03	5 29
5	7 19	5 43	7 11	6 08	6 46	6 28	6 10	6 46	5 41	7 03	5 28	7 21	5 33	7 27	5 50	7 13	6 06	6 42	6 21	6 06	6 41	5 37	7 04	5 29
6	7 19	5 44	7 11	6 09	6 45	6 29	6 09	6 47	5 41	7 04	5 28	7 21	5 34	7 27	5 50	7 12	6 06	6 40	6 21	6 05	6 42	5 37	7 05	5 29
7	7 19	5 44	7 10	6 10	6 44	6 30	6 08	6 47	5 40	7 05	5 27	7 22	5 34	7 27	5 51	7 11	6 07	6 39	6 22	6 04	6 42	5 36	7 05	5 29
8	7 19	5 45	7 09	6 10	6 42	6 30	6 07	6 48	5 39	7 05	5 27	7 22	5 35	7 27	5 51	7 10	6 07	6 38	6 23	6 03	6 43	5 35	7 06	5 29
9	7 19	5 46	7 09	6 11	6 41	6 31	6 06	6 48	5 38	7 06	5 27	7 23	5 35	7 26	5 52	7 10	6 08	6 37	6 23	6 02	6 44	5 35	7 07	5 30
10	7 19	5 47	7 08	6 12	6 40	6 31	6 05	6 49	5 38	7 06	5 27	7 23	5 36	7 26	5 52	7 09	6 08	6 36	6 24	6 01	6 45	5 34	7 08	5 30
11	7 19	5 47	7 07	6 13	6 39	6 32	6 04	6 49	5 37	7 07	5 27	7 23	5 36	7 26	5 53	7 08	6 09	6 35	6 24	6 00	6 45	5 34	7 08	5 30
12	7 19	5 48	7 06	6 13	6 38	6 33	6 03	6 50	5 36	7 08	5 27	7 24	5 37	7 26	5 53	7 07	6 09	6 33	6 25	5 58	6 46	5 33	7 09	5 30
13	7 19	5 49	7 06	6 14	6 37	6 33	6 02	6 51	5 36	7 08	5 27	7 24	5 37	7 25	5 54	7 06	6 10	6 32	6 25	5 57	6 47	5 33	7 10	5 31
14	7 19	5 50	7 05	6 15	6 36	6 34	6 01	6 51	5 35	7 09	5 27	7 24	5 38	7 25	5 55	7 05	6 10	6 31	6 26	5 56	6 48	5 32	7 10	5 31
15	7 19	5 51	7 04	6 16	6 35	6 34	6 00	6 52	5 35	7 09	5 27	7 25	5 38	7 25	5 55	7 04	6 11	6 30	6 27	5 55	6 48	5 32	7 11	5 31
16	7 19	5 51	7 03	6 16	6 33	6 35	5 59	6 52	5 34	7 10	5 28	7 25	5 39	7 24	5 56	7 03	6 11	6 29	6 27	5 54	6 49	5 31	7 11	5 32
17	7 19	5 52	7 02	6 17	6 32	6 36	5 58	6 53	5 34	7 11	5 28	7 25	5 39	7 24	5 56	7 02	6 12	6 27	6 28	5 53	6 50	5 31	7 12	5 32
18	7 19	5 53	7 02	6 18	6 31	6 36	5 57	6 53	5 33	7 11	5 28	7 26	5 40	7 24	5 57	7 01	6 12	6 26	6 28	5 52	6 51	5 31	7 13	5 33
19	7 19	5 54	7 01	6 18	6 30	6 37	5 56	6 54	5 33	7 12	5 28	7 26	5 40	7 23	5 58	7 00	6 13	6 25	6 29	5 51	6 52	5 30	7 13	5 33
20	7 19	5 55	7 00	6 19	6 29	6 37	5 55	6 55	5 32	7 12	5 28	7 26	5 41	7 23	5 58	6 59	6 13	6 24	6 30	5 50	6 52	5 30	7 14	5 34
21	7 18	5 56	6 59	6 20	6 28	6 38	5 54	6 55	5 32	7 13	5 28	7 26	5 41	7 22	5 59	6 58	6 14	6 23	6 30	5 49	6 53	5 29	7 14	5 34
22	7 18	5 56	6 58	6 21	6 27	6 38	5 53	6 56	5 31	7 14	5 29	7 26	5 42	7 22	5 59	6 57	6 14	6 21	6 31	5 48	6 54	5 29	7 15	5 35
23	7 18	5 57	6 57	6 21	6 25	6 39	5 52	6 56	5 31	7 14	5 29	7 27	5 42	7 21	6 00	6 56	6 15	6 20	6 32	5 48	6 55	5 29	7 15	5 35
24	7 17	5 58	6 56	6 22	6 24	6 39	5 51	6 57	5 30	7 15	5 29	7 27	5 43	7 21	6 00	6 55	6 15	6 19	6 32	5 47	6 56	5 29	7 15	5 36
25	7 17	5 59	6 55	6 23	6 23	6 40	5 50	6 58	5 30	7 15	5 29	7 27	5 43	7 20	6 01	6 54	6 16	6 18	6 33	5 46	6 56	5 29	7 16	5 36
26	7 16	6 00	6 54	6 23	6 22	6 41	5 49	6 58	5 29	7 16	5 30	7 27	5 44	7 20	6 01	6 53	6 16	6 17	6 34	5 45	6 57	5 29	7 16	5 37
27	7 16	6 01	6 53	6 24	6 21	6 41	5 48	6 59	5 29	7 17	5 30	7 27	5 44	7 19	6 02	6 52	6 17	6 15	6 34	5 44	6 58	5 29	7 17	5 37
28	7 16	6 01	6 52	6 25	6 20	6 42	5 47	7 00	5 29	7 17	5 31	7 27	5 45	7 19	6 02	6 51	6 17	6 14	6 35	5 43	6 59	5 28	7 17	5 38
29	7 15	6 02			6 18	6 42	5 46	7 00	5 28	7 18	5 31	7 27	5 45	7 18	6 02	6 50	6 18	6 13	6 36	5 42	7 00	5 28	7 18	5 38
30	7 15	6 03			6 17	6 43	5 45	7 00	5 28	7 18	5 31	7 27	5 46	7 18	6 03	6 48	6 18	6 12	6 36	5 42	7 00	5 28	7 18	5 39
31	7 14	6 04			6 16	6 43			5 28	7 18			5 47	7 16	6 03	6 47			6 37	5 41			7 18	5 40

Add one hour for daylight time, if and when in use.
East Bound - Subtract 1 min/10 mi from center   West Bound - Add 1 min/10 mi from center

ORLANDO, FLORIDA

THE OVERLOAD COMPANION 2017 © FREDA BARBER BOOTH

Astronomical Applications Dept
Location: W084 17, N30 26

Rise and Set for the Sun for 2017
TALLAHASSEE, FLORIDA

U. S. Naval Observatory, Washington, DC
Eastern Standard Time

	JAN AM	JAN PM	FEB AM	FEB PM	MAR AM	MAR PM	APR AM	APR PM	MAY AM	MAY PM	JUN AM	JUN PM	JUL AM	JUL PM	AUG AM	AUG PM	SEP AM	SEP PM	OCT AM	OCT PM	NOV AM	NOV PM	DEC AM	DEC PM
1	7 34	5 47	7 28	6 13	7 03	6 36	6 26	6 56	5 53	7 16	5 35	7 35	5 39	7 43	5 56	7 31	6 14	6 59	6 31	6 22	6 52	5 49	7 17	5 36
2	7 34	5 48	7 28	6 14	7 02	6 37	6 24	6 57	5 52	7 16	5 35	7 35	5 39	7 43	5 56	7 30	6 15	6 58	6 32	6 21	6 53	5 48	7 18	5 36
3	7 34	5 49	7 27	6 15	7 01	6 38	6 23	6 58	5 51	7 17	5 35	7 36	5 40	7 43	5 57	7 29	6 15	6 57	6 32	6 19	6 54	5 48	7 18	5 36
4	7 35	5 50	7 27	6 16	6 59	6 39	6 22	6 58	5 51	7 18	5 35	7 36	5 40	7 43	5 58	7 28	6 16	6 56	6 33	6 18	6 54	5 47	7 19	5 36
5	7 35	5 50	7 26	6 17	6 58	6 39	6 21	6 59	5 50	7 18	5 35	7 37	5 41	7 43	5 58	7 28	6 16	6 54	6 33	6 17	6 55	5 46	7 20	5 36
6	7 35	5 51	7 25	6 18	6 57	6 40	6 20	7 00	5 49	7 19	5 35	7 37	5 41	7 43	5 59	7 27	6 17	6 53	6 34	6 16	6 56	5 45	7 21	5 36
7	7 35	5 52	7 24	6 18	6 56	6 41	6 19	7 00	5 48	7 20	5 35	7 38	5 42	7 43	5 59	7 26	6 17	6 52	6 35	6 15	6 57	5 45	7 21	5 36
8	7 35	5 53	7 24	6 19	6 56	6 41	6 17	7 01	5 47	7 20	5 35	7 38	5 42	7 43	6 00	7 25	6 18	6 51	6 35	6 13	6 58	5 44	7 22	5 37
9	7 35	5 53	7 23	6 20	6 54	6 42	6 16	7 01	5 47	7 21	5 34	7 39	5 42	7 42	6 01	7 24	6 19	6 49	6 36	6 12	6 58	5 43	7 23	5 37
10	7 35	5 54	7 22	6 21	6 52	6 43	6 15	7 02	5 46	7 22	5 34	7 39	5 43	7 42	6 01	7 23	6 19	6 48	6 36	6 11	6 59	5 42	7 24	5 38
11	7 35	5 55	7 21	6 22	6 51	6 43	6 14	7 03	5 45	7 22	5 34	7 40	5 44	7 42	6 02	7 22	6 20	6 47	6 37	6 10	7 00	5 42	7 24	5 38
12	7 35	5 56	7 20	6 23	6 50	6 44	6 13	7 03	5 45	7 23	5 34	7 40	5 44	7 42	6 02	7 21	6 20	6 46	6 38	6 09	7 01	5 41	7 25	5 38
13	7 35	5 57	7 20	6 23	6 49	6 44	6 12	7 04	5 44	7 23	5 34	7 40	5 45	7 41	6 03	7 20	6 21	6 44	6 38	6 08	7 02	5 40	7 26	5 39
14	7 35	5 58	7 19	6 24	6 48	6 45	6 10	7 05	5 43	7 24	5 35	7 41	5 45	7 41	6 04	7 19	6 21	6 43	6 39	6 07	7 03	5 40	7 26	5 39
15	7 35	5 58	7 18	6 25	6 46	6 46	6 09	7 05	5 43	7 25	5 35	7 41	5 46	7 41	6 04	7 18	6 22	6 42	6 40	6 05	7 03	5 39	7 27	5 39
16	7 35	5 59	7 17	6 26	6 45	6 46	6 08	7 06	5 42	7 25	5 35	7 42	5 46	7 40	6 05	7 17	6 22	6 41	6 40	6 04	7 04	5 39	7 27	5 40
17	7 34	6 00	7 16	6 27	6 44	6 47	6 07	7 06	5 41	7 26	5 35	7 42	5 47	7 40	6 06	7 16	6 23	6 39	6 41	6 03	7 05	5 39	7 28	5 40
18	7 34	6 01	7 15	6 27	6 43	6 47	6 06	7 07	5 41	7 27	5 35	7 42	5 47	7 39	6 06	7 15	6 24	6 38	6 42	6 02	7 06	5 38	7 29	5 40
19	7 34	6 02	7 14	6 28	6 42	6 48	6 05	7 08	5 40	7 27	5 35	7 42	5 48	7 39	6 07	7 14	6 24	6 37	6 42	6 01	7 07	5 38	7 29	5 40
20	7 34	6 03	7 13	6 29	6 40	6 49	6 04	7 08	5 40	7 28	5 35	7 42	5 49	7 38	6 07	7 13	6 25	6 36	6 43	6 00	7 08	5 38	7 30	5 41
21	7 34	6 04	7 12	6 30	6 39	6 50	6 03	7 09	5 39	7 29	5 36	7 43	5 49	7 38	6 08	7 12	6 25	6 34	6 44	5 59	7 08	5 38	7 30	5 41
22	7 33	6 05	7 11	6 31	6 38	6 50	6 02	7 10	5 39	7 29	5 36	7 43	5 50	7 37	6 08	7 11	6 26	6 33	6 45	5 58	7 09	5 37	7 31	5 42
23	7 33	6 05	7 10	6 31	6 37	6 51	6 01	7 10	5 38	7 30	5 36	7 43	5 50	7 37	6 09	7 10	6 26	6 32	6 45	5 57	7 10	5 37	7 31	5 42
24	7 32	6 06	7 09	6 32	6 35	6 52	6 00	7 11	5 38	7 31	5 36	7 43	5 51	7 36	6 10	7 09	6 27	6 31	6 46	5 56	7 11	5 37	7 32	5 43
25	7 32	6 07	7 08	6 33	6 34	6 52	5 59	7 12	5 38	7 32	5 37	7 43	5 52	7 35	6 10	7 08	6 27	6 29	6 47	5 55	7 12	5 37	7 32	5 43
26	7 32	6 08	7 07	6 33	6 33	6 53	5 58	7 12	5 37	7 32	5 37	7 43	5 52	7 35	6 11	7 06	6 28	6 28	6 47	5 54	7 13	5 36	7 32	5 44
27	7 31	6 09	7 06	6 34	6 32	6 53	5 57	7 13	5 37	7 32	5 37	7 43	5 53	7 34	6 11	7 05	6 29	6 27	6 48	5 53	7 13	5 36	7 33	5 44
28	7 31	6 10	7 05	6 35	6 31	6 54	5 56	7 14	5 37	7 33	5 38	7 43	5 53	7 34	6 12	7 04	6 29	6 25	6 49	5 52	7 14	5 36	7 33	5 45
29	7 30	6 11			6 29	6 55	5 55	7 14	5 36	7 33	5 38	7 43	5 54	7 33	6 12	7 03	6 30	6 24	6 50	5 52	7 15	5 36	7 33	5 46
30	7 30	6 12			6 28	6 55	5 54	7 15	5 36	7 34	5 38	7 43	5 54	7 32	6 13	7 02	6 30	6 23	6 51	5 51	7 16	5 36	7 34	5 46
31	7 29	6 12			6 27	6 56			5 36	7 34			5 55	7 31	6 14	7 00			6 51	5 50			7 34	5 47

Add one hour for daylight time, if and when in use.
East Bound - Subtract 1 min/10 mi from center   West Bound - Add 1 min/10 mi from center

TALLAHASSEE, FLORIDA

THE OVERLOAD COMPANION 2017 © FREDA BARBER BOOTH

Astronomical Applications Dept
Location: W084 25, N33 46

Rise and Set for the Sun for 2017
ATLANTA, GEORGIA

U. S. Naval Observatory, Washington, DC
Eastern Standard Time

	JAN AM	JAN PM	FEB AM	FEB PM	MAR AM	MAR PM	APR AM	APR PM	MAY AM	MAY PM	JUN AM	JUN PM	JUL AM	JUL PM	AUG AM	AUG PM	SEP AM	SEP PM	OCT AM	OCT PM	NOV AM	NOV PM	DEC AM	DEC PM
1	7 42	5 40	7 35	6 08	7 05	6 35	6 24	6 59	5 48	7 21	5 28	7 43	5 31	7 52	5 50	7 37	6 12	7 02	6 32	6 21	6 57	5 45	7 25	5 29
2	7 43	5 41	7 34	6 09	7 04	6 35	6 23	6 59	5 47	7 22	5 28	7 44	5 31	7 52	5 51	7 37	6 12	7 01	6 33	6 20	6 58	5 44	7 26	5 29
3	7 43	5 41	7 33	6 10	7 03	6 36	6 22	7 00	5 46	7 23	5 27	7 45	5 32	7 52	5 51	7 36	6 13	7 00	6 34	6 19	6 59	5 43	7 26	5 29
4	7 43	5 42	7 32	6 11	7 02	6 37	6 20	7 01	5 46	7 24	5 27	7 45	5 32	7 52	5 52	7 35	6 14	6 58	6 35	6 17	7 00	5 42	7 27	5 29
5	7 43	5 43	7 32	6 12	7 00	6 38	6 19	7 02	5 45	7 24	5 27	7 46	5 33	7 52	5 53	7 34	6 15	6 57	6 35	6 16	7 01	5 41	7 28	5 29
6	7 43	5 44	7 31	6 13	6 59	6 39	6 18	7 02	5 44	7 25	5 27	7 46	5 33	7 52	5 54	7 33	6 15	6 56	6 36	6 15	7 02	5 40	7 29	5 29
7	7 43	5 45	7 30	6 14	6 58	6 40	6 17	7 03	5 43	7 26	5 27	7 47	5 34	7 51	5 54	7 32	6 16	6 54	6 37	6 13	7 03	5 40	7 30	5 29
8	7 43	5 45	7 29	6 15	6 57	6 40	6 15	7 04	5 42	7 27	5 27	7 47	5 34	7 51	5 55	7 31	6 17	6 53	6 38	6 12	7 04	5 39	7 30	5 29
9	7 43	5 46	7 28	6 16	6 55	6 41	6 14	7 05	5 41	7 28	5 27	7 48	5 35	7 51	5 56	7 30	6 18	6 52	6 38	6 11	7 05	5 38	7 31	5 29
10	7 43	5 47	7 27	6 17	6 54	6 42	6 13	7 05	5 40	7 28	5 27	7 48	5 35	7 51	5 56	7 29	6 18	6 50	6 39	6 09	7 05	5 37	7 32	5 30
11	7 43	5 48	7 26	6 18	6 53	6 43	6 11	7 06	5 39	7 29	5 27	7 48	5 36	7 50	5 57	7 28	6 19	6 49	6 40	6 08	7 06	5 37	7 32	5 30
12	7 43	5 49	7 25	6 19	6 51	6 44	6 10	7 07	5 38	7 30	5 27	7 49	5 36	7 50	5 58	7 26	6 19	6 48	6 41	6 07	7 07	5 36	7 33	5 30
13	7 43	5 50	7 24	6 20	6 50	6 44	6 09	7 08	5 37	7 31	5 27	7 49	5 37	7 49	5 59	7 25	6 20	6 46	6 42	6 06	7 08	5 35	7 34	5 30
14	7 43	5 51	7 23	6 21	6 49	6 45	6 08	7 08	5 36	7 31	5 27	7 49	5 37	7 49	5 59	7 24	6 21	6 45	6 43	6 04	7 09	5 35	7 35	5 31
15	7 42	5 52	7 22	6 22	6 47	6 46	6 06	7 09	5 35	7 32	5 27	7 50	5 38	7 49	6 00	7 23	6 21	6 43	6 44	6 03	7 10	5 34	7 35	5 31
16	7 42	5 53	7 21	6 22	6 46	6 47	6 05	7 10	5 34	7 33	5 27	7 50	5 38	7 48	6 01	7 22	6 22	6 42	6 44	6 02	7 11	5 34	7 36	5 31
17	7 42	5 54	7 20	6 23	6 45	6 47	6 04	7 11	5 33	7 34	5 27	7 50	5 39	7 48	6 01	7 21	6 23	6 41	6 45	6 01	7 12	5 33	7 37	5 32
18	7 42	5 55	7 19	6 24	6 43	6 48	6 03	7 11	5 33	7 34	5 28	7 51	5 39	7 47	6 02	7 20	6 24	6 39	6 46	6 00	7 13	5 33	7 37	5 32
19	7 41	5 56	7 18	6 25	6 42	6 49	6 02	7 12	5 32	7 35	5 28	7 51	5 40	7 47	6 03	7 19	6 24	6 38	6 47	5 58	7 14	5 32	7 38	5 33
20	7 41	5 56	7 17	6 26	6 41	6 50	6 00	7 13	5 31	7 36	5 28	7 51	5 41	7 46	6 04	7 18	6 25	6 36	6 48	5 57	7 15	5 32	7 38	5 33
21	7 41	5 57	7 16	6 27	6 39	6 50	5 59	7 14	5 30	7 36	5 28	7 52	5 41	7 45	6 04	7 16	6 25	6 35	6 48	5 56	7 16	5 32	7 39	5 33
22	7 40	5 58	7 15	6 28	6 38	6 51	5 58	7 14	5 32	7 37	5 28	7 52	5 42	7 45	6 05	7 15	6 26	6 34	6 49	5 55	7 17	5 31	7 39	5 34
23	7 40	5 59	7 14	6 29	6 37	6 52	5 57	7 15	5 31	7 38	5 28	7 52	5 43	7 44	6 06	7 14	6 27	6 32	6 49	5 54	7 18	5 31	7 40	5 34
24	7 39	6 00	7 13	6 30	6 35	6 53	5 56	7 16	5 31	7 39	5 28	7 52	5 44	7 44	6 06	7 13	6 27	6 31	6 50	5 53	7 18	5 30	7 40	5 35
25	7 39	6 01	7 12	6 30	6 34	6 53	5 55	7 17	5 30	7 40	5 29	7 52	5 45	7 43	6 07	7 12	6 28	6 29	6 51	5 52	7 19	5 30	7 41	5 36
26	7 38	6 02	7 10	6 31	6 33	6 54	5 54	7 17	5 30	7 40	5 29	7 52	5 46	7 42	6 08	7 10	6 29	6 28	6 52	5 51	7 20	5 30	7 41	5 36
27	7 38	6 03	7 09	6 32	6 31	6 55	5 53	7 18	5 29	7 41	5 29	7 52	5 46	7 42	6 08	7 09	6 29	6 27	6 53	5 50	7 21	5 30	7 42	5 37
28	7 37	6 04	7 08	6 33	6 30	6 56	5 51	7 19	5 29	7 42	5 30	7 52	5 47	7 41	6 09	7 08	6 30	6 25	6 54	5 49	7 22	5 29	7 42	5 38
29	7 37	6 05			6 28	6 56	5 50	7 20	5 29	7 42	5 30	7 52	5 48	7 40	6 10	7 06	6 31	6 24	6 55	5 48	7 23	5 29	7 42	5 38
30	7 36	6 06			6 27	6 57	5 49	7 21	5 29	7 42	5 31	7 52	5 49	7 39	6 10	7 05	6 32	6 23	6 56	5 47	7 24	5 29	7 42	5 39
31	7 35	6 07			6 26	6 58			5 28	7 43			5 49	7 38	6 11	7 04			6 56	5 46			7 42	5 40

Add one hour for daylight time, if and when in use.
East Bound - Subtract 1 min/10 mi from center   West Bound - Add 1 min/10 mi from center

ATLANTA, GEORGIA

Astronomical Applications Dept
Location: W116 13, N43 37

Rise and Set for the Sun for 2017
BOISE, IDAHO

U. S. Naval Observatory, Washington, DC
Mountain Standard Time

	JAN AM	JAN PM	FEB AM	FEB PM	MAR AM	MAR PM	APR AM	APR PM	MAY AM	MAY PM	JUN AM	JUN PM	JUL AM	JUL PM	AUG AM	AUG PM	SEP AM	SEP PM	OCT AM	OCT PM	NOV AM	NOV PM	DEC AM	DEC PM
1	8 18	5 19	8 02	5 56	7 20	6 34	6 25	7 12	5 37	7 48	5 06	8 20	5 08	8 30	5 35	8 07	6 09	7 19	6 43	6 25	7 21	5 35	7 59	5 09
2	8 18	5 19	8 01	5 57	7 19	6 36	6 24	7 14	5 35	7 49	5 06	8 21	5 08	8 30	5 36	8 06	6 10	7 17	6 44	6 23	7 23	5 34	8 00	5 09
3	8 18	5 20	8 01	5 58	7 17	6 37	6 22	7 15	5 34	7 50	5 05	8 21	5 09	8 29	5 37	8 04	6 11	7 16	6 45	6 21	7 24	5 32	8 01	5 09
4	8 18	5 21	7 59	6 00	7 15	6 38	6 20	7 16	5 32	7 51	5 05	8 22	5 09	8 29	5 38	8 03	6 13	7 14	6 47	6 19	7 25	5 31	8 02	5 08
5	8 18	5 22	7 58	6 01	7 15	6 40	6 18	7 17	5 31	7 53	5 04	8 23	5 10	8 29	5 39	8 02	6 14	7 12	6 48	6 18	7 27	5 30	8 03	5 08
6	8 18	5 23	7 57	6 02	7 14	6 41	6 18	7 18	5 30	7 54	5 04	8 24	5 11	8 28	5 40	8 00	6 15	7 10	6 49	6 16	7 28	5 29	8 04	5 08
7	8 18	5 24	7 56	6 02	7 12	6 42	6 17	7 20	5 29	7 55	5 04	8 24	5 11	8 28	5 41	7 59	6 16	7 08	6 50	6 14	7 29	5 27	8 05	5 08
8	8 18	5 25	7 55	6 04	7 10	6 42	6 15	7 20	5 27	7 56	5 04	8 25	5 12	8 27	5 42	7 58	6 17	7 07	6 51	6 12	7 31	5 26	8 06	5 08
9	8 18	5 27	7 53	6 05	7 08	6 43	6 13	7 21	5 26	7 57	5 04	8 25	5 13	8 27	5 44	7 56	6 18	7 05	6 53	6 11	7 32	5 25	8 07	5 08
10	8 18	5 27	7 52	6 07	7 07	6 45	6 11	7 22	5 25	7 58	5 03	8 25	5 14	8 27	5 45	7 55	6 19	7 03	6 54	6 09	7 33	5 24	8 08	5 08
11	8 17	5 28	7 51	6 08	7 05	6 46	6 10	7 23	5 24	7 59	5 03	8 26	5 15	8 26	5 46	7 53	6 20	7 01	6 55	6 07	7 34	5 23	8 09	5 09
12	8 17	5 29	7 50	6 09	7 03	6 47	6 08	7 24	5 23	8 01	5 03	8 26	5 15	8 26	5 47	7 52	6 22	6 59	6 56	6 06	7 36	5 22	8 09	5 09
13	8 17	5 30	7 48	6 11	7 01	6 48	6 06	7 25	5 21	8 02	5 03	8 27	5 16	8 25	5 48	7 50	6 23	6 58	6 57	6 04	7 37	5 21	8 10	5 09
14	8 16	5 31	7 47	6 12	7 00	6 49	6 05	7 27	5 20	8 03	5 03	8 27	5 17	8 24	5 49	7 49	6 24	6 56	6 59	6 02	7 38	5 20	8 11	5 09
15	8 16	5 32	7 45	6 13	6 58	6 51	6 03	7 28	5 19	8 04	5 03	8 28	5 18	8 24	5 50	7 47	6 25	6 54	7 00	6 01	7 40	5 19	8 12	5 09
16	8 15	5 33	7 44	6 15	6 56	6 52	6 01	7 29	5 18	8 05	5 03	8 28	5 19	8 23	5 51	7 46	6 26	6 52	7 01	5 59	7 41	5 18	8 12	5 10
17	8 15	5 35	7 42	6 16	6 54	6 53	6 00	7 30	5 18	8 06	5 03	8 29	5 19	8 23	5 52	7 44	6 27	6 50	7 02	5 57	7 42	5 17	8 13	5 10
18	8 14	5 36	7 41	6 17	6 52	6 54	5 58	7 31	5 17	8 07	5 03	8 29	5 20	8 22	5 54	7 43	6 28	6 48	7 03	5 56	7 43	5 17	8 14	5 10
19	8 13	5 37	7 40	6 19	6 51	6 56	5 56	7 33	5 16	8 08	5 03	8 29	5 21	8 21	5 55	7 41	6 29	6 47	7 05	5 54	7 45	5 16	8 14	5 11
20	8 13	5 38	7 38	6 20	6 49	6 57	5 55	7 34	5 15	8 09	5 03	8 30	5 22	8 20	5 56	7 40	6 31	6 45	7 06	5 52	7 46	5 15	8 15	5 11
21	8 12	5 40	7 36	6 21	6 47	6 58	5 53	7 35	5 14	8 10	5 04	8 30	5 22	8 19	5 57	7 38	6 32	6 43	7 07	5 51	7 47	5 14	8 15	5 11
22	8 11	5 41	7 35	6 23	6 45	6 59	5 52	7 36	5 14	8 11	5 04	8 30	5 23	8 19	5 58	7 36	6 33	6 41	7 08	5 49	7 48	5 14	8 16	5 12
23	8 11	5 42	7 33	6 24	6 43	7 00	5 50	7 37	5 13	8 12	5 04	8 30	5 24	8 18	5 59	7 35	6 34	6 39	7 10	5 48	7 50	5 13	8 16	5 12
24	8 10	5 44	7 32	6 25	6 42	7 02	5 48	7 39	5 12	8 13	5 04	8 30	5 25	8 17	6 00	7 33	6 35	6 37	7 11	5 46	7 51	5 12	8 17	5 13
25	8 09	5 45	7 30	6 27	6 40	7 03	5 47	7 40	5 11	8 14	5 05	8 30	5 26	8 16	6 01	7 31	6 36	6 36	7 12	5 45	7 52	5 12	8 17	5 14
26	8 08	5 46	7 29	6 28	6 38	7 04	5 45	7 41	5 10	8 15	5 05	8 30	5 27	8 15	6 03	7 30	6 37	6 34	7 14	5 43	7 53	5 11	8 17	5 14
27	8 07	5 48	7 27	6 29	6 36	7 05	5 44	7 42	5 10	8 16	5 05	8 30	5 28	8 14	6 04	7 28	6 38	6 32	7 15	5 42	7 54	5 11	8 18	5 15
28	8 06	5 49	7 25	6 31	6 34	7 06	5 42	7 43	5 09	8 17	5 06	8 30	5 29	8 13	6 05	7 26	6 40	6 30	7 16	5 40	7 56	5 10	8 18	5 16
29	8 05	5 52	7 24	6 32	6 31	7 09	5 41	7 44	5 08	8 17	5 06	8 30	5 31	8 11	6 06	7 24	6 41	6 28	7 17	5 39	7 57	5 10	8 18	5 17
30	8 04	5 53			6 29	7 10	5 39	7 46	5 08	8 18	5 07	8 30	5 32	8 10	6 07	7 23	6 42	6 27	7 19	5 38	7 58	5 09	8 18	5 18
31	8 03	5 54			6 27	7 11			5 07	8 19			5 33	8 09	6 08	7 21			7 20	5 36			8 18	5 18

Add one hour for daylight time, if and when in use.
East Bound - Subtract 1 min/10 mi from center   West Bound - Add 1 min/10 mi from center

BOISE, IDAHO

THE OVERLOAD COMPANION 2017 © FREDA BARBER BOOTH

Astronomical Applications Dept
Location: W089 39, N39 48

Rise and Set for the Sun for 2017
SPRINGFIELD, ILLINOIS

U. S. Naval Observatory, Washington, DC
Central Standard Time

	JAN AM	JAN PM	FEB AM	FEB PM	MAR AM	MAR PM	APR AM	APR PM	MAY AM	MAY PM	JUN AM	JUN PM	JUL AM	JUL PM	AUG AM	AUG PM	SEP AM	SEP PM	OCT AM	OCT PM	NOV AM	NOV PM	DEC AM	DEC PM
1	7 20	4 44	7 07	5 18	6 31	5 51	5 42	6 23	4 58	6 53	4 32	7 21	4 34	7 31	4 58	7 11	5 27	6 29	5 55	5 40	6 28	4 56	7 01	4 34
2	7 20	4 45	7 06	5 19	6 29	5 52	5 40	6 24	4 57	6 54	4 32	7 22	4 35	7 30	4 59	7 10	5 28	6 27	5 56	5 39	6 29	4 55	7 02	4 34
3	7 20	4 46	7 05	5 20	6 28	5 53	5 39	6 25	4 56	6 55	4 32	7 22	4 35	7 30	5 00	7 09	5 29	6 26	5 57	5 37	6 30	4 54	7 03	4 34
4	7 20	4 47	7 04	5 21	6 26	5 54	5 37	6 26	4 55	6 56	4 31	7 23	4 36	7 30	5 01	7 08	5 30	6 24	5 58	5 35	6 31	4 53	7 04	4 34
5	7 20	4 48	7 03	5 22	6 25	5 56	5 36	6 27	4 54	6 57	4 31	7 24	4 37	7 30	5 02	7 07	5 31	6 23	5 59	5 34	6 32	4 52	7 05	4 34
6	7 20	4 49	7 02	5 24	6 23	5 57	5 34	6 28	4 53	6 58	4 31	7 24	4 37	7 29	5 03	7 06	5 32	6 21	6 00	5 32	6 34	4 50	7 06	4 34
7	7 20	4 50	7 01	5 25	6 22	5 58	5 32	6 29	4 51	6 59	4 30	7 25	4 38	7 29	5 04	7 04	5 33	6 19	6 01	5 31	6 35	4 49	7 07	4 34
8	7 20	4 51	7 00	5 26	6 20	5 59	5 31	6 30	4 50	7 00	4 30	7 25	4 38	7 29	5 04	7 03	5 34	6 18	6 02	5 29	6 36	4 48	7 08	4 34
9	7 20	4 52	6 59	5 27	6 19	6 00	5 29	6 31	4 49	7 01	4 30	7 26	4 39	7 28	5 05	7 02	5 35	6 16	6 03	5 27	6 37	4 48	7 09	4 34
10	7 20	4 53	6 58	5 28	6 17	6 01	5 28	6 32	4 48	7 02	4 30	7 27	4 40	7 28	5 06	7 01	5 35	6 14	6 04	5 26	6 38	4 47	7 10	4 34
11	7 19	4 54	6 57	5 30	6 16	6 02	5 26	6 33	4 47	7 03	4 30	7 27	4 41	7 28	5 07	6 59	5 36	6 13	6 05	5 24	6 39	4 46	7 11	4 34
12	7 19	4 55	6 55	5 31	6 14	6 03	5 25	6 34	4 46	7 04	4 30	7 27	4 41	7 27	5 08	6 58	5 37	6 11	6 06	5 23	6 41	4 45	7 12	4 35
13	7 19	4 56	6 54	5 32	6 12	6 04	5 23	6 35	4 45	7 05	4 30	7 28	4 42	7 27	5 09	6 57	5 38	6 10	6 07	5 21	6 42	4 44	7 12	4 35
14	7 19	4 57	6 53	5 33	6 11	6 05	5 22	6 36	4 44	7 06	4 30	7 28	4 43	7 26	5 10	6 55	5 39	6 08	6 08	5 20	6 43	4 43	7 13	4 35
15	7 18	4 58	6 52	5 34	6 09	6 06	5 20	6 37	4 43	7 07	4 30	7 29	4 43	7 25	5 11	6 54	5 39	6 06	6 09	5 18	6 44	4 42	7 14	4 35
16	7 18	4 59	6 50	5 35	6 08	6 07	5 19	6 38	4 42	7 08	4 30	7 29	4 44	7 25	5 12	6 53	5 40	6 05	6 10	5 17	6 45	4 42	7 14	4 36
17	7 17	5 00	6 49	5 37	6 06	6 08	5 17	6 39	4 42	7 09	4 30	7 29	4 45	7 24	5 13	6 51	5 41	6 03	6 12	5 16	6 46	4 41	7 15	4 36
18	7 17	5 01	6 48	5 38	6 04	6 09	5 16	6 40	4 41	7 10	4 30	7 30	4 46	7 24	5 14	6 50	5 42	6 01	6 13	5 14	6 47	4 40	7 15	4 36
19	7 16	5 02	6 47	5 39	6 03	6 10	5 14	6 41	4 40	7 11	4 30	7 30	4 47	7 23	5 15	6 49	5 43	6 00	6 14	5 13	6 48	4 40	7 16	4 37
20	7 16	5 04	6 45	5 40	6 01	6 11	5 13	6 42	4 39	7 12	4 30	7 30	4 47	7 22	5 16	6 47	5 44	5 58	6 15	5 11	6 50	4 39	7 16	4 37
21	7 15	5 05	6 44	5 41	6 00	6 12	5 12	6 43	4 39	7 12	4 31	7 30	4 48	7 21	5 17	6 46	5 45	5 56	6 16	5 10	6 51	4 38	7 17	4 38
22	7 15	5 06	6 42	5 42	5 58	6 13	5 10	6 44	4 38	7 13	4 31	7 30	4 49	7 21	5 18	6 44	5 46	5 55	6 17	5 08	6 52	4 38	7 17	4 38
23	7 14	5 07	6 41	5 43	5 56	6 14	5 09	6 45	4 37	7 14	4 31	7 30	4 50	7 20	5 19	6 43	5 47	5 53	6 18	5 07	6 53	4 37	7 17	4 39
24	7 13	5 08	6 40	5 45	5 55	6 15	5 07	6 46	4 36	7 15	4 32	7 31	4 51	7 19	5 20	6 41	5 48	5 51	6 19	5 06	6 54	4 37	7 18	4 39
25	7 13	5 09	6 38	5 46	5 53	6 16	5 06	6 47	4 36	7 16	4 32	7 31	4 52	7 18	5 21	6 40	5 49	5 50	6 20	5 05	6 55	4 36	7 18	4 40
26	7 12	5 11	6 37	5 47	5 52	6 17	5 05	6 48	4 35	7 17	4 32	7 31	4 53	7 17	5 22	6 38	5 51	5 48	6 21	5 03	6 56	4 36	7 19	4 40
27	7 11	5 12	6 35	5 48	5 50	6 18	5 03	6 49	4 35	7 17	4 33	7 31	4 53	7 16	5 22	6 37	5 51	5 47	6 22	5 02	6 57	4 36	7 19	4 41
28	7 10	5 13	6 34	5 49	5 48	6 19	5 02	6 50	4 34	7 18	4 33	7 31	4 54	7 15	5 23	6 35	5 52	5 45	6 23	5 01	6 58	4 35	7 19	4 42
29	7 10	5 14			5 47	6 20	5 01	6 51	4 34	7 19	4 33	7 31	4 55	7 14	5 24	6 34	5 53	5 43	6 25	4 59	6 59	4 35	7 19	4 43
30	7 09	5 15			5 45	6 21	5 00	6 52	4 33	7 20	4 34	7 31	4 56	7 13	5 25	6 32	5 54	5 42	6 26	4 58	7 00	4 35	7 20	4 43
31	7 08	5 16			5 44	6 22			4 33	7 20			4 57	7 12	5 26	6 31			6 27	4 57			7 20	4 44

Add one hour for daylight time, if and when in use.
East Bound - Subtract 1 min/10 mi from center   West Bound - Add 1 min/10 mi from center

SPRINGFIELD, ILLINOIS

Astronomical Applications Dept
Location: W086 08, N39 47

Rise and Set for the Sun for 2017
INDIANAPOLIS, INDIANA

U. S. Naval Observatory, Washington, DC
Eastern Standard Time

	JAN AM	JAN PM	FEB AM	FEB PM	MAR AM	MAR PM	APR AM	APR PM	MAY AM	MAY PM	JUN AM	JUN PM	JUL AM	JUL PM	AUG AM	AUG PM	SEP AM	SEP PM	OCT AM	OCT PM	NOV AM	NOV PM	DEC AM	DEC PM
1	8 06	5 30	7 53	6 04	7 17	6 37	6 28	7 09	5 44	7 39	5 18	8 07	5 20	8 16	5 44	7 57	6 13	7 15	6 41	6 26	7 14	5 42	7 47	5 20
2	8 06	5 31	7 52	6 05	7 15	6 38	6 26	7 10	5 43	7 40	5 18	8 08	5 21	8 16	5 45	7 56	6 14	7 13	6 42	6 24	7 15	5 41	7 48	5 20
3	8 06	5 32	7 51	6 06	7 14	6 39	6 25	7 11	5 42	7 41	5 18	8 08	5 21	8 16	5 46	7 55	6 15	7 12	6 43	6 23	7 16	5 40	7 49	5 20
4	8 06	5 33	7 50	6 07	7 12	6 40	6 23	7 12	5 41	7 42	5 17	8 09	5 22	8 16	5 47	7 54	6 16	7 10	6 44	6 21	7 17	5 39	7 50	5 20
5	8 06	5 34	7 49	6 08	7 11	6 42	6 22	7 13	5 40	7 43	5 17	8 10	5 23	8 16	5 48	7 53	6 17	7 09	6 45	6 20	7 18	5 37	7 51	5 20
6	8 06	5 35	7 48	6 10	7 09	6 43	6 20	7 14	5 39	7 44	5 17	8 10	5 23	8 15	5 49	7 52	6 18	7 07	6 46	6 18	7 20	5 36	7 52	5 20
7	8 06	5 36	7 47	6 11	7 08	6 44	6 18	7 15	5 37	7 45	5 16	8 11	5 24	8 15	5 50	7 50	6 19	7 05	6 47	6 17	7 21	5 35	7 53	5 20
8	8 06	5 37	7 46	6 12	7 06	6 45	6 17	7 16	5 36	7 46	5 16	8 11	5 24	8 15	5 50	7 49	6 20	7 04	6 48	6 15	7 22	5 34	7 54	5 20
9	8 06	5 38	7 45	6 13	7 05	6 46	6 15	7 17	5 35	7 47	5 16	8 12	5 25	8 14	5 51	7 48	6 20	7 02	6 49	6 13	7 23	5 33	7 54	5 20
10	8 06	5 39	7 44	6 14	7 03	6 47	6 14	7 18	5 34	7 48	5 16	8 12	5 26	8 14	5 52	7 47	6 21	7 00	6 50	6 12	7 24	5 32	7 55	5 20
11	8 05	5 40	7 43	6 16	7 02	6 48	6 12	7 19	5 33	7 49	5 16	8 13	5 26	8 13	5 53	7 45	6 22	6 59	6 51	6 10	7 25	5 31	7 56	5 20
12	8 05	5 41	7 41	6 17	7 00	6 49	6 11	7 20	5 32	7 50	5 16	8 13	5 27	8 13	5 54	7 44	6 23	6 57	6 52	6 09	7 26	5 31	7 57	5 20
13	8 05	5 42	7 40	6 18	6 58	6 50	6 09	7 21	5 31	7 51	5 16	8 14	5 28	8 12	5 55	7 43	6 24	6 56	6 53	6 07	7 28	5 30	7 58	5 20
14	8 04	5 43	7 39	6 19	6 57	6 51	6 08	7 22	5 30	7 52	5 16	8 14	5 29	8 12	5 56	7 41	6 25	6 54	6 54	6 06	7 29	5 29	7 58	5 21
15	8 04	5 44	7 38	6 20	6 55	6 52	6 06	7 23	5 29	7 53	5 16	8 15	5 29	8 11	5 57	7 40	6 26	6 52	6 55	6 04	7 30	5 28	7 59	5 21
16	8 04	5 45	7 36	6 21	6 54	6 53	6 05	7 24	5 29	7 54	5 16	8 15	5 30	8 11	5 58	7 39	6 27	6 51	6 56	6 03	7 31	5 28	8 00	5 21
17	8 03	5 46	7 35	6 23	6 52	6 54	6 03	7 25	5 28	7 55	5 16	8 15	5 31	8 10	5 59	7 37	6 28	6 49	6 57	6 02	7 32	5 27	8 00	5 22
18	8 03	5 47	7 34	6 24	6 50	6 55	6 02	7 26	5 27	7 56	5 16	8 16	5 32	8 09	6 00	7 36	6 29	6 47	6 59	6 00	7 33	5 26	8 01	5 22
19	8 02	5 48	7 33	6 25	6 49	6 56	6 00	7 27	5 26	7 57	5 16	8 16	5 33	8 09	6 01	7 35	6 30	6 46	7 00	5 59	7 34	5 25	8 01	5 23
20	8 02	5 50	7 31	6 26	6 47	6 57	5 59	7 28	5 25	7 58	5 16	8 16	5 33	8 08	6 02	7 33	6 31	6 44	7 01	5 57	7 35	5 25	8 02	5 23
21	8 01	5 51	7 30	6 27	6 46	6 58	5 58	7 29	5 24	7 58	5 17	8 16	5 34	8 07	6 03	7 32	6 32	6 42	7 02	5 56	7 37	5 24	8 02	5 23
22	8 01	5 52	7 28	6 28	6 44	6 59	5 56	7 30	5 24	7 59	5 17	8 16	5 35	8 06	6 04	7 30	6 33	6 41	7 03	5 55	7 38	5 24	8 02	5 24
23	8 00	5 53	7 27	6 29	6 42	7 00	5 55	7 31	5 23	8 00	5 17	8 17	5 36	8 06	6 05	7 29	6 34	6 39	7 04	5 53	7 39	5 23	8 03	5 25
24	7 59	5 54	7 26	6 31	6 41	7 01	5 53	7 32	5 22	8 01	5 18	8 17	5 37	8 05	6 06	7 27	6 35	6 37	7 05	5 52	7 40	5 23	8 03	5 25
25	7 59	5 55	7 24	6 32	6 39	7 02	5 52	7 33	5 22	8 02	5 18	8 17	5 38	8 04	6 06	7 26	6 35	6 36	7 06	5 51	7 41	5 22	8 04	5 26
26	7 58	5 56	7 23	6 33	6 38	7 03	5 51	7 34	5 21	8 03	5 18	8 17	5 38	8 03	6 07	7 24	6 36	6 34	7 07	5 49	7 42	5 22	8 05	5 26
27	7 57	5 58	7 21	6 34	6 36	7 04	5 49	7 35	5 21	8 03	5 19	8 17	5 39	8 02	6 08	7 23	6 37	6 33	7 08	5 48	7 43	5 21	8 05	5 27
28	7 56	5 59	7 20	6 35	6 34	7 05	5 48	7 36	5 20	8 04	5 19	8 17	5 40	8 01	6 09	7 21	6 38	6 31	7 09	5 47	7 44	5 21	8 05	5 28
29	7 56	6 00			6 33	7 06	5 47	7 37	5 20	8 05	5 19	8 17	5 41	8 00	6 10	7 20	6 39	6 29	7 10	5 45	7 45	5 21	8 05	5 29
30	7 55	6 01			6 31	7 07	5 46	7 38	5 19	8 06	5 20	8 17	5 42	8 00	6 11	7 18	6 40	6 28	7 12	5 44	7 46	5 21	8 06	5 29
31	7 54	6 02			6 29	7 08			5 19	8 06			5 43	7 59	6 12	7 16			7 13	5 43			8 06	5 30

Add one hour for daylight time, if and when in use.
East Bound - Subtract 1 min/10 mi from center   West Bound - Add 1 min/10 mi from center

INDIANAPOLIS, INDIANA

THE OVERLOAD COMPANION 2017 © FREDA BARBER BOOTH

Astronomical Applications Dept
Location: W093 38, N41 36

Rise and Set for the Sun for 2017
DES MOINES, IOWA

U. S. Naval Observatory, Washington, DC
Central Standard Time

	JAN AM	JAN PM	FEB AM	FEB PM	MAR AM	MAR PM	APR AM	APR PM	MAY AM	MAY PM	JUN AM	JUN PM	JUL AM	JUL PM	AUG AM	AUG PM	SEP AM	SEP PM	OCT AM	OCT PM	NOV AM	NOV PM	DEC AM	DEC PM
1	7 41	4 55	7 27	5 30	6 48	6 06	5 57	6 40	5 11	7 13	4 43	7 43	4 44	7 52	5 10	7 31	5 41	6 47	6 12	5 55	6 47	5 09	7 22	4 45
2	7 41	4 56	7 26	5 31	6 47	6 07	5 55	6 42	5 09	7 14	4 42	7 43	4 45	7 52	5 11	7 30	5 42	6 45	6 13	5 54	6 48	5 07	7 23	4 45
3	7 41	4 57	7 25	5 32	6 45	6 08	5 53	6 43	5 08	7 15	4 42	7 44	4 46	7 52	5 12	7 29	5 43	6 43	6 14	5 52	6 50	5 06	7 24	4 45
4	7 41	4 57	7 24	5 34	6 44	6 09	5 52	6 44	5 07	7 16	4 41	7 45	4 46	7 52	5 13	7 28	5 44	6 42	6 15	5 50	6 51	5 05	7 25	4 44
5	7 41	4 58	7 23	5 35	6 42	6 10	5 50	6 45	5 06	7 17	4 41	7 46	4 47	7 51	5 14	7 27	5 45	6 40	6 16	5 49	6 52	5 04	7 26	4 44
6	7 41	4 59	7 22	5 36	6 40	6 12	5 48	6 46	5 04	7 18	4 41	7 46	4 47	7 51	5 15	7 25	5 46	6 38	6 17	5 47	6 53	5 03	7 27	4 44
7	7 41	5 00	7 20	5 37	6 39	6 13	5 47	6 47	5 03	7 19	4 40	7 47	4 48	7 51	5 16	7 24	5 47	6 37	6 18	5 45	6 54	5 02	7 28	4 44
8	7 41	5 01	7 19	5 39	6 37	6 14	5 45	6 48	5 02	7 21	4 40	7 47	4 49	7 50	5 17	7 23	5 48	6 35	6 19	5 44	6 56	5 01	7 29	4 44
9	7 41	5 02	7 18	5 40	6 35	6 15	5 43	6 49	5 01	7 22	4 40	7 48	4 49	7 50	5 18	7 22	5 49	6 33	6 21	5 42	6 57	5 00	7 30	4 44
10	7 41	5 03	7 17	5 41	6 34	6 16	5 42	6 50	5 00	7 23	4 40	7 48	4 50	7 49	5 19	7 20	5 50	6 32	6 22	5 40	6 58	4 59	7 31	4 44
11	7 41	5 04	7 16	5 42	6 32	6 17	5 40	6 51	4 59	7 24	4 40	7 49	4 51	7 49	5 20	7 19	5 51	6 30	6 23	5 39	6 59	4 58	7 32	4 45
12	7 40	5 06	7 14	5 44	6 30	6 18	5 39	6 52	4 58	7 25	4 40	7 49	4 52	7 49	5 21	7 17	5 52	6 28	6 24	5 37	7 00	4 57	7 32	4 45
13	7 40	5 07	7 13	5 45	6 29	6 20	5 37	6 54	4 57	7 26	4 40	7 50	4 52	7 48	5 22	7 16	5 53	6 26	6 25	5 36	7 02	4 56	7 33	4 45
14	7 40	5 08	7 12	5 46	6 27	6 21	5 35	6 55	4 56	7 27	4 40	7 50	4 53	7 47	5 23	7 15	5 54	6 25	6 26	5 34	7 03	4 55	7 34	4 45
15	7 39	5 09	7 10	5 48	6 25	6 22	5 34	6 56	4 55	7 28	4 40	7 51	4 54	7 47	5 24	7 13	5 55	6 23	6 27	5 32	7 04	4 54	7 35	4 46
16	7 39	5 10	7 09	5 49	6 24	6 23	5 32	6 57	4 54	7 29	4 40	7 51	4 55	7 46	5 25	7 12	5 56	6 21	6 28	5 31	7 05	4 53	7 35	4 46
17	7 38	5 11	7 08	5 50	6 22	6 24	5 31	6 58	4 53	7 30	4 40	7 51	4 56	7 45	5 26	7 10	5 57	6 19	6 29	5 29	7 06	4 52	7 36	4 46
18	7 38	5 12	7 06	5 51	6 20	6 25	5 29	6 59	4 52	7 31	4 40	7 52	4 56	7 45	5 27	7 09	5 58	6 18	6 31	5 28	7 08	4 52	7 37	4 46
19	7 37	5 14	7 05	5 52	6 19	6 26	5 28	7 00	4 51	7 32	4 40	7 52	4 57	7 44	5 28	7 07	5 59	6 16	6 32	5 26	7 09	4 51	7 37	4 47
20	7 37	5 15	7 03	5 54	6 17	6 27	5 26	7 01	4 50	7 33	4 40	7 52	4 58	7 43	5 29	7 06	6 00	6 14	6 33	5 25	7 10	4 50	7 38	4 47
21	7 36	5 16	7 02	5 55	6 15	6 28	5 25	7 02	4 49	7 34	4 41	7 52	4 59	7 42	5 30	7 04	6 01	6 12	6 34	5 23	7 11	4 50	7 38	4 48
22	7 35	5 17	7 01	5 56	6 14	6 30	5 23	7 03	4 48	7 35	4 41	7 52	5 00	7 41	5 31	7 03	6 02	6 11	6 35	5 22	7 12	4 49	7 39	4 48
23	7 35	5 18	6 59	5 57	6 12	6 31	5 22	7 04	4 47	7 36	4 41	7 53	5 01	7 41	5 32	7 01	6 03	6 09	6 36	5 21	7 14	4 48	7 39	4 48
24	7 34	5 20	6 58	5 59	6 10	6 32	5 20	7 06	4 47	7 37	4 41	7 53	5 02	7 40	5 33	7 00	6 04	6 07	6 38	5 19	7 15	4 48	7 39	4 49
25	7 33	5 21	6 56	6 00	6 08	6 33	5 19	7 07	4 46	7 38	4 42	7 53	5 03	7 39	5 34	6 58	6 05	6 06	6 39	5 18	7 16	4 47	7 40	4 50
26	7 32	5 22	6 55	6 01	6 07	6 34	5 17	7 08	4 46	7 39	4 42	7 53	5 04	7 38	5 35	6 57	6 06	6 04	6 40	5 16	7 17	4 47	7 40	4 51
27	7 31	5 23	6 53	6 02	6 05	6 35	5 16	7 09	4 45	7 40	4 42	7 53	5 05	7 37	5 36	6 55	6 07	6 02	6 41	5 15	7 18	4 46	7 40	4 51
28	7 31	5 25	6 51	6 03	6 03	6 36	5 15	7 10	4 45	7 41	4 43	7 53	5 06	7 36	5 37	6 53	6 08	6 00	6 42	5 14	7 19	4 46	7 41	4 52
29	7 30	5 26			6 02	6 37	5 13	7 11	4 44	7 42	4 43	7 53	5 07	7 35	5 38	6 52	6 10	5 59	6 44	5 12	7 20	4 46	7 41	4 53
30	7 29	5 27			6 00	6 38	5 12	7 12	4 44	7 43	4 44	7 53	5 08	7 34	5 39	6 50	6 11	5 57	6 45	5 11	7 21	4 45	7 41	4 54
31	7 28	5 28			5 58	6 39			4 43	7 42			5 09	7 33	5 40	6 48			6 46	5 10			7 41	4 55

Add one hour for daylight time, if and when in use.
East Bound - Subtract 1 min/10 mi from center   West Bound - Add 1 min/10 mi from center

DES MOINES, IOWA

Astronomical Applications Dept
Location: W095 41, N39 02

Rise and Set for the Sun for 2017
TOPEKA, KANSAS

U. S. Naval Observatory, Washington, DC
Central Standard Time

	JAN AM	JAN PM	FEB AM	FEB PM	MAR AM	MAR PM	APR AM	APR PM	MAY AM	MAY PM	JUN AM	JUN PM	JUL AM	JUL PM	AUG AM	AUG PM	SEP AM	SEP PM	OCT AM	OCT PM	NOV AM	NOV PM	DEC AM	DEC PM
1	7 42	5 11	7 30	5 43	6 54	6 16	6 06	6 47	5 24	7 16	4 59	7 43	5 01	7 52	5 24	7 34	5 52	6 52	6 19	6 05	6 51	5 21	7 23	5 01
2	7 42	5 12	7 29	5 45	6 53	6 17	6 05	6 48	5 23	7 17	4 58	7 44	5 01	7 52	5 25	7 33	5 53	6 51	6 20	6 03	6 52	5 20	7 24	5 00
3	7 42	5 12	7 28	5 46	6 52	6 18	6 03	6 49	5 22	7 18	4 58	7 44	5 02	7 52	5 26	7 31	5 54	6 49	6 21	6 01	6 53	5 19	7 25	5 00
4	7 42	5 13	7 27	5 47	6 50	6 19	6 02	6 50	5 21	7 19	4 58	7 45	5 03	7 52	5 27	7 30	5 55	6 48	6 22	6 00	6 54	5 18	7 26	5 00
5	7 42	5 14	7 26	5 48	6 49	6 20	6 00	6 51	5 19	7 20	4 57	7 46	5 03	7 52	5 27	7 29	5 56	6 46	6 23	5 58	6 55	5 17	7 27	5 00
6	7 42	5 15	7 25	5 49	6 47	6 21	5 59	6 52	5 18	7 21	4 57	7 46	5 04	7 51	5 28	7 28	5 57	6 45	6 24	5 57	6 56	5 16	7 28	5 00
7	7 42	5 16	7 24	5 50	6 46	6 22	5 57	6 53	5 17	7 22	4 57	7 47	5 04	7 51	5 29	7 27	5 57	6 43	6 25	5 55	6 57	5 15	7 29	5 00
8	7 42	5 17	7 23	5 52	6 44	6 23	5 56	6 54	5 16	7 23	4 57	7 47	5 05	7 50	5 30	7 26	5 58	6 41	6 26	5 54	6 59	5 14	7 30	5 00
9	7 42	5 18	7 22	5 53	6 43	6 24	5 54	6 55	5 15	7 24	4 57	7 48	5 06	7 50	5 31	7 25	5 59	6 40	6 27	5 52	7 00	5 13	7 30	5 00
10	7 42	5 19	7 21	5 54	6 41	6 25	5 53	6 56	5 14	7 25	4 57	7 48	5 06	7 50	5 32	7 23	6 00	6 38	6 28	5 51	7 01	5 12	7 31	5 00
11	7 41	5 20	7 19	5 55	6 39	6 26	5 51	6 57	5 13	7 26	4 57	7 49	5 07	7 49	5 33	7 22	6 01	6 37	6 29	5 49	7 02	5 11	7 32	5 01
12	7 41	5 21	7 18	5 56	6 38	6 27	5 50	6 58	5 12	7 27	4 57	7 49	5 08	7 49	5 34	7 21	6 02	6 35	6 30	5 48	7 03	5 11	7 33	5 01
13	7 41	5 22	7 17	5 57	6 36	6 28	5 48	6 59	5 11	7 28	4 57	7 49	5 08	7 49	5 35	7 20	6 03	6 33	6 31	5 46	7 04	5 10	7 34	5 01
14	7 41	5 23	7 16	5 58	6 35	6 29	5 47	7 00	5 10	7 28	4 56	7 50	5 09	7 48	5 36	7 18	6 04	6 32	6 32	5 45	7 05	5 09	7 34	5 01
15	7 40	5 24	7 15	6 00	6 33	6 30	5 45	7 01	5 09	7 29	4 56	7 50	5 10	7 47	5 37	7 17	6 05	6 30	6 33	5 43	7 06	5 08	7 35	5 01
16	7 40	5 25	7 13	6 01	6 32	6 31	5 44	7 02	5 09	7 30	4 56	7 50	5 11	7 47	5 38	7 16	6 05	6 29	6 34	5 42	7 07	5 07	7 36	5 02
17	7 40	5 26	7 12	6 02	6 30	6 32	5 43	7 03	5 08	7 31	4 56	7 51	5 11	7 46	5 38	7 14	6 06	6 27	6 35	5 40	7 09	5 07	7 36	5 02
18	7 39	5 27	7 11	6 03	6 29	6 33	5 41	7 03	5 07	7 32	4 57	7 51	5 12	7 46	5 39	7 13	6 07	6 25	6 36	5 39	7 10	5 06	7 37	5 03
19	7 39	5 28	7 10	6 04	6 27	6 34	5 40	7 04	5 06	7 33	4 57	7 51	5 13	7 45	5 40	7 11	6 08	6 24	6 37	5 38	7 11	5 05	7 37	5 03
20	7 38	5 30	7 08	6 05	6 25	6 35	5 38	7 05	5 05	7 34	4 57	7 52	5 14	7 44	5 41	7 10	6 09	6 22	6 38	5 36	7 12	5 05	7 38	5 03
21	7 38	5 31	7 07	6 06	6 24	6 36	5 37	7 06	5 05	7 35	4 57	7 52	5 14	7 43	5 42	7 09	6 10	6 20	6 39	5 35	7 13	5 04	7 38	5 04
22	7 37	5 32	7 06	6 07	6 22	6 37	5 36	7 07	5 04	7 36	4 57	7 52	5 15	7 43	5 43	7 07	6 11	6 19	6 40	5 34	7 14	5 04	7 39	5 04
23	7 36	5 33	7 04	6 08	6 21	6 38	5 34	7 08	5 03	7 37	4 58	7 52	5 16	7 42	5 44	7 06	6 12	6 17	6 41	5 32	7 15	5 03	7 39	5 05
24	7 36	5 34	7 03	6 10	6 19	6 39	5 33	7 09	5 03	7 37	4 58	7 52	5 17	7 41	5 45	7 04	6 13	6 16	6 42	5 31	7 16	5 03	7 40	5 05
25	7 35	5 35	7 02	6 11	6 17	6 40	5 32	7 10	5 02	7 38	4 58	7 53	5 18	7 40	5 46	7 03	6 14	6 14	6 43	5 30	7 17	5 02	7 40	5 06
26	7 34	5 36	7 00	6 12	6 16	6 41	5 30	7 11	5 02	7 39	4 59	7 53	5 19	7 39	5 47	7 01	6 15	6 12	6 44	5 28	7 18	5 02	7 41	5 07
27	7 34	5 38	6 59	6 13	6 14	6 42	5 29	7 12	5 01	7 39	4 59	7 53	5 19	7 38	5 48	7 00	6 15	6 11	6 45	5 27	7 19	5 02	7 41	5 07
28	7 33	5 39	6 57	6 14	6 13	6 43	5 28	7 13	5 00	7 40	4 59	7 53	5 20	7 38	5 48	6 58	6 16	6 09	6 46	5 26	7 20	5 01	7 41	5 08
29	7 32	5 40			6 11	6 44	5 26	7 14	5 00	7 41	5 00	7 53	5 21	7 37	5 49	6 57	6 17	6 08	6 48	5 25	7 21	5 01	7 41	5 08
30	7 31	5 41			6 10	6 45	5 25	7 15	5 00	7 42	5 00	7 52	5 22	7 36	5 50	6 55	6 18	6 06	6 49	5 24	7 22	5 01	7 42	5 09
31	7 31	5 42			6 08	6 46			4 59	7 42			5 23	7 35	5 51	6 54			6 50	5 22			7 42	5 11

Add one hour for daylight time, if and when in use.

East Bound - Subtract 1 min/10 mi from center   West Bound - Add 1 min/10 mi from center

TOPEKA, KANSAS

Astronomical Applications Dept
Location: W084 29, N38 04

Rise and Set for the Sun for 2017
LEXINGTON, KENTUCKY

U. S. Naval Observatory, Washington, DC
Eastern Standard Time

	JAN AM	JAN PM	FEB AM	FEB PM	MAR AM	MAR PM	APR AM	APR PM	MAY AM	MAY PM	JUN AM	JUN PM	JUL AM	JUL PM	AUG AM	AUG PM	SEP AM	SEP PM	OCT AM	OCT PM	NOV AM	NOV PM	DEC AM	DEC PM
1	7 54	5 29	7 43	6 01	7 09	6 32	6 22	7 02	5 41	7 29	5 17	7 55	5 19	8 05	5 41	7 47	6 08	7 07	6 34	6 20	7 04	5 38	7 36	5 18
2	7 54	5 30	7 42	6 02	7 08	6 33	6 21	7 02	5 40	7 30	5 16	7 56	5 20	8 04	5 42	7 46	6 09	7 05	6 35	6 19	7 05	5 37	7 37	5 18
3	7 54	5 30	7 41	6 03	7 06	6 34	6 19	7 03	5 39	7 31	5 16	7 57	5 20	8 04	5 43	7 45	6 10	7 04	6 36	6 17	7 06	5 36	7 38	5 18
4	7 54	5 31	7 40	6 04	7 05	6 35	6 18	7 04	5 38	7 32	5 16	7 57	5 21	8 04	5 44	7 44	6 11	7 02	6 37	6 16	7 08	5 35	7 39	5 18
5	7 55	5 32	7 39	6 05	7 03	6 36	6 16	7 05	5 37	7 33	5 16	7 58	5 21	8 04	5 45	7 42	6 12	7 01	6 38	6 14	7 09	5 34	7 39	5 18
6	7 55	5 33	7 38	6 06	7 02	6 37	6 15	7 06	5 36	7 34	5 15	7 58	5 22	8 04	5 46	7 41	6 12	6 59	6 39	6 13	7 10	5 33	7 40	5 18
7	7 55	5 34	7 37	6 07	7 00	6 38	6 13	7 07	5 35	7 35	5 15	7 59	5 22	8 03	5 46	7 40	6 13	6 58	6 40	6 11	7 11	5 32	7 41	5 18
8	7 55	5 35	7 36	6 08	6 59	6 39	6 12	7 08	5 34	7 36	5 15	8 00	5 23	8 03	5 47	7 39	6 14	6 56	6 40	6 10	7 12	5 31	7 42	5 18
9	7 54	5 36	7 35	6 10	6 57	6 40	6 10	7 09	5 33	7 37	5 15	8 00	5 23	8 03	5 48	7 38	6 15	6 54	6 41	6 08	7 13	5 30	7 43	5 18
10	7 54	5 37	7 34	6 11	6 56	6 41	6 09	7 10	5 32	7 38	5 15	8 01	5 24	8 02	5 49	7 37	6 16	6 53	6 42	6 07	7 14	5 30	7 44	5 19
11	7 54	5 38	7 33	6 12	6 54	6 42	6 08	7 11	5 31	7 39	5 15	8 01	5 25	8 02	5 50	7 36	6 17	6 51	6 43	6 05	7 15	5 29	7 44	5 19
12	7 54	5 39	7 32	6 13	6 53	6 43	6 06	7 12	5 30	7 40	5 15	8 01	5 26	8 01	5 51	7 34	6 18	6 50	6 44	6 04	7 16	5 28	7 45	5 19
13	7 54	5 40	7 31	6 14	6 51	6 44	6 05	7 13	5 29	7 41	5 15	8 02	5 26	8 01	5 52	7 33	6 18	6 48	6 45	6 02	7 17	5 27	7 46	5 19
14	7 53	5 41	7 30	6 15	6 50	6 45	6 03	7 14	5 28	7 42	5 15	8 02	5 27	8 00	5 53	7 32	6 19	6 47	6 46	6 01	7 18	5 26	7 47	5 20
15	7 53	5 42	7 29	6 16	6 48	6 46	6 02	7 15	5 27	7 43	5 15	8 03	5 28	8 00	5 53	7 31	6 20	6 45	6 47	6 00	7 19	5 26	7 47	5 20
16	7 53	5 43	7 27	6 17	6 47	6 47	6 00	7 15	5 26	7 44	5 15	8 03	5 28	7 59	5 54	7 29	6 21	6 44	6 48	5 58	7 20	5 25	7 48	5 20
17	7 52	5 44	7 26	6 18	6 45	6 48	5 59	7 16	5 25	7 45	5 15	8 03	5 29	7 59	5 55	7 28	6 22	6 42	6 49	5 57	7 21	5 24	7 49	5 20
18	7 52	5 45	7 25	6 19	6 44	6 49	5 58	7 17	5 25	7 46	5 15	8 03	5 30	7 58	5 56	7 27	6 23	6 40	6 50	5 55	7 23	5 24	7 49	5 21
19	7 51	5 46	7 24	6 20	6 42	6 49	5 56	7 18	5 24	7 46	5 15	8 04	5 31	7 58	5 57	7 25	6 24	6 39	6 51	5 54	7 24	5 23	7 50	5 21
20	7 51	5 47	7 22	6 22	6 41	6 50	5 55	7 19	5 23	7 47	5 15	8 04	5 31	7 57	5 58	7 24	6 24	6 37	6 52	5 53	7 25	5 22	7 50	5 22
21	7 51	5 48	7 21	6 23	6 39	6 51	5 54	7 20	5 22	7 48	5 16	8 04	5 32	7 56	5 59	7 23	6 25	6 36	6 53	5 51	7 26	5 22	7 51	5 22
22	7 50	5 49	7 20	6 24	6 38	6 52	5 52	7 21	5 22	7 49	5 16	8 04	5 33	7 55	6 00	7 21	6 26	6 34	6 54	5 50	7 27	5 21	7 51	5 23
23	7 49	5 50	7 19	6 25	6 36	6 53	5 51	7 22	5 21	7 50	5 16	8 04	5 34	7 55	6 00	7 20	6 27	6 33	6 55	5 49	7 28	5 21	7 52	5 23
24	7 49	5 52	7 17	6 26	6 35	6 54	5 50	7 23	5 20	7 51	5 16	8 05	5 34	7 54	6 01	7 18	6 28	6 31	6 56	5 48	7 29	5 21	7 52	5 24
25	7 48	5 53	7 16	6 27	6 33	6 55	5 48	7 24	5 20	7 52	5 16	8 05	5 35	7 53	6 02	7 17	6 29	6 29	6 57	5 46	7 30	5 20	7 52	5 24
26	7 48	5 54	7 15	6 28	6 32	6 56	5 47	7 25	5 19	7 52	5 17	8 05	5 36	7 52	6 03	7 15	6 30	6 28	6 58	5 45	7 31	5 20	7 53	5 25
27	7 47	5 55	7 13	6 29	6 30	6 57	5 46	7 26	5 19	7 53	5 17	8 05	5 37	7 51	6 04	7 14	6 31	6 26	6 59	5 44	7 32	5 19	7 53	5 26
28	7 46	5 56	7 12	6 30	6 28	6 58	5 45	7 27	5 18	7 54	5 18	8 05	5 38	7 50	6 05	7 13	6 31	6 25	7 00	5 43	7 33	5 19	7 53	5 26
29	7 45	5 57			6 27	6 59	5 44	7 28	5 18	7 55	5 18	8 05	5 39	7 50	6 06	7 11	6 32	6 23	7 01	5 42	7 34	5 19	7 54	5 27
30	7 45	5 58			6 25	7 00	5 42	7 28	5 18	7 55	5 19	8 05	5 40	7 49	6 06	7 10	6 33	6 22	7 02	5 40	7 35	5 19	7 54	5 28
31	7 44	5 59			6 24	7 01			5 17	7 55			5 40	7 48	6 07	7 08			7 03	5 39			7 54	5 29

Add one hour for daylight time, if and when in use.
East Bound - Subtract 1 min/10 mi from center   West Bound - Add 1 min/10 mi from center

LEXINGTON, KENTUCKY

Astronomical Applications Dept
Location: W085 45, N38 13

Rise and Set for the Sun for 2017
LOUISVILLE, KENTUCKY

U. S. Naval Observatory, Washington, DC
Eastern Standard Time

	JAN AM	JAN PM	FEB AM	FEB PM	MAR AM	MAR PM	APR AM	APR PM	MAY AM	MAY PM	JUN AM	JUN PM	JUL AM	JUL PM	AUG AM	AUG PM	SEP AM	SEP PM	OCT AM	OCT PM	NOV AM	NOV PM	DEC AM	DEC PM
1	8 00	5 33	7 48	6 05	7 14	6 37	6 27	7 07	5 46	7 35	5 21	8 01	5 24	8 10	5 46	7 52	6 13	7 12	6 39	6 25	7 10	5 43	7 41	5 23
2	8 00	5 34	7 47	6 06	7 13	6 38	6 26	7 08	5 45	7 36	5 21	8 02	5 24	8 10	5 47	7 51	6 14	7 10	6 40	6 24	7 11	5 42	7 42	5 23
3	8 00	5 35	7 46	6 08	7 11	6 39	6 24	7 09	5 44	7 37	5 21	8 02	5 25	8 10	5 48	7 50	6 15	7 09	6 41	6 22	7 12	5 41	7 43	5 23
4	8 00	5 36	7 46	6 09	7 10	6 40	6 23	7 09	5 42	7 38	5 20	8 03	5 25	8 09	5 49	7 49	6 16	7 07	6 42	6 20	7 13	5 40	7 44	5 23
5	8 00	5 37	7 45	6 10	7 08	6 41	6 21	7 10	5 41	7 38	5 20	8 03	5 26	8 09	5 49	7 48	6 16	7 06	6 43	6 19	7 14	5 39	7 45	5 23
6	8 00	5 38	7 44	6 11	7 07	6 42	6 20	7 11	5 40	7 39	5 20	8 04	5 26	8 09	5 50	7 47	6 17	7 04	6 44	6 17	7 15	5 38	7 46	5 23
7	8 00	5 39	7 43	6 12	7 05	6 43	6 18	7 12	5 39	7 40	5 20	8 04	5 27	8 09	5 51	7 46	6 18	7 03	6 45	6 16	7 16	5 37	7 47	5 23
8	8 00	5 39	7 42	6 13	7 04	6 44	6 17	7 13	5 38	7 41	5 20	8 05	5 28	8 08	5 52	7 44	6 19	7 01	6 46	6 14	7 17	5 36	7 48	5 23
9	8 00	5 40	7 41	6 14	7 02	6 45	6 15	7 14	5 37	7 42	5 19	8 06	5 28	8 08	5 53	7 43	6 20	7 00	6 47	6 13	7 18	5 35	7 48	5 23
10	8 00	5 41	7 40	6 15	7 01	6 46	6 14	7 15	5 36	7 43	5 19	8 06	5 29	8 08	5 54	7 42	6 21	6 58	6 48	6 12	7 19	5 34	7 49	5 23
11	8 00	5 42	7 38	6 17	6 59	6 47	6 12	7 16	5 35	7 44	5 19	8 06	5 30	8 07	5 55	7 41	6 22	6 56	6 48	6 10	7 20	5 33	7 50	5 23
12	7 59	5 43	7 37	6 18	6 58	6 48	6 11	7 17	5 34	7 45	5 19	8 07	5 30	8 07	5 56	7 40	6 23	6 55	6 49	6 09	7 21	5 33	7 51	5 23
13	7 59	5 44	7 36	6 19	6 56	6 49	6 09	7 18	5 33	7 46	5 19	8 07	5 31	8 06	5 56	7 38	6 23	6 53	6 50	6 07	7 23	5 32	7 51	5 24
14	7 59	5 45	7 35	6 20	6 55	6 50	6 08	7 19	5 33	7 47	5 19	8 08	5 32	8 06	5 57	7 37	6 24	6 52	6 51	6 06	7 24	5 31	7 52	5 24
15	7 58	5 46	7 34	6 21	6 53	6 51	6 07	7 20	5 32	7 48	5 19	8 08	5 32	8 05	5 58	7 36	6 25	6 50	6 52	6 04	7 25	5 30	7 53	5 24
16	7 58	5 48	7 33	6 22	6 52	6 52	6 05	7 21	5 31	7 48	5 19	8 08	5 33	8 05	5 59	7 35	6 26	6 49	6 53	6 03	7 26	5 30	7 53	5 24
17	7 58	5 49	7 31	6 23	6 50	6 53	6 04	7 22	5 30	7 49	5 19	8 09	5 34	8 04	6 00	7 33	6 27	6 47	6 54	6 02	7 27	5 29	7 54	5 25
18	7 57	5 50	7 30	6 24	6 49	6 54	6 02	7 23	5 29	7 50	5 20	8 09	5 35	8 04	6 01	7 32	6 28	6 45	6 55	6 00	7 28	5 28	7 55	5 25
19	7 57	5 51	7 29	6 25	6 47	6 55	6 01	7 23	5 29	7 51	5 20	8 09	5 35	8 03	6 02	7 31	6 29	6 44	6 56	5 59	7 29	5 28	7 55	5 26
20	7 56	5 52	7 28	6 26	6 46	6 55	6 00	7 24	5 28	7 52	5 20	8 09	5 36	8 02	6 03	7 29	6 29	6 42	6 57	5 58	7 30	5 27	7 56	5 26
21	7 56	5 53	7 26	6 27	6 44	6 56	5 58	7 25	5 27	7 53	5 20	8 10	5 37	8 02	6 03	7 28	6 30	6 41	6 58	5 56	7 31	5 27	7 56	5 27
22	7 55	5 54	7 25	6 29	6 43	6 57	5 57	7 26	5 26	7 53	5 20	8 10	5 38	8 01	6 04	7 26	6 31	6 39	6 59	5 55	7 32	5 26	7 57	5 27
23	7 55	5 55	7 24	6 30	6 41	6 58	5 56	7 27	5 26	7 54	5 21	8 10	5 38	8 00	6 05	7 25	6 32	6 38	7 00	5 54	7 33	5 26	7 57	5 28
24	7 54	5 56	7 22	6 31	6 40	6 59	5 54	7 28	5 25	7 55	5 21	8 10	5 39	7 59	6 06	7 24	6 33	6 36	7 01	5 52	7 34	5 25	7 58	5 28
25	7 54	5 57	7 21	6 32	6 38	7 00	5 53	7 29	5 25	7 56	5 21	8 10	5 40	7 58	6 07	7 22	6 34	6 34	7 02	5 51	7 35	5 25	7 58	5 29
26	7 53	5 58	7 20	6 33	6 36	7 01	5 52	7 30	5 24	7 56	5 22	8 10	5 41	7 58	6 08	7 21	6 35	6 33	7 03	5 50	7 36	5 24	7 58	5 30
27	7 52	6 00	7 18	6 34	6 35	7 02	5 51	7 31	5 24	7 57	5 22	8 10	5 42	7 57	6 09	7 19	6 36	6 31	7 04	5 49	7 37	5 24	7 59	5 30
28	7 51	6 01	7 17	6 35	6 33	7 03	5 49	7 32	5 23	7 58	5 22	8 10	5 43	7 56	6 10	7 18	6 36	6 30	7 05	5 48	7 38	5 24	7 59	5 31
29	7 51	6 02			6 32	7 04	5 48	7 33	5 23	7 59	5 23	8 10	5 43	7 55	6 10	7 16	6 37	6 28	7 06	5 46	7 39	5 24	7 59	5 32
30	7 50	6 03			6 30	7 05	5 47	7 34	5 22	7 59	5 23	8 10	5 44	7 54	6 11	7 15	6 38	6 27	7 08	5 45	7 40	5 23	7 59	5 32
31	7 49	6 04			6 29	7 06			5 22	8 00			5 45	7 53	6 12	7 13			7 09	5 44			8 00	5 33

Add one hour for daylight time, if and when in use.

East Bound - Subtract 1 min/10 mi from center   West Bound - Add 1 min/10 mi from center

LOUISVILLE, KENTUCKY

THE OVERLOAD COMPANION 2017 © FREDA BARBER BOOTH

Astronomical Applications Dept
Location: W084 29, N38 04

Rise and Set for the Sun for 2017
LEXINGTON, KENTUCKY

U. S. Naval Observatory, Washington, DC
Eastern Standard Time

	JAN		FEB		MAR		APR		MAY		JUN		JUL		AUG		SEP		OCT		NOV		DEC	
	AM	PM	AM	PM	AM	PM	AM	PM	AM	PM	AM	PM	AM	PM	AM	PM	AM	PM	AM	PM	AM	PM	AM	PM
1	7 54	5 29	7 43	6 01	7 09	6 32	6 22	7 02	5 41	7 29	5 17	7 55	5 19	8 05	5 41	7 47	6 08	7 07	6 34	6 20	7 04	5 38	7 36	5 18
2	7 54	5 30	7 42	6 02	7 08	6 33	6 21	7 02	5 40	7 30	5 16	7 56	5 20	8 04	5 42	7 46	6 09	7 05	6 35	6 19	7 05	5 37	7 37	5 18
3	7 54	5 30	7 41	6 03	7 06	6 34	6 19	7 03	5 39	7 31	5 16	7 57	5 20	8 04	5 43	7 45	6 10	7 04	6 36	6 17	7 06	5 36	7 38	5 18
4	7 54	5 31	7 40	6 04	7 05	6 35	6 18	7 04	5 38	7 32	5 16	7 57	5 21	8 04	5 44	7 44	6 11	7 02	6 37	6 16	7 08	5 35	7 39	5 18
5	7 55	5 32	7 39	6 05	7 03	6 36	6 16	7 05	5 37	7 33	5 16	7 58	5 21	8 04	5 45	7 42	6 12	7 01	6 38	6 14	7 09	5 34	7 39	5 18
6	7 55	5 33	7 38	6 06	7 02	6 37	6 15	7 06	5 36	7 34	5 15	7 58	5 22	8 04	5 46	7 41	6 12	6 59	6 39	6 13	7 10	5 33	7 40	5 18
7	7 55	5 34	7 37	6 07	7 00	6 38	6 13	7 07	5 35	7 35	5 15	7 59	5 22	8 03	5 46	7 40	6 13	6 58	6 40	6 11	7 11	5 32	7 41	5 18
8	7 55	5 35	7 36	6 08	6 59	6 39	6 12	7 08	5 34	7 36	5 15	8 00	5 23	8 03	5 47	7 39	6 14	6 56	6 40	6 10	7 12	5 31	7 42	5 18
9	7 54	5 36	7 35	6 10	6 57	6 40	6 10	7 09	5 33	7 37	5 15	8 00	5 23	8 03	5 48	7 38	6 15	6 54	6 41	6 08	7 13	5 30	7 43	5 19
10	7 54	5 37	7 34	6 11	6 56	6 41	6 09	7 10	5 32	7 38	5 15	8 01	5 24	8 03	5 49	7 37	6 16	6 53	6 42	6 07	7 14	5 30	7 44	5 19
11	7 54	5 38	7 33	6 12	6 54	6 42	6 08	7 11	5 31	7 39	5 15	8 01	5 24	8 02	5 50	7 36	6 17	6 51	6 43	6 05	7 15	5 29	7 45	5 19
12	7 54	5 39	7 32	6 13	6 53	6 43	6 06	7 12	5 30	7 39	5 15	8 01	5 25	8 02	5 51	7 34	6 18	6 50	6 44	6 04	7 16	5 28	7 45	5 19
13	7 54	5 40	7 31	6 14	6 51	6 44	6 05	7 13	5 29	7 40	5 15	8 02	5 26	8 01	5 52	7 33	6 18	6 48	6 45	6 02	7 17	5 27	7 46	5 19
14	7 53	5 41	7 30	6 15	6 50	6 45	6 03	7 14	5 28	7 41	5 15	8 02	5 26	8 01	5 53	7 32	6 19	6 47	6 46	6 01	7 18	5 26	7 47	5 20
15	7 53	5 42	7 29	6 16	6 48	6 46	6 02	7 15	5 27	7 42	5 15	8 02	5 27	8 00	5 53	7 31	6 20	6 45	6 46	6 00	7 19	5 26	7 47	5 20
16	7 53	5 43	7 27	6 17	6 47	6 47	6 00	7 16	5 26	7 43	5 15	8 03	5 28	7 59	5 54	7 29	6 21	6 44	6 47	5 58	7 20	5 25	7 48	5 20
17	7 52	5 44	7 26	6 18	6 45	6 48	5 59	7 16	5 25	7 44	5 15	8 03	5 29	7 59	5 55	7 28	6 22	6 42	6 48	5 57	7 21	5 24	7 49	5 20
18	7 52	5 45	7 25	6 19	6 44	6 49	5 58	7 17	5 25	7 45	5 15	8 03	5 29	7 58	5 56	7 27	6 23	6 40	6 49	5 55	7 23	5 24	7 49	5 21
19	7 51	5 46	7 24	6 20	6 42	6 49	5 56	7 18	5 24	7 46	5 15	8 04	5 30	7 58	5 57	7 25	6 24	6 39	6 50	5 54	7 24	5 23	7 50	5 21
20	7 51	5 47	7 22	6 22	6 41	6 50	5 55	7 19	5 23	7 46	5 15	8 04	5 31	7 57	5 58	7 24	6 24	6 37	6 51	5 53	7 25	5 22	7 50	5 22
21	7 51	5 48	7 21	6 23	6 39	6 51	5 54	7 20	5 22	7 47	5 16	8 04	5 32	7 56	5 59	7 23	6 25	6 36	6 52	5 51	7 26	5 22	7 51	5 22
22	7 50	5 49	7 20	6 24	6 38	6 52	5 52	7 21	5 22	7 48	5 16	8 04	5 32	7 55	6 00	7 21	6 26	6 34	6 53	5 50	7 27	5 21	7 51	5 23
23	7 49	5 50	7 19	6 25	6 36	6 53	5 51	7 22	5 21	7 49	5 16	8 04	5 33	7 55	6 00	7 20	6 27	6 33	6 54	5 49	7 28	5 21	7 52	5 23
24	7 49	5 52	7 17	6 26	6 35	6 54	5 50	7 23	5 20	7 50	5 16	8 04	5 34	7 54	6 01	7 18	6 28	6 31	6 55	5 48	7 29	5 20	7 52	5 24
25	7 48	5 53	7 16	6 27	6 33	6 55	5 48	7 24	5 19	7 51	5 17	8 05	5 35	7 53	6 02	7 17	6 29	6 29	6 56	5 46	7 30	5 20	7 52	5 25
26	7 48	5 54	7 15	6 28	6 32	6 56	5 47	7 25	5 19	7 52	5 17	8 05	5 36	7 52	6 03	7 15	6 30	6 28	6 57	5 45	7 31	5 20	7 53	5 25
27	7 47	5 55	7 13	6 29	6 30	6 57	5 46	7 26	5 19	7 53	5 17	8 05	5 37	7 51	6 04	7 14	6 31	6 26	6 58	5 44	7 32	5 19	7 53	5 26
28	7 46	5 56	7 12	6 30	6 28	6 58	5 45	7 27	5 18	7 54	5 18	8 05	5 38	7 50	6 05	7 13	6 31	6 25	6 59	5 43	7 33	5 19	7 53	5 26
29	7 45	5 57			6 27	6 59	5 44	7 28	5 18	7 54	5 18	8 05	5 39	7 50	6 06	7 11	6 32	6 23	7 00	5 42	7 34	5 19	7 54	5 27
30	7 45	5 58			6 25	7 00	5 42	7 28	5 18	7 55	5 19	8 05	5 40	7 49	6 06	7 10	6 33	6 22	7 02	5 40	7 35	5 19	7 54	5 28
31	7 44	5 59			6 24	7 01			5 17	7 55			5 40	7 48	6 07	7 08			7 03	5 39			7 54	5 29

Add one hour for daylight time, if and when in use.
East Bound - Subtract 1 min/10 mi from center   West Bound - Add 1 min/10 mi from center

LEXINGTON, KENTUCKY

THE OVERLOAD COMPANION 2017 © FREDA BARBER BOOTH

Astronomical Applications Dept
Location: W091 08, N30 27

Rise and Set for the Sun for 2017
BATON ROUGE, LOUISIANA

U. S. Naval Observatory, Washington, DC
Central Standard Time

	JAN		FEB		MAR		APR		MAY		JUN		JUL		AUG		SEP		OCT		NOV		DEC	
	AM	PM	AM	PM	AM	PM	AM	PM	AM	PM	AM	PM	AM	PM	AM	PM	AM	PM	AM	PM	AM	PM	AM	PM
1	7 01	5 15	6 56	5 41	6 30	6 04	5 53	6 24	5 21	6 43	5 03	7 02	5 06	7 11	5 23	6 58	5 42	6 27	5 58	5 49	6 19	5 16	6 44	5 03
2	7 02	5 15	6 55	5 42	6 29	6 04	5 52	6 24	5 20	6 44	5 03	7 03	5 07	7 11	5 24	6 57	5 42	6 25	5 59	5 48	6 20	5 16	6 45	5 03
3	7 02	5 16	6 55	5 42	6 28	6 05	5 51	6 25	5 19	6 44	5 02	7 03	5 07	7 11	5 24	6 57	5 43	6 24	6 00	5 47	6 21	5 15	6 46	5 03
4	7 02	5 17	6 54	5 43	6 27	6 06	5 49	6 26	5 18	6 45	5 02	7 03	5 07	7 11	5 25	6 56	5 43	6 23	6 00	5 46	6 22	5 14	6 47	5 03
5	7 02	5 18	6 53	5 44	6 26	6 07	5 48	6 26	5 17	6 46	5 02	7 04	5 08	7 10	5 26	6 55	5 44	6 22	6 01	5 44	6 23	5 13	6 47	5 03
6	7 02	5 18	6 53	5 45	6 25	6 07	5 47	6 27	5 16	6 46	5 02	7 04	5 08	7 10	5 26	6 54	5 44	6 21	6 01	5 43	6 23	5 13	6 48	5 04
7	7 02	5 19	6 52	5 46	6 23	6 08	5 46	6 28	5 16	6 47	5 02	7 05	5 08	7 10	5 27	6 54	5 45	6 19	6 02	5 42	6 24	5 12	6 49	5 04
8	7 02	5 20	6 51	5 47	6 22	6 09	5 45	6 28	5 15	6 48	5 02	7 05	5 09	7 10	5 27	6 53	5 45	6 18	6 03	5 41	6 25	5 11	6 50	5 04
9	7 03	5 21	6 50	5 48	6 21	6 09	5 44	6 29	5 14	6 48	5 02	7 06	5 09	7 10	5 28	6 52	5 46	6 17	6 03	5 40	6 26	5 11	6 50	5 04
10	7 03	5 22	6 50	5 48	6 20	6 10	5 42	6 29	5 13	6 49	5 02	7 06	5 10	7 09	5 29	6 51	5 47	6 16	6 04	5 38	6 27	5 10	6 51	5 04
11	7 03	5 22	6 49	5 49	6 19	6 11	5 41	6 30	5 13	6 50	5 02	7 07	5 11	7 09	5 29	6 50	5 47	6 14	6 05	5 37	6 28	5 09	6 52	5 05
12	7 03	5 23	6 48	5 50	6 17	6 11	5 40	6 31	5 12	6 50	5 02	7 07	5 11	7 09	5 30	6 49	5 48	6 13	6 05	5 36	6 28	5 09	6 52	5 05
13	7 02	5 24	6 47	5 51	6 16	6 12	5 39	6 31	5 11	6 51	5 02	7 08	5 12	7 09	5 30	6 48	5 48	6 12	6 06	5 35	6 29	5 08	6 53	5 05
14	7 02	5 25	6 46	5 52	6 15	6 13	5 38	6 32	5 11	6 52	5 02	7 08	5 12	7 08	5 31	6 47	5 49	6 11	6 06	5 34	6 30	5 08	6 54	5 06
15	7 02	5 26	6 45	5 52	6 14	6 13	5 37	6 33	5 10	6 52	5 02	7 08	5 13	7 08	5 32	6 46	5 49	6 09	6 07	5 33	6 31	5 07	6 54	5 06
16	7 02	5 27	6 44	5 53	6 13	6 14	5 36	6 33	5 09	6 53	5 02	7 09	5 14	7 08	5 32	6 45	5 50	6 08	6 08	5 32	6 32	5 07	6 55	5 07
17	7 02	5 28	6 44	5 54	6 11	6 14	5 35	6 34	5 09	6 54	5 02	7 09	5 14	7 07	5 33	6 44	5 50	6 07	6 08	5 31	6 33	5 06	6 55	5 07
18	7 02	5 28	6 43	5 55	6 10	6 15	5 33	6 35	5 08	6 54	5 02	7 09	5 15	7 07	5 33	6 43	5 51	6 05	6 09	5 30	6 33	5 06	6 56	5 07
19	7 01	5 29	6 42	5 56	6 09	6 16	5 32	6 35	5 08	6 55	5 03	7 09	5 15	7 06	5 34	6 42	5 51	6 04	6 10	5 29	6 34	5 06	6 57	5 07
20	7 01	5 30	6 41	5 56	6 08	6 16	5 31	6 36	5 07	6 56	5 03	7 10	5 16	7 06	5 35	6 40	5 52	6 03	6 11	5 27	6 35	5 05	6 57	5 08
21	7 01	5 31	6 40	5 57	6 07	6 17	5 30	6 36	5 07	6 56	5 03	7 10	5 16	7 05	5 35	6 39	5 53	6 02	6 11	5 26	6 36	5 05	6 58	5 08
22	7 00	5 32	6 39	5 58	6 05	6 18	5 29	6 37	5 06	6 57	5 03	7 10	5 17	7 05	5 36	6 38	5 53	6 00	6 12	5 25	6 37	5 05	6 58	5 09
23	7 00	5 33	6 38	5 58	6 04	6 18	5 28	6 38	5 06	6 57	5 03	7 10	5 18	7 04	5 36	6 37	5 54	5 59	6 13	5 24	6 38	5 04	6 59	5 09
24	7 00	5 34	6 37	5 59	6 03	6 19	5 27	6 38	5 05	6 58	5 04	7 10	5 18	7 04	5 37	6 36	5 54	5 58	6 13	5 24	6 38	5 04	6 59	5 10
25	6 59	5 35	6 36	6 00	6 02	6 20	5 26	6 39	5 05	6 58	5 04	7 11	5 19	7 03	5 38	6 35	5 55	5 57	6 14	5 23	6 39	5 04	6 59	5 11
26	6 59	5 35	6 35	6 01	6 00	6 20	5 25	6 40	5 05	6 59	5 04	7 11	5 20	7 03	5 38	6 34	5 55	5 55	6 15	5 22	6 40	5 04	7 00	5 11
27	6 58	5 36	6 33	6 02	5 59	6 21	5 24	6 40	5 04	7 00	5 04	7 11	5 20	7 02	5 39	6 33	5 56	5 54	6 16	5 21	6 41	5 04	7 00	5 12
28	6 58	5 37	6 32	6 02	5 58	6 22	5 23	6 41	5 04	7 00	5 04	7 11	5 21	7 01	5 39	6 31	5 57	5 53	6 16	5 20	6 42	5 04	7 00	5 12
29	6 57	5 38			5 57	6 22	5 22	6 42	5 04	7 01	5 05	7 11	5 21	7 01	5 40	6 30	5 57	5 52	6 17	5 19	6 43	5 03	7 01	5 13
30	6 57	5 39			5 56	6 23	5 21	6 42	5 03	7 01	5 05	7 11	5 22	7 00	5 40	6 29	5 58	5 50	6 18	5 18	6 43	5 03	7 01	5 14
31	6 56	5 40			5 54	6 23			5 03	7 02			5 23	6 59	5 41	6 28			6 19	5 17			7 01	5 15

Add one hour for daylight time, if and when in use.

East Bound - Subtract 1 min/10 mi from center   West Bound - Add 1 min/10 mi from center

BATON ROUGE, LOUISIANA

THE OVERLOAD COMPANION 2017 © FREDA BARBER BOOTH

Astronomical Applications Dept
Location: W069 46, N44 19

Rise and Set for the Sun for 2017
AUGUSTA, MAINE

U. S. Naval Observatory, Washington, DC
Eastern Standard Time

	JAN AM	JAN PM	FEB AM	FEB PM	MAR AM	MAR PM	APR AM	APR PM	MAY AM	MAY PM	JUN AM	JUN PM	JUL AM	JUL PM	AUG AM	AUG PM	SEP AM	SEP PM	OCT AM	OCT PM	NOV AM	NOV PM	DEC AM	DEC PM
1	7 15	4 10	6 58	4 48	6 15	5 28	5 19	6 07	4 29	6 44	3 58	7 17	3 59	7 27	4 27	7 03	5 02	6 14	5 37	5 19	6 17	4 28	6 55	4 01
2	7 15	4 11	6 57	4 49	6 14	5 29	5 18	6 08	4 28	6 45	3 57	7 17	4 00	7 26	4 28	7 02	5 04	6 13	5 39	5 17	6 18	4 27	6 56	4 01
3	7 15	4 12	6 55	4 51	6 12	5 30	5 16	6 09	4 27	6 46	3 57	7 18	4 00	7 26	4 29	7 01	5 05	6 11	5 40	5 15	6 19	4 25	6 58	4 01
4	7 15	4 13	6 54	4 52	6 10	5 32	5 14	6 11	4 25	6 47	3 57	7 19	4 01	7 26	4 30	6 59	5 06	6 09	5 41	5 13	6 21	4 24	6 59	4 00
5	7 15	4 14	6 53	4 54	6 08	5 33	5 12	6 12	4 24	6 48	3 56	7 20	4 02	7 26	4 31	6 58	5 07	6 07	5 42	5 12	6 22	4 23	7 00	4 00
6	7 15	4 15	6 52	4 55	6 07	5 34	5 10	6 13	4 22	6 50	3 56	7 20	4 02	7 25	4 33	6 57	5 08	6 05	5 43	5 10	6 24	4 21	7 01	4 00
7	7 15	4 16	6 51	4 56	6 05	5 36	5 09	6 14	4 21	6 51	3 56	7 21	4 03	7 25	4 34	6 55	5 09	6 04	5 45	5 08	6 25	4 20	7 02	4 00
8	7 14	4 17	6 49	4 58	6 03	5 37	5 07	6 16	4 20	6 52	3 55	7 22	4 04	7 24	4 35	6 54	5 11	6 02	5 46	5 06	6 26	4 19	7 03	4 00
9	7 14	4 18	6 48	4 59	6 01	5 38	5 05	6 17	4 19	6 53	3 55	7 22	4 05	7 24	4 36	6 52	5 12	6 00	5 47	5 04	6 28	4 18	7 04	4 00
10	7 14	4 19	6 47	5 01	6 00	5 40	5 03	6 18	4 17	6 54	3 55	7 23	4 05	7 23	4 37	6 51	5 13	5 58	5 48	5 03	6 29	4 17	7 05	4 00
11	7 14	4 21	6 45	5 02	5 58	5 41	5 02	6 19	4 16	6 55	3 55	7 23	4 06	7 22	4 38	6 49	5 14	5 56	5 50	5 01	6 30	4 16	7 06	4 00
12	7 13	4 22	6 44	5 03	5 56	5 42	5 00	6 20	4 15	6 57	3 55	7 24	4 07	7 22	4 39	6 48	5 15	5 54	5 51	4 59	6 32	4 15	7 07	4 00
13	7 13	4 23	6 42	5 05	5 54	5 43	4 58	6 22	4 14	6 58	3 54	7 24	4 08	7 22	4 41	6 46	5 16	5 52	5 52	4 58	6 33	4 14	7 08	4 00
14	7 12	4 24	6 41	5 06	5 52	5 45	4 56	6 23	4 13	6 59	3 54	7 25	4 09	7 21	4 42	6 45	5 17	5 51	5 53	4 56	6 34	4 13	7 08	4 01
15	7 12	4 25	6 40	5 08	5 51	5 46	4 55	6 24	4 12	7 00	3 54	7 25	4 10	7 20	4 43	6 43	5 19	5 49	5 55	4 54	6 36	4 12	7 09	4 01
16	7 11	4 27	6 38	5 09	5 49	5 47	4 53	6 25	4 11	7 01	3 54	7 25	4 10	7 20	4 44	6 42	5 20	5 47	5 56	4 52	6 37	4 11	7 10	4 01
17	7 11	4 28	6 37	5 10	5 47	5 48	4 51	6 27	4 09	7 02	3 55	7 26	4 11	7 19	4 45	6 40	5 21	5 45	5 57	4 51	6 38	4 10	7 10	4 01
18	7 10	4 29	6 35	5 12	5 45	5 50	4 50	6 28	4 08	7 03	3 55	7 26	4 12	7 18	4 46	6 38	5 22	5 43	5 58	4 49	6 39	4 09	7 11	4 02
19	7 10	4 30	6 33	5 13	5 43	5 51	4 48	6 29	4 08	7 04	3 55	7 26	4 13	7 17	4 47	6 37	5 23	5 41	6 00	4 47	6 41	4 08	7 11	4 02
20	7 09	4 32	6 32	5 14	5 41	5 52	4 46	6 30	4 07	7 05	3 55	7 27	4 14	7 16	4 49	6 35	5 24	5 39	6 01	4 46	6 42	4 07	7 12	4 02
21	7 09	4 33	6 30	5 16	5 40	5 53	4 45	6 31	4 06	7 06	3 55	7 27	4 15	7 15	4 50	6 34	5 26	5 37	6 02	4 44	6 43	4 06	7 12	4 03
22	7 08	4 34	6 29	5 17	5 38	5 55	4 43	6 33	4 05	7 07	3 55	7 27	4 16	7 14	4 51	6 32	5 27	5 36	6 04	4 43	6 45	4 06	7 12	4 04
23	7 07	4 36	6 27	5 18	5 36	5 56	4 41	6 34	4 04	7 08	3 55	7 27	4 17	7 13	4 52	6 30	5 28	5 34	6 05	4 41	6 46	4 05	7 13	4 04
24	7 06	4 37	6 25	5 20	5 34	5 57	4 40	6 35	4 03	7 09	3 56	7 27	4 18	7 12	4 53	6 28	5 29	5 32	6 06	4 40	6 47	4 04	7 13	4 05
25	7 05	4 38	6 24	5 21	5 32	5 58	4 38	6 36	4 02	7 10	3 56	7 27	4 19	7 11	4 54	6 27	5 30	5 30	6 08	4 38	6 48	4 04	7 13	4 05
26	7 04	4 40	6 22	5 23	5 30	6 00	4 37	6 38	4 02	7 11	3 56	7 27	4 20	7 10	4 56	6 25	5 31	5 28	6 09	4 37	6 50	4 03	7 14	4 06
27	7 03	4 41	6 21	5 24	5 29	6 01	4 35	6 39	4 01	7 12	3 57	7 27	4 21	7 09	4 57	6 23	5 33	5 26	6 10	4 35	6 51	4 03	7 14	4 07
28	7 02	4 42	6 19	5 25	5 27	6 02	4 34	6 40	4 00	7 13	3 57	7 27	4 23	7 08	4 58	6 22	5 34	5 24	6 11	4 34	6 52	4 02	7 14	4 08
29	7 01	4 44			5 25	6 03	4 32	6 41	4 00	7 14	3 58	7 27	4 24	7 07	4 59	6 20	5 35	5 23	6 13	4 32	6 53	4 02	7 15	4 08
30	7 00	4 45			5 23	6 04	4 31	6 42	3 59	7 15	3 58	7 27	4 25	7 06	5 00	6 18	5 36	5 21	6 14	4 31	6 54	4 01	7 15	4 09
31	6 59	4 47			5 21	6 06			3 58	7 16			4 26	7 04	5 01	6 16			6 15	4 29			7 15	4 10

Add one hour for daylight time, if and when in use.

East Bound - Subtract 1 min/10 mi from center   West Bound - Add 1 min/10 mi from center

AUGUSTA, MAINE

THE OVERLOAD COMPANION 2017 © FREDA BARBER BOOTH

Astronomical Applications Dept
Location: W076 30, N38 58

Rise and Set for the Sun for 2017
ANNAPOLIS, MARYLAND

U. S. Naval Observatory, Washington, DC
Eastern Standard Time

	JAN AM	JAN PM	FEB AM	FEB PM	MAR AM	MAR PM	APR AM	APR PM	MAY AM	MAY PM	JUN AM	JUN PM	JUL AM	JUL PM	AUG AM	AUG PM	SEP AM	SEP PM	OCT AM	OCT PM	NOV AM	NOV PM	DEC AM	DEC PM
1	7 25	4 54	7 13	5 27	6 38	5 59	5 50	6 30	5 07	6 59	4 42	7 26	4 44	7 35	5 07	7 17	5 35	6 36	6 02	5 48	6 34	5 05	7 06	4 44
2	7 25	4 55	7 12	5 28	6 36	6 00	5 48	6 31	5 06	7 00	4 42	7 27	4 45	7 35	5 08	7 16	5 36	6 34	6 03	5 46	6 35	5 04	7 07	4 44
3	7 25	4 56	7 11	5 29	6 35	6 01	5 47	6 32	5 05	7 01	4 41	7 27	4 45	7 35	5 09	7 15	5 37	6 33	6 04	5 45	6 36	5 03	7 08	4 44
4	7 25	4 57	7 10	5 30	6 33	6 02	5 45	6 33	5 04	7 02	4 41	7 27	4 46	7 35	5 10	7 14	5 38	6 31	6 05	5 43	6 37	5 02	7 09	4 44
5	7 25	4 58	7 09	5 31	6 32	6 03	5 44	6 34	5 03	7 03	4 41	7 28	4 47	7 35	5 11	7 12	5 39	6 29	6 06	5 42	6 38	5 01	7 10	4 44
6	7 25	4 59	7 08	5 33	6 30	6 04	5 42	6 35	5 02	7 04	4 41	7 29	4 47	7 34	5 12	7 11	5 40	6 28	6 07	5 40	6 39	5 00	7 11	4 44
7	7 25	4 59	7 07	5 34	6 29	6 05	5 41	6 36	5 01	7 05	4 40	7 29	4 48	7 34	5 13	7 10	5 41	6 26	6 08	5 39	6 41	4 59	7 12	4 44
8	7 25	5 00	7 06	5 35	6 27	6 06	5 39	6 37	5 00	7 06	4 40	7 30	4 48	7 34	5 14	7 09	5 42	6 25	6 09	5 37	6 42	4 58	7 13	4 44
9	7 25	5 01	7 05	5 36	6 26	6 08	5 38	6 38	4 59	7 07	4 40	7 30	4 49	7 33	5 14	7 08	5 42	6 23	6 10	5 36	6 43	4 57	7 13	4 44
10	7 25	5 02	7 04	5 37	6 24	6 09	5 36	6 39	4 58	7 08	4 40	7 31	4 50	7 33	5 15	7 06	5 43	6 21	6 11	5 34	6 44	4 56	7 14	4 44
11	7 25	5 03	7 03	5 38	6 23	6 10	5 35	6 40	4 57	7 09	4 40	7 32	4 51	7 33	5 16	7 05	5 44	6 20	6 12	5 33	6 45	4 55	7 15	4 44
12	7 24	5 04	7 01	5 39	6 21	6 11	5 33	6 41	4 56	7 10	4 40	7 32	4 51	7 32	5 17	7 04	5 45	6 18	6 13	5 31	6 46	4 54	7 16	4 44
13	7 24	5 05	7 00	5 41	6 20	6 12	5 32	6 42	4 55	7 11	4 40	7 33	4 52	7 32	5 18	7 03	5 46	6 17	6 14	5 30	6 47	4 53	7 17	4 44
14	7 24	5 06	6 59	5 42	6 18	6 13	5 30	6 43	4 54	7 12	4 40	7 33	4 52	7 31	5 19	7 01	5 47	6 15	6 15	5 28	6 48	4 52	7 17	4 45
15	7 23	5 07	6 58	5 43	6 17	6 14	5 29	6 44	4 53	7 12	4 40	7 33	4 53	7 31	5 20	7 00	5 48	6 13	6 16	5 27	6 49	4 52	7 18	4 45
16	7 23	5 09	6 57	5 44	6 15	6 15	5 27	6 45	4 52	7 13	4 40	7 34	4 54	7 30	5 21	6 59	5 49	6 12	6 17	5 25	6 50	4 51	7 19	4 45
17	7 23	5 10	6 55	5 45	6 13	6 16	5 26	6 46	4 51	7 14	4 40	7 34	4 54	7 30	5 22	6 57	5 50	6 10	6 18	5 24	6 52	4 50	7 19	4 46
18	7 22	5 11	6 54	5 46	6 12	6 17	5 24	6 47	4 50	7 15	4 40	7 34	4 55	7 29	5 23	6 56	5 51	6 09	6 19	5 22	6 53	4 50	7 20	4 46
19	7 22	5 12	6 53	5 47	6 10	6 18	5 23	6 48	4 50	7 16	4 40	7 35	4 56	7 28	5 24	6 55	5 52	6 07	6 20	5 21	6 54	4 49	7 20	4 46
20	7 21	5 13	6 52	5 48	6 09	6 19	5 22	6 49	4 49	7 17	4 41	7 35	4 57	7 27	5 25	6 53	5 53	6 05	6 21	5 20	6 55	4 48	7 21	4 47
21	7 21	5 14	6 50	5 50	6 07	6 20	5 20	6 50	4 48	7 18	4 41	7 35	4 58	7 27	5 26	6 52	5 54	6 04	6 22	5 18	6 56	4 48	7 21	4 47
22	7 20	5 15	6 49	5 51	6 06	6 21	5 19	6 51	4 47	7 19	4 41	7 35	4 59	7 26	5 27	6 50	5 55	6 02	6 23	5 17	6 57	4 47	7 22	4 48
23	7 20	5 16	6 48	5 52	6 04	6 22	5 18	6 52	4 46	7 20	4 42	7 35	4 59	7 25	5 28	6 49	5 56	6 01	6 24	5 16	6 58	4 47	7 22	4 48
24	7 19	5 17	6 46	5 53	6 02	6 23	5 16	6 53	4 46	7 21	4 42	7 36	5 00	7 24	5 29	6 48	5 57	5 59	6 25	5 14	6 59	4 46	7 23	4 49
25	7 18	5 19	6 45	5 54	6 01	6 24	5 15	6 54	4 45	7 22	4 42	7 36	5 01	7 23	5 30	6 46	5 58	5 57	6 26	5 13	7 00	4 46	7 23	4 50
26	7 18	5 20	6 43	5 55	5 59	6 25	5 14	6 55	4 44	7 23	4 43	7 36	5 02	7 22	5 31	6 45	5 59	5 56	6 27	5 12	7 01	4 46	7 23	4 50
27	7 17	5 21	6 42	5 56	5 58	6 26	5 12	6 56	4 44	7 23	4 43	7 36	5 03	7 22	5 32	6 43	6 00	5 54	6 28	5 11	7 02	4 45	7 24	4 51
28	7 16	5 22	6 41	5 57	5 56	6 26	5 11	6 57	4 43	7 24	4 43	7 36	5 04	7 21	5 32	6 42	6 01	5 53	6 29	5 09	7 03	4 45	7 24	4 52
29	7 15	5 23			5 55	6 27	5 10	6 57	4 43	7 24	4 44	7 36	5 04	7 20	5 33	6 40	6 01	5 51	6 30	5 08	7 04	4 45	7 24	4 52
30	7 14	5 24			5 53	6 28	5 09	6 58	4 43	7 25	4 44	7 35	5 05	7 19	5 33	6 39	6 01	5 49	6 31	5 07	7 05	4 44	7 25	4 53
31	7 14	5 26			5 51	6 29			4 43	7 25			5 06	7 18	5 34	6 37			6 33	5 06			7 25	4 54

Add one hour for daylight time, if and when in use.

Close accuracy within 10 miles from center of this location - if further than 10 miles, add/subtract 1 minute per 10 miles

ANNAPOLIS, MARYLAND

THE OVERLOAD COMPANION 2017 © FREDA BARBER BOOTH

Astronomical Applications Dept
Location: W077 43, N39 38

Rise and Set for the Sun for 2017
HAGERSTOWN, MARYLAND

U. S. Naval Observatory, Washington, DC
Eastern Standard Time

	JAN AM	JAN PM	FEB AM	FEB PM	MAR AM	MAR PM	APR AM	APR PM	MAY AM	MAY PM	JUN AM	JUN PM	JUL AM	JUL PM	AUG AM	AUG PM	SEP AM	SEP PM	OCT AM	OCT PM	NOV AM	NOV PM	DEC AM	DEC PM
1	7 32	4 57	7 19	5 30	6 43	6 04	5 54	6 35	5 11	7 05	4 45	7 33	4 47	7 42	5 11	7 23	5 39	6 41	6 08	5 53	6 40	5 08	7 13	4 47
2	7 32	4 58	7 18	5 31	6 42	6 05	5 53	6 36	5 10	7 06	4 45	7 34	4 48	7 42	5 11	7 22	5 40	6 40	6 08	5 51	6 41	5 07	7 14	4 47
3	7 32	4 59	7 17	5 33	6 40	6 06	5 51	6 37	5 09	7 07	4 44	7 34	4 48	7 42	5 12	7 21	5 41	6 38	6 09	5 49	6 42	5 06	7 15	4 47
4	7 32	5 00	7 16	5 34	6 39	6 07	5 50	6 38	5 07	7 08	4 44	7 35	4 49	7 42	5 13	7 20	5 42	6 36	6 10	5 48	6 43	5 05	7 16	4 47
5	7 32	5 01	7 15	5 35	6 37	6 08	5 48	6 39	5 06	7 09	4 44	7 36	4 49	7 42	5 14	7 19	5 43	6 35	6 11	5 46	6 44	5 04	7 17	4 47
6	7 32	5 01	7 14	5 36	6 36	6 09	5 46	6 40	5 05	7 10	4 44	7 36	4 50	7 41	5 15	7 18	5 44	6 33	6 12	5 45	6 46	5 03	7 18	4 47
7	7 32	5 02	7 13	5 37	6 34	6 10	5 45	6 41	5 04	7 11	4 43	7 37	4 51	7 41	5 16	7 16	5 45	6 32	6 13	5 43	6 47	5 02	7 19	4 47
8	7 32	5 03	7 12	5 39	6 33	6 11	5 43	6 42	5 03	7 12	4 43	7 37	4 51	7 41	5 17	7 15	5 46	6 30	6 14	5 41	6 48	5 01	7 19	4 47
9	7 32	5 04	7 11	5 40	6 31	6 12	5 42	6 43	5 02	7 13	4 43	7 38	4 52	7 40	5 18	7 14	5 47	6 28	6 15	5 40	6 49	5 00	7 20	4 47
10	7 31	5 05	7 10	5 41	6 29	6 13	5 40	6 44	5 01	7 14	4 43	7 38	4 53	7 40	5 19	7 13	5 48	6 27	6 16	5 38	6 50	4 59	7 21	4 47
11	7 31	5 06	7 09	5 42	6 28	6 14	5 39	6 45	5 00	7 15	4 43	7 39	4 53	7 39	5 20	7 11	5 49	6 25	6 17	5 37	6 51	4 58	7 22	4 47
12	7 31	5 07	7 07	5 43	6 26	6 15	5 37	6 46	4 59	7 16	4 43	7 39	4 54	7 39	5 21	7 10	5 50	6 23	6 18	5 35	6 52	4 57	7 23	4 47
13	7 31	5 08	7 06	5 44	6 25	6 16	5 36	6 47	4 58	7 17	4 43	7 40	4 55	7 38	5 22	7 09	5 51	6 22	6 19	5 34	6 54	4 57	7 23	4 47
14	7 30	5 10	7 05	5 46	6 23	6 17	5 34	6 48	4 57	7 18	4 43	7 40	4 55	7 38	5 23	7 07	5 52	6 20	6 20	5 32	6 55	4 56	7 24	4 48
15	7 30	5 11	7 04	5 47	6 22	6 18	5 33	6 49	4 56	7 19	4 43	7 40	4 56	7 37	5 24	7 06	5 52	6 19	6 22	5 31	6 56	4 55	7 25	4 48
16	7 30	5 12	7 03	5 48	6 20	6 19	5 31	6 50	4 55	7 20	4 43	7 41	4 57	7 37	5 25	7 05	5 53	6 17	6 23	5 29	6 57	4 54	7 25	4 48
17	7 29	5 13	7 01	5 49	6 18	6 20	5 30	6 51	4 54	7 21	4 43	7 41	4 58	7 36	5 25	7 03	5 54	6 15	6 24	5 28	6 58	4 54	7 26	4 48
18	7 29	5 14	7 00	5 50	6 17	6 21	5 28	6 52	4 54	7 22	4 43	7 41	4 58	7 35	5 26	7 02	5 55	6 14	6 25	5 27	6 59	4 53	7 27	4 49
19	7 28	5 15	6 59	5 51	6 15	6 22	5 27	6 53	4 53	7 23	4 43	7 42	4 59	7 35	5 27	7 01	5 56	6 12	6 26	5 25	7 00	4 52	7 27	4 49
20	7 28	5 16	6 57	5 53	6 14	6 23	5 26	6 54	4 52	7 24	4 43	7 42	5 00	7 34	5 28	6 59	5 57	6 10	6 27	5 24	7 01	4 52	7 28	4 50
21	7 27	5 17	6 56	5 54	6 12	6 24	5 24	6 55	4 51	7 25	4 44	7 42	5 01	7 33	5 29	6 58	5 58	6 09	6 28	5 22	7 02	4 51	7 28	4 50
22	7 27	5 18	6 55	5 55	6 10	6 25	5 23	6 56	4 51	7 26	4 44	7 42	5 02	7 32	5 30	6 56	5 59	6 07	6 29	5 21	7 04	4 50	7 29	4 51
23	7 26	5 20	6 53	5 56	6 09	6 26	5 21	6 57	4 50	7 26	4 44	7 42	5 02	7 32	5 31	6 55	6 00	6 05	6 30	5 20	7 05	4 50	7 29	4 51
24	7 25	5 21	6 52	5 57	6 07	6 27	5 20	6 58	4 49	7 27	4 44	7 42	5 03	7 31	5 32	6 53	6 01	6 04	6 31	5 18	7 06	4 49	7 30	4 52
25	7 25	5 22	6 50	5 58	6 06	6 28	5 19	6 59	4 49	7 28	4 45	7 43	5 04	7 30	5 33	6 52	6 02	6 02	6 32	5 17	7 07	4 49	7 30	4 53
26	7 24	5 23	6 49	5 59	6 04	6 29	5 17	7 00	4 48	7 28	4 45	7 43	5 05	7 29	5 34	6 50	6 03	6 01	6 33	5 16	7 08	4 49	7 30	4 53
27	7 23	5 24	6 48	6 00	6 02	6 30	5 16	7 01	4 47	7 29	4 45	7 43	5 06	7 28	5 35	6 49	6 04	5 59	6 34	5 15	7 09	4 48	7 31	4 54
28	7 22	5 25	6 46	6 01	6 01	6 31	5 15	7 02	4 47	7 30	4 46	7 43	5 07	7 27	5 36	6 47	6 05	5 57	6 35	5 13	7 10	4 48	7 31	4 55
29	7 22	5 27			5 59	6 32	5 14	7 03	4 46	7 31	4 46	7 43	5 08	7 26	5 37	6 46	6 06	5 56	6 37	5 12	7 11	4 48	7 31	4 55
30	7 21	5 28			5 58	6 33	5 12	7 04	4 46	7 31	4 47	7 42	5 09	7 25	5 38	6 44	6 07	5 54	6 38	5 11	7 12	4 47	7 31	4 56
31	7 20	5 29			5 56	6 34			4 45	7 32			5 10	7 24	5 39	6 43			6 39	5 10			7 32	4 57

Add one hour for daylight time, if and when in use.

Close accuracy within 10 miles from center of this location - if further than 10 miles, add/subtract 1 minute per 10 miles

HAGERSTOWN, MARYLAND

THE OVERLOAD COMPANION 2017 © FREDA BARBER BOOTH

Astronomical Applications Dept
Location: W071 05, N42 19

Rise and Set for the Sun for 2017
BOSTON, MASSACHUSETTS

U. S. Naval Observatory, Washington, DC
Eastern Standard Time

	JAN AM	JAN PM	FEB AM	FEB PM	MAR AM	MAR PM	APR AM	APR PM	MAY AM	MAY PM	JUN AM	JUN PM	JUL AM	JUL PM	AUG AM	AUG PM	SEP AM	SEP PM	OCT AM	OCT PM	NOV AM	NOV PM	DEC AM	DEC PM
1	7 13	4 23	6 58	4 59	6 19	5 35	5 27	6 10	4 39	6 44	4 10	7 15	4 12	7 25	4 37	7 03	5 10	6 18	5 42	5 25	6 18	4 37	6 54	4 13
2	7 14	4 24	6 57	5 00	6 18	5 36	5 25	6 12	4 38	6 45	4 10	7 15	4 12	7 25	4 38	7 02	5 11	6 16	5 43	5 24	6 19	4 36	6 55	4 13
3	7 14	4 25	6 55	5 01	6 16	5 37	5 23	6 13	4 37	6 46	4 09	7 16	4 13	7 24	4 39	7 01	5 12	6 14	5 44	5 22	6 20	4 35	6 56	4 12
4	7 14	4 26	6 54	5 03	6 14	5 38	5 21	6 14	4 35	6 47	4 09	7 17	4 13	7 24	4 40	7 00	5 13	6 13	5 45	5 20	6 22	4 34	6 57	4 12
5	7 13	4 27	6 53	5 04	6 13	5 39	5 20	6 15	4 34	6 49	4 09	7 18	4 14	7 24	4 41	6 59	5 14	6 11	5 46	5 19	6 23	4 33	6 58	4 12
6	7 13	4 28	6 52	5 05	6 11	5 41	5 18	6 16	4 33	6 50	4 08	7 18	4 15	7 23	4 42	6 57	5 15	6 09	5 47	5 17	6 24	4 31	6 59	4 12
7	7 13	4 29	6 51	5 07	6 09	5 42	5 16	6 17	4 32	6 51	4 08	7 19	4 15	7 23	4 43	6 56	5 16	6 08	5 48	5 15	6 25	4 30	7 00	4 12
8	7 13	4 30	6 50	5 08	6 08	5 43	5 15	6 18	4 31	6 52	4 08	7 19	4 16	7 23	4 44	6 55	5 17	6 06	5 49	5 14	6 27	4 29	7 01	4 12
9	7 13	4 31	6 48	5 09	6 06	5 44	5 13	6 19	4 29	6 53	4 08	7 20	4 17	7 22	4 46	6 53	5 18	6 04	5 51	5 12	6 28	4 28	7 02	4 12
10	7 13	4 32	6 47	5 11	6 04	5 45	5 11	6 21	4 28	6 54	4 07	7 21	4 17	7 22	4 47	6 52	5 19	6 02	5 52	5 10	6 29	4 27	7 03	4 12
11	7 12	4 33	6 46	5 12	6 03	5 46	5 10	6 22	4 27	6 55	4 07	7 21	4 18	7 21	4 48	6 51	5 20	6 01	5 53	5 09	6 30	4 26	7 03	4 12
12	7 12	4 34	6 45	5 13	6 01	5 48	5 08	6 23	4 26	6 56	4 07	7 21	4 19	7 21	4 49	6 49	5 21	5 59	5 54	5 07	6 32	4 25	7 04	4 12
13	7 12	4 35	6 43	5 14	5 59	5 49	5 06	6 24	4 25	6 57	4 07	7 22	4 20	7 20	4 50	6 48	5 22	5 57	5 55	5 05	6 33	4 24	7 05	4 12
14	7 11	4 36	6 42	5 16	5 58	5 50	5 05	6 25	4 24	6 58	4 07	7 22	4 20	7 20	4 51	6 46	5 23	5 55	5 56	5 04	6 34	4 23	7 06	4 13
15	7 11	4 37	6 40	5 17	5 56	5 51	5 03	6 26	4 23	6 59	4 07	7 23	4 21	7 19	4 52	6 45	5 25	5 54	5 57	5 02	6 35	4 22	7 07	4 13
16	7 10	4 39	6 39	5 18	5 54	5 52	5 02	6 27	4 22	7 00	4 07	7 23	4 22	7 18	4 53	6 43	5 26	5 52	5 59	5 00	6 37	4 21	7 07	4 13
17	7 10	4 40	6 38	5 20	5 53	5 53	5 00	6 28	4 21	7 01	4 07	7 24	4 23	7 18	4 54	6 42	5 27	5 50	6 00	4 59	6 38	4 21	7 08	4 13
18	7 09	4 41	6 36	5 21	5 51	5 55	4 58	6 30	4 20	7 02	4 07	7 24	4 24	7 17	4 55	6 40	5 28	5 48	6 01	4 57	6 39	4 20	7 08	4 14
19	7 09	4 42	6 35	5 22	5 49	5 56	4 57	6 31	4 19	7 03	4 07	7 24	4 25	7 16	4 56	6 39	5 29	5 47	6 02	4 56	6 40	4 19	7 09	4 14
20	7 08	4 44	6 33	5 23	5 47	5 57	4 55	6 32	4 18	7 04	4 08	7 24	4 26	7 15	4 57	6 37	5 30	5 45	6 03	4 54	6 41	4 18	7 10	4 15
21	7 07	4 45	6 32	5 25	5 46	5 58	4 54	6 33	4 17	7 05	4 08	7 25	4 27	7 15	4 58	6 36	5 31	5 43	6 04	4 53	6 43	4 18	7 10	4 15
22	7 06	4 46	6 30	5 26	5 44	5 59	4 52	6 34	4 17	7 06	4 08	7 25	4 27	7 14	4 59	6 34	5 32	5 41	6 06	4 51	6 44	4 17	7 11	4 16
23	7 06	4 47	6 29	5 27	5 42	6 00	4 51	6 35	4 16	7 07	4 08	7 25	4 28	7 13	5 00	6 33	5 33	5 39	6 07	4 50	6 45	4 16	7 11	4 16
24	7 05	4 49	6 27	5 28	5 40	6 01	4 49	6 36	4 15	7 08	4 09	7 25	4 29	7 12	5 01	6 31	5 34	5 38	6 08	4 48	6 46	4 16	7 12	4 17
25	7 04	4 50	6 26	5 30	5 39	6 03	4 48	6 37	4 14	7 09	4 09	7 25	4 30	7 11	5 02	6 29	5 35	5 36	6 09	4 47	6 47	4 15	7 12	4 17
26	7 03	4 51	6 24	5 31	5 37	6 04	4 46	6 39	4 14	7 10	4 09	7 25	4 31	7 10	5 03	6 28	5 36	5 34	6 10	4 46	6 48	4 15	7 12	4 18
27	7 02	4 52	6 23	5 32	5 35	6 05	4 45	6 40	4 13	7 11	4 09	7 25	4 32	7 09	5 05	6 26	5 37	5 32	6 12	4 44	6 50	4 14	7 13	4 19
28	7 02	4 54	6 21	5 33	5 33	6 06	4 44	6 41	4 12	7 11	4 10	7 25	4 33	7 08	5 06	6 25	5 38	5 31	6 13	4 43	6 51	4 14	7 13	4 19
29	7 01	4 55			5 32	6 07	4 42	6 42	4 12	7 12	4 11	7 25	4 34	7 07	5 07	6 23	5 39	5 29	6 14	4 41	6 52	4 13	7 13	4 20
30	7 00	4 56			5 30	6 08	4 41	6 43	4 11	7 13	4 11	7 25	4 35	7 06	5 08	6 21	5 41	5 27	6 15	4 40	6 53	4 13	7 13	4 21
31	6 59	4 58			5 28	6 09			4 11	7 14			4 36	7 05	5 09	6 20			6 17	4 39			7 13	4 22

Add one hour for daylight time, if and when in use.

Close accuracy within 10 miles from center of this location - if further than 10 miles, add/subtract 1 minute per 10 miles

BOSTON, MASSACHUSETTS

THE OVERLOAD COMPANION 2017 © FREDA BARBER BOOTH

Astronomical Applications Dept
Location: W084 34, N42 43

Rise and Set for the Sun for 2017
LANSING, MICHIGAN

U. S. Naval Observatory, Washington, DC
Eastern Standard Time

	JAN AM	JAN PM	FEB AM	FEB PM	MAR AM	MAR PM	APR AM	APR PM	MAY AM	MAY PM	JUN AM	JUN PM	JUL AM	JUL PM	AUG AM	AUG PM	SEP AM	SEP PM	OCT AM	OCT PM	NOV AM	NOV PM	DEC AM	DEC PM
1	8 09	5 15	7 53	5 51	7 13	6 28	6 20	7 05	5 32	7 39	5 03	8 10	5 04	8 20	5 30	7 58	6 04	7 12	6 36	6 19	7 13	5 30	7 49	5 05
2	8 09	5 16	7 52	5 52	7 11	6 30	6 18	7 06	5 31	7 40	5 02	8 11	5 05	8 20	5 31	7 57	6 05	7 10	6 37	6 17	7 14	5 29	7 50	5 05
3	8 09	5 17	7 51	5 54	7 10	6 31	6 16	7 07	5 29	7 41	5 02	8 12	5 05	8 20	5 32	7 56	6 06	7 08	6 38	6 15	7 15	5 28	7 52	5 05
4	8 09	5 18	7 50	5 55	7 08	6 32	6 14	7 08	5 28	7 43	5 01	8 12	5 06	8 19	5 34	7 54	6 07	7 07	6 39	6 13	7 17	5 26	7 53	5 05
5	8 09	5 19	7 49	5 56	7 06	6 33	6 13	7 10	5 27	7 44	5 01	8 13	5 07	8 19	5 35	7 53	6 08	7 05	6 41	6 12	7 18	5 25	7 54	5 05
6	8 09	5 20	7 48	5 58	7 05	6 35	6 11	7 11	5 26	7 45	5 01	8 14	5 07	8 19	5 36	7 52	6 09	7 03	6 42	6 10	7 19	5 24	7 54	5 04
7	8 08	5 21	7 46	5 59	7 03	6 36	6 09	7 12	5 24	7 46	5 00	8 14	5 08	8 18	5 37	7 50	6 10	7 01	6 43	6 08	7 20	5 23	7 55	5 04
8	8 08	5 22	7 45	6 00	7 01	6 37	6 08	7 13	5 23	7 47	5 00	8 15	5 09	8 18	5 38	7 49	6 11	7 00	6 44	6 07	7 22	5 22	7 56	5 04
9	8 08	5 23	7 44	6 02	7 00	6 38	6 06	7 14	5 22	7 48	5 00	8 15	5 09	8 17	5 39	7 48	6 12	6 58	6 45	6 05	7 23	5 21	7 57	5 05
10	8 08	5 24	7 43	6 03	6 58	6 39	6 04	7 15	5 21	7 49	5 00	8 16	5 10	8 17	5 40	7 46	6 13	6 56	6 46	6 03	7 24	5 20	7 58	5 05
11	8 08	5 25	7 41	6 04	6 56	6 41	6 03	7 16	5 20	7 50	5 00	8 17	5 11	8 16	5 41	7 45	6 14	6 54	6 47	6 02	7 26	5 19	7 59	5 05
12	8 07	5 26	7 40	6 05	6 55	6 42	6 01	7 18	5 18	7 51	5 00	8 17	5 12	8 16	5 42	7 44	6 15	6 52	6 49	6 00	7 27	5 18	8 00	5 05
13	8 07	5 27	7 39	6 07	6 53	6 43	5 59	7 19	5 17	7 52	5 00	8 17	5 12	8 15	5 43	7 42	6 16	6 51	6 50	5 58	7 28	5 17	8 01	5 05
14	8 06	5 28	7 37	6 08	6 51	6 44	5 58	7 20	5 16	7 53	5 00	8 18	5 13	8 15	5 44	7 41	6 17	6 49	6 51	5 57	7 29	5 16	8 01	5 05
15	8 06	5 29	7 36	6 09	6 49	6 45	5 56	7 21	5 15	7 55	5 00	8 18	5 14	8 14	5 45	7 39	6 19	6 47	6 52	5 55	7 31	5 15	8 02	5 06
16	8 06	5 31	7 35	6 11	6 48	6 46	5 54	7 22	5 14	7 56	5 00	8 19	5 15	8 13	5 46	7 38	6 20	6 45	6 53	5 53	7 32	5 14	8 03	5 06
17	8 05	5 32	7 33	6 12	6 46	6 48	5 53	7 23	5 13	7 57	5 00	8 19	5 16	8 12	5 47	7 36	6 21	6 44	6 54	5 52	7 33	5 13	8 03	5 06
18	8 05	5 33	7 32	6 13	6 44	6 49	5 51	7 24	5 12	7 58	5 00	8 19	5 17	8 12	5 49	7 35	6 22	6 42	6 56	5 50	7 34	5 12	8 04	5 07
19	8 04	5 34	7 30	6 15	6 42	6 50	5 50	7 26	5 11	7 59	5 00	8 20	5 18	8 11	5 50	7 33	6 23	6 40	6 57	5 49	7 36	5 12	8 04	5 07
20	8 03	5 35	7 29	6 16	6 41	6 51	5 48	7 27	5 11	8 00	5 00	8 20	5 19	8 10	5 51	7 31	6 24	6 38	6 58	5 47	7 37	5 11	8 05	5 07
21	8 03	5 37	7 27	6 17	6 39	6 52	5 47	7 28	5 10	8 01	5 00	8 20	5 19	8 09	5 52	7 30	6 25	6 36	6 59	5 46	7 38	5 10	8 06	5 08
22	8 02	5 38	7 26	6 18	6 37	6 53	5 45	7 29	5 09	8 02	5 01	8 20	5 20	8 08	5 53	7 28	6 26	6 35	7 00	5 44	7 39	5 10	8 06	5 08
23	8 01	5 39	7 24	6 20	6 35	6 55	5 44	7 30	5 09	8 03	5 01	8 20	5 21	8 08	5 54	7 27	6 27	6 33	7 02	5 43	7 40	5 09	8 06	5 09
24	8 00	5 41	7 23	6 21	6 34	6 56	5 42	7 31	5 08	8 04	5 01	8 20	5 22	8 07	5 55	7 25	6 28	6 31	7 03	5 41	7 42	5 08	8 07	5 09
25	8 00	5 42	7 21	6 22	6 32	6 57	5 41	7 32	5 07	8 05	5 02	8 20	5 23	8 06	5 56	7 23	6 29	6 29	7 04	5 40	7 43	5 08	8 07	5 10
26	7 59	5 43	7 19	6 23	6 30	6 58	5 39	7 34	5 06	8 06	5 02	8 20	5 24	8 05	5 57	7 22	6 30	6 27	7 05	5 38	7 44	5 07	8 08	5 11
27	7 58	5 44	7 18	6 25	6 28	6 59	5 38	7 35	5 05	8 07	5 03	8 20	5 25	8 04	5 58	7 20	6 32	6 26	7 07	5 37	7 45	5 07	8 08	5 11
28	7 57	5 46	7 16	6 26	6 27	7 00	5 36	7 36	5 05	8 07	5 03	8 20	5 26	8 02	5 59	7 18	6 33	6 24	7 08	5 36	7 46	5 06	8 08	5 12
29	7 56	5 47			6 25	7 02	5 35	7 37	5 04	8 08	5 04	8 20	5 27	8 01	6 00	7 17	6 34	6 22	7 09	5 34	7 47	5 06	8 08	5 13
30	7 55	5 48			6 23	7 03	5 33	7 38	5 04	8 09	5 04	8 20	5 28	8 00	6 01	7 15	6 35	6 20	7 10	5 33	7 48	5 06	8 08	5 14
31	7 54	5 50			6 21	7 04			5 03	8 09			5 29	7 59	6 02	7 13			7 12	5 31			8 09	5 15

Add one hour for daylight time, if and when in use.

Close accuracy within 10 miles from center of this location - if further than 10 miles, add/subtract 1 minute per 10 miles

LANSING, MICHIGAN

THE OVERLOAD COMPANION 2017 © FREDA BARBER BOOTH

Astronomical Applications Dept
Location: W093 16, N44 58

Rise and Set for the Sun for 2017
MINNEAPOLIS, MINNESOTA

U. S. Naval Observatory, Washington, DC
Central Standard Time

	JAN AM	JAN PM	FEB AM	FEB PM	MAR AM	MAR PM	APR AM	APR PM	MAY AM	MAY PM	JUN AM	JUN PM	JUL AM	JUL PM	AUG AM	AUG PM	SEP AM	SEP PM	OCT AM	OCT PM	NOV AM	NOV PM	DEC AM	DEC PM
1	7 51	4 42	7 33	5 20	6 50	6 01	5 53	6 42	5 02	7 19	4 30	7 53	4 31	8 03	4 59	7 39	5 36	6 49	6 12	5 53	6 52	5 01	7 32	4 33
2	7 51	4 43	7 32	5 22	6 48	6 03	5 51	6 43	5 00	7 20	4 29	7 54	4 31	8 03	5 00	7 38	5 37	6 47	6 13	5 51	6 54	4 59	7 33	4 33
3	7 51	4 44	7 31	5 23	6 46	6 04	5 49	6 44	4 59	7 22	4 29	7 55	4 32	8 03	5 01	7 36	5 38	6 45	6 14	5 49	6 55	4 58	7 34	4 32
4	7 51	4 45	7 30	5 25	6 45	6 05	5 47	6 45	4 57	7 23	4 28	7 55	4 33	8 02	5 03	7 35	5 39	6 44	6 15	5 47	6 56	4 56	7 35	4 32
5	7 51	4 46	7 28	5 26	6 43	6 07	5 45	6 47	4 56	7 24	4 28	7 56	4 33	8 02	5 04	7 33	5 41	6 42	6 17	5 45	6 58	4 55	7 36	4 32
6	7 51	4 47	7 27	5 28	6 41	6 08	5 44	6 48	4 55	7 25	4 27	7 57	4 34	8 02	5 05	7 32	5 42	6 40	6 18	5 43	6 59	4 54	7 37	4 32
7	7 51	4 48	7 26	5 29	6 39	6 09	5 42	6 49	4 53	7 27	4 27	7 57	4 35	8 01	5 06	7 31	5 43	6 38	6 19	5 41	7 00	4 53	7 38	4 32
8	7 51	4 49	7 25	5 31	6 37	6 11	5 40	6 50	4 52	7 28	4 27	7 58	4 35	8 01	5 07	7 29	5 44	6 36	6 20	5 40	7 02	4 51	7 39	4 32
9	7 50	4 50	7 23	5 32	6 36	6 12	5 38	6 52	4 51	7 29	4 27	7 59	4 36	8 00	5 08	7 28	5 45	6 34	6 22	5 38	7 03	4 50	7 40	4 32
10	7 50	4 51	7 22	5 33	6 34	6 13	5 36	6 53	4 50	7 30	4 26	7 59	4 37	8 00	5 10	7 26	5 46	6 32	6 23	5 36	7 05	4 49	7 41	4 32
11	7 50	4 52	7 20	5 35	6 32	6 15	5 35	6 54	4 48	7 31	4 26	8 00	4 38	7 59	5 11	7 25	5 48	6 30	6 24	5 34	7 06	4 48	7 42	4 32
12	7 49	4 54	7 19	5 36	6 30	6 16	5 33	6 55	4 47	7 33	4 26	8 00	4 39	7 58	5 12	7 23	5 49	6 29	6 26	5 33	7 07	4 47	7 42	4 32
13	7 49	4 55	7 17	5 38	6 28	6 17	5 31	6 57	4 46	7 34	4 26	8 01	4 40	7 58	5 13	7 22	5 50	6 27	6 27	5 31	7 09	4 46	7 43	4 32
14	7 48	4 56	7 16	5 39	6 26	6 19	5 29	6 58	4 45	7 35	4 26	8 01	4 41	7 57	5 14	7 20	5 51	6 25	6 28	5 29	7 10	4 45	7 44	4 32
15	7 48	4 57	7 15	5 41	6 25	6 20	5 28	6 59	4 44	7 36	4 26	8 02	4 41	7 56	5 16	7 18	5 52	6 23	6 29	5 27	7 11	4 44	7 45	4 32
16	7 47	4 59	7 13	5 42	6 23	6 21	5 26	7 00	4 43	7 37	4 26	8 02	4 42	7 56	5 17	7 17	5 54	6 21	6 31	5 26	7 13	4 43	7 45	4 33
17	7 47	5 00	7 11	5 43	6 21	6 22	5 24	7 02	4 41	7 38	4 26	8 02	4 43	7 55	5 18	7 15	5 55	6 19	6 32	5 24	7 14	4 42	7 46	4 33
18	7 46	5 01	7 10	5 45	6 19	6 24	5 22	7 03	4 40	7 39	4 26	8 03	4 44	7 54	5 19	7 14	5 56	6 17	6 33	5 22	7 15	4 41	7 47	4 33
19	7 45	5 03	7 08	5 46	6 17	6 25	5 21	7 04	4 39	7 40	4 26	8 03	4 45	7 53	5 20	7 12	5 57	6 15	6 35	5 20	7 17	4 40	7 47	4 34
20	7 45	5 04	7 07	5 48	6 15	6 26	5 19	7 05	4 38	7 42	4 26	8 03	4 46	7 52	5 21	7 10	5 58	6 13	6 36	5 19	7 18	4 39	7 48	4 34
21	7 44	5 05	7 05	5 49	6 13	6 28	5 17	7 07	4 38	7 43	4 26	8 03	4 47	7 51	5 23	7 09	6 00	6 11	6 37	5 17	7 19	4 39	7 48	4 35
22	7 43	5 07	7 03	5 50	6 11	6 29	5 16	7 08	4 37	7 44	4 27	8 03	4 48	7 50	5 24	7 07	6 01	6 09	6 39	5 16	7 21	4 38	7 49	4 35
23	7 42	5 08	7 02	5 52	6 10	6 30	5 14	7 09	4 36	7 45	4 27	8 04	4 49	7 49	5 25	7 05	6 02	6 08	6 40	5 14	7 22	4 37	7 49	4 36
24	7 41	5 09	7 00	5 53	6 08	6 31	5 12	7 11	4 35	7 46	4 27	8 04	4 50	7 48	5 26	7 03	6 03	6 06	6 41	5 12	7 23	4 36	7 50	4 36
25	7 41	5 11	6 59	5 55	6 06	6 33	5 11	7 12	4 34	7 47	4 28	8 04	4 51	7 47	5 27	7 02	6 04	6 04	6 43	5 11	7 24	4 36	7 50	4 37
26	7 40	5 12	6 57	5 56	6 04	6 34	5 09	7 13	4 33	7 48	4 28	8 04	4 53	7 46	5 29	7 00	6 06	6 02	6 44	5 09	7 26	4 35	7 50	4 38
27	7 39	5 13	6 55	5 57	6 02	6 35	5 08	7 14	4 33	7 49	4 29	8 04	4 54	7 45	5 30	6 58	6 07	6 00	6 45	5 08	7 27	4 35	7 51	4 39
28	7 38	5 15	6 53	5 59	6 00	6 36	5 06	7 16	4 32	7 49	4 29	8 04	4 55	7 44	5 31	6 56	6 08	5 58	6 47	5 06	7 28	4 34	7 51	4 39
29	7 37	5 16			5 58	6 38	5 05	7 17	4 31	7 50	4 30	8 03	4 56	7 43	5 32	6 55	6 09	5 56	6 48	5 05	7 29	4 34	7 51	4 40
30	7 35	5 18			5 57	6 39	5 03	7 18	4 31	7 51	4 30	8 03	4 57	7 41	5 33	6 53	6 10	5 54	6 49	5 03	7 30	4 33	7 51	4 41
31	7 34	5 19			5 55	6 40			4 30	7 52			4 58	7 40	5 35	6 51			6 51	5 02			7 51	4 42

Add one hour for daylight time, if and when in use.

Close accuracy within 10 miles from center of this location - if further than 10 miles, add/subtract 1 minute per 10 miles

MINNEAPOLIS, MINNESOTA

THE OVERLOAD COMPANION 2017 © FREDA BARBER BOOTH

Astronomical Applications Dept
Location: W090 12, N32 19

Rise and Set for the Sun for 2017
JACKSON, MISSISSIPPI

U. S. Naval Observatory, Washington, DC
Central Standard Time

	JAN AM	JAN PM	FEB AM	FEB PM	MAR AM	MAR PM	APR AM	APR PM	MAY AM	MAY PM	JUN AM	JUN PM	JUL AM	JUL PM	AUG AM	AUG PM	SEP AM	SEP PM	OCT AM	OCT PM	NOV AM	NOV PM	DEC AM	DEC PM
1	7 02	5 07	6 55	5 34	6 28	5 59	5 48	6 21	5 14	6 42	4 55	7 03	4 58	7 12	5 16	6 58	5 36	6 24	5 55	5 45	6 18	5 10	6 45	4 55
2	7 02	5 07	6 55	5 35	6 26	6 00	5 47	6 22	5 13	6 43	4 54	7 04	4 58	7 12	5 17	6 57	5 37	6 23	5 56	5 44	6 19	5 09	6 45	4 55
3	7 02	5 08	6 54	5 36	6 25	6 00	5 46	6 22	5 12	6 44	4 54	7 04	4 59	7 11	5 17	6 56	5 37	6 22	5 56	5 42	6 20	5 08	6 46	4 55
4	7 03	5 09	6 53	5 37	6 24	6 01	5 45	6 23	5 11	6 44	4 54	7 04	4 59	7 11	5 18	6 55	5 38	6 21	5 57	5 41	6 21	5 07	6 47	4 55
5	7 03	5 10	6 52	5 38	6 23	6 02	5 43	6 24	5 10	6 45	4 54	7 05	5 00	7 11	5 19	6 54	5 39	6 19	5 58	5 40	6 22	5 07	6 48	4 55
6	7 03	5 10	6 52	5 38	6 22	6 03	5 42	6 25	5 09	6 46	4 54	7 05	5 00	7 11	5 19	6 54	5 39	6 18	5 59	5 38	6 23	5 06	6 49	4 56
7	7 03	5 11	6 51	5 39	6 20	6 03	5 41	6 25	5 09	6 47	4 54	7 06	5 01	7 11	5 20	6 53	5 40	6 17	5 59	5 37	6 24	5 05	6 49	4 56
8	7 03	5 12	6 50	5 40	6 19	6 04	5 40	6 26	5 08	6 47	4 54	7 06	5 01	7 11	5 21	6 52	5 41	6 15	6 00	5 36	6 24	5 04	6 50	4 56
9	7 03	5 13	6 49	5 41	6 18	6 05	5 38	6 27	5 07	6 48	4 54	7 07	5 02	7 10	5 21	6 51	5 41	6 14	6 01	5 35	6 25	5 04	6 51	4 56
10	7 03	5 14	6 48	5 42	6 17	6 06	5 37	6 27	5 06	6 49	4 53	7 07	5 02	7 10	5 22	6 50	5 42	6 13	6 01	5 33	6 26	5 03	6 52	4 56
11	7 03	5 15	6 47	5 43	6 15	6 06	5 36	6 28	5 05	6 49	4 53	7 07	5 03	7 09	5 23	6 49	5 43	6 11	6 02	5 32	6 27	5 02	6 52	4 57
12	7 03	5 15	6 47	5 44	6 14	6 07	5 35	6 29	5 05	6 50	4 53	7 08	5 03	7 09	5 23	6 48	5 43	6 10	6 03	5 31	6 28	5 02	6 53	4 57
13	7 03	5 16	6 46	5 45	6 13	6 08	5 33	6 29	5 04	6 51	4 53	7 08	5 04	7 09	5 24	6 47	5 44	6 09	6 03	5 30	6 29	5 01	6 54	4 57
14	7 03	5 17	6 45	5 46	6 12	6 08	5 32	6 30	5 03	6 52	4 54	7 09	5 04	7 08	5 25	6 46	5 44	6 07	6 04	5 29	6 30	5 01	6 55	4 58
15	7 02	5 18	6 44	5 46	6 10	6 09	5 31	6 31	5 03	6 53	4 54	7 09	5 05	7 08	5 25	6 45	5 45	6 06	6 05	5 27	6 31	5 00	6 55	4 58
16	7 02	5 19	6 43	5 47	6 09	6 10	5 30	6 32	5 02	6 53	4 54	7 10	5 06	7 08	5 26	6 43	5 46	6 05	6 06	5 26	6 32	5 00	6 56	4 58
17	7 02	5 20	6 42	5 48	6 08	6 11	5 29	6 32	5 01	6 54	4 54	7 10	5 06	7 07	5 27	6 42	5 46	6 03	6 06	5 25	6 32	4 59	6 56	4 58
18	7 02	5 21	6 41	5 49	6 06	6 11	5 28	6 33	5 01	6 55	4 54	7 10	5 07	7 07	5 27	6 41	5 47	6 02	6 07	5 24	6 33	4 59	6 57	4 59
19	7 01	5 22	6 40	5 50	6 05	6 12	5 26	6 34	5 00	6 56	4 54	7 10	5 07	7 06	5 28	6 40	5 47	6 01	6 08	5 23	6 34	4 58	6 57	4 59
20	7 01	5 23	6 39	5 51	6 04	6 13	5 25	6 34	4 59	6 56	4 54	7 11	5 08	7 06	5 29	6 39	5 48	5 59	6 09	5 22	6 35	4 58	6 58	5 00
21	7 01	5 24	6 38	5 52	6 03	6 13	5 24	6 35	4 59	6 57	4 54	7 11	5 09	7 05	5 29	6 38	5 49	5 58	6 09	5 21	6 36	4 58	6 58	5 00
22	7 00	5 25	6 37	5 52	6 01	6 14	5 23	6 36	4 58	6 57	4 55	7 11	5 09	7 05	5 30	6 37	5 49	5 57	6 10	5 20	6 37	4 57	6 59	5 01
23	7 00	5 25	6 36	5 53	6 00	6 14	5 22	6 36	4 58	6 58	4 55	7 11	5 10	7 04	5 30	6 35	5 50	5 55	6 11	5 19	6 38	4 57	6 59	5 01
24	7 00	5 26	6 35	5 54	5 59	6 15	5 21	6 37	4 57	6 59	4 55	7 11	5 11	7 04	5 31	6 34	5 51	5 54	6 12	5 18	6 39	4 57	7 00	5 02
25	6 59	5 27	6 33	5 55	5 57	6 16	5 20	6 38	4 57	7 00	4 56	7 11	5 11	7 03	5 32	6 33	5 51	5 53	6 13	5 17	6 39	4 57	7 00	5 02
26	6 59	5 28	6 32	5 56	5 56	6 17	5 19	6 39	4 56	7 00	4 56	7 12	5 12	7 02	5 32	6 32	5 52	5 51	6 13	5 16	6 40	4 56	7 00	5 03
27	6 58	5 29	6 31	5 56	5 55	6 17	5 18	6 39	4 56	7 01	4 56	7 12	5 12	7 02	5 33	6 31	5 53	5 50	6 14	5 15	6 41	4 56	7 01	5 04
28	6 58	5 30	6 30	5 57	5 54	6 18	5 17	6 40	4 56	7 01	4 57	7 12	5 13	7 01	5 34	6 29	5 53	5 49	6 15	5 14	6 42	4 56	7 01	5 04
29	6 57	5 31			5 52	6 19	5 16	6 41	4 56	7 02	4 57	7 12	5 14	7 00	5 34	6 28	5 54	5 47	6 16	5 13	6 43	4 56	7 01	5 05
30	6 56	5 32			5 51	6 20	5 15	6 41	4 55	7 02	4 57	7 12	5 15	6 59	5 35	6 27	5 54	5 46	6 17	5 12	6 44	4 55	7 02	5 06
31	6 56	5 33			5 50	6 20			4 55	7 03			5 15	6 59	5 36	6 26			6 17	5 11			7 02	5 06

Add one hour for daylight time, if and when in use.

Close accuracy within 10 miles from center of this location - if further than 10 miles, add/subtract 1 minute per 10 miles

JACKSON, MISSISSIPPI

THE OVERLOAD COMPANION 2017 © FREDA BARBER BOOTH

Astronomical Applications Dept
Location: W093 17, N37 12

Rise and Set for the Sun for 2017
SPRINGFIELD, MISSOURI

U. S. Naval Observatory, Washington, DC
Central Standard Time

	JAN AM	JAN PM	FEB AM	FEB PM	MAR AM	MAR PM	APR AM	APR PM	MAY AM	MAY PM	JUN AM	JUN PM	JUL AM	JUL PM	AUG AM	AUG PM	SEP AM	SEP PM	OCT AM	OCT PM	NOV AM	NOV PM	DEC AM	DEC PM
1	7 27	5 06	7 16	5 37	6 43	6 08	5 58	6 36	5 18	7 03	4 54	7 28	4 57	7 37	5 18	7 20	5 44	6 41	6 09	5 56	6 38	5 15	7 09	4 56
2	7 27	5 07	7 16	5 39	6 42	6 09	5 57	6 37	5 17	7 04	4 54	7 29	4 57	7 37	5 19	7 19	5 45	6 40	6 10	5 54	6 39	5 14	7 10	4 56
3	7 27	5 08	7 15	5 40	6 41	6 10	5 55	6 38	5 16	7 05	4 54	7 29	4 58	7 37	5 20	7 18	5 46	6 38	6 11	5 53	6 40	5 13	7 11	4 56
4	7 27	5 09	7 14	5 41	6 39	6 11	5 54	6 39	5 15	7 06	4 53	7 30	4 58	7 37	5 21	7 17	5 47	6 37	6 12	5 51	6 41	5 12	7 11	4 56
5	7 27	5 10	7 13	5 42	6 38	6 12	5 52	6 40	5 14	7 07	4 53	7 31	4 59	7 36	5 22	7 16	5 48	6 35	6 12	5 50	6 42	5 11	7 12	4 56
6	7 27	5 11	7 12	5 43	6 36	6 13	5 51	6 41	5 13	7 07	4 53	7 31	5 00	7 36	5 23	7 15	5 48	6 34	6 13	5 48	6 43	5 10	7 13	4 56
7	7 27	5 11	7 11	5 44	6 35	6 14	5 49	6 42	5 12	7 08	4 53	7 32	5 00	7 36	5 23	7 14	5 49	6 32	6 14	5 47	6 44	5 09	7 14	4 56
8	7 27	5 12	7 10	5 45	6 34	6 14	5 48	6 42	5 11	7 09	4 53	7 32	5 01	7 36	5 24	7 13	5 50	6 31	6 15	5 45	6 45	5 08	7 15	4 56
9	7 27	5 13	7 09	5 46	6 32	6 15	5 46	6 43	5 10	7 10	4 53	7 33	5 01	7 35	5 25	7 11	5 51	6 29	6 16	5 44	6 46	5 07	7 16	4 56
10	7 27	5 14	7 08	5 47	6 31	6 16	5 45	6 44	5 09	7 11	4 53	7 33	5 02	7 35	5 26	7 10	5 52	6 28	6 17	5 42	6 48	5 06	7 16	4 56
11	7 27	5 15	7 07	5 48	6 29	6 17	5 44	6 45	5 08	7 12	4 52	7 34	5 03	7 35	5 27	7 09	5 52	6 26	6 18	5 41	6 49	5 06	7 17	4 56
12	7 27	5 16	7 06	5 49	6 28	6 18	5 42	6 46	5 07	7 13	4 52	7 34	5 03	7 34	5 28	7 08	5 53	6 25	6 19	5 40	6 50	5 05	7 18	4 56
13	7 27	5 17	7 05	5 50	6 26	6 19	5 41	6 47	5 06	7 14	4 52	7 34	5 04	7 34	5 28	7 07	5 54	6 23	6 20	5 38	6 51	5 04	7 19	4 57
14	7 26	5 18	7 04	5 52	6 25	6 20	5 39	6 48	5 05	7 15	4 52	7 35	5 05	7 33	5 29	7 06	5 55	6 21	6 21	5 37	6 52	5 03	7 19	4 57
15	7 26	5 19	7 03	5 53	6 23	6 21	5 38	6 49	5 04	7 15	4 52	7 35	5 05	7 33	5 30	7 04	5 56	6 20	6 22	5 36	6 53	5 03	7 20	4 57
16	7 26	5 20	7 01	5 54	6 22	6 22	5 37	6 50	5 03	7 16	4 52	7 36	5 06	7 32	5 31	7 03	5 56	6 18	6 22	5 34	6 54	5 02	7 21	4 58
17	7 25	5 21	7 00	5 55	6 20	6 23	5 35	6 51	5 03	7 17	4 53	7 36	5 07	7 32	5 32	7 02	5 57	6 17	6 23	5 33	6 55	5 01	7 21	4 58
18	7 25	5 22	6 59	5 56	6 19	6 24	5 34	6 51	5 02	7 18	4 53	7 36	5 07	7 31	5 33	7 00	5 58	6 15	6 24	5 32	6 56	5 01	7 22	4 58
19	7 25	5 23	6 58	5 57	6 17	6 25	5 33	6 52	5 01	7 19	4 53	7 36	5 08	7 30	5 33	6 59	5 59	6 14	6 25	5 30	6 57	5 00	7 22	4 59
20	7 24	5 24	6 57	5 58	6 16	6 26	5 31	6 53	5 01	7 19	4 53	7 37	5 09	7 30	5 34	6 58	6 00	6 12	6 26	5 29	6 58	5 00	7 23	4 59
21	7 24	5 25	6 55	5 59	6 14	6 26	5 30	6 54	5 00	7 20	4 53	7 37	5 10	7 29	5 35	6 56	6 01	6 11	6 27	5 28	6 59	4 59	7 23	5 00
22	7 23	5 27	6 54	6 00	6 13	6 27	5 29	6 55	4 59	7 21	4 53	7 37	5 10	7 28	5 36	6 55	6 01	6 09	6 28	5 26	7 00	4 59	7 24	5 00
23	7 23	5 28	6 53	6 01	6 11	6 28	5 27	6 56	4 59	7 22	4 54	7 37	5 11	7 28	5 37	6 54	6 02	6 08	6 29	5 25	7 01	4 58	7 24	5 01
24	7 22	5 29	6 52	6 02	6 10	6 29	5 26	6 57	4 58	7 22	4 54	7 37	5 12	7 27	5 38	6 52	6 03	6 06	6 30	5 24	7 02	4 58	7 25	5 01
25	7 21	5 30	6 50	6 03	6 08	6 30	5 25	6 58	4 57	7 23	4 55	7 37	5 13	7 26	5 38	6 51	6 04	6 05	6 31	5 23	7 03	4 57	7 25	5 02
26	7 21	5 31	6 49	6 04	6 07	6 31	5 24	6 59	4 57	7 24	4 55	7 37	5 14	7 26	5 39	6 50	6 05	6 03	6 32	5 22	7 04	4 57	7 26	5 03
27	7 20	5 32	6 48	6 05	6 05	6 32	5 23	7 00	4 56	7 25	4 56	7 37	5 14	7 25	5 40	6 48	6 06	6 02	6 33	5 20	7 05	4 57	7 26	5 03
28	7 19	5 33	6 46	6 06	6 04	6 33	5 21	7 00	4 56	7 26	4 56	7 37	5 15	7 24	5 41	6 47	6 06	6 00	6 34	5 19	7 06	4 57	7 26	5 04
29	7 19	5 34			6 02	6 34	5 20	7 01	4 56	7 26	4 56	7 37	5 16	7 23	5 42	6 45	6 07	5 59	6 35	5 18	7 07	4 56	7 26	5 05
30	7 18	5 35			6 01	6 34	5 19	7 02	4 55	7 27	4 56	7 37	5 17	7 22	5 42	6 44	6 08	5 57	6 36	5 17	7 08	4 56	7 27	5 05
31	7 17	5 36			6 00	6 35			4 55	7 27			5 18	7 21	5 43	6 42			6 37	5 16			7 27	5 06

Add one hour for daylight time, if and when in use.

Close accuracy within 10 miles from center of this location - if further than 10 miles, add/subtract 1 minute per 10 miles

SPRINGFIELD, MISSOURI

Astronomical Applications Dept
Location: W112 02, N46 35

Rise and Set for the Sun for 2017
HELENA, MONTANA

U. S. Naval Observatory, Washington, DC
Mountain Standard Time

	JAN AM	JAN PM	FEB AM	FEB PM	MAR AM	MAR PM	APR AM	APR PM	MAY AM	MAY PM	JUN AM	JUN PM	JUL AM	JUL PM	AUG AM	AUG PM	SEP AM	SEP PM	OCT AM	OCT PM	NOV AM	NOV PM	DEC AM	DEC PM
1	8 12	4 51	7 52	5 31	7 06	6 15	6 06	6 58	5 13	7 38	4 38	8 14	4 39	8 25	5 09	7 58	5 49	7 06	6 28	6 07	7 11	5 12	7 52	4 42
2	8 12	4 52	7 51	5 33	7 05	6 16	6 04	6 59	5 11	7 40	4 38	8 15	4 40	8 24	5 11	7 57	5 50	7 04	6 29	6 05	7 12	5 10	7 54	4 42
3	8 12	4 53	7 50	5 35	7 03	6 18	6 03	7 01	5 10	7 41	4 37	8 16	4 41	8 24	5 12	7 56	5 51	7 02	6 30	6 03	7 14	5 09	7 55	4 42
4	8 12	4 54	7 49	5 36	7 01	6 19	6 01	7 02	5 08	7 42	4 37	8 17	4 41	8 24	5 13	7 54	5 53	7 00	6 32	6 01	7 15	5 08	7 56	4 41
5	8 12	4 55	7 47	5 38	6 59	6 21	5 59	7 03	5 07	7 44	4 36	8 18	4 42	8 23	5 14	7 53	5 54	6 58	6 33	5 59	7 17	5 06	7 57	4 41
6	8 12	4 56	7 46	5 39	6 57	6 22	5 57	7 05	5 05	7 45	4 36	8 18	4 43	8 23	5 16	7 51	5 55	6 56	6 34	5 57	7 18	5 05	7 58	4 41
7	8 12	4 57	7 44	5 41	6 55	6 23	5 55	7 06	5 04	7 46	4 36	8 19	4 43	8 22	5 17	7 50	5 57	6 54	6 36	5 55	7 20	5 04	7 59	4 41
8	8 11	4 58	7 43	5 42	6 53	6 25	5 53	7 07	5 02	7 48	4 35	8 20	4 44	8 22	5 18	7 48	5 58	6 52	6 37	5 53	7 21	5 02	8 00	4 41
9	8 11	5 00	7 42	5 44	6 51	6 26	5 51	7 09	5 01	7 49	4 35	8 20	4 45	8 21	5 19	7 47	5 59	6 50	6 38	5 51	7 22	5 01	8 01	4 41
10	8 11	5 01	7 40	5 45	6 49	6 28	5 49	7 10	5 00	7 50	4 35	8 21	4 46	8 20	5 21	7 45	6 00	6 48	6 40	5 49	7 24	5 00	8 02	4 41
11	8 10	5 02	7 39	5 47	6 48	6 29	5 47	7 12	4 58	7 51	4 34	8 21	4 47	8 20	5 22	7 44	6 02	6 46	6 41	5 48	7 25	4 59	8 03	4 41
12	8 10	5 03	7 37	5 48	6 46	6 31	5 45	7 13	4 57	7 53	4 34	8 22	4 48	8 19	5 23	7 42	6 03	6 44	6 42	5 46	7 27	4 57	8 04	4 41
13	8 09	5 04	7 36	5 50	6 44	6 32	5 44	7 14	4 56	7 54	4 34	8 23	4 49	8 18	5 25	7 40	6 04	6 43	6 44	5 44	7 28	4 56	8 05	4 41
14	8 09	5 06	7 34	5 51	6 42	6 33	5 42	7 16	4 55	7 55	4 34	8 23	4 50	8 18	5 26	7 39	6 05	6 41	6 45	5 42	7 30	4 55	8 06	4 41
15	8 08	5 07	7 32	5 53	6 40	6 35	5 40	7 17	4 53	7 56	4 34	8 23	4 51	8 17	5 27	7 37	6 07	6 39	6 47	5 40	7 31	4 54	8 07	4 41
16	8 08	5 08	7 31	5 54	6 38	6 36	5 38	7 18	4 52	7 57	4 34	8 24	4 52	8 16	5 28	7 35	6 08	6 37	6 48	5 38	7 33	4 53	8 07	4 41
17	8 07	5 10	7 29	5 56	6 36	6 37	5 36	7 20	4 51	7 59	4 34	8 24	4 53	8 16	5 30	7 34	6 09	6 35	6 49	5 37	7 34	4 52	8 08	4 42
18	8 06	5 11	7 28	5 57	6 34	6 39	5 35	7 21	4 50	8 00	4 34	8 24	4 54	8 15	5 31	7 32	6 11	6 33	6 51	5 35	7 35	4 51	8 08	4 42
19	8 06	5 12	7 26	5 59	6 32	6 40	5 33	7 22	4 49	8 01	4 35	8 25	4 55	8 14	5 32	7 30	6 12	6 31	6 52	5 33	7 37	4 50	8 09	4 43
20	8 05	5 14	7 24	6 00	6 30	6 42	5 31	7 24	4 48	8 02	4 35	8 25	4 56	8 13	5 33	7 28	6 13	6 29	6 54	5 31	7 38	4 49	8 09	4 43
21	8 04	5 15	7 22	6 02	6 28	6 43	5 29	7 25	4 47	8 03	4 35	8 25	4 57	8 12	5 35	7 26	6 14	6 27	6 55	5 30	7 40	4 48	8 09	4 44
22	8 03	5 17	7 21	6 03	6 26	6 44	5 27	7 26	4 46	8 04	4 35	8 25	4 58	8 11	5 36	7 25	6 16	6 25	6 56	5 28	7 41	4 48	8 10	4 44
23	8 02	5 18	7 19	6 05	6 24	6 46	5 26	7 28	4 45	8 05	4 35	8 25	4 59	8 10	5 37	7 23	6 17	6 23	6 58	5 26	7 42	4 47	8 11	4 45
24	8 01	5 20	7 17	6 06	6 22	6 47	5 24	7 29	4 44	8 07	4 36	8 25	5 00	8 08	5 39	7 21	6 18	6 21	6 59	5 25	7 44	4 46	8 11	4 45
25	8 00	5 21	7 15	6 08	6 20	6 48	5 22	7 30	4 43	8 08	4 36	8 25	5 01	8 07	5 40	7 19	6 20	6 19	7 01	5 23	7 45	4 45	8 11	4 46
26	7 59	5 22	7 14	6 09	6 18	6 50	5 21	7 32	4 42	8 09	4 36	8 25	5 02	8 06	5 41	7 17	6 21	6 17	7 02	5 21	7 46	4 45	8 12	4 47
27	7 58	5 24	7 12	6 11	6 16	6 51	5 19	7 33	4 42	8 10	4 37	8 25	5 04	8 05	5 42	7 15	6 22	6 15	7 04	5 20	7 47	4 44	8 12	4 47
28	7 57	5 25	7 10	6 12	6 14	6 53	5 17	7 34	4 41	8 11	4 37	8 25	5 05	8 04	5 44	7 14	6 24	6 13	7 05	5 18	7 49	4 44	8 11	4 48
29	7 56	5 27			6 12	6 54	5 16	7 36	4 40	8 12	4 38	8 25	5 06	8 02	5 45	7 12	6 25	6 11	7 06	5 16	7 50	4 43	8 12	4 49
30	7 55	5 28			6 10	6 55	5 14	7 37	4 40	8 12	4 38	8 25	5 07	8 01	5 46	7 10	6 26	6 09	7 08	5 15	7 51	4 43	8 12	4 50
31	7 54	5 30			6 08	6 57			4 39	8 13			5 08	8 00	5 48	7 08			7 09	5 13			8 12	4 51

Add one hour for daylight time, if and when in use.

Close accuracy within 10 miles from center of this location - if further than 10 miles, add/subtract 1 minute per 10 miles

HELENA, MONTANA

THE OVERLOAD COMPANION 2017 © FREDA BARBER BOOTH

Astronomical Applications Dept
Location: W100 46, N41 08

Rise and Set for the Sun for 2017
NORTH PLATTE, NEBRASKA

U. S. Naval Observatory, Washington, DC
Central Standard Time

	JAN AM	JAN PM	FEB AM	FEB PM	MAR AM	MAR PM	APR AM	APR PM	MAY AM	MAY PM	JUN AM	JUN PM	JUL AM	JUL PM	AUG AM	AUG PM	SEP AM	SEP PM	OCT AM	OCT PM	NOV AM	NOV PM	DEC AM	DEC PM
1	8 08	5 25	7 54	5 59	7 16	6 35	6 25	7 09	5 40	7 41	5 13	8 10	5 15	8 19	5 39	7 59	6 10	7 15	6 40	6 24	7 15	5 38	7 50	5 15
2	8 08	5 26	7 53	6 01	7 15	6 36	6 24	7 10	5 39	7 42	5 12	8 10	5 15	8 19	5 40	7 58	6 11	7 13	6 41	6 22	7 16	5 37	7 51	5 15
3	8 09	5 27	7 52	6 02	7 13	6 37	6 22	7 11	5 38	7 43	5 12	8 11	5 16	8 19	5 41	7 57	6 12	7 11	6 42	6 21	7 17	5 36	7 52	5 15
4	8 09	5 27	7 51	6 03	7 12	6 38	6 21	7 12	5 36	7 44	5 11	8 12	5 16	8 19	5 42	7 55	6 13	7 10	6 43	6 19	7 18	5 34	7 53	5 14
5	8 09	5 28	7 50	6 04	7 10	6 39	6 19	7 13	5 35	7 45	5 11	8 12	5 17	8 18	5 43	7 54	6 14	7 08	6 45	6 17	7 20	5 33	7 53	5 14
6	8 08	5 29	7 49	6 06	7 09	6 40	6 17	7 14	5 34	7 46	5 11	8 13	5 17	8 18	5 44	7 53	6 15	7 06	6 46	6 16	7 21	5 32	7 54	5 14
7	8 08	5 30	7 48	6 07	7 07	6 42	6 16	7 15	5 33	7 47	5 11	8 14	5 18	8 18	5 45	7 52	6 16	7 05	6 47	6 14	7 22	5 31	7 55	5 14
8	8 08	5 31	7 47	6 08	7 05	6 43	6 14	7 16	5 32	7 48	5 10	8 14	5 19	8 17	5 46	7 50	6 17	7 03	6 48	6 13	7 23	5 30	7 56	5 14
9	8 08	5 32	7 46	6 09	7 04	6 44	6 12	7 17	5 31	7 49	5 10	8 15	5 19	8 17	5 47	7 49	6 18	7 01	6 49	6 11	7 24	5 29	7 57	5 14
10	8 08	5 33	7 45	6 11	7 02	6 45	6 11	7 18	5 30	7 50	5 10	8 15	5 20	8 17	5 48	7 48	6 19	7 00	6 50	6 09	7 26	5 28	7 58	5 15
11	8 08	5 34	7 43	6 12	7 00	6 46	6 09	7 19	5 28	7 51	5 10	8 16	5 21	8 16	5 49	7 46	6 20	6 58	6 51	6 08	7 27	5 27	7 59	5 15
12	8 07	5 36	7 42	6 13	6 59	6 47	6 08	7 20	5 27	7 52	5 10	8 16	5 22	8 16	5 50	7 45	6 21	6 56	6 52	6 06	7 28	5 26	7 59	5 15
13	8 07	5 37	7 41	6 14	6 57	6 48	6 06	7 22	5 26	7 53	5 10	8 17	5 22	8 15	5 51	7 44	6 22	6 55	6 53	6 05	7 29	5 25	8 00	5 15
14	8 07	5 38	7 39	6 16	6 56	6 49	6 05	7 23	5 25	7 54	5 10	8 17	5 23	8 14	5 52	7 42	6 23	6 53	6 54	6 03	7 30	5 24	8 01	5 15
15	8 06	5 39	7 38	6 17	6 54	6 50	6 03	7 24	5 24	7 55	5 10	8 18	5 24	8 14	5 53	7 41	6 24	6 51	6 55	6 01	7 32	5 24	8 02	5 16
16	8 06	5 40	7 37	6 18	6 52	6 52	6 01	7 25	5 23	7 56	5 10	8 18	5 25	8 13	5 54	7 40	6 25	6 50	6 56	6 00	7 33	5 23	8 02	5 16
17	8 05	5 41	7 36	6 19	6 51	6 53	6 00	7 26	5 23	7 57	5 10	8 18	5 26	8 13	5 55	7 38	6 26	6 48	6 58	5 58	7 34	5 22	8 03	5 16
18	8 05	5 42	7 34	6 20	6 49	6 54	5 58	7 27	5 22	7 58	5 10	8 19	5 26	8 12	5 56	7 37	6 27	6 46	6 59	5 57	7 35	5 21	8 04	5 17
19	8 04	5 43	7 33	6 22	6 47	6 55	5 57	7 28	5 21	7 59	5 10	8 19	5 27	8 11	5 57	7 35	6 28	6 44	7 00	5 56	7 36	5 21	8 04	5 17
20	8 04	5 45	7 31	6 23	6 46	6 56	5 55	7 29	5 20	8 00	5 11	8 19	5 28	8 10	5 58	7 34	6 29	6 43	7 01	5 54	7 37	5 20	8 05	5 18
21	8 03	5 46	7 30	6 24	6 44	6 57	5 54	7 30	5 19	8 01	5 11	8 19	5 29	8 09	5 59	7 32	6 30	6 41	7 02	5 53	7 39	5 19	8 05	5 18
22	8 03	5 47	7 28	6 25	6 42	6 58	5 53	7 31	5 19	8 02	5 11	8 19	5 30	8 09	5 59	7 31	6 31	6 39	7 03	5 51	7 40	5 19	8 06	5 18
23	8 02	5 48	7 27	6 26	6 41	6 59	5 51	7 32	5 18	8 02	5 11	8 20	5 31	8 08	6 00	7 29	6 32	6 38	7 04	5 50	7 41	5 18	8 06	5 19
24	8 01	5 49	7 26	6 28	6 39	7 00	5 50	7 33	5 17	8 03	5 12	8 20	5 32	8 07	6 01	7 28	6 33	6 36	7 05	5 48	7 42	5 18	8 06	5 20
25	8 00	5 51	7 24	6 29	6 37	7 01	5 48	7 34	5 17	8 04	5 12	8 20	5 33	8 06	6 02	7 26	6 34	6 34	7 07	5 47	7 43	5 17	8 06	5 20
26	8 00	5 52	7 23	6 30	6 35	7 02	5 47	7 35	5 16	8 05	5 12	8 20	5 34	8 05	6 03	7 24	6 35	6 32	7 08	5 46	7 44	5 17	8 07	5 21
27	7 59	5 53	7 21	6 31	6 34	7 03	5 45	7 36	5 15	8 06	5 13	8 20	5 35	8 04	6 04	7 23	6 36	6 31	7 09	5 44	7 45	5 17	8 07	5 22
28	7 58	5 54	7 20	6 32	6 32	7 04	5 44	7 38	5 15	8 07	5 13	8 20	5 35	8 03	6 05	7 21	6 37	6 29	7 10	5 43	7 46	5 16	8 08	5 22
29	7 57	5 56			6 30	7 06	5 43	7 39	5 14	8 07	5 14	8 20	5 36	8 02	6 06	7 20	6 38	6 27	7 11	5 42	7 47	5 16	8 08	5 23
30	7 56	5 57			6 29	7 07	5 41	7 40	5 14	8 08	5 14	8 19	5 37	8 01	6 07	7 18	6 39	6 26	7 12	5 40	7 48	5 15	8 08	5 24
31	7 55	5 58			6 27	7 08			5 13	8 09			5 38	8 00	6 09	7 16			7 14	5 39			8 08	5 25

Add one hour for daylight time, if and when in use.

Close accuracy within 10 miles from center of this location - if further than 10 miles, add/subtract 1 minute per 10 miles

NORTH PLATTE, NEBRASKA

THE OVERLOAD COMPANION 2017 © FREDA BARBER BOOTH

Astronomical Applications Dept
Location: W119 47, N39 09

Rise and Set for the Sun for 2017
CARSON CITY, NEVADA

U. S. Naval Observatory, Washington, DC
Pacific Standard Time

	JAN AM	JAN PM	FEB AM	FEB PM	MAR AM	MAR PM	APR AM	APR PM	MAY AM	MAY PM	JUN AM	JUN PM	JUL AM	JUL PM	AUG AM	AUG PM	SEP AM	SEP PM	OCT AM	OCT PM	NOV AM	NOV PM	DEC AM	DEC PM
1	7 18	4 47	7 06	5 20	6 31	5 52	5 43	6 23	5 00	6 53	4 35	7 20	4 37	7 29	5 00	7 10	5 28	6 29	5 56	5 41	6 27	4 57	7 00	4 37
2	7 19	4 48	7 05	5 21	6 29	5 53	5 41	6 24	4 59	6 54	4 34	7 20	4 38	7 29	5 01	7 09	5 29	6 27	5 57	5 39	6 29	4 56	7 01	4 37
3	7 19	4 49	7 04	5 22	6 28	5 54	5 40	6 25	4 58	6 55	4 34	7 21	4 38	7 29	5 02	7 08	5 30	6 26	5 58	5 38	6 30	4 55	7 02	4 36
4	7 19	4 49	7 03	5 23	6 26	5 56	5 38	6 26	4 57	6 56	4 34	7 21	4 39	7 28	5 03	7 07	5 31	6 24	5 59	5 36	6 31	4 54	7 03	4 36
5	7 19	4 50	7 02	5 24	6 25	5 57	5 36	6 27	4 55	6 57	4 33	7 22	4 39	7 28	5 04	7 06	5 32	6 22	6 00	5 34	6 32	4 53	7 04	4 36
6	7 19	4 51	7 01	5 25	6 23	5 58	5 35	6 28	4 54	6 58	4 33	7 23	4 40	7 28	5 05	7 05	5 33	6 21	6 00	5 33	6 33	4 52	7 05	4 36
7	7 19	4 52	7 00	5 27	6 22	5 59	5 33	6 29	4 53	6 59	4 33	7 23	4 40	7 28	5 05	7 03	5 34	6 19	6 01	5 31	6 34	4 51	7 05	4 36
8	7 19	4 53	6 59	5 28	6 20	6 00	5 32	6 30	4 52	7 00	4 33	7 24	4 41	7 27	5 06	7 02	5 35	6 18	6 02	5 30	6 35	4 50	7 06	4 36
9	7 18	4 54	6 58	5 29	6 19	6 01	5 30	6 31	4 51	7 00	4 33	7 24	4 42	7 27	5 07	7 01	5 36	6 16	6 03	5 28	6 36	4 49	7 07	4 36
10	7 18	4 55	6 57	5 30	6 17	6 02	5 29	6 32	4 50	7 01	4 33	7 25	4 42	7 27	5 08	7 00	5 36	6 15	6 04	5 27	6 37	4 48	7 08	4 36
11	7 18	4 56	6 56	5 31	6 16	6 03	5 27	6 33	4 49	7 02	4 33	7 25	4 43	7 26	5 09	6 59	5 37	6 13	6 05	5 25	6 39	4 48	7 09	4 37
12	7 18	4 57	6 55	5 32	6 14	6 04	5 26	6 34	4 48	7 03	4 32	7 26	4 44	7 26	5 10	6 57	5 38	6 11	6 06	5 24	6 40	4 47	7 10	4 37
13	7 18	4 58	6 54	5 34	6 13	6 05	5 24	6 35	4 47	7 04	4 32	7 26	4 44	7 25	5 11	6 56	5 39	6 10	6 07	5 22	6 41	4 46	7 10	4 37
14	7 17	4 59	6 52	5 35	6 11	6 06	5 23	6 36	4 46	7 05	4 32	7 27	4 45	7 25	5 12	6 55	5 40	6 08	6 08	5 21	6 42	4 45	7 11	4 37
15	7 17	5 00	6 51	5 36	6 10	6 07	5 21	6 37	4 46	7 06	4 32	7 27	4 46	7 24	5 13	6 53	5 41	6 06	6 09	5 19	6 43	4 44	7 12	4 38
16	7 17	5 01	6 50	5 37	6 08	6 08	5 20	6 38	4 45	7 07	4 33	7 27	4 47	7 23	5 14	6 52	5 42	6 05	6 10	5 18	6 44	4 44	7 12	4 38
17	7 16	5 02	6 49	5 38	6 06	6 09	5 19	6 39	4 44	7 08	4 33	7 28	4 47	7 23	5 15	6 51	5 43	6 03	6 11	5 17	6 45	4 43	7 13	4 38
18	7 16	5 04	6 47	5 39	6 05	6 10	5 17	6 40	4 43	7 09	4 33	7 28	4 48	7 22	5 16	6 49	5 44	6 02	6 12	5 15	6 46	4 42	7 14	4 39
19	7 15	5 05	6 46	5 40	6 03	6 11	5 16	6 41	4 42	7 10	4 33	7 28	4 49	7 22	5 16	6 48	5 45	6 00	6 13	5 14	6 47	4 42	7 14	4 39
20	7 15	5 06	6 45	5 41	6 02	6 12	5 14	6 42	4 41	7 10	4 33	7 29	4 50	7 21	5 17	6 47	5 46	5 58	6 15	5 12	6 49	4 41	7 15	4 40
21	7 14	5 07	6 43	5 43	6 00	6 13	5 13	6 43	4 41	7 11	4 33	7 29	4 51	7 20	5 18	6 45	5 46	5 57	6 16	5 11	6 50	4 40	7 15	4 40
22	7 14	5 08	6 42	5 44	5 58	6 14	5 12	6 44	4 40	7 12	4 34	7 29	4 52	7 19	5 19	6 44	5 47	5 55	6 17	5 10	6 51	4 40	7 16	4 41
23	7 13	5 09	6 41	5 45	5 57	6 15	5 10	6 45	4 39	7 13	4 34	7 29	4 53	7 18	5 20	6 42	5 48	5 54	6 18	5 08	6 52	4 39	7 16	4 41
24	7 12	5 10	6 39	5 46	5 55	6 16	5 09	6 46	4 39	7 14	4 34	7 29	4 54	7 17	5 21	6 41	5 49	5 52	6 19	5 07	6 53	4 39	7 16	4 42
25	7 12	5 11	6 38	5 47	5 54	6 17	5 08	6 47	4 38	7 15	4 35	7 29	4 55	7 16	5 22	6 39	5 50	5 50	6 20	5 06	6 54	4 38	7 16	4 42
26	7 11	5 13	6 37	5 48	5 52	6 18	5 06	6 48	4 38	7 15	4 35	7 29	4 56	7 15	5 23	6 38	5 51	5 49	6 21	5 05	6 55	4 38	7 17	4 43
27	7 10	5 14	6 35	5 49	5 51	6 19	5 05	6 49	4 37	7 16	4 35	7 29	4 56	7 14	5 24	6 36	5 52	5 47	6 22	5 03	6 56	4 38	7 17	4 44
28	7 09	5 15	6 34	5 50	5 49	6 20	5 04	6 50	4 36	7 17	4 36	7 29	4 57	7 13	5 25	6 35	5 53	5 45	6 23	5 02	6 57	4 37	7 17	4 44
29	7 09	5 16			5 47	5 47	5 03	6 51	4 36	7 18	4 36	7 29	4 57	7 13	5 26	6 33	5 54	5 44	6 24	5 01	6 58	4 37	7 18	4 45
30	7 08	5 17			5 46	6 22	5 01	6 52	4 36	7 18	4 37	7 29	4 58	7 12	5 27	6 32	5 55	5 42	6 25	5 00	6 59	4 37	7 18	4 46
31	7 07	5 18			5 44	6 23			4 35	7 19			4 59	7 11	5 27	6 30			6 26	4 59			7 18	4 47

Add one hour for daylight time, if and when in use.

Close accuracy within 10 miles from center of this location - if further than 10 miles, add/subtract 1 minute per 10 miles

CARSON CITY, NEVADA

THE OVERLOAD COMPANION 2017 © FREDA BARBER BOOTH

Astronomical Applications Dept
Location: W071 32, N43 13

Rise and Set for the Sun for 2017
CONCORD, NEW HAMPSHIRE

U. S. Naval Observatory, Washington, DC
Eastern Standard Time

	JAN AM	JAN PM	FEB AM	FEB PM	MAR AM	MAR PM	APR AM	APR PM	MAY AM	MAY PM	JUN AM	JUN PM	JUL AM	JUL PM	AUG AM	AUG PM	SEP AM	SEP PM	OCT AM	OCT PM	NOV AM	NOV PM	DEC AM	DEC PM
1	7 18	4 21	7 02	4 58	6 21	5 36	5 27	6 13	4 39	6 48	4 09	7 20	4 10	7 30	4 37	19 07	5 11	6 20	5 44	5 26	6 22	4 37	6 59	4 12
2	7 18	4 22	7 01	4 59	6 20	5 37	5 25	6 14	4 38	6 49	4 08	7 20	4 11	7 30	4 38	19 06	5 12	6 18	5 45	5 25	6 23	4 36	7 00	4 11
3	7 18	4 23	7 00	5 00	6 18	5 38	5 24	6 16	4 36	6 51	4 08	7 21	4 11	7 29	4 39	19 05	5 13	6 17	5 46	5 23	6 24	4 35	7 01	4 11
4	7 18	4 24	6 59	5 02	6 16	5 40	5 22	6 17	4 35	6 52	4 08	7 22	4 12	7 29	4 40	19 03	5 14	6 15	5 48	5 21	6 26	4 33	7 02	4 11
5	7 18	4 25	6 58	5 03	6 15	5 41	5 20	6 18	4 34	6 53	4 07	7 23	4 13	7 29	4 41	19 02	5 15	6 13	5 49	5 19	6 27	4 32	7 03	4 11
6	7 18	4 26	6 57	5 04	6 13	5 42	5 19	6 19	4 32	6 54	4 07	7 23	4 13	7 28	4 42	19 01	5 16	6 11	5 50	5 18	6 28	4 31	7 04	4 11
7	7 18	4 27	6 55	5 06	6 11	5 43	5 17	6 20	4 31	6 55	4 07	7 24	4 14	7 28	4 43	19 00	5 17	6 10	5 51	5 16	6 29	4 30	7 05	4 11
8	7 18	4 28	6 54	5 07	6 10	5 45	5 15	6 21	4 30	6 56	4 06	7 25	4 15	7 28	4 45	6 58	5 19	6 08	5 52	5 14	6 31	4 29	7 06	4 11
9	7 17	4 29	6 53	5 08	6 08	5 46	5 13	6 23	4 29	6 57	4 06	7 25	4 16	7 27	4 46	6 57	5 20	6 06	5 53	5 12	6 32	4 28	7 07	4 11
10	7 17	4 30	6 52	5 10	6 06	5 47	5 12	6 24	4 27	6 58	4 06	7 26	4 16	7 27	4 47	6 55	5 21	6 04	5 55	5 11	6 33	4 26	7 08	4 11
11	7 17	4 31	6 50	5 11	6 04	5 48	5 10	6 25	4 26	7 00	4 06	7 26	4 17	7 27	4 48	6 54	5 22	6 03	5 56	5 09	6 35	4 25	7 09	4 11
12	7 17	4 32	6 49	5 12	6 03	5 50	5 08	6 26	4 25	7 01	4 06	7 27	4 18	7 26	4 49	6 53	5 23	6 01	5 57	5 07	6 36	4 24	7 10	4 11
13	7 16	4 33	6 48	5 14	6 01	5 51	5 07	6 27	4 24	7 02	4 06	7 27	4 19	7 25	4 50	6 51	5 24	5 59	5 58	5 06	6 37	4 23	7 11	4 12
14	7 16	4 35	6 46	5 15	5 59	5 52	5 05	6 28	4 23	7 03	4 06	7 28	4 19	7 24	4 51	6 50	5 25	5 57	5 59	5 04	6 38	4 22	7 12	4 12
15	7 15	4 36	6 45	5 16	5 57	5 53	5 03	6 30	4 22	7 04	4 06	7 28	4 20	7 24	4 52	6 48	5 26	5 55	6 00	5 02	6 40	4 22	7 13	4 12
16	7 15	4 37	6 43	5 18	5 56	5 54	5 02	6 31	4 21	7 05	4 06	7 28	4 21	7 23	4 53	6 47	5 27	5 53	6 02	5 01	6 41	4 21	7 14	4 13
17	7 14	4 38	6 42	5 19	5 54	5 56	5 00	6 32	4 20	7 06	4 06	7 29	4 22	7 22	4 54	6 45	5 28	5 52	6 03	4 59	6 42	4 20	7 15	4 13
18	7 14	4 39	6 40	5 20	5 52	5 57	4 58	6 33	4 19	7 08	4 06	7 29	4 23	7 21	4 55	6 43	5 30	5 50	6 05	4 58	6 44	4 19	7 15	4 13
19	7 13	4 41	6 39	5 22	5 50	5 58	4 57	6 34	4 18	7 09	4 06	7 29	4 24	7 20	4 57	6 42	5 31	5 48	6 05	4 56	6 45	4 18	7 16	4 14
20	7 13	4 42	6 37	5 23	5 49	5 59	4 55	6 35	4 17	7 10	4 06	7 30	4 25	7 20	4 58	6 40	5 32	5 46	6 07	4 54	6 46	4 17	7 16	4 14
21	7 12	4 43	6 36	5 24	5 47	6 00	4 54	6 37	4 16	7 11	4 06	7 30	4 26	7 19	4 59	6 39	5 33	5 44	6 08	4 53	6 47	4 17	7 16	4 15
22	7 11	4 44	6 34	5 26	5 45	6 01	4 52	6 38	4 15	7 12	4 07	7 30	4 27	7 18	5 00	6 37	5 34	5 43	6 09	4 51	6 48	4 16	7 16	4 15
23	7 10	4 46	6 33	5 27	5 43	6 03	4 51	6 39	4 15	7 13	4 07	7 30	4 28	7 17	5 01	6 35	5 35	5 41	6 10	4 50	6 50	4 15	7 17	4 16
24	7 10	4 47	6 31	5 28	5 41	6 04	4 49	6 40	4 14	7 14	4 07	7 30	4 29	7 16	5 02	6 34	5 36	5 39	6 12	4 48	6 51	4 15	7 16	4 16
25	7 09	4 48	6 30	5 30	5 40	6 05	4 48	6 41	4 13	7 15	4 08	7 30	4 30	7 15	5 03	6 32	5 37	5 37	6 13	4 47	6 52	4 14	7 16	4 17
26	7 08	4 50	6 28	5 31	5 38	6 06	4 46	6 42	4 12	7 16	4 08	7 30	4 31	7 14	5 04	6 30	5 38	5 35	6 14	4 45	6 53	4 14	7 17	4 17
27	7 07	4 51	6 26	5 32	5 36	6 07	4 45	6 44	4 12	7 17	4 08	7 30	4 32	7 13	5 05	6 29	5 40	5 34	6 15	4 44	6 54	4 13	7 17	4 18
28	7 06	4 52	6 25	5 33	5 34	6 08	4 43	6 45	4 11	7 18	4 09	7 30	4 33	7 12	5 06	6 27	5 41	5 32	6 17	4 43	6 56	4 13	7 18	4 18
29	7 05	4 54			5 33	6 10	4 42	6 46	4 10	7 17	4 09	7 30	4 34	7 11	5 08	6 25	5 42	5 30	6 18	4 41	6 57	4 12	7 18	4 19
30	7 04	4 55			5 31	6 11	4 40	6 47	4 10	7 18	4 10	7 30	4 35	7 10	5 09	6 24	5 43	5 28	6 19	4 40	6 58	4 12	7 18	4 20
31	7 03	4 56			5 29	6 12			4 09	7 19			4 36	7 08	5 10	6 22			6 20	4 39			7 18	4 21

Add one hour for daylight time, if and when in use.

Close accuracy within 10 miles from center of this location - if further than 10 miles, add/subtract 1 minute per 10 miles

CONCORD, NEW HAMPSHIRE

THE OVERLOAD COMPANION 2017 © FREDA BARBER BOOTH

Astronomical Applications Dept
Location: W074 46, N40 13

Rise and Set for the Sun for 2017
TRENTON, NEW JERSEY

U. S. Naval Observatory, Washington, DC
Eastern Standard Time

	JAN AM	JAN PM	FEB AM	FEB PM	MAR AM	MAR PM	APR AM	APR PM	MAY AM	MAY PM	JUN AM	JUN PM	JUL AM	JUL PM	AUG AM	AUG PM	SEP AM	SEP PM	OCT AM	OCT PM	NOV AM	NOV PM	DEC AM	DEC PM
1	7 22	4 44	7 08	5 17	6 32	5 51	5 42	6 24	4 58	6 55	4 31	7 23	4 34	7 32	4 57	7 13	5 27	6 30	5 56	5 40	6 29	4 56	7 03	4 34
2	7 22	4 44	7 07	5 18	6 30	5 52	5 41	6 25	4 57	6 56	4 31	7 24	4 34	7 32	4 58	7 12	5 28	6 28	5 57	5 39	6 30	4 55	7 04	4 33
3	7 22	4 45	7 06	5 20	6 29	5 54	5 39	6 26	4 56	6 57	4 31	7 24	4 35	7 32	4 59	7 10	5 29	6 27	5 58	5 37	6 31	4 53	7 05	4 33
4	7 22	4 46	7 05	5 21	6 27	5 55	5 37	6 27	4 54	6 58	4 30	7 25	4 35	7 32	5 00	7 09	5 30	6 25	5 59	5 36	6 33	4 52	7 06	4 33
5	7 22	4 47	7 04	5 22	6 26	5 56	5 36	6 28	4 53	6 59	4 30	7 25	4 36	7 31	5 01	7 08	5 31	6 23	6 00	5 34	6 34	4 51	7 07	4 33
6	7 22	4 48	7 03	5 23	6 24	5 57	5 34	6 29	4 52	7 00	4 30	7 26	4 36	7 31	5 02	7 07	5 32	6 22	6 01	5 32	6 35	4 50	7 08	4 33
7	7 22	4 49	7 02	5 24	6 23	5 58	5 33	6 30	4 51	7 01	4 30	7 27	4 37	7 31	5 03	7 06	5 33	6 20	6 02	5 31	6 36	4 49	7 08	4 33
8	7 22	4 50	7 01	5 26	6 21	5 59	5 31	6 31	4 50	7 02	4 29	7 27	4 38	7 31	5 04	7 05	5 34	6 19	6 03	5 29	6 37	4 48	7 09	4 33
9	7 21	4 51	7 00	5 27	6 19	6 00	5 29	6 32	4 49	7 03	4 29	7 28	4 38	7 30	5 05	7 03	5 35	6 17	6 04	5 28	6 38	4 47	7 10	4 33
10	7 21	4 52	6 59	5 28	6 18	6 01	5 28	6 33	4 48	7 04	4 29	7 28	4 39	7 30	5 06	7 02	5 36	6 15	6 05	5 26	6 40	4 46	7 11	4 33
11	7 21	4 53	6 58	5 29	6 16	6 02	5 26	6 34	4 47	7 05	4 29	7 29	4 40	7 29	5 07	7 01	5 37	6 14	6 06	5 25	6 41	4 45	7 12	4 33
12	7 21	4 54	6 57	5 30	6 15	6 03	5 25	6 35	4 46	7 06	4 29	7 29	4 40	7 29	5 08	6 59	5 38	6 12	6 07	5 23	6 42	4 44	7 13	4 33
13	7 21	4 55	6 55	5 32	6 13	6 04	5 23	6 36	4 45	7 07	4 29	7 30	4 41	7 28	5 09	6 58	5 38	6 10	6 08	5 22	6 43	4 43	7 13	4 34
14	7 20	4 56	6 54	5 33	6 11	6 05	5 22	6 37	4 44	7 08	4 29	7 30	4 42	7 28	5 10	6 57	5 39	6 09	6 09	5 20	6 44	4 43	7 14	4 34
15	7 20	4 57	6 53	5 34	6 10	6 06	5 20	6 38	4 43	7 09	4 29	7 30	4 43	7 27	5 11	6 55	5 40	6 07	6 10	5 18	6 45	4 42	7 15	4 34
16	7 19	4 58	6 52	5 35	6 08	6 07	5 19	6 39	4 42	7 10	4 29	7 31	4 43	7 27	5 12	6 54	5 41	6 05	6 11	5 17	6 46	4 41	7 15	4 35
17	7 19	4 59	6 50	5 36	6 07	6 08	5 17	6 40	4 41	7 11	4 29	7 31	4 44	7 26	5 13	6 53	5 42	6 04	6 12	5 16	6 48	4 40	7 16	4 35
18	7 18	5 01	6 49	5 38	6 05	6 09	5 16	6 41	4 40	7 11	4 29	7 31	4 45	7 25	5 14	6 51	5 43	6 02	6 13	5 14	6 49	4 40	7 17	4 35
19	7 18	5 02	6 48	5 39	6 03	6 10	5 14	6 42	4 39	7 12	4 29	7 32	4 46	7 24	5 15	6 50	5 44	6 00	6 15	5 13	6 50	4 39	7 17	4 36
20	7 17	5 03	6 46	5 40	6 02	6 11	5 13	6 43	4 39	7 13	4 30	7 32	4 47	7 24	5 16	6 48	5 45	5 59	6 16	5 11	6 51	4 38	7 18	4 36
21	7 17	5 04	6 45	5 41	6 00	6 12	5 11	6 44	4 38	7 14	4 30	7 32	4 48	7 23	5 17	6 47	5 46	5 57	6 17	5 10	6 52	4 38	7 19	4 37
22	7 16	5 05	6 43	5 42	5 58	6 13	5 10	6 45	4 37	7 15	4 30	7 32	4 48	7 22	5 18	6 45	5 47	5 55	6 18	5 08	6 53	4 37	7 19	4 37
23	7 16	5 06	6 42	5 43	5 57	6 14	5 09	6 46	4 36	7 16	4 30	7 33	4 49	7 21	5 19	6 44	5 48	5 54	6 19	5 07	6 54	4 37	7 20	4 38
24	7 15	5 08	6 41	5 45	5 55	6 15	5 07	6 47	4 36	7 16	4 31	7 33	4 50	7 20	5 20	6 42	5 49	5 52	6 20	5 06	6 55	4 36	7 20	4 38
25	7 14	5 09	6 39	5 46	5 54	6 16	5 06	6 48	4 35	7 17	4 31	7 33	4 51	7 20	5 21	6 41	5 50	5 50	6 21	5 04	6 57	4 36	7 20	4 39
26	7 13	5 10	6 38	5 47	5 52	6 17	5 05	6 49	4 34	7 18	4 31	7 33	4 52	7 19	5 22	6 39	5 51	5 49	6 22	5 03	6 58	4 35	7 20	4 40
27	7 13	5 11	6 36	5 48	5 50	6 18	5 03	6 50	4 34	7 19	4 32	7 33	4 53	7 18	5 23	6 38	5 52	5 47	6 23	5 02	6 59	4 35	7 21	4 40
28	7 12	5 12	6 35	5 49	5 49	6 20	5 02	6 52	4 33	7 20	4 32	7 33	4 54	7 17	5 24	6 36	5 53	5 45	6 25	5 01	7 00	4 34	7 21	4 41
29	7 11	5 14			5 47	6 21	5 01	6 53	4 33	7 21	4 33	7 33	4 55	7 16	5 24	6 35	5 54	5 44	6 26	4 59	7 01	4 34	7 21	4 42
30	7 10	5 15			5 45	6 22	4 59	6 54	4 32	7 21	4 33	7 32	4 56	7 15	5 25	6 33	5 55	5 42	6 27	4 58	7 02	4 34	7 21	4 43
31	7 09	5 16			5 44	6 23			4 32	7 22			4 56	7 14	5 26	6 31			6 28	4 57			7 21	4 43

Add one hour for daylight time, if and when in use.

Close accuracy within 10 miles from center of this location - if further than 10 miles, add/subtract 1 minute per 10 miles

TRENTON, NEW JERSEY

THE OVERLOAD COMPANION 2017 © FREDA BARBER BOOTH

Astronomical Applications Dept
Location: W105 57, N35 40

Rise and Set for the Sun for 2017
SANTA FE, NEW MEXICO

U. S. Naval Observatory, Washington, DC
Mountain Standard Time

Day	JAN AM	JAN PM	FEB AM	FEB PM	MAR AM	MAR PM	APR AM	APR PM	MAY AM	MAY PM	JUN AM	JUN PM	JUL AM	JUL PM	AUG AM	AUG PM	SEP AM	SEP PM	OCT AM	OCT PM	NOV AM	NOV PM	DEC AM	DEC PM
1	7 13	5 01	7 04	5 31	6 33	6 00	5 50	6 26	5 11	6 51	4 49	7 15	4 52	7 23	5 12	7 07	5 36	6 30	5 59	5 47	6 26	5 08	6 56	4 50
2	7 14	5 02	7 03	5 32	6 32	6 00	5 48	6 27	5 10	6 52	4 49	7 15	4 52	7 23	5 13	7 06	5 37	6 29	6 00	5 45	6 27	5 07	6 56	4 50
3	7 14	5 03	7 03	5 33	6 30	6 01	5 47	6 28	5 09	6 53	4 49	7 16	4 53	7 23	5 14	7 05	5 38	6 27	6 01	5 44	6 28	5 06	6 57	4 50
4	7 14	5 04	7 02	5 34	6 29	6 02	5 45	6 28	5 08	6 54	4 48	7 16	4 53	7 23	5 15	7 04	5 39	6 26	6 02	5 42	6 29	5 05	6 58	4 50
5	7 14	5 04	7 01	5 35	6 28	6 03	5 44	6 29	5 07	6 54	4 48	7 17	4 54	7 23	5 15	7 03	5 39	6 25	6 02	5 41	6 30	5 04	6 59	4 50
6	7 14	5 05	7 00	5 36	6 26	6 04	5 43	6 30	5 06	6 55	4 48	7 17	4 54	7 23	5 16	7 02	5 40	6 23	6 03	5 40	6 31	5 03	7 00	4 50
7	7 14	5 06	6 59	5 37	6 25	6 05	5 41	6 31	5 05	6 56	4 48	7 18	4 55	7 22	5 17	7 01	5 41	6 22	6 04	5 38	6 32	5 02	7 01	4 50
8	7 14	5 07	6 58	5 38	6 24	6 06	5 40	6 32	5 04	6 57	4 48	7 18	4 55	7 22	5 18	7 00	5 42	6 20	6 05	5 37	6 33	5 01	7 02	4 50
9	7 14	5 08	6 57	5 39	6 22	6 07	5 38	6 33	5 03	6 58	4 47	7 19	4 56	7 22	5 19	6 59	5 42	6 19	6 06	5 36	6 34	5 00	7 02	4 51
10	7 14	5 09	6 56	5 40	6 21	6 08	5 37	6 34	5 02	6 58	4 47	7 19	4 57	7 22	5 19	6 58	5 43	6 17	6 07	5 34	6 35	4 59	7 03	4 51
11	7 14	5 10	6 55	5 41	6 19	6 08	5 36	6 35	5 02	6 59	4 47	7 20	4 57	7 22	5 20	6 57	5 44	6 16	6 07	5 33	6 36	4 59	7 04	4 51
12	7 14	5 11	6 54	5 42	6 18	6 09	5 34	6 36	5 01	7 00	4 47	7 20	4 58	7 21	5 21	6 56	5 45	6 14	6 08	5 31	6 37	4 58	7 04	4 51
13	7 13	5 12	6 53	5 43	6 17	6 10	5 33	6 37	5 00	7 01	4 47	7 20	4 59	7 21	5 22	6 55	5 45	6 13	6 09	5 30	6 38	4 57	7 05	4 51
14	7 13	5 13	6 52	5 44	6 15	6 11	5 32	6 38	4 59	7 02	4 47	7 21	4 59	7 20	5 22	6 54	5 46	6 11	6 10	5 29	6 39	4 56	7 06	4 52
15	7 13	5 14	6 51	5 45	6 14	6 12	5 30	6 38	4 58	7 02	4 47	7 21	5 00	7 19	5 23	6 52	5 47	6 10	6 11	5 28	6 40	4 57	7 07	4 52
16	7 13	5 15	6 50	5 46	6 12	6 13	5 29	6 39	4 58	7 03	4 47	7 22	5 01	7 19	5 24	6 51	5 48	6 09	6 12	5 26	6 41	4 56	7 07	4 52
17	7 12	5 16	6 49	5 47	6 11	6 14	5 28	6 40	4 57	7 04	4 48	7 22	5 01	7 18	5 25	6 50	5 48	6 07	6 13	5 25	6 42	4 55	7 08	4 53
18	7 12	5 17	6 48	5 48	6 09	6 14	5 27	6 41	4 56	7 05	4 48	7 22	5 02	7 18	5 26	6 49	5 49	6 06	6 13	5 24	6 43	4 55	7 08	4 53
19	7 12	5 18	6 47	5 49	6 08	6 15	5 25	6 42	4 56	7 06	4 48	7 23	5 03	7 17	5 26	6 48	5 50	6 04	6 14	5 22	6 44	4 54	7 09	4 54
20	7 11	5 19	6 45	5 50	6 07	6 16	5 24	6 43	4 55	7 06	4 48	7 23	5 03	7 17	5 27	6 46	5 51	6 03	6 15	5 21	6 45	4 54	7 09	4 54
21	7 11	5 20	6 44	5 51	6 05	6 17	5 23	6 43	4 54	7 07	4 48	7 23	5 04	7 16	5 28	6 45	5 51	6 01	6 16	5 20	6 46	4 53	7 10	4 55
22	7 10	5 21	6 43	5 52	6 04	6 18	5 22	6 44	4 54	7 08	4 49	7 23	5 05	7 15	5 29	6 44	5 52	6 00	6 17	5 19	6 47	4 53	7 10	4 55
23	7 10	5 22	6 42	5 53	6 02	6 19	5 20	6 45	4 53	7 09	4 49	7 23	5 05	7 15	5 29	6 42	5 53	5 58	6 18	5 18	6 48	4 52	7 11	4 56
24	7 09	5 23	6 41	5 54	6 01	6 19	5 19	6 46	4 53	7 09	4 49	7 23	5 06	7 14	5 30	6 41	5 54	5 57	6 19	5 16	6 49	4 52	7 11	4 56
25	7 09	5 24	6 39	5 55	5 59	6 20	5 18	6 47	4 52	7 10	4 50	7 24	5 07	7 13	5 31	6 40	5 54	5 55	6 20	5 15	6 50	4 52	7 12	4 57
26	7 08	5 25	6 38	5 56	5 58	6 21	5 17	6 47	4 52	7 11	4 50	7 24	5 08	7 12	5 32	6 38	5 55	5 54	6 21	5 14	6 51	4 51	7 12	4 57
27	7 08	5 26	6 37	5 57	5 57	6 22	5 16	6 48	4 51	7 12	4 50	7 24	5 08	7 12	5 33	6 37	5 56	5 52	6 22	5 13	6 52	4 51	7 12	4 58
28	7 07	5 27	6 36	5 58	5 55	6 23	5 15	6 49	4 51	7 12	4 51	7 24	5 09	7 11	5 33	6 36	5 57	5 51	6 23	5 12	6 53	4 51	7 13	4 59
29	7 06	5 28			5 54	6 23	5 13	6 49	4 50	7 13	4 51	7 24	5 10	7 10	5 34	6 34	5 58	5 50	6 24	5 11	6 54	4 51	7 13	4 59
30	7 06	5 29			5 52	6 24	5 12	6 50	4 50	7 13	4 52	7 24	5 11	7 09	5 35	6 33	5 58	5 48	6 24	5 10	6 55	4 51	7 13	5 00
31	7 05	5 30			5 51	6 25			4 49	7 14			5 12	7 08	5 36	6 32			6 25	5 09			7 13	5 01

Add one hour for daylight time, if and when in use.

Close accuracy within 10 miles from center of this location - if further than 10 miles, add/subtract 1 minute per 10 miles

SANTA FE, NEW MEXICO

THE OVERLOAD COMPANION 2017 © FREDA BARBER BOOTH

Astronomical Applications Dept
Location: W073 47, N42 40

Rise and Set for the Sun for 2017
ALBANY, NEW YORK

U. S. Naval Observatory, Washington, DC
Eastern Standard Time

	JAN AM	JAN PM	FEB AM	FEB PM	MAR AM	MAR PM	APR AM	APR PM	MAY AM	MAY PM	JUN AM	JUN PM	JUL AM	JUL PM	AUG AM	AUG PM	SEP AM	SEP PM	OCT AM	OCT PM	NOV AM	NOV PM	DEC AM	DEC PM
1	7 25	4 32	7 10	5 08	6 30	5 45	5 37	6 22	4 49	6 56	4 20	7 27	4 21	7 37	4 47	7 15	5 20	6 29	5 53	5 36	6 30	4 47	7 06	4 22
2	7 25	4 33	7 09	5 09	6 28	5 47	5 35	6 23	4 48	6 57	4 19	7 28	4 22	7 36	4 48	7 14	5 22	6 27	5 54	5 34	6 31	4 46	7 07	4 22
3	7 25	4 34	7 08	5 11	6 27	5 48	5 33	6 24	4 46	6 58	4 19	7 28	4 22	7 36	4 49	7 12	5 23	6 25	5 55	5 32	6 32	4 45	7 08	4 22
4	7 25	4 35	7 07	5 12	6 25	5 49	5 31	6 25	4 45	6 59	4 18	7 29	4 23	7 36	4 51	7 11	5 24	6 23	5 56	5 30	6 33	4 44	7 09	4 22
5	7 25	4 36	7 05	5 13	6 23	5 50	5 30	6 26	4 44	7 00	4 18	7 30	4 24	7 36	4 52	7 10	5 25	6 22	5 57	5 29	6 35	4 42	7 10	4 22
6	7 25	4 37	7 04	5 15	6 22	5 51	5 28	6 27	4 43	7 02	4 18	7 30	4 24	7 35	4 53	7 09	5 26	6 20	5 58	5 27	6 36	4 41	7 11	4 22
7	7 25	4 38	7 03	5 16	6 20	5 53	5 26	6 29	4 41	7 03	4 18	7 31	4 25	7 35	4 54	7 07	5 27	6 18	6 00	5 25	6 37	4 40	7 12	4 21
8	7 25	4 39	7 02	5 17	6 18	5 54	5 25	6 30	4 40	7 04	4 17	7 32	4 26	7 35	4 55	7 06	5 28	6 16	6 01	5 24	6 38	4 39	7 13	4 21
9	7 25	4 40	7 01	5 18	6 17	5 55	5 23	6 31	4 39	7 05	4 17	7 32	4 26	7 34	4 56	7 05	5 29	6 15	6 02	5 22	6 40	4 38	7 14	4 21
10	7 25	4 41	6 59	5 20	6 15	5 56	5 21	6 32	4 38	7 06	4 17	7 33	4 27	7 34	4 57	7 03	5 30	6 13	6 03	5 20	6 41	4 37	7 15	4 22
11	7 25	4 42	6 58	5 21	6 13	5 57	5 20	6 33	4 37	7 07	4 17	7 33	4 28	7 33	4 58	7 02	5 31	6 11	6 04	5 19	6 42	4 36	7 16	4 22
12	7 24	4 43	6 57	5 22	6 11	5 59	5 18	6 34	4 36	7 08	4 17	7 34	4 29	7 33	4 59	7 00	5 32	6 09	6 05	5 17	6 44	4 35	7 17	4 22
13	7 24	4 44	6 55	5 24	6 10	6 00	5 16	6 35	4 34	7 09	4 17	7 34	4 30	7 32	5 00	6 59	5 33	6 08	6 06	5 15	6 45	4 34	7 18	4 22
14	7 23	4 45	6 54	5 25	6 08	6 01	5 15	6 37	4 33	7 10	4 17	7 35	4 30	7 31	5 01	6 57	5 34	6 06	6 08	5 14	6 46	4 33	7 19	4 22
15	7 23	4 46	6 53	5 26	6 06	6 02	5 13	6 38	4 32	7 11	4 17	7 35	4 31	7 31	5 02	6 56	5 35	6 04	6 09	5 12	6 47	4 32	7 19	4 23
16	7 22	4 48	6 51	5 28	6 05	6 03	5 11	6 39	4 31	7 12	4 17	7 35	4 32	7 30	5 03	6 54	5 37	6 02	6 10	5 10	6 49	4 31	7 20	4 23
17	7 22	4 49	6 50	5 29	6 03	6 04	5 10	6 40	4 30	7 13	4 17	7 36	4 33	7 29	5 04	6 53	5 38	6 00	6 11	5 09	6 50	4 30	7 21	4 23
18	7 21	4 50	6 49	5 30	6 01	6 06	5 08	6 41	4 30	7 14	4 17	7 36	4 34	7 29	5 05	6 51	5 39	5 59	6 12	5 07	6 51	4 29	7 21	4 24
19	7 21	4 51	6 47	5 32	5 59	6 07	5 07	6 42	4 29	7 15	4 17	7 36	4 35	7 28	5 07	6 50	5 40	5 57	6 14	5 06	6 52	4 29	7 22	4 24
20	7 20	4 52	6 46	5 33	5 58	6 08	5 05	6 43	4 28	7 16	4 17	7 36	4 36	7 27	5 08	6 48	5 41	5 55	6 15	5 04	6 53	4 28	7 22	4 24
21	7 19	4 54	6 44	5 34	5 56	6 09	5 04	6 45	4 27	7 17	4 17	7 37	4 37	7 26	5 09	6 47	5 42	5 53	6 16	5 03	6 55	4 27	7 22	4 25
22	7 19	4 55	6 43	5 35	5 54	6 10	5 02	6 46	4 26	7 18	4 18	7 37	4 37	7 25	5 10	6 45	5 43	5 52	6 17	5 01	6 56	4 27	7 23	4 25
23	7 18	4 56	6 41	5 37	5 52	6 11	5 01	6 47	4 25	7 19	4 18	7 37	4 38	7 24	5 11	6 44	5 44	5 50	6 18	5 00	6 57	4 26	7 23	4 26
24	7 17	4 58	6 40	5 38	5 51	6 13	4 59	6 48	4 25	7 20	4 18	7 37	4 39	7 23	5 12	6 42	5 45	5 48	6 20	4 58	6 58	4 25	7 24	4 27
25	7 16	4 59	6 38	5 39	5 49	6 14	4 58	6 49	4 24	7 21	4 19	7 37	4 40	7 22	5 13	6 40	5 46	5 46	6 21	4 57	6 59	4 25	7 24	4 27
26	7 16	5 00	6 36	5 40	5 47	6 15	4 56	6 50	4 23	7 22	4 19	7 37	4 41	7 21	5 14	6 39	5 47	5 44	6 22	4 55	7 01	4 24	7 24	4 28
27	7 15	5 01	6 35	5 42	5 45	6 16	4 55	6 51	4 22	7 23	4 19	7 37	4 42	7 20	5 15	6 37	5 48	5 43	6 23	4 54	7 02	4 24	7 25	4 29
28	7 14	5 03	6 33	5 43	5 44	6 17	4 53	6 53	4 22	7 24	4 20	7 37	4 43	7 19	5 16	6 35	5 50	5 41	6 25	4 53	7 03	4 23	7 25	4 29
29	7 13	5 04			5 42	5 18	4 52	6 54	4 21	7 24	4 20	7 37	4 44	7 18	5 17	6 34	5 51	5 39	6 26	4 51	7 04	4 23	7 25	4 30
30	7 12	5 05			5 40	6 19	4 50	6 55	4 21	7 25	4 21	7 37	4 45	7 17	5 18	6 32	5 52	5 37	6 27	4 50	7 05	4 23	7 25	4 31
31	7 11	5 07			5 38	6 21			4 20	7 26			4 46	7 16	5 19	6 30			6 28	4 49			7 25	4 32

Add one hour for daylight time, if and when in use.

Close accuracy within 10 miles from center of this location - if further than 10 miles, add/subtract 1 minute per 10 miles

ALBANY, NEW YORK

THE OVERLOAD COMPANION 2017 © FREDA BARBER BOOTH

Astronomical Applications Dept
Location: W078 51, N42 55

Rise and Set for the Sun for 2017
BUFFALO, NEW YORK

U. S. Naval Observatory, Washington, DC
Eastern Standard Time

	JAN AM	JAN PM	FEB AM	FEB PM	MAR AM	MAR PM	APR AM	APR PM	MAY AM	MAY PM	JUN AM	JUN PM	JUL AM	JUL PM	AUG AM	AUG PM	SEP AM	SEP PM	OCT AM	OCT PM	NOV AM	NOV PM	DEC AM	DEC PM
1	7 46	4 51	7 31	5 28	6 50	6 05	5 57	6 42	5 09	7 17	4 39	7 48	4 41	7 58	5 07	7 36	5 40	6 49	6 13	5 56	6 50	5 07	7 27	4 42
2	7 47	4 52	7 30	5 29	6 49	6 07	5 55	6 43	5 07	7 18	4 39	7 49	4 41	7 58	5 08	7 34	5 42	6 47	6 14	5 54	6 52	5 06	7 28	4 42
3	7 47	4 53	7 29	5 30	6 47	6 08	5 53	6 45	5 06	7 19	4 38	7 49	4 42	7 57	5 09	7 33	5 43	6 46	6 15	5 52	6 53	5 04	7 29	4 41
4	7 47	4 54	7 27	5 32	6 45	6 09	5 51	6 46	5 05	7 20	4 38	7 50	4 42	7 57	5 10	7 32	5 44	6 44	6 17	5 51	6 54	5 03	7 30	4 41
5	7 46	4 55	7 26	5 33	6 44	6 10	5 50	6 47	5 03	7 21	4 38	7 51	4 43	7 57	5 11	7 31	5 45	6 42	6 18	5 49	6 56	5 02	7 31	4 41
6	7 46	4 56	7 25	5 34	6 42	6 12	5 48	6 48	5 02	7 22	4 37	7 52	4 43	7 56	5 12	7 29	5 46	6 40	6 19	5 47	6 57	5 01	7 32	4 41
7	7 46	4 57	7 24	5 36	6 40	6 13	5 46	6 49	5 01	7 24	4 37	7 52	4 44	7 56	5 13	7 28	5 47	6 39	6 20	5 45	6 58	5 00	7 33	4 41
8	7 46	4 58	7 23	5 37	6 39	6 14	5 45	6 50	5 00	7 25	4 37	7 53	4 45	7 56	5 14	7 27	5 48	6 37	6 21	5 44	6 59	4 59	7 34	4 41
9	7 46	4 59	7 21	5 38	6 37	6 15	5 43	6 52	4 59	7 26	4 37	7 53	4 46	7 55	5 16	7 25	5 49	6 35	6 22	5 42	7 01	4 58	7 35	4 41
10	7 46	5 00	7 20	5 40	6 35	6 16	5 41	6 53	4 57	7 27	4 36	7 54	4 47	7 55	5 17	7 24	5 50	6 33	6 24	5 40	7 02	4 56	7 36	4 41
11	7 45	5 01	7 19	5 41	6 34	6 18	5 40	6 54	4 56	7 28	4 36	7 55	4 47	7 54	5 18	7 23	5 51	6 32	6 25	5 39	7 03	4 55	7 37	4 41
12	7 45	5 02	7 18	5 42	6 32	6 19	5 38	6 55	4 55	7 29	4 36	7 55	4 48	7 54	5 19	7 21	5 52	6 30	6 26	5 37	7 04	4 54	7 38	4 41
13	7 45	5 04	7 16	5 44	6 30	6 20	5 36	6 56	4 54	7 30	4 36	7 55	4 49	7 53	5 20	7 20	5 53	6 28	6 27	5 35	7 06	4 53	7 38	4 42
14	7 44	5 05	7 15	5 45	6 28	6 21	5 35	6 57	4 53	7 31	4 36	7 56	4 50	7 52	5 21	7 18	5 55	6 26	6 28	5 34	7 07	4 52	7 39	4 42
15	7 44	5 06	7 13	5 46	6 27	6 22	5 33	6 58	4 52	7 32	4 36	7 56	4 51	7 52	5 22	7 17	5 56	6 24	6 29	5 32	7 08	4 52	7 40	4 42
16	7 43	5 07	7 12	5 48	6 25	6 24	5 31	7 00	4 51	7 33	4 36	7 57	4 52	7 51	5 23	7 15	5 57	6 23	6 31	5 30	7 09	4 51	7 40	4 42
17	7 43	5 08	7 11	5 49	6 23	6 25	5 30	7 01	4 50	7 34	4 36	7 57	4 52	7 50	5 24	7 14	5 58	6 21	6 32	5 29	7 11	4 50	7 41	4 43
18	7 42	5 10	7 09	5 50	6 21	6 26	5 28	7 02	4 49	7 35	4 36	7 57	4 53	7 50	5 25	7 12	5 59	6 19	6 33	5 27	7 12	4 49	7 42	4 43
19	7 42	5 11	7 08	5 51	6 20	6 27	5 27	7 03	4 48	7 36	4 36	7 57	4 54	7 49	5 26	7 11	6 00	6 17	6 34	5 26	7 13	4 48	7 42	4 43
20	7 41	5 12	7 06	5 53	6 18	6 28	5 25	7 04	4 47	7 37	4 36	7 58	4 55	7 48	5 27	7 09	6 01	6 15	6 35	5 24	7 14	4 48	7 43	4 44
21	7 40	5 13	7 05	5 54	6 16	6 29	5 23	7 05	4 46	7 38	4 36	7 58	4 56	7 47	5 29	7 07	6 02	6 14	6 37	5 23	7 16	4 47	7 43	4 44
22	7 40	5 15	7 03	5 55	6 14	6 31	5 22	7 06	4 46	7 39	4 37	7 58	4 57	7 46	5 30	7 06	6 03	6 12	6 38	5 21	7 17	4 46	7 44	4 45
23	7 39	5 16	7 02	5 57	6 12	6 32	5 20	7 08	4 45	7 40	4 37	7 58	4 58	7 45	5 31	7 04	6 04	6 10	6 39	5 20	7 18	4 46	7 44	4 45
24	7 38	5 17	7 00	5 58	6 11	6 33	5 19	7 09	4 44	7 41	4 37	7 58	4 59	7 45	5 32	7 03	6 05	6 08	6 40	5 18	7 19	4 45	7 45	4 46
25	7 37	5 18	6 58	5 59	6 09	6 34	5 17	7 10	4 43	7 42	4 38	7 58	5 00	7 43	5 33	7 01	6 07	6 06	6 42	5 17	7 20	4 44	7 45	4 46
26	7 36	5 20	6 57	6 00	6 07	6 35	5 16	7 11	4 43	7 43	4 38	7 58	5 01	7 42	5 34	6 59	6 08	6 05	6 43	5 15	7 22	4 44	7 45	4 47
27	7 36	5 21	6 55	6 02	6 05	6 36	5 14	7 12	4 42	7 44	4 38	7 58	5 02	7 41	5 35	6 58	6 09	6 03	6 44	5 14	7 23	4 43	7 45	4 47
28	7 35	5 22	6 54	6 03	6 04	6 38	5 13	7 13	4 41	7 45	4 39	7 58	5 03	7 40	5 36	6 56	6 10	6 01	6 45	5 12	7 24	4 43	7 46	4 48
29	7 34	5 24			6 02	6 39	5 12	7 14	4 41	7 46	4 39	7 58	5 04	7 39	5 37	6 54	6 11	5 59	6 47	5 11	7 25	4 43	7 46	4 49
30	7 33	5 25			6 00	6 40	5 10	7 16	4 40	7 46	4 40	7 58	5 05	7 38	5 38	6 53	6 12	5 58	6 48	5 10	7 26	4 42	7 46	4 50
31	7 32	5 26			5 58	6 41			4 40	7 47			5 06	7 37	5 39	6 51			6 49	5 08			7 46	4 51

Add one hour for daylight time, if and when in use.

Close accuracy within 10 miles from center of this location - if further than 10 miles, add/subtract 1 minute per 10 miles

BUFFALO, NEW YORK

THE OVERLOAD COMPANION 2017 © FREDA BARBER BOOTH

Astronomical Applications Dept
Location: W082 34, N35 35

Rise and Set for the Sun for 2017
ASHEVILLE, NORTH CAROLINA

U. S. Naval Observatory, Washington, DC
Eastern Standard Time

	JAN AM	JAN PM	FEB AM	FEB PM	MAR AM	MAR PM	APR AM	APR PM	MAY AM	MAY PM	JUN AM	JUN PM	JUL AM	JUL PM	AUG AM	AUG PM	SEP AM	SEP PM	OCT AM	OCT PM	NOV AM	NOV PM	DEC AM	DEC PM
1	7 40	5 28	7 30	5 57	6 59	6 26	6 16	6 52	5 38	7 17	5 16	7 41	5 19	7 50	5 39	7 34	6 03	6 57	6 26	6 13	6 53	5 35	7 22	5 17
2	7 40	5 29	7 30	5 59	6 58	6 27	6 15	6 53	5 37	7 18	5 16	7 41	5 19	7 50	5 40	7 33	6 04	6 55	6 26	6 12	6 54	5 34	7 23	5 17
3	7 40	5 29	7 29	6 00	6 57	6 28	6 13	6 54	5 36	7 19	5 15	7 42	5 19	7 50	5 40	7 32	6 04	6 54	6 27	6 10	6 55	5 33	7 24	5 17
4	7 40	5 30	7 28	6 01	6 55	6 29	6 12	6 55	5 35	7 20	5 15	7 43	5 20	7 49	5 41	7 31	6 05	6 52	6 28	6 09	6 56	5 32	7 24	5 17
5	7 40	5 31	7 27	6 02	6 54	6 30	6 10	6 56	5 34	7 20	5 15	7 43	5 21	7 49	5 42	7 30	6 06	6 51	6 29	6 08	6 57	5 31	7 25	5 17
6	7 40	5 32	7 26	6 03	6 53	6 30	6 09	6 56	5 33	7 21	5 15	7 44	5 21	7 49	5 43	7 29	6 07	6 50	6 30	6 06	6 58	5 30	7 26	5 17
7	7 40	5 33	7 25	6 04	6 51	6 31	6 08	6 57	5 32	7 22	5 14	7 44	5 22	7 49	5 44	7 28	6 07	6 48	6 30	6 05	6 58	5 29	7 27	5 17
8	7 40	5 34	7 25	6 05	6 50	6 32	6 06	6 58	5 31	7 23	5 14	7 45	5 22	7 48	5 44	7 27	6 08	6 47	6 31	6 03	6 59	5 28	7 28	5 17
9	7 40	5 34	7 24	6 06	6 49	6 33	6 05	6 59	5 30	7 24	5 14	7 45	5 23	7 48	5 45	7 26	6 09	6 45	6 32	6 02	7 00	5 27	7 28	5 17
10	7 40	5 35	7 23	6 07	6 47	6 34	6 04	7 00	5 29	7 25	5 14	7 46	5 23	7 48	5 46	7 25	6 10	6 44	6 33	6 01	7 01	5 27	7 29	5 18
11	7 40	5 36	7 22	6 08	6 46	6 35	6 02	7 01	5 28	7 25	5 14	7 46	5 24	7 47	5 46	7 23	6 10	6 42	6 34	5 59	7 02	5 26	7 30	5 18
12	7 40	5 37	7 21	6 09	6 44	6 36	6 01	7 01	5 27	7 26	5 14	7 47	5 25	7 47	5 47	7 22	6 11	6 41	6 35	5 58	7 03	5 25	7 31	5 18
13	7 40	5 38	7 20	6 10	6 43	6 37	6 00	7 02	5 27	7 27	5 14	7 47	5 25	7 47	5 48	7 21	6 12	6 39	6 35	5 57	7 04	5 24	7 31	5 18
14	7 40	5 39	7 19	6 11	6 42	6 37	5 58	7 03	5 26	7 28	5 14	7 47	5 26	7 46	5 49	7 20	6 13	6 38	6 36	5 55	7 05	5 24	7 32	5 19
15	7 39	5 40	7 17	6 12	6 40	6 38	5 57	7 04	5 25	7 29	5 14	7 48	5 26	7 46	5 50	7 19	6 13	6 37	6 37	5 54	7 06	5 23	7 33	5 19
16	7 39	5 41	7 16	6 13	6 39	6 39	5 56	7 05	5 24	7 29	5 14	7 48	5 27	7 45	5 51	7 18	6 14	6 35	6 38	5 53	7 07	5 23	7 33	5 19
17	7 39	5 42	7 15	6 14	6 37	6 40	5 54	7 05	5 24	7 30	5 14	7 48	5 28	7 45	5 51	7 16	6 15	6 34	6 39	5 52	7 08	5 22	7 34	5 19
18	7 38	5 43	7 14	6 15	6 36	6 41	5 53	7 06	5 23	7 31	5 15	7 49	5 29	7 44	5 52	7 15	6 16	6 32	6 40	5 50	7 09	5 21	7 35	5 20
19	7 38	5 44	7 13	6 16	6 35	6 42	5 52	7 07	5 22	7 32	5 15	7 49	5 29	7 44	5 53	7 14	6 16	6 31	6 41	5 49	7 10	5 20	7 35	5 20
20	7 38	5 45	7 12	6 17	6 33	6 42	5 51	7 08	5 22	7 33	5 15	7 49	5 30	7 43	5 54	7 13	6 17	6 29	6 42	5 48	7 11	5 20	7 36	5 21
21	7 37	5 46	7 11	6 18	6 32	6 43	5 49	7 09	5 21	7 33	5 15	7 49	5 31	7 42	5 55	7 11	6 18	6 28	6 42	5 47	7 12	5 20	7 36	5 21
22	7 37	5 47	7 09	6 19	6 30	6 44	5 48	7 10	5 20	7 34	5 15	7 49	5 31	7 42	5 55	7 10	6 19	6 26	6 43	5 45	7 13	5 19	7 37	5 22
23	7 37	5 48	7 08	6 19	6 29	6 45	5 47	7 10	5 20	7 35	5 16	7 50	5 32	7 41	5 56	7 09	6 19	6 25	6 44	5 44	7 14	5 19	7 37	5 22
24	7 36	5 49	7 07	6 20	6 27	6 46	5 46	7 11	5 19	7 36	5 16	7 50	5 33	7 40	5 57	7 08	6 20	6 23	6 45	5 43	7 15	5 19	7 38	5 23
25	7 36	5 50	7 06	6 21	6 26	6 47	5 45	7 12	5 19	7 36	5 16	7 50	5 34	7 40	5 58	7 06	6 21	6 22	6 46	5 42	7 16	5 18	7 38	5 23
26	7 35	5 51	7 05	6 22	6 25	6 47	5 43	7 13	5 18	7 37	5 17	7 50	5 34	7 39	5 59	7 05	6 22	6 20	6 47	5 41	7 17	5 18	7 38	5 24
27	7 34	5 52	7 03	6 23	6 23	6 48	5 42	7 14	5 18	7 38	5 17	7 50	5 35	7 38	6 00	7 04	6 22	6 19	6 48	5 40	7 18	5 18	7 39	5 25
28	7 33	5 53	7 02	6 24	6 22	6 49	5 41	7 15	5 17	7 39	5 17	7 50	5 36	7 37	6 01	7 02	6 23	6 18	6 49	5 39	7 19	5 18	7 39	5 25
29	7 33	5 54			6 20	6 50	5 40	7 15	5 17	7 39	5 18	7 50	5 37	7 36	6 01	7 01	6 24	6 16	6 50	5 38	7 20	5 17	7 39	5 26
30	7 32	5 55			6 19	6 51	5 39	7 16	5 16	7 40	5 18	7 50	5 37	7 35	6 02	6 59	6 25	6 15	6 51	5 37	7 21	5 17	7 39	5 27
31	7 31	5 56			6 17	6 52			5 16	7 40			5 38	7 35	6 02	6 58			6 52	5 36			7 40	5 28

Add one hour for daylight time, if and when in use.

Close accuracy within 10 miles from center of this location - if further than 10 miles, add/subtract 1 minute per 10 miles

ASHEVILLE, NORTH CAROLINA

THE OVERLOAD COMPANION 2017 © FREDA BARBER BOOTH

Astronomical Applications Dept
Location: W078 39, N35 47

Rise and Set for the Sun for 2017
RALEIGH, NORTH CAROLINA

U. S. Naval Observatory, Washington, DC
Eastern Standard Time

	JAN AM	JAN PM	FEB AM	FEB PM	MAR AM	MAR PM	APR AM	APR PM	MAY AM	MAY PM	JUN AM	JUN PM	JUL AM	JUL PM	AUG AM	AUG PM	SEP AM	SEP PM	OCT AM	OCT PM	NOV AM	NOV PM	DEC AM	DEC PM
1	7 25	5 12	7 15	5 41	6 44	6 10	6 00	6 37	5 22	7 02	5 00	7 26	5 02	7 35	5 23	7 18	5 47	6 41	6 10	5 58	6 37	5 19	7 07	5 01
2	7 25	5 12	7 14	5 43	6 43	6 11	5 59	6 38	5 21	7 03	4 59	7 26	5 03	7 35	5 24	7 18	5 48	6 40	6 11	5 56	6 38	5 18	7 07	5 01
3	7 25	5 13	7 14	5 44	6 41	6 12	5 58	6 38	5 20	7 04	4 59	7 27	5 03	7 34	5 24	7 17	5 48	6 38	6 12	5 55	6 39	5 17	7 08	5 01
4	7 25	5 14	7 13	5 45	6 40	6 13	5 56	6 39	5 19	7 04	4 59	7 27	5 04	7 34	5 25	7 16	5 49	6 37	6 12	5 53	6 40	5 16	7 09	5 01
5	7 25	5 15	7 12	5 46	6 39	6 14	5 55	6 40	5 18	7 05	4 59	7 28	5 04	7 34	5 26	7 15	5 50	6 36	6 13	5 52	6 41	5 15	7 10	5 01
6	7 25	5 16	7 11	5 47	6 37	6 15	5 53	6 41	5 17	7 06	4 58	7 28	5 05	7 34	5 26	7 14	5 50	6 34	6 14	5 50	6 42	5 14	7 11	5 01
7	7 25	5 17	7 10	5 48	6 36	6 16	5 52	6 42	5 16	7 07	4 58	7 29	5 05	7 34	5 27	7 13	5 51	6 33	6 15	5 49	6 43	5 13	7 12	5 01
8	7 25	5 17	7 09	5 49	6 34	6 16	5 51	6 43	5 15	7 08	4 58	7 30	5 06	7 33	5 28	7 11	5 52	6 31	6 16	5 48	6 44	5 12	7 13	5 01
9	7 25	5 18	7 08	5 50	6 33	6 17	5 49	6 43	5 14	7 09	4 58	7 30	5 07	7 33	5 29	7 10	5 53	6 30	6 17	5 46	6 45	5 11	7 13	5 01
10	7 25	5 19	7 07	5 51	6 32	6 18	5 48	6 44	5 13	7 09	4 58	7 30	5 07	7 33	5 29	7 09	5 54	6 28	6 18	5 45	6 46	5 10	7 14	5 01
11	7 25	5 20	7 06	5 52	6 30	6 19	5 46	6 45	5 12	7 10	4 58	7 31	5 08	7 32	5 30	7 08	5 55	6 27	6 19	5 44	6 47	5 10	7 15	5 01
12	7 25	5 21	7 05	5 53	6 29	6 20	5 45	6 46	5 11	7 11	4 58	7 31	5 08	7 32	5 31	7 07	5 55	6 25	6 19	5 42	6 48	5 09	7 16	5 02
13	7 25	5 22	7 04	5 54	6 28	6 21	5 44	6 47	5 11	7 12	4 58	7 32	5 09	7 32	5 32	7 06	5 56	6 24	6 20	5 41	6 49	5 08	7 16	5 02
14	7 24	5 23	7 03	5 55	6 26	6 22	5 42	6 48	5 10	7 13	4 58	7 32	5 10	7 31	5 32	7 05	5 57	6 22	6 21	5 40	6 50	5 08	7 17	5 02
15	7 24	5 24	7 02	5 56	6 25	6 23	5 41	6 48	5 09	7 14	4 58	7 33	5 10	7 31	5 33	7 04	5 58	6 21	6 22	5 38	6 51	5 07	7 18	5 02
16	7 24	5 25	7 01	5 57	6 23	6 23	5 40	6 49	5 08	7 14	4 58	7 33	5 11	7 30	5 34	7 02	5 58	6 19	6 23	5 37	6 52	5 06	7 18	5 03
17	7 24	5 26	7 00	5 58	6 22	6 24	5 39	6 50	5 07	7 15	4 58	7 33	5 12	7 30	5 35	7 01	5 59	6 18	6 23	5 36	6 53	5 06	7 19	5 03
18	7 23	5 27	6 59	5 59	6 20	6 25	5 37	6 51	5 07	7 16	4 58	7 33	5 12	7 29	5 36	7 00	6 00	6 17	6 24	5 34	6 54	5 05	7 19	5 04
19	7 23	5 28	6 58	6 00	6 19	6 26	5 36	6 52	5 06	7 17	4 58	7 34	5 13	7 28	5 36	6 59	6 01	6 15	6 25	5 33	6 55	5 05	7 20	5 04
20	7 22	5 29	6 56	6 01	6 18	6 27	5 35	6 53	5 05	7 18	4 59	7 34	5 14	7 28	5 37	6 57	6 01	6 14	6 26	5 32	6 56	5 04	7 21	5 04
21	7 22	5 30	6 55	6 02	6 16	6 28	5 33	6 53	5 05	7 18	4 59	7 34	5 14	7 27	5 38	6 56	6 02	6 12	6 27	5 31	6 57	5 04	7 21	5 05
22	7 21	5 31	6 54	6 03	6 15	6 28	5 32	6 54	5 04	7 19	4 59	7 34	5 15	7 27	5 39	6 55	6 03	6 11	6 28	5 30	6 58	5 03	7 22	5 05
23	7 21	5 32	6 53	6 04	6 13	6 29	5 31	6 55	5 04	7 20	4 59	7 34	5 16	7 26	5 40	6 53	6 04	6 09	6 29	5 28	6 59	5 03	7 22	5 06
24	7 20	5 33	6 52	6 05	6 12	6 30	5 30	6 56	5 03	7 21	4 59	7 35	5 16	7 25	5 41	6 52	6 04	6 08	6 30	5 27	7 00	5 03	7 22	5 07
25	7 20	5 34	6 50	6 06	6 10	6 31	5 29	6 57	5 03	7 22	5 00	7 35	5 17	7 25	5 41	6 51	6 05	6 06	6 31	5 26	7 01	5 02	7 23	5 07
26	7 19	5 35	6 49	6 06	6 09	6 32	5 27	6 58	5 02	7 22	5 00	7 35	5 18	7 24	5 42	6 49	6 06	6 05	6 32	5 25	7 02	5 02	7 23	5 08
27	7 19	5 36	6 48	6 07	6 07	6 33	5 26	6 58	5 02	7 23	5 00	7 35	5 19	7 23	5 43	6 48	6 07	6 03	6 33	5 24	7 03	5 02	7 23	5 09
28	7 18	5 37	6 47	6 08	6 06	6 33	5 25	6 59	5 01	7 23	5 01	7 35	5 19	7 22	5 44	6 47	6 08	6 02	6 33	5 23	7 04	5 01	7 24	5 09
29	7 17	5 38			6 05	6 34	5 24	7 00	5 01	7 24	5 01	7 35	5 20	7 22	5 45	6 45	6 08	6 00	6 34	5 22	7 05	5 01	7 24	5 10
30	7 17	5 39			6 03	6 35	5 23	7 01	5 00	7 24	5 02	7 35	5 21	7 21	5 45	6 44	6 09	5 59	6 35	5 21	7 06	5 01	7 24	5 11
31	7 16	5 40			6 02	6 36			5 00	7 25			5 22	7 19	5 46	6 43			6 36	5 20			7 25	5 11

Add one hour for daylight time, if and when in use.

Close accuracy within 10 miles from center of this location - if further than 10 miles, add/subtract 1 minute per 10 miles

RALEIGH, NORTH CAROLINA

THE OVERLOAD COMPANION 2017 © FREDA BARBER BOOTH

Astronomical Applications Dept
Rise and Set for the Sun for 2017
U. S. Naval Observatory, Washington, DC
Location: W100 47, N46 49
BISMARCK, NORTH DAKOTA
Central Standard Time

	JAN		FEB		MAR		APR		MAY		JUN		JUL		AUG		SEP		OCT		NOV		DEC	
	AM	PM	AM	PM	AM	PM	AM	PM	AM	PM	AM	PM	AM	PM	AM	PM	AM	PM	AM	PM	AM	PM	AM	PM
1	8 28	5 05	8 08	5 46	7 22	6 30	6 21	7 13	5 27	7 54	4 52	8 30	4 53	8 41	5 24	8 14	6 03	7 21	6 43	6 22	7 26	5 27	8 08	4 56
2	8 28	5 06	8 07	5 47	7 20	6 31	6 19	7 14	5 26	7 55	4 52	8 31	4 54	8 40	5 25	8 13	6 05	7 19	6 44	6 20	7 28	5 25	8 09	4 56
3	8 28	5 07	8 05	5 49	7 18	6 33	6 17	7 16	5 24	7 57	4 51	8 32	4 55	8 40	5 26	8 11	6 06	7 17	6 45	6 18	7 29	5 24	8 10	4 56
4	8 28	5 08	8 04	5 50	7 16	6 34	6 15	7 17	5 23	7 58	4 51	8 33	4 55	8 40	5 28	8 10	6 07	7 16	6 47	6 16	7 31	5 22	8 12	4 55
5	8 28	5 09	8 03	5 52	7 14	6 35	6 14	7 19	5 21	7 59	4 50	8 33	4 56	8 39	5 29	8 08	6 09	7 14	6 48	6 14	7 32	5 21	8 13	4 55
6	8 28	5 10	8 01	5 54	7 12	6 37	6 12	7 20	5 20	8 01	4 50	8 34	4 57	8 39	5 30	8 07	6 10	7 12	6 49	6 12	7 34	5 19	8 14	4 55
7	8 27	5 11	8 00	5 55	7 10	6 38	6 10	7 21	5 18	8 02	4 50	8 35	4 57	8 38	5 31	8 05	6 11	7 10	6 51	6 10	7 35	5 18	8 15	4 55
8	8 27	5 12	7 59	5 57	7 08	6 40	6 08	7 23	5 17	8 03	4 49	8 36	4 58	8 38	5 33	8 04	6 13	7 08	6 52	6 08	7 37	5 17	8 16	4 55
9	8 27	5 14	7 57	5 58	7 07	6 41	6 06	7 24	5 15	8 04	4 49	8 36	4 59	8 37	5 34	8 02	6 14	7 06	6 53	6 06	7 38	5 15	8 17	4 55
10	8 27	5 15	7 56	6 00	7 05	6 43	6 04	7 25	5 14	8 06	4 49	8 37	5 00	8 37	5 35	8 01	6 15	7 04	6 55	6 04	7 40	5 14	8 18	4 55
11	8 26	5 16	7 54	6 01	7 03	6 44	6 02	7 27	5 13	8 07	4 49	8 37	5 01	8 36	5 36	7 59	6 16	7 02	6 56	6 02	7 41	5 13	8 19	4 55
12	8 26	5 17	7 53	6 03	7 01	6 45	6 00	7 28	5 11	8 08	4 49	8 38	5 02	8 35	5 38	7 57	6 18	7 00	6 58	6 01	7 42	5 12	8 19	4 55
13	8 25	5 19	7 51	6 04	6 59	6 47	5 58	7 30	5 10	8 09	4 48	8 38	5 03	8 35	5 39	7 56	6 19	6 58	6 59	5 59	7 44	5 11	8 20	4 55
14	8 25	5 20	7 50	6 06	6 57	6 48	5 56	7 31	5 09	8 11	4 48	8 39	5 04	8 34	5 40	7 54	6 20	6 56	7 00	5 57	7 45	5 10	8 21	4 55
15	8 24	5 21	7 48	6 07	6 55	6 50	5 55	7 32	5 08	8 12	4 48	8 39	5 05	8 33	5 42	7 52	6 22	6 54	7 02	5 55	7 47	5 08	8 22	4 55
16	8 23	5 23	7 46	6 09	6 53	6 51	5 53	7 34	5 07	8 13	4 48	8 40	5 06	8 32	5 43	7 51	6 23	6 52	7 03	5 53	7 48	5 07	8 23	4 56
17	8 23	5 24	7 45	6 10	6 51	6 52	5 51	7 35	5 05	8 14	4 48	8 40	5 07	8 31	5 44	7 49	6 24	6 50	7 05	5 51	7 50	5 06	8 23	4 56
18	8 22	5 25	7 43	6 12	6 49	6 54	5 49	7 36	5 04	8 16	4 48	8 40	5 08	8 30	5 45	7 47	6 25	6 48	7 06	5 50	7 51	5 05	8 24	4 56
19	8 21	5 27	7 41	6 13	6 47	6 55	5 47	7 38	5 03	8 17	4 49	8 41	5 09	8 30	5 47	7 46	6 27	6 46	7 07	5 48	7 52	5 04	8 24	4 57
20	8 20	5 28	7 40	6 15	6 45	6 57	5 46	7 39	5 02	8 18	4 49	8 41	5 10	8 29	5 48	7 44	6 28	6 44	7 09	5 46	7 54	5 04	8 25	4 57
21	8 20	5 30	7 38	6 16	6 43	6 58	5 44	7 40	5 01	8 19	4 49	8 41	5 11	8 28	5 49	7 42	6 29	6 42	7 10	5 44	7 55	5 03	8 25	4 58
22	8 19	5 31	7 36	6 18	6 41	6 59	5 42	7 42	5 00	8 20	4 49	8 41	5 12	8 26	5 51	7 40	6 31	6 40	7 12	5 43	7 57	5 02	8 26	4 58
23	8 18	5 32	7 34	6 19	6 39	7 01	5 40	7 43	4 59	8 21	4 50	8 41	5 13	8 25	5 52	7 38	6 32	6 38	7 13	5 41	7 58	5 02	8 26	4 59
24	8 17	5 34	7 33	6 21	6 37	7 02	5 39	7 45	4 58	8 22	4 50	8 41	5 14	8 24	5 53	7 36	6 33	6 36	7 15	5 39	7 59	5 01	8 27	4 59
25	8 16	5 35	7 31	6 22	6 35	7 03	5 37	7 46	4 58	8 23	4 50	8 41	5 15	8 23	5 54	7 35	6 35	6 34	7 16	5 38	8 01	5 00	8 27	5 00
26	8 15	5 37	7 29	6 24	6 33	7 05	5 35	7 47	4 57	8 24	4 51	8 41	5 17	8 22	5 56	7 33	6 36	6 32	7 17	5 36	8 02	5 00	8 27	5 01
27	8 14	5 38	7 27	6 25	6 31	7 06	5 34	7 49	4 56	8 25	4 51	8 41	5 18	8 21	5 57	7 31	6 37	6 30	7 19	5 34	8 03	4 59	8 28	5 02
28	8 13	5 40	7 25	6 27	6 29	7 08	5 32	7 50	4 55	8 26	4 52	8 41	5 19	8 19	5 58	7 29	6 39	6 28	7 20	5 33	8 04	4 58	8 28	5 02
29	8 12	5 41			6 27	7 09	5 30	7 51	4 54	8 27	4 52	8 41	5 20	8 18	6 00	7 27	6 40	6 26	7 22	5 31	8 06	4 58	8 28	5 03
30	8 10	5 43			6 25	7 10	5 29	7 53	4 54	8 28	4 53	8 41	5 21	8 17	6 01	7 25	6 41	6 24	7 23	5 30	8 07	4 57	8 28	5 04
31	8 09	5 44			6 23	7 12			4 53	8 29			5 23	8 16	6 02	7 23			7 25	5 28			8 28	5 05

Add one hour for daylight time, if and when in use.

Close accuracy within 10 miles from center of this location - if further than 10 miles, add/subtract 1 minute per 10 miles

BISMARCK, NORTH DAKOTA

THE OVERLOAD COMPANION 2017 © FREDA BARBER BOOTH

Astronomical Applications Dept
Location: W082 59, N39 59

Rise and Set for the Sun for 2017
COLUMBUS, OHIO

U. S. Naval Observatory, Washington, DC
Eastern Standard Time

	JAN AM	JAN PM	FEB AM	FEB PM	MAR AM	MAR PM	APR AM	APR PM	MAY AM	MAY PM	JUN AM	JUN PM	JUL AM	JUL PM	AUG AM	AUG PM	SEP AM	SEP PM	OCT AM	OCT PM	NOV AM	NOV PM	DEC AM	DEC PM
1	7 54	5 17	7 41	5 51	7 04	6 24	6 15	6 57	5 31	7 27	5 05	7 55	5 07	8 04	5 31	7 45	6 00	7 03	6 29	6 13	7 02	5 29	7 35	5 07
2	7 54	5 18	7 40	5 52	7 03	6 26	6 14	6 58	5 30	7 28	5 05	7 56	5 08	8 04	5 32	7 44	6 01	7 01	6 30	6 12	7 03	5 28	7 36	5 07
3	7 54	5 19	7 39	5 53	7 01	6 27	6 12	6 59	5 29	7 29	5 04	7 56	5 08	8 04	5 33	7 43	6 02	6 59	6 31	6 10	7 04	5 27	7 37	5 07
4	7 54	5 20	7 38	5 54	7 00	6 28	6 10	7 00	5 28	7 30	5 04	7 57	5 09	8 04	5 34	7 42	6 03	6 58	6 32	6 09	7 05	5 26	7 38	5 07
5	7 54	5 21	7 37	5 55	6 58	6 29	6 09	7 01	5 27	7 31	5 04	7 58	5 09	8 04	5 35	7 41	6 04	6 56	6 33	6 07	7 06	5 25	7 39	5 07
6	7 54	5 22	7 36	5 57	6 57	6 30	6 07	7 02	5 26	7 32	5 03	7 58	5 10	8 03	5 36	7 39	6 05	6 55	6 34	6 05	7 07	5 23	7 40	5 07
7	7 54	5 23	7 35	5 58	6 55	6 31	6 06	7 03	5 24	7 33	5 03	7 59	5 11	8 03	5 37	7 38	6 06	6 53	6 35	6 04	7 08	5 22	7 41	5 07
8	7 54	5 24	7 34	5 59	6 54	6 32	6 04	7 04	5 23	7 34	5 03	7 59	5 11	8 03	5 37	7 37	6 07	6 51	6 36	6 02	7 10	5 21	7 42	5 07
9	7 54	5 25	7 33	6 00	6 52	6 33	6 03	7 05	5 22	7 35	5 03	8 00	5 12	8 02	5 38	7 36	6 08	6 50	6 37	6 01	7 11	5 20	7 42	5 07
10	7 53	5 26	7 31	6 01	6 51	6 34	6 01	7 06	5 21	7 36	5 03	8 00	5 13	8 02	5 39	7 34	6 09	6 48	6 38	5 59	7 12	5 19	7 43	5 07
11	7 53	5 27	7 30	6 03	6 49	6 35	5 59	7 07	5 20	7 37	5 03	8 01	5 13	8 01	5 40	7 33	6 10	6 46	6 39	5 58	7 13	5 18	7 44	5 07
12	7 53	5 28	7 29	6 04	6 47	6 36	5 58	7 08	5 19	7 38	5 03	8 01	5 14	8 01	5 41	7 32	6 11	6 45	6 40	5 56	7 14	5 17	7 45	5 07
13	7 53	5 29	7 28	6 05	6 46	6 37	5 56	7 09	5 18	7 39	5 03	8 02	5 15	8 00	5 42	7 31	6 12	6 43	6 41	5 55	7 15	5 16	7 46	5 08
14	7 52	5 30	7 27	6 06	6 44	6 38	5 55	7 10	5 17	7 40	5 03	8 02	5 15	8 00	5 43	7 29	6 13	6 41	6 42	5 53	7 17	5 15	7 46	5 08
15	7 52	5 31	7 25	6 07	6 43	6 39	5 53	7 11	5 16	7 41	5 03	8 03	5 16	7 59	5 44	7 28	6 14	6 40	6 43	5 52	7 18	5 15	7 47	5 08
16	7 52	5 32	7 24	6 09	6 41	6 40	5 52	7 12	5 15	7 42	5 03	8 03	5 17	7 59	5 45	7 26	6 15	6 38	6 44	5 50	7 19	5 14	7 48	5 09
17	7 51	5 33	7 23	6 10	6 39	6 41	5 50	7 13	5 14	7 43	5 03	8 03	5 18	7 58	5 46	7 25	6 16	6 36	6 45	5 49	7 20	5 13	7 49	5 09
18	7 51	5 34	7 21	6 11	6 38	6 43	5 49	7 14	5 14	7 44	5 03	8 04	5 19	7 57	5 47	7 24	6 17	6 35	6 46	5 47	7 21	5 13	7 49	5 09
19	7 50	5 35	7 20	6 12	6 36	6 44	5 47	7 15	5 13	7 45	5 03	8 04	5 19	7 57	5 48	7 22	6 18	6 33	6 47	5 46	7 22	5 12	7 50	5 10
20	7 50	5 36	7 19	6 13	6 35	6 45	5 46	7 16	5 12	7 45	5 03	8 04	5 20	7 56	5 49	7 21	6 19	6 31	6 48	5 44	7 23	5 12	7 50	5 10
21	7 49	5 38	7 17	6 14	6 33	6 46	5 45	7 17	5 11	7 46	5 03	8 04	5 21	7 55	5 50	7 19	6 20	6 30	6 49	5 43	7 24	5 11	7 51	5 11
22	7 49	5 39	7 16	6 15	6 31	6 47	5 43	7 18	5 11	7 47	5 03	8 05	5 22	7 54	5 51	7 18	6 21	6 28	6 50	5 42	7 26	5 11	7 51	5 11
23	7 48	5 40	7 15	6 17	6 30	6 48	5 42	7 19	5 10	7 48	5 04	8 05	5 23	7 54	5 52	7 16	6 22	6 27	6 51	5 40	7 27	5 10	7 52	5 12
24	7 47	5 41	7 13	6 18	6 28	6 49	5 41	7 20	5 09	7 49	5 04	8 05	5 24	7 53	5 53	7 15	6 23	6 25	6 52	5 39	7 28	5 10	7 52	5 12
25	7 47	5 42	7 12	6 19	6 26	6 50	5 39	7 21	5 09	7 50	5 05	8 05	5 25	7 52	5 54	7 13	6 24	6 23	6 53	5 38	7 29	5 10	7 52	5 13
26	7 46	5 43	7 10	6 20	6 25	6 51	5 38	7 22	5 08	7 51	5 05	8 05	5 25	7 51	5 55	7 12	6 25	6 22	6 54	5 36	7 30	5 09	7 53	5 13
27	7 45	5 45	7 09	6 21	6 23	6 52	5 37	7 23	5 07	7 52	5 06	8 05	5 26	7 50	5 56	7 10	6 26	6 20	6 55	5 35	7 31	5 09	7 53	5 14
28	7 44	5 46	7 07	6 22	6 22	6 53	5 35	7 24	5 07	7 53	5 06	8 05	5 27	7 49	5 57	7 09	6 27	6 18	6 57	5 34	7 32	5 08	7 53	5 15
29	7 43	5 47			6 20	6 54	5 34	7 25	5 06	7 53	5 07	8 05	5 28	7 48	5 58	7 07	6 27	6 17	6 58	5 33	7 33	5 08	7 53	5 15
30	7 43	5 48			6 18	6 55	5 33	7 26	5 06	7 54	5 07	8 05	5 29	7 47	5 59	7 06	6 28	6 15	6 59	5 31	7 34	5 07	7 54	5 16
31	7 42	5 49			6 17	6 56			5 05	7 54			5 30	7 46	5 59	7 04			7 00	5 30			7 54	5 17

Add one hour for daylight time, if and when in use.

Close accuracy within 10 miles from center of this location - if further than 10 miles, add/subtract 1 minute per 10 miles

COLUMBUS, OHIO

THE OVERLOAD COMPANION 2017 © FREDA BARBER BOOTH

Astronomical Applications Dept

Rise and Set for the Sun for 2017
BOISE CITY, OKLAHOMA

U. S. Naval Observatory, Washington, DC
Central Standard Time

Location: W102 31, N36 44

	JAN AM	JAN PM	FEB AM	FEB PM	MAR AM	MAR PM	APR AM	APR PM	MAY AM	MAY PM	JUN AM	JUN PM	JUL AM	JUL PM	AUG AM	AUG PM	SEP AM	SEP PM	OCT AM	OCT PM	NOV AM	NOV PM	DEC AM	DEC PM
1	8 03	5 45	7 52	6 15	7 20	6 45	6 35	7 13	5 56	7 39	5 33	8 04	5 35	8 13	5 56	7 56	6 22	7 17	6 46	6 33	7 14	5 52	7 44	5 34
2	8 03	5 45	7 52	6 16	7 19	6 46	6 34	7 14	5 55	7 40	5 32	8 04	5 36	8 13	5 57	7 55	6 22	7 16	6 47	6 31	7 15	5 51	7 45	5 34
3	8 03	5 46	7 51	6 17	7 17	6 47	6 32	7 15	5 53	7 41	5 32	8 05	5 36	8 12	5 58	7 54	6 23	7 15	6 47	6 30	7 16	5 50	7 46	5 34
4	8 03	5 47	7 50	6 18	7 16	6 48	6 31	7 15	5 52	7 42	5 32	8 05	5 37	8 12	5 59	7 53	6 24	7 13	6 48	6 28	7 17	5 50	7 47	5 34
5	8 03	5 48	7 49	6 20	7 14	6 49	6 29	7 16	5 51	7 43	5 31	8 06	5 37	8 12	6 00	7 52	6 25	7 12	6 49	6 27	7 18	5 49	7 48	5 34
6	8 03	5 49	7 48	6 21	7 13	6 50	6 28	7 17	5 50	7 43	5 31	8 07	5 38	8 12	6 00	7 51	6 26	7 10	6 50	6 25	7 19	5 48	7 49	5 34
7	8 03	5 50	7 47	6 22	7 12	6 51	6 27	7 18	5 49	7 44	5 31	8 07	5 38	8 11	6 01	7 50	6 26	7 09	6 51	6 24	7 20	5 47	7 50	5 34
8	8 03	5 51	7 46	6 23	7 10	6 52	6 25	7 19	5 48	7 45	5 31	8 08	5 39	8 11	6 02	7 49	6 27	7 07	6 52	6 22	7 21	5 46	7 51	5 34
9	8 03	5 51	7 45	6 24	7 09	6 53	6 24	7 20	5 47	7 46	5 31	8 08	5 39	8 11	6 03	7 47	6 28	7 06	6 53	6 21	7 22	5 45	7 51	5 34
10	8 03	5 52	7 44	6 25	7 07	6 53	6 22	7 21	5 47	7 47	5 31	8 09	5 40	8 11	6 04	7 46	6 29	7 04	6 54	6 20	7 23	5 44	7 52	5 34
11	8 03	5 53	7 43	6 26	7 06	6 54	6 21	7 22	5 46	7 48	5 31	8 09	5 40	8 10	6 04	7 45	6 30	7 03	6 54	6 18	7 25	5 43	7 53	5 34
12	8 02	5 54	7 42	6 27	7 05	6 55	6 19	7 22	5 45	7 49	5 31	8 10	5 41	8 10	6 05	7 44	6 30	7 01	6 55	6 17	7 26	5 43	7 54	5 35
13	8 02	5 55	7 41	6 28	7 03	6 56	6 18	7 23	5 44	7 49	5 31	8 10	5 41	8 10	6 06	7 43	6 31	7 00	6 56	6 15	7 27	5 42	7 54	5 35
14	8 02	5 56	7 40	6 29	7 02	6 57	6 17	7 24	5 43	7 50	5 31	8 10	5 42	8 09	6 07	7 42	6 32	6 58	6 57	6 14	7 28	5 41	7 55	5 35
15	8 02	5 57	7 39	6 30	7 00	6 58	6 15	7 25	5 42	7 51	5 31	8 11	5 43	8 09	6 08	7 40	6 33	6 57	6 58	6 13	7 29	5 41	7 56	5 35
16	8 01	5 58	7 38	6 31	6 59	6 59	6 14	7 26	5 41	7 52	5 31	8 11	5 44	8 08	6 09	7 39	6 34	6 55	6 59	6 11	7 30	5 40	7 56	5 36
17	8 01	5 59	7 36	6 32	6 57	7 00	6 13	7 27	5 41	7 53	5 31	8 11	5 45	8 08	6 09	7 38	6 34	6 54	7 00	6 10	7 31	5 39	7 57	5 36
18	8 01	6 00	7 35	6 33	6 56	7 01	6 11	7 28	5 40	7 54	5 31	8 12	5 46	8 07	6 10	7 37	6 35	6 52	7 01	6 09	7 32	5 39	7 57	5 37
19	8 00	6 01	7 34	6 34	6 54	7 02	6 10	7 29	5 39	7 54	5 31	8 12	5 46	8 06	6 11	7 35	6 36	6 51	7 02	6 08	7 33	5 38	7 58	5 37
20	8 00	6 02	7 33	6 35	6 53	7 03	6 09	7 29	5 38	7 55	5 31	8 12	5 47	8 06	6 12	7 34	6 37	6 49	7 03	6 06	7 34	5 38	7 59	5 38
21	7 59	6 03	7 32	6 36	6 51	7 04	6 08	7 30	5 38	7 56	5 32	8 12	5 48	8 05	6 13	7 33	6 38	6 48	7 04	6 05	7 35	5 37	7 59	5 38
22	7 59	6 04	7 30	6 37	6 50	7 04	6 06	7 31	5 37	7 57	5 32	8 12	5 49	8 04	6 13	7 31	6 38	6 46	7 04	6 04	7 36	5 37	8 00	5 39
23	7 58	6 06	7 29	6 38	6 48	7 05	6 05	7 32	5 36	7 58	5 32	8 13	5 49	8 04	6 14	7 30	6 39	6 45	7 05	6 03	7 37	5 36	8 00	5 40
24	7 58	6 07	7 28	6 39	6 47	7 06	6 04	7 33	5 36	7 58	5 33	8 13	5 50	8 03	6 15	7 29	6 40	6 43	7 06	6 01	7 38	5 36	8 01	5 40
25	7 57	6 08	7 27	6 40	6 45	7 07	6 03	7 34	5 35	7 59	5 33	8 13	5 51	8 02	6 16	7 27	6 41	6 42	7 07	6 00	7 39	5 35	8 01	5 41
26	7 57	6 09	7 25	6 41	6 44	7 08	6 01	7 35	5 35	8 00	5 33	8 13	5 52	8 01	6 17	7 26	6 42	6 40	7 08	5 59	7 40	5 35	8 01	5 41
27	7 56	6 10	7 24	6 42	6 42	7 08	6 00	7 36	5 34	8 00	5 34	8 13	5 53	8 01	6 18	7 25	6 42	6 39	7 09	5 58	7 41	5 35	8 02	5 42
28	7 55	6 11	7 23	6 43	6 41	7 09	5 59	7 37	5 34	8 01	5 34	8 13	5 53	8 00	6 19	7 23	6 43	6 37	7 10	5 57	7 42	5 35	8 02	5 42
29	7 55	6 12			6 40	7 10	5 58	7 37	5 34	8 02	5 34	8 13	5 54	7 59	6 19	7 22	6 44	6 36	7 11	5 56	7 43	5 34	8 02	5 43
30	7 54	6 13			6 38	7 11	5 57	7 38	5 33	8 02	5 35	8 13	5 55	7 58	6 20	7 20	6 45	6 34	7 12	5 55	7 44	5 34	8 02	5 44
31	7 53	6 14			6 37	7 12			5 33	8 03			5 56	7 57	6 21	7 19			7 13	5 54			8 03	5 44

Add one hour for daylight time, if and when in use.

Close accuracy within 10 miles from center of this location - if further than 10 miles, add/subtract 1 minute per 10 miles

BOISE CITY, OKLAHOMA

THE OVERLOAD COMPANION 2017 © FREDA BARBER BOOTH

Astronomical Applications Dept
Rise and Set for the Sun for 2017
OKLAHOMA CITY, OKLAHOMA
Location: W097 32, N35 29

U. S. Naval Observatory, Washington, DC
Central Standard Time

	JAN AM	JAN PM	FEB AM	FEB PM	MAR AM	MAR PM	APR AM	APR PM	MAY AM	MAY PM	JUN AM	JUN PM	JUL AM	JUL PM	AUG AM	AUG PM	SEP AM	SEP PM	OCT AM	OCT PM	NOV AM	NOV PM	DEC AM	DEC PM
1	7 39	5 28	7 30	5 58	6 59	6 26	6 16	6 52	5 38	7 17	5 16	7 40	5 19	7 49	5 39	7 33	6 03	6 56	6 25	6 13	6 52	5 35	7 21	5 17
2	7 39	5 29	7 29	5 59	6 58	6 27	6 15	6 53	5 37	7 18	5 16	7 41	5 19	7 49	5 40	7 32	6 04	6 55	6 26	6 12	6 53	5 34	7 22	5 17
3	7 40	5 30	7 29	6 00	6 57	6 28	6 13	6 54	5 36	7 19	5 15	7 42	5 20	7 49	5 41	7 31	6 04	6 54	6 27	6 10	6 54	5 33	7 23	5 17
4	7 40	5 30	7 28	6 01	6 55	6 29	6 12	6 55	5 35	7 19	5 15	7 42	5 20	7 49	5 41	7 30	6 05	6 52	6 28	6 09	6 55	5 32	7 24	5 17
5	7 40	5 31	7 27	6 02	6 54	6 30	6 10	6 55	5 34	7 20	5 15	7 43	5 21	7 49	5 42	7 29	6 06	6 51	6 29	6 07	6 56	5 31	7 25	5 17
6	7 40	5 32	7 26	6 03	6 53	6 30	6 09	6 56	5 33	7 21	5 15	7 43	5 21	7 49	5 43	7 28	6 07	6 49	6 29	6 06	6 57	5 30	7 26	5 17
7	7 40	5 33	7 25	6 04	6 51	6 31	6 08	6 57	5 32	7 22	5 15	7 44	5 22	7 48	5 44	7 27	6 07	6 48	6 30	6 05	6 58	5 29	7 27	5 17
8	7 40	5 34	7 24	6 05	6 50	6 32	6 06	6 58	5 31	7 23	5 14	7 44	5 22	7 48	5 44	7 26	6 08	6 46	6 31	6 03	6 59	5 28	7 28	5 18
9	7 40	5 35	7 23	6 06	6 48	6 33	6 05	6 59	5 30	7 23	5 14	7 45	5 23	7 48	5 45	7 25	6 09	6 45	6 32	6 02	7 00	5 27	7 29	5 18
10	7 40	5 36	7 22	6 07	6 47	6 34	6 04	7 00	5 29	7 24	5 14	7 45	5 24	7 47	5 46	7 24	6 10	6 44	6 33	6 01	7 01	5 27	7 30	5 18
11	7 40	5 36	7 21	6 08	6 46	6 35	6 02	7 00	5 28	7 25	5 14	7 46	5 24	7 47	5 47	7 23	6 10	6 42	6 34	5 59	7 02	5 26	7 30	5 18
12	7 40	5 37	7 20	6 09	6 44	6 36	6 01	7 01	5 27	7 26	5 14	7 46	5 25	7 47	5 48	7 22	6 11	6 41	6 34	5 58	7 03	5 25	7 31	5 18
13	7 39	5 38	7 19	6 10	6 43	6 36	6 00	7 02	5 27	7 27	5 14	7 46	5 25	7 46	5 48	7 21	6 12	6 39	6 35	5 57	7 04	5 25	7 32	5 19
14	7 39	5 39	7 18	6 11	6 41	6 37	5 58	7 03	5 26	7 27	5 14	7 47	5 26	7 46	5 49	7 20	6 13	6 38	6 36	5 55	7 05	5 24	7 33	5 19
15	7 39	5 40	7 17	6 12	6 40	6 38	5 57	7 04	5 25	7 28	5 14	7 47	5 27	7 45	5 50	7 18	6 13	6 36	6 37	5 54	7 06	5 23	7 34	5 19
16	7 39	5 41	7 16	6 13	6 39	6 39	5 56	7 04	5 24	7 29	5 14	7 47	5 27	7 45	5 51	7 17	6 14	6 35	6 38	5 53	7 07	5 23	7 34	5 19
17	7 39	5 42	7 15	6 14	6 37	6 40	5 54	7 05	5 23	7 30	5 15	7 48	5 28	7 45	5 52	7 16	6 15	6 33	6 39	5 52	7 08	5 22	7 35	5 20
18	7 38	5 43	7 14	6 15	6 36	6 41	5 53	7 06	5 22	7 31	5 15	7 48	5 29	7 44	5 53	7 15	6 16	6 32	6 40	5 50	7 09	5 21	7 35	5 20
19	7 38	5 44	7 13	6 16	6 34	6 42	5 52	7 07	5 22	7 31	5 15	7 48	5 29	7 43	5 54	7 14	6 17	6 30	6 40	5 49	7 10	5 21	7 36	5 20
20	7 37	5 45	7 12	6 17	6 33	6 42	5 51	7 08	5 21	7 32	5 15	7 49	5 30	7 43	5 54	7 12	6 18	6 29	6 41	5 48	7 11	5 20	7 36	5 21
21	7 37	5 46	7 10	6 18	6 32	6 43	5 49	7 09	5 20	7 33	5 15	7 49	5 31	7 42	5 55	7 11	6 18	6 28	6 42	5 47	7 12	5 20	7 36	5 21
22	7 36	5 47	7 09	6 19	6 30	6 44	5 48	7 09	5 20	7 34	5 15	7 49	5 32	7 42	5 56	7 10	6 19	6 26	6 43	5 45	7 13	5 20	7 37	5 22
23	7 36	5 48	7 08	6 20	6 29	6 45	5 47	7 10	5 19	7 35	5 16	7 49	5 33	7 41	5 57	7 09	6 20	6 25	6 44	5 44	7 14	5 19	7 37	5 22
24	7 35	5 49	7 07	6 20	6 27	6 46	5 46	7 11	5 18	7 35	5 16	7 49	5 33	7 40	5 58	7 07	6 21	6 23	6 45	5 43	7 15	5 19	7 37	5 23
25	7 35	5 50	7 06	6 21	6 26	6 47	5 45	7 12	5 18	7 36	5 16	7 49	5 34	7 39	5 59	7 06	6 22	6 22	6 46	5 42	7 16	5 19	7 38	5 24
26	7 34	5 51	7 05	6 22	6 24	6 48	5 43	7 13	5 17	7 37	5 17	7 49	5 35	7 39	6 00	7 05	6 22	6 20	6 47	5 41	7 17	5 18	7 38	5 24
27	7 34	5 52	7 04	6 23	6 23	6 49	5 42	7 13	5 17	7 38	5 17	7 49	5 36	7 38	6 01	7 03	6 23	6 19	6 48	5 40	7 18	5 18	7 38	5 25
28	7 33	5 53	7 03	6 24	6 22	6 50	5 41	7 14	5 17	7 38	5 18	7 49	5 36	7 37	6 01	7 02	6 24	6 17	6 49	5 39	7 19	5 18	7 38	5 26
29	7 32	5 55			6 20	6 51	5 40	7 15	5 16	7 39	5 18	7 49	5 37	7 36	6 02	7 01	6 25	6 16	6 50	5 38	7 20	5 18	7 39	5 26
30	7 32	5 56			6 19	6 51	5 39	7 16	5 16	7 40	5 18	7 49	5 37	7 35	6 02	6 59	6 25	6 15	6 51	5 37	7 20	5 17	7 39	5 27
31	7 31	5 57			6 17	6 51			5 16	7 40			5 38	7 34	6 02	6 58			6 51	5 36			7 39	5 28

Add one hour for daylight time, if and when in use.
Close accuracy within 10 miles from center of this location - if further than 10 miles, add/subtract 1 minute per 10 miles

OKLAHOMA CITY, OKLAHOMA

THE OVERLOAD COMPANION 2017 © FREDA BARBER BOOTH

Astronomical Applications Dept
Location: W122 39, N45 31

Rise and Set for the Sun for 2017
PORTLAND, OREGON

U. S. Naval Observatory, Washington, DC
Pacific Standard Time

	JAN AM	JAN PM	FEB AM	FEB PM	MAR AM	MAR PM	APR AM	APR PM	MAY AM	MAY PM	JUN AM	JUN PM	JUL AM	JUL PM	AUG AM	AUG PM	SEP AM	SEP PM	OCT AM	OCT PM	NOV AM	NOV PM	DEC AM	DEC PM
1	7 51	4 38	7 32	5 17	6 48	5 58	5 50	6 40	4 58	7 18	4 25	7 53	4 26	8 03	4 55	7 38	5 33	6 47	6 10	5 50	6 51	4 57	7 31	4 29
2	7 51	4 39	7 31	5 18	6 46	6 00	5 48	6 41	4 56	7 19	4 24	7 53	4 27	8 03	4 56	7 36	5 34	6 45	6 11	5 48	6 52	4 55	7 32	4 28
3	7 51	4 39	7 30	5 20	6 44	6 01	5 46	6 42	4 55	7 21	4 24	7 54	4 27	8 02	4 58	7 35	5 35	6 43	6 12	5 46	6 54	4 54	7 33	4 28
4	7 51	4 40	7 28	5 21	6 42	6 03	5 44	6 44	4 53	7 22	4 23	7 55	4 28	8 02	4 59	7 34	5 36	6 42	6 13	5 44	6 55	4 53	7 34	4 28
5	7 51	4 41	7 27	5 23	6 41	6 04	5 42	6 45	4 52	7 23	4 23	7 56	4 29	8 02	5 00	7 32	5 38	6 40	6 15	5 42	6 57	4 51	7 35	4 27
6	7 50	4 43	7 26	5 24	6 39	6 05	5 40	6 46	4 51	7 24	4 23	7 56	4 29	8 01	5 01	7 31	5 39	6 38	6 16	5 40	6 58	4 50	7 36	4 27
7	7 50	4 44	7 24	5 26	6 37	6 07	5 39	6 47	4 49	7 26	4 22	7 57	4 30	8 01	5 02	7 29	5 40	6 36	6 17	5 38	6 59	4 49	7 37	4 27
8	7 50	4 45	7 23	5 27	6 35	6 08	5 37	6 49	4 48	7 27	4 22	7 58	4 31	8 00	5 03	7 28	5 41	6 34	6 19	5 37	7 01	4 47	7 38	4 27
9	7 50	4 46	7 22	5 28	6 33	6 09	5 35	6 50	4 47	7 28	4 22	7 58	4 32	8 00	5 05	7 26	5 42	6 32	6 20	5 35	7 02	4 46	7 39	4 27
10	7 49	4 47	7 20	5 30	6 31	6 11	5 33	6 51	4 45	7 29	4 22	7 59	4 33	7 59	5 06	7 25	5 44	6 30	6 21	5 33	7 04	4 45	7 40	4 27
11	7 49	4 48	7 19	5 31	6 30	6 12	5 31	6 53	4 44	7 31	4 21	7 59	4 33	7 59	5 07	7 23	5 45	6 28	6 22	5 31	7 05	4 44	7 41	4 27
12	7 49	4 49	7 17	5 33	6 28	6 13	5 29	6 54	4 43	7 32	4 21	8 00	4 34	7 58	5 08	7 22	5 46	6 26	6 24	5 29	7 06	4 43	7 42	4 27
13	7 48	4 51	7 16	5 34	6 26	6 15	5 28	6 55	4 42	7 33	4 21	8 00	4 35	7 57	5 10	7 20	5 47	6 24	6 25	5 28	7 08	4 42	7 43	4 27
14	7 48	4 52	7 14	5 36	6 24	6 16	5 26	6 56	4 40	7 34	4 21	8 01	4 36	7 57	5 11	7 19	5 49	6 22	6 26	5 26	7 09	4 41	7 44	4 28
15	7 47	4 53	7 13	5 37	6 22	6 17	5 24	6 58	4 39	7 35	4 21	8 01	4 37	7 56	5 12	7 17	5 50	6 20	6 28	5 24	7 11	4 40	7 44	4 28
16	7 47	4 54	7 11	5 39	6 20	6 19	5 22	6 59	4 38	7 37	4 21	8 02	4 38	7 55	5 13	7 15	5 51	6 18	6 29	5 22	7 12	4 39	7 45	4 28
17	7 46	4 56	7 10	5 40	6 18	6 20	5 21	7 00	4 37	7 38	4 21	8 02	4 39	7 54	5 14	7 14	5 52	6 17	6 30	5 20	7 13	4 38	7 46	4 28
18	7 45	4 57	7 08	5 42	6 16	6 21	5 19	7 02	4 36	7 39	4 21	8 02	4 40	7 53	5 16	7 12	5 53	6 15	6 32	5 19	7 15	4 37	7 46	4 29
19	7 45	4 58	7 07	5 43	6 14	6 23	5 17	7 03	4 35	7 40	4 21	8 03	4 41	7 52	5 17	7 10	5 55	6 13	6 33	5 17	7 16	4 36	7 47	4 29
20	7 44	5 00	7 05	5 44	6 13	6 24	5 15	7 04	4 34	7 41	4 22	8 03	4 42	7 51	5 18	7 09	5 56	6 11	6 34	5 15	7 17	4 35	7 48	4 30
21	7 43	5 01	7 03	5 46	6 11	6 25	5 14	7 05	4 33	7 42	4 22	8 03	4 43	7 51	5 19	7 07	5 57	6 09	6 36	5 14	7 19	4 34	7 48	4 30
22	7 42	5 02	7 02	5 47	6 09	6 27	5 12	7 07	4 32	7 43	4 22	8 03	4 44	7 50	5 20	7 05	5 58	6 07	6 37	5 12	7 20	4 34	7 48	4 31
23	7 41	5 04	7 00	5 49	6 07	6 28	5 10	7 08	4 31	7 44	4 22	8 03	4 45	7 48	5 22	7 03	6 00	6 05	6 39	5 10	7 21	4 33	7 49	4 31
24	7 40	5 05	6 58	5 50	6 05	6 29	5 09	7 09	4 30	7 45	4 23	8 03	4 46	7 47	5 23	7 02	6 01	6 03	6 40	5 09	7 23	4 32	7 49	4 32
25	7 40	5 07	6 57	5 51	6 03	6 31	5 07	7 11	4 29	7 46	4 23	8 03	4 47	7 46	5 24	7 00	6 02	6 01	6 41	5 07	7 24	4 31	7 50	4 33
26	7 39	5 08	6 55	5 53	6 01	6 32	5 06	7 12	4 29	7 47	4 24	8 03	4 48	7 45	5 25	6 58	6 03	5 59	6 43	5 06	7 25	4 31	7 50	4 33
27	7 38	5 10	6 53	5 54	5 59	6 33	5 04	7 13	4 28	7 48	4 24	8 03	4 49	7 44	5 27	6 56	6 05	5 57	6 44	5 04	7 26	4 30	7 50	4 34
28	7 37	5 11	6 51	5 56	5 57	6 34	5 02	7 14	4 27	7 49	4 24	8 03	4 51	7 43	5 28	6 54	6 06	5 55	6 45	5 03	7 28	4 30	7 50	4 35
29	7 35	5 12			5 55	5 57	5 01	7 16	4 27	7 50	4 25	8 03	4 52	7 42	5 29	6 53	6 07	5 53	6 47	5 01	7 29	4 29	7 51	4 36
30	7 34	5 14			5 54	6 37	4 59	7 17	4 26	7 51	4 26	8 03	4 53	7 40	5 30	6 51	6 08	5 51	6 48	5 00	7 30	4 29	7 51	4 36
31	7 33	5 15			5 52	6 38			4 25	7 52			4 54	7 39	5 31	6 49			6 50	4 58			7 51	4 37

Add one hour for daylight time, if and when in use.

Close accuracy within 10 miles from center of this location - if further than 10 miles, add/subtract 1 minute per 10 miles

PORTLAND, OREGON

Astronomical Applications Dept
Location: W075 09, N40 00

Rise and Set for the Sun for 2017
PHILADELPHIA, PENNSYLVANIA

U. S. Naval Observatory, Washington, DC
Eastern Standard Time

Day	JAN AM	JAN PM	FEB AM	FEB PM	MAR AM	MAR PM	APR AM	APR PM	MAY AM	MAY PM	JUN AM	JUN PM	JUL AM	JUL PM	AUG AM	AUG PM	SEP AM	SEP PM	OCT AM	OCT PM	NOV AM	NOV PM	DEC AM	DEC PM
1	7 22	4 46	7 09	5 19	6 33	5 53	5 44	6 25	5 00	6 56	4 34	7 24	4 36	7 33	4 59	7 14	5 29	6 31	5 57	5 42	6 30	4 58	7 04	4 36
2	7 23	4 47	7 09	5 20	6 32	5 54	5 42	6 26	4 59	6 57	4 33	7 24	4 36	7 33	5 00	7 13	5 30	6 30	5 58	5 40	6 31	4 56	7 05	4 36
3	7 23	4 47	7 08	5 22	6 30	5 55	5 41	6 27	4 58	6 58	4 33	7 25	4 37	7 33	5 01	7 11	5 31	6 28	5 59	5 39	6 33	4 55	7 06	4 35
4	7 23	4 48	7 07	5 23	6 29	5 56	5 39	6 28	4 56	6 59	4 33	7 25	4 37	7 33	5 02	7 10	5 32	6 26	6 00	5 37	6 34	4 54	7 07	4 35
5	7 23	4 49	7 06	5 24	6 27	5 57	5 37	6 29	4 55	7 00	4 32	7 26	4 38	7 32	5 03	7 09	5 33	6 25	6 01	5 36	6 35	4 53	7 08	4 35
6	7 23	4 50	7 05	5 25	6 26	5 58	5 36	6 30	4 54	7 01	4 32	7 27	4 38	7 32	5 04	7 08	5 34	6 23	6 02	5 34	6 36	4 52	7 08	4 35
7	7 23	4 51	7 03	5 26	6 24	6 00	5 34	6 31	4 53	7 02	4 32	7 27	4 39	7 32	5 05	7 07	5 34	6 22	6 03	5 33	6 37	4 51	7 09	4 35
8	7 22	4 52	7 02	5 28	6 22	6 01	5 33	6 33	4 52	7 03	4 32	7 28	4 39	7 31	5 06	7 06	5 35	6 20	6 04	5 31	6 38	4 50	7 10	4 35
9	7 22	4 53	7 01	5 29	6 21	6 02	5 31	6 34	4 51	7 04	4 32	7 28	4 40	7 31	5 07	7 04	5 36	6 18	6 05	5 29	6 39	4 49	7 11	4 35
10	7 22	4 54	7 00	5 30	6 19	6 03	5 30	6 35	4 50	7 05	4 32	7 29	4 40	7 31	5 08	7 03	5 37	6 17	6 06	5 28	6 41	4 48	7 12	4 35
11	7 22	4 55	6 59	5 31	6 18	6 04	5 28	6 36	4 49	7 06	4 31	7 30	4 41	7 31	5 09	7 02	5 38	6 15	6 07	5 26	6 42	4 47	7 13	4 36
12	7 22	4 56	6 58	5 32	6 16	6 05	5 27	6 37	4 48	7 07	4 31	7 30	4 42	7 30	5 10	7 01	5 39	6 13	6 08	5 25	6 43	4 46	7 13	4 36
13	7 21	4 57	6 57	5 34	6 15	6 06	5 25	6 38	4 47	7 08	4 31	7 31	4 42	7 30	5 11	6 59	5 40	6 12	6 09	5 23	6 44	4 46	7 14	4 36
14	7 21	4 58	6 55	5 35	6 13	6 07	5 24	6 39	4 46	7 09	4 31	7 31	4 43	7 29	5 12	6 58	5 41	6 10	6 11	5 22	6 45	4 45	7 15	4 36
15	7 21	4 59	6 54	5 36	6 11	6 08	5 22	6 40	4 45	7 10	4 31	7 32	4 44	7 29	5 13	6 57	5 42	6 08	6 12	5 20	6 46	4 44	7 16	4 36
16	7 21	5 00	6 53	5 37	6 10	6 09	5 21	6 41	4 44	7 11	4 31	7 32	4 45	7 28	5 14	6 55	5 43	6 07	6 13	5 19	6 47	4 43	7 16	4 37
17	7 20	5 02	6 52	5 38	6 08	6 10	5 19	6 42	4 43	7 12	4 31	7 33	4 46	7 27	5 15	6 54	5 44	6 05	6 14	5 17	6 49	4 42	7 17	4 37
18	7 20	5 03	6 50	5 39	6 06	6 11	5 18	6 43	4 42	7 13	4 32	7 33	4 47	7 26	5 16	6 52	5 45	6 03	6 15	5 16	6 50	4 41	7 18	4 38
19	7 19	5 04	6 49	5 41	6 05	6 12	5 16	6 44	4 42	7 14	4 32	7 33	4 48	7 25	5 17	6 51	5 46	6 02	6 16	5 14	6 51	4 41	7 18	4 38
20	7 19	5 05	6 48	5 42	6 03	6 13	5 15	6 45	4 41	7 15	4 32	7 34	4 49	7 25	5 18	6 49	5 47	6 00	6 17	5 13	6 52	4 40	7 19	4 39
21	7 18	5 06	6 46	5 43	6 02	6 14	5 13	6 46	4 40	7 16	4 32	7 34	4 50	7 24	5 19	6 48	5 48	5 59	6 18	5 12	6 53	4 40	7 19	4 39
22	7 18	5 07	6 45	5 44	6 00	6 15	5 12	6 47	4 39	7 17	4 32	7 34	4 51	7 23	5 20	6 47	5 49	5 57	6 19	5 10	6 54	4 39	7 20	4 39
23	7 17	5 08	6 43	5 45	5 58	6 16	5 11	6 48	4 39	7 18	4 33	7 35	4 51	7 22	5 21	6 45	5 50	5 55	6 20	5 09	6 55	4 39	7 20	4 40
24	7 16	5 10	6 42	5 46	5 57	6 17	5 09	6 49	4 38	7 19	4 33	7 35	4 52	7 21	5 22	6 44	5 51	5 54	6 21	5 08	6 56	4 38	7 20	4 41
25	7 15	5 11	6 41	5 47	5 55	6 18	5 08	6 50	4 37	7 20	4 33	7 35	4 53	7 20	5 23	6 42	5 52	5 52	6 22	5 06	6 57	4 38	7 21	4 41
26	7 15	5 12	6 39	5 49	5 54	6 19	5 06	6 51	4 37	7 21	4 33	7 35	4 54	7 19	5 24	6 41	5 53	5 50	6 23	5 05	6 59	4 37	7 21	4 42
27	7 14	5 13	6 38	5 50	5 52	6 20	5 05	6 52	4 36	7 22	4 34	7 35	4 55	7 19	5 25	6 39	5 54	5 49	6 25	5 04	7 00	4 37	7 21	4 43
28	7 13	5 14	6 36	5 51	5 50	6 21	5 04	6 53	4 36	7 23	4 34	7 35	4 56	7 18	5 26	6 38	5 55	5 47	6 26	5 02	7 01	4 37	7 21	4 43
29	7 12	5 16			5 49	5 52	5 03	6 54	4 35	7 24	4 34	7 35	4 57	7 17	5 26	6 36	5 55	5 45	6 27	5 01	7 02	4 36	7 22	4 44
30	7 11	5 17			5 47	6 23	5 01	6 55	4 35	7 22	4 35	7 35	4 58	7 16	5 27	6 34	5 56	5 44	6 28	5 00	7 03	4 36	7 22	4 45
31	7 10	5 18			5 45	6 24			4 34	7 23			4 59	7 15	5 28	6 33			6 29	4 59			7 22	4 46

Add one hour for daylight time, if and when in use.

Close accuracy within 10 miles from center of this location - if further than 10 miles, add/subtract 1 minute per 10 miles

PHILADELPHIA, PENNSYLVANIA

THE OVERLOAD COMPANION 2017 © FREDA BARBER BOOTH

Astronomical Applications Dept
Location: W079 58, N40 26

Rise and Set for the Sun for 2017
PITTSBURGH, PENNSYLVANIA

U. S. Naval Observatory, Washington, DC
Eastern Standard Time

	JAN AM	JAN PM	FEB AM	FEB PM	MAR AM	MAR PM	APR AM	APR PM	MAY AM	MAY PM	JUN AM	JUN PM	JUL AM	JUL PM	AUG AM	AUG PM	SEP AM	SEP PM	OCT AM	OCT PM	NOV AM	NOV PM	DEC AM	DEC PM
1	7 43	5 04	7 30	5 38	6 53	6 12	6 03	6 45	5 18	7 16	4 52	7 44	4 54	7 54	5 18	7 34	5 48	6 51	6 17	18 01	6 50	5 16	7 24	4 54
2	7 43	5 05	7 29	5 39	6 51	6 13	6 01	6 46	5 17	7 17	4 51	7 45	4 54	7 54	5 19	7 33	5 49	6 49	6 18	18 00	6 51	5 15	7 25	4 54
3	7 43	5 05	7 28	5 40	6 50	6 14	6 00	6 47	5 16	7 18	4 51	7 46	4 55	7 53	5 20	7 32	5 50	6 48	6 19	5 58	6 53	5 14	7 26	4 53
4	7 43	5 06	7 27	5 41	6 48	6 15	5 58	6 48	5 15	7 19	4 51	7 46	4 55	7 53	5 21	7 31	5 51	6 46	6 20	5 56	6 54	5 13	7 27	4 53
5	7 43	5 07	7 26	5 42	6 47	6 16	5 56	6 49	5 14	7 20	4 50	7 47	4 56	7 53	5 22	7 29	5 52	6 44	6 21	5 55	6 55	5 12	7 28	4 53
6	7 43	5 08	7 25	5 44	6 45	6 18	5 55	6 50	5 12	7 21	4 50	7 48	4 56	7 53	5 22	7 28	5 52	6 43	6 22	5 53	6 56	5 10	7 29	4 53
7	7 43	5 09	7 24	5 45	6 44	6 19	5 53	6 51	5 11	7 22	4 50	7 48	4 57	7 52	5 23	7 27	5 53	6 41	6 23	5 52	6 57	5 09	7 30	4 53
8	7 43	5 10	7 22	5 46	6 42	6 20	5 52	6 52	5 10	7 23	4 50	7 49	4 58	7 52	5 24	7 26	5 54	6 40	6 24	5 50	6 58	5 08	7 31	4 53
9	7 43	5 11	7 21	5 47	6 40	6 21	5 50	6 53	5 09	7 24	4 49	7 49	4 58	7 52	5 25	7 25	5 55	6 38	6 25	5 48	7 00	5 07	7 32	4 53
10	7 43	5 12	7 20	5 49	6 39	6 22	5 48	6 54	5 08	7 25	4 49	7 50	4 59	7 51	5 26	7 23	5 56	6 36	6 26	5 47	7 01	5 06	7 33	4 53
11	7 43	5 13	7 19	5 50	6 37	6 23	5 47	6 55	5 07	7 26	4 49	7 50	5 00	7 51	5 27	7 22	5 57	6 35	6 27	5 45	7 02	5 05	7 33	4 54
12	7 42	5 14	7 18	5 51	6 36	6 24	5 45	6 56	5 06	7 27	4 49	7 50	5 01	7 50	5 28	7 21	5 58	6 33	6 28	5 44	7 03	5 05	7 34	4 54
13	7 42	5 15	7 17	5 52	6 34	6 25	5 44	6 57	5 05	7 28	4 49	7 51	5 01	7 50	5 29	7 19	5 59	6 31	6 29	5 42	7 04	5 04	7 35	4 54
14	7 42	5 16	7 15	5 53	6 32	6 26	5 42	6 58	5 04	7 29	4 49	7 52	5 02	7 49	5 30	7 18	6 00	6 30	6 30	5 41	7 05	5 03	7 36	4 54
15	7 41	5 17	7 14	5 55	6 31	6 27	5 41	6 59	5 03	7 30	4 49	7 52	5 03	7 49	5 31	7 17	6 01	6 28	6 31	5 39	7 07	5 02	7 36	4 55
16	7 41	5 19	7 13	5 56	6 29	6 28	5 39	7 01	5 02	7 31	4 49	7 52	5 04	7 48	5 32	7 15	6 02	6 26	6 32	5 38	7 08	5 01	7 37	4 55
17	7 40	5 20	7 11	5 57	6 27	6 29	5 38	7 02	5 01	7 32	4 49	7 53	5 04	7 47	5 33	7 14	6 03	6 25	6 33	5 36	7 09	5 01	7 38	4 55
18	7 40	5 21	7 10	5 58	6 26	6 30	5 36	7 03	5 00	7 33	4 49	7 53	5 05	7 47	5 34	7 12	6 04	6 23	6 35	5 35	7 10	5 00	7 38	4 55
19	7 39	5 22	7 09	5 59	6 24	6 31	5 35	7 04	4 59	7 34	4 49	7 53	5 06	7 46	5 35	7 11	6 05	6 21	6 36	5 33	7 11	4 59	7 39	4 56
20	7 39	5 23	7 07	6 01	6 22	6 33	5 33	7 05	4 59	7 35	4 50	7 54	5 07	7 45	5 36	7 09	6 06	6 19	6 37	5 32	7 12	4 59	7 39	4 56
21	7 38	5 24	7 06	6 02	6 21	6 34	5 32	7 06	4 58	7 36	4 50	7 54	5 08	7 45	5 37	7 08	6 07	6 18	6 38	5 30	7 13	4 58	7 40	4 57
22	7 38	5 25	7 05	6 03	6 19	6 35	5 31	7 07	4 57	7 37	4 50	7 54	5 09	7 44	5 38	7 06	6 08	6 16	6 39	5 29	7 15	4 58	7 40	4 57
23	7 37	5 27	7 03	6 04	6 18	6 36	5 29	7 08	4 57	7 38	4 50	7 54	5 09	7 43	5 39	7 05	6 09	6 14	6 40	5 28	7 16	4 57	7 41	4 58
24	7 36	5 28	7 02	6 05	6 16	6 37	5 28	7 09	4 56	7 38	4 51	7 54	5 10	7 42	5 40	7 03	6 10	6 13	6 41	5 26	7 17	4 57	7 41	4 58
25	7 36	5 29	7 00	6 06	6 14	6 38	5 26	7 10	4 55	7 39	4 51	7 54	5 11	7 41	5 41	7 02	6 11	6 11	6 42	5 25	7 18	4 56	7 42	4 59
26	7 35	5 30	6 59	6 07	6 13	6 39	5 25	7 11	4 55	7 40	4 51	7 54	5 12	7 40	5 42	7 00	6 12	6 09	6 43	5 24	7 19	4 56	7 42	5 00
27	7 34	5 31	6 57	6 09	6 11	6 40	5 24	7 12	4 54	7 41	4 52	7 54	5 13	7 39	5 43	6 59	6 13	6 08	6 45	5 22	7 20	4 55	7 42	5 00
28	7 33	5 33	6 56	6 10	6 09	6 41	5 22	7 13	4 53	7 42	4 52	7 54	5 14	7 38	5 44	6 57	6 14	6 06	6 46	5 21	7 21	4 55	7 41	5 01
29	7 32	5 34			6 08	6 42	5 21	7 14	4 53	7 42	4 53	7 54	5 15	7 37	5 45	6 56	6 15	6 04	6 47	5 20	7 22	4 54	7 42	5 02
30	7 32	5 35			6 06	6 43	5 20	7 15	4 53	7 43	4 53	7 54	5 16	7 36	5 46	6 54	6 16	6 03	6 48	5 18	7 23	4 54	7 43	5 03
31	7 31	5 36			6 04	6 44			4 52	7 44			5 17	7 35	5 47	6 53			6 49	5 17			7 43	5 04

Add one hour for daylight time, if and when in use.

Close accuracy within 10 miles from center of this location - if further than 10 miles, add/subtract 1 minute per 10 miles

PITTSBURGH, PENNSYLVANIA

Astronomical Applications Dept
Location: W071 26, N41 49

Rise and Set for the Sun for 2017
PROVIDENCE, RHODE ISLAND

U. S. Naval Observatory, Washington, DC
Eastern Standard Time

	JAN AM	JAN PM	FEB AM	FEB PM	MAR AM	MAR PM	APR AM	APR PM	MAY AM	MAY PM	JUN AM	JUN PM	JUL AM	JUL PM	AUG AM	AUG PM	SEP AM	SEP PM	OCT AM	OCT PM	NOV AM	NOV PM	DEC AM	DEC PM
1	7 13	4 25	6 59	5 00	6 20	5 37	5 28	6 12	4 41	6 45	4 13	7 15	4 15	7 24	4 40	7 03	5 12	6 18	5 43	5 27	6 19	4 39	6 54	4 16
2	7 13	4 26	6 58	5 02	6 18	5 38	5 26	6 13	4 40	6 46	4 13	7 15	4 15	7 24	4 41	7 02	5 13	6 17	5 44	5 25	6 20	4 38	6 55	4 15
3	7 13	4 27	6 57	5 03	6 17	5 39	5 24	6 14	4 39	6 47	4 12	7 16	4 16	7 24	4 42	7 01	5 14	6 15	5 45	5 23	6 21	4 37	6 56	4 15
4	7 13	4 28	6 55	5 04	6 15	5 40	5 23	6 15	4 38	6 48	4 12	7 17	4 17	7 24	4 43	7 00	5 15	6 13	5 46	5 21	6 22	4 36	6 57	4 15
5	7 13	4 29	6 54	5 06	6 13	5 41	5 21	6 16	4 36	6 49	4 12	7 17	4 17	7 23	4 44	6 58	5 16	6 12	5 47	5 20	6 24	4 35	6 58	4 15
6	7 13	4 30	6 53	5 07	6 12	5 43	5 19	6 17	4 35	6 50	4 11	7 18	4 18	7 23	4 45	6 57	5 17	6 10	5 49	5 18	6 25	4 34	6 59	4 15
7	7 13	4 31	6 52	5 08	6 10	5 44	5 18	6 18	4 34	6 51	4 11	7 19	4 18	7 23	4 46	6 56	5 18	6 08	5 50	5 16	6 26	4 32	7 00	4 15
8	7 13	4 32	6 51	5 09	6 08	5 45	5 16	6 19	4 33	6 52	4 11	7 19	4 19	7 22	4 47	6 55	5 19	6 06	5 51	5 15	6 27	4 31	7 01	4 15
9	7 13	4 33	6 50	5 11	6 07	5 46	5 14	6 21	4 32	6 53	4 10	7 20	4 20	7 22	4 48	6 53	5 20	6 05	5 52	5 13	6 28	4 30	7 02	4 15
10	7 13	4 34	6 48	5 12	6 05	5 47	5 13	6 22	4 31	6 54	4 10	7 20	4 21	7 21	4 49	6 52	5 21	6 03	5 53	5 12	6 30	4 29	7 03	4 15
11	7 12	4 35	6 47	5 13	6 03	5 48	5 11	6 23	4 29	6 55	4 10	7 21	4 21	7 21	4 50	6 51	5 22	6 01	5 54	5 10	6 31	4 28	7 03	4 15
12	7 12	4 36	6 46	5 14	6 02	5 49	5 10	6 24	4 28	6 56	4 10	7 21	4 22	7 20	4 51	6 49	5 23	5 59	5 55	5 08	6 32	4 27	7 04	4 15
13	7 12	4 37	6 45	5 16	6 00	5 51	5 08	6 25	4 27	6 57	4 10	7 22	4 23	7 20	4 52	6 48	5 24	5 58	5 56	5 07	6 33	4 26	7 05	4 16
14	7 11	4 38	6 43	5 17	5 58	5 52	5 06	6 26	4 26	6 58	4 09	7 22	4 24	7 19	4 53	6 46	5 25	5 56	5 57	5 05	6 35	4 26	7 06	4 16
15	7 11	4 39	6 42	5 18	5 57	5 53	5 05	6 27	4 25	6 59	4 09	7 23	4 24	7 19	4 54	6 45	5 26	5 54	5 59	5 04	6 36	4 25	7 06	4 16
16	7 10	4 41	6 41	5 20	5 55	5 54	5 03	6 28	4 24	7 00	4 09	7 23	4 25	7 18	4 55	6 44	5 27	5 53	6 00	5 02	6 37	4 24	7 07	4 16
17	7 10	4 42	6 39	5 21	5 53	5 55	5 02	6 29	4 23	7 01	4 09	7 23	4 26	7 17	4 57	6 42	5 28	5 51	6 01	5 00	6 38	4 23	7 08	4 17
18	7 09	4 43	6 38	5 22	5 52	5 56	5 00	6 30	4 22	7 02	4 10	7 23	4 27	7 17	4 58	6 41	5 29	5 49	6 02	4 59	6 39	4 22	7 08	4 17
19	7 09	4 44	6 36	5 23	5 50	5 57	4 59	6 32	4 21	7 03	4 10	7 24	4 28	7 16	4 59	6 39	5 30	5 47	6 03	4 57	6 41	4 22	7 09	4 18
20	7 08	4 45	6 35	5 25	5 48	5 58	4 57	6 33	4 20	7 04	4 10	7 24	4 29	7 16	5 00	6 38	5 32	5 46	6 04	4 56	6 42	4 21	7 09	4 18
21	7 08	4 47	6 34	5 26	5 47	6 00	4 56	6 34	4 19	7 05	4 10	7 24	4 30	7 15	5 01	6 36	5 33	5 44	6 05	4 54	6 43	4 20	7 10	4 19
22	7 07	4 48	6 32	5 27	5 45	6 01	4 54	6 35	4 18	7 06	4 11	7 24	4 31	7 14	5 02	6 34	5 34	5 42	6 07	4 53	6 44	4 20	7 10	4 19
23	7 06	4 49	6 31	5 28	5 43	6 02	4 53	6 36	4 17	7 07	4 11	7 24	4 31	7 13	5 03	6 33	5 35	5 40	6 08	4 52	6 45	4 19	7 11	4 20
24	7 06	4 50	6 29	5 29	5 41	6 03	4 51	6 37	4 17	7 08	4 11	7 25	4 32	7 12	5 04	6 31	5 36	5 39	6 09	4 50	6 46	4 18	7 11	4 20
25	7 05	4 52	6 28	5 31	5 40	6 04	4 50	6 38	4 16	7 09	4 12	7 25	4 33	7 11	5 05	6 30	5 37	5 37	6 10	4 49	6 48	4 18	7 12	4 21
26	7 04	4 53	6 26	5 32	5 38	6 05	4 48	6 39	4 15	7 10	4 12	7 25	4 34	7 10	5 06	6 28	5 38	5 35	6 11	4 47	6 49	4 17	7 12	4 21
27	7 03	4 54	6 25	5 33	5 36	6 06	4 47	6 40	4 15	7 11	4 13	7 25	4 35	7 09	5 07	6 26	5 39	5 33	6 13	4 46	6 50	4 17	7 12	4 22
28	7 02	4 55	6 23	5 34	5 35	6 07	4 46	6 41	4 15	7 11	4 13	7 25	4 36	7 08	5 08	6 25	5 40	5 32	6 14	4 45	6 51	4 17	7 13	4 23
29	7 01	4 57			5 33	6 08	4 44	6 43	4 14	7 12	4 14	7 25	4 37	7 07	5 09	6 23	5 41	5 30	6 15	4 43	6 52	4 16	7 13	4 23
30	7 01	4 58			5 31	6 10	4 43	6 44	4 14	7 13	4 14	7 25	4 38	7 05	5 10	6 22	5 42	5 28	6 16	4 42	6 53	4 16	7 13	4 24
31	7 00	4 59			5 29	6 11			4 14	7 14			4 39	7 04	5 11	6 20			6 17	4 41			7 13	4 25

Add one hour for daylight time, if and when in use.

Close accuracy within 10 miles from center of this location - if further than 10 miles, add/subtract 1 minute per 10 miles

PROVIDENCE, RHODE ISLAND

Astronomical Applications Dept
Rise and Set for the Sun for 2017
U. S. Naval Observatory, Washington, DC
Location: W081 00, N34 01
COLUMBIA, SOUTH CAROLINA
Eastern Standard Time

	JAN AM	JAN PM	FEB AM	FEB PM	MAR AM	MAR PM	APR AM	APR PM	MAY AM	MAY PM	JUN AM	JUN PM	JUL AM	JUL PM	AUG AM	AUG PM	SEP AM	SEP PM	OCT AM	OCT PM	NOV AM	NOV PM	DEC AM	DEC PM
1	7 29	5 26	7 21	5 54	6 52	6 21	6 11	6 45	5 34	7 08	5 14	7 30	5 17	7 39	5 36	7 24	5 58	6 49	6 19	6 08	6 44	5 31	7 12	5 15
2	7 30	5 26	7 21	5 55	6 51	6 22	6 09	6 46	5 33	7 09	5 13	7 31	5 17	7 39	5 37	7 23	5 59	6 48	6 20	6 06	6 45	5 30	7 13	5 15
3	7 30	5 27	7 20	5 56	6 50	6 23	6 08	6 47	5 32	7 10	5 13	7 32	5 18	7 39	5 37	7 23	5 59	6 46	6 20	6 05	6 46	5 29	7 13	5 15
4	7 30	5 28	7 19	5 57	6 48	6 23	6 07	6 47	5 31	7 11	5 13	7 32	5 18	7 39	5 38	7 22	6 00	6 45	6 21	6 03	6 47	5 28	7 14	5 15
5	7 30	5 29	7 18	5 58	6 47	6 24	6 05	6 48	5 30	7 11	5 13	7 33	5 18	7 39	5 39	7 21	6 01	6 44	6 22	6 02	6 48	5 27	7 15	5 15
6	7 30	5 29	7 17	5 59	6 46	6 25	6 04	6 49	5 30	7 12	5 13	7 33	5 19	7 39	5 39	7 20	6 01	6 42	6 23	6 01	6 49	5 26	7 16	5 15
7	7 30	5 30	7 17	6 00	6 44	6 26	6 03	6 50	5 29	7 13	5 12	7 34	5 19	7 38	5 40	7 19	6 02	6 41	6 23	5 59	6 50	5 26	7 17	5 15
8	7 30	5 31	7 16	6 01	6 43	6 27	6 01	6 50	5 28	7 14	5 12	7 34	5 20	7 38	5 41	7 18	6 03	6 40	6 24	5 58	6 50	5 25	7 17	5 15
9	7 30	5 32	7 15	6 02	6 42	6 27	6 00	6 51	5 27	7 14	5 12	7 35	5 21	7 38	5 42	7 17	6 03	6 38	6 25	5 57	6 51	5 24	7 18	5 15
10	7 30	5 33	7 14	6 03	6 40	6 28	5 59	6 52	5 26	7 15	5 12	7 35	5 21	7 38	5 42	7 16	6 04	6 37	6 26	5 56	6 52	5 23	7 19	5 15
11	7 30	5 34	7 13	6 04	6 39	6 29	5 58	6 53	5 25	7 16	5 12	7 36	5 22	7 38	5 43	7 15	6 05	6 35	6 26	5 54	6 53	5 23	7 20	5 15
12	7 30	5 35	7 12	6 05	6 38	6 30	5 56	6 54	5 24	7 17	5 12	7 36	5 22	7 37	5 44	7 14	6 06	6 34	6 27	5 53	6 54	5 22	7 20	5 16
13	7 30	5 36	7 11	6 06	6 37	6 31	5 55	6 54	5 24	7 17	5 12	7 36	5 23	7 37	5 45	7 12	6 06	6 33	6 28	5 52	6 55	5 21	7 21	5 16
14	7 30	5 37	7 10	6 07	6 35	6 31	5 54	6 55	5 23	7 18	5 12	7 37	5 24	7 36	5 45	7 11	6 07	6 31	6 29	5 51	6 56	5 21	7 22	5 16
15	7 29	5 38	7 09	6 08	6 34	6 32	5 53	6 56	5 22	7 19	5 12	7 37	5 24	7 36	5 46	7 10	6 08	6 30	6 30	5 49	6 57	5 20	7 22	5 17
16	7 29	5 38	7 08	6 08	6 32	6 33	5 51	6 57	5 22	7 20	5 12	7 37	5 25	7 35	5 47	7 09	6 08	6 28	6 30	5 48	6 58	5 20	7 23	5 17
17	7 29	5 39	7 07	6 09	6 31	6 34	5 50	6 57	5 21	7 20	5 13	7 38	5 25	7 35	5 47	7 08	6 09	6 27	6 31	5 47	6 59	5 19	7 24	5 18
18	7 29	5 40	7 06	6 10	6 30	6 35	5 49	6 58	5 20	7 21	5 13	7 38	5 26	7 34	5 48	7 07	6 10	6 26	6 32	5 46	7 00	5 18	7 24	5 18
19	7 28	5 41	7 05	6 11	6 28	6 35	5 48	6 59	5 20	7 22	5 13	7 38	5 27	7 34	5 49	7 06	6 10	6 24	6 33	5 44	7 01	5 18	7 25	5 19
20	7 28	5 42	7 04	6 12	6 27	6 36	5 46	7 00	5 19	7 23	5 13	7 38	5 27	7 33	5 50	7 04	6 11	6 23	6 34	5 43	7 02	5 18	7 25	5 19
21	7 27	5 43	7 03	6 13	6 26	6 37	5 45	7 00	5 18	7 23	5 13	7 38	5 28	7 32	5 50	7 03	6 12	6 21	6 34	5 42	7 03	5 17	7 26	5 20
22	7 27	5 44	7 02	6 14	6 24	6 38	5 44	7 01	5 18	7 24	5 14	7 39	5 29	7 32	5 51	7 02	6 12	6 20	6 35	5 41	7 04	5 17	7 26	5 20
23	7 27	5 45	7 00	6 15	6 23	6 38	5 43	7 02	5 17	7 25	5 14	7 39	5 29	7 31	5 52	7 01	6 13	6 19	6 36	5 40	7 04	5 17	7 27	5 21
24	7 26	5 46	6 59	6 16	6 22	6 39	5 42	7 03	5 17	7 26	5 14	7 39	5 30	7 30	5 53	7 00	6 14	6 17	6 37	5 39	7 05	5 16	7 27	5 21
25	7 26	5 47	6 58	6 17	6 20	6 40	5 41	7 04	5 16	7 26	5 14	7 39	5 31	7 30	5 53	6 59	6 15	6 16	6 38	5 37	7 06	5 16	7 28	5 22
26	7 25	5 48	6 57	6 17	6 19	6 41	5 39	7 04	5 16	7 27	5 15	7 39	5 32	7 29	5 54	6 58	6 15	6 14	6 39	5 36	7 07	5 16	7 28	5 23
27	7 25	5 49	6 56	6 18	6 17	6 41	5 38	7 05	5 15	7 28	5 15	7 39	5 32	7 28	5 54	6 56	6 16	6 13	6 40	5 35	7 08	5 15	7 29	5 23
28	7 24	5 50	6 55	6 19	6 16	6 42	5 37	7 06	5 15	7 28	5 15	7 39	5 33	7 28	5 55	6 54	6 17	6 12	6 40	5 34	7 09	5 15	7 29	5 24
29	7 23	5 51			6 15	6 43	5 36	7 07	5 15	7 29	5 16	7 39	5 34	7 27	5 56	6 53	6 17	6 10	6 41	5 34	7 10	5 15	7 29	5 24
30	7 23	5 52			6 13	6 44	5 35	7 07	5 14	7 29	5 16	7 39	5 34	7 26	5 57	6 52	6 18	6 09	6 42	5 33	7 11	5 15	7 29	5 25
31	7 22	5 53			6 12	6 44			5 14	7 30			5 35	7 25	5 57	6 50			6 43	5 32			7 29	5 25

Add one hour for daylight time, if and when in use.
Close accuracy within 10 miles from center of this location - if further than 10 miles, add/subtract 1 minute per 10 miles

COLUMBIA, SOUTH CAROLINA

THE OVERLOAD COMPANION 2017 © FREDA BARBER BOOTH

Astronomical Applications Dept
Location: W098 29, N45 28

Rise and Set for the Sun for 2017
ABERDEEN, SOUTH DAKOTA

U. S. Naval Observatory, Washington, DC
Central Standard Time

	JAN AM	JAN PM	FEB AM	FEB PM	MAR AM	MAR PM	APR AM	APR PM	MAY AM	MAY PM	JUN AM	JUN PM	JUL AM	JUL PM	AUG AM	AUG PM	SEP AM	SEP PM	OCT AM	OCT PM	NOV AM	NOV PM	DEC AM	DEC PM
1	8 14	5 01	7 55	5 40	7 11	6 22	6 13	7 03	5 21	7 41	4 49	8 16	4 50	8 26	5 19	8 01	5 56	7 10	6 33	6 13	7 14	5 20	7 54	4 52
2	8 14	5 02	7 54	5 42	7 09	6 23	6 11	7 04	5 20	7 43	4 48	8 16	4 50	8 26	5 20	8 00	5 57	7 09	6 34	6 11	7 16	5 19	7 55	4 52
3	8 14	5 03	7 53	5 43	7 08	6 24	6 09	7 05	5 18	7 44	4 48	8 17	4 51	8 25	5 21	7 58	5 58	7 07	6 35	6 09	7 17	5 17	7 56	4 51
4	8 14	5 04	7 52	5 45	7 06	6 26	6 08	7 07	5 17	7 45	4 47	8 18	4 52	8 25	5 22	7 57	6 00	7 05	6 37	6 07	7 18	5 16	7 57	4 51
5	8 14	5 05	7 50	5 46	7 04	6 27	6 06	7 08	5 16	7 46	4 47	8 19	4 52	8 25	5 23	7 56	6 01	7 03	6 38	6 06	7 20	5 15	7 58	4 51
6	8 14	5 06	7 49	5 47	7 02	6 29	6 04	7 09	5 14	7 48	4 46	8 19	4 53	8 24	5 24	7 54	6 02	7 01	6 39	6 04	7 21	5 13	8 00	4 51
7	8 13	5 07	7 48	5 49	7 00	6 30	6 02	7 11	5 13	7 49	4 46	8 20	4 54	8 24	5 26	7 53	6 03	6 59	6 40	6 02	7 23	5 12	8 01	4 51
8	8 13	5 08	7 46	5 50	6 59	6 31	6 00	7 12	5 11	7 50	4 46	8 21	4 54	8 23	5 27	7 51	6 05	6 57	6 42	6 00	7 24	5 11	8 01	4 51
9	8 13	5 09	7 45	5 52	6 57	6 33	5 58	7 13	5 10	7 51	4 45	8 21	4 55	8 23	5 28	7 50	6 06	6 55	6 43	5 58	7 25	5 10	8 02	4 51
10	8 13	5 10	7 44	5 53	6 55	6 34	5 57	7 14	5 09	7 52	4 45	8 22	4 56	8 22	5 29	7 48	6 07	6 54	6 44	5 56	7 27	5 09	8 03	4 51
11	8 12	5 12	7 42	5 55	6 53	6 35	5 55	7 16	5 08	7 54	4 45	8 23	4 57	8 22	5 30	7 47	6 08	6 52	6 46	5 55	7 28	5 07	8 04	4 51
12	8 12	5 13	7 41	5 56	6 51	6 37	5 53	7 17	5 06	7 55	4 45	8 23	4 57	8 21	5 32	7 45	6 09	6 50	6 47	5 53	7 29	5 06	8 05	4 51
13	8 11	5 14	7 39	5 58	6 49	6 38	5 51	7 18	5 05	7 56	4 45	8 24	4 58	8 20	5 33	7 44	6 11	6 48	6 48	5 51	7 31	5 05	8 06	4 51
14	8 11	5 15	7 38	5 59	6 47	6 39	5 49	7 20	5 04	7 57	4 45	8 24	4 59	8 20	5 34	7 42	6 12	6 46	6 50	5 49	7 32	5 04	8 07	4 51
15	8 10	5 17	7 36	6 01	6 45	6 41	5 48	7 21	5 03	7 58	4 45	8 24	5 00	8 19	5 35	7 40	6 13	6 44	6 51	5 47	7 34	5 03	8 07	4 52
16	8 10	5 18	7 35	6 02	6 44	6 42	5 46	7 22	5 02	8 00	4 45	8 25	5 00	8 18	5 37	7 39	6 14	6 42	6 52	5 46	7 35	5 02	8 08	4 52
17	8 09	5 19	7 33	6 03	6 42	6 43	5 44	7 23	5 01	8 01	4 45	8 25	5 01	8 17	5 38	7 37	6 15	6 40	6 54	5 44	7 36	5 01	8 09	4 52
18	8 08	5 20	7 32	6 05	6 40	6 45	5 42	7 25	5 00	8 02	4 46	8 26	5 02	8 16	5 39	7 35	6 17	6 38	6 55	5 42	7 38	5 00	8 09	4 53
19	8 08	5 22	7 30	6 06	6 38	6 46	5 41	7 26	4 59	8 03	4 46	8 26	5 03	8 16	5 40	7 34	6 18	6 36	6 56	5 41	7 39	4 59	8 10	4 53
20	8 07	5 23	7 28	6 08	6 36	6 47	5 39	7 27	4 58	8 04	4 46	8 26	5 04	8 15	5 41	7 32	6 19	6 34	6 58	5 39	7 40	4 59	8 11	4 53
21	8 06	5 25	7 27	6 09	6 34	6 49	5 37	7 29	4 57	8 05	4 46	8 26	5 05	8 14	5 43	7 30	6 20	6 32	6 59	5 37	7 42	4 58	8 11	4 54
22	8 05	5 26	7 25	6 11	6 32	6 50	5 36	7 30	4 56	8 06	4 46	8 26	5 06	8 13	5 44	7 29	6 22	6 30	7 00	5 36	7 43	4 57	8 11	4 54
23	8 05	5 27	7 23	6 12	6 30	6 51	5 34	7 31	4 55	8 07	4 46	8 27	5 07	8 12	5 45	7 27	6 23	6 28	7 02	5 34	7 44	4 56	8 12	4 55
24	8 04	5 29	7 22	6 13	6 28	6 52	5 32	7 32	4 54	8 08	4 46	8 27	5 09	8 11	5 46	7 25	6 24	6 26	7 03	5 32	7 46	4 56	8 12	4 55
25	8 03	5 30	7 20	6 15	6 26	6 54	5 31	7 34	4 53	8 09	4 47	8 27	5 10	8 09	5 48	7 23	6 25	6 25	7 04	5 31	7 47	4 55	8 13	4 56
26	8 02	5 32	7 18	6 16	6 25	6 55	5 29	7 35	4 52	8 10	4 47	8 27	5 11	8 08	5 49	7 21	6 27	6 23	7 06	5 29	7 48	4 55	8 13	4 57
27	8 01	5 33	7 16	6 18	6 23	6 56	5 27	7 36	4 52	8 11	4 47	8 27	5 12	8 07	5 50	7 20	6 28	6 21	7 07	5 28	7 49	4 54	8 13	4 58
28	8 00	5 34	7 15	6 19	6 21	6 58	5 26	7 38	4 51	8 12	4 48	8 26	5 13	8 06	5 51	7 18	6 29	6 19	7 09	5 26	7 51	4 53	8 13	4 58
29	7 59	5 36			6 19	6 59	5 24	7 39	4 50	8 13	4 48	8 26	5 14	8 05	5 52	7 16	6 30	6 17	7 10	5 25	7 52	4 53	8 14	4 59
30	7 58	5 37			6 17	7 00	5 23	7 40	4 50	8 14	4 49	8 26	5 15	8 04	5 54	7 14	6 32	6 15	7 11	5 23	7 53	4 52	8 14	5 00
31	7 56	5 39			6 15	7 01			4 49	8 15			5 17	8 02	5 55	7 12			7 13	5 22			8 14	5 01

Add one hour for daylight time, if and when in use.

Close accuracy within 10 miles from center of this location - if further than 10 miles, add/subtract 1 minute per 10 miles

ABERDEEN, SOUTH DAKOTA

THE OVERLOAD COMPANION 2017 © FREDA BARBER BOOTH

Astronomical Applications Dept

Rise and Set for the Sun for 2017
RAPID CITY, SOUTH DAKOTA

U. S. Naval Observatory, Washington, DC
Mountain Standard Time

Location: W103 14, N44 04

	JAN AM	JAN PM	FEB AM	FEB PM	MAR AM	MAR PM	APR AM	APR PM	MAY AM	MAY PM	JUN AM	JUN PM	JUL AM	JUL PM	AUG AM	AUG PM	SEP AM	SEP PM	OCT AM	OCT PM	NOV AM	NOV PM	DEC AM	DEC PM
1	7 28	4 25	7 11	5 03	6 29	5 42	5 33	6 21	4 44	6 57	4 13	7 30	4 14	7 40	4 42	7 16	5 17	6 28	5 51	5 33	6 30	4 42	7 08	4 16
2	7 28	4 26	7 10	5 04	6 27	5 43	5 31	6 22	4 42	6 58	4 12	7 30	4 15	7 39	4 43	7 15	5 18	6 26	5 52	5 31	6 32	4 41	7 10	4 15
3	7 28	4 27	7 09	5 05	6 25	5 45	5 30	6 23	4 41	6 59	4 12	7 31	4 15	7 39	4 44	7 14	5 19	6 24	5 54	5 29	6 33	4 40	7 11	4 15
4	7 28	4 28	7 07	5 07	6 24	5 46	5 28	6 24	4 39	7 01	4 12	7 32	4 16	7 39	4 45	7 12	5 20	6 22	5 55	5 27	6 34	4 38	7 12	4 15
5	7 28	4 29	7 06	5 08	6 22	5 47	5 26	6 26	4 38	7 02	4 11	7 33	4 16	7 38	4 46	7 11	5 21	6 21	5 56	5 25	6 36	4 37	7 13	4 15
6	7 28	4 30	7 05	5 09	6 20	5 48	5 24	6 27	4 37	7 03	4 11	7 33	4 17	7 38	4 47	7 10	5 22	6 19	5 57	5 24	6 37	4 36	7 14	4 15
7	7 28	4 31	7 04	5 11	6 18	5 50	5 23	6 28	4 36	7 04	4 10	7 34	4 18	7 38	4 48	7 08	5 24	6 17	5 58	5 22	6 38	4 35	7 15	4 15
8	7 28	4 32	7 02	5 12	6 17	5 51	5 21	6 29	4 34	7 05	4 10	7 35	4 19	7 37	4 49	7 07	5 25	6 15	6 00	5 20	6 40	4 33	7 16	4 15
9	7 27	4 33	7 01	5 14	6 15	5 52	5 19	6 30	4 33	7 06	4 10	7 35	4 19	7 37	4 50	7 05	5 26	6 13	6 01	5 18	6 41	4 32	7 16	4 15
10	7 27	4 34	7 00	5 15	6 13	5 54	5 17	6 32	4 32	7 08	4 10	7 36	4 20	7 36	4 52	7 04	5 27	6 11	6 02	5 17	6 42	4 31	7 17	4 15
11	7 27	4 35	6 58	5 16	6 11	5 55	5 16	6 33	4 31	7 09	4 09	7 36	4 21	7 36	4 53	7 02	5 28	6 10	6 03	5 15	6 44	4 30	7 18	4 15
12	7 26	4 36	6 57	5 18	6 10	5 56	5 14	6 34	4 29	7 10	4 09	7 37	4 22	7 35	4 54	7 01	5 29	6 08	6 05	5 13	6 45	4 29	7 19	4 15
13	7 26	4 38	6 56	5 19	6 08	5 57	5 12	6 35	4 28	7 11	4 09	7 37	4 23	7 34	4 55	6 59	5 30	6 06	6 06	5 11	6 46	4 28	7 20	4 15
14	7 26	4 39	6 54	5 21	6 06	5 59	5 10	6 37	4 27	7 12	4 09	7 38	4 23	7 34	4 56	6 58	5 32	6 04	6 07	5 10	6 48	4 27	7 21	4 15
15	7 25	4 40	6 53	5 22	6 04	6 00	5 09	6 38	4 26	7 13	4 09	7 38	4 24	7 33	4 57	6 56	5 33	6 02	6 08	5 08	6 49	4 26	7 21	4 16
16	7 25	4 41	6 51	5 23	6 02	6 01	5 07	6 39	4 25	7 14	4 09	7 38	4 25	7 32	4 58	6 55	5 34	6 00	6 10	5 06	6 50	4 25	7 22	4 16
17	7 24	4 43	6 50	5 25	6 01	6 03	5 05	6 40	4 24	7 15	4 09	7 39	4 26	7 32	5 00	6 53	5 35	5 59	6 11	5 05	6 51	4 24	7 23	4 17
18	7 23	4 44	6 48	5 26	5 59	6 04	5 04	6 41	4 23	7 16	4 09	7 39	4 27	7 31	5 01	6 52	5 36	5 57	6 12	5 03	6 53	4 23	7 23	4 17
19	7 22	4 45	6 47	5 27	5 57	6 05	5 02	6 43	4 22	7 17	4 10	7 39	4 28	7 30	5 02	6 50	5 37	5 55	6 13	5 02	6 54	4 22	7 24	4 18
20	7 22	4 46	6 45	5 29	5 55	6 06	5 00	6 44	4 21	7 18	4 10	7 40	4 29	7 29	5 03	6 48	5 38	5 53	6 15	5 00	6 55	4 22	7 24	4 19
21	7 21	4 48	6 44	5 30	5 53	6 07	4 59	6 45	4 20	7 19	4 10	7 40	4 30	7 28	5 04	6 47	5 40	5 51	6 16	4 58	6 57	4 21	7 25	4 19
22	7 20	4 49	6 42	5 31	5 51	6 08	4 57	6 46	4 19	7 20	4 10	7 40	4 31	7 27	5 05	6 45	5 41	5 49	6 17	4 57	6 58	4 20	7 25	4 20
23	7 20	4 50	6 41	5 33	5 50	6 10	4 56	6 47	4 18	7 21	4 11	7 40	4 32	7 26	5 06	6 43	5 42	5 47	6 18	4 55	6 59	4 20	7 26	4 20
24	7 19	4 52	6 39	5 34	5 48	6 11	4 54	6 49	4 18	7 22	4 11	7 40	4 33	7 25	5 08	6 42	5 43	5 46	6 20	4 54	7 00	4 19	7 26	4 21
25	7 18	4 53	6 37	5 35	5 46	6 12	4 53	6 50	4 17	7 23	4 11	7 40	4 34	7 24	5 09	6 40	5 44	5 44	6 21	4 52	7 01	4 18	7 26	4 22
26	7 17	4 54	6 36	5 37	5 44	6 13	4 51	6 51	4 16	7 25	4 12	7 40	4 35	7 23	5 10	6 38	5 45	5 42	6 22	4 51	7 03	4 18	7 27	4 22
27	7 16	4 56	6 34	5 38	5 42	6 15	4 49	6 52	4 16	7 26	4 12	7 40	4 36	7 22	5 11	6 37	5 47	5 40	6 24	4 49	7 04	4 17	7 27	4 23
28	7 15	4 57	6 32	5 39	5 41	6 16	4 48	6 53	4 15	7 27	4 13	7 40	4 37	7 21	5 12	6 35	5 48	5 38	6 25	4 48	7 05	4 17	7 27	4 23
29	7 14	4 58			5 39	6 17	4 47	6 55	4 14	7 27	4 13	7 40	4 38	7 20	5 13	6 33	5 49	5 36	6 26	4 46	7 06	4 16	7 28	4 24
30	7 13	5 00			5 37	6 18	4 45	6 56	4 14	7 28	4 13	7 40	4 39	7 19	5 14	6 31	5 50	5 35	6 28	4 45	7 07	4 16	7 28	4 24
31	7 12	5 01			5 35	6 19			4 13	7 29			4 40	7 17	5 16	6 30			6 29	4 44			7 28	4 25

Add one hour for daylight time, if and when in use.

Close accuracy within 10 miles from center of this location - if further than 10 miles, add/subtract 1 minute per 10 miles

RAPID CITY, SOUTH DAKOTA

THE OVERLOAD COMPANION 2017 © FREDA BARBER BOOTH

Astronomical Applications Dept
Location: W083 56, N35 59

Rise and Set for the Sun for 2017
KNOXVILLE, TENNESSEE

U. S. Naval Observatory, Washington, DC
Eastern Standard Time

	JAN AM	JAN PM	FEB AM	FEB PM	MAR AM	MAR PM	APR AM	APR PM	MAY AM	MAY PM	JUN AM	JUN PM	JUL AM	JUL PM	AUG AM	AUG PM	SEP AM	SEP PM	OCT AM	OCT PM	NOV AM	NOV PM	DEC AM	DEC PM
1	7 46	5 32	7 37	6 02	7 05	6 31	6 21	6 58	5 43	7 23	5 20	7 47	5 23	7 56	5 44	7 40	6 08	7 03	6 31	6 19	6 59	5 39	7 28	5 22
2	7 46	5 33	7 36	6 03	7 04	6 32	6 20	6 59	5 42	7 24	5 20	7 48	5 23	7 56	5 44	7 39	6 09	7 01	6 32	6 17	7 00	5 38	7 29	5 22
3	7 47	5 34	7 35	6 04	7 03	6 33	6 19	7 00	5 41	7 25	5 20	7 49	5 24	7 56	5 45	7 38	6 09	7 00	6 33	6 16	7 01	5 38	7 30	5 21
4	7 47	5 35	7 34	6 05	7 01	6 34	6 17	7 01	5 40	7 26	5 19	7 49	5 24	7 56	5 46	7 37	6 10	6 58	6 34	6 14	7 02	5 37	7 31	5 21
5	7 47	5 35	7 33	6 06	7 00	6 35	6 16	7 01	5 39	7 27	5 19	7 50	5 25	7 56	5 47	7 36	6 11	6 57	6 34	6 13	7 03	5 36	7 32	5 21
6	7 47	5 36	7 33	6 08	6 58	6 36	6 14	7 02	5 38	7 28	5 19	7 50	5 26	7 56	5 48	7 35	6 12	6 55	6 35	6 11	7 04	5 35	7 33	5 21
7	7 47	5 37	7 32	6 09	6 57	6 37	6 13	7 03	5 37	7 28	5 19	7 51	5 26	7 56	5 48	7 34	6 13	6 54	6 36	6 10	7 05	5 34	7 33	5 21
8	7 47	5 38	7 31	6 10	6 56	6 38	6 12	7 04	5 36	7 29	5 19	7 51	5 27	7 55	5 49	7 33	6 13	6 52	6 37	6 09	7 06	5 33	7 34	5 22
9	7 47	5 39	7 30	6 11	6 54	6 38	6 10	7 05	5 35	7 30	5 19	7 52	5 27	7 55	5 50	7 32	6 14	6 51	6 38	6 07	7 07	5 32	7 35	5 22
10	7 47	5 40	7 29	6 12	6 53	6 39	6 09	7 06	5 34	7 31	5 19	7 52	5 28	7 54	5 51	7 31	6 15	6 50	6 39	6 06	7 08	5 31	7 36	5 22
11	7 47	5 41	7 28	6 13	6 52	6 40	6 07	7 06	5 33	7 32	5 19	7 53	5 28	7 54	5 52	7 30	6 16	6 48	6 40	6 05	7 09	5 31	7 37	5 22
12	7 47	5 42	7 27	6 14	6 50	6 41	6 06	7 07	5 32	7 33	5 19	7 53	5 29	7 54	5 52	7 29	6 16	6 47	6 41	6 03	7 10	5 30	7 37	5 22
13	7 47	5 43	7 26	6 15	6 49	6 42	6 05	7 08	5 31	7 33	5 19	7 53	5 29	7 53	5 53	7 27	6 17	6 45	6 42	6 02	7 11	5 29	7 38	5 23
14	7 46	5 44	7 25	6 16	6 47	6 43	6 03	7 09	5 30	7 34	5 19	7 54	5 30	7 53	5 54	7 26	6 18	6 44	6 43	6 01	7 12	5 29	7 39	5 23
15	7 46	5 45	7 23	6 17	6 46	6 44	6 02	7 10	5 30	7 35	5 19	7 54	5 31	7 52	5 55	7 25	6 19	6 42	6 44	5 59	7 13	5 28	7 39	5 23
16	7 46	5 46	7 22	6 18	6 44	6 45	6 01	7 11	5 29	7 36	5 19	7 54	5 32	7 52	5 55	7 24	6 19	6 41	6 44	5 58	7 14	5 27	7 40	5 23
17	7 45	5 47	7 21	6 19	6 43	6 45	5 59	7 11	5 28	7 37	5 19	7 55	5 32	7 51	5 56	7 23	6 20	6 39	6 45	5 57	7 15	5 27	7 41	5 24
18	7 45	5 48	7 20	6 20	6 42	6 46	5 58	7 12	5 27	7 38	5 19	7 55	5 33	7 51	5 57	7 21	6 21	6 38	6 46	5 55	7 16	5 26	7 41	5 24
19	7 44	5 49	7 19	6 21	6 40	6 47	5 57	7 13	5 26	7 38	5 19	7 55	5 34	7 50	5 58	7 20	6 22	6 36	6 47	5 54	7 17	5 26	7 42	5 25
20	7 44	5 50	7 18	6 22	6 39	6 48	5 56	7 14	5 25	7 39	5 19	7 56	5 34	7 49	5 59	7 19	6 23	6 35	6 48	5 53	7 18	5 25	7 42	5 25
21	7 44	5 51	7 17	6 23	6 37	6 49	5 54	7 15	5 25	7 40	5 20	7 56	5 35	7 49	5 59	7 17	6 23	6 33	6 48	5 52	7 19	5 25	7 43	5 26
22	7 43	5 52	7 15	6 24	6 36	6 50	5 53	7 16	5 24	7 41	5 20	7 56	5 36	7 48	6 00	7 16	6 24	6 32	6 49	5 51	7 20	5 24	7 43	5 26
23	7 43	5 53	7 14	6 25	6 34	6 51	5 52	7 17	5 24	7 42	5 20	7 56	5 37	7 47	6 01	7 15	6 25	6 30	6 50	5 49	7 21	5 24	7 43	5 27
24	7 42	5 54	7 13	6 26	6 33	6 52	5 51	7 17	5 23	7 43	5 20	7 56	5 37	7 47	6 02	7 13	6 26	6 29	6 51	5 48	7 22	5 23	7 44	5 27
25	7 41	5 55	7 12	6 27	6 31	6 53	5 50	7 18	5 23	7 43	5 21	7 56	5 38	7 46	6 03	7 12	6 26	6 27	6 52	5 47	7 23	5 23	7 44	5 28
26	7 41	5 56	7 10	6 27	6 30	6 54	5 48	7 19	5 22	7 44	5 21	7 56	5 39	7 45	6 03	7 11	6 27	6 26	6 53	5 46	7 24	5 22	7 45	5 28
27	7 40	5 57	7 09	6 28	6 29	6 55	5 47	7 20	5 22	7 45	5 21	7 56	5 40	7 44	6 04	7 09	6 28	6 24	6 54	5 45	7 25	5 22	7 45	5 29
28	7 40	5 58	7 08	6 29	6 27	6 55	5 46	7 21	5 21	7 46	5 22	7 56	5 40	7 44	6 05	7 08	6 29	6 23	6 55	5 44	7 25	5 22	7 45	5 29
29	7 39	5 59			6 26	6 56	5 45	7 22	5 21	7 46	5 22	7 56	5 41	7 43	6 06	7 07	6 30	6 22	6 56	5 43	7 26	5 22	7 46	5 30
30	7 38	6 00			6 24	6 56	5 45	7 22	5 21	7 47	5 22	7 56	5 42	7 42	6 06	7 05	6 30	6 20	6 57	5 42	7 27	5 22	7 46	5 31
31	7 37	6 01			6 23	6 57			5 21	7 47			5 43	7 41	6 07	7 04			6 58	5 40			7 46	5 32

Add one hour for daylight time, if and when in use.

Close accuracy within 10 miles from center of this location - if further than 10 miles, add/subtract 1 minute per 10 miles

KNOXVILLE, TENNESSEE

Astronomical Applications Dept
Location: W089 59, N35 07

Rise and Set for the Sun for 2017
MEMPHIS, TENNESSEE

U. S. Naval Observatory, Washington, DC
Central Standard Time

	JAN AM	JAN PM	FEB AM	FEB PM	MAR AM	MAR PM	APR AM	APR PM	MAY AM	MAY PM	JUN AM	JUN PM	JUL AM	JUL PM	AUG AM	AUG PM	SEP AM	SEP PM	OCT AM	OCT PM	NOV AM	NOV PM	DEC AM	DEC PM
1	7 08	4 59	6 59	5 28	6 29	5 56	5 46	6 22	5 08	6 46	4 47	7 09	4 50	7 18	5 10	7 02	5 33	6 26	5 55	5 43	6 22	5 05	6 50	4 48
2	7 08	4 59	6 59	5 29	6 27	5 57	5 45	6 23	5 07	6 47	4 47	7 10	4 50	7 18	5 10	7 02	5 34	6 25	5 56	5 42	6 23	5 04	6 51	4 48
3	7 09	5 00	6 58	5 30	6 26	5 58	5 43	6 23	5 06	6 48	4 46	7 10	4 51	7 18	5 11	7 01	5 34	6 23	5 57	5 40	6 24	5 03	6 52	4 48
4	7 09	5 01	6 57	5 31	6 25	5 59	5 42	6 24	5 05	6 49	4 46	7 11	4 51	7 18	5 12	7 00	5 35	6 22	5 57	5 39	6 25	5 02	6 53	4 48
5	7 09	5 02	6 56	5 32	6 24	6 00	5 41	6 25	5 04	6 49	4 46	7 12	4 52	7 18	5 13	6 59	5 36	6 20	5 58	5 38	6 25	5 01	6 54	4 48
6	7 09	5 03	6 55	5 33	6 22	6 00	5 39	6 26	5 03	6 50	4 46	7 12	4 52	7 17	5 13	6 58	5 37	6 19	5 59	5 36	6 26	5 00	6 55	4 48
7	7 09	5 04	6 54	5 34	6 21	6 01	5 38	6 27	5 02	6 51	4 45	7 13	4 53	7 17	5 14	6 57	5 37	6 18	6 00	5 35	6 27	5 00	6 55	4 48
8	7 09	5 04	6 53	5 35	6 20	6 02	5 36	6 27	5 02	6 52	4 45	7 13	4 53	7 17	5 15	6 56	5 38	6 16	6 01	5 33	6 28	4 59	6 56	4 48
9	7 09	5 05	6 53	5 36	6 18	6 03	5 35	6 28	5 01	6 53	4 45	7 14	4 54	7 17	5 16	6 55	5 39	6 15	6 01	5 32	6 29	4 58	6 57	4 48
10	7 09	5 06	6 52	5 37	6 17	6 04	5 34	6 29	5 00	6 53	4 45	7 14	4 54	7 16	5 16	6 53	5 40	6 13	6 02	5 31	6 30	4 57	6 58	4 49
11	7 09	5 07	6 51	5 38	6 15	6 05	5 32	6 30	4 59	6 54	4 45	7 15	4 55	7 16	5 17	6 52	5 40	6 12	6 03	5 29	6 31	4 56	6 58	4 49
12	7 08	5 08	6 50	5 39	6 14	6 06	5 31	6 31	4 58	6 55	4 45	7 15	4 56	7 16	5 18	6 51	5 41	6 10	6 04	5 28	6 32	4 56	6 59	4 49
13	7 08	5 09	6 49	5 40	6 13	6 06	5 30	6 31	4 57	6 56	4 45	7 15	4 56	7 15	5 19	6 50	5 42	6 09	6 05	5 27	6 33	4 55	7 00	4 49
14	7 08	5 10	6 48	5 41	6 11	6 07	5 29	6 32	4 57	6 57	4 45	7 16	4 57	7 15	5 19	6 49	5 43	6 08	6 06	5 26	6 34	4 54	7 01	4 50
15	7 08	5 11	6 47	5 42	6 10	6 08	5 27	6 33	4 56	6 58	4 45	7 16	4 57	7 14	5 20	6 48	5 43	6 06	6 06	5 24	6 35	4 54	7 01	4 50
16	7 08	5 12	6 45	5 43	6 08	6 09	5 26	6 34	4 55	6 59	4 45	7 16	4 58	7 14	5 21	6 47	5 44	6 05	6 07	5 23	6 36	4 53	7 02	4 50
17	7 07	5 13	6 44	5 44	6 07	6 10	5 25	6 35	4 54	6 59	4 45	7 17	4 59	7 13	5 22	6 45	5 45	6 03	6 08	5 22	6 37	4 53	7 02	4 51
18	7 07	5 14	6 43	5 45	6 06	6 10	5 23	6 35	4 54	7 00	4 46	7 17	4 59	7 13	5 22	6 44	5 45	6 02	6 09	5 20	6 38	4 52	7 03	4 51
19	7 07	5 15	6 42	5 46	6 04	6 11	5 22	6 36	4 53	7 00	4 46	7 17	5 00	7 12	5 23	6 43	5 46	6 00	6 10	5 19	6 39	4 52	7 04	4 51
20	7 06	5 16	6 41	5 47	6 03	6 12	5 21	6 37	4 52	7 01	4 46	7 17	5 01	7 12	5 24	6 42	5 47	5 59	6 11	5 18	6 40	4 51	7 04	4 52
21	7 06	5 17	6 40	5 48	6 01	6 13	5 20	6 38	4 52	7 02	4 46	7 18	5 01	7 11	5 25	6 41	5 48	5 57	6 12	5 17	6 41	4 51	7 04	4 52
22	7 05	5 18	6 39	5 49	6 00	6 14	5 19	6 39	4 51	7 03	4 46	7 18	5 02	7 10	5 25	6 39	5 48	5 56	6 12	5 16	6 42	4 51	7 05	4 53
23	7 05	5 19	6 37	5 50	5 59	6 15	5 17	6 39	4 51	7 03	4 46	7 18	5 03	7 10	5 26	6 38	5 49	5 55	6 13	5 15	6 43	4 50	7 05	4 53
24	7 04	5 20	6 36	5 51	5 57	6 15	5 16	6 40	4 50	7 04	4 47	7 18	5 04	7 09	5 27	6 37	5 50	5 53	6 14	5 13	6 44	4 50	7 06	4 54
25	7 04	5 21	6 35	5 52	5 56	6 16	5 15	6 41	4 50	7 05	4 47	7 18	5 04	7 08	5 28	6 35	5 51	5 52	6 15	5 12	6 45	4 49	7 06	4 54
26	7 03	5 22	6 34	5 52	5 54	6 17	5 14	6 42	4 49	7 05	4 47	7 18	5 05	7 07	5 28	6 34	5 51	5 50	6 16	5 11	6 46	4 49	7 07	4 55
27	7 03	5 23	6 33	5 53	5 53	6 18	5 13	6 43	4 49	7 06	4 48	7 18	5 06	7 07	5 29	6 33	5 52	5 49	6 17	5 10	6 47	4 49	7 07	4 56
28	7 02	5 24	6 31	5 54	5 52	6 19	5 12	6 44	4 48	7 07	4 48	7 18	5 07	7 06	5 30	6 31	5 53	5 47	6 18	5 09	6 48	4 48	7 07	4 56
29	7 01	5 25			5 50	5 55	5 11	6 44	4 48	7 07	4 48	7 18	5 07	7 05	5 31	6 30	5 54	5 46	6 19	5 08	6 48	4 48	7 08	4 57
30	7 01	5 26			5 49	6 20	5 09	6 45	4 47	7 08	4 49	7 18	5 08	7 04	5 31	6 29	5 54	5 45	6 20	5 07	6 49	4 48	7 08	4 58
31	7 00	5 27			5 47	6 21			4 47	7 09			5 09	7 03	5 32	6 27			6 21	5 06			7 08	4 59

Add one hour for daylight time, if and when in use.

Close accuracy within 10 miles from center of this location - if further than 10 miles, add/subtract 1 minute per 10 miles

MEMPHIS, TENNESSEE

Astronomical Applications Dept
Location: W086 46, N36 10

Rise and Set for the Sun for 2017
NASHVILLE, TENNESSEE

U. S. Naval Observatory, Washington, DC
Central Standard Time

	JAN AM	JAN PM	FEB AM	FEB PM	MAR AM	MAR PM	APR AM	APR PM	MAY AM	MAY PM	JUN AM	JUN PM	JUL AM	JUL PM	AUG AM	AUG PM	SEP AM	SEP PM	OCT AM	OCT PM	NOV AM	NOV PM	DEC AM	DEC PM
1	6 58	4 43	6 48	5 13	6 17	5 42	5 33	6 09	4 54	6 35	4 31	6 59	4 34	7 08	4 55	6 52	5 19	6 14	5 43	5 30	6 10	4 50	6 40	4 33
2	6 58	4 44	6 48	5 14	6 15	5 43	5 31	6 10	4 53	6 36	4 31	7 00	4 34	7 08	4 55	6 51	5 20	6 13	5 43	5 28	6 11	4 49	6 41	4 32
3	6 58	4 45	6 47	5 15	6 14	5 44	5 30	6 11	4 52	6 37	4 31	7 00	4 35	7 08	4 56	6 50	5 21	6 11	5 44	5 27	6 12	4 49	6 42	4 32
4	6 58	4 46	6 46	5 16	6 13	5 45	5 28	6 12	4 51	6 38	4 30	7 01	4 35	7 08	4 57	6 49	5 21	6 10	5 45	5 26	6 13	4 48	6 43	4 32
5	6 59	4 46	6 45	5 17	6 11	5 46	5 27	6 13	4 50	6 38	4 30	7 02	4 36	7 08	4 58	6 48	5 22	6 08	5 46	5 24	6 14	4 47	6 44	4 32
6	6 59	4 47	6 44	5 19	6 10	5 47	5 25	6 14	4 49	6 39	4 30	7 02	4 36	7 07	4 59	6 47	5 23	6 07	5 47	5 23	6 15	4 46	6 44	4 32
7	6 59	4 48	6 43	5 20	6 08	5 48	5 24	6 15	4 48	6 40	4 30	7 03	4 37	7 07	4 59	6 46	5 24	6 05	5 48	5 21	6 16	4 45	6 45	4 32
8	6 59	4 49	6 42	5 21	6 07	5 49	5 23	6 16	4 47	6 41	4 30	7 03	4 37	7 07	5 00	6 45	5 25	6 04	5 48	5 20	6 17	4 44	6 46	4 32
9	6 59	4 50	6 41	5 22	6 06	5 50	5 21	6 16	4 46	6 42	4 29	7 04	4 38	7 06	5 01	6 44	5 25	6 02	5 49	5 19	6 18	4 43	6 47	4 33
10	6 58	4 51	6 40	5 23	6 04	5 51	5 20	6 17	4 45	6 43	4 29	7 04	4 38	7 06	5 02	6 42	5 26	6 01	5 50	5 17	6 19	4 42	6 48	4 33
11	6 58	4 52	6 39	5 24	6 03	5 52	5 19	6 18	4 44	6 44	4 29	7 05	4 39	7 06	5 02	6 41	5 27	5 59	5 51	5 16	6 20	4 42	6 48	4 33
12	6 58	4 53	6 38	5 25	6 01	5 52	5 17	6 19	4 43	6 44	4 29	7 05	4 39	7 05	5 03	6 40	5 28	5 58	5 52	5 14	6 21	4 41	6 49	4 33
13	6 58	4 54	6 37	5 26	6 00	5 53	5 16	6 20	4 42	6 45	4 29	7 06	4 40	7 05	5 03	6 39	5 28	5 57	5 53	5 13	6 22	4 40	6 50	4 34
14	6 58	4 55	6 36	5 27	5 59	5 54	5 14	6 20	4 41	6 46	4 29	7 06	4 41	7 04	5 04	6 38	5 29	5 55	5 54	5 12	6 23	4 39	6 50	4 34
15	6 57	4 56	6 35	5 28	5 57	5 55	5 13	6 21	4 41	6 47	4 29	7 06	4 41	7 04	5 05	6 37	5 30	5 54	5 54	5 10	6 24	4 39	6 51	4 34
16	6 57	4 57	6 34	5 29	5 56	5 56	5 12	6 22	4 40	6 48	4 29	7 06	4 42	7 04	5 06	6 35	5 31	5 52	5 55	5 09	6 25	4 38	6 52	4 34
17	6 57	4 58	6 33	5 30	5 54	5 57	5 11	6 23	4 39	6 48	4 30	7 07	4 43	7 03	5 06	6 34	5 31	5 51	5 56	5 08	6 26	4 38	6 52	4 35
18	6 57	4 59	6 32	5 31	5 53	5 58	5 09	6 24	4 38	6 49	4 30	7 07	4 43	7 02	5 07	6 33	5 32	5 49	5 57	5 07	6 27	4 37	6 53	4 35
19	6 56	5 00	6 30	5 32	5 51	5 58	5 08	6 25	4 38	6 50	4 30	7 07	4 44	7 02	5 08	6 32	5 33	5 48	5 58	5 05	6 28	4 36	6 53	4 36
20	6 56	5 01	6 29	5 33	5 50	5 59	5 07	6 26	4 37	6 51	4 30	7 07	4 45	7 01	5 09	6 30	5 34	5 46	5 59	5 04	6 29	4 36	6 54	4 36
21	6 55	5 02	6 28	5 34	5 49	6 00	5 05	6 26	4 36	6 52	4 30	7 08	4 45	7 01	5 10	6 29	5 35	5 45	6 00	5 03	6 30	4 35	6 55	4 36
22	6 55	5 03	6 27	5 35	5 47	6 01	5 04	6 27	4 36	6 52	4 31	7 08	4 46	7 00	5 11	6 28	5 35	5 43	6 01	5 02	6 31	4 35	6 55	4 37
23	6 54	5 04	6 26	5 36	5 46	6 02	5 03	6 28	4 35	6 53	4 31	7 08	4 47	6 59	5 12	6 26	5 36	5 42	6 02	5 00	6 32	4 35	6 55	4 38
24	6 54	5 05	6 24	5 37	5 44	6 03	5 02	6 29	4 35	6 54	4 31	7 08	4 48	6 58	5 13	6 25	5 37	5 40	6 03	4 59	6 33	4 34	6 56	4 38
25	6 53	5 06	6 23	5 38	5 43	6 04	5 01	6 30	4 34	6 55	4 31	7 08	4 49	6 58	5 14	6 24	5 38	5 39	6 04	4 58	6 34	4 34	6 56	4 39
26	6 53	5 07	6 22	5 39	5 41	6 04	4 59	6 31	4 34	6 56	4 32	7 08	4 50	6 57	5 14	6 22	5 39	5 37	6 05	4 57	6 35	4 34	6 57	4 39
27	6 52	5 08	6 21	5 40	5 40	6 05	4 58	6 31	4 33	6 57	4 32	7 08	4 51	6 56	5 15	6 21	5 39	5 36	6 06	4 56	6 36	4 33	6 57	4 40
28	6 51	5 09	6 19	5 41	5 38	6 06	4 57	6 32	4 33	6 57	4 32	7 08	4 51	6 55	5 16	6 20	5 40	5 34	6 07	4 55	6 37	4 33	6 57	4 41
29	6 51	5 10			5 37	6 07	4 56	6 33	4 32	6 58	4 33	7 08	4 52	6 54	5 17	6 18	5 41	5 33	6 08	4 54	6 38	4 33	6 58	4 41
30	6 50	5 11			5 35	6 08	4 55	6 34	4 32	6 58	4 33	7 08	4 53	6 54	5 18	6 17	5 42	5 31	6 08	4 53	6 39	4 33	6 58	4 42
31	6 49	5 12			5 34	6 09			4 31	6 59			4 54	6 53	5 18	6 15			6 09	4 52			6 58	4 43

Add one hour for daylight time, if and when in use.

Close accuracy within 10 miles from center of this location - if further than 10 miles, add/subtract 1 minute per 10 miles

NASHVILLE, TENNESSEE

THE OVERLOAD COMPANION 2017 © FREDA BARBER BOOTH

Astronomical Applications Dept
Location: W101 51, N35 12

Rise and Set for the Sun for 2017
AMARILLO, TEXAS

U. S. Naval Observatory, Washington, DC
Central Standard Time

	JAN AM	JAN PM	FEB AM	FEB PM	MAR AM	MAR PM	APR AM	APR PM	MAY AM	MAY PM	JUN AM	JUN PM	JUL AM	JUL PM	AUG AM	AUG PM	SEP AM	SEP PM	OCT AM	OCT PM	NOV AM	NOV PM	DEC AM	DEC PM
1	7 56	5 46	7 47	6 15	7 16	6 43	6 33	7 09	5 56	7 34	5 34	7 57	5 37	8 06	5 57	7 50	6 20	7 13	6 43	6 30	7 09	5 52	7 38	5 35
2	7 56	5 47	7 46	6 16	7 15	6 44	6 32	7 10	5 55	7 35	5 34	7 58	5 37	8 06	5 58	7 49	6 21	7 12	6 43	6 29	7 10	5 51	7 39	5 35
3	7 56	5 48	7 45	6 17	7 14	6 45	6 31	7 11	5 54	7 35	5 33	7 58	5 38	8 06	5 58	7 48	6 22	7 11	6 44	6 28	7 11	5 50	7 40	5 35
4	7 56	5 48	7 44	6 18	7 12	6 46	6 29	7 12	5 53	7 36	5 33	7 59	5 38	8 05	5 59	7 47	6 23	7 09	6 45	6 26	7 12	5 49	7 41	5 35
5	7 56	5 49	7 44	6 19	7 11	6 47	6 28	7 13	5 52	7 37	5 33	7 59	5 39	8 05	6 00	7 46	6 23	7 08	6 46	6 25	7 13	5 49	7 41	5 35
6	7 56	5 50	7 43	6 21	7 10	6 48	6 26	7 13	5 51	7 38	5 33	8 00	5 39	8 05	6 01	7 45	6 24	7 06	6 47	6 23	7 14	5 48	7 42	5 35
7	7 56	5 51	7 42	6 22	7 08	6 49	6 25	7 14	5 50	7 39	5 33	8 00	5 40	8 05	6 01	7 44	6 25	7 05	6 47	6 22	7 15	5 47	7 43	5 35
8	7 56	5 52	7 41	6 23	7 07	6 50	6 24	7 15	5 49	7 39	5 33	8 01	5 40	8 05	6 02	7 43	6 25	7 04	6 48	6 21	7 16	5 46	7 44	5 35
9	7 56	5 53	7 40	6 24	7 06	6 50	6 22	7 16	5 48	7 40	5 33	8 01	5 41	8 04	6 03	7 42	6 26	7 02	6 49	6 19	7 17	5 45	7 45	5 36
10	7 56	5 54	7 39	6 25	7 04	6 51	6 21	7 17	5 47	7 41	5 32	8 02	5 42	8 04	6 04	7 41	6 27	7 01	6 50	6 18	7 18	5 45	7 46	5 36
11	7 56	5 54	7 38	6 26	7 03	6 52	6 20	7 17	5 46	7 42	5 32	8 02	5 42	8 04	6 05	7 40	6 28	6 59	6 51	6 17	7 19	5 44	7 46	5 36
12	7 56	5 55	7 37	6 27	7 01	6 53	6 18	7 18	5 45	7 43	5 32	8 03	5 43	8 03	6 05	7 39	6 28	6 58	6 51	6 15	7 20	5 43	7 47	5 37
13	7 56	5 56	7 36	6 28	7 00	6 54	6 17	7 19	5 45	7 43	5 32	8 03	5 43	8 03	6 06	7 38	6 29	6 56	6 52	6 14	7 21	5 42	7 48	5 38
14	7 56	5 57	7 35	6 29	6 59	6 55	6 16	7 20	5 44	7 44	5 32	8 03	5 44	8 02	6 07	7 37	6 30	6 55	6 53	6 13	7 22	5 42	7 48	5 38
15	7 55	5 58	7 34	6 29	6 57	6 56	6 15	7 21	5 43	7 45	5 32	8 04	5 45	8 02	6 08	7 35	6 31	6 54	6 54	6 12	7 23	5 41	7 49	5 37
16	7 55	5 59	7 33	6 30	6 56	6 56	6 13	7 21	5 42	7 46	5 32	8 04	5 45	8 01	6 08	7 34	6 31	6 52	6 55	6 10	7 24	5 40	7 50	5 38
17	7 55	6 00	7 32	6 31	6 55	6 57	6 12	7 22	5 42	7 47	5 33	8 04	5 46	8 01	6 09	7 33	6 32	6 51	6 56	6 09	7 25	5 40	7 50	5 38
18	7 55	6 01	7 31	6 32	6 53	6 58	6 11	7 23	5 41	7 47	5 33	8 05	5 47	8 00	6 10	7 32	6 33	6 49	6 57	6 08	7 26	5 39	7 51	5 38
19	7 54	6 02	7 30	6 33	6 52	6 59	6 09	7 24	5 40	7 48	5 33	8 05	5 47	8 00	6 11	7 31	6 34	6 48	6 57	6 07	7 27	5 39	7 51	5 39
20	7 54	6 03	7 28	6 34	6 50	7 00	6 08	7 25	5 40	7 49	5 33	8 05	5 48	7 59	6 11	7 29	6 34	6 46	6 58	6 05	7 28	5 38	7 52	5 39
21	7 53	6 04	7 27	6 35	6 49	7 00	6 07	7 25	5 39	7 50	5 33	8 05	5 49	7 59	6 12	7 28	6 35	6 45	6 59	6 04	7 29	5 38	7 52	5 40
22	7 53	6 05	7 26	6 36	6 47	7 01	6 06	7 26	5 38	7 50	5 34	8 05	5 49	7 58	6 13	7 27	6 36	6 43	7 00	6 03	7 30	5 38	7 53	5 40
23	7 52	6 06	7 25	6 37	6 46	7 02	6 05	7 27	5 38	7 51	5 34	8 06	5 50	7 57	6 14	7 25	6 37	6 42	7 01	6 02	7 31	5 37	7 53	5 41
24	7 52	6 07	7 24	6 38	6 45	7 03	6 03	7 28	5 37	7 52	5 34	8 06	5 51	7 57	6 14	7 24	6 37	6 40	7 02	6 01	7 32	5 37	7 54	5 42
25	7 51	6 08	7 23	6 39	6 43	7 04	6 02	7 29	5 37	7 52	5 35	8 06	5 52	7 56	6 15	7 23	6 38	6 39	7 02	6 00	7 32	5 36	7 54	5 42
26	7 51	6 09	7 21	6 40	6 42	7 04	6 01	7 30	5 36	7 53	5 35	8 06	5 52	7 55	6 16	7 22	6 39	6 38	7 03	5 58	7 33	5 36	7 55	5 43
27	7 50	6 10	7 20	6 41	6 40	7 05	6 00	7 30	5 36	7 54	5 35	8 06	5 53	7 54	6 17	7 20	6 40	6 36	7 04	5 57	7 34	5 36	7 55	5 44
28	7 50	6 11	7 19	6 42	6 39	7 06	5 59	7 31	5 35	7 55	5 36	8 06	5 54	7 53	6 18	7 19	6 40	6 35	7 05	5 56	7 35	5 36	7 55	5 44
29	7 49	6 12			6 38	7 07	5 58	7 32	5 35	7 55	5 36	8 06	5 55	7 53	6 18	7 18	6 41	6 33	7 06	5 55	7 36	5 36	7 55	5 45
30	7 48	6 13			6 36	7 08	5 57	7 33	5 35	7 56	5 36	8 06	5 55	7 52	6 19	7 16	6 42	6 32	7 07	5 54	7 37	5 35	7 56	5 45
31	7 48	6 14			6 35	7 08			5 34	7 56			5 56	7 51	6 20	7 15			7 08	5 53			7 56	5 46

Add one hour for daylight time, if and when in use.

Close accuracy within 10 miles from center of this location - if further than 10 miles, add/subtract 1 minute per 10 miles

AMARILLO, TEXAS

THE OVERLOAD COMPANION 2017 © FREDA BARBER BOOTH

Astronomical Applications Dept
Location: W097 44, N30 17

Rise and Set for the Sun for 2017
AUSTIN, TEXAS

U. S. Naval Observatory, Washington, DC
Central Standard Time

	JAN AM	JAN PM	FEB AM	FEB PM	MAR AM	MAR PM	APR AM	APR PM	MAY AM	MAY PM	JUN AM	JUN PM	JUL AM	JUL PM	AUG AM	AUG PM	SEP AM	SEP PM	OCT AM	OCT PM	NOV AM	NOV PM	DEC AM	DEC PM
1	7 27	5 41	7 22	6 07	6 56	6 30	6 19	6 50	5 47	7 09	5 30	7 28	5 33	7 37	5 50	7 24	6 08	6 53	6 25	6 16	6 46	5 43	7 10	5 30
2	7 28	5 42	7 21	6 08	6 55	6 31	6 18	6 51	5 46	7 10	5 29	7 29	5 33	7 37	5 50	7 23	6 09	6 52	6 25	6 14	6 46	5 42	7 11	5 30
3	7 28	5 43	7 21	6 09	6 54	6 32	6 17	6 51	5 45	7 10	5 29	7 29	5 34	7 37	5 51	7 23	6 09	6 50	6 26	6 13	6 47	5 41	7 12	5 30
4	7 28	5 44	7 20	6 10	6 53	6 32	6 16	6 52	5 45	7 11	5 29	7 30	5 34	7 37	5 52	7 22	6 10	6 49	6 26	6 12	6 48	5 41	7 13	5 30
5	7 28	5 44	7 19	6 11	6 52	6 33	6 15	6 53	5 44	7 12	5 29	7 30	5 35	7 36	5 52	7 21	6 10	6 48	6 27	6 11	6 49	5 40	7 13	5 30
6	7 28	5 45	7 19	6 12	6 51	6 34	6 14	6 53	5 43	7 12	5 29	7 31	5 35	7 36	5 53	7 21	6 11	6 47	6 28	6 10	6 50	5 39	7 14	5 30
7	7 28	5 46	7 18	6 12	6 50	6 34	6 12	6 54	5 42	7 13	5 29	7 31	5 36	7 36	5 53	7 20	6 11	6 46	6 28	6 08	6 50	5 39	7 15	5 30
8	7 28	5 47	7 17	6 13	6 48	6 35	6 11	6 54	5 41	7 14	5 29	7 32	5 36	7 36	5 54	7 19	6 12	6 44	6 29	6 07	6 51	5 38	7 16	5 31
9	7 29	5 48	7 16	6 14	6 47	6 36	6 10	6 55	5 41	7 14	5 29	7 32	5 37	7 36	5 55	7 18	6 12	6 43	6 30	6 06	6 52	5 37	7 16	5 31
10	7 29	5 48	7 16	6 15	6 46	6 36	6 09	6 56	5 40	7 15	5 29	7 33	5 37	7 35	5 55	7 18	6 13	6 42	6 30	6 05	6 53	5 37	7 17	5 31
11	7 29	5 49	7 15	6 16	6 45	6 37	6 08	6 56	5 39	7 16	5 29	7 33	5 38	7 35	5 56	7 16	6 13	6 41	6 31	6 04	6 54	5 36	7 18	5 31
12	7 28	5 50	7 14	6 17	6 44	6 38	6 07	6 57	5 39	7 16	5 29	7 33	5 38	7 35	5 56	7 16	6 14	6 39	6 31	6 03	6 54	5 36	7 18	5 32
13	7 28	5 51	7 13	6 17	6 43	6 38	6 05	6 58	5 38	7 17	5 29	7 34	5 39	7 35	5 57	7 15	6 14	6 38	6 32	6 01	6 55	5 35	7 19	5 32
14	7 28	5 52	7 12	6 18	6 41	6 39	6 04	6 58	5 37	7 18	5 29	7 34	5 39	7 34	5 58	7 14	6 15	6 37	6 33	6 00	6 56	5 35	7 20	5 33
15	7 28	5 53	7 11	6 19	6 40	6 40	6 03	6 59	5 37	7 18	5 29	7 34	5 40	7 34	5 58	7 13	6 16	6 36	6 33	5 59	6 57	5 34	7 20	5 33
16	7 28	5 53	7 11	6 20	6 39	6 40	6 02	7 00	5 36	7 19	5 29	7 34	5 40	7 34	5 59	7 12	6 16	6 34	6 34	5 58	6 58	5 34	7 21	5 33
17	7 28	5 54	7 10	6 21	6 38	6 41	6 01	7 01	5 35	7 20	5 29	7 35	5 41	7 33	5 59	7 11	6 17	6 33	6 35	5 57	6 59	5 34	7 22	5 34
18	7 28	5 55	7 09	6 21	6 37	6 41	6 00	7 01	5 35	7 20	5 29	7 35	5 41	7 33	6 00	7 09	6 18	6 32	6 35	5 56	6 59	5 33	7 22	5 34
19	7 27	5 56	7 08	6 22	6 35	6 42	5 59	7 02	5 34	7 21	5 29	7 35	5 42	7 32	6 01	7 08	6 18	6 31	6 36	5 55	7 00	5 33	7 23	5 35
20	7 27	5 57	7 07	6 23	6 34	6 43	5 58	7 02	5 34	7 21	5 29	7 35	5 42	7 32	6 01	7 07	6 19	6 29	6 37	5 54	7 01	5 32	7 23	5 35
21	7 27	5 58	7 06	6 24	6 33	6 43	5 57	7 03	5 33	7 22	5 30	7 36	5 43	7 31	6 02	7 06	6 19	6 28	6 37	5 53	7 02	5 32	7 24	5 35
22	7 27	5 59	7 05	6 24	6 32	6 44	5 56	7 03	5 33	7 23	5 30	7 36	5 43	7 31	6 03	7 05	6 20	6 27	6 38	5 52	7 03	5 31	7 24	5 36
23	7 26	5 59	7 04	6 25	6 30	6 45	5 55	7 04	5 32	7 23	5 30	7 36	5 44	7 30	6 03	7 04	6 20	6 25	6 39	5 51	7 04	5 31	7 25	5 36
24	7 26	6 00	7 04	6 26	6 29	6 45	5 54	7 05	5 32	7 24	5 31	7 36	5 44	7 30	6 04	7 03	6 21	6 24	6 40	5 50	7 04	5 31	7 25	5 37
25	7 25	6 01	7 03	6 26	6 28	6 46	5 53	7 05	5 32	7 25	5 31	7 37	5 45	7 29	6 05	7 01	6 22	6 23	6 41	5 48	7 05	5 31	7 25	5 37
26	7 25	6 02	7 02	6 27	6 27	6 46	5 52	7 06	5 31	7 26	5 31	7 37	5 46	7 28	6 05	7 00	6 22	6 22	6 42	5 47	7 06	5 31	7 26	5 38
27	7 25	6 03	7 01	6 28	6 26	6 47	5 51	7 06	5 31	7 26	5 32	7 37	5 47	7 28	6 06	6 59	6 23	6 20	6 43	5 46	7 07	5 30	7 26	5 39
28	7 24	6 04	7 00	6 28	6 24	6 48	5 50	7 07	5 31	7 27	5 32	7 37	5 47	7 27	6 06	6 58	6 24	6 19	6 43	5 46	7 08	5 30	7 26	5 39
29	7 24	6 05			6 23	6 48	5 49	7 08	5 30	7 27	5 32	7 37	5 48	7 26	6 07	6 56	6 24	6 18	6 44	5 45	7 09	5 30	7 27	5 40
30	7 23	6 06			6 22	6 49	5 48	7 08	5 30	7 28	5 33	7 37	5 49	7 26	6 07	6 55		6 17	6 45	5 44		5 30	7 27	5 41
31	7 22	6 06			6 21	6 50			5 30	7 28			5 49	7 25	6 07	6 54			6 45				7 27	5 41

Add one hour for daylight time, if and when in use.

Close accuracy within 10 miles from center of this location - if further than 10 miles, add/subtract 1 minute per 10 miles

AUSTIN, TEXAS

THE OVERLOAD COMPANION 2017 © FREDA BARBER BOOTH

Astronomical Applications Dept
Location: W106 25, N31 47

Rise and Set for the Sun for 2017
EL PASO, TEXAS

U.S. Naval Observatory, Washington, DC
Mountain Standard Time

	JAN AM	JAN PM	FEB AM	FEB PM	MAR AM	MAR PM	APR AM	APR PM	MAY AM	MAY PM	JUN AM	JUN PM	JUL AM	JUL PM	AUG AM	AUG PM	SEP AM	SEP PM	OCT AM	OCT PM	NOV AM	NOV PM	DEC AM	DEC PM
1	7 06	5 13	6 59	5 40	6 32	6 04	5 53	6 26	5 20	6 46	5 01	7 07	5 04	7 15	5 22	7 02	5 42	6 29	6 00	5 50	6 23	5 16	6 48	5 01
2	7 06	5 13	6 58	5 41	6 31	6 05	5 52	6 26	5 19	6 47	5 01	7 07	5 04	7 15	5 22	7 01	5 42	6 28	6 01	5 49	6 23	5 15	6 49	5 01
3	7 06	5 14	6 58	5 41	6 30	6 06	5 51	6 27	5 18	6 48	5 00	7 08	5 05	7 15	5 23	7 00	5 43	6 26	6 01	5 47	6 24	5 14	6 50	5 01
4	7 06	5 15	6 57	5 42	6 29	6 06	5 50	6 28	5 17	6 48	5 00	7 08	5 05	7 15	5 24	6 59	5 43	6 25	6 02	5 46	6 25	5 13	6 51	5 01
5	7 06	5 16	6 56	5 43	6 27	6 07	5 48	6 28	5 16	6 49	5 00	7 09	5 06	7 15	5 24	6 58	5 44	6 24	6 03	5 45	6 26	5 12	6 52	5 02
6	7 06	5 16	6 56	5 44	6 26	6 07	5 47	6 29	5 15	6 50	5 00	7 09	5 06	7 15	5 25	6 57	5 45	6 22	6 03	5 44	6 27	5 12	6 52	5 02
7	7 06	5 17	6 55	5 45	6 25	6 08	5 46	6 30	5 14	6 51	5 00	7 10	5 07	7 14	5 26	6 57	5 45	6 21	6 04	5 42	6 28	5 11	6 53	5 02
8	7 07	5 18	6 54	5 46	6 24	6 09	5 45	6 30	5 14	6 51	5 00	7 10	5 07	7 14	5 26	6 56	5 46	6 20	6 05	5 41	6 28	5 10	6 54	5 02
9	7 07	5 19	6 53	5 47	6 23	6 10	5 44	6 31	5 13	6 52	5 00	7 11	5 08	7 14	5 27	6 55	5 46	6 19	6 05	5 40	6 29	5 10	6 55	5 02
10	7 07	5 20	6 52	5 48	6 21	6 11	5 42	6 32	5 12	6 53	5 00	7 11	5 08	7 14	5 28	6 54	5 47	6 17	6 06	5 39	6 30	5 09	6 55	5 03
11	7 07	5 21	6 52	5 49	6 20	6 11	5 41	6 32	5 11	6 53	5 00	7 11	5 09	7 13	5 28	6 53	5 48	6 16	6 07	5 37	6 31	5 08	6 56	5 03
12	7 06	5 22	6 51	5 49	6 19	6 12	5 40	6 33	5 10	6 54	5 00	7 12	5 09	7 13	5 29	6 52	5 48	6 15	6 07	5 36	6 32	5 08	6 57	5 03
13	7 06	5 22	6 50	5 50	6 18	6 13	5 39	6 34	5 10	6 55	5 00	7 12	5 10	7 13	5 30	6 51	5 49	6 13	6 08	5 35	6 33	5 07	6 58	5 03
14	7 06	5 23	6 49	5 51	6 16	6 13	5 38	6 34	5 09	6 55	5 00	7 13	5 11	7 12	5 30	6 50	5 49	6 12	6 09	5 34	6 34	5 07	6 58	5 04
15	7 06	5 24	6 48	5 52	6 15	6 14	5 36	6 35	5 08	6 56	5 00	7 13	5 11	7 12	5 31	6 49	5 50	6 11	6 09	5 33	6 35	5 06	6 59	5 04
16	7 06	5 25	6 47	5 53	6 14	6 15	5 35	6 36	5 08	6 57	5 00	7 13	5 12	7 12	5 32	6 48	5 51	6 09	6 10	5 32	6 35	5 05	6 59	5 04
17	7 06	5 26	6 46	5 54	6 13	6 16	5 34	6 37	5 07	6 57	5 00	7 13	5 13	7 11	5 32	6 46	5 51	6 08	6 11	5 31	6 36	5 05	7 00	5 05
18	7 05	5 27	6 45	5 55	6 11	6 16	5 33	6 37	5 07	6 58	5 00	7 14	5 13	7 11	5 33	6 45	5 52	6 07	6 12	5 29	6 37	5 05	7 00	5 05
19	7 05	5 28	6 44	5 55	6 10	6 17	5 32	6 38	5 06	6 59	5 00	7 14	5 14	7 10	5 33	6 44	5 52	6 05	6 12	5 28	6 38	5 04	7 01	5 05
20	7 05	5 29	6 43	5 56	6 09	6 18	5 31	6 39	5 05	6 59	5 00	7 14	5 14	7 10	5 34	6 43	5 53	6 04	6 13	5 27	6 39	5 04	7 01	5 06
21	7 05	5 30	6 42	5 57	6 07	6 18	5 30	6 39	5 05	7 00	5 01	7 14	5 15	7 09	5 35	6 42	5 54	6 03	6 14	5 26	6 40	5 03	7 02	5 06
22	7 04	5 30	6 41	5 58	6 06	6 19	5 29	6 40	5 04	7 01	5 01	7 14	5 15	7 09	5 35	6 41	5 54	6 02	6 15	5 25	6 41	5 03	7 02	5 07
23	7 04	5 31	6 40	5 59	6 05	6 20	5 28	6 41	5 04	7 02	5 01	7 14	5 16	7 08	5 36	6 40	5 55	6 00	6 15	5 24	6 42	5 03	7 03	5 07
24	7 03	5 32	6 39	5 59	6 04	6 20	5 27	6 42	5 03	7 02	5 02	7 15	5 17	7 07	5 37	6 39	5 55	5 59	6 16	5 23	6 42	5 03	7 03	5 08
25	7 03	5 33	6 38	6 00	6 02	6 21	5 25	6 42	5 03	7 03	5 02	7 15	5 17	7 07	5 37	6 37	5 56	5 58	6 17	5 22	6 43	5 02	7 04	5 09
26	7 02	5 34	6 37	6 01	6 01	6 22	5 24	6 43	5 02	7 04	5 02	7 15	5 18	7 06	5 38	6 36	5 57	5 56	6 18	5 21	6 44	5 02	7 04	5 09
27	7 02	5 35	6 36	6 02	6 00	6 22	5 23	6 44	5 02	7 04	5 03	7 15	5 19	7 05	5 38	6 35	5 57	5 55	6 18	5 20	6 45	5 02	7 04	5 10
28	7 01	5 36	6 34	6 03	5 59	6 23	5 22	6 45	5 02	7 05	5 03	7 15	5 19	7 05	5 39	6 34	5 58	5 54	6 19	5 19	6 46	5 02	7 05	5 10
29	7 01	5 37			5 57	6 24	5 21	6 45	5 02	7 06	5 03	7 15	5 20	7 04	5 40	6 33	5 59	5 52	6 20	5 18	6 47	5 02	7 05	5 11
30	7 00	5 38			5 56	6 24	5 21	6 46	5 01	7 06	5 04	7 15	5 20	7 03	5 40	6 31	5 59	5 51	6 21	5 17	6 47	5 02	7 05	5 12
31	7 00	5 39			5 55	6 25			5 01	7 06			5 21	7 02	5 41	6 30			6 22	5 16			7 06	5 13

Add one hour for daylight time, if and when in use.

Close accuracy within 10 miles from center of this location - if further than 10 miles, add/subtract 1 minute per 10 miles

EL PASO, TEXAS

THE OVERLOAD COMPANION 2017 © FREDA BARBER BOOTH

Astronomical Applications Dept
Location: W111 52, N40 46

Rise and Set for the Sun for 2017
SALT LAKE CITY, UTAH

U. S. Naval Observatory, Washington, DC
Mountain Standard Time

	JAN AM	JAN PM	FEB AM	FEB PM	MAR AM	MAR PM	APR AM	APR PM	MAY AM	MAY PM	JUN AM	JUN PM	JUL AM	JUL PM	AUG AM	AUG PM	SEP AM	SEP PM	OCT AM	OCT PM	NOV AM	NOV PM	DEC AM	DEC PM
1	7 52	5 10	7 38	5 45	7 01	6 19	6 10	6 53	5 25	7 24	4 58	7 53	5 00	8 03	5 25	7 42	5 55	6 59	6 25	6 09	6 59	5 23	7 33	5 00
2	7 52	5 11	7 37	5 46	6 59	6 21	6 08	6 54	5 24	7 25	4 58	7 54	5 01	8 02	5 26	7 41	5 56	6 57	6 26	6 07	7 00	5 22	7 34	5 00
3	7 52	5 12	7 36	5 47	6 57	6 22	6 07	6 55	5 23	7 26	4 57	7 54	5 01	8 02	5 27	7 40	5 57	6 55	6 27	6 05	7 01	5 21	7 35	5 00
4	7 52	5 13	7 35	5 48	6 56	6 23	6 05	6 56	5 22	7 27	4 57	7 55	5 02	8 02	5 28	7 39	5 58	6 54	6 28	6 04	7 02	5 20	7 36	5 00
5	7 52	5 14	7 34	5 50	6 54	6 24	6 04	6 57	5 20	7 28	4 57	7 56	5 02	8 02	5 28	7 38	5 59	6 52	6 29	6 02	7 03	5 18	7 37	5 00
6	7 52	5 15	7 33	5 51	6 53	6 25	6 02	6 58	5 19	7 30	4 57	7 56	5 03	8 01	5 29	7 36	6 00	6 51	6 30	6 00	7 04	5 17	7 38	5 00
7	7 52	5 16	7 32	5 52	6 51	6 26	6 00	6 59	5 18	7 31	4 56	7 57	5 04	8 01	5 30	7 35	6 01	6 49	6 31	5 59	7 06	5 16	7 39	5 00
8	7 52	5 17	7 31	5 53	6 50	6 27	5 59	7 00	5 17	7 32	4 56	7 58	5 04	8 01	5 31	7 34	6 02	6 47	6 32	5 57	7 07	5 15	7 39	5 00
9	7 51	5 18	7 29	5 55	6 48	6 28	5 57	7 01	5 16	7 33	4 56	7 58	5 05	8 00	5 32	7 33	6 03	6 46	6 33	5 56	7 08	5 14	7 40	5 00
10	7 51	5 19	7 28	5 56	6 46	6 29	5 56	7 02	5 15	7 34	4 56	7 59	5 06	8 00	5 33	7 31	6 04	6 44	6 34	5 54	7 09	5 13	7 41	5 01
11	7 51	5 20	7 27	5 57	6 45	6 31	5 54	7 03	5 14	7 35	4 56	7 59	5 06	7 59	5 34	7 30	6 05	6 42	6 35	5 52	7 10	5 12	7 42	5 01
12	7 51	5 21	7 26	5 58	6 43	6 32	5 52	7 04	5 13	7 36	4 56	8 00	5 07	7 59	5 35	7 29	6 06	6 41	6 36	5 51	7 12	5 11	7 43	5 01
13	7 50	5 22	7 25	5 59	6 41	6 33	5 51	7 05	5 12	7 37	4 56	8 00	5 08	7 58	5 36	7 27	6 07	6 39	6 37	5 49	7 13	5 10	7 44	5 02
14	7 50	5 23	7 23	6 01	6 40	6 34	5 49	7 07	5 11	7 38	4 56	8 00	5 09	7 58	5 37	7 26	6 08	6 37	6 38	5 48	7 14	5 09	7 44	5 02
15	7 50	5 24	7 22	6 02	6 38	6 35	5 48	7 08	5 10	7 39	4 56	8 01	5 10	7 57	5 38	7 25	6 09	6 35	6 39	5 46	7 15	5 08	7 45	5 02
16	7 49	5 25	7 21	6 03	6 37	6 36	5 46	7 09	5 09	7 40	4 56	8 01	5 10	7 56	5 39	7 23	6 10	6 34	6 40	5 45	7 16	5 08	7 46	5 03
17	7 49	5 27	7 19	6 04	6 35	6 37	5 45	7 10	5 08	7 41	4 56	8 01	5 11	7 56	5 40	7 22	6 11	6 32	6 41	5 43	7 17	5 07	7 46	5 03
18	7 48	5 28	7 18	6 05	6 33	6 38	5 43	7 11	5 07	7 42	4 56	8 02	5 12	7 55	5 41	7 20	6 12	6 30	6 42	5 42	7 19	5 06	7 47	5 04
19	7 48	5 29	7 17	6 07	6 32	6 39	5 42	7 12	5 06	7 43	4 56	8 02	5 13	7 54	5 42	7 19	6 13	6 29	6 43	5 40	7 20	5 06	7 47	5 04
20	7 47	5 30	7 15	6 08	6 30	6 40	5 40	7 13	5 05	7 44	4 56	8 02	5 14	7 54	5 43	7 17	6 14	6 27	6 44	5 39	7 21	5 05	7 48	5 05
21	7 47	5 31	7 14	6 09	6 28	6 41	5 39	7 14	5 05	7 45	4 56	8 02	5 14	7 53	5 44	7 16	6 15	6 25	6 45	5 37	7 22	5 05	7 48	5 05
22	7 46	5 32	7 12	6 10	6 27	6 42	5 37	7 15	5 04	7 46	4 56	8 03	5 15	7 52	5 45	7 14	6 16	6 24	6 46	5 36	7 23	5 04	7 49	5 05
23	7 45	5 34	7 11	6 11	6 25	6 43	5 36	7 16	5 03	7 47	4 56	8 03	5 16	7 52	5 46	7 13	6 17	6 22	6 47	5 35	7 24	5 04	7 49	5 06
24	7 45	5 35	7 10	6 12	6 23	6 45	5 35	7 17	5 02	7 48	4 57	8 03	5 17	7 51	5 47	7 11	6 18	6 20	6 48	5 33	7 25	5 03	7 49	5 06
25	7 44	5 36	7 08	6 14	6 22	6 46	5 33	7 18	5 02	7 48	4 57	8 03	5 18	7 50	5 48	7 10	6 19	6 19	6 49	5 32	7 27	5 03	7 50	5 06
26	7 43	5 37	7 07	6 15	6 20	6 47	5 32	7 19	5 01	7 49	4 57	8 03	5 19	7 49	5 49	7 08	6 20	6 17	6 51	5 31	7 28	5 03	7 50	5 07
27	7 42	5 38	7 05	6 16	6 18	6 48	5 31	7 20	5 01	7 50	4 57	8 03	5 20	7 48	5 50	7 07	6 21	6 15	6 52	5 29	7 29	5 02	7 50	5 08
28	7 42	5 40	7 04	6 17	6 17	6 49	5 29	7 21	5 00	7 51	4 58	8 03	5 21	7 47	5 51	7 05	6 22	6 13	6 53	5 28	7 30	5 01	7 51	5 08
29	7 41	5 41			6 15	6 50	5 28	7 22	5 00	7 52	4 58	8 03	5 22	7 46	5 52	7 04	6 23	6 12	6 54	5 27	7 31	5 01	7 51	5 09
30	7 40	5 42			6 13	6 51	5 27	7 23	4 59	7 52	4 59	8 03	5 23	7 45	5 53	7 02	6 24	6 10	6 55	5 25	7 32	5 01	7 51	5 09
31	7 39	5 43			6 12	6 52			4 59	7 53			5 24	7 43	5 54	7 00			6 57	5 24			7 52	5 10

Add one hour for daylight time, if and when in use.

Close accuracy within 10 miles from center of this location - if further than 10 miles, add/subtract 1 minute per 10 miles

SALT LAKE CITY, UTAH

THE OVERLOAD COMPANION 2017 © FREDA BARBER BOOTH

Astronomical Applications Dept
Rise and Set for the Sun for 2017
U. S. Naval Observatory, Washington, DC
Location: W072 34, N44 16
MONTPELIER, VERMONT
Eastern Standard Time

	JAN AM	JAN PM	FEB AM	FEB PM	MAR AM	MAR PM	APR AM	APR PM	MAY AM	MAY PM	JUN AM	JUN PM	JUL AM	JUL PM	AUG AM	AUG PM	SEP AM	SEP PM	OCT AM	OCT PM	NOV AM	NOV PM	DEC AM	DEC PM
1	7 26	4 22	7 09	4 59	6 27	5 39	5 31	6 18	4 41	6 55	4 09	7 28	4 11	7 38	4 38	7 14	5 14	6 26	5 49	5 30	6 28	4 39	7 06	4 12
2	7 26	4 23	7 08	5 01	6 25	5 40	5 29	6 19	4 39	6 56	4 09	7 28	4 11	7 37	4 39	7 13	5 15	6 24	5 50	5 28	6 29	4 38	7 07	4 12
3	7 26	4 23	7 06	5 02	6 23	5 42	5 27	6 21	4 38	6 57	4 08	7 29	4 12	7 37	4 41	7 12	5 16	6 22	5 51	5 26	6 31	4 37	7 08	4 12
4	7 26	4 24	7 05	5 04	6 21	5 43	5 25	6 22	4 36	6 58	4 08	7 30	4 12	7 37	4 42	7 10	5 17	6 20	5 52	5 25	6 32	4 35	7 10	4 12
5	7 26	4 25	7 04	5 05	6 20	5 44	5 23	6 23	4 35	6 59	4 08	7 31	4 13	7 37	4 43	7 09	5 18	6 18	5 53	5 23	6 33	4 34	7 11	4 12
6	7 26	4 26	7 03	5 06	6 18	5 46	5 22	6 24	4 34	7 01	4 07	7 31	4 14	7 36	4 44	7 08	5 20	6 16	5 55	5 21	6 35	4 33	7 12	4 11
7	7 26	4 27	7 02	5 08	6 16	5 47	5 20	6 25	4 32	7 02	4 07	7 32	4 14	7 36	4 45	7 06	5 21	6 15	5 56	5 19	6 36	4 32	7 13	4 11
8	7 25	4 29	7 00	5 09	6 14	5 48	5 18	6 27	4 31	7 03	4 07	7 33	4 15	7 35	4 46	7 05	5 22	6 13	5 57	5 17	6 37	4 30	7 14	4 11
9	7 25	4 30	6 59	5 11	6 13	5 49	5 16	6 28	4 30	7 04	4 06	7 33	4 16	7 35	4 47	7 03	5 23	6 11	5 58	5 16	6 39	4 29	7 15	4 11
10	7 25	4 31	6 58	5 12	6 11	5 51	5 15	6 29	4 29	7 05	4 06	7 34	4 17	7 34	4 48	7 02	5 24	6 09	6 00	5 14	6 40	4 28	7 16	4 11
11	7 25	4 32	6 56	5 13	6 09	5 52	5 13	6 30	4 28	7 06	4 06	7 34	4 18	7 34	4 50	7 00	5 25	6 07	6 01	5 12	6 41	4 27	7 17	4 11
12	7 24	4 33	6 55	5 15	6 07	5 53	5 11	6 32	4 26	7 08	4 06	7 35	4 18	7 33	4 51	6 59	5 26	6 05	6 02	5 10	6 43	4 26	7 18	4 11
13	7 24	4 34	6 54	5 16	6 05	5 55	5 09	6 33	4 25	7 09	4 06	7 35	4 19	7 33	4 52	6 57	5 28	6 04	6 03	5 09	6 44	4 25	7 18	4 12
14	7 23	4 35	6 52	5 17	6 04	5 56	5 08	6 34	4 24	7 10	4 06	7 36	4 20	7 32	4 53	6 56	5 29	6 02	6 05	5 07	6 45	4 24	7 19	4 12
15	7 23	4 37	6 51	5 19	6 02	5 57	5 06	6 35	4 23	7 11	4 06	7 36	4 21	7 31	4 54	6 54	5 30	6 00	6 06	5 05	6 47	4 23	7 20	4 12
16	7 22	4 38	6 49	5 20	6 00	5 58	5 04	6 36	4 22	7 12	4 06	7 36	4 22	7 30	4 55	6 53	5 31	5 58	6 07	5 04	6 48	4 22	7 21	4 12
17	7 22	4 39	6 48	5 22	5 58	6 00	5 03	6 38	4 21	7 13	4 06	7 37	4 23	7 30	4 56	6 51	5 32	5 56	6 08	5 02	6 49	4 21	7 21	4 13
18	7 21	4 40	6 46	5 23	5 56	6 01	5 01	6 39	4 20	7 14	4 06	7 37	4 24	7 29	4 58	6 50	5 33	5 54	6 10	5 00	6 51	4 20	7 22	4 13
19	7 20	4 42	6 45	5 24	5 54	6 02	4 59	6 40	4 19	7 15	4 06	7 37	4 25	7 28	4 59	6 48	5 34	5 52	6 11	4 59	6 52	4 19	7 22	4 14
20	7 20	4 43	6 43	5 26	5 53	6 03	4 58	6 41	4 18	7 16	4 06	7 38	4 26	7 27	5 00	6 46	5 36	5 51	6 12	4 57	6 53	4 19	7 22	4 14
21	7 19	4 44	6 41	5 27	5 51	6 05	4 56	6 43	4 17	7 17	4 06	7 38	4 27	7 26	5 01	6 45	5 37	5 49	6 13	4 56	6 54	4 18	7 23	4 15
22	7 18	4 46	6 40	5 28	5 49	6 06	4 54	6 44	4 16	7 18	4 06	7 38	4 28	7 25	5 02	6 43	5 38	5 47	6 15	4 54	6 56	4 17	7 23	4 15
23	7 17	4 47	6 38	5 30	5 47	6 07	4 53	6 45	4 15	7 19	4 06	7 38	4 29	7 24	5 03	6 41	5 39	5 45	6 16	4 52	6 57	4 16	7 23	4 16
24	7 17	4 48	6 37	5 31	5 45	6 08	4 51	6 46	4 15	7 20	4 06	7 38	4 30	7 23	5 05	6 40	5 40	5 43	6 17	4 51	6 58	4 16	7 24	4 16
25	7 16	4 50	6 35	5 32	5 43	6 09	4 50	6 47	4 14	7 21	4 07	7 38	4 31	7 22	5 06	6 38	5 41	5 41	6 19	4 49	6 59	4 15	7 24	4 17
26	7 15	4 51	6 33	5 34	5 42	6 11	4 48	6 49	4 13	7 22	4 07	7 38	4 32	7 21	5 07	6 36	5 43	5 39	6 20	4 48	7 01	4 15	7 25	4 18
27	7 14	4 52	6 32	5 35	5 40	6 12	4 47	6 50	4 12	7 23	4 08	7 38	4 33	7 20	5 08	6 34	5 44	5 37	6 21	4 46	7 02	4 14	7 25	4 18
28	7 13	4 54	6 30	5 36	5 38	6 13	4 45	6 51	4 12	7 24	4 09	7 38	4 34	7 19	5 09	6 33	5 45	5 36	6 23	4 45	7 03	4 14	7 25	4 19
29	7 12	4 55			5 36	6 14	4 44	6 52	4 11	7 25	4 09	7 38	4 35	7 18	5 10	6 31	5 46	5 34	6 24	4 43	7 04	4 13	7 26	4 20
30	7 11	4 57			5 34	6 16	4 42	6 54	4 10	7 26	4 10	7 38	4 36	7 17	5 11	6 29	5 47	5 32	6 25	4 42	7 05	4 13	7 26	4 21
31	7 10	4 58			5 32	6 17			4 10	7 27			4 37	7 15	5 13	6 27			6 27	4 41			7 26	4 21

Add one hour for daylight time, if and when in use.

Close accuracy within 10 miles from center of this location - if further than 10 miles, add/subtract 1 minute per 10 miles

MONTPELIER, VERMONT

THE OVERLOAD COMPANION 2017 © FREDA BARBER BOOTH

Astronomical Applications Dept
Rise and Set for the Sun for 2017
U. S. Naval Observatory, Washington, DC
Location: W081 58, N36 43
ABINGDON, VIRGINIA
Eastern Standard Time

	JAN AM	JAN PM	FEB AM	FEB PM	MAR AM	MAR PM	APR AM	APR PM	MAY AM	MAY PM	JUN AM	JUN PM	JUL AM	JUL PM	AUG AM	AUG PM	SEP AM	SEP PM	OCT AM	OCT PM	NOV AM	NOV PM	DEC AM	DEC PM
1	7 40	5 22	7 30	5 53	6 58	6 23	6 13	6 51	5 34	7 17	5 10	7 42	5 13	7 51	5 34	7 34	5 59	6 55	6 24	6 10	6 52	5 30	7 22	5 12
2	7 41	5 23	7 29	5 54	6 57	6 24	6 12	6 52	5 32	7 18	5 10	7 42	5 13	7 50	5 35	7 33	6 00	6 54	6 24	6 09	6 53	5 29	7 23	5 12
3	7 41	5 24	7 29	5 55	6 55	6 25	6 10	6 52	5 31	7 18	5 10	7 43	5 14	7 50	5 36	7 32	6 01	6 52	6 25	6 08	6 54	5 28	7 24	5 12
4	7 41	5 25	7 28	5 56	6 54	6 26	6 09	6 53	5 30	7 19	5 10	7 43	5 14	7 50	5 37	7 31	6 02	6 51	6 26	6 06	6 55	5 27	7 25	5 12
5	7 41	5 26	7 27	5 57	6 52	6 27	6 07	6 54	5 29	7 20	5 09	7 44	5 15	7 50	5 37	7 30	6 03	6 50	6 27	6 05	6 56	5 26	7 26	5 12
6	7 41	5 27	7 26	5 58	6 51	6 28	6 06	6 55	5 28	7 21	5 09	7 44	5 16	7 50	5 38	7 29	6 03	6 48	6 28	6 03	6 57	5 26	7 27	5 12
7	7 41	5 27	7 25	5 59	6 50	6 28	6 04	6 56	5 27	7 22	5 09	7 45	5 16	7 49	5 39	7 28	6 04	6 47	6 29	6 02	6 58	5 25	7 27	5 12
8	7 41	5 28	7 24	6 01	6 48	6 29	6 03	6 57	5 26	7 23	5 09	7 46	5 17	7 49	5 40	7 26	6 05	6 45	6 30	6 00	6 59	5 24	7 28	5 12
9	7 41	5 29	7 23	6 02	6 47	6 30	6 02	6 58	5 25	7 24	5 09	7 46	5 17	7 49	5 41	7 25	6 06	6 44	6 30	5 59	7 00	5 23	7 29	5 12
10	7 41	5 30	7 22	6 03	6 45	6 31	6 00	6 58	5 24	7 25	5 09	7 46	5 18	7 48	5 41	7 24	6 07	6 42	6 31	5 58	7 01	5 22	7 30	5 12
11	7 41	5 31	7 21	6 04	6 44	6 32	5 59	6 59	5 23	7 25	5 09	7 47	5 18	7 48	5 42	7 23	6 07	6 41	6 32	5 56	7 02	5 21	7 31	5 13
12	7 40	5 32	7 20	6 05	6 42	6 33	5 57	7 00	5 23	7 26	5 09	7 47	5 19	7 48	5 43	7 22	6 08	6 39	6 33	5 55	7 03	5 21	7 31	5 13
13	7 40	5 33	7 19	6 06	6 41	6 34	5 56	7 01	5 22	7 27	5 09	7 48	5 20	7 47	5 44	7 21	6 09	6 38	6 34	5 53	7 04	5 20	7 32	5 13
14	7 40	5 34	7 18	6 07	6 40	6 35	5 55	7 02	5 21	7 28	5 09	7 48	5 20	7 47	5 45	7 19	6 10	6 36	6 35	5 52	7 05	5 19	7 33	5 14
15	7 39	5 35	7 17	6 08	6 38	6 36	5 53	7 03	5 20	7 29	5 09	7 48	5 21	7 46	5 46	7 18	6 11	6 35	6 36	5 51	7 06	5 18	7 33	5 14
16	7 39	5 36	7 15	6 09	6 37	6 37	5 52	7 04	5 19	7 30	5 09	7 49	5 22	7 46	5 46	7 17	6 11	6 33	6 37	5 49	7 07	5 18	7 34	5 14
17	7 39	5 37	7 14	6 10	6 35	6 38	5 51	7 05	5 19	7 30	5 09	7 49	5 22	7 45	5 47	7 16	6 12	6 32	6 38	5 48	7 08	5 17	7 35	5 14
18	7 39	5 38	7 13	6 11	6 34	6 38	5 49	7 06	5 18	7 31	5 09	7 49	5 23	7 45	5 48	7 14	6 13	6 30	6 39	5 47	7 09	5 17	7 35	5 15
19	7 38	5 39	7 12	6 12	6 32	6 39	5 48	7 06	5 17	7 32	5 09	7 50	5 24	7 44	5 49	7 13	6 14	6 28	6 39	5 46	7 10	5 16	7 36	5 15
20	7 38	5 40	7 11	6 13	6 31	6 40	5 47	7 07	5 16	7 33	5 09	7 50	5 25	7 43	5 50	7 12	6 15	6 27	6 40	5 44	7 11	5 15	7 36	5 15
21	7 37	5 41	7 10	6 14	6 29	6 41	5 45	7 08	5 16	7 34	5 10	7 50	5 26	7 43	5 50	7 11	6 15	6 25	6 41	5 43	7 12	5 15	7 37	5 16
22	7 37	5 42	7 08	6 15	6 28	6 42	5 44	7 09	5 15	7 34	5 10	7 50	5 26	7 42	5 51	7 09	6 16	6 24	6 42	5 42	7 13	5 15	7 37	5 16
23	7 36	5 43	7 07	6 16	6 26	6 43	5 43	7 10	5 14	7 35	5 10	7 51	5 27	7 41	5 52	7 08	6 17	6 22	6 43	5 41	7 14	5 14	7 38	5 17
24	7 36	5 44	7 06	6 17	6 25	6 44	5 42	7 11	5 14	7 36	5 10	7 51	5 28	7 41	5 53	7 07	6 18	6 21	6 44	5 39	7 15	5 14	7 38	5 17
25	7 35	5 45	7 04	6 18	6 23	6 45	5 41	7 12	5 13	7 37	5 11	7 51	5 29	7 40	5 54	7 05	6 19	6 19	6 45	5 38	7 16	5 14	7 39	5 18
26	7 35	5 47	7 03	6 19	6 22	6 46	5 39	7 12	5 13	7 37	5 11	7 51	5 29	7 39	5 55	7 04	6 19	6 18	6 46	5 37	7 17	5 13	7 39	5 19
27	7 34	5 48	7 02	6 20	6 20	6 47	5 38	7 13	5 12	7 38	5 12	7 51	5 30	7 38	5 56	7 02	6 20	6 16	6 47	5 36	7 18	5 13	7 39	5 19
28	7 33	5 49	7 01	6 21	6 19	6 47	5 37	7 14	5 12	7 39	5 12	7 51	5 31	7 37	5 57	7 01	6 21	6 15	6 48	5 35	7 19	5 13	7 40	5 20
29	7 32	5 50			6 17	6 48	5 36	7 15	5 11	7 40	5 12	7 51	5 32	7 36	5 58	7 00	6 22	6 13	6 49	5 34	7 20	5 12	7 40	5 21
30	7 32	5 51			6 16	6 49	5 35	7 16	5 11	7 40	5 13	7 51	5 32	7 36	5 58	6 58	6 23	6 12	6 50	5 32	7 21	5 12	7 40	5 21
31	7 31	5 52			6 15	6 50			5 11	7 41			5 33	7 35	5 59	6 57			6 51	5 31			7 40	5 22

Add one hour for daylight time, if and when in use.

Close accuracy within 10 miles from center of this location - if further than 10 miles, add/subtract 1 minute per 10 miles

ABINGDON, VIRGINIA

THE OVERLOAD COMPANION 2017 © FREDA BARBER BOOTH

Astronomical Applications Dept

Rise and Set for the Sun for 2017
RICHMOND, VIRGINIA

U. S. Naval Observatory, Washington, DC
Eastern Standard Time

Location: W077 28, N37 32

	JAN AM	JAN PM	FEB AM	FEB PM	MAR AM	MAR PM	APR AM	APR PM	MAY AM	MAY PM	JUN AM	JUN PM	JUL AM	JUL PM	AUG AM	AUG PM	SEP AM	SEP PM	OCT AM	OCT PM	NOV AM	NOV PM	DEC AM	DEC PM
1	7 25	5 02	7 14	5 33	6 40	6 04	5 55	6 33	5 14	7 00	4 50	7 26	4 53	7 35	5 14	7 17	5 41	6 38	6 06	5 52	6 35	5 11	7 06	4 52
2	7 25	5 03	7 13	5 35	6 39	6 05	5 53	6 34	5 13	7 01	4 50	7 26	4 53	7 35	5 15	7 16	5 41	6 37	6 07	5 51	6 36	5 10	7 07	4 52
3	7 25	5 04	7 12	5 36	6 38	6 06	5 52	6 35	5 12	7 02	4 49	7 27	4 54	7 35	5 16	7 15	5 42	6 35	6 08	5 49	6 37	5 09	7 08	4 51
4	7 25	5 05	7 11	5 37	6 36	6 07	5 50	6 36	5 11	7 03	4 49	7 28	4 54	7 34	5 17	7 14	5 43	6 34	6 08	5 48	6 38	5 08	7 09	4 51
5	7 25	5 05	7 10	5 38	6 35	6 08	5 49	6 37	5 10	7 04	4 49	7 28	4 55	7 34	5 18	7 13	5 44	6 32	6 09	5 46	6 40	5 07	7 10	4 51
6	7 25	5 06	7 09	5 39	6 33	6 09	5 47	6 38	5 09	7 05	4 49	7 29	4 55	7 34	5 19	7 12	5 45	6 31	6 10	5 45	6 41	5 06	7 11	4 51
7	7 25	5 07	7 08	5 40	6 32	6 10	5 46	6 39	5 08	7 06	4 49	7 29	4 56	7 34	5 19	7 11	5 46	6 29	6 11	5 43	6 42	5 05	7 12	4 51
8	7 25	5 08	7 07	5 41	6 31	6 11	5 44	6 40	5 07	7 07	4 48	7 30	4 56	7 33	5 20	7 10	5 46	6 28	6 12	5 42	6 43	5 04	7 12	4 51
9	7 25	5 09	7 06	5 42	6 29	6 12	5 43	6 41	5 06	7 07	4 48	7 30	4 57	7 33	5 21	7 09	5 47	6 26	6 13	5 40	6 44	5 03	7 13	4 52
10	7 25	5 10	7 05	5 43	6 28	6 13	5 41	6 42	5 05	7 08	4 48	7 31	4 58	7 33	5 22	7 08	5 48	6 25	6 14	5 39	6 45	5 02	7 14	4 52
11	7 25	5 11	7 04	5 44	6 26	6 14	5 40	6 43	5 04	7 09	4 48	7 31	4 58	7 32	5 23	7 06	5 49	6 23	6 15	5 38	6 46	5 02	7 15	4 52
12	7 24	5 12	7 03	5 46	6 25	6 15	5 39	6 44	5 03	7 10	4 48	7 32	4 59	7 32	5 24	7 05	5 50	6 21	6 16	5 36	6 47	5 01	7 16	4 52
13	7 24	5 13	7 02	5 47	6 23	6 16	5 37	6 45	5 02	7 11	4 48	7 32	5 00	7 31	5 24	7 04	5 51	6 20	6 17	5 35	6 48	5 00	7 16	4 53
14	7 24	5 14	7 01	5 48	6 22	6 17	5 36	6 46	5 01	7 12	4 48	7 33	5 00	7 31	5 25	7 03	5 51	6 18	6 18	5 33	6 49	4 59	7 17	4 53
15	7 24	5 15	7 00	5 49	6 20	6 18	5 34	6 47	5 00	7 13	4 48	7 33	5 01	7 30	5 26	7 02	5 52	6 17	6 18	5 32	6 50	4 59	7 18	4 53
16	7 23	5 16	6 59	5 50	6 19	6 19	5 33	6 47	4 59	7 14	4 48	7 33	5 02	7 30	5 27	7 00	5 53	6 15	6 19	5 31	6 51	4 58	7 18	4 53
17	7 23	5 17	6 57	5 51	6 17	6 19	5 32	6 48	4 59	7 14	4 48	7 34	5 02	7 29	5 28	6 59	5 54	6 14	6 20	5 29	6 52	4 57	7 19	4 54
18	7 23	5 18	6 56	5 52	6 16	6 20	5 30	6 49	4 58	7 15	4 48	7 34	5 03	7 29	5 29	6 58	5 55	6 12	6 21	5 28	6 53	4 57	7 19	4 54
19	7 22	5 19	6 55	5 53	6 14	6 21	5 29	6 50	4 57	7 16	4 49	7 34	5 04	7 28	5 30	6 56	5 56	6 11	6 22	5 27	6 54	4 56	7 20	4 54
20	7 22	5 20	6 54	5 54	6 13	6 22	5 28	6 50	4 56	7 17	4 49	7 34	5 05	7 27	5 30	6 55	5 56	6 09	6 23	5 25	6 55	4 56	7 21	4 55
21	7 21	5 21	6 52	5 55	6 11	6 23	5 26	6 51	4 56	7 18	4 49	7 34	5 05	7 27	5 31	6 54	5 57	6 08	6 24	5 24	6 56	4 55	7 21	4 55
22	7 21	5 22	6 51	5 56	6 10	6 24	5 25	6 52	4 55	7 19	4 49	7 34	5 06	7 26	5 32	6 52	5 58	6 06	6 25	5 23	6 57	4 55	7 22	4 56
23	7 20	5 23	6 50	5 57	6 08	6 25	5 24	6 53	4 54	7 19	4 50	7 34	5 07	7 25	5 33	6 51	5 59	6 04	6 26	5 21	6 58	4 54	7 22	4 56
24	7 19	5 24	6 49	5 58	6 07	6 26	5 22	6 54	4 54	7 20	4 50	7 34	5 08	7 24	5 34	6 50	6 00	6 03	6 27	5 20	6 59	4 54	7 22	4 57
25	7 19	5 25	6 47	5 59	6 05	6 27	5 21	6 55	4 53	7 21	4 50	7 35	5 09	7 24	5 35	6 48	6 01	6 01	6 28	5 19	7 00	4 53	7 23	4 58
26	7 18	5 26	6 46	6 00	6 04	6 28	5 20	6 56	4 53	7 22	4 51	7 35	5 09	7 23	5 36	6 47	6 01	6 00	6 29	5 18	7 01	4 53	7 23	4 58
27	7 18	5 27	6 45	6 01	6 02	6 29	5 19	6 57	4 52	7 22	4 51	7 35	5 10	7 22	5 36	6 45	6 02	5 58	6 30	5 17	7 02	4 53	7 24	4 59
28	7 17	5 28	6 43	6 02	6 01	6 29	5 17	6 58	4 52	7 23	4 51	7 35	5 11	7 21	5 37	6 44	6 03	5 57	6 31	5 15	7 03	4 52	7 24	5 00
29	7 16	5 29			5 59	6 30	5 16	6 58	4 51	7 24	4 52	7 35	5 12	7 20	5 38	6 42	6 04	5 55	6 32	5 14	7 04	4 52	7 24	5 00
30	7 15	5 31			5 58	6 31	5 15	6 59	4 51	7 24	4 52	7 35	5 13	7 19	5 39	6 41	6 05	5 54	6 33	5 13	7 05	4 52	7 24	5 01
31	7 15	5 32			5 56	6 32			4 50	7 25			5 13	7 18	5 40	6 40			6 34	5 12			7 25	5 02

Add one hour for daylight time, if and when in use.

Close accuracy within 10 miles from center of this location - if further than 10 miles, add/subtract 1 minute per 10 miles

RICHMOND, VIRGINIA

THE OVERLOAD COMPANION 2017 © FREDA BARBER BOOTH

Astronomical Applications Dept
Location: W122 20, N47 38

Rise and Set for the Sun for 2017
SEATTLE, WASHINGTON

U. S. Naval Observatory, Washington, DC
Pacific Standard Time

	JAN AM	JAN PM	FEB AM	FEB PM	MAR AM	MAR PM	APR AM	APR PM	MAY AM	MAY PM	JUN AM	JUN PM	JUL AM	JUL PM	AUG AM	AUG PM	SEP AM	SEP PM	OCT AM	OCT PM	NOV AM	NOV PM	DEC AM	DEC PM
1	7 58	4 28	7 36	5 10	6 49	5 55	5 47	6 40	4 51	7 22	4 15	8 10	4 16	8 10	4 48	7 43	5 29	6 49	6 09	5 47	6 54	4 51	7 37	4 20
2	7 58	4 29	7 35	5 11	6 47	5 57	5 45	6 42	4 50	7 24	4 15	8 10	4 17	8 10	4 49	7 41	5 30	6 47	6 11	5 45	6 56	4 49	7 39	4 19
3	7 58	4 30	7 34	5 13	6 45	5 58	5 43	6 43	4 48	7 25	4 14	8 10	4 17	8 10	4 50	7 40	5 31	6 45	6 12	5 43	6 57	4 48	7 40	4 19
4	7 57	4 31	7 32	5 15	6 43	6 00	5 41	6 44	4 46	7 26	4 14	8 09	4 18	8 09	4 51	7 38	5 33	6 43	6 13	5 41	6 59	4 46	7 41	4 18
5	7 57	4 32	7 31	5 16	6 41	6 01	5 39	6 46	4 45	7 28	4 13	8 09	4 19	8 09	4 53	7 37	5 34	6 41	6 15	5 39	7 00	4 45	7 42	4 18
6	7 57	4 33	7 30	5 18	6 39	6 03	5 37	6 47	4 43	7 29	4 13	8 08	4 19	8 08	4 54	7 35	5 35	6 39	6 16	5 37	7 02	4 43	7 43	4 18
7	7 57	4 34	7 28	5 19	6 37	6 04	5 35	6 49	4 42	7 31	4 12	8 08	4 20	8 08	4 55	7 34	5 37	6 36	6 18	5 35	7 03	4 42	7 44	4 18
8	7 57	4 36	7 27	5 21	6 35	6 06	5 33	6 50	4 41	7 32	4 12	8 07	4 21	8 07	4 57	7 32	5 38	6 34	6 19	5 33	7 05	4 41	7 45	4 18
9	7 56	4 37	7 25	5 23	6 33	6 07	5 31	6 51	4 39	7 33	4 12	8 07	4 22	8 07	4 58	7 31	5 39	6 32	6 20	5 32	7 07	4 39	7 46	4 18
10	7 56	4 38	7 24	5 24	6 31	6 08	5 29	6 53	4 38	7 35	4 11	8 06	4 23	8 06	4 59	7 29	5 41	6 30	6 22	5 30	7 08	4 38	7 47	4 18
11	7 55	4 39	7 22	5 26	6 29	6 10	5 27	6 54	4 36	7 36	4 11	8 06	4 24	8 06	5 01	7 27	5 42	6 28	6 23	5 28	7 10	4 37	7 48	4 18
12	7 55	4 41	7 20	5 27	6 27	6 11	5 25	6 56	4 35	7 37	4 11	8 05	4 25	8 05	5 02	7 26	5 43	6 26	6 25	5 26	7 11	4 36	7 49	4 18
13	7 54	4 42	7 19	5 29	6 25	6 13	5 23	6 57	4 34	7 39	4 11	8 04	4 26	8 04	5 03	7 24	5 45	6 24	6 26	5 24	7 13	4 34	7 50	4 18
14	7 54	4 43	7 17	5 30	6 23	6 14	5 21	6 59	4 32	7 40	4 11	8 04	4 27	8 03	5 05	7 22	5 46	6 22	6 28	5 22	7 14	4 33	7 51	4 18
15	7 53	4 45	7 16	5 32	6 21	6 16	5 19	7 00	4 31	7 41	4 11	8 09	4 28	8 02	5 06	7 20	5 47	6 20	6 29	5 20	7 15	4 32	7 51	4 19
16	7 52	4 46	7 14	5 34	6 19	6 17	5 17	7 01	4 30	7 42	4 11	8 10	4 29	8 02	5 07	7 19	5 49	6 18	6 31	5 18	7 17	4 31	7 52	4 19
17	7 52	4 47	7 12	5 35	6 17	6 19	5 16	7 03	4 29	7 44	4 11	8 10	4 30	8 01	5 09	7 17	5 50	6 16	6 32	5 16	7 18	4 30	7 53	4 19
18	7 51	4 49	7 10	5 37	6 15	6 20	5 14	7 04	4 28	7 45	4 11	8 10	4 31	8 00	5 10	7 15	5 51	6 14	6 33	5 14	7 20	4 29	7 54	4 20
19	7 50	4 50	7 09	5 38	6 13	6 22	5 12	7 06	4 26	7 46	4 11	8 10	4 32	7 59	5 11	7 13	5 53	6 12	6 35	5 13	7 21	4 28	7 54	4 20
20	7 49	4 52	7 07	5 40	6 11	6 23	5 10	7 07	4 25	7 47	4 11	8 11	4 33	7 58	5 13	7 11	5 54	6 10	6 36	5 11	7 23	4 27	7 55	4 20
21	7 48	4 53	7 05	5 41	6 09	6 24	5 08	7 08	4 24	7 48	4 11	8 11	4 34	7 57	5 14	7 10	5 56	6 08	6 38	5 09	7 24	4 26	7 55	4 21
22	7 48	4 55	7 03	5 43	6 07	6 26	5 06	7 10	4 23	7 49	4 12	8 11	4 35	7 56	5 15	7 08	5 57	6 06	6 39	5 07	7 26	4 25	7 56	4 21
23	7 47	4 56	7 02	5 44	6 05	6 27	5 05	7 11	4 22	7 51	4 12	8 11	4 37	7 54	5 17	7 06	5 58	6 04	6 41	5 06	7 27	4 24	7 56	4 22
24	7 46	4 58	7 00	5 46	6 03	6 29	5 03	7 13	4 21	7 52	4 12	8 11	4 38	7 53	5 18	7 04	6 00	6 02	6 42	5 04	7 28	4 24	7 56	4 23
25	7 45	4 59	6 58	5 48	6 01	6 30	5 01	7 14	4 20	7 53	4 13	8 11	4 39	7 52	5 19	7 02	6 01	6 00	6 44	5 02	7 30	4 23	7 57	4 24
26	7 44	5 01	6 56	5 49	5 59	6 32	4 59	7 15	4 19	7 54	4 13	8 11	4 40	7 51	5 21	7 00	6 02	5 58	6 45	5 00	7 31	4 22	7 57	4 24
27	7 42	5 02	6 54	5 51	5 57	6 33	4 58	7 17	4 18	7 55	4 14	8 11	4 41	7 50	5 22	6 58	6 04	5 56	6 47	4 59	7 32	4 22	7 57	4 25
28	7 41	5 04	6 52	5 52	5 55	6 34	4 56	7 18	4 17	7 56	4 14	8 11	4 43	7 48	5 23	6 56	6 05	5 53	6 48	4 57	7 34	4 21	7 58	4 26
29	7 40	5 05			5 53	6 36	4 54	7 20	4 17	7 57	4 15	8 11	4 44	7 47	5 25	6 54	6 06	5 51	6 50	4 55	7 35	4 21	7 58	4 27
30	7 39	5 07			5 51	6 37	4 53	7 21	4 17	7 58	4 15	8 11	4 45	7 46	5 26	6 52	6 08	5 49	6 51	4 54	7 36	4 20	7 58	4 27
31	7 38	5 08			5 49	6 39			4 16	7 59			4 46	7 44	5 27	6 50			6 53	4 52			7 58	4 28

Add one hour for daylight time, if and when in use.

Close accuracy within 10 miles from center of this location - if further than 10 miles, add/subtract 1 minute per 10 miles

SEATTLE, WASHINGTON

Astronomical Applications Dept
Location: W117 25, N47 40

Rise and Set for the Sun for 2017
SPOKANE, WASHINGTON

U. S. Naval Observatory, Washington, DC
Pacific Standard Time

	JAN AM	JAN PM	FEB AM	FEB PM	MAR AM	MAR PM	APR AM	APR PM	MAY AM	MAY PM	JUN AM	JUN PM	JUL AM	JUL PM	AUG AM	AUG PM	SEP AM	SEP PM	OCT AM	OCT PM	NOV AM	NOV PM	DEC AM	DEC PM
1	7 38	4 08	7 17	4 50	6 29	5 35	5 27	6 20	4 31	7 03	3 55	7 40	3 56	7 51	4 28	7 23	5 09	6 29	5 50	5 28	6 35	4 31	7 18	4 00
2	7 38	4 09	7 15	4 52	6 27	5 37	5 25	6 22	4 30	7 04	3 55	7 41	3 57	7 51	4 29	7 22	5 10	6 27	5 51	5 26	6 36	4 29	7 19	3 59
3	7 38	4 10	7 14	4 53	6 25	5 38	5 23	6 23	4 28	7 06	3 54	7 42	3 57	7 50	4 30	7 20	5 12	6 25	5 52	5 24	6 38	4 28	7 20	3 59
4	7 38	4 11	7 13	4 55	6 23	5 40	5 21	6 25	4 27	7 07	3 54	7 43	3 58	7 50	4 32	7 19	5 13	6 23	5 54	5 22	6 39	4 27	7 21	3 59
5	7 38	4 12	7 11	4 56	6 21	5 41	5 19	6 26	4 25	7 08	3 53	7 44	3 59	7 49	4 33	7 17	5 14	6 21	5 55	5 20	6 41	4 25	7 23	3 58
6	7 38	4 13	7 10	4 58	6 19	5 43	5 17	6 28	4 24	7 10	3 53	7 44	4 00	7 49	4 34	7 16	5 16	6 19	5 57	5 18	6 42	4 24	7 24	3 58
7	7 37	4 15	7 09	5 00	6 17	5 44	5 15	6 29	4 22	7 11	3 53	7 45	4 00	7 49	4 36	7 14	5 17	6 17	5 58	5 16	6 44	4 22	7 25	3 58
8	7 37	4 16	7 07	5 01	6 15	5 46	5 13	6 30	4 21	7 12	3 52	7 46	4 01	7 48	4 37	7 13	5 18	6 15	5 59	5 14	6 45	4 21	7 26	3 58
9	7 37	4 17	7 06	5 03	6 13	5 47	5 11	6 32	4 19	7 14	3 52	7 47	4 02	7 47	4 38	7 11	5 20	6 13	6 01	5 12	6 47	4 20	7 27	3 58
10	7 36	4 18	7 04	5 04	6 11	5 49	5 09	6 33	4 18	7 15	3 52	7 47	4 03	7 47	4 39	7 09	5 21	6 11	6 02	5 10	6 48	4 18	7 28	3 58
11	7 36	4 19	7 02	5 06	6 09	5 50	5 07	6 35	4 16	7 16	3 52	7 48	4 04	7 46	4 41	7 08	5 22	6 09	6 04	5 08	6 50	4 17	7 29	3 58
12	7 35	4 21	7 01	5 08	6 07	5 52	5 05	6 36	4 15	7 18	3 51	7 48	4 05	7 45	4 42	7 06	5 24	6 07	6 05	5 06	6 51	4 16	7 29	3 58
13	7 35	4 22	6 59	5 09	6 05	5 53	5 03	6 37	4 14	7 19	3 51	7 49	4 06	7 45	4 43	7 04	5 25	6 05	6 07	5 04	6 53	4 15	7 30	3 58
14	7 34	4 23	6 58	5 11	6 03	5 55	5 02	6 39	4 13	7 20	3 51	7 49	4 07	7 44	4 45	7 03	5 26	6 03	6 08	5 02	6 54	4 13	7 31	3 58
15	7 34	4 25	6 56	5 12	6 01	5 56	5 00	6 40	4 11	7 21	3 51	7 50	4 08	7 43	4 46	7 01	5 28	6 01	6 09	5 00	6 56	4 12	7 32	3 58
16	7 33	4 26	6 54	5 14	5 59	5 58	4 58	6 42	4 10	7 23	3 51	7 50	4 09	7 42	4 47	6 59	5 29	5 58	6 11	4 58	6 57	4 11	7 33	3 59
17	7 32	4 28	6 53	5 15	5 57	5 59	4 56	6 43	4 09	7 24	3 51	7 50	4 10	7 42	4 49	6 57	5 30	5 56	6 12	4 57	6 59	4 10	7 33	3 59
18	7 31	4 29	6 51	5 17	5 55	6 00	4 54	6 45	4 08	7 25	3 51	7 51	4 11	7 41	4 50	6 56	5 32	5 54	6 14	4 55	7 00	4 09	7 34	3 59
19	7 31	4 30	6 49	5 18	5 53	6 02	4 52	6 46	4 07	7 26	3 51	7 51	4 12	7 39	4 51	6 54	5 33	5 52	6 15	4 53	7 02	4 08	7 35	4 00
20	7 30	4 32	6 47	5 20	5 51	6 03	4 50	6 47	4 06	7 28	3 51	7 51	4 13	7 38	4 53	6 52	5 34	5 50	6 17	4 51	7 03	4 07	7 35	4 00
21	7 29	4 33	6 46	5 22	5 49	6 05	4 49	6 49	4 04	7 29	3 52	7 51	4 14	7 37	4 54	6 50	5 36	5 48	6 18	4 49	7 05	4 06	7 36	4 01
22	7 28	4 35	6 44	5 23	5 47	6 06	4 47	6 50	4 03	7 30	3 52	7 52	4 15	7 36	4 56	6 48	5 37	5 46	6 20	4 48	7 06	4 05	7 36	4 01
23	7 27	4 36	6 42	5 25	5 45	6 08	4 45	6 52	4 03	7 31	3 52	7 52	4 17	7 35	4 57	6 46	5 39	5 44	6 21	4 46	7 07	4 05	7 36	4 02
24	7 26	4 38	6 40	5 26	5 43	6 09	4 43	6 53	4 02	7 32	3 53	7 52	4 18	7 34	4 58	6 44	5 40	5 42	6 23	4 44	7 09	4 04	7 37	4 02
25	7 25	4 39	6 38	5 28	5 41	6 10	4 41	6 54	4 01	7 33	3 53	7 52	4 19	7 33	5 00	6 43	5 41	5 40	6 24	4 42	7 10	4 03	7 37	4 03
26	7 24	4 41	6 37	5 29	5 39	6 12	4 40	6 56	4 00	7 35	3 53	7 52	4 20	7 31	5 01	6 41	5 43	5 38	6 26	4 41	7 11	4 02	7 37	4 04
27	7 23	4 42	6 35	5 31	5 37	6 13	4 38	6 57	3 59	7 36	3 54	7 52	4 21	7 30	5 02	6 39	5 44	5 36	6 27	4 39	7 13	4 02	7 37	4 05
28	7 22	4 44	6 33	5 32	5 35	6 15	4 36	6 59	3 58	7 37	3 54	7 52	4 23	7 29	5 04	6 37	5 45	5 34	6 29	4 37	7 14	4 01	7 38	4 05
29	7 21	4 45			5 33	6 16	4 35	7 00	3 59	7 37	3 55	7 51	4 24	7 27	5 05	6 35	5 47	5 32	6 30	4 36	7 15	4 01	7 38	4 06
30	7 19	4 47			5 31	6 18	4 33	7 01	3 57	7 38	3 56	7 51	4 25	7 26	5 06	6 33	5 48	5 30	6 32	4 34	7 17	4 00	7 38	4 07
31	7 18	4 49			5 29	6 19			3 56	7 39			4 26	7 25	5 08	6 31			6 33	4 33			7 38	4 08

Add one hour for daylight time, if and when in use.

Close accuracy within 10 miles from center of this location - if further than 10 miles, add/subtract 1 minute per 10 miles

SPOKANE, WASHINGTON

THE OVERLOAD COMPANION 2017 © FREDA BARBER BOOTH

Astronomical Applications Dept
Location: W081 38, N38 21

Rise and Set for the Sun for 2017
CHARLESTON, WEST VIRGINIA

U. S. Naval Observatory, Washington, DC
Eastern Standard Time

	JAN AM	JAN PM	FEB AM	FEB PM	MAR AM	MAR PM	APR AM	APR PM	MAY AM	MAY PM	JUN AM	JUN PM	JUL AM	JUL PM	AUG AM	AUG PM	SEP AM	SEP PM	OCT AM	OCT PM	NOV AM	NOV PM	DEC AM	DEC PM
1	7 44	5 16	7 32	5 49	6 58	6 20	6 11	6 50	5 29	7 18	5 04	7 45	5 07	7 54	5 29	7 36	5 56	6 56	6 23	6 09	6 53	5 26	7 25	5 06
2	7 44	5 17	7 31	5 50	6 56	6 21	6 09	6 51	5 28	7 19	5 04	7 45	5 07	7 54	5 30	7 35	5 57	6 54	6 24	6 07	6 54	5 25	7 26	5 06
3	7 44	5 18	7 30	5 51	6 55	6 22	6 08	6 52	5 27	7 20	5 04	7 46	5 08	7 54	5 31	7 34	5 58	6 52	6 25	6 05	6 56	5 24	7 27	5 06
4	7 44	5 19	7 29	5 52	6 53	6 23	6 06	6 53	5 26	7 21	5 04	7 47	5 08	7 54	5 32	7 33	5 59	6 51	6 25	6 04	6 57	5 23	7 28	5 06
5	7 44	5 20	7 28	5 53	6 52	6 24	6 05	6 54	5 25	7 22	5 03	7 47	5 09	7 53	5 33	7 32	6 00	6 49	6 26	6 02	6 58	5 22	7 29	5 06
6	7 44	5 21	7 27	5 54	6 51	6 25	6 03	6 55	5 24	7 23	5 03	7 48	5 09	7 53	5 34	7 31	6 01	6 48	6 27	6 01	6 59	5 21	7 30	5 06
7	7 44	5 22	7 26	5 55	6 49	6 26	6 02	6 56	5 23	7 24	5 03	7 48	5 10	7 53	5 34	7 29	6 02	6 46	6 28	5 59	7 00	5 20	7 31	5 06
8	7 44	5 23	7 25	5 56	6 48	6 27	6 00	6 57	5 21	7 25	5 03	7 49	5 11	7 52	5 35	7 28	6 03	6 45	6 29	5 58	7 01	5 19	7 31	5 06
9	7 44	5 24	7 24	5 58	6 46	6 28	5 59	6 58	5 20	7 26	5 03	7 49	5 11	7 52	5 36	7 27	6 03	6 43	6 30	5 56	7 02	5 18	7 32	5 06
10	7 44	5 25	7 23	5 59	6 45	6 29	5 57	6 59	5 19	7 27	5 02	7 50	5 12	7 52	5 37	7 26	6 04	6 42	6 31	5 55	7 03	5 17	7 33	5 06
11	7 43	5 26	7 22	6 00	6 43	6 30	5 56	7 00	5 19	7 28	5 02	7 50	5 13	7 51	5 38	7 25	6 05	6 40	6 32	5 54	7 04	5 16	7 34	5 06
12	7 43	5 27	7 21	6 01	6 42	6 31	5 54	7 01	5 18	7 29	5 02	7 51	5 13	7 51	5 39	7 23	6 06	6 38	6 33	5 52	7 05	5 16	7 35	5 06
13	7 43	5 28	7 20	6 02	6 40	6 32	5 53	7 02	5 17	7 30	5 02	7 51	5 14	7 50	5 40	7 22	6 07	6 37	6 34	5 51	7 06	5 15	7 35	5 07
14	7 43	5 29	7 19	6 03	6 39	6 33	5 51	7 03	5 16	7 31	5 02	7 52	5 15	7 50	5 41	7 21	6 08	6 35	6 35	5 49	7 07	5 14	7 36	5 07
15	7 42	5 30	7 18	6 04	6 37	6 34	5 50	7 04	5 15	7 31	5 02	7 52	5 15	7 49	5 42	7 20	6 09	6 34	6 36	5 48	7 09	5 14	7 37	5 07
16	7 42	5 31	7 16	6 05	6 35	6 35	5 49	7 05	5 14	7 32	5 02	7 52	5 16	7 49	5 42	7 18	6 09	6 32	6 37	5 46	7 10	5 13	7 37	5 08
17	7 42	5 32	7 15	6 06	6 34	6 36	5 47	7 06	5 13	7 33	5 02	7 53	5 17	7 48	5 43	7 17	6 10	6 31	6 38	5 45	7 11	5 12	7 38	5 08
18	7 41	5 33	7 14	6 08	6 32	6 37	5 46	7 07	5 12	7 34	5 02	7 53	5 18	7 48	5 44	7 16	6 11	6 29	6 39	5 44	7 12	5 12	7 38	5 08
19	7 41	5 34	7 13	6 09	6 31	6 38	5 44	7 08	5 11	7 35	5 03	7 53	5 18	7 47	5 45	7 14	6 12	6 27	6 40	5 42	7 13	5 11	7 39	5 09
20	7 40	5 35	7 11	6 10	6 29	6 39	5 43	7 09	5 11	7 36	5 03	7 53	5 19	7 46	5 46	7 13	6 13	6 26	6 41	5 41	7 14	5 10	7 40	5 09
21	7 40	5 36	7 10	6 11	6 28	6 40	5 42	7 10	5 10	7 36	5 03	7 54	5 20	7 46	5 47	7 11	6 14	6 24	6 42	5 40	7 15	5 10	7 40	5 10
22	7 39	5 37	7 09	6 12	6 26	6 41	5 40	7 11	5 10	7 37	5 03	7 54	5 21	7 45	5 48	7 10	6 15	6 23	6 43	5 38	7 16	5 09	7 40	5 10
23	7 39	5 38	7 07	6 13	6 25	6 42	5 39	7 12	5 09	7 38	5 03	7 54	5 22	7 44	5 49	7 09	6 16	6 21	6 44	5 37	7 17	5 09	7 41	5 11
24	7 38	5 39	7 06	6 14	6 23	6 43	5 38	7 13	5 08	7 39	5 04	7 54	5 22	7 44	5 49	7 07	6 16	6 19	6 45	5 36	7 18	5 08	7 41	5 11
25	7 37	5 41	7 05	6 15	6 22	6 44	5 37	7 14	5 08	7 40	5 04	7 54	5 23	7 43	5 50	7 06	6 17	6 18	6 46	5 35	7 19	5 08	7 42	5 12
26	7 37	5 42	7 03	6 16	6 20	6 45	5 35	7 15	5 07	7 40	5 04	7 54	5 24	7 42	5 51	7 04	6 18	6 16	6 47	5 33	7 20	5 08	7 42	5 13
27	7 36	5 43	7 02	6 17	6 18	6 46	5 34	7 16	5 07	7 41	5 04	7 54	5 25	7 41	5 52	7 03	6 19	6 15	6 48	5 32	7 21	5 07	7 43	5 13
28	7 35	5 44	7 01	6 18	6 17	6 47	5 33	7 17	5 06	7 42	5 05	7 54	5 26	7 40	5 53	7 01	6 20	6 13	6 49	5 31	7 22	5 07	7 43	5 14
29	7 34	5 45			6 15	6 48	5 32	7 18	5 06	7 43	5 05	7 54	5 26	7 39	5 54	7 00	6 21	6 12	6 50	5 30	7 23	5 07	7 43	5 15
30	7 34	5 46			6 14	6 48	5 30	7 18	5 06	7 44	5 06	7 54	5 27	7 38	5 55	6 59	6 22	6 10	6 51	5 29	7 24	5 06	7 43	5 16
31	7 33	5 47			6 12	6 49			5 05	7 44			5 28	7 37	5 56	6 57			6 52	5 27			7 44	5 16

Add one hour for daylight time, if and when in use.

Close accuracy within 10 miles from center of this location - if further than 10 miles, add/subtract 1 minute per 10 miles

CHARLESTON, WEST VIRGINIA

THE OVERLOAD COMPANION 2017 © FREDA BARBER BOOTH

Rise and Set for the Sun for 2017
MILWAUKEE, WISCONSIN

Astronomical Applications Dept
Location: W087 57, N43 03
U. S. Naval Observatory, Washington, DC
Central Standard Time

	JAN AM	JAN PM	FEB AM	FEB PM	MAR AM	MAR PM	APR AM	APR PM	MAY AM	MAY PM	JUN AM	JUN PM	JUL AM	JUL PM	AUG AM	AUG PM	SEP AM	SEP PM	OCT AM	OCT PM	NOV AM	NOV PM	DEC AM	DEC PM
1	7 23	4 27	7 07	5 04	6 27	5 42	5 33	6 19	4 45	6 54	4 15	7 25	4 17	7 35	4 43	7 12	5 17	6 26	5 50	5 32	6 27	4 43	7 04	4 18
2	7 23	4 28	7 06	5 05	6 25	5 43	5 31	6 20	4 44	6 55	4 15	7 26	4 17	7 35	4 44	7 11	5 18	6 24	5 51	5 30	6 28	4 42	7 05	4 18
3	7 23	4 29	7 05	5 06	6 24	5 44	5 29	6 21	4 42	6 56	4 14	7 26	4 18	7 34	4 45	7 10	5 19	6 22	5 52	5 29	6 30	4 41	7 06	4 17
4	7 23	4 30	7 04	5 08	6 22	5 45	5 28	6 22	4 41	6 57	4 14	7 27	4 18	7 34	4 46	7 09	5 20	6 20	5 53	5 27	6 31	4 39	7 07	4 17
5	7 23	4 31	7 03	5 09	6 20	5 47	5 26	6 23	4 40	6 58	4 13	7 28	4 19	7 34	4 47	7 07	5 21	6 19	5 54	5 25	6 32	4 38	7 08	4 17
6	7 23	4 32	7 02	5 10	6 19	5 48	5 24	6 25	4 38	6 59	4 13	7 28	4 20	7 33	4 48	7 06	5 22	6 17	5 55	5 23	6 34	4 37	7 09	4 17
7	7 23	4 33	7 01	5 12	6 17	5 49	5 23	6 26	4 37	7 00	4 13	7 29	4 20	7 33	4 50	7 05	5 23	6 15	5 57	5 22	6 35	4 36	7 10	4 17
8	7 23	4 34	6 59	5 13	6 15	5 50	5 21	6 27	4 36	7 01	4 13	7 30	4 21	7 33	4 51	7 03	5 24	6 13	5 58	5 20	6 36	4 35	7 11	4 17
9	7 23	4 35	6 58	5 14	6 13	5 52	5 19	6 28	4 35	7 03	4 13	7 30	4 22	7 32	4 52	7 02	5 25	6 12	5 59	5 18	6 37	4 34	7 12	4 17
10	7 22	4 36	6 57	5 16	6 12	5 53	5 17	6 29	4 33	7 04	4 12	7 31	4 23	7 32	4 53	7 01	5 27	6 10	6 00	5 16	6 39	4 32	7 13	4 17
11	7 22	4 37	6 55	5 17	6 10	5 54	5 16	6 30	4 32	7 05	4 12	7 31	4 23	7 31	4 54	6 59	5 28	6 08	6 01	5 15	6 40	4 31	7 14	4 18
12	7 22	4 38	6 54	5 18	6 08	5 55	5 14	6 32	4 31	7 06	4 12	7 32	4 24	7 31	4 55	6 58	5 29	6 06	6 02	5 13	6 41	4 30	7 14	4 18
13	7 21	4 40	6 53	5 20	6 06	5 56	5 12	6 33	4 30	7 07	4 12	7 32	4 25	7 30	4 56	6 56	5 30	6 04	6 04	5 11	6 42	4 29	7 15	4 19
14	7 21	4 41	6 51	5 21	6 05	5 58	5 11	6 34	4 29	7 08	4 12	7 33	4 26	7 29	4 57	6 55	5 31	6 03	6 05	5 10	6 44	4 29	7 16	4 19
15	7 21	4 42	6 50	5 22	6 03	5 59	5 09	6 35	4 28	7 09	4 12	7 33	4 27	7 29	4 58	6 53	5 32	6 01	6 06	5 08	6 45	4 28	7 17	4 20
16	7 20	4 43	6 49	5 24	6 01	6 00	5 07	6 36	4 27	7 10	4 12	7 33	4 27	7 28	4 59	6 52	5 33	5 59	6 07	5 07	6 46	4 27	7 17	4 20
17	7 20	4 44	6 47	5 25	5 59	6 01	5 06	6 37	4 26	7 11	4 12	7 34	4 28	7 27	5 00	6 50	5 34	5 57	6 08	5 05	6 48	4 26	7 18	4 21
18	7 19	4 46	6 46	5 26	5 58	6 02	5 04	6 39	4 25	7 12	4 12	7 34	4 29	7 26	5 01	6 49	5 35	5 55	6 10	5 03	6 49	4 25	7 19	4 21
19	7 19	4 47	6 44	5 28	5 56	6 04	5 03	6 40	4 24	7 13	4 12	7 34	4 30	7 26	5 03	6 47	5 36	5 54	6 11	5 02	6 50	4 24	7 19	4 22
20	7 18	4 48	6 43	5 29	5 54	6 05	5 01	6 41	4 23	7 14	4 12	7 35	4 31	7 25	5 04	6 46	5 37	5 52	6 12	5 00	6 51	4 24	7 20	4 22
21	7 18	4 49	6 41	5 30	5 52	6 06	5 00	6 42	4 22	7 15	4 13	7 35	4 32	7 24	5 05	6 44	5 39	5 50	6 13	4 59	6 52	4 23	7 20	4 23
22	7 17	4 51	6 40	5 32	5 51	6 07	4 58	6 43	4 21	7 16	4 13	7 35	4 33	7 23	5 06	6 42	5 40	5 48	6 15	4 57	6 54	4 22	7 21	4 23
23	7 16	4 52	6 38	5 33	5 49	6 08	4 56	6 44	4 20	7 17	4 13	7 35	4 34	7 22	5 07	6 41	5 41	5 46	6 16	4 56	6 55	4 22	7 21	4 24
24	7 15	4 53	6 37	5 34	5 47	6 09	4 55	6 45	4 20	7 18	4 13	7 35	4 35	7 21	5 08	6 39	5 42	5 45	6 17	4 54	6 56	4 21	7 22	4 25
25	7 14	4 55	6 35	5 35	5 45	6 11	4 53	6 47	4 19	7 19	4 14	7 35	4 36	7 20	5 09	6 37	5 43	5 43	6 18	4 53	6 57	4 20	7 22	4 25
26	7 13	4 56	6 33	5 37	5 44	6 12	4 51	6 48	4 18	7 20	4 14	7 35	4 37	7 19	5 10	6 36	5 44	5 41	6 19	4 51	6 58	4 20	7 22	4 26
27	7 12	4 57	6 32	5 38	5 42	6 13	4 49	6 49	4 18	7 21	4 15	7 35	4 38	7 18	5 11	6 34	5 45	5 39	6 21	4 50	7 00	4 19	7 22	4 26
28	7 11	4 58	6 30	5 39	5 40	6 14	4 48	6 50	4 17	7 22	4 15	7 35	4 39	7 17	5 12	6 32	5 46	5 37	6 22	4 48	7 01	4 19	7 23	4 27
29	7 10	5 00			5 38	6 15	4 46	6 51	4 17	7 22	4 16	7 35	4 40	7 16	5 13	6 31	5 47	5 36	6 23	4 47	7 02	4 19	7 23	4 25
30	7 09	5 01			5 36	6 16	4 46	6 52	4 16	7 23	4 16	7 35	4 41	7 15	5 15	6 29	5 49	5 34	6 25	4 46	7 03	4 18	7 23	4 26
31	7 08	5 02			5 35	6 18			4 16	7 24			4 42	7 14	5 16	6 27			6 26	4 44			7 23	4 27

Add one hour for daylight time, if and when in use.

Close accuracy within 10 miles from center of this location - if further than 10 miles, add/subtract 1 minute per 10 miles

MILWAUKEE, WISCONSIN

THE OVERLOAD COMPANION 2017 © FREDA BARBER BOOTH

Rise and Set for the Sun for 2017
CASPER, WYOMING

Astronomical Applications Dept
Location: W106 19, N42 50

U. S. Naval Observatory, Washington, DC
Mountain Standard Time

	JAN AM	JAN PM	FEB AM	FEB PM	MAR AM	MAR PM	APR AM	APR PM	MAY AM	MAY PM	JUN AM	JUN PM	JUL AM	JUL PM	AUG AM	AUG PM	SEP AM	SEP PM	OCT AM	OCT PM	NOV AM	NOV PM	DEC AM	DEC PM
1	7 36	4 42	7 20	5 18	6 40	5 55	5 46	6 32	4 59	7 07	4 29	7 38	4 31	7 47	4 57	7 25	5 31	6 39	6 03	5 46	6 40	4 57	7 17	4 32
2	7 36	4 42	7 19	5 19	6 38	5 57	5 45	6 33	4 57	7 08	4 29	7 38	4 31	7 47	4 58	7 24	5 32	6 37	6 04	5 44	6 42	4 56	7 18	4 32
3	7 36	4 43	7 18	5 20	6 37	5 58	5 43	6 34	4 56	7 09	4 28	7 39	4 32	7 47	4 59	7 23	5 33	6 35	6 05	5 42	6 43	4 54	7 19	4 32
4	7 36	4 44	7 17	5 22	6 35	5 59	5 41	6 36	4 55	7 10	4 28	7 40	4 33	7 47	5 00	7 22	5 34	6 34	6 07	5 40	6 44	4 53	7 20	4 31
5	7 36	4 45	7 16	5 23	6 33	6 00	5 40	6 37	4 53	7 11	4 28	7 41	4 33	7 46	5 01	7 20	5 35	6 32	6 08	5 39	6 45	4 52	7 21	4 31
6	7 36	4 46	7 15	5 24	6 32	6 02	5 38	6 38	4 52	7 12	4 27	7 41	4 34	7 46	5 02	7 19	5 36	6 30	6 09	5 37	6 47	4 51	7 22	4 31
7	7 36	4 47	7 14	5 26	6 30	6 03	5 36	6 39	4 51	7 13	4 27	7 42	4 35	7 46	5 04	7 18	5 37	6 28	6 10	5 35	6 48	4 50	7 23	4 31
8	7 36	4 48	7 12	5 27	6 28	6 04	5 34	6 40	4 50	7 14	4 27	7 43	4 35	7 45	5 05	7 16	5 38	6 27	6 11	5 33	6 49	4 49	7 24	4 31
9	7 36	4 49	7 11	5 28	6 27	6 05	5 33	6 41	4 49	7 16	4 27	7 43	4 36	7 45	5 06	7 15	5 39	6 25	6 12	5 32	6 50	4 47	7 25	4 31
10	7 35	4 50	7 10	5 30	6 25	6 06	5 31	6 43	4 47	7 17	4 26	7 44	4 37	7 44	5 07	7 14	5 40	6 23	6 13	5 30	6 52	4 46	7 26	4 31
11	7 35	4 52	7 08	5 31	6 23	6 08	5 29	6 44	4 46	7 18	4 26	7 44	4 38	7 44	5 08	7 12	5 41	6 21	6 15	5 28	6 53	4 45	7 26	4 31
12	7 35	4 53	7 07	5 32	6 22	6 09	5 28	6 45	4 45	7 19	4 26	7 45	4 39	7 43	5 09	7 11	5 42	6 19	6 16	5 27	6 54	4 44	7 27	4 31
13	7 34	4 54	7 06	5 34	6 20	6 10	5 26	6 46	4 44	7 20	4 26	7 45	4 39	7 43	5 10	7 09	5 43	6 18	6 17	5 25	6 56	4 43	7 28	4 32
14	7 34	4 55	7 04	5 35	6 18	6 11	5 24	6 47	4 43	7 21	4 26	7 45	4 40	7 42	5 11	7 08	5 45	6 16	6 18	5 23	6 57	4 42	7 29	4 32
15	7 33	4 56	7 03	5 36	6 16	6 12	5 23	6 48	4 42	7 22	4 26	7 46	4 41	7 41	5 12	7 06	5 46	6 14	6 19	5 22	6 58	4 42	7 29	4 32
16	7 33	4 57	7 02	5 38	6 15	6 14	5 21	6 49	4 41	7 23	4 26	7 46	4 42	7 41	5 13	7 05	5 47	6 12	6 20	5 20	6 59	4 41	7 30	4 33
17	7 32	4 59	7 00	5 39	6 13	6 15	5 20	6 51	4 40	7 24	4 26	7 47	4 43	7 40	5 14	7 03	5 48	6 10	6 22	5 19	7 01	4 40	7 31	4 33
18	7 32	5 00	6 59	5 40	6 11	6 16	5 18	6 52	4 39	7 25	4 26	7 47	4 43	7 39	5 15	7 02	5 49	6 09	6 23	5 17	7 02	4 39	7 31	4 33
19	7 31	5 01	6 57	5 42	6 09	6 17	5 16	6 53	4 38	7 26	4 26	7 47	4 44	7 38	5 16	7 00	5 50	6 07	6 24	5 15	7 03	4 38	7 32	4 33
20	7 31	5 02	6 56	5 43	6 08	6 18	5 15	6 54	4 37	7 27	4 27	7 47	4 45	7 38	5 18	6 59	5 51	6 05	6 25	5 14	7 04	4 38	7 32	4 34
21	7 30	5 03	6 54	5 44	6 06	6 19	5 13	6 55	4 36	7 28	4 27	7 47	4 46	7 37	5 19	6 57	5 52	6 03	6 27	5 12	7 05	4 37	7 33	4 34
22	7 29	5 05	6 53	5 45	6 04	6 21	5 12	6 56	4 36	7 29	4 27	7 47	4 47	7 36	5 20	6 55	5 53	6 02	6 28	5 11	7 07	4 36	7 33	4 34
23	7 29	5 06	6 51	5 47	6 02	6 22	5 10	6 57	4 35	7 30	4 27	7 48	4 48	7 35	5 21	6 54	5 54	6 00	6 29	5 09	7 08	4 36	7 34	4 35
24	7 28	5 07	6 50	5 48	6 01	6 23	5 09	6 59	4 34	7 31	4 28	7 48	4 49	7 34	5 22	6 52	5 55	5 58	6 30	5 08	7 09	4 35	7 34	4 36
25	7 27	5 09	6 48	5 49	5 59	6 24	5 07	7 00	4 33	7 32	4 28	7 48	4 50	7 33	5 23	6 51	5 56	5 56	6 31	5 06	7 10	4 35	7 34	4 36
26	7 26	5 10	6 47	5 50	5 57	6 25	5 06	7 01	4 32	7 33	4 28	7 48	4 51	7 32	5 24	6 49	5 58	5 54	6 33	5 05	7 11	4 34	7 34	4 37
27	7 25	5 11	6 45	5 52	5 55	6 26	5 04	7 02	4 32	7 34	4 29	7 48	4 52	7 31	5 25	6 47	5 59	5 53	6 34	5 04	7 12	4 34	7 35	4 37
28	7 24	5 12	6 43	5 53	5 53	6 28	5 03	7 03	4 31	7 35	4 29	7 48	4 53	7 30	5 26	6 46	6 00	5 51	6 35	5 02	7 14	4 33	7 35	4 38
29	7 23	5 14			5 52	6 29	5 01	7 04	4 31	7 35	4 30	7 48	4 54	7 29	5 27	6 44	6 01	5 49	6 36	5 01	7 15	4 33	7 35	4 39
30	7 22	5 15			5 50	6 30	5 00	7 05	4 30	7 36	4 30	7 48	4 55	7 28	5 28	6 42	6 02	5 47	6 38	5 00	7 16	4 32	7 36	4 40
31	7 21	5 16			5 48	6 31			4 30	7 37			4 56	7 26	5 29	6 40			6 39	4 58			7 36	4 41

Add one hour for daylight time, if and when in use.

Close accuracy within 10 miles from center of this location - if further than 10 miles, add/subtract 1 minute per 10 miles

CASPER, WYOMING

THE OVERLOAD COMPANION 2017 © FREDA BARBER BOOTH

MARCH 2017

SUNDAY	MONDAY	TUESDAY	WEDNESDAY	THURSDAY	FRIDAY	SATURDAY
			1	2	3	4
5	6	7	8	9	10	11
12	13	14	15	16	17	18
19	20	21	22	23	24	25
26	27	28	29	30	31	

APRIL 2017

SUNDAY	MONDAY	TUESDAY	WEDNESDAY	THURSDAY	FRIDAY	SATURDAY
						1
2	3	4	5	6	7	8
9	10	11	12	13	14	15
16	17	18	19	20	21	22
23	24	25	26	27	28	29
30						

THE OVERLOAD COMPANION 2017 © FREDA BARBER BOOTH - PILOTCARSTODAY.COM

MAY 2017

SUNDAY	MONDAY	TUESDAY	WEDNESDAY	THURSDAY	FRIDAY	SATURDAY
	1	2	3	4	5	6
7	8	9	10	11	12	13
14	15	16	17	18	19	20
21	22	23	24	25	26	27
28	29	30	31			

JUNE 2017

SUNDAY	MONDAY	TUESDAY	WEDNESDAY	THURSDAY	FRIDAY	SATURDAY
			1	2	3	
4	5	6	7	8	9	10
11	12	13	14	15	16	17
18	19	20	21	22	23	24
25	26	27	28	29	30	

THE OVERLOAD COMPANION 2017 © FREDA BARBER BOOTH - PILOTCARSTODAY.COM

JULY 2017

SUNDAY	MONDAY	TUESDAY	WEDNESDAY	THURSDAY	FRIDAY	SATURDAY
						1
2	3	4	5	6	7	8
9	10	11	12	13	14	15
16	17	18	19	20	21	22
23	24	25	26	27	28	29
30	31					

AUGUST 2017

SUNDAY	MONDAY	TUESDAY	WEDNESDAY	THURSDAY	FRIDAY	SATURDAY
		1	2	3	4	5
6	7	8	9	10	11	12
13	14	15	16	17	18	19
20	21	22	23	24	25	26
27	28	29	30	31		

THE OVERLOAD COMPANION 2017 © FREDA BARBER BOOTH - PILOTCARSTODAY.COM

SEPTEMBER 2017

SUNDAY	MONDAY	TUESDAY	WEDNESDAY	THURSDAY	FRIDAY	SATURDAY
					1	2
3	4	5	6	7	8	9
10	11	12	13	14	15	16
17	18	19	20	21	22	23
24	25	26	27	28	29	30

OCTOBER 2017

SUNDAY	MONDAY	TUESDAY	WEDNESDAY	THURSDAY	FRIDAY	SATURDAY
1	2	3	4	5	6	7
8	9	10	11	12	13	14
15	16	17	18	19	20	21
22	23	24	25	26	27	28
29	30	31				

NOVEMBER 2017

SUNDAY	MONDAY	TUESDAY	WEDNESDAY	THURSDAY	FRIDAY	SATURDAY
			1	2	3	4
5	6	7	8	9	10	11
12	13	14	15	16	17	18
19	20	21	22	23	24	25
26	27	28	29	30		

DECEMBER 2017

SUNDAY	MONDAY	TUESDAY	WEDNESDAY	THURSDAY	FRIDAY	SATURDAY
					1	2
3	4	5	6	7	8	9
10	11	12	13	14	15	16
17	18	19	20	21	22	23
24	25	26	27	28	29	30
31						

JANUARY 2018

SUNDAY	MONDAY	TUESDAY	WEDNESDAY	THURSDAY	FRIDAY	SATURDAY
	1	2	3	4	5	6
7	8	9	10	11	12	13
14	15	16	17	18	19	20
21	22	23	24	25	26	27
28	29	30	31			

FEBRUARY 2018

SUNDAY	MONDAY	TUESDAY	WEDNESDAY	THURSDAY	FRIDAY	SATURDAY
			1	2	3	
4	5	6	7	8	9	10
11	12	13	14	15	16	17
18	19	20	21	22	23	24
25	26	27	28			

THE OVERLOAD COMPANION 2017 © FREDA BARBER BOOTH - PILOTCARSTODAY.COM

FORMS AND RECORD KEEPING FOR PILOT CAR COMPANIES

The following pages are for you to cut out, make copies and use for your business needs.

MORE PRODUCTS WE OFFER

Invoice - Custom-Designed for your business - **$15**
Invoice on Spreadsheet - Custom Designed - **$30**
Manual Entry Book - **$20**
EZ Record Keeping on Microsoft™ Excel (Does the Math for you) **$20**

Visit pilotcarstoday.com TODAY for more information!

EZ RECORD KEEPING FOR PILOT CARS
© 2013,2014,2015,2016,2016 Freda Barber Booth

** COLLECTION AGENCIES MAY HELP YOU COLLECT UNPAID INVOICES ONLY IF YOU HAVE A SIGNED TRIP AGREEMENT

TRIP AGREEMENT

Between

Auth. Rep _____   Auth. Rep: _____
_____   Company: _____
_____   Address: _____
_____   Phone: _____
_____   Fax: _____
_____

Driver: _____ Truck # _____ Load # _____

Driver Phone: _____   Estimated miles if Mini or Day Run _____

Dimensions: _____ H _____ W _____ L _____ WEGHT _____ PO# _____

Escort 1 - Pick-up Location: _____   Drop: _____
Notes: _____

Escort 2 - Pick-up Location: _____   Drop: _____
Notes: _____

Escort 3 - Pick-up Location: _____   Drop: _____
Notes: _____

RATES

PER MILE _____   MINI _____   DAY _____

                                                  NEXT DAY RETURN FEE _____ (OVERNIGHT)

DELAY/HR _____   NO-GO _____   LAYOVER _____
(Time starts after 2 hrs/day)   REFER TO "ADDITIONAL TERMS"

Early termination of trip due to truck malfunction, permit problems: Refer to Delay, Mini or Day Rate whichever applies:

ADDITIONAL TERMS/RATES: [   ]

TERMS OF PAYMENT

As per agreement, contracting company agrees to pay in full to: _____ the total balance due within _____ days from date of completion of trip. Payments not received within this time will be considered late and a late charge of 10% of total bill will be added to the total amount due per 30 days unpaid. If not paid after 45 days, it will be considered "theft of service" and will be submitted for legal prosecution.

Payment may be made using following methods: Cash, Company Check, CC, Comcheck, EFS

Additional Terms: _____
_____

These terms must be adhered to as written. Any changes in rates or trip must be amended and signed.

I _____ have the authority to quote rates and to authorize payment as agreed in this contract. I understand that any changes made to his agreement will require and addendum to be signed and attached and this page will be declared as "page 1 of (2, 3, etc)" as needed until escort has been released from this assignment. We agree to pay by method of _____.

(X) _____   Date _____

(X) _____   Date _____

INVOICE / RECEIPT

COMPANY:

PHONE:

INVOICE #		FAX:

DATE: (BEGIN) (END)	DUTY	QTY	CHARGE
DRIVER:	MILES		$
DRIVER'S COMPANY (if different)	DAY RUN		$
PHONE	MINI		$
DIMENSIONS WD H L WT	LAYOVER		$
PO #	NIGHTS		$
TRUCK #	NO-GO		$
PICK-UP	HR DELAY		$
DROP	OTHER		$
Driver Furnished Copy of Permit(s)? Y N	PAY THIS AMOUNT →		$
Odometer Begin End			

NOTES/COMMENTS

Detail of Escort Duties (Do not pay from this section)

Date	Escort	Pickup	Drop	Miles	Day	Mini	No-Go	Overnight

Thank you for your business!

We have given our best to ensure good service and to make ourselves available to your company. When money is held, our business cannot run smoothly. Please allow us to be available to other companies as we were available to yours by remitting payment as agreed. "Late Payment" fees may apply (See PRE-TRIP Agreement)

Please make payment to:

Acceptable form of payment: Cash, Credit Card, Company Check, EFS, ComChek

PAID	$	METHOD	(X)

X) _____
   TRUCK DRIVER   Date

X) _____
   PILOT CAR DRIVER   Date

Invoice Design ©2014 Freda Barber Booth / 817-583-5503

Louisiana Department of Transportation and Development
P.O. Box 94042
Baton Rouge, Louisiana 70804-9042
Attention: Truck Permit Section
Fax Number: 225-377-7108
Application for:

Escort Vehicle Permit   **Out of state $10.00 per vehicle**   **No fee for in state**

Please enclose a check, money order, credit card information below or DOTD charge account number

Issued to Customer Number:	Paid by Customer Number:
EFFECTIVE DATE FOR PERMIT:	

Company Name: _____	Vehicle Owner: _____
Address: _____	Address: _____
City: _____ State: __ Zip: ____	City: _____ State: __ Zip: ____
Phone: _____	Phone: _____
Fax Number:	Email:

Complete name and address if to be mailed other than above:

Insurance Company:	Insurance Policy Number:

Insurance coverage in the amount shown below must be maintained for the duration of this Permit
Property Damage: Liability Coverage:
($50,000.00 Minimum)   ($100,000.00 Minimum)

VEHICLE INFORMATION

Make	Model	Year	Serial Number	License	License State	License Year

CREDIT CARD INFO (if applicable):

Card Type: € Visa   € MasterCard   € American Express

| Card Number: | Expiration Date: |
| Name on Credit Card: | Phone# of Cardholder: |

*******************************THIS IS NOT A PERMIT*******************************

_____   _____
Signature of applicant   Date

COLORADO DEPARTMENT OF TRANSPORTATION
4201 East Arkansas Avenue, Suite 290
Denver, CO 80222

1-800-350-3765 or 303-757-9539
Fax 303-757-9719

COLORADO ROUTE SURVEY

*This Route Survey must accompany a Colorado Transport Permit Application for all vehicles/loads that exceed 17' 6" in height or 130' in length

Date Survey conducted:
Month / Day / Year

Applicant and/or Company Name (print):	Telephone:
Applicant Address (print Street/PO Box, City, State, Zip):	Person submitting application:
Company performing survey (print):	Contact name (Survey company):
Company performing survey address (print Street/PO Box, City, State, Zip):	Telephone:

Shipment consists of:

Gross weight:	No. of axles:	Distance first to last axle:	Overall length:	Trailer length:
Front overhang:	Rear overhang:	Height (actual):	Width:	

The CGVW and/or axle group weights cannot exceed the limits indicated on the Bridge Weight Limit Restriction map.

lbs.
Ft'-in"
Axles 1 2 3 4 5 6 7 8 9

lbs.
Ft'-in"
Axles 10 11 12 13 14 15 16 17 18

Starting point in Colorado:	Ending point in Colorado:

REQUESTED ROUTE with Mile point references (attach additional sheets, as necessary)
(The routing must be complete, including all city streets and/or county roads for the proposed line of travel.)
☐ Route verified to the latest Restrictions report for limitations that may affect the movement of this vehicle/load - www.dot.state.co.us/truckpermits/Restrictions.htm

Potential Staging location(s)

POTENTIAL GRADE CONFLICTS (i.e. railroad crossing, speed bumps, etc)	CLEARANCE CONCERNS (attach Utility clearance letters, as needed)

EMERGENCY CONTACT NUMBERS (keep available in case an incident occurs)

LAW ENFORCEMENT	RAILROAD	UTILITIES

I declare under penalty of perjury in the second degree, and any other applicable state or federal laws, that the statements made on this document are true and complete to the best of my knowledge.

Applicant Signature (**Required**):

Date:
CDOT Form #1384 (04/11)

FORM OS-1A
Rev.10/08

STATE OF OHIO
DEPARTMENT OF TRANSPORTATION

LIMITATIONS/PROVISIONS ON THE USE OF A SPECIAL HAULING PERMIT
THIS IS A TWO-SIDED FORM AND MUST BE CARRIED IN ITS ENTIRETY

GENERAL LIMITATIONS

1. A copy of the valid Special Hauling Permit (SHP) as issued by the Ohio Department of Transportation (ODOT) shall be in the possession of the driver at all times during the progress of transportation and shall be shown on demand to any law enforcement officer, employee of the Ohio State Highway Patrol or to any employee of ODOT. The driver is responsible to identify and present the precise copy of the SHP covering the movement of the load being transported. The SHP shall be clearly legible, free of any markings, writing, symbol, logo, letterhead, characters or inscriptions that are not part of the SHP as transmitted by ODOT (an additional tele-facsimile header is allowed).

2. The permission granted restricts the movement of the vehicle(s) or object(s) to the highways specified, between the points designated, and within the time allotted. Permittee is responsible to check the route for abnormal, changed, or unknown/unusual conditions which may exist during any move. **Permission to travel county or township roads, local streets not part of the State Highway System, or the Ohio Turnpike must be obtained from the proper authorities.**

3. No vehicle(s) or object(s) being transported under a **SHP** shall be left parked on the roadway either day or night except in case of an emergency, in which case adequate protection shall be provided for the traveling public. The vehicle(s) shall not be loaded or unloaded within the limits of the highway.

4. The operator of the vehicle must comply with all laws, rules, regulations or credentials covering:
   The movement of traffic over highways and streets.
   Commercial Motor Vehicle operations (I.R.P., C.D.L., I.F.T.A., U.C.R., Load Securement, etc.)

5. **SHP's** will not generally be issued for built-up loads that are divisible into legal loads or loads that have not been loaded to the least over dimension or the least overweight. Miscellaneous items may, however, be transported on the same vehicle with an over dimensional piece or pieces so long as the miscellaneous items do not add to the over dimension. It is not necessary to identify these miscellaneous items. If, in the event of an extenuating circumstance, a **SHP** is issued for a divisible load in which two or more pieces add to the over dimension or overweight, such load will be adequately described.

6. A **SHP is void** at any time road, weather or traffic conditions make travel unsafe, as determined by the State Highway Patrol or local law enforcement.

7. Movement of mobile homes, manufactured structures, office trailers, and park model recreational vehicles is prohibited when wind velocity exceeds 25 mph on the roadway or 15 mph on bridges.

OPERATING LIMITATIONS

1. No vehicle(s) or object(s) being transported under a **SHP** shall travel in convoy with any other oversize/overweight vehicle or vehicle and load. Convoying is defined as operating within 500' of any other permitted vehicle that is traveling in front and in the same direction as said vehicle.

2. Every vehicle operating under a **SHP** when traveling on freeways, expressways, multi-lane undivided highways, shall remain in the extreme right-hand lane of said highway except as necessary to maintain continuous through movement, to make left turns or exits or to pass other vehicles.

3. Any load with an overall height in excess of **14 feet 10 inches** shall be required to coordinate the move with the owners of all overhead signs, signals, utilities, etc., which may obstruct safe, clear movement.

4. Reductions in legal weight posted on roadways or bridges must be obeyed. Contact the Permit Office immediately if your route includes legal load reductions.

DAYS/HOURS OF OPERATION

1. Overweight vehicle/loads that are not over dimensional, traveling under the authority of a **SHP**, will not be restricted as to travel hours or days so long as the overweight vehicle/load can move without obstructing the normal flow of the traffic.

2. With the exception of permitted legal dimensioned overweight vehicle/loads noted in 1. above, vehicle/loads traveling under the authority of a **SHP** shall be prohibited from movement on the following days/ weekends: **New Year's Day, Good Friday, Memorial Day, Independence Day, Labor Day, Thanksgiving Day and Christmas Day.** Prohibitions begin at noon the day preceding and continue until one-half hour before sunrise the day following the holiday or holiday weekend, with the exception of Good Friday, when the prohibition is Sunrise on Good Friday to Sunrise the following Monday.

3. Movement of all vehicles/loads in **excess of twelve feet** in width shall be prohibited within Butler, Clermont, Cuyahoga, Delaware, Fairfield, Franklin, Geauga, Hamilton, Lake, Licking, Lorain, Lucas, Madison, Mahoning, Medina, Montgomery, Pickaway, Stark, Summit, Union, Warren and Wood Counties between the hours of 6:30 a.m. and 9:00 a.m. and 4:30 p.m. and 6:00 p.m. Monday through Friday.

4. Movement of all vehicles/loads in **excess of twelve feet** in width **shall be prohibited** during the following travel times:
   Saturday from 3 P.M. until ½ hour before sunrise on the following Sunday.
   Sunday from 3 P.M. until ½ hour before sunrise on the following Monday.
   Friday from 3 P.M. until ½ hour before sunrise on the following Saturday (April 1 through November 30).
   These time limitations are in addition to items 2 and 3 of the **Days/Hours of Operation**, above.

5. With the exception of limits noted in 1., 2., 3., and 4. above, permitted vehicles/loads may move daylight hours, Sunday through Saturday. Daylight hours are defined as one-half hour before sunrise until one-half hour after sunset.

WARNING FLAGS AND SIGNS

1. Warning flags shall be displayed on all over dimensional vehicles and loads. Warning flags shall be 18 inches square, red or orange in color, in good repair and free of printing or other markings and shall be securely fastened by at least one corner or securely mounted on a staff.

2. Over width vehicles and loads shall bear two flags at the widest extremities of the vehicle or load as well as one flag at each corner of the vehicle or load. Warning flags are not required to be displayed on the tractor.

3. Over length vehicles and loads or vehicles and loads with a rear overhang of 4 feet or greater shall display a single flag at the extreme rear if the over length or projecting part is two feet wide or less. Two flags shall be displayed if the over length or projecting portion is wider than two feet and the flags should be located to indicate maximum width.

4. Warning signs, when required, shall be in good repair, shall read "**OVERSIZE LOAD**" and shall be at least 7 feet long and 18 inches high. The sign's background shall be yellow with black lettering. Letters shall be at least 10 inches high with a 1.41 inch brush stroke. If series E Modified is used, the brush stroke is to be two inches.

5. **OVERSIZE LOAD** signs shall be displayed on any vehicle or vehicle/load:
    exceeding the maximum legal length limit as set in the Ohio Revised Code, section 5577.05.
    with an overall width of **10 feet or greater**,
    with an overall height in excess of **14 feet 6 inches.**
When required, **OVERSIZE LOAD** signs, shall be displayed on the front and rear of the over dimensioned vehicle or vehicle/load.

LIGHTING

1. **All** permitted vehicle's standard vehicle lighting must be in operating order: **THE HEADLIGHTS MUST BE ON DURING THE MOVEMENT OF ANY OVER DIMENSION VEHICLE/LOAD.**

2. **PERMITTED VEHICLE SPECIAL LIGHTING-** Clearance and side marker lights, in addition to the standard lights required by law, need not mark the extremities of an oversize load unless it is specially authorized to move at night or when visibility is less than 1000 feet, in which case, the additional lighting shall be displayed in the manner described in the **OPERATIONAL REQUIREMENTS** section of the **SHP OPERATIONAL GUIDE.**

PRIVATE ESCORT VEHICLES

1. Private Escort vehicles, when required by a **SHP** to accompany an over dimensional or overweight vehicle or vehicle/load, shall be required to display a warning sign, yellow with black letters, reading **"OVERSIZE LOAD"**. The sign shall be 5 feet long by 12 inches high with 8 inch high letters and shall be in good repair. Escort vehicles shall also be required to maintain radio communication with the operator of the permitted vehicle and shall also be required to be equipped with a roof mounted amber flashing or rotating light(s). Driver of the escort vehicle is to act as a flagger when needed. The Driver of an escort vehicle shall not serve as an operator of other vehicles or equipment while escorting a vehicle/load operating under a SHP. Unless otherwise specified on the SHP, Public Safety/Law Enforcement Vehicles shall not be considered to be Private Escorts.

2. **One rear** escort vehicle shall be required for the transportation of any vehicle/load with **a permitted length in excess of 90 feet**.

3. **One lead** (rear on multiple lane highways) escort vehicle shall be required for the transportation of any vehicle/load **with a permitted width in excess of 13 feet.**

4. **One lead** escort vehicle equipped with a **height sensing device** shall be required for the transportation of any vehicle/load with **a permitted height in excess of 14 feet 6 inches.**

5. **One lead and one rear** escort shall be required on any vehicle/load with a permitted **width in excess of 14 feet 6 inches,** or on any vehicle/load with a permitted **height in excess of 14 feet 10 inches.**

6. If more than one of the conditions set forth in numbers 2 through 4 above are met, (for example, a load with a permitted width exceeding 13 feet and a permitted length exceeding 90 feet) **two escorts** (one lead and one rear) shall be required.

7. Front and rear escort vehicles, when required, shall maintain a safe operating distance consistent with existing traffic conditions between the vehicle/load being escorted and the escort vehicle.

8. Escort vehicles shall be a single unit vehicle with unobstructed vision from the front and rear. Escort Vehicles when accompanying a vehicle/load operating under a SHP shall not tow a trailer or another vehicle, or haul equipment which extends beyond the dimensions of the escort vehicle.

PENALTIES FOR VIOLATION

1. Failure to comply with the **SHP** provisions or the general provisions (**OS-1A**), or exceeding the gross vehicle weight or exceeding an axle or axle group weight (by more than 2000 lbs.) or exceeding the dimensions granted, or operating on dates or times, or upon highways other than assigned, or whenever the SHP does not adequately describe the vehicle /load, **shall render the SHP null and void and the operator of the vehicle will be subject to enforcement action,** as provided in sections 5577.02 to 5577.05 inclusive, of the Ohio Revised Code.

2. A SHP should not be voided when a vehicle exceeds a granted axle weight by 2000 lbs or less, provided that the vehicle does not exceed the gross vehicle weight granted by the **SHP**. The enforcing officer shall instruct the driver to bring the vehicle into compliance with the **SHP** prior to substantial movement. If the load cannot be brought into compliance, the load may not move until a revised **SHP** is obtained. Should the vehicle be moved prior to the vehicle being brought into compliance or prior to a revised **SHP** being obtained, the **SHP shall be rendered null and void and the operator will be subject to enforcement action** as provided in sections 5577.02 to 5577.05 inclusive, of the Ohio Revised Code.

3. Moving violations for offenses that are relevant to the safe movement of a Commercial Motor Vehicle (for example, Speed, Reckless Operation, DUI, Improper Lane Change, etc.) **shall render the SHP null and void, and the operator subject to additional enforcement action.**

These limitations and provisions describe the general requirements placed on the operation of over dimension and overweight vehicles traveling on Ohio's highways, and are in addition to specific provisions stated on the SHP or its attachments. **For reference or detailed information, please refer to the** *Special Hauling Permits Operational Guide or contact the* **Office of Highway Management, Special Hauling Permit Section.**

M-936ARS (3-09)

pennsylvania
DEPARTMENT OF TRANSPORTATION
www.dot.state.pa.us

APPLICATION - ROUTE SURVEY

THIS SURVEY IS VALID FOR 21 DAYS FROM
DATE SURVEY IS PHYSICALLY PERFORMED

Application ID#: _____

The routes shown below for the movement of a _____
(Load Description)

having a Gross Weight of _____ pounds and Maximum Dimensions of

Length: _____ FT. _____ IN.   Width: _____ FT. _____ IN.   Height: _____ FT. _____ IN.

moving from:

ORIGIN   PA County   PA Town (optional)   State

State Route: _____   Direction: _____

Point of Interest ☐   Starting Point   Miles/Direction from Intersect
Intersection ☐

DESTINATION   PA County   PA Town (optional)   State

State Route: _____   Direction: _____

Point of Interest ☐   Ending Point   Miles/Direction from Intersect
Intersection ☐

have been **physically** surveyed on _____ and it is hereby certified by:
(Date survey performed)

_____   _____
(Company Performing Survey)   (Person Performing Survey)

for: _____
(Responsible Motor Carrier Name)

that (1) there is safe and sufficient clearance throughout the entire proposed routing as detailed below, (2) turns at all intersections can be traversed, (3) all overhead structures can be traveled under, (4) steep grades can be traversed, (5) cities are identified, (6) all parking and stop-off locations are identified, (7) the vehicle Gross Weight does not exceed any highway or bridge posted weight limit, (8) the survey has been **physically** performed by actually driving the entire proposed routes, (9) State Routes are identified by SR number, (10) local roads and streets and other non-PA state highways are listed in (parentheses) for routing continuity, and that authorization for their use will be obtained by the applicant from the appropriate authority.

Detailed proposed routing: _____

_____

_____

Attach additional 8 1/2 x 11 sheet(s) if necessary

Upon request, submit digital photos of each "turning" intersection and each structure that has less than three inches of vertical clearance (measured from pavement) and identify proposed travel lanes at these locations.

Surveyor Signature(s): _____   Date: _____

Surveyor Phone Number: (_____) _____   Fax Number: (_____) _____

**FALSE INFORMATION GIVEN ON THE PERMIT APPLICATION SHALL AUTOMATICALLY INVALIDATE THE PERMIT.
THIS DOCUMENT MUST BE COMPLETED BY SURVEYOR**

MONTH _____ YEAR _____

DAY	INVOICE NO.	COMPANY	DATE PAID	PAYMENT TYPE	BEGINNING BALANCE	PAID	END BALANCE
1							
2							
3							
4							
5							
6							
7							
8							
9							
10							
11							
12							
13							
14							
15							
16							
17							
18							
19							
20							
21							
22							
23							
24							
25							
26							
27							
28							
29							
30							
31							
				TOTALS			

_____   _____
MONTH   YEAR

DAY	INVOICE NO.	COMPANY / BROKER / DRIVER INVOICED	PICK UP	DROP	DEAD HEAD	PERSONAL	LOADED
1							
2							
3							
4							
5							
6							
7							
8							
9							
10							
11							
12							
13							
14							
15							
16							
17							
18							
19							
20							
21							
22							
23							
24							
25							
26							
27							
28							
29							
30							
31							
				TOTALS			

MONTH _____ YEAR _____

DAY	INVOICE NO.	MILES	RATE/MILE	CHARGED MILEAGE	CHARGED NO-GO	CHARGED MINI	OVER NIGHT LAYOVER	CHARGED PER DAY	CHARGED DELAY	DAILY TOTALS
1										
2										
3										
4										
5										
6										
7										
8										
9										
10										
11										
12										
13										
14										
15										
16										
17										
18										
19										
20										
21										
22										
23										
24										
25										
26										
27										
28										
29										
30										
31										
			TOTALS							

MONTH _____   YEAR _____

DAY	INVOICE NO.	FUEL MAINT	FOOD	MOTEL	EQUIPMENT SUPPLIES	TOTAL EXPENSE
1						
2						
3						
4						
5						
6						
7						
8						
9						
10						
11						
12						
13						
14						
15						
16						
17						
18						
19						
20						
21						
22						
23						
24						
25						
26						
27						
28						
29						
30						
31						
TOTALS						

CENTURY FINANCE

CASH TODAY!

FACTORING MADE EASY FOR AMERICA'S TRUCKERS

1-888-684-7195

Made in the USA
San Bernardino, CA
03 March 2017